NAG HAMMADI STUDIES

VOLUME XXXI

NAG HAMMADI STUDIES

EDITED BY

MARTIN KRAUSE-JAMES M. ROBINSON
FREDERIK WISSE

IN CONJUNCTION WITH

ALEXANDER BÖHLIG-JEAN DORESSE-SØREN GIVERSEN
HANS JONAS-RODOLPHE KASSER-PAHOR LABIB
GEORGE W. MACRAE†-JACQUES-É. MÉNARD
TORGNY SÄVE-SÖDERBERGH
WILLEM CORNELIS VAN UNNIK†-R. McL. WILSON
JAN ZANDEE†

XXXI

GENERAL EDITOR OF THE COPTIC GNOSTIC LIBRARY
JAMES M. ROBINSON

THE COPTIC GNOSTIC LIBRARY

EDITED WITH ENGLISH TRANSLATION, INTRODUCTION AND NOTES
published under the auspices of
THE INSTITUTE FOR ANTIQUITY AND CHRISTIANITY

NAG HAMMADI CODEX VIII

CONTRIBUTORS
BENTLY LAYTON
MARVIN W. MEYER
JOHN H. SIEBER
FREDERICK WISSE

VOLUME EDITOR
JOHN H. SIEBER

E. J. BRILL
LEIDEN · NEW YORK · KØBENHAVN · KÖLN
1991

The paper in this book meets te guidelines for permanence and durability of the Committee on Production Guidelines for Book Longevity of the Council on Library Resources.

ISSN 0169-7749
ISBN 90 04 09477 6

TABLE OF CONTENTS

Foreword   James M. Robinson vii

Preface   John H. Sieber xi

Table of Tractates in the Nag Hammadi Library xiii

Abbreviations and Short Titles xv

Sigla xxxv

NAG HAMMADI CODEX VIII

Introduction to Codex VIII .3
    Bentley Layton
NHC VIII,*1*: *Zostrianos*
    Introduction by John H. Sieber 7
    Text and Transcriptional Notes by Bentley Layton 30
    Translation and Translation Notes by John H. Sieber 31
NHC VIII,2: *Letter of Peter to Philip*
    Introduction by Marvin W. Meyer 227
    Text, Translation and Notes by Frederik Wisse 234
    Commentary by Marvin W. Meyer 234
Indices to *Zostrianos*
    Coptic Words 255
    Greek Words 271
    Proper Names 277
Indices to the *Letter of Peter to Philip*
    Coptic Words 281
    Greek Words 287
    Proper Names 289
Ancient Works and Authors 291
Modern Authors 301

FOREWORD

"The Coptic Gnostic Library" is a complete edition of the Nag Hammadi Codices, of Papyrus Berolinensis 8502, and of the Askew and Bruce Codices, comprising a critical text with English translations, introductions, notes, and indices. Its aim is to present these texts in a uniform edition that will promptly follow the appearance of *The Facsimile Edition of the Nag Hammadi Codices* and that can be a basis for more detailed technical and interpretive investigations. Further studies of this sort are expected to appear in the monograph series Nag Hammadi Studies of which the present edition is a part.

The Gnostic religion was not only a force that interacted with early Christianity and Judaism in their formative periods, but also a significant religious position in its own right. General acceptance of this modern insight had been seriously impeded by the scarcity of original source material. Now this situation has been decisively altered. It is thus under a sense of obligation imposed by the discovery of these largely unique documents that the present edition has been prepared.

This edition is a project of the Institute for Antiquity and Christianity, Claremont, California. The translation team consists of Harold W. Attridge, J. S. B. Barns, Hans-Gebhard Bethge, Alexander Bohlig, James Brashler, G.M. Browne, Roger A. Bullard, Peter A. Dirkse, Stephen Emmel, Joseph A. Gibbons, Soren Giversen, Charles W. Hedrick, Wesley W. Isenberg, T. O. Lambdin, Bentley Layton, Violet MacDermot, George W. MacRae, Dieter Mueller, William R. Murdock, Douglas M. Parrott, Birger A. Pearson, Malcolm L. Pell, James M. Robinson, William C. Robinson, Jr., William R. Schoedel, J. C. Shelton, John H. Sieber, John D. Turner, Francis E. Williams, R. McL. Wilson, Orval S. Wintermute, Frederik Wisse, and Jan Zandee.

The project was initiated in 1966 with only a limited number of tractates accessible, but rapidly developed as the texts became increasingly available. It was first planned that Birger A. Pearson would be volume editor for a volume containing Codices VIII and IX. It was at this stage that preliminary announcements were made in *New Testament Studies* 16 (1969/70), 185-90, and *Novum Testamentum* 12 (1970), 83-85, reprinted in *Essays on the Coptic Gnostic Library* (Leiden: Brill, 1970). But then a decision to exclude Codex X from the last volume, planned originally to include Codices X-XIII, led to the decision to publish Codices IX and X together under the editorship of Pearson and Codex VIII separately. Originally Bentley Layton took over the role of volume editor for Codex VIII, in which capacity he made valuable contributions to the reconstruction of the page sequence and provided the definitive transcription. Then the volume editorship was assumed for a time by Charles W. Hedrick, who then turned it over to John H. Sieber.

After it was decided to include in Nag Hammadi Studies a new English edition of the other Coptic gnostic codices known previously, the Askew and Bruce Codices, the publisher included them in the Coptic Gnostic Library to make it complete.

The volumes and the editors of the Coptic Gnostic Library are as follows: *Nag Hammadi Codex I (The Jung Codex)*, Volume 1: *Introduction, Texts and Translation*; Volume 2: *Notes*, volume editor Harold W. Attridge, NHS 22 and 23, 1985; *Nag Hammadi Codices II,1 and IV,1: The Apocryphon of John, Long Recension*, edited by Frederik Wisse, NHS 32, in preparation; *Nag Hammadi Codex II,2-7, together with XIII,2*, Brit. Lib. Or. 4926 (I), and P. Oxy. 1,654,655*, Volume I: *Gospel According to Thomas, Gospel According to Philip, Hypostasis of the Archons, and Indexes*; Volume 2: *On the Origin of the World, Expository Treatise On the Soul, Book of Thomas the Contender*, edited by Bentley Layton, NHS 20 and 21, 1989; *Nag Hammadi Codex III,1 and Papyrus Berolinensis 8502,2: The Apocryphon of John, Short Recension*, edited by Peter Nagel, NHS 33, in preparation; *Nag Hammadi Codices III,2 and IV,2: The Gospel of the Egyptians (The Holy Book of the Great Invisible Spirit)*, edited by Alexander Bohlig and Frederik Wisse in cooperation with Pahor Labib, NHS 4, 1975; *Nag Hammadi Codices III,3-4 and V,1 with Papyrus Berolinensis 8502,3 and Oxyrhynchus Papyrus 1081: Eugnostos and The Sophia of Jesus Christ*, edited and translated by Douglas M. Parrott, NHS 27, in the press; *Nag Hammadi Codex III,5: The Dialogue of the Savior*, volume editor Stephen Emmel, NHS 26, 1984; *Nag Hammadi Codices V,2-5 and VI with Papyrus Berolinensis 8502,1 and 4*, volume editor Douglas M. Parrott, NHS 11, 1979; *Nag Hammadi Codex VII*, volume editor Birger A. Pearson, NHS 30, in preparation; *Nag Hammadi Codex VIII*, volume editor John H. Sieber, NHS 31, 1991; *Nag Hammadi Codices IX and X*, volume editor Birger A Pearson, NHS 15, 1981; *Nag Hammadi Codices XI, XII and XIII*, volume editor Charles W. Hedrick, NHS 28, 1990; *Nag Hammadi Codices: Greek and Coptic Papyri from the Cartonnage of the Covers*, edited by J. W. B. Barns, G. M. Browne, and J. C. Shelton, NHS 16, 1981; *Pistis Sophia*, text edited by Carl Schmidt, translation and notes by Violet Mac Dermot, volume editor R. McL. Wilson, NHS 9, 1978; *The Books of Jehu and the Untitled Text in the Bruce Codex*, text edited by Carl Schmidt, translation and notes by Violet VacDermot, volume editor R. McL. Wilson, NHS 13, 1978. Thus, as now envisaged, the full scope of the edition is seventeen volumes.

An English translation of all 13 Nag Hammadi Codices and P. Berol. 8502 has also been published in 1977 in a single volume, *The Nag*

Hammadi Library in English, by E. J. Brill and Harper & Row. A first paperback edition of that preprint augmented by the inclusion of Yale inv. 1784 of the Beinecke Library at NHC III 145/146 (p. 238) appeared in 1981 at Harper and Row and in 1984 at E. J. Brill. It was not possible to include there subsequent improvements in translations. A third, completely revised edition appeared in 1988 at E. J. Brill and Harper and Row. The translation appearing in the present volume is the substantially revised translation used in the third edition.

The team research of the project has been supported primarily through the Institute for Antiquity and Christianity by the National Endowment for the Humanities, the American Philosophical Society, the John Simon Guggenheim Memorial Foundation, and Claremont Graduate School; and through the American Research Center in Egypt by the Smithsonian Institution. Members of the project have participated in the preparatory work of the Technical Sub-Committee of the International Committtee for the Nag Hammadi Codices, which has been done at the Coptic Museum in Cairo under the sponsorship of the Arab Republic of Egypt and UNESCO. The extensive work on the reassembly of fragments, the reconstruction of page sequence, and the collation of the transcriptions by the originals not only served the immediate needs of the facsimile edition, but also provided a basis for a critical edition. Without such generous support and such mutual cooperation of all parties concerned this edition could not have been prepared. Therefore we wish to express our sincere gratitude to alll who have been involved.

A special word of thanks is due to the Egyptian and UNESCO officials through whose assistance the work has been carried on: Gamal Mokhtar, President until 1977 of the Egyptian Antiquities Organization and our gracious and able host in Egypt; Pahor Labib, Victor Girgis, Mounir Basta, Directors Emeriti, and Dr. Gawdat Gabra, currently Director of the Coptic Museum, who together have guided the work on the manuscript material; Samiha Abd El-Shaheed, First Curator for Manuscripts at the Coptic Museum, who is personally responsible for the codices and was constantly by our side in the library of the Coptic Museum; and, at UNESCO, N. Bammate, Deputy Assistant Director General for the Social Sciences, Human Sciences, and Culture until 1978, who has guided the UNESCO planning since its beginning, and Dina Zeidan, specialist in the Arab Program of the Division of Cultural Studies, who has always proved ready with gracious assistance and helpful advice.

We also wish to acknowledge our great indebtedness to the administration of Brill during the years in which this volume was in preparation, F. C. Wieder, Jr., Director Emeritus, the late T. A. Edridge, Dr. W.

Backhuys, Director Emeritus, and Drs. M. G. Elisabeth Venekamp, Vice-President, who is in charge of Nag Hammadi Studies for Brill.

James M. Robinson

PREFACE

This volume has been produced through the cooperative efforts of many people. James M. Robinson guided the project and wrote the foreword. Bentley Layton produced the Codex introduction, the transcription of the text, and the notes for *Zostrianos*. I prepared the introduction, translation, and commentary notes for *Zostrianos*. Both sets of notes to *Zostrianos* have been combined with Layton's textual notes usually given as the first part of common entries. Since both Layton and I reviewed each other's work extensively, the finished product is in a real sense the work of both of us. We wish to thank the many others who provided assistance and advice over the years, especially Stephen Emmel, Charles W. Hedrick, Malcolm Peel, Birger Pearson, and Fredrik Wisse. For the *Letter of Peter to Philip* Frederik Wisse produced the transcription of the text, its notes, and translation; Marvin W. Meyer prepared the introduction and the commentary notes. Preliminary editorial work was done by Charles W. Hedrick, and the initial word indices were prepared by David Embree. I have done the final editing of all the materials and have guided the production of the camera-ready copy.

This project was supported by many institutions. Much of the work of the contributors on the original manuscript of Codex VIII was carried out under the auspices of the Technical Subcommittee for the Publication of the Nag Hammadi Codices of UNESCO and the Egyptian Antiquities Organization of the Arab Republic of Egypt. The sponsor of the project was the Institute for Antiquity and Christianity of the Claremont Graduate School. Financial support for the editor over the years has come from the National Endowment for the Humanities, the Society of Biblical Literature, the American Theosophical Society, the American Council of Learned Societies, and Luther College.

The camera-ready copy for this volume was prepared using Macintosh computers at Luther College, Decorah, Iowa. The editor thanks the many people in Luther's computer center and publications office who supported and contributed to the project, with special thanks to Dale Nimrod, Steve Demuth, and Debra Shook for their technical assistance, and to Greg Vanney, Publications Director. Heather Bronner of publications did a marvelous job in setting the pages, copyediting the final draft and producing the postscript version of the Coptic font; without her dedication and skills this volume might never have appeared at all and would have been much poorer in any case. The initial files were prepared using Microsoft Word; Pagemaker was used to compose the pages. The English font is Palatino; the Greek font is SuperGreek from Linguists

Software; the Coptic is a postscript font based in part on the Nag
Hammadi bitmap font from Linguists.

Finally, I want to thank my wife Katrinka and our children Anne
and Hans for their patience and their support during the many years of
this project. To them this volume, which they thought would never be
finished, is dedicated.

John H. Sieber
Luther College
May 31, 1991

TABLE OF TRACTATES IN THE
COPTIC GNOSTIC LIBRARY

The following table lists, for the thirteen Nag Hammadi Codices and Papyrus Berolinensis 8502, the codex and tractate numbers, the tractate titles as used in this edition (the titles found in the tractates themselves, sometimes simplified and standardized, or, when the tractate bears no surviving title, one supplied by the editors), and the abbreviations of these titles. The abbreviations in parentheses are used only in this volume, for the sake of brevity.

I,*1*	*The Prayer of the Apostle Paul*	*Pr. Paul*
I,*2*	*The Apocryphon of James*	*Ap. Jas.*
I,*3*	*The Gospel of Truth*	*Gos. Truth*
I,*4*	*The Treatise on the Resurrection*	*Treat. Res.*
I,*5*	*The Tripartite Tractate*	*Tri. Trac.*
II,*1*	*The Apocryphon of John*	*Ap. John*
II,*2*	*The Gospel of Thomas*	*Gos. Thom.*
II,*3*	*The Gospel of Philip*	*Gos. Phil.*
II,*4*	*The Hypostasis of the Archons*	*Hyp. Arch.*
II,*5*	*On the Origin of the World*	*Orig. World*
II,*6*	*The Exegesis on the Soul*	*Exeg. Soul*
II,*7*	*The Book of Thomas the Contender*	*Thom. Cont.*
III,*1*	*The Apocryphon of John*	*Ap. John*
III,*2*	*The Gospel of the Egyptians*	*Gos. Eg.*
III,*3*	*Eugnostos the Blessed*	*Eugnostos (Eug)*
III,*4*	*The Sophia of Jesus Christ*	*Soph. Jes. Chr. (SJC)*
III,*5*	*The Dialogue of the Savior*	*Dial. Sav.*
IV,*1*	*The Apocryphon of John*	*Ap. John*
IV,*2*	*The Gospel of the Egyptians*	*Gos. Eg.*
V,*1*	*Eugnostos the Blessed*	*Eugnostos (Eug)*
V,*2*	*The Apocalypse of Paul*	*Apoc. Paul*
V,*3*	*The (First) Apocalypse of James*	*1 Apoc. Jas.*
V,*4*	*The (Second) Apocalypse of James*	*2 Apoc. Jas.*
V,*5*	*The Apocalypse of Adam*	*Apoc. Adam*
VI,*1*	*The Acts of Peter and the Twelve Apostles*	*Acts Pet. 12 Apost.*
VI,*2*	*The Thunder: Perfect Mind*	*Thund.*
VI,*3*	*Authoritative Teaching*	*Auth. Teach.*
VI,*4*	*The Concept of our Great Power*	*Great Pow.*
VI,*5*	*Plato, Republic 588b–589b*	*Plato Rep.*
VI,*6*	*The Discourse on the Eighth and Ninth*	*Disc. 8–9*
VI,*7*	*The Prayer of Thanksgiving*	*Pr. Thanks.*
VI,*8*	*Asclepius 21–29*	*Asclepius*
VII,*1*	*The Paraphrase of Shem*	*Paraph. Shem*
VII,*2*	*The Second Treatise of the Great Seth*	*Treat. Seth*
VII,*3*	*Apocalypse of Peter*	*Apoc. Pet.*
VII,*4*	*The Teachings of Silvanus*	*Teach. Silv.*

VII,5	*The Three Steles of Seth*	*Steles Seth*
VIII,1	*Zostrianos*	*Zost.*
VIII,2	*The Letter of Peter to Philip*	*Ep. Pet. Phil.*
IX,1	*Melchizedek*	*Melch.*
IX,2	*The Thought of Norea*	*Norea*
IX,3	*The Testimony of Truth*	*Testim. Truth*
X	*Marsanes*	*Marsanes*
XI,1	*The Interpretation of Knowledge*	*Interp. Know.*
XI,2	*A Valentinian Exposition*	*Val. Exp.*
XI,2a	*On the Anointing*	*On Anoint.*
XI,2b	*On Baptism A*	*On Bap. A*
XI,2c	*On Baptism B*	*On Bap. B*
XI,2d	*On the Eucharist A*	*On Euch. A*
XI,2e	*On the Eucharist B*	*On Euch. B*
XI,3	*Allogenes*	*Allogenes*
XI,4	*Hypsiphrone*	*Hypsiph.*
XII,1	*The Sentences of Sextus*	*Sent. Sextus*
XII,2	*The Gospel of Truth*	*Gos. Truth*
XII,3	*Fragments*	*Frm.*
XIII,1	*Trimorphic Protennoia*	*Trim. Prot.*
XIII,2	*On the Origin of the World*	*Orig. World*
BG,1	*The Gospel of Mary*	*Gos. Mary*
BG,2	*The Apocryphon of John*	*Ap. John*
BG,3	*The Sophia of Jesus Christ*	*Soph. Jes. Chr. (SJC)*
BG,4	*The Act of Peter*	*Act Pet.*

ABBREVIATIONS AND SHORT TITLES

1. Abbreviations of Biblical and Related Works

a. Old Testament

Deut	Deuteronomy	Num	Numbers
Gen	Genesis	Ps	Psalms

b. New Testament

1 Cor	1 Corinthians	2 Pet	2 Pete
2 Cor	2 Corinthians	Rev	Revelation
Eph	Ephesians	Rom	Romans
Heb	Hebrews	1 Thess	1 Thessalonians
Matt	Matthew	2 Thess	2 Thessalonians
Phil	Philippians	1 Tim	1 Timothy
1 Pet	1 Peter		

c. Apocrypha and Pseudepigrapha

Adam and Eve	The Books of Adam and Eve
Apoc. Seth	The Apocalypse of Seth
Barn	The Epistle of Barnabas
Ep. Apost.	Epitula Apostolorum
Gos. Eb.	Gospel of the Ebionites
Wis	The Wisdom of Solomon

2. Other Works

Aland, *Gnosis*

Aland, B., ed. *Gnosis: Festschrift für Hans Jonas.* Göttingen: Vandenhoeck & Ruprecht, 1978.

Anderson, "2 Enoch"

Anderson, F., "2 (Slavonic Apocalypse of) Enoch," in Charlesworthy, *Pseudepigrapha*, 1, 91-100.

Angus, *Mystery-Religions and Chrisitantiy*

Angus, S. *The Mystery-Religions and Christianity*. The University Library of Comparative Religion.

New Hyde Park, New York: University Books, 1966.

Armstrong, *Cambridge History*

Armstrong, A.H., ed. *The Cambridge History of Later Greek and Early Medieval Philosophy*. Cambridge: University Press, 1967.

Armstrong, "Gnosis and Greek Philosophy"

Armstrong, A.H. "Gnosis and Greek Philosophy," in Aland, *Gnosis*, 7-124.

Arnobius

Arnobius of Sicca, *The Case Against the Pagans*.

BAG2

Bauer, W., Arndt, W.F. and Gingrich, F.W. *Greek-English Lexicon of the New Testament. Second Edition*. Chicago: University of Chicago Press, 19.

Barns-Browne-Shelton, *Nag Hammadi Codices: Cartonnage*

Barns, J.W.B., Brown, G.M. and Shelton, J.C., eds. *Nag Hammadi Codices. Greek and Coptic Papyri from the Cartonnage of the Covers*. NHS 16. Leiden: E.J. Brill, 1981.

BASP

Bulletin of the American Society of Papyrologists.

Baynes, *Coptic Gnostic Treatise*

Baynes, C.A. *A Coptic Gnostic Treatise Contained in the Codex Brucianus (Bruce MS 96, Bod. Lib. Oxford): A Translation from the Coptic; Transcription and Commentary*. Cambridge: University Press, 1933.

BCNH

Bibliothèque copte de Nag Hammadi.

Berliner Arbeitskreis, "Die Bedeutung"

Berliner Arbeitskreis für Koptische-gnostische Schriften, "Die Bedeutung der Texte von Nag

Hammadi für die Moderne Gnosisforschung," in K.-W. Tröger, ed. *Gnosis und Neues Testament. Studien aus Religionswissenschaft und Theologie.* Berlin: Evangelische Verlagsanstalt, 1973, 13-76.

Bethge, "Der sogennante Brief"

Bethge, H.-G. "Der sogennante 'Brief des Petrus and Philippus': Die zweite 'Schrift' aus Nag-Hammadi-Codex VIII, eingeleitet und übersetzt vom Berliner Arbeitskreis für koptisch-gnostische Schriften," *ThLz* 103 (1978), 161-70.

Bethge, "Der Brief des Petrus an Philippus"

Bethge, H. G. "'Der Brief des Petrus an Philippus': Ein neutestamentliches Apokryphon aus dem Fund von Nag Hammadi (NHC VIII, 2)," Unpublished doctoral dissertation, Humboldt Universität, Berlin, 1984.

Bianchi, *Le origini dello gnosticismo*

Bianchi, U. *Le origini dello gnosticismo: Colloquio di Messina 13-18 Aprile 1966. Testi e discussioni.* (Supplements to *Numen* 12.) Leiden: Brill, 1967.

Bidez-Cumont, *Zoroastre, Ostanès et Hystaspe*

Bidez, J. and Cumont, F. *Les mages hellénisés. Zoroastre, Ostanès et Hystaspe d'après la tradition grecque.* 2 volumes. Paris: Société d'Éditions "Les Belles Lettres," 1938.

Böhlig-Wisse, *Gospel of the Egyptians*

Böhlig, A. and Wisse, F., eds. *Nag Hammadi Codices III, 2 and IV, 2. The Gospel of the Egyptians (The*

	Holy Book of the Great Invisible Spirit). NHS 4. Leiden: E.J. Brill, 1975.
Bousset, *Kyrios Christos*	Bousset, W. *Kyrios Christos. A History of the Belief in Christ from the Beginnings of Christianity to Irenaeus.* Translated by J.E. Steely. Nashville/New York: Abingdon, 1970 (German 1913).
Bultmann, "ἐλπίς"	Bultmann, R. "ἐλπίς," s.v., *TDNT*, vol. 2.
Charlesworthy, *Pseudepigrapha*	Charlesworthy, J. ed., *Pseudepigrapha: Volume 1, Apocalyptic Literature and Testaments.* Garden City: Doubleday & Company, 1983.
Clem., *Strom.*	Clement of Alexandria. *Stromata.*
Collins, *Apocalypse*	Collins, J., ed. *Apocalypse: The Morphology of a Genre. Semeia* 14. Missoula, MT: Society of Biblical Literature, 1979)
Collins, "Morphology"	Collins, J. "Introduction: Towards the Morphology of a Genre." in Collins, *Apocalypse,* 1-20.
Colpe, "Heidnische, jüdische und christliche Überlieferung VI"	Colpe, C. "Heidnische, jüdische und christliche Überlieferung in der Schriften aus Nag Hammadi VI," *JAC* 20 (1977), 149-70.
Crum	Crum, W.E. *A Coptic Dictionary.* Oxford: Clarendon, 1939.
Davidson, *Angels*	Davidson, G.A. *Dictionary of Angels: Including the Fallen Angels.* N.Y.: Free Press, 1967.

Dillon, *Middle Platonists*

Dillon, J. *The Middle Platonists: 80 B.C. to A.D. 200.* Ithaca: Cornell University Press, 1977.

Dillon, "Pleroma and Noetic Cosmos"

Dillon, J. "Pleroma and Noetic Cosmos." in Wallis, *Neoplatonism and Gnosticism.*

Dodds, *Les Sources de Plotin*

Dodds, E.R., ed. *Les Sources de Plotin. Dix exposés et discussions par E.R. Dodds [et al.] Vandoeuvres-Genève 21-29 août 1959.* Entretiens sur l'antiquité classique 5. Genève: Fondation Hardt, 1960.

Dodds, "Numenius and Ammonius"

Dodds, E.R. "Numenius and Ammonius," in Dodds, *Les Sources de Plotin,* 3-61.

Dodds, *Pagan and Christian*

Dodds, E.R. *Pagan and Christian in an Age of Anxiety; Some Aspects of Religious Experience from Marcus Aurelius to Constantine.* Cambridge: University Press, 1965.

Dodds, *Proclus: Theology*

Dodds, E.R., ed. *Proclus: The Elements of Theology. A Revised Text with Translation, Introduction and Commentary.* 2nd ed. Oxford: Clarendon, 1963 (originally appeared 1933).

Doresse, "Les apocalypses de Zoroastre"

Doresse, J. "Les Apocalypses de Zoroastre, de Zostrien, de Nicothée... (Porphyre, *Vie de Plotin,* §16)," in Malinine, *Coptic Studies,* 255-263.

Doresse, *Les livres secrets,*

Doresse, J. *Les livres secrets des gnostiques d' Égypt.* 2 vols. Paris: Plon, 1958-59.

Emmel, "Photographic Evidence"

Emmel, S. "Unique Photograph Evidence for Nag Hammadi Texts: CG V-VIII," *BASP* 16 (1979), 179-191.

Epiph., *Pan.*

Epiphanius, *Panarion*.

Facsimile Edition

Robinson, J.M., et al. *The Facsimile Edition of the Nag Hammadi Codices.* Published under the auspices of the Department of Antiquities of the Arab Republic of Egypt in conjunction with UNESCO. 12 volumes. Leiden: Brill, 1972-84.

Essays

Essays on the Coptic Gnostic Library. Essays by George McRae, W. C. Robinson, Jr., W. R. Schoedel, Frederik Wisse and Malcom Peel. Leiden: Brill, 1970. (Offprint *NovT* XII,2.)

Fallon, "Gnostic Apocalypses"

Fallon, F. "The Gnostic Apocalypses," in Collins, *Apocalypse*, 123-158.

Foerster, Gnosis

Foester, W. Gnosis: *A Selection of Gnostic Texts*. Translated and edited by R. Mcl. Wilson. 2 vols. Oxford: Clarendon, 1972-74.

Hadot, "Etre, vie, pensée
   chez Plotin"

Hadot, P. "Etre, vie, pensée chez Plotin et avant Plotin," in Dodds, *Les Sources de Plotin,* 107-157.

Hadot, *Marius Victorinus*

Hadot, P. *Marius Victorinus: recherches sur sa vie et ses œuvres.* Paris: Études augustiniennes, 1971.

Hedrick, "Christian Motifs"

Hedrick, C.W. "Christian Motifs in the *Gospel of the Egyptians*:

Method and Motive," *NovT* 23(1981), 242-60.

Hedrick & Hodgson, *Nag Hammadi, Gnosticism*

Hedrick, C. & Hodgson, R. eds., *Nag Hammadi, Gnosticism, and Early Christianity*. Peabody, Mass.: Hendrickson Publishers, 1986.

Hengel, *Judaism and Hellenism*

Hengel, M. *Judaism and Hellenism*. Trans. J. Bowden from 2nd ed. Philadelphia: Fortress Press, 1974.

Henry-Hadot, *Claudius Marius Victor*

Henry, P. and Hadot, P., eds. *Claudius Marius Victor. Traités théologiques sur la Trinité*. Sources chrétienne 68-69. 2 volumes. Paris: Éditions du Cerf, 1960.

Henry-Schwyzer, *Plotinus: Opera*

Henry, P. and H.-R. Schwyzer, eds. *Plotinus: Opera*. 2 volumes. Paris: Desclée de Brouwer, 1951-59.

Hinz, "Zoroaster"

Hinz, W. "Zoroaster," *RAC*, 19A, cols. 774-84.

Hipp. *Ref.*

Hippolytus, *Refutatio*.

Ign., *Rom.*

Ignatius, *ad Romanos*.

Ign., Smyrn.

Ignatius, *ad Smyrnaeos*.

Iren. *Adv. Haer.*

Irenaeus, *Adversus Haereses*.

Jackson, *Zoroaster*

Jackson, A.V. *Zoroaster*. N.Y.: Columbia University Press, 1926.

JAC

Jahrbuch für Antike und Christentum.

JBL

Journal of Biblical Literature.

Jonas, "Delimitation of the Gnostic Phenomenon"

Jonas, H. "Delimitation of the Gnostic Phenomenon-Typological and Historical," in Bianchi, *Le origini dello gnosticismo*, 90-104.

Jonas, "Gnosticism and Modern Nihilism"

Jonas, H. "Gnosticism and Mod-Nihilism," *Social Research 19* (1952), 430-52.

Jonas, *Gnosis und spätantiker Geist*

Jonas, H. *Gnosis und spätantiker Geist*. 2 volumes. Göttingen: Vandenhoeck & Ruprecht, 1964-66.

Jonas, *Gnostic Religion*

Jonas, H. *The Gnostic Religion: The Message of the Alien God and the Beginnings of Christianity*. Boston: Beacon, 1963.

Klijin, *Seth*

Klijin, A.F.J., *Seth in Jewish, Christian and Gnostic Literature*. Leiden: Brill, 1977. (Supplements to *NovT*, XLVI.)

Koschorke, *Die Polemik der Gnostiker*

Koschorke, K. Die *Polemik der Gnostiker gegen das kirchliche Christentum: Unter besonderer Berücksichtigung der Nag-Hammadi-Traktate "Apokalypse des Petrus" (NHC VII,3) und "Testimonium Veritatis" (NHC IX,3)*. NHS 12. Leiden: E.J. Brill, 1978.

Koschorke, "Eine gnostische Paraphrase"

Koschorke, K. "Eine gnostische Paraphrase des johanneischen Prologs: Zur Interpretation von 'Epistula Petri ad Philippum' (NHC VIII,2) 136,16-137,4," *VC* 33 (1979), 383-92.

Koschorke, "Eine gnostische Pfingstpredigt"

Koschorke, K. "Eine gnostische Pfingstpredigt: Zur Auseinandersetzung zwischen gnostischem und kirchlichem Christentum am Beispeil der 'Epistula Petri ad Philippum' (NHC VIII,2)," *ZThK* 74 (1977), 323-43.

Krause-Labib, *Gnostische und hermetische Schriften*

Krause, M. and Labib, P. *Gnostische und hermetische Schriften aus Codex II und Codex VI.* Abhandlungen des Deutschen Archäologischen Instituts Kairo. Koptische Reihe 2. Glückstadt: J.J. Augustin, 1971 (appeared 1972).

Lampe, *Lexicon*

Lampe, G., ed. *A Patristic Greek Lexicon.* Oxford: Clarendon, 1961.

Layton, *Gnostic Scriptures*

Layton, B. *The Gnostic Scriptures: A New Translation with Annotations and Introductions.* New York, Doubleday, 1987.

Layton, *Rediscovery of Gnosticism*

Layton, B., ed. *The Rediscovery of Gnosticism: Proceedings of the International Conference on Gnosticism at Yale, New Haven, Connecticut, March 28-31, 1978.* Supplements to Numen 41. 2 volumes. Leiden: E.J. Brill, 1978-81.

Luttikhuizen, "The Letter of Peter to Philip"

Luttikhuizen, G.P. "The Letter of Peter to Philip and the New Testament," in Wilson, *Nag Hammadi and Gnosis*, 96-102.

Malinine, *Coptic Studies*

Malinine, M., ed. *Coptic Studies in Honor of Walter Ewing Crum.* Bulletin of the Byzantine Institute 2. Boston: The Byzantine Institute, 1950.

McCracken, *Arnobius of Sicca*

McCracken, G.E. *Arnobius of Sicca: The Case against the Pagans.* Ancient Christian Writers 7-8. 2 volumes. Westminster, Maryland: Newman, 1949.

Ménard, *La Lettre de Pierre à Philippe*

Ménard, J.-É. *La Lettre de Pierre à Philippe. BCNH,* Section "Textes," 1. Quebec: Les presses de l'Université Laval, 1977.

Ménard, "La Lettre de Pierre à Philippe"

Ménard, J.-É. "La Lettre de Pierre à Philippe," in Aland, *Gnosis,* 449-463.

Ménard, "Pierre à Philippe: sa structure"

Ménard, J.-É. "La Lettre de Pierre à Philippe: sa structure," in Wilson, *Nag Hammadi and Gnosis,* 103-7.

Meyer, *The Letter of Peter to Philip*

Meyer, M.W. *The Letter of Peter to Philip: Text, Translation, and Commentary.* SBLDS 53. Chico: Scholars Press, 1981.

Meyer, "The Light and Voice on the Damascus Road"

Meyer, M. W. "The Light and Voice on the Damascus Road," *Foundations and Facets Forum* 2 (1986), 27-35.

NHLE

Robinson, J.M., gen. ed., *The Nag Hammadi Library in English.* Translated by Members of the Coptic Gnostic Library Project of the Institute for Antiquity and Christianity. San Francisco/Cambridge/Hagerstown/Philadelphia/New York/London/Mexico City/Sao Paulo/Sydney: Harper and Row, 1977.

NHS

Nickelsburg, "Traditions in the Apocalypse of Adam"

Nag Hammadi Studies.

Nickelsburg, G.W.E. "Some Related Traditions in the Apocalypse of Adam. The Books of Adam and Eve, and I Enoch." in Layton, *Rediscovery of Gnosticism,* 2, 515-539.

NovT

Novum Testamentum.

PL

Patrologia Latina.

Pagels, "Visions, Appearances and Apostolic Authority"

Pagels, E. "Visions, Appearances and Apostolic Authority: Gnostic and Orthodox Traditions," in Aland, *Gnosis,* 415-430.

Parrott, "Gnostic and Orthodox Disciples"

Parrott, D.M. "Gnostic and Orthodox Disciples in the Second and Third Centuries," in Hedrick-Hodgson, *Nag Hammadi, Gnosticism,* 193-219.

Pearson, "Biblical Exegesis"

Pearson, B. "Biblical Exegesis in Gnostic Literature." in H. Stone, ed., *Armenian and Biblical Studies* (*Sion,* Supplement 1). Jerusalem: Armenian Patriarchate, 1976, 70-80.

Pearson, "Marsanes"

Pearson, B. "Marsanes," in B. Pearson, ed. *Nag Hammadi Codices IX and X.* NHS 15. Leiden: Brill, 1981, 229-250.

Pearson, "The Tractate Marsanes"

Pearson, B. "The Tractate Marsanes (NHC X) and the Platonic Tradition," in Aland, *Gnosis,* 373-384.

Perkins, *Gnostic Diaolog*	Perkins, Pheme. *The Gnostic Dialog: The Early Church and the Crisis of Gnosticism*. New York: Paulist Press, 1980.
Plato, *Phaedo*	Plato, *Phaedo*.
Plato, *Phaedrus*	Plato, *Phaedrus*.
Plato, *Resp.*	Plato, *Respublica*.
Plato, *Symposium*	Plato, *Symposium*.
Plato, *Tim.*	Plato, *Timaeus*.
Plot. *Enn.*	Plotinus, *Enneads*.
Porph. *Vit. Plot.*	Porphyry, *Vita Plotini*.
Ps.-Clem.	Pseudo-Clement, *Epistula Petri*.
Ptolemy, *Letter to Flora*	Ptolemy, *Letter to Flora*.
Puech, *En quête de la gnose:I*	Puech, H.-Ch. *En quête de la gnose. Volume 1: La Gnose et le temps et autre essais*. Bibliothèque des Sciences Humaine. Paris: Gallimard, 1978.
Puech, "Les nouveaux écrits gnostiques"	Puech, H.-C. "Les nouveaux écrits gnostiques découverts en Haute-Égypte (premier inventaire et essai d'identification)," in Malinine, *Coptic Studies*, 91-154.
Puech, "Plotin et les gnostiques"	Puech, H.-Ch. "Plotin et les gnostiques," in Dodds, *Les Sources de Plotin*, 161-190.
RAC	Pauly-Wissowa, *Real-Encyclopädie der Classischen Altertumswissenschaft*, Neuerarbeitung.

RSPhTh

Revue des sciences philosophiques et
théologiques.

Robinson, "Codicology"

Robinson, J.M. "On the
Codicology of the Nag Hammadi
Codices," in J.-É. Ménard, ed. *Les
textes de Nag Hammadi: Colloque
du Centre d'Histoire des Religions
(Strasbourg, 23-25 Octobre 1974).*
NHS 7. Leiden: E.J. Brill, 1975, 15-
31.

Robinson, "Discovery"

Robinson, J.M. "The Discovery of
the Nag Hammadi Codices," *Biblical Archaeologist* 42(1979), 206-24.

Robinson, *Facsimile Edition:
Introduction*

Robinson, J. M. *The Facsimile
Edition of the Nag Hammadi Codices:
Introduction.* Leiden: E. J. Brill,
1984.

Robinson, "From the Cliff to
Cairo"

Robinson, J.M. "From the Cliff
to Cairo. The Story of the Discoverers and the Middlemen of the
Nag Hammadi Codices," in B.
Barc, ed. *Colloque international sur
les textes de Nag Hammadi (Québec,
22-25 août 1978).* Québec:
Université Laval, 1981, 21-58.

Robinson, "Three Steles of Seth"

Robinson, J.M. "The Three Steles
of Seth and the Gnostics of
Plotinus," in G. Widengren, ed.
*Proceedings of the International
Colloquium on Gnosticism:
Stockholm, August 20-25, 1973.*
Kungl. Vitterhets Historie och
Antikvitets Akademiens,
Handlingar, Filologisk-filosofiska
serien 17. Stockholm: Almqvist &
Wiksell; Leiden: E.J. Brill, 1977,
132-142.

Rudolf, *Gnosis*

Rudolf, K. *Gnosis: The Nature & History of Gnosticism.* Trans. and ed. by R. McLachan Wilson. San Francisco: Harper & Row, 1987.

SBLDS

Society of Biblical Literature Dissertation Series.

Schenke, "Das Sethianische System"

Schenke, H.-M. "Das Sethianische System nach Nag-Hammadi-Handschriften," in P.Nagel, ed. *Sturdia Coptica.* Berlin: Akademie, 1974, 165-173.

Schenke, "Gnostic Sethianism"

Schenke, H.-M. "The Phenomenon and Significance of Gnostic Sethianism," in Layton, *Rediscovery of Gnosticism*, 2, 588-616.

Schenke, "Middle Egyptian Dialect"

Schenke, H.-U. "On the Middle Egyptian Dialect of the Coptic Language," *Enchoria* 8 (1978), 43*(89)-(104)58*.

Schmidt, *Gnostische Schriften*

Schmidt, C., ed. *Gnostische Schriften in Koptischer Sprache aus dem Codex Brucianus.* TU 8. Leipzig: Hinrichs, 1892.

Schmidt, "Irenaeus und seine Quelle in adv. haer. I.29."

Schmidt, C. "Irenaeus und seine Quelle in adv. haer. I.29," in A. Harnack, H. Diels, K. Holl, P. Gennrich, and E. Kautzch, eds. *Philotesia. Paul Kleinert zum LXX. Geburtstag.* Berlin: Trowizsch, 1907, 315-336.

Schmidt-MacDermott, *Jehu and the Untitled Text*

Schmidt, C., ed. and MacDermott, V., trans. *The Books of Jeu and the Untitled Text in the Bruce Codex.* NHS 13. Leiden: E.J. Brill, 1978.

Schneemelcher, *Neutestamentliche Apokryphen*

Schneemelcher, W. ed. *Neutestamentliche Apokryphen in deutsche Übersetzung hersg. von Edgar Hennecke*. 3 vollig neuarb. Auflage hrsg. von Wilhelm Schneemelcher. Tübigen: Mohr (Siebeck), 1959-64.

Scholer, *Nag Hammadi Bibliography.*

Scholer, D.M. *Nag Hammadi Bibliography 1948-1969. NHS 1.* Leiden: E.J. Brill, 1971.

Schweizer, "Slaves of the Elements"

Schweizer, E. "Slaves of the Elements and Worshippers," *JBL* 107 (1988), 455-68.

Scopello, "Zostrianos and the Book of the Secrets of Enoch"

Scopello, M. "The Apocalypse of Zostrianos and the Book of the Secrets of Enoch," *VC* 34 (1980), 376-85.

Scopello, "Un rituel idéal d'intronisation"

Scopello, M. "Un rituel idéal d'intronisation dans trois textes gnostiques de Nag Hammadi," in R.Mcl.Wilson, *Nag Hammadi and Gnosis*, 91-95.

Sevrin, *Le dossier baptismal séthien*

Sevrin, J.-M. *Le dossier baptismal séthien: études sur la sacramentaire gnostique*. Bibliothèque copte de Nag Hammadi, Section "Études," no. 2. Quebec: Les Université Laval, 1986.

Sieber, "Barbelo Aeon as Sophia"

Sieber, J.H. "The Barbelo Aeon as Sophia in Zostrianos and Related Tractates," in Layton, *Rediscovery of Gnosticism*, 2, 788-795.

Sieber, "Introduction to Zostrianos"

Sieber, J.H. "An Introduction to the Tractate *Zostrianos from Nag Hammadi*," *NovT* 15(1973), 233-40.

Tardieu, "*Les Trois Stèles de Seth*"

Tardieu, M. "*Les Trois Stèles de Seth*: Un écrit gnostique retrouvé à Nag Hammadi," *RSPhTh* 57 (1973), 545-75.

TDNT

Theological Dictionary of the New Testament.

ThLZ

Theologische Literaturzeitung.

Thompson, *Acts*

Thompson, H.F.H. *The Coptic Version of the Acts of the Apostles and the Pauline Epistles, in the Sahidic Dialect.* Cambridge: University Press, 1932.

Tröger, "Doketistische Christologie in Nag-Hammadi-Texten"

Tröger, K.-W. "Doketistische Christologie in Nag-Hammadi-Texten: Ein Beitrag zum Doketismus in frühchristlicher Zeit," *Kairos* 19 (1977), 45-52.

TU

Texte und Untersuchungen zur Geschichte der altchristlichen Literatur.

Tuckett, *Nag Hammadi*

Tuckett, C.M. *Nag Hammadi and the Gospel Tradition: Synoptic Tradition in the Nag Hammadi Library.* Edinburgh: T. & T. Clark, 1986.

Turner, "Gnosticism and Platonism"

Turner, J. "Gnosticism and Platonism: The Platonizing Texts from Nag Hammadi in the relation to later Plaonic Literature," in Wallis, *Neoplatonism and Gnosticism.*

Turner, "Gnostic Threefold Path"

Turner, J.D. "The Gnostic Three fold Path to Enlightenment: The Ascent of Mind and the Descent of Wisdom," *NovT* 22 (1980), 324-51.

Turner, "Sethian Gnosticism"

Turner, J. "Sethian Gnosticism: A Literary History," in Hedrick & Hodgson, *Nag Hammadi, Gnosticism*, 55-86.

VC

Vigiliae Christianae.

Wallis, *Neoplatonism and Gnosticism*

Wallis, R. T., ed. *Neoplatonism and Gnosticism*. Studies in Neoplatonism: Ancient and Modern, 5, general ed. R. Baine Harris. Stoneybrook, N.Y.: SUNY Press, in press.

Wallis, "Numenius and Gnosticism"

Wallis, R. T. "Numenius and Gnosticism," in Wallis, *Neoplatonism and Gnosticism*.

Widengren, *Gnostic Attitude*

Widengren, G. *The Gnostic Attitude*. Translated and edited by B. Pearson. Santa Barbara: Institute of Religious Studies, University of California, 1973.

Widengren, "Les origines du gnosticisme"

Widengren, G. "Les origines du gnosticisme et l'histoire des religions," in Bianchi, *Le origini dello gnosticismo*, 28-60.

Williams, *The Immovable Race*

Williams, M. A., *The Immovable Race*. Leiden: Brill, 1985.

Wilson, *Nag Hammadi and Gnosis*

Wilson, R. McL., ed. *Nag Hammadi and Gnosis: Papers Read at the First International Congress of Coptology* (Cairo, December 1976). NHS 14. Leiden: E.J. Brill, 1978.

Wire-Turner, "Allogenes"

Wire, A. and Turner, J. "Allogenes," in *Nag Hammadi Codices XI, XII, XIII*, 1990.

Wisse, "Letter of Peter to Philip"

Wisse, F. "The Letter of Peter to Philip (VIII,2)," in NHLE, 394-398.

Wisse, "Nag Hammadi and the Heresiologists"

Wisse, F. "The Hag Hammadi Library and the Heresiologists," VC 25(1971), 205-23.

Wisse, "Sethians and the Nag Hammadi Library"

Wisse, F. "The Sethians and the Nag Hammadi Library," in L.C. McGaughy, ed., The Society of Biblical Literature One Hundred Eighth Annual Meeting. Book of Seminar Papers. Friday-Tuesday, 1-5 September 1972 Century Plaza Hotel-Los Angeles, CA. 2 volumes. Missoula, Mont.: Society of Biblical Literature, 1972, 2, 601-607.

Wisse, "Stalking Those Elusive Sethians"

Wisse, F. "Stalking Those Elusive Sethians," in Layton, Rediscovery of Gnosticism, 2, 563-576.

Wisse-Meyer, "The Letter of Peter to Philip"

Wisse, F. and Meyer, M. W. "The Letter of Peter to Philip," in The Nag Hammadi Library in English, ed. J. M. Robinson. 2nd ed. Leiden: Brill; San Francisco, Harper & Row.

Zaehner, Zurvan

Zaehner, R.C., Zurvan: A Zoroastrian Dilemma. Oxford: Clarendon, 1935.

Zandee, Terminology of Plotinus

Zandee, J. The Terminology of Plotinus and of Some Gnostic Writings, Mainly the Fourth Treatise of the Jung Codex. Vitgaven van het Nederlands Historisch-Archaeologisch Institute te Istanbul II. Nederlands Historisch-Archaeologisch Institut in het Nabije Oosten, 1961.

| Ziegler, "Zostrianos" | Ziegler, K. "Zostrianos," in *RAC*, 19A, col. 853. |
| ZThK | *Zeitschrift für Theologie und Kirche.* |

3. Other Abbreviations

A	Codex VIII in its original leaf sequence.
BG	Papyrus Berolinensis Gnosticus
Bo.	Boharic
Cf./cf.	compare
col(s).	column(s)
cod.	codex
esp.	especially
passim	many places
ca.	*circa*
fem.	feminine
inv.	inventory
κτλ.	and the rest
Lit./lit.	literally
Ms.	manuscript
n(n).	note(s)
NT	New Testament
p(p).	page(s)
pl.	plate(s)
par.	parallel
s.v.	*sub verbo*
Sah.	Sahidic
seq.	and the following
sic	just as the original
viz.	videlicet, namely
vs.	versus, against

SIGLA

[ ] or [	lacuna in manuscript
[ ]	lacuna of unspecified length
ddd[	lacuna of unspecified length after
[. . .]	lacuna long enough to suit d *standard* letters (N being the standard) and 3 interliteral spaces; [. . . .], 4 letters; and 4 spaces etc.
ddd[. . .],	lacuna of 3´ standard letters
ddd[. . .	at least 4 (or 3´) standard letters at the end of a damaged line
[[. . .]]	text deleted or canceled by scribe
. . .	traces of 3 unidentified letters
ḁḁḁ	palaeographically ambiguous letter traces
<u>v</u>	*vacat*; blank space for 1 standard letter (N) and 1 interliteral space in the manuscript; for 2 letters and 2 spaces; etc.
<ddd>	Text *added* by modern editor; a conjecture
{ddd}	Text *deleted* by modern editor; a conjecture
CO(N)	Resolution of an abbreviation in the manuscript, i.e.
–	Hyphen at the end of line indicates that the immediately preceding letter(s) form(s) a unit with the immediately following letter(s).

CODEX VIII

INTRODUCTION TO CODEX VIII

<small>PHYSICAL DESCRIPTION</small>

Nag Hammadi Codex VIII (CG VIII, NHC VIII). Cairo, Coptic Museum, Department of Manuscripts, inv. 10550. Formerly the manuscript was numbered Codex VII by Doresse-Mina, IX by Puech, and IV by Doresse, *Les Livres secrets* (see Robinson, *Facsimile Edition: Codex VIII*, pp. vii and ix). Papyrus codex, very imperfect. Original folios were 242 mm high by 147 mm wide. Prior to conservation many leaves or leaf fragments of the codex were in several pieces; these have now been repaired. The text block was attached to its ancient binding (or in loose fragments) until 1961; now it has been completely disbound, and the quire sheets (cut apart into leaves in 1961, but then rejoined between 1970-76) are conserved in plexiglas frames, numbered by the ancient codex page numbers. The ancient binding is conserved separately (inv. 10550). One hundred twenty-six fragments of cartonnage have been removed from the binding and are also conserved separately (see *Facsimile Edition: Cartonnage*, 59-70; Barns-Browne-Shelton, *Nag Hammadi Codices: Cartonnage*, 87-102, transcribing 43 fragments; 83 other fragments were too small to be transcribed). Originally the text block (in a single quire) consisted of 74 leaves of which two were flyleaves, two were stubs, and two formed a blank protective bifolium at the center of the quire; of these, 70 leaves (many imperfect) have survived of which two are flyleaves, one a stub, one a blank protective leaf at the center; together with 119 unidentified fragments, mostly very small. Traces of ancient pagination appear in the head fore-edge corners: [ⲁ̄]-[ⲍ̄ⲏ̄], (one leaf wanting), [ⲟ̄ⲁ̄] (blank)-[ⲣ̄ⲏ̄], (two leaves wanting), [ⲣ̄ⲓ̄ⲧ̄]-[ⲣ̄ⲙ̄]; the pagination included the two blank leaves at the center of the quire, but not the flyleaves or stubs. The text block has been ruined by insects, rotting, and at the fold by the corrosive influence of the leather binding; leaves occasionally show offset (leaving traces useful for restoration of lost text), stains, or rubbing. In general, less papyrus survives near the fold than at the fore-edge, and the ruin is most complete about half way through the text. According to all indications the manuscript was already in this ruinous state when it was discovered in 1945 (see *Facsimile Edition: Codex VIII*, pl. 3-6). Various small parts of the leaves that have been lost or have deteriorated since about 1949 are still attested in early photographic records; this evidence was incorporated into the *Facsimile Edition: Codex VIII* and has been collated by Emmel, "Photographic Evidence." On the structure of the manuscript see also Robinson, "Codicology," and *Facsimile Edition: Introduction*, 32-70.

CONTENTS

The codex contains an untitled miscellany comprising two works, one non-Christian and the other Christian, in a Sahidic (Crypto-Bohairic) Coptic version. The spelling and morphology of the text usually correspond to classical Sahidic practice (e.g., that of the Chester Beatty *Acts* edited by H. Thompson), but the syntax and to a lesser degree the lexicon are often non-Sahidic, coinciding with Bohairic.

1. (p. 1) Ζωστριάνος· Λόγοι ἀληθείας Ζωστριάνου· θεός (sic) ἀληθείας· Λόγοι Ζωροάστρου] "Zostrianos: Oracles of Truth of Zostrianos—God of Truth—Oracles [of] Zoroaster" (132,6-9). The state of preservation is very poor. Pages 71-72 are blank. Ends p. 132.

2. (p. 132) ΤΕΠΙСΤΟΛΗ ΜΠΕΤΡΟС ΕΤΑЧϪΟΟЧС ΜΦΙΛΙΠΠΟС "The Epistle of Peter that He Sent to Philip" (132,10-11). The text is mostly complete. It may be an excerpt from a larger work, preceded by a caption. Ends p. 140.

Secondary literature on these texts is listed exhaustively by Scholer, *Nag Hammadi Bibliography*, with annual supplements.

There is no colophon. A few corrections have been made by the original copyist (cf. 7,14; 30,20; 118,5); there are no other annotations. The provenance of the codex is unknown; it was discovered near Hamra Dom opposite Nag Hammadi, Egypt. It is dated to the fourth century C.E. by its association with the other Nag Hammadi manuscripts, and possibly not earlier than the early or middle part of that century on the basis of cartonnage removed from the ancient binding (see Shelton [with hesitation] in Barns-Browne-Shelton, *Nag Hammadi Codices: Cartonnage*, 88).

FORMAT

Collation: (A)[74] a single quire codex (A17 [stub], A37 [blank protective leaf], A57-58 wanting; including front flyleaf, pp. 1-30, 31-68, 71-108, 113-140, back flyleaf. A17 and A67 were stubs conjungate with A58 and A8 respectively. A1 (flyleaf), A17 (stub), A37-38 (protective leaves at center fold), A67 (stub), A74 (flyleaf) were blank. There were no catchwords or headlines.

Papyrus: Two of the rolls from which the codex was constructed are of a papyrus that was relatively thin and therefore of fine quality; two other rolls (Nos. 3-4, used to copy the middle of the text) were relatively thick and opaque (on the relation of the stationer's stock rolls to the structure of the text block, see Robinson in *Facsimile Edition: Codex VIII*, pp. xv, xvii). The fiber directions of the leaves is A1-37 ↓/→ , A38-74 →/↓. The bottom of A9 (pp. 15-16) was patched in antiquity.

Script (cf. *Facsimile Edition: Codex VIII;* Krause-Labib, *Gnostische und hermetische Schriften,* pl. 11): Letters are upright or slightly left-sloping, thick-and-thin style, with 3-stroke Ϻ, round Є Ϲ, narrow Ο (pinched and sloping from upper left to lower right), tall ⲣ ϥ, short (and, at end of line, occasionally tall) ⲧ, and two forms of Ϭ. Ligature is used. The height and compactness of the script varies from passage to passage. 10 lines = ca. 77 mm. Black ink was used throughout.

Major sections of text are set off by paragraphus signs (forked or straight), coordinated with dicola written in the text. Connective *(Bindestrich)* superlineation is used, often curved or terminating in knobs. Noteworthy peculiarities are the stroke connecting Єⲓ in the word "come" and ⲟⲓ in ⲟⲓⲧⲛ, ⲟⲓⲋⲁⲛ, ⲟⲓ H, and ⲟⲓⲛⲁ. Proper names and compendia are marked by a continuous superlinear stroke. Only the strokes above proper names are printed in this edition.

Morpheme dividers are attached to ⲡ and ⲧ, giving ⲡ̇ and ⲧ̇. Letters ⲁ and Є are often ornamentally extended at end of line. Rhetorical punctuation (distinction of cola) is marked by a half-raised point (·). ï is common. The usual compendia for *nomina sacra* appear in the text; note also K̅Λ̅C̅ = καλυπτός, X̅P̅C̅ = χρηστός. One also finds ⲏ (Greek conjunction) with a smooth breathing mark above it, sometimes resembling the letter "Y" rotated 90 degrees to the left. At end of lines final letters or penultimate *omicron* are on rare occasion written small, and final vowels plus ⲛ are optionally abbreviated; $-\overline{ⲁ}$ (11,9) and $-ⲟ\overline{ⲧ}$ (79,17) being attested. Titles (p. 132) are set off by ornamental horizontal rules and diple signs. Each tractate concludes with a dicolon and diple or diple obelisme signs. The long title of Tractate 1 is written in a Greek numerical cipher (see commentary on 132,7-9). No colors or other decorations are used.

Layout: The written area averages ca. 206 x 112 mm (but with considerable variation) and is in a single column of 22-32 lines. There are no initials or ekthesis. The left margin is often irregular. Lines are often not straight, and only rarely are perpendicular to the left margin.

HISTORY

On the history of the manuscript, see Robinson, "Discovery" and "From the Cliff to Cairo."

ZOSTRIANOS (NHC VIII,*1*)
INTRODUCTION

Doresse, "Les apocalypses de Zoroastre"; Layton, *Gnostic Scriptures*; Pearson, "Marsanes"; Perkins, *Gnostic Dialog*; Puech, "Plotin et les gnostiques"; Robinson, "Three Steles of Seth"; Scopello, "Un rituel idéal d'intronisation"; Sevrin, *Le dossier baptismal séthien*; Sieber, "Barbelo Aeon as Sophia"; Sieber, "Introduction to Zostrianos"; Turner, "Gnostic Threefold Path"; Turner, "Sethian Gnosticism"; Williams, *The Immovable Race*, pp. 69-102.

The Contents of the Tractate

GENERAL INTRODUCTION

Zostrianos (NHC VIII,*1*) is the pseudonymous account of an otherworldly journey by Zostrianos, a kinsman of Zoroaster. Probably written late in the second century C.E. or early in the third, perhaps in Alexandria, it reflects a non-Christian Sethian gnosis heavily influenced by Middle Platonism.

The tractate opens with a narrative section, told in the first person, that introduces Zostrianos as a possessor of the truth and knowledge of life. In despair over his bondage in this world, he asks how this evil world came into existence from the eternal, non-existing Spirit. Interpreting angels then lead Zostrianos through the heavenly world and reveal to him its secret gnosis. At each level of his ascent he undergoes a ritual baptism through which he is transformed; then, knowledge suitable to that stage of his perfection is revealed to him. The content of the knowledge consists of the names and the interrelationships of the heavenly beings of each level. When all has been revealed to him, he descends to the perceptible world and writes his newly-acquired knowledge on three wooden tablets for the benefit of those to be saved. The tractate concludes with Zostrianos preaching a short homily in which he urges his readers to escape their bondage to matter and to return to the Spirit from which they have come.

DRAMATIS PERSONAE

1. Zostrianos and the interpreting angels

a. Zostrianos: The reputed kinsman of Zoroaster and the central character of the narrative. He makes a journey through the heavenly realms, returns, and leaves his teachings as a saving knowledge for the seed of Seth. He is a "redeemed redeemer" figure and supposedly the author of the tractate.

b. Authrounis: The angelic interpreter who leads Zostrianos through the lowest levels of the Autogenes aeon; perhaps he is to be identified with the Light Harmozel (see 127,7).

c. Ephesech: The angelic interpreter who for most of the first half of the book provides the knowledge about the Autogenes aeon; perhaps he is to be identified with the heavenly Seth. He is also called the "Perfect Child."

d. Yoel/Youel: The angelic interpreter who leads Zostrianos through the Protophanes aeon; she is also called the "male virgin glory" and "she who belongs to the glories." She may be the consort of the Kalyptos aeon.

e. Salamex: The angelic interpreter for the last half of the book; he is also one of the "Lights in Thought."

2. The Heavenly World

a. The Invisible Spirit: The name for the chief deity from which all else has emanated, hence the frequent designation Three-Powered.

b. The Barbelo Aeon: The collective name for the intermediate realm between the Spirit and the physical world; she is one aeon yet has or is three aeons (see 2.c.d.e). She is usually called the virgin Barbelo, but also Thought, First Thought, and gnosis of the Spirit as she is the first emanation from the Spirit.

c. The Kalyptos Aeon: The first aeon of Barbelo; the name means the "hidden" or "veiled" one and is abbreviated as K̄Ā̄C̄. Described as "unborn," he is identified with the philosophical category "Existence." He has four constituent Lights: Harmedon, Diphanes, Malsedon, and Solmis.

d. The Protophanes Aeon: The second aeon of Barbelo; the name means "first-visible" or "first-appearing." He is often called the male perfect Mind and is identified with the philosophical category "Mind." He has four Lights: Solmis, Akremon, Amrosios, and [Seldao].

e. The Autogenes Aeon: The third aeon of Barbelo; the name means "self-begotten." He is often called "divine" and is identified with the philosophical category "Life." He has four Lights: Harmozel, Oroiael, Daveithe, and Eleleth. As the aeon who occupies the lowest level in Barbelo he is responsible together with Sophia (his consort?) for the creation of the physical universe. His lower "levels" are called the ethereal Earth, the Exile, and the Repentance. The heavenly Adam (Geradamas) and Seth (Setheus) are also constituent parts of the Autogenes.

OUTLINE

1. Introduction (1,1-2,7)

Zostrianos introduces himself as an ascetic seeking the separation of spirit (light) from matter (darkness) and struggling with adversaries.

2. The Call, Redemption and Ascent of Zostrianos (2,7-7,22)

The Perfect Child Ephesech appears to him in a vision. Zostrianos raises philosophical questions about the origin of this world from the nether world. With Ephesech as a guide his soul begins its heavenly journey and ascends through the ethereal Earth into the Autogenes aeon. At each level of his ascent he is baptized and transformed.

3. The Revelations from Authrounios (7,22-13,6)

After his initiation into the Autogenes aeon, Zostrianos asks a new set of questions about the levels through which he has passed. Authrounios' replies introduce the concept that each lower level is a poorer copy of the one above it, a process that eventually produced the physical world. They also include a brief and fragmentary reference to the fall of Sophia and the creation of this world by its archon. Of particular interest is the way in which the emanation process explains the origin of different kinds of souls.

4. The Revelations from Ephesech (13,7-57,12)

Zostrianos calls upon Ephesech for further help in understanding the mixed nature of the All or Universe. The new revelation is a somewhat redundant description of the Autogenes, but it serves to introduce the philosophical categories of Existence, Mind, and Life with which the Barbelo aeons are identified. Anthropology is a major topic, i.e., a concern over the differences between the souls that can be saved and those that cannot be. The section concludes with the fifth baptism of Zostrianos in the Autogenes aeon, completing his identification with it.

5. The Revelations from Youel (57,13-63,17)

Youel next leads Zostrianos through the Protophanes aeon. A series of baptisms introduce him to its gnosis. The account is much briefer than that for the Autogenes aeon and is now very poorly preserved.

6. The revelations from Salamex (63,17-129,1)

Following the instructions of Youel, Zostrianos calls for further revelations. Although the poor condition of the manuscript makes it impossible to be certain, this is probably the final set of revelations in the tractate. The contents include a description of the Kalyptos aeon, of Barbelo and her aeons, and of the Spirit. It concludes with a review of the Barbelo aeons. At the end Zostrianos is told that he has now learned things of which even the gods are ignorant.

7. The Descent of Zostrianos and Deposit of the Gnosis (129,2-132,5)

Zostrianos descends through the aeons and writes his gnosis on three tablets for the use of the elect. Finally he re-enters his physical body and preaches a Gnostic homily in which he urges rejection of the material world and acceptance of a kind father.

8. Titles (132,6-9)

Two subscript titles provide the title *Zostrianos* and the link with the traditions concerning the magus Zoroaster.

Genre and Title

GENRE

Zostrianos is a non-historical, otherworldly apocalypse. Unlike Jewish and Christian apocalypses which have the secrets of history as their main concern, non-historical apocalypses have as their prime interests life after death and knowledge of the otherworld. The earliest such story extant in Greek literature is that of Er (Plato, *Resp.*, X). The purpose of the revelation received by Zostrianos is to provide an otherworldly gnosis as the means of salvation for the chosen race of Seth. Towards this end the book describes the mystical experiences of Zostrianos, and the names and relationships of the inhabitants of the otherworld through which every soul must pass. At the same time a negative judgment is pronounced against this world and its ruler, and their ultimate destruction is affirmed. This combination of a primary concern for cosmology with a secondary one for personal eschatology is typical for apocalypses of this type (see Collins, "Morphology," 15; Fallon, "Gnostic Apocalypses," 137-138; Perkins, *Gnostic Dialog,* 25-73; cf. Hengel, *Judaism and Hellenism,* 1, 210-218).

In terms of genre, though not in content, *Zostrianos* is quite like some later Jewish apocalypses from the O.T. Pseudepigrapha. It provides some close parallels to chapters 17-36 of *I Enoch* and to the *Books of Adam and Eve*. It seems to share with *II Enoch* (Slavonic) not only a general heavenly journey framework but also specific phrases and formulas, although the lack of consensus about a date and provenance for II Enoch makes the value of this evidence uncertain. The *Paraphrase of Shem* (NHC VII, *I*) and *Apocalypse of Paul* (NHC V, 2) provide the close genre parallels from Nag Hammadi. (See Scopello, "*Zostrianos* and the Book of the Secrets of Enoch," 376-85; Perkins, *Gnostic Dialog,* 25 n. 1; Anderson, "2 Enoch"; cf. Hengel, *Judaism and Hellenism,* 1, 202-206; the *Apocalypse of Seth* which is briefly quoted in the *Mani Codex* (50,8-52,7) may also have belonged to this genre.)

TITLE

The title *Zostrianos* is provided by two subscript titles, the first of which reads simply "Zostrianos" (132,6). That name appears five other times in the extant text (1,2; 3,31; 14,1; 64,11; 128,15), as well as once more in the second subscript title. It is a fitting title for the work as Zostrianos is presented as its central character and author.

The second subscript (132,7-9) is in the form of a cryptogram. It immediately follows the first subscript and is separated from it by decorative marks. The solution to the cryptogram was recognized by Doresse as one used in Theban convents of a later period. When deciphered it reads: "Teachings of Zostrianos. God of Truth. Teachings of Zoroaster." (Doresse, "Les apocalypses de Zoroastre," 255-263). The purpose of this second subscript title was to certify the teachings of the book as authentic wisdom from the East and thus to enhance the authority of the book. It did so by linking the unfamiliar name of Zostrianos with that of his famous ancestor Zoroaster (see Sieber, "Introduction to Zostrianos," 233-236; Puech, "Plotin et les gnostiques," 167; Colpe, "Heidnische, jüdische und christliche Überlieferung VI," 155-157; Berliner Arbeitskreis, "Die Bedeutung," 65; see also Ziegler, "Zostrianos," col. 853; Bidez-cumont, *Zoroastre, Ostanes et Hystaspe*, 1.41-55; Jackson, *Zoroaster*; Hinz, "Zoroaster," 19A, cols. 774-784; cf. Hengel, *Judaism and Hellenism*, 1, 211-213).

Doresse's early conclusion that this second subscript gives the tractate the title "Apocalypse of Zoroaster and Zostrianos" cannot be maintained. Clement of Alexandria (*Strom.* I.15) mentions secret books of Zoroaster which were in use in Alexandria in his time by the followers of Prodicus. The *Apocryphon of John* (NHC II 19,8-10) also knows a book of Zoroaster, but *Zostrianos* does not furnish the type of information which it ascribes to that work. Thus, the book of Zoroaster must have been a totally different work from this Nag Hammadi tractate. That conclusion is supported further by evidence from Porphyry's *Vit. Plot.* 16 (quoted below). He tells of certain Gnostic books known to and opposed by Plotinus, his teacher. Among them were "Revelations" in the names of Zoroaster, Zostrianos, Nicotheos, Allogenes, and Messos. Since Plotinus assigned a different pupil to refute each of these books, the titles Zostrianos and Zoroaster in his list certainly refer to two books, not one.

A second ancient testimony to the name Zostrianos is from Arnobius' *The Case Against the Pagans*. It refers to him as a relative of Zoroaster and calls him a magus (for the Latin text see Bidez-cumont, *Zoroastre, Ostanes, et Hystaspe*, 2. 15; for its interpretation see McCracken, *Arnobius of Sicca,*

1,294, nn. 258-60; Orelli in PL, 5, 788, understood Pamphylius as a fourth Zoroaster and emended the unfamiliar name Zostrianos to Ostanes). The passage which is dated to the late third or early fourth century C.E. says (my translation):

Well, then! Let there come through the fiery region, I beg you, a Zoroaster, a magician from a remote land, provided that we accept Hermippus as an authority. Also let that Bactrian come along, about whose affairs Ctesias expounds in the first book of his histories; and Armenius, the grandson of Zostrianos and Pamphylian friend of Cyrus . . .

Although the passage is a confusing one, it is clear that Arnobius thought of Armenius and Zostrianos as part of the lineage of Zoroaster. Thus, placing the name Zoroaster in the second subscript served to present the tractate to readers of late antiquity as part of the ancient, secret teachings of the East. The Zoroaster-Armenius tradition was in turn connected to the story of Er in Plato (*Resp.*, X, 614b-621d). Er, a fallen warrior, is said to have travelled in the spirit to the nether world. He returns to his body just prior to its burial to relate his knowledge about the immortality of the soul. Clement of Alexandria understood Er to be the same person as the magician Armenius/Zoroaster (*Strom.* V, 14). It is possible that the same traditions which linked the name of Zostrianos to those of Zoroaster and Armenius also provided the suggestion that Zostrianos' secret knowledge had been acquired on an otherworldly journey.

The Gnostic Character of the Tractate
The transmission of gnosis or knowledge was the primary purpose of the tractate. The narrative of the heavenly journey provided a framework in which that knowledge could be communicated. The world-view of the text is thoroughly Gnostic in character as it assumes a basic dualism between matter which is inherently evil, and spirit which is inherently good. In *Zostrianos* this basic dualism is explicitly expressed in terms of contrasts between matter and spirit, darkness and light, body and soul, femaleness and maleness. Humanity is viewed as a microcosm of the universe, having souls or spirits trapped in material bodies. The release of the soul from its painful bondage in matter is to be obtained through the knowledge conveyed to Zostrianos who had previously prepared himself through extreme ascetic disciplines. This gnosis sent from above was intended to awaken the realization that one is an alien here and belongs to another world. Zostrianos is both a lost soul and a

redeemer who brings gnosis back after his salvation. Since the Gnostic message was one of spirit saving spirit, the exhortations of the concluding homily in *Zostrianos* to awaken one's inner-self (god) to god are typical of the intention of the entire book (see Jonas, *Gnostic Religion* ; Jonas, *Gnosis und Spätantikergeist*; Jonas, "Delimitation of the gnostic phenomenon"; Rudolf, *Gnosis*; Widengren, *Gnostic Attitude*; Widengren, "Les origines du gnosticism," 37-42).

The fundamental Gnostic attitude was that matter in and of itself is evil and the cause of all other evils. In *Zostrianos* this conviction finds expression in a variety of ways. The imprisonment of the soul within a physical body is one of the most frequent. The body is said to bring darkness (1,10-11); pain and suffering (46,2-15); powerlessness (26,9-11); death (123,6-8); and ignorance (130,7). Another familiar theme is bondage to the perceptible world (3,22-23); to femaleness (1,13; 131,6); and to the body (46,6-9; 131,10-12). Matter is changeable (5,9) and without limits (46,5-6). Those who are in this world think that matter is eternal when in truth it is perishable (9,4-6). The world and its creator are under condemnation (1,16-19; 9,12-15; 128,7-14; 131,23-24). The meaning of salvation is to be rescued from the body (4,24-25); the world (4,26; 46,15-31); and its ruler (4,25-31; 130,10-12). Spirit is good. In *Zostrianos* the ultimate good, the Three-Powered Invisible Spirit, is the source of all that is (17,12-13); it is perfection and silence (24,12-17), simple and undivided (79,16-24; 87,6-19), unseen, and self-existent (128,20-25). Souls can find their true selves by setting themselves straight (1,30-31; 2,8); by discovering the infinite part of their matter (1,15-16); and by seeking a resting place worthy of spirit (2,13; 3,20-21). In their escape souls use the knowledge revealed to Zostrianos by the angels (4,11-17); Seth (30,9-14); powers and glories (24,6-9. 18-20; 46,15-31); and a savior (131,14-16).

The mythological aeons occupy spatial positions in the heavenly world between spirit and matter and represent an attempt to bridge the gulf between them. From the opening questions of Zostrianos to those near the end, a major concern of the book is to explain how the manifold universe has derived from one non-existing source (2,24-30; 8,1-17; 20,4-15; 22,2-4; 45,1-30; 48,3-29; 64,11-22; 117,15-19; 128,19-22). The aeon systems in *Zostrianos* provide a mythological solution to that puzzle. Each aeon is produced by an overflow or emanation from the one above it; each is created in the image of its source; each successive image is a somewhat less than perfect representation of its source. In the first step the Barbelo aeon comes forth from the Spirit (81,8-83,1). As the First Thought of the Spirit, Barbelo knows Spirit as her source (81,19-20; 118,9-11); yet, she herself divides into three aeons, a sign of imperfection

(82,13-83,1), while Spirit remains undivided (118,1-5). The first aeon, the Kalyptos (The Hidden or Veiled One), is the pattern for the other two (20,4-15). The Protophanes aeon (The First-Visible One) ranks higher than the Autogenes aeon (the Self-Begotten One), as is shown by the hierarchically structured blessings which are located throughout the text. Each of these major aeons in turn has a multitude of constituent parts called powers, glories, waters, lights, and the like. Much of the gnosis concerns the Autogenes aeon. Sophia (Wisdom), a part of Autogenes, produces through her error the physical world (9,16-11,14); at the same time salvation comes from the Autogenes in the form of Seth (30,9-14). Thus, *Zostrianos* represents the kind of Gnosticism which Jonas called Syrian or Alexandrian (see Jonas, *Gnostic Religion*, 105, 130-32, 236-237; cf. Widengren, *Gnostic Attitude*, 18-20). Prior to the discovery of the Nag Hammadi Library, this type of Gnosticism was represented by the Hermetic literature and by several varieties of Christian Gnosticism. Its major features are its conviction that evil has its origin in the divine itself and the resulting speculation about how that could be so; its typical solution for this dilemma is the kind of emanation theory contained in *Zostrianos* which thus provides us with a philosophical exemplar for Syrian Gnosticism.

The gnosis is a secret knowledge partly because it came through revelations and partly because it was intended only for a select group. That group is described by several designations within the text: it is the "living elect" (1,7; 130,4); the "male race" (7,6), the "all-perfect race" (20,2-3). In terms of Zostrianos' story the group is referred to as "those of my age and afterwards" (1,5-6) and "my race" (3,15; cf. 4,14). It is "this race" (24,23) when contrasted with those who are not part of the elect; they are called "others" or "the others" (27,19). More specifically, the elect are identified as the "children of Seth" (7,8-9) or the "seed of Seth" (130,16-17). The heavenly Seth is the "father" of the group (30,9-14; 51,14-16), while his father Adam is referred to as "forefather" (6,22). That this group evidently participated in cultic practices is shown by the liturgical materials that are scattered throughout the book. The homily at the end of the book reads like a model sermon for such a community (130,16-132,5). Elsewhere are formulas for giving blessings (e.g., 6,21-26), words of acclamation and praise such as the phrase "you are one" which is to be repeated three times (e.g., 51,23-25), and magical vowel combinations (e.g., 118,18.21). Furthermore, one evidently became a member of the group by means of baptisms similar to those reported for Zostrianos. If so, each level of Zostrianos' ascent represents one stage in the initiation process. A discussion of the meaning of the waters (22,3-23,17) equates the attainment of a specific level of knowledge with a washing in the waters of each of the Barbelo aeons. This combination of baptism and new self understanding is what is reported of Zostrianos: he is baptized, receives revelations, and is transformed (e.g., 6,7-21) at each stage of his ascent. After his fourth baptism Zostrianos is said to have become a "perfect angel (7,19)." The term τέλειος (perfect) is one used in some of the mystery religions for the first stage of the initiation process (see BAG 2, s.v., 809,2b; cf. Bousset, *Kyrios Christos*, 260, n. 58; Angus, *Mystery Religions and Christianity*, 76-107). Taken together, the two sections on baptism in *Zostrianos* (5,11-7,22; 15,1-25,22) suggest a cultic background for some of the contents of *Zostrianos* (see Schenke, "Gnostic Sethianism," 602-607; Sevrin, *Le dossier baptismal séthien*, 224-251; Robinson, "Three Steles of Seth," 538-539; Scopello, "Un rituel idéal d'intonisation"; cf. Nicklesburg, "Traditions in the Apocalpyse of Adam").

The larger question of how *Zostrianos'* Gnostic views are related to what is known from other writings is quite complex. Its answer is clearest with respect to three other tractates from Nag Hammadi with which *Zostrianos* shares mythologoumena and a philosophical orientation, *The Three Steles of Seth* (NHC VII, 5), *Marsanes* (NHC X), and *Allogenes* (NHC XI, 3). These four tractates have in turn some strong mythological ties to several of the Christian Gnostic works, especially the *Gospel of the Egyptians* (NHC III, 2 and IV, 2) and the *Apocryphon of John* (NHC II, I; III, I; IV, I; BG8502, 2). Similar but less clear parallels are found between them and the *Untitled Text* in the Bruce Codex.

Allogenes, the *Three Steles of Seth*, and *Marsanes* have heavenly worlds quite similar to that of *Zostrianos* (see Pearson, "Marsanes"; Robinson, "Three Steles of Seth"; Turner, "Gnostic Threefold Path"; Sieber, "Barbelo aeon as Sophia"). The chief deity in *Allogenes* is called the Invisible Spirit (e.g., *Allogenes* XI 66,34; cf. *Marsanes* X 4,15-17), although its Three-Powered One seems to be a separate entity (e.g., *Allogenes* XI 47,9; cf. *Marsanes* X 6,18-19). In the *Three Steles of Seth* the chief deity is not named but is addressed as "Spirit" (*Steles Seth* VII 125,6-25) and Three-Powered One (*Steles Seth* VII 121,31). From Spirit comes the Barbelo aeon (*Steles Seth* VII 121,25-30; *Allogenes* XI 45,28-30) who is herself the source of three aeons named Kalyptos, Protophanes, and Autogenes (*Steles Seth* VII 122,4-123,5; *Marsanes* X 9,1-3; *Allogenes* XI 45,31-46,35). In *Allogenes* these aeons are specifically identified with the philosophical triad of Existence-Mind-Life, just as in *Zostrianos* (see below). Even lists of rather esoteric heavenly beings are similar (e.g., *Steles Seth* VII 126,1-17; *Zost.* VIII 88,9-13; and *Allogenes* XI 54,26-31). Group designations and the roles of the respective revealers are also comparable. The *Three Steles of Seth* refers to Seth as the father of the elect, living, immovable race (*Steles Seth* VII 118,13.17). Allogenes receives a gnosis for the "worthy generation" (*Allogenes* XI 52,21-25; cf. *Zost.* VIII 1,5-7 and 130,3-4; *Marsanes* X 6,15-16) and "for those who are worthy after you" (*Allogenes* XI 68,16-20). Like Zostrianos, Allogenes ascends in order to bring knowledge to earth (*Allogenes* XI 58,26-69,20; cf. *Marsanes* X 8,18-25). Youel, one of the major interpreting angels in *Zostrianos*, also speaks to Allogenes, and she is called "the one who belongs to all the glories" in both books (e.g., *Zost.* VIII 53,13-14; 57,13-15; *Allogenes* XI 50,20-25; 55,17-20). In addition these tractates use similar types of liturgical materials; for example, *Allogenes* XI 52,13-15 has anointings comparable to the washings of *Zost.* VIII 62,11-24, while *Marsanes* has seals to break (*Marsanes* X 2,12-4,23). The *Three Steles of Seth* has prayers and words of praise including especially the thrice repeated "you are one" (e.g., *Steles Seth* VII 125,23-25). Though the parallels between these four tractates are not totally consistent, they are of sufficient number and depth to conclude that all four are representatives of the same Gnostic tradition, especially since they also share an intention to understand gnosis in philosophical ways.

The *Gospel of the Egyptians* (NHC III, 2 and IV, 2) shares some of the same mythologoumena, in particular many of the names connected with the Autogenes and Barbelo aeons and with the Invisible Spirit (*Gos.Eg.* III 52,1-54,11; III 61,23-62,11; cf. *Zost.* VIII 127,15-128,7). It also speaks of the immovable, living race of Seth (e.g., *Gos.Eg.* III 51,5-9; cf. *Zost.* VIII 30,4-14), of baptisms and purifying waters (*Gos. Eg.* III 64,9-20), of a light-cloud and Sophia (*Gos.Eg.* III 56,22-57,5; cf. *Zost.* VIII 4,20-5,10), of Youel and Esephech (Ephesech in *Zostrianos*) as interpreting angels (e.g., *Gos.Eg.* III 50,16-56,2; cf. *Zost.* VIII 56,24-57,20). At the same time there are significant differences between these two works. Two aeons of the Barbelo in *Zostrianos*, Kalyptos, and Protophanes, do not appear at all in the *Gospel of the Egyptians*, and the Autogenes in the *Gospel of the Egyptians* is an independent aeon, not part of the Barbelo. Also the tripartite character of Barbelo is lacking; instead, there is a triad consisting of Spirit (Father), Barbelo (Mother), and Autogenes (Son) (*Gos.Eg.* III 41,23-48,8). This Son is identified with Christ (e.g., *Gos.Eg.* III 44,23), and other Christian terms frequently appear, often as further titles for mythological beings. Although a detailed comparison of these two tractates remains to be done, they appear to represent a non-Christian and a Christianized version of the same Gnostic traditions (see Hedrick, "Christian Motifs"; Bohlig-Wisse, *Gospel of the Egyptians*, 46).

The *Apocryphon of John* (NHC II, *I*; III, *I*; IV, *I*; BG8502, 2) also has a few parallels with *Zostrianos*. The presentation of the Spirit, Barbelo, and Autogenes in its opening pages (*Ap.John* II 2,25-9,25) provides in Christian dress some of the cosmology found in *Zostrianos,* but the extensive interest in Yaldabaoth, Adam and Eve, and the Genesis creation accounts that occupy the succeeding sections of the *Apocryphon of John* are at best only alluded to *Zostrianos.* To a still smaller degree *Trimorphic Protennoia* (NHC XIII, *I*); *Melchizadek* (NHC IX, *I*); *Hypostasis of the Archons* (NHC II, *4*); the *Apocalypse of Adam* (NHC V, 5); and the *Thought of Norea* (NHC IX, 2) show some similarilities. Finally, *Zostrianos* bears some resemblance to several sections of the *Untitled Text* from the Bruce Codex (Schmidt's text, *Gnostische Schriften,* is reprinted in Schmidt-MacDermott, *Jehu and the Untitled Text,* 214-317, with a less useful English translation; see also Baynes, *Coptic Gnostic Treatise*). The *Untitled Text* refers to Setheus, the Three-Powered One, the places of the Autogenes, and the names of the watchers Gamaliel and Strempsuchos (see Schmidt-MacDermot, *Jehu and the Untitled Text,* 238,26-239,27). Another passage mentions Michar and Micheus and the copies called the ethereal Earth, the Exile, and the Repentance (see Schmidt-MacDermot, *Jehu and the Untitled Text,* 263,11-264,6). In chapter 15 the Kalyptos aeon appears but as an aeon of the self-father having ten powers and nine enneads (see Schmidt-McDermot, *Jehu and the Untitled Text,* 255,15-26). Such major differences with *Zostrianos* are so often the case that the mythological world of the *Untitled Text* is, in the end, quite unlike that of *Zostrianos.*

The writings of the Christian heresiologists prove to be of little value in helping to identify the group of Gnostics from which *Zostrianos* and its related books may have come (see Wisse, "Nag Hammadi and the Heresiologists"; Wisse, "Sethians and the Nag Hammadi Library"; Wisse, "Stalking those Elusive Sethians"; cf. Schmidt, "Ireneus und seine Quelle in *Adv. Haer.* I. 29"). Ireneus (*Adv. Haer.* I, 29) identifies as Barbeloites a group with teachings somewhat like those in the *Apocryphon of John,* yet much of what he describes is quite unlike *Zostrianos.* The same can be said of the information from Ireneus' *Adv. Haer.* I, 30 and its expansion in Epiphanius' *Pan.* II, 39, "On the Sethians." Epiphanius says, for example, that the Sethians trace their race from Seth, Adam's son, and that they have books in the name of Seth, Allogenes, and other men. But serious problems arise if one attempts to identify this Sethian group as the one that produced and/or used tractates such as *Zostrianos.* The new texts speak of a heavenly mother, for example, but Epiphanius does not refer to Mirothea or Barbelo. The interest of Epiphanius' Sethians in the Cain-Abel and Noah cycles from Genesis is applicable to the *Apocalypse of Adam* (NHC V, 5), or the *Hypostasis of the Archons* (NHC II, 4), but not to *Zostrianos.* Epiphanius' account adds to the problem by reporting much the same information about his next group the Archontics (*Pan.*, II, 40). (See Schmidt, *Gnostische Schriften*, 602, who concluded that the *Untitled Text* was produced by the Archontics.) On the other hand, an account in Hippolytus (*Ref.* V) ascribes totally different teachings to the Sethians, teachings related to those found in the *Paraphrase of Shem* (NHC VII, *I*). Such contradictory sets of evidence indicate that the Fathers often wrote on the basis of scanty information; however, to conclude as Wisse does that these books were literary productions with no connections to specific Gnostic groups is improbable (see Wisse, "Stalking those Elusive Sethians," 571-76).

Schenke and others have isolated from these tractates a set of common traits for a sect based on the sharing of cultic materials, the names divine figures and of the group designation "the seed of Seth" (see Schenke, "Gnostic Sethianism"; Schenke, "Das sethianische System"; Pearson, "Marsanes," 241-244; Turner, "Sethian Gnosticism"; cf. Colpe, "Heidnische, jüdische und christliche Überlieferung VI," 161-70). The evidence from *Zostrianos* supports that conclusion: 1) its liturgical materials are best understood as cultic in origin; 2) it gives a name (the seed or race of Seth) to its adherents; 3) its traditions about the heavenly world are shared in substantive ways with several other tractates. There must not have been an organized Sethian Gnostic "church" or a system of "orthodox" doctrine as none of the texts Schenke identifies as Sethian have all the traits he identifies, some do not even mention Seth. Rather, there must have been different groups of Gnostics who used in a free way a common set of Gnostic traditions for the description of the other world. Since personal revelations and experience were more authoritative for Gnostic Christians than adherence to Churchly tradition, perhaps pagan Gnostics were not so faithful to their traditions either (cf. Pagels, "Visions, Appearances, and Apostolic Authority," 427-429). Some of these Gnostics evidently intended to be Christians, others Platonic philosophers, others Hermeticists, etc. Together they shared some common cultic and mythological conceptions. Whether these disparate groups also shared a feeling of kinship or a common self-designation such as "Sethians" with one another is still unclear.

At present it is sufficient to say that *Zostrianos* bears a close relationship to several other documents from Nag Hammadi and that their common contents provide help in understanding each of the respective books. Since most of them make reference to Seth in some way, it is convenient to designate them as "Sethian," even though the persons and groups that produced the individual texts may not have had ties with one another.

The Philosophical Traditions

Zostrianos presents its mythological gnosis as philosophical knowledge. The key philosophical text for the mystical ascent of the soul came from Plato's *Symposium* (210a-212), and the topic was a common one for Middle Platonism. The concerns about the emanation of matter from spirit in *Zostrianos* also depend largely on philosophical categories that derive ultimately from Plato. Many of the Greek loan words in the Coptic of *Zostrianos* are familiar as technical terminology to those who know the writings of Plotinus and his predecessors, and *Zostrianos* identifies the mythological aeons of Barbelo with the philosophical triad of Existence, Life, and Mind, known best from later neo-Platonic writers. In order to understand *Zostrianos*, therefore, it is necessary to explore the philosophical milieu to which it was related.

The discussion must begin with Chapter 16 of Porphyry's *Vit. Plot.* (see Henry-Schwyzer, *Plotinus: Opera* 1.21-22, for the Greek text). The relevant passage reads (my translation):

At that time there were many Christians and some others, and they (the others) were sectarians who had withdrawn from the ancient philosophy, students of Adelphius and Acquilinus. They possessed most of the writings of Alexander the Libyan, Philocomes, Demostratus, and Lydos and cited revelations by Zoroaster, Zostrianos, Nikotheos, Allogenes, Messos, and other such men. They have deceived many, yet it is they themselves who are deceived by thinking that Plato did not approach the depths of intellectual being. Therefore, after he himself had produced many refutations for the benefit of his associates and had also written a book "Against the Gnostics," he assigned the rest to us for criticism. Amelius put forward almost forty books in writing against the book of Zostrianos. As for me, I Porphyry produced many refutations against that one called Zoroaster, showing it altogether to be an illegitimate and recent book, constructed by those who were members of the sect to give them the distinction of being the teachings of the ancient Zoroaster which they had chosen to venerate.

As Porphyry explicitly mentions Christians, previous interpreters have often assumed that the entire paragraph referred to Gnostic Christians and so translated "At the time of Plotinus there were Christians and others, and they (i.e., Christians) were sectarians..." (γεγόναι δὲ κατ αὐτὸν τῶν χριστιανῶν πολλοὶ μὲν καὶ ἄλλοι, αἱρετικοὶ δὲ ἐκ τῆς παλαιᾶς φιλοσοφίας). However, since neither *Allogenes* nor *Zostrianos* is explicitly Christian (see below), the Greek must now be understood as referring to two groups, many Christians (χριστιανῶν πολλοὶ μὲν), and others who are sectarian philosophers (αἱρετικοὶ δέ) (cf. Puech, "Plotin et les Gnostiques," 175-77; Schmidt, *Gnostische Scriften*, 614). The dispute between Plotinus and those Gnostic sectarian philosophers was largely one about canonical authority. Plotinus argued that true philosophers cite only Plato as the ultimate authority, while his Gnostic opponents depended on books ascribed to other authorities. Porphyry says that they "brought forward" (πρφέροντες) their books. Although in the light of his later statement that he refuted *Zoroaster* as recent and illegitimate this term could mean that they wrote the books, the more likely sense is that they cited them as authorities against Plato (cf. Schmidt, *Gnostische Schriften*, 614). Since everyone assumed that only ancient books were authoritative, it was important to show that the sources of his opponents were of recent origin.

Zostrianos is certainly the book of that name known to Porphyry (so also Layton, *Gnostic Scriptures*, 121; Perkins, *Gnostic Dialog*, 12-13, 40; Dillon, "Pleroma and Noetic Cosmos"; Wallis, "Numenius and Gnosticism"; Pearson, "Marsanes," 244-250). He knew of a book titled *Zostrianos* which contained secret revelations and which pretended to be philosophical in orientation, an accurate description of NHC VIII, I. Although Porphyry himself does not provide us with specific information about the contents of the books which he names, the frequent use of philosophical vocabulary in *Zostrianos* provides one type of evidence for identifying our *Zostrianos* with the one Prophyry knew. Among the more frequently occurring technical terms in *Zostrianos* are ἀρχή (principle or origin), οὐσία (substance or essence), εἴκον (image), εἶδος (form or species), τάξις (arrangement or order), κόσμος αἰσθητός/αἴσθησις (perceptible world), τέλειος (perfect). Sometimes this technical vocabulary is preserved in Coptic translation, such as ⲡⲓⲟⲛⲧⲱⲥ ⲉⲧϣⲟⲟⲡ for τὸ ὄντως ὄν (the really existing one). These terms and others like them are part of the common vocabulary of the Middle Platonists and Plotinus (cf. Zandee, *Terminology of Plotinus*; Tardieu, "Les trois steles de Seth," 565-567). M. Williams (*The Immovable Race*, pp. 69-102) has pointed out another significant contact between *Zostrianos* and those same Platonists, the concept of "standing." After each of Zostrianos' five baptisms he receives a new identity, then he stands, and finally he blesses. Williams has traced the idea of "standing" back to Plato (esp. to *Phaedo* 83A; *Phaedrus* 246Aff) and shown that its use by Plotinus and others describes the stability of the soul during its ascent into the transcendent realms. Plotinus in particular uses the term in the sense of "stand at rest" for the soul which in its mystical ascent has left behind discursive reasoning and has turned towards the One (e.g., *Enn.* III. 8.6.). Though *Zostrianos* may also draw on a Jewish apocalyptic background for this idea, its appearance is another piece of evidence that *Zostrianos* comes from Plotinus' philosophical milieu. Fortunately, Plotinus himself in his essay "Against the Gnostics" (*Enn.* II.9) provides us with fairly specific information about the teachings of his Gnostic opponents. A comparison of its contents with *Zostrianos* reveals several striking comparisons. The "ethereal Earth" (e.g., *Zost.* 5,18; 8,11) is that new earth which Plotinus condemns at *Enn.*II. 9.5.23-26. A little later (*Enn.* II. 9.6.1-6) Plotinus argues that the Gnostics have spoiled the perfection of the three hypostases and invented a new terminology by introducing extraneous emanations called παροικήσεις (Exiles), ἀντίτυποι (Copies), and μετάνοιαι (Repentances). This unusual combination of terms occurs together several times in *Zostrianos* (5,17-29; 8,13-17; 12,11-15; 27,15-28,5; 31,6-9; 43,12-19). In connection with these new hypostases the Gnostics discuss the differences in souls (*Enn.* II. 9.6.28-62) instead of counting the World Soul as the third hypostasis. At *Zost.* 26,19-28,30 (cf. 42,20-46,18) the topic is the differences of soul and the context that of the souls that exist in the Exile and Repentance. According to *Enn.* II. 9.6.59-63 the Gnostics wrongly censure the maker of this world, just what one finds at *Zost.* 9,12-15. The Gnostics make wisdom (Sophia) the cause of the origin of this world (*Enn.* II 9.10.19-24) as *Zostrianos* does (9,16-17; 27,9-12). When they do so, they speak of forming the world as "the reflection of a reflection" (*Enn.* II. 9.27-28); *Zost.* 10,4 uses precisely those terms to describe the work of the archon of this world. Both the closeness of these parallels between *Zostrianos* and Plotinus' *Enneads* and the fact that the terms involved often appear in the same order in both texts make it certain that this tractate was the book (or a version of the book) known to Plotinus'school and refuted his student Amelius.

The philosophical intention of *Zostrianos* and its use by Gnostics known to Plotinus might suggest that it was written by someone with close ties to Plotinus. He himself indicates that there were Gnostics within his own circle of friends (*Enn.* II 9.10); however, it would seem that forgeries of a very recent origin would have been easier to refute than the prodigious efforts required by Plotinus and his students. More significantly, a comparison of *Zostrianos'* content with Plotinus' writings reveals little that suggests that its author was in active conversation with Plotinus. The particular genius of Plotinus' thought was the understanding that there are three, and only three, levels of reality. Beyond everything that makes up the physical world, he postulated an utterly transcendent First Principle called The One (τὸ ἕν), a term used earlier by the Neopythagoreans. From the One emanated a second level called Mind (νοῦς) which is both Thought and the object of Thought. As the latter, it contains the individual Platonic forms (εἶδος) from which all particulars in this world derive. Soul (ψυχή), the third level, is derived from Mind. As the intermediary between Mind and the perceptible world in which we live, Soul looks both towards Mind and Nature. These three levels of being are, according to Plotinus, logically or hierarchically structured, but they are not be to understood as being separated in time or space. All three are present in everything at the same time. Although *Zostrianos* shares a considerable vocabulary and a general viewpoint with Plotinus, there is no evidence that it was written in direct opposition with positions held by him. Like Plotinus, *Zostrianos* posits a transcendent First Principle and occasionally uses the terms "the one" (79,25; 81,20; 118,15) and "the good" (117,15-17). Nonetheless, *Zostrianos* does not argue against Plotinus' insistence on the complete separation of Spirit and Mind, for at 58,16-20 the Spirit is called an intellectual power, a knower and a fore-knower. That kind of first principle is more like those known from Plotinus' predecessors, the Middle Platonists, than from Plotinus himself. The same is true of the use of terms such as "unreachable" and "ineffable." A similar result is obtained in searching for evidence that the concept of Barbelo in *Zostrianos* was influenced by the Plotinian hypostasis called Mind. Barbelo is called Thought (83,9-10), First Thought (24,12), knowledge (118,11), and one of her constituent aeons (Protophanes) is identified with Mind. But her other two aeons, the Kalyptos and the Autogenes, as well as a myriad of other constituent beings neither reflect Plotinus' thinking, nor are they offered as substitutes for it. Plotinus' third level of being, Soul, is not mentioned in *Zostrianos*. The Autogenes aeon is something like Soul in that it is responsible for the perceptible world, yet the Autogenes is clearly not a separate hypostasis on the order of Soul. The concern in *Zostrianos* is not over Soul, but over the different kinds of souls imprisoned in this world. Furthermore, the entire emanation process is seen by *Zostrianos* as evil (1,16-19; 9,6-15; 10,4-17). Plotinus' contention (e.g., *Enn.* II 9.13) that the process must be good because each lower level depends on the higher level above it is not refuted by logical argument in *Zostrianos*.

Even in those philosophical areas where *Zostrianos* and Plotinus are in general agreement, there are significant differences between them. They agree in general about using the process of emanation to understand the relationship of matter to spirit, but they do not employ the same analogies to describe it. Plotinus favors analogies based on the sun giving off light or fire heat (e.g., *Enn.* II. 7.20-50; II 1.8.1-15); *Zostrianos* refers to a fountain that overflows (17,4-13). Moreover, Plotinus wishes to understand emanation logically (e.g., *Enn.* II 9.14.37-43), not temporally or spatially as does *Zostrianos*, and for him all three hypostases are everywhere present (e.g., *Enn.* II 9. 16.15-33). The aeons in *Zostrianos*, its stories about the creation and destruction of this world, and its additions of other hypostases are all aimed at providing as much spatial distance as possible between the Spirit and matter (e.g., 129,22-130,7). Thus, while there are many similarities of thought between *Zostrianos* and that of Plotinus, they do not appear to be the result of an immediate confrontation between its author and Plotinus (vs. Perkins, *Gnostic Dialog*, 71, who thinks *Zostrianos* may have originated as a critique of Plotinus' mysticism).

It is much more likely that *Zostrianos'* author was part of the same late Middle Platonic era from which Plotinus emerged. Its agreement with the terms and issues raised by Albinus, Moderatus, and Numenius from about 150 C.E. and on are especially striking. These similarities extend along four basic lines: the attempt to distinguish a god higher than the world of forms or ideas; speculation about the four elements; acceptance of demons as lower gods; uneasiness over calling this world good. In each case *Zostrianos* reveals a concern both for the type of question under debate and for the terminology being employed in it (see esp. the articles by Merlan, Chadwick, and Armstrong in Armstrong, *Cambridge History*; Dillon, *Middle Platonists*; Armstrong "Gnosis and Greek Philosophy"; Dodds, "Numenius and Ammonius"; Dodds, *Pagan and Christian*; Wallis, *Neoplatonism*, 12-36). The attempt to distinguish a chief deity from the world of forms is known from about the middle of the second century C.E. on. Albinus anticipated Plotinus' triad of the One, Mind, and Soul by accepting without argument the proposition that ideas are the thoughts of god, who is ineffable and unreachable. Yet at other times Albinus evidently identified god with active intelligence so that he did not make this an absolute distinction (see Dillon, *Middle Platonists*, 267-306). Moderatus and Numenius both pursued the question by attempting to reconcile Plato with Pythagorean thought. Moderatus understood Plato to have posited three realms other than the physical world: the One which is above all being and substance, the ideas, and the psyche. The matter of which the physical world consists is a reflection or a shadow of the One and the Ideas. Numenius also understood Socrates and Plato to have taught a doctrine of three gods, and he sought to bolster his arguments with teachings from eastern sources such as Judaism and Zoroastrianism. Numenius called the chief deity goodness, first intelligence, the one-that-is. His second god is a duality that contemplates the chief deity on the one hand and uses the "ideas" to create the physical world on the other. Indeed the role of Numenius' second god is almost identical to that of Barbelo in *Zostrianos*, although Barbelo is a triad, not a duality. In *Zostrianos* the Spirit, as knower and fore-knower, is also more like the chief deity of these Middle

Platonic philosophers, than like the One of Plotinus. Although these
philosophers may not have conceived the doctrine of this chief deity as
clearly as Plotinus was to do later, the Gnostics of the period (such as
Valentinus) were already doing so in their own terms. Therefore, we find
the closest parallels to these concepts from *Zostrianos* in late second
century philosophers and Gnostics.

The task of interpreting Plato's talk about the creation of this world
by a demiurge in *Tim.* 28c began with Aristotle and continued on
through the Neoplatonists. Most Middle Platonists accepted Aristotle's
opinion that the cosmos was eternal. The question of how the physical
world could participate in the intellectual was a major concern. As we
have seen, *Zostrianos* also wrestles with this problem (e.g., 2,24-3,13). The
use of the four elements (earth, air, fire, and water) as an aid in explaining
the process was one of the ways in which Aristotelian and Stoic elements
were blended to interpret the demiurge passage (see Schweizer, "Slaves
of the Elements," esp. 456-464). In *Zostrianos* these four elements appear
in the sections which discuss the vast array of ideas in each of the Barbelo
aeons (e.g., 48,3-7; 55,13-19; 113,9-10). The belief in lower gods or spirits,
called demons (daimons), was a part of Platonic philosophy from the
fourth century B.C.E. These spirits served as the intermediaries between
this world and the world of ideas. Some demons were thought to be evil
(and hence were the cause of evil in the world); others were good. Some
had always been incorporeal; others were the souls of the dead who had
once inhabited bodies. *Zostrianos* makes several references to such
demons (e.g., 43,1-12). Although the world was considered as mostly
good by the majority of Platonists, from at least the second century C.E.
some writers were not very eager to affirm its goodness. Numenius,
taking a position later rejected by Plotinus, argued for an evil cosmic soul
identified with matter, while Celsus believed that matter itself was the
source of evil. Although these philosophical positions differ from the
Gnostic attitude (i.e., that both matter itself and the entire process
leading to it is evil), they serve to show that the question about the
goodness of the world was being addressed by Middle Platonists. The
negative evaluation of the cosmos and its creator in *Zostrianos* is a
Gnostic view of the same issue.

As a representative of the Middle Platonic period, *Zostrianos* provides evidence for the pre-Plotinian origin of the triad Existence-Mind-
Life employed by later Neoplatonic writers to explain the functioning of
Plotinus' second hypostasis, Mind. E.R. Dodds discussed its appearance
in the works of Proclus, who wrote in the fifth century C.E. (see Dodds,
Proclus:Theology, 90-91, 252-53). More recently Hadot traced it back into
the fourth century in the writings of Marius Victorinus (see Hadot,

Marius Victorinus). Then, in a 1977 essay Hadot reviewed the evidence for this triad in the writings of Plotinus and argued that it was not something new in his thought (see Hadot, "Etre, vie, pensée chez Plotin," 107-141). Instead, he suggested that the triad was part of the standard summaries of Platonic thought available at that time. The main objection to his thesis at that time was that he lacked documentary evidence for the pre-Plotinian existence of the triad. James M. Robinson was the first to suggest that the Nag Hammadi Library had supplied the evidence that Hadot had lacked (see Robinson, "Three Steles," 132-142). In discussing the appearance of the triad in *Allogenes* and *Zostrianos* he argued that the proceedings at which Hadot's paper had been presented would have greatly benefited from an earlier publication of those Nag Hammadi materials. Further study has substantiated that opinion (see Sieber, "Barbelo aeon as Sophia"; Turner, "Gnostic Threefold Path"; Wire-Turner, "Allogenes"; Pearson, "Marsanes"; Pearson, "The Tractate Marsanes"). Key passages in *Zostrianos* identify the Barbelo aeons with the philosophical triad as follows: the Kalyptos aeon is Existence, the Protophanes aeon is Mind (also called Blessedness and Knowledge), and the Autogenes aeon is Life or Vitality (see esp. 15,1-18,10). They are three and yet one, as they are in those later Neoplatonic authors.

The Composition of the Tractate

DATE

The close relationships between *Zostrianos* and Middle Platonism demonstrate that it must have been written either in the last half of the second century C.E. or quite early in the third century. It cannot have been composed much later than 215 C.E. since according to Porphyry it was in use in Rome sometime between years 244 and 265-266 C.E. (265 C.E. marks Plotinus' arrival in Rome, and in 266 he assigned the tractate to Amelius for refutation). Other considerations make a late second century dating more likely. Groups of Gnostics were being refuted as early as 150 C.E. Clement of Alexandria (*Strom.* I.15) mentions both Alexander and Prodicus who use the book of Zoroaster. None of the Gnostic authors mentioned by Porphyry can be identified with certainty, although it is possible that Porphyry's Alexander the Libyan may be identified with the Alexander mentioned by Clement (cf. Schmidt, *Gnostische Schriften*, 629-630). In ca. 185 C.E. Ireneus knew of Gnostic teachings in which the names for aeons and lights similar to those found in the *Apocryphon of John* and *Zostrianos*. Moreover, the other Gnostic books with which *Zostrianos* is most closely allied have been independently dated in the latter half of the second century or early in the third.

PROVENANCE

While one cannot be certain about the matter of provenance, Alexandria in Egypt is a likely place for its composition (cf. Perkins, *Gnostic Dialogue*, 40). That city was a "melting pot" for a wide variety of religious and philosophical thought during this period, as the Christian writings of Justin, Clement, and Origen demonstrate. Platonic philosophy was popular there; Plotinus studied it there under Ammonius early in the third century C.E. We know also that some of the Gnostics living in Alexandria probably came from Syria, and that the city had a large Jewish population.

The original language of *Zostrianos* was Greek. A number of constructions in the Coptic text can only be understood on the assumption of a Greek original. First, there are several instances in which the Coptic definite article is separated from its noun by several words or phrases (e.g., 5,26-27; 12,12-13), a familiar Greek construction but "impossible" in Coptic. Second, ⲁⲩⲱ is used as the indicator of the apodosis of a condition in the way the Greek καί functions (e.g., 31,18-19). Third, ϣⲟⲣⲡ is used to translate προ, as in ϣⲟⲣⲡ ⲛ ϣⲟⲟⲡ = προεῖναι (2,31) and ϣⲟⲣⲡ ⲛ ⲉⲓⲟⲧⲉ for προπάτωρ (3,18). Fourth, many literal translations from the Greek are employed such as placing the Coptic definite article before a Greek preposition as in ⲛⲓⲕⲁⲧⲁ ⲟⲩⲁ = οἱ καθ᾽ ἕν (127,3.11-12.14). The Coptic of *Zostrianos* deviates considerably from later standard Sahidic usage, and its translation of the Greek quite literal. The translator prefered to translate Greek participles with the Coptic circumstantial (e.g., 2,28-33) even when at times temporal forms (rare in *Zostrianos*) could have been used. Often the Coptic is confused as if translator had lost his way (the Greek original was probably somewhat obtuse because of its philosophical bent). The difficulties of the Coptic translation plus the loss of text due to lacunae combine at times to produce nearly untranslatable sections in the manuscript. Because of these several problems, the English translation offered for this edition is often quite literal as well.

Zostrianos appears to be the work of a single author. There is considerable continuity of thought and construction between the opening narrative of the book and that at its conclusion. The contents of the revelations are arranged in a logical order which corresponds to the aeon levels, first in an ascending order, then a descending one. The repetitious nature of the body of the text is evidently due to the use for didactic reasons of sets of traditional materials to expand the description of the heavenly world. The most evident example of the use of such a source by the author of the text is the addition of the revelatory material between 7,22 and 53,15. At 7,22, after a series of four baptisms narrated in a concise, formulaic style, Zostrianos begins to ask a series of philosophical questions. These questions—there are seven sets of them in all in the tractate—are themselves probably derived from Gnostic traditions (Perkins, *Gnostic Dialog*, 55-56, 86-88). Only after the lengthy revelations from Authrounios and Ephesech about the Autogenes aeon system do we come at 53,15 to a fifth baptism, yet it is reported using the same formula as that used earlier on pages 6-7, and this fifth baptism is followed by still another description of the Autogenes aeon. Thus it appears that into an account of an ascent with five baptisms the author has inserted additional materials. This pattern of composition seems to have been followed in the later sections of the book as well, although it cannot be clearly traced because of the extensive damage to the middle portion of the manuscript. Other sources are difficult to detect with so much of the tractate missing. Many of the hymnic and magical elements may have been appropriated from elsewhere and adapted for use in this work. The concluding homily was probably borrowed from another source since it makes a general appeal to gnosis without a single specific reference to the aeon system revealed in the tractate, while references in the homily to a "gentle father" and to his sending of a redeemer are found only in the homily. The homily's rhetorical style and its balance between parensis and proclamation suggest that it may have been a model homily which the author appropriated and adapted.

As he intended, the author's identity remains a mystery. His use of the pseudonym Zostrianos enabled him to claim access to a tradition of truth more ancient and authoritative than that of Plato. Our most certain conclusion about him is that he must have been a Gnostic who sought to understand his gnosis philosophically. Some have argued that the author might have been a Christian. Layton, basing his opinion on the traditional understanding of Porphyry's passage, thinks that the author could have been a Christian writing in a "pseudo-Zoroastrian mode" (see Layton, *Gnostic Scriptures*, 121-122). Perkins sees the warning against being baptized with death in the concluding homily as an attack on Christian baptism (see Perkins, *Gnostic Dialogue*, 25-26, 89-90). Yet on the whole, there is very little in the text to indicate an active interest in things Christian on the part of the author. Not once in the extant text is Christ named (the x̄p̄c̄ of 131,14 is for χπστός), not even in those Autogenes passages that have explicitly Christian parallels in other tractates. A brief mention of one who cannot suffer but does so at 48,27-29 could be a reference to Christ's suffering, but it is not explicitly so. Apart from a few allusions to the N.T. the author betrays no special interest in it. The best of those allusions, a reference to the Pauline triad of faith, hope, and love at 28,20-22, reveals only the kind of non-Christian knowledge of the N.T.

that began to appear at the middle of the second century (cf. Dodds, *Pagan and Christian*, 102-138). Since the contents of *Zostrianos* reveal so little interest in Christianity, it is unlikely that its author was a Christian (see Sieber, "Introduction to Zostrianos"; cf. Tuckett, *Nag Hammadi*, 14-15). Nor does the author seem to have been Jewish since the tractate betrays no particular interest in Judaism. Although some of the names of the heavenly beings are obviously Hebrew in their origin (e.g., Daveithe and Gamaliel), this book contains none of the midrashic material that appears in some of the other Nag Hammadi tractates. The author knows and repeats some Jewish ideas, such as the creation of the world by a word (9,2-4), but he does not allude the Genesis accounts of creation. He seems familiar with the form of the Enoch literature yet does not use its content. As both the Christian and Jewish elements in *Zostrianos* survive only in a secondary way, they probably came to its author through the general culture, although they may be the residue from earlier stages of Sethianism (see Turner, "Sethian Gnosticism," 59-85, who argues that the Sethians originated as a Jewish baptismal sect, then successively became Christians and Platonists). In any case, the book itself is most accurately described as the representative of a non-Christian, non-Jewish, philosophical Gnosticism.

The author wrote for an audience that interpreted its cultic experience in terms of traditional Greek philosophy. Such an attempt at a syncretism of religion and philosophy was typical for the late second century C.E. Justin Martyr's attempt to use philosophical categories provides a Christian example of the same tendency. In this instance the author tried to combine a tradition of mythological aeons from Gnostic circles with philosophical categories, although the stress remained on the mythological. Aeons are blessed and addressed, and possession of their names is understood to provide magical access to the otherworld, while intellectual argument of the type known from Plotinus is mostly lacking. Though the author of *Zostrianos* certainly believed himself a true and faithful interpreter of Plato, modern readers will undoubtedly find themselves sympathetic to Porphyry's complaint that he had in fact abandoned the ancient philosophy.

[ⲁ]

```
     [ . . . . . .]ⲉ ⲛⲧⲉ ⲡⲉ .[ . . .] ⲛ ⲛⲓϣⲁϫⲉ
2    [ . . . . . .]ⲟⲛⲅ ϣⲁ ⲉⲛ[ⲉⲅ] ⲛⲁⲓ̈ ⲁⲛⲟⲕ
     [ . . . . . . . . . . . . . . .]ⲩ ⳨ⲱ̄ⲥ̄[ⲧⲣⲓⲁⲛ—]
4    [ⲟⲥ .] . .[ . . . .] .ⲥ̄ .[ . .]ⲥ̄ⲁ ⲙⲛ ⲓ̈ⲟⲗⲁⲟⲥ
     [ⲉⲧ]ⲁ̣ⲓ̈ϣⲱⲡⲉ ⲅⲙ ⲡ[ⲓ̈ⲕ]ⲟⲥⲙⲟⲥ ⲛ ⲛⲁⲓ̈
6    [ⲉⲧ]ⲉ ⲛ ⲧⲁⲅⲟⲩ ⲙⲛ [ⲛⲏ] ⲉⲧⲙⲛⲛⲥⲱⲉⲓ
     [ⲛⲓ]ⲥ̇ⲱⲧⲡ ⲉⲧⲟⲛⲅ· ϥ̇ⲟⲛⲅ ⲛ̇ϭⲓ ⲡⲛⲟⲩⲧⲉ
8    [ . . . .] ⲧⲙⲉ ⲅⲛ ⲟⲩⲙⲛⲧⲙⲉ ⲛ ⲧⲁⲡⲙⲉ
     [ⲙⲛ ⲟ]ⲩⲥⲟⲟⲩⲛ ⲁⲛⲟⲕ ⲙⲛ <ⲟⲩ>ⲟⲩⲟⲉⲓⲛ ϣⲁ
10   [ⲉⲛ]ⲉⲅ· ⲉⲧⲁⲉⲓⲡⲱⲣϫ ⲙ ⲡⲓⲥⲱⲙⲁⲧⲓ
     [ⲕ]ⲟⲛ ⲛ ⲕⲁⲕⲉ ⲉⲧⲛⲅⲣⲁⲓ̈ ⲛⲅⲏⲧ̇ ⲙⲛ ⲡⲓ—
12   [ⲯ]ⲩⲭⲓⲕⲟⲛ ⲛ ⲭⲁⲟⲩⲥ ⲅⲛ ⲟⲩⲛⲟⲩⲥ
     ⲙⲛ ϯⲙⲛⲧⲥⲅⲓⲙⲉ ⲛⲛ ⲉⲡⲓⲑⲩⲙⲓⲁ
14   [ .]ⲁ̣ⲓ̈ ⲉⲧⲅⲛ ⲡⲓⲕⲁⲕⲉ· ⲉⲙⲡⲓⲣ ⲅⲱⲃ ϭⲉ
     ⲉⲣⲟⲥ· ⲉⲧⲁⲉⲓϭⲓⲛⲉ ⲙ ⲡⲓⲁⲧⲛ ⲁⲣⲏϫϥ
16   ⲛⲧⲉ ⲧⲁⲅⲩⲗⲏ· ⲁⲩⲱ ⲁⲉⲓⲥⲟⲅⲉ ⲛ ϯ—
     [ⲕⲧ]ⲓⲥⲓⲥ ⲉⲧⲙⲟⲟⲩⲧ̇ ⲉⲧⲅⲣⲁⲓ̈ ⲛⲅⲏⲧ̇
18   [ⲙ]ⲛ ⲡⲓⲕⲟⲥⲙⲟⲕⲣⲁⲧⲱⲣ ⲛ ⲛⲟⲩⲧⲉ
     ⲛⲛ ⲉⲥⲑⲏⲧⲟⲛ· ⲉⲁⲉ[ⲓ]ϯ ⲅⲛ ⲟⲩϭⲟⲙ
20   ⲛⲛ ⲟⲩⲟⲉⲓϣ ⲛⲧⲉ ⲡⲧⲏⲣϥ ⲛ ⲛⲏ ⲉ—
     ⲧⲛⲧⲁ[ⲩ] ⲙⲙⲁⲩ ⲙ ⲙⲉⲣⲓⲕⲟⲛ ⲛ ϣⲙ—
22   ⲙⲟ· ⲉⲉⲓ̈ⲅⲓ ⲧⲟⲟⲧ̇ ⲉ ⲛⲉⲩⲅⲃⲏⲩⲧⲉ ⲛ
```

A single copy of the text is known to survive. Some of its readings can now be distinguished only with the aid of ultraviolet light. Textual evidence now attested only by photographs is cited according to Emmel's sigla (Emmel, "Photographic Evidence").

1,1-2,7   *Introduction of Zostrianos*

1   The following text was read solely from blotting on the facing flyleaf; cf. *Facsimile Edition: Codex VIII*, pl. B: line 1,]ⲉ ⲛⲧⲉ ⲡⲉ .[. . .]ⲛ and final ⲉ at the end of the line; line 2,] ⲟⲛⲅ ϣⲁ ⲉⲛ[.

1,1-3   E.g., [ⲡϫⲱⲱⲙ]ⲉ or [ⲡⲓϫⲱⲱⲙ]ⲉ ⲛⲧⲉ ⲡⲉⲟ[ⲟⲩ] ⲛ ⲛⲓϣⲁϫⲉ /[ⲙ ⲡⲏ ⲉⲧ]ⲟⲛⲅ ϣⲁ ⲉⲛ[ⲉⲅ] ⲛⲁⲓ̈ ⲁⲛⲟⲕ/[ⲉⲧⲁⲓ̈ⲥⲅⲣⲁⲓ̈ ⲙⲙⲟ]ⲩ; or in line 2 possibly [ⲛ ⲛⲏ ⲉⲧ]. [The glorious book] of the words [of the one who] lives forever, [which] I Zostrianos [wrote].

1,1   .[, an angular junction of two strokes at midline (read with ultraviolet light), suggestive of ⲫ but also compatible with the left of a pinched ⲟ or ⲥ; too high to be the angle of ⲅ.

1,2   ]ⲟⲛⲅ, read (from blotting) in December 1971 while flyleaf still adhered to inner surface of the upper cover; text was subsequently damaged and now reads only]ⲛⲅ | or ⲡⲁ̣ⲓ̈.

1,3   No supralinear stroke above ⳨ⲱⲥ[Iⲥ, or else ⲟ̣.

[1]

[   ] of the [   ] of the words
2   [   ] live forever, these things I] Zos[trianos]
     [
4   [   ] and Iolaos
     when I was in the world (κόσμος) for the sake of
6   these of my age and [those] (coming) after me,
     [the] living elect. God lives!
8   I [   ] the truth with truth
     [and] knowledge and eternal
10   light. After I parted from the
     somatic (σωματικόν) darkness in me and
12   the psychic (ψυχικόν) chaos (χάος) in mind (νοῦς)
     and the feminine desire (ἐπιθυμία)
14   [ ] in the darkness, I did not make use of it
     again. After I had found the infinite
16   (side) of my matter (ὕλη) and reproved the
     dead creation (κτίσις) within me
18   and the divine cosmocrater (κοσμωκράτωρ)
     of the perceptible (αἰσθητόν) (world), I preached
20   powerfully about the All to those
     with alien parts (μερικόν).
22   Although I tried their ways

1,4   .] . .[, these ink traces (bottoms of three vertical strokes) are incompatible
       with ⲡϢⲎⲢⲉ Ⲛ or ⲡϢⲎⲢⲉ Ⲛⲓ.ⲥ .[. .]ⲓⲁ, traces of a proper name with
       a supralinear stroke above it; first ink trace is from Ⲏ, Ϥ, or Ⲛ; second trace,
       from Ⲧ, Ⲏ, Ϥ, Ⲕ, Ⲛ, or possibly Ⲃ.
1,5   ⲉⲧⲁ̈ⲓ´ = Sahidic Ⲛⲧⲉⲣⲉϥ´.
1,6   Sahidic ⲉⲧ ⲟ Ⲛ; cf. Bohairic Ⲛⲧⲉϥϭⲟⲧ.
1,8   E.g., [ϯϫⲱ Ⲛ] (with slight crowding); cf. Eph 4:15 I Bohairic, ⲦⲀϥⲘⲎϥ;
       cf. 24,20; 117,10.
1,9-10 Possibly emend [ⲀⲚⲞⲔ] ⲘⲚ ‹ⲞⲨ›ⲞⲨⲞⲉⲓⲚ Ϣⲁ [ⲉⲚ]ⲉϩ· ‹ⲀⲚⲞⲔ›
       ⲉⲦⲀⲉⲓ´, etc.
1,9   Not room for [ⲀⲨⲰ ⲟ]I ‹ⲞⲨ›, copyist's careless omission.
1,12   I.e., ⲭⲀⲞⲤ.
1,13   Circumflex over the group ϩ Ϥ I lit., the femaleness of desire;
       cf. 1 Apoc. Jas. V 24,27ff.
1,14   E.g., [Ⲧ]Ⲁ̈ⲓ or [Ⲛ]Ⲁ̈ⲓ.
1,15   ⲀⲦⲚⲀⲣⲎϫ = ἄληπτος; cf. 16,5-7.
1,19   −ⲦⲞⲚ, sic.
1,21   Ⲙ, particle of the direct object.
1,22   Circumflex over the group ϩϤ I see 25,4n.

ⲚⲀⲨ ⲞⲨⲔⲞⲨⲈⲤ· Ⲙ ⲠⲢⲎⲦⲈ ⲈⲦⲀ–
24 ⲦⲀⲚⲀⲄⲔⲎ ⲚⲦⲈ ⲠⲤⲀⲠⲞ ⲚⲦ Ⲉ ⲠⲈⲦ–
ⲦⲞⲨⲞⲚⲨ· ⲈⲘⲠⲤⲰⲔ ⲨⲦⲎⲞⲨ ⲢⲰ
26 ⲈⲚⲈⲨ· ⲀⲖⲖⲀ Ⲛ ⲞⲨⲞⲈⲤⲰ ⲚⲤⲘ
ⲚⲈⲨⲠⲰⲢⲬ ⲘⲘⲞⲒ ⲚⲤⲀⲂⲞⲖ ⲘⲘⲞⲞⲨ
28 ⲈⲤⲰⲰⲠⲈ ⲈⲂⲞⲖ ⲨⲤⲦⲞⲞⲦⲨ Ⲛ ⲞⲨ–
[. .]ⲤⲈ ⲈⲨⲞⲨⲀⲀⲂ· ⲀⲨⲰ ⲈⲨⲘⲞⲬⲄ
30 [Ⲉ]ⲦⲀⲒⲤⲞⲞⲨⲦⲚ Ⲛ ⲦⲀⲮⲨⲬⲎ ⲚⲚ ⲀⲦ–
ⲔⲀⲄⲤⲀ ⲈⲂⲞⲖ· ⲀⲨⲰ ⲀⲈⲤ† ⳠⲞⲘ

Ⲃ̄

Ⲙ ⲠⲤⲚⲞⲈⲢ[ⲞⲚ
2 ⲀⲨⲰ ⲀⲈⲤ[
ⲨⲘ ⲠⲤⲚⲔ[––––] Ⲛ Ⲕ[. .] . .[
4 Ⲙ ⲠⲀⲚⲞⲨⲦ[Ⲉ
[. . .] ⲈⲀⲈⲤⲢ Ⳝ[. . . .] ⲠⲒ . . .]ⲀⲚⲦ[. . . . . .
6 ⳠⲘⳠⲞⲘ ⳠⲚ [Ⲟ]ⲨⲠⲚⲀ ⲈⲨⲞⲨⲀⲀ[Ⲃ· ⲠⲎ]
ⲈⲦⲬⲞⳞⲈ [Ⲉ ⲚⲞ]ⲨⲦⲈ· ⲀⲨⲰ Ⲁ[Ⲩ . . . .
8 ⳠⲤⲬⲰⲈⲤ ⲘⲀⲨⲀⲀⲦ ⲈⲈⲤⳞⲞⲞⲦⲰ[Ⲛ ⲀⲨⲰ]
ⲀⲈⲤⲚⲀⲨ Ⲉ ⲠⲤⲦⲈⲖⲤⲞⳞ Ⲛ ⲀⲖⲞ[Ⲩ . . . . . .
10 ⲠⲈ ⲚⲦⲞⲨ· ⲀⲨⲰ ⲘⲚ ⲠⲎ ⲈⲦ .[. . . Ⲛ ⲞⲨ–]
ⲘⲎⲎⲰⲈ Ⲛ ⳞⲞⲠ ⲘⲚ ⲞⲨⲀⲦⲞ Ⲛ Ⲣ[ⲎⲦⲈ ⲈⲨ–]
12 ⲞⲨⲞⲚⳠ ⲚⲀⲒ ⲈⲂⲞⲖ· Ⲙ ⲠⲈⲨⲢⲎⲦⲈ Ⲟ[ⲨⲈⲤ–]
ⲰⲦ ⲈⲨⲞⲨⲰⳞ· ⲈⲈⲤⲔⲰⲦⲈ ⲚⲤⲀ Ⲡ[ⳞⳠⲞ–]
14 ⲞⲨⲦ Ⲛ ⲈⲤⲰⲦ ⲚⲦⲈ ⲚⲀⲒ ⲦⲎⲢⲞⲨ [ⲚⲎ ⲈⲦ–]
ⳠⲚ ⲞⲨⲈⲚⲚⲞⳞⲀ ⲘⲚ ⲞⲨⲈⳞⲐⲎⳞⲤⳞ Ⳡ[Ⲛ ⲞⲨ–]
16 ⲈⳞⲀⲞⳞ ⲀⲨⲰ ⲞⲨⳞⲈⲚⲞⳞ ⲘⲚ ⲞⲨ[ⲘⲈ–]
ⲢⲞⳞ ⲀⲨⲰ ⲞⲨⲠⲦⲎⲢⲨ ⲘⲚ ⲠⲎ Ⲉ[ⲦⲀ–]

1,26-27 Cf.3,14-19. What tradition Zostrianos is rejecting here (Judaism, Christianity, another variety of Gnosticism, Platonism) is unclear. See also Perkins, *Gnostic Dialog*, 80-81.

1,28 ⲉ, curved trace as from upper left of ⲉ | ⲓ̈ only one dot of the trema survives; possibly ⲉ[ⲁ]ⲓ̈´, but elsewhere this is spelled ⲉⲁⲉⲥ´ | circumflex over the group ⳠⲤ.

1,29 ⳽, a characteristic trace from bottom right of this letter; it has a serif, as often on this page | e.g., [ⲘⲤ]ⳞⲈ; [ⳠⲤ]ⳞⲈ perhaps would not fill the lacuna.

1,31 ⲀⲨⲰ, taken as *καί* introducing apodosis.

2 The following text was read from blotting on the facing page (p. 3): pagination, Ⲃ̄; line 1, Ⲙ ⲠⲤⲚⲞⲈⲢ[; line 2, ⲀⲨⲰ; end of line 3,]Ⲛ Ⲕ[.] . .[.

2,3 Cod. ⲠⲤⲚ .[, the Ⲛ has a supralinear stroke and the following trace is from ⲁ, ⲕ, or Ⲛ | end of line, Ⲕ[Ⲟ]ⳞⲘ[ⳞⲔⲞⲚ]?

2,5 E.g., Ⳡ[ⲞⲦⲈ; (Ⳡ[ⲰⲂ] is too short) | ⲁ, or else Ⲙ.

2,6 Cf. Luke 1:80; Rom 4:20.

for a little while as
24 the necessity (ἀνάγκη) of birth brought me
into the visible world, I was never pleased with
26 them; instead (ἀλλά), I always
separated myself from them
28 because I came into being through
a holy [ ].
30 When I, a mixed one, had set straight my sinless (-κακία)
soul (ψυχή), then I strengthened
2
the intellectual (νοερόν) [
2 and I [
in the [
4 of my God [
[   ] I having done [
6 grow strong in a holy spirit (πνεῦμα)
higher than god. [
8 upon me alone as I was setting myself straight, [and]
I saw the perfect (τέλειος) child [
10 [   ]. With him who [
many times and many [ways, he]
12 appeared to me as a
loving [father] when I was seeking the
14 [male] father of all these [who are]
in thought (ἔννοια) and perception (αἴσθησις) in
16 form (εἶδος), race (γένος), [region (μέρος)],
(in) an All and one [that]

2,7-7,22 *The Call, Redemption and Ascent of Zostrianos*
2,7   I.e., higher than the god who created this world; see also 13,5; 34,15; cf.
          Apoc.Adam V 64,16-19.
2,9   E.g., [ⲩ ⲉⲩϢ Ⲏⲣⲉ] ǀ for perfect child, cf. 13,6; 30,4-6.
2,10   After ⲉⲧ̄, only a trace of a supralinear stroke; e.g., ⲉ̄ⲧ̄Ⲛ[Ⲙⲁⳓ or
          ⲉⲧⲘ[Ⲙⲁⲩ; length of lacuna is uncertain.
2,11   Or, [ⲟⲩ'].
2,12   Or, ọ[Ⲛ ⲟⲩⲥ].
2,13-14   Loving father, perhaps the heavenly Seth; cf. 30,9-14.
2,14   Ⲛⲁï ⲦⲎⲣⲟⲩ, probably a collective body of spiritual beings (not the
          universe).
2,15   Not Ⲙ[Ⲛ.
2,17   Cf. *Apoc.Pet.* VII 82,26-83,8.

18　ＭＡϩＴＥ ＡＵⲰ ＥＴＯⲨＡＭＡϩＴＥ ＭＭ[ＯϤ]
　　ＭＮ ＯⲨＣⲰＭＡ ＡⲨⲰ ＯⲨＡＴＣⲰ[ＭＡ]
20　ＭＮ ＯⲨＯⲨＣＩＡ ＡⲨⲰ ＯⲨϩⲨＡＮ Ｍ[Ｎ ＮＥＴ–]
　　ＮＴＥⲨ ＴＨＰＯⲨ· ＡⲨⲰ ϯϩⲨⲠＡＰⰉＩＣ [ＥＣ–]
22　ＭＯⰅＫ ＮＭＡⲨ ＭＮ ⲠＮＯⲨＴＥ ＮＴＥ
　　{ⲠＥＩ}ⲠⰉＫⲰＣ ＮＮ ＡⲨＭＩＣＥ ＭＮ ϯϬＯＭ [ＥＴＮ–]
24　ＴＯＯＴＯⲨ ＴＨＰＯⲨ· ＡⲨⲰ ϯϩⲨⲠＡＰⰅＩ[Ｃ]
　　ⰅＥ ⲠⲰＣ ＮＥⲦϢＯＯⲠ ＥϩＥＮＥＢＯⲆ ϩＭ
26　ⲠＥⲰＮ ＮＴＥ ＮＥⲦϢＯＯⲠ ＮＥ ＥＢＯⲆ
　　ϩＮ ＯⲨⲠＮⲀ ＮＮ ＡⲨＮＡⲨ ＥＰＯϤ ＡⲨⲰ ＮＮ Ａ[ϯ–]
28　ⲠⲰϢＥ ＮＮ ＡⲨＴＯⲨＥＮＨＣ ＥϩＥＮⲦ Ｎ [ＥＩ–]
　　ＮＥ ＮＮ ＡⲨＭ[Ｉ]ϬＥ ＥⲨＮＴＡⲨ ＭＭＡⲨ
30　ＮＮ ＯⲨＡＰＸＨ ＥＣＣＯＴⲠⲀ Ｅ ϯϩⲨⲠＡＰＸ[ＩＣ]
　　ＡⲨⲰ ＥⲨＰ ϢＯＰⲠⲀ Ｎ ϢＯＯⲠ [Ｅ ＮＡＩ ＴＨ–]
32　ＰＯⲨ· ＥＡⲨϢⲰⲠＥ ⰅＥ Ｍ ⲠⰃＫ[ＯＣＭＯＣ]
　　Ｈ ⲠⲰＣ ＮＨ ＥＴＯⲨＢＨϤ ＭＮ ＮＡＩ ＴＨ[ＰＯⲨ]

　　　　　　　　　　　　　　　　　　　　　Ｃ̅

　　[. . . . . ＮＡ]ＮＯⲨϤ· ⲠＡＩ
2　　[. . . . .]Ａ[. . . . . . .] ＡⲨⲰ ＮⲀＯＥⰅ–
　　[ϬＥ Ａ]ⲨⲰ ⰅＥ ＡϢ [ⲠＥ ⲠＴ]ＯⲠＯＣ Ｎ[Ｔ]Ｅ
4　　[ⲠＨ Ｅ]ⲦＭＭＡⲨ· Ｈ ＯⲨ Ｎ ＡＰＸＨ ＥＴＮＴＡϤ
　　[ＭＭＡ]Ⲩ· Ｈ Ｎ ＡϢ Ｎ ＰＨＴＥ ⲠⰅＥＢＯⲆ ＭＭＯϤ
6　　[ＥϤ]ϢＯＯⲠ ＮＡϤ ＭＮ [ＮＡＩ] ＴＨＰＯⲨ· Ｈ ⲠⲰＣ–
　　[ＥϤϢⲰ]ⲠＥ Ｎ ϩＡⲠⲆＯⲨＮ ＥⲨϢＥＢＩＨＯⲨⲦ
8　　[ＥＰＯϤ] ＭＡⲨＡＡϤ· ＥϤϢＯＯⲠⲀ Ｎ ＯⲨϩⲨ–
　　[ⲠＡ]ＰＸＩＣ ＭＮ ＯⲨＥＩⰅＯＣ· ＡⲨⲰ ＯⲨＭＮⲦ–
10　[Ｍ]ＡＫＡＰＩＯＣ· ＡⲨⲰ ＥϤϯ Ｎ ＯⲨϬＯＭ ＥϤ–
　　[Ｏ]Ｎϩ ϩＭ ⲠⲰＮϩ· Ｈ Ｎ ＡϢ Ｎ ＰＨＴＥ ϯϩⲨ–
12　[Ⲡ]ＡＰＸＩＣ ＥＴＥ ＮＣϢＯＯⲠⲀ ＡＮ ＡＣＯⲨ–
　　ⲰＮϩ ＥＢＯⲆ ϩＮ ＯⲨϬＯＭ ＥＣϢＯＯⲠ:
14　[Ｎ]ＡＩ ⰅＥ ＥＥＩϢＯⰅＮＥ Ｅ ＥＩＭＥ ＥＰＯ[Ｏ]Ⲩ·
　　[Ａ]ⲨⲰ ＮＥＩＥ[Ｉ]ＮＥ ＥϩＰＡＩ Ｍ ＭＨＮＥ ＫＡＴＡ
16　ⲠⲦⲰⲛ ＮＴＥ ⲠＡＧＥＮＯＣ Ｍ ⲠＮＯⲨＴＥ

2,21　Or, ϯϩⲨⲠＡＰＸＩＣ ＭＯⲨⰉＫ ＮＭＡⲨ.
2,23　For {ⲠＥＩ}, cf. 13,2; or else, ⲠＥＩ{ⲠＩ}Ｋ̅Ｌ̅Ｃ̅, cf. 18,10 | for Ｋ̅Ｌ̅Ｃ̅,
　　　　see 15,12n.
2,25ff　The text is obscure.
2,28　I.e., ϩＥＮϢＯＭⲦ.
2,30　ϯϩⲨⲠ, error for ϯϩⲨⲠ´.
2,32　Ｋ[, only the bottom of a vertical stroke survives.

18   restrains and is restrained,
      (in) a body (σῶμα) yet without a body (-σῶμα),
20   (in) essence (οὐσία), matter (ὕλη) and [those who]
      belong to all these. It is with
22   them and the divine, unborn
      Kalyptos (καλυπτός) and the power [in] them all that
24   existence (ὕπαρξις) is mixed. (About) existence (ὕπαρξις):
      How (πῶς) do those who exist, coming from
26   the aeon (αἰών) of those who exist- from
      an invisible, undivided and
28   self-begotten (αὐτογενής) Spirit (πνεῦμα) as
      three unborn images, have
30   an origin (ἀρχή) better than existence (ὕπαρξις)?
      They exist prior [to] all [these],
32   yet (δέ) they have become the [world (κόσμος)].
      How (ἤ πῶς) are those opposite it and all these

                                3

      [   ] good, he
2   [   ] and an
      [excuse.] What is [that one's] place (τόπος)?
4   What (+δέ) is his origin (ἀρχή)?
      How (+ἤ) does the one from him
6   belong to him and all these? How (ἤ πῶς)
      [does he come into existence] as simple (ἁπλοῦν)
8   (yet) differing [from] himself? He exists as
      existence (ὕπαρξις), form (εἶδος), and
10   blessedness (-μακάριος), yet by giving strength he
      is alive with life. How (+ἤ)
12   has the existence (ὕπαρξις) which does not exist
      appeared from a power that exists?"
14   While (+δέ) pondering these things to understand them,
      then after the custom of my race (γένος)
16   I kept bringing them up daily to the god

---

3   The underlined letter in the following text was read primarily from blotting
           on the facing page (p. 2): line 32, ⲣⲏⲧⲉ.
3,3-13   That one, he, etc., antecedent unknown.
3,5   Not ἤ.
3,10-11   Or, in giving strength he is alive with life.
3,14   Or, ‹ⲛ›ⲉⲉⲓϣⲟⲝⲛⲉ.
3,15   For the figurative use of ⲉⲓⲛⲉ, cf. 44,24.

[N]ⲧⲉ ⲛⲁⲉⲓⲟⲧⲉ· ⲛⲉⲓϫⲱ ⲙ ⲡⲥⲙⲟⲩ ⲛ–
18 [ⲧ]ⲉ ⲛⲁⲓ̈ ⲧⲏⲣⲟⲩ· ⲛⲁϣⲟⲣⲡ̄ ⲛ ⲉⲓⲟⲧⲉ
[ⲧ]ⲁⲣ ⲙⲛ ⲛⲁⲉⲓⲟⲧⲉ ⲉⲧⲁⲩⲕⲱⲧⲉ ⲁⲩϭⲓⲛⲉ
20 ⲁⲛⲟⲕ ⲇⲉ ⲙⲡⲓⲕⲁ ⲧⲟⲟⲧ ⲉⲃⲟⲗ ⲉⲉⲓⲣ ⲁⲓⲧⲓ
ⲛⲥⲁ ⲟ[ⲩ]ⲙⲁ ⲛ ⲙⲧⲟⲛ ⲉϥⲙⲡϣⲁ ⲙ ⲡⲁⲡⲛⲁ·
22 ⲉⲙⲡ[ⲁ]ⲧⲟⲩⲥⲟⲛϩ̄ⲧ ϩⲙ ⲡⲓⲥⲉⲑⲛⲧⲟⲛ
ⲛ ⲕⲟⲥⲙⲟⲥ· ⲁⲩⲱ ⲧⲟⲧⲉ ⲉⲓ̈ⲙⲟⲕϩ ⲛ ϩⲏⲧ
24 ⲉⲙⲁⲧⲉ ⲁⲩⲱ ⲉⲉⲓⲟⲕⲙ ⲉⲧⲃⲉ ϯⲙⲛⲧ–
ⲕⲟⲩⲉ[ⲓ] ⲛ ϩⲏⲧ ⲉⲧⲕⲱⲧⲉ ⲉⲣⲟⲉⲓ· ⲁⲉⲓⲣ
26 ⲧⲟⲗⲙⲁ ⲉ ⲉⲓⲣⲉ ⲛ ⲟⲩ[ⲗ]ⲁⲁⲩ ⲁⲩⲱ ⲉ ⲧⲁ–
ⲁ̄ⲧ ⲛ ⲛⲓⲑⲏⲣⲓⲟⲛ ⲛ[ⲧ]ⲉ ϯⲉⲣⲏⲙⲟⲥ·
28 ⲉϩⲣⲁⲓ̈ ⲉⲩⲧⲁⲕⲟ ⲉϥⲛⲁϣⲧ̄· ⲁϥⲁϩⲉⲣⲁⲧϥ̄
ⲛⲁⲓ̈ [ⲛ]ϭⲓ ⲡⲁⲅⲅⲉⲗⲟⲥ ⲛⲧⲉ ϯⲅⲛⲱⲥⲓⲥ ⲛⲧⲉ
30 [ⲡⲓⲟⲩⲟ]ⲉⲓⲛ ϣⲁ ⲉⲛⲉϩ· ⲁⲩⲱ ⲡⲉϫⲁϥ ⲛⲁⲓ̈
[ϫⲉ] ⲍⲱⲥⲧⲣⲓⲛⲉ· ⲉⲧⲃⲉ ⲟⲩ ⲁⲕⲗⲓⲃⲉ ⲙ
32 [ⲡⲓ]ⲣⲏⲧⲉ ⲉⲕⲉ ⲛⲛ ⲁⲧⲙⲙⲉ ⲉ ⲛⲓⲛⲁϭ ⲛ ϣⲁ ⲉⲛⲉϩ
Δ
ⲉⲧⲥⲁϩⲣⲁ[ⲓ̈
2 ⲉⲣⲟⲕ ⲁⲛ[
ⲁⲩⲱ ⲉⲧⲃ[ⲉ . . . .]ⲧⲁⲩⲟⲕⲉⲡ[. . . . .
4 ⲁ[.] ϫⲉ ⲉⲕⲉⲛ[ⲟ]ⲩ[ϩ]ⲙ ⲧⲉⲛⲟⲩ· ⲙ[. . . .
ⲡⲉ ⲣⲱ ϩⲛ ⲧⲁⲕⲟ ⲉⲛⲉϩ· ⲟⲩⲇⲉ [. . . . .
6 ⲙⲉ ⲉ ⲛⲏ ⲉⲧⲕⲥⲟⲟⲩⲛ ⲙⲙⲟⲟⲩ [ϩⲓⲛⲁ]
ϫⲉ ⲉⲕⲉⲛⲟⲩ[ϩ]ⲙ ⲛ ϩⲉⲛⲕⲟⲟⲩⲉ· ⲛ[ⲏ ⲉⲧⲉ–]
8 ⲡⲓⲱⲧ̄ ⲛⲧ[ⲉ] ⲛⲓϫⲓⲥⲉ ⲛⲁⲥⲟⲧⲡⲟ[ⲩ ⲕⲙⲉ–]
ⲉⲧⲉ ⲟⲛ ϫⲉ ⲛⲧⲕ ⲡⲓⲱⲧ ⲛⲧⲉ ⲡ[ⲉⲕⲅⲉⲛⲟⲥ]
10 ⲏ ϫⲉ ⲓ̈ⲟⲗⲁⲟⲥ ⲡⲉ ⲡⲉⲕⲉⲓⲱⲧ· ⲟⲩ[. . .
ⲟⲩⲁⲅⲅⲉⲗⲟⲥ ⲛⲧⲉ ⲡⲛⲟⲩⲧⲉ ⲉⲁ[. . .
12 ⲉⲓⲧ ⲛⲁⲕ ⲉⲃⲟⲗ ϩⲓⲧⲛ ϩⲉⲛⲣⲱⲙⲉ ⲉ[ⲩⲟⲩ–]
ⲁⲁⲃ· ⲁⲙⲟⲩ ⲛⲧⲥⲓⲛⲉ ⲉⲃⲟⲗ ϩⲛ ⲛ[ⲁⲓ̈]
14 ⲛⲁⲓ̈ ⲉⲧⲕⲛⲁⲕⲟⲧⲕ ⲉⲣⲟⲟⲩ ⲟⲛ ⲛ ⲕⲉ[ⲥⲟⲡ]
ϩⲓⲛⲁ ϫⲉ ⲉⲕⲁⲧⲁϣⲉ ⲟⲉⲓϣ ⲛ ⲟⲩⲅⲉⲛ[ⲉⲁ]

3,26-28   For suicide as a common ascetic practice in late antiquity, see Perkins, *Gnostic Dialog*, 89.

3,27   Cod. ⲑⲏⲣⲓⲟⲛ̄, supralinear stroke in error ǀ cf. Ps 74:19.

3,28-29   Cf. Luke 1:9; Acts 27:24.

3,31   Cf. Porph. *Vit.Plot.* 16.

3,32   [ⲡⲓ], error for ⲡⲉⲓ̈ as at 46,30 ǀ the eternals, divine beings who were thought to have had no beginning or ending (mortals who became divine were called immortals); cf. *Apoc.Adam* V 64,15.

4,3   ]ⲧ, or else]ⲡ.

of my fathers. I kept praising
18 them all, for (γάρ) my fore-fathers
and fathers who sought found.
20 As for me (+δέ), I did not cease seeking (αἰτεῖν)
a place of repose worthy of my spirit (πνεῦμα)
22 where I would not be bound in the perceptible (αἰσθητόν)
world (κόσμος). Then (τότε), as I was deeply
24 troubled and gloomy because of the
discouragement which surrounded me,
26 I dared (τολμᾶν) to act and
to deliver myself to the wild beasts (θηρίον) of the
28 desert (ἐρῆμος) for a violent death. There stood
before me the angel (ἄγγελος) of the knowledge (γνῶσις)
30 of eternal light. He said to me,
"Zostrianos, why have you gone mad
32 as if you were ignorant of the great eternals
4
who are above? [
2 you [
and concerning [
4 that you are now saved, [
[   ] in eternal death, nor (οὐδέ) [
6 [   ] those whom you know
in order to [(+ἵνα)] save others,
8 my father's chosen elect? [Do you]
[suppose] that you are the father of [your race (γένος)]
10 or (ἤ) that Iolaos is your father, a [   ]
angel (ἄγγελος) of god [
12 you through holy men?
Come and pass through each
14 of [these]. You will return to them another [time]
to (ἵνα) preach to a living [race (γενέα)],

4,4   ἀ[.], ἀ read from blotting on the facing page (at 5,18) | for ⲝⲉ ⲉˊ = ⲉˊ,
        cf. 83, 20.
4,5   E.g., [Ⲙⲡϥⲉⲓˊ].
4,8-9   Or, [ⲧ ⲉⲕⲙⲉ]/ⲉⲧⲉ.
4,9-10 Cf. Deut 32:6; Ps 89:26.
4,9   Or, ⲡ[ⲉⲓ̈ⲧⲉⲛⲟⲥ].
4,12   ⲉⲓⲧ̄ read from blotting on the facing page (at 5,9).
4,15   Sahidic, ⲉⲕⲉⲧⲁϣⲉ.

16 ЄСОΝϨ· ⲁⲩⲱ ⲚⲦⲚΟⲨϨⲘ Ⲛ ⲚⲎ ⲈⲦ[Ⲙ–]
     ⲠⲰⲀ· ⲁⲩⲱ ⲚⲤϮ ϬΟⲘ Ⲛ ⲚⲤⲰⲦ[Ⲡ]
18 ⲆⲈ ΟⲨΝΟϬ ⲠⲈ ⲠⲤⲀⲦⲰⲚ ⲚⲦⲈ ⲠⲤⲈ[ⲰⲚ]
     ⲁⲩⲱ ⲆⲈ ΟⲨⲔΟⲨⲈⲤ ⲠⲈ ⲠⲤⲬⲢΟΝΟ[Ⲥ Ⲙ]
20 ⲠⲈⲒⲘⲀ· ⲚⲀⲒ ⲆⲈ ⲚⲦⲈⲢⲈⳒⳜΟΟⲨ Ⲛ[ⲀⲒ]
     ⲀΝΟⲔ ϨⲚ ΟⲨΝΟϬ Ⲛ ⲒⲎⲤ ⲘⲚ ΟⲨΝΟ[Ϭ Ⲛ]
22 ΟⲨⲢΟⲦ̇ Ⲛ ϨⲎ[Ⲧ] ⲀⲈⲤⲀⲖⲈ ⲚⲘⲘⲀⳒ ⲈϨⲢ[ⲀⲒ]
     ⲈⲨΝΟϬ Ⲛ ⲔⲖΟΟⲖⲈ Ⲛ ΟⲨΟⲈ[Ⲥ]Ⲛ ⲀⲈⲤⲔ[Ⲱ]
24 Ⲙ ⲠⲀⲠⲖⲀⲤⲘⲀ ϨⲤⳜⲘ ⲠⲔⲀ[Ϩ] ⲈⲨⲀⲢⲈ[Ϩ]
     ⲈⲢΟⳒ ⲈⲂΟⲖ ϨⲤⲦⲚ ϨⲈΝⲈΟΟⲨ· ⲁⲩⲱ ⲁ[Ⲛ–]
26 ΝΟⲨϨⲘ Ⲉ̄ⲂΟⲖ [Ϩ]Ⲙ ⲠⲤⲔΟⲤⲘΟⲤ ⲦⲎⲢⳒ
     ⲘⲚ ⲠⲤ̄Ⲧ̄ Ⲛ[Ⲛ] ⲈⲰⲚ ⲈⲦⲰΟΟⲠ
28 ΝϨⲎⲦⳒ [ⲘⲚ ΝΟ]ⲨⲘⲚⲦⲀⲄⲄⲈⲖΟⲤ
     ⲘⲠΟⲨΝⲀⲨ ⲈⲢΟⲚ[·] ⲁⲩⲱ ⲠΟⲨⲀⲢ–
30 ⲬⲰⲚ ⲀⳒⲰⲦΟⲢⲦⲢ̄ ϨⲀⲐⲎ Ⲛ Ⲧ[ⲈΝϨⲤⲎ Ⲙ]
     ⲘΟΟⲰⲈ· ϮϬⲎⲠⲈ ⲄⲀⲢ Ⲛ ΟⲨ[ΟⲈⲤⲚ]

                              Ⲉ̄

     [.]ⲦⲚ[. . . . .] .[. . . .] ⲈⲤⲤΟⲦⲠ̄
2 ΝϨΟ[ⲨΟ Ⲉ ⲔΟ]Ⲥ̇ⲘⲤⲔ[ΟΝ ΝⲤ]Ⲙ· ⲈⲨⲀⲦ–
     ⲰⲀⳜⲈ ⲘⲘΟⳒ ⲠⲈ Ⲡ[Ⲉ]ⳜⲤⲀ ⲈⲤϮ ΟⲨΟ–
4 [Ⲉ]Ⲥ[Ⲛ] ⲈⲨⲚⲦⲀⲤ Ⲛ ΟⲨϬΟⲘ ⲈⲤⳜⲤ ⲘΟ–
     [ⲈⲤⲦ Ϩ]ⲎⲦΟⲨ Ⲛ ϨⲈⲚⲠ̄Ⲛ̄Ⲁ̄ ⲈⲦΟⲨⲀⲀⲂ
6 [ⲈⲤⲰ]ΟΟⲠ̄ Ⲛ ΟⲨⲠⲚ[Ⲁ] Ⲛ ⲢⲈⳒⲦⲀΝϨΟ·
     [ⲘⲚ] ΟⲨⲰⲀⳜⲈ Ⲛ ΝΟⲈⲢΟⲚ· Ⲙ ⲠⲢⲎⲦⲈ
8 [ⲀⲚ Ⲛ] ⲚⲎ ⲈⲦⲰΟΟⲠ ϨⲘ ⲠⲤⲔΟⲤⲘΟⲤ
     [. .] .Ⲥ ⲚⲦⲈ ΟⲨϨⲨⲖⲎ ⲈⲰⲀⲤⲰⲤⲂⲈ
10 [Ⲙ]Ⲛ̇ ΟⲨⲰⲀⳜⲈ ⲈⲰⲀⳒⲦⲰϬⲚ· ⲁⲩⲱ
     [Ⲧ]ΟⲦⲈ ⲀⲈⲤⲤΟⲨⲰⲚ ϮϬΟⲘ ⲈⲦⲰΟ–
12 [Ο]Ⲡ̄ ΝϨⲎⲦ ⲆⲈ ⲚⲈⲤⲔⲎ ϨⲤⳜⲚ ⲠⲤⲔⲀⲔⲈ
     [Ⲉ]ⲨΝⲦⲀⲤ ⲘⲘⲀⲨ Ⲙ ⲠⲤΟⲨΟⲈⲤΝ ⲦⲎⲢⳒ·
14 [Ⲁ]ⲈⲤⳜⲤ ⲰⲘⳒ Ⲙ ⲠⲤⲘⲀ ⲈⲦⲘⲘⲀⲨ· ⲁⲩⲱ

4,19-20   Or, the time [of] this world is short; cf. 131,19-20.
4,19   There is an extraneous ink trace before the letter Ⲭ, possibly blotting from the facing page.
4,23   Ⲕ, or else Ⲏ, Ⲥ, or Ⲛ Ⲓ in *Gos.Eg.* III 49,1-7, a light-cloud is identified with Mirothea; see also *Ap.John* II 10,14ff and *Paraph.Shem.* VII 7,11ff; cf. Mark 9:7 par; Acts 1:9; I Thess 4:17; 1 Cor 10:1-2; Rev 11:17.
4,24   For πλάσμα as physical body, see B. Pearson, "Biblical Exegesis," 72; cf. 2 Cor 12:2-3.
4,25   For glories as hypostasized thoughts, see 46,22-31.
4,27   Ⲡ̄Ⲥ̄Ⲧ̄ read with UV lamp; cf. *Gos.Eg.* III 64,4 = IV 75,18-19 Ⅰ cf. *Ap.John* II 10,14ff; *Gos.Eg.* III 64,4; *Apoc.Adam* V 77,27ff; Ps 43.

16   to save those who are
      worthy and to strengthen the elect,
18   for great is the struggle (ἀγών) of the age (αἰών),
      but time (χρόνος) [in] this world is short."
20   When (+δέ) he had said this [to me],
      I very quickly and very
22   gladly went up with him
      into a great light cloud. I [cast]
24   my body (πλάσμα) upon the earth
      to be guarded by glories. [We] were
26   rescued from the whole world (κόσμος)
      and the thirteen aeons (αἰών)
28   in it and their angelic (-ἄγγελος) beings.
      They did not see us, but their
30   archon (ἄρχων) was disturbed at [our]
      [passage,] for (γάρ) the light-cloud

                                                    5

      [   ] it is better
2   than any [worldly (κοσμικόν)] thing.]
      With its ineffable beauty
4   it shines brightly
      [guiding] pure spirits (πνεῦμα)
6   as a spirit-savior (-πνεῦμα)
      and an intellectual (νοερόν) word,
8   [not] like those things in the world (κόσμος)
      [   ] with changeable matter (ὕλη)
10   and an upsetting word.
      Then (τότε) I knew that the power
12   in me was set over the darkness
      because it contained the whole light.
14   I was baptized there, and

4,29-30   Cf. 130,10-12.
4,29   For ⲉⲙ̄ⲡⲟⲧ.
4,31-5,1 E.g., ⲟ̅ⲩ̅[ⲟⲉⲓⲛ/ⲉ]ⲧ; or ⲟ̅ⲩ̅[ⲟⲉⲓⲛ ⲛ/ⲁ]ⲧ.
5,1   Lit., she, probably the light-cloud.
5,2   ⲟ̣ⲓ̣, overlaid with blotting from the facing page.
5,3   Or, because of its ineffable beauty.
5,5   ⲛⲧⲉ ⲡⲁ̅ⲩ̅ⲧⲟⲅⲉⲛⲏⲥ might be expected.
5,9   ⲓⲟ̣, or ⲓϭ̣, or ⲓⲉ̣ (but not ligatured to ⲓ).
5,11   The baptisms recounted here through 7,22 may represent the ritual baptisms
          of the group that produced Zostrianos. Cf. Schenke, "Sethianism," 602-607;
          Scopella, "Un rituel ideal d'intronisation," 91-95; cf. 2 Enoch 22:8-10.

[ⲁ]ⲉⲓⲍⲓ ⲡⲓⲛⲉ ⲛ ⲛⲓⲉⲟⲟⲩ ⲉⲧϩⲙ ⲡⲙⲁ

16 [ⲉ]ⲧⲙⲙⲁⲩ· ⲁⲉⲓϣⲱⲡⲉ ⲙ ⲡⲣⲏⲧⲉ ⲛ
[ⲟ]ⲩⲁ ⲙⲙⲟⲟⲩ· ⲁⲉⲓⲥⲓⲛⲉ ⲉⲃⲟⲗ ϩⲙ ⲡⲓ-

18 [ⲕⲁϩ] ⲛ ⲁⲏⲣ· ⲁⲩⲱ ⲁⲉⲓⲥⲓⲛⲉ ⲛ ⲛⲓⲁⲛ-
[ⲧⲓⲧⲩ]ⲡⲟⲥ ⲛⲛ ⲉⲱ[ⲛ]· ⲉⲁⲉⲓⲱⲙⲥ

20 [ⲙ ⲡⲙⲁ] ⲉⲧⲙⲙⲁⲩ ⲛ ⲥⲁϣϥ ⲛ ⲥⲟⲡ
[ⲛ ⲟⲩⲙⲟⲟ]ⲩ ⲉϥⲟⲛϩ ⲕⲁⲧⲁ ⲡⲟⲩⲁ ⲡⲟⲩⲁ

22 [ⲛⲧⲉ ⲛⲓ]ⲉⲱⲛ· ⲉⲙⲡⲓⲕ[ⲁ ⲧ]ⲟⲟⲧ ϣⲁⲛ-
[ϯⲛⲁⲩ] ⲉ ⲙⲙⲟⲟⲩ [ⲧ]ⲏⲣ[ⲟⲩ ⲉ] ⲟⲩⲥⲟⲡ

24 [ⲁⲩⲱ] ⲁⲓⲉⲓ ⲉϩⲣⲁⲓ ⲉ [ϯⲟⲛⲧⲱ]ⲥ ⲉⲧϣⲟ-
[ⲟⲡ] ⲙ ⲡⲁⲣⲟⲓⲕⲏⲥⲓⲥ ⲁ[ⲓ̈]ⲍⲓ ⲱⲙⲥ ⲁⲩⲱ

26 [. . . . .] .[ⲕⲟ]ⲥⲙⲟⲥ· ⲁⲓⲉⲓ ⲉϩⲣⲁⲓ ⲉ ϯⲟⲛ-
[ⲧⲱⲥ ⲉ]ⲧϣⲟⲟⲡ ⲙ ⲙⲉⲧⲁⲛⲟⲓⲁ

28 [ⲁⲩⲱ ⲁⲉⲓ]ⲍⲓ ⲱⲙⲥ ⲙ ⲡⲙⲁ ⲉⲧⲙⲙⲁⲩ
[ⲛ ϥⲧ]ⲟⲟⲩ ⲛ ⲥⲟⲡ· ⲁⲉⲓⲥⲓⲛⲉ ⲙ ⲡⲓ-

ⲋ̄

ⲙⲉϩⲥⲟⲟⲩ [ⲛ ⲉⲱⲛ] ⲍ[. . . . .] . . .[. .

2 ⲁⲩⲱ ⲁⲓⲉⲓ [ⲉϩⲣⲁⲓ] ⲉ ⲛⲓⲉ .[. . . . . .] . . .[.
ⲁⲓ̈ⲁϩⲉⲣⲁⲧ ⲙ[ⲙⲁ]ⲩ ⲉⲁⲉⲓⲛⲁⲩ ⲉⲧⲟⲩⲟⲉ[ⲓⲛ ⲛ-]

4 ⲧⲉ ⲧⲙⲉ· ⲉϥϣⲟⲟⲡ ⲟⲛⲧⲱⲥ ⲉⲃ[ⲟ]ⲗ ϩⲛ [ⲟⲩ-]
ⲛⲟⲩⲛⲉ ⲛⲧⲁϥ ⲛ ⲁⲩⲧⲟⲅⲉⲛⲏⲥ ⲙⲓ[ⲛ ϩⲉⲛ-]

6 ⲛⲟϭ ⲛ ⲁⲅⲅⲉⲗⲟⲥ ⲙⲛ ϩⲉⲛⲉⲟⲟ[ⲩ . . . .
ⲉ ⲡⲱⲓ· ⲁⲩ[ⲱ ⲁ]ⲉⲓⲍⲓ ⲱⲙⲥ ⲉ ⲡ[ⲣⲁⲛ ⲙ]

8 ⲡⲓⲁⲩⲧⲟⲅⲉⲛⲏⲥ ⲛ ⲛⲟⲩⲧⲉ ⲉ[ⲃⲟⲗ ϩⲓⲧⲟ-]
ⲟⲧⲟⲩ ⲛ ⲛⲓϭⲟⲙ ⲛ̄ⲏ̄ ⲉⲧϣⲟⲟⲡ [ϩⲓⲍⲛ ϩⲉⲛ-]

10 ⲙⲟⲟⲩ ⲉⲧⲟⲛϩ ⲙ̄ⲓ̄ⲭ̄ⲁ̄ⲣ̄ ⲙⲛ ⲙ̄ⲓ̄[ⲭⲉⲩⲥ]
ⲁⲩⲱ ⲁⲉⲓⲧⲃⲃⲟ ⲉⲃⲟⲗ ϩⲓⲧⲟⲟⲧϥ ⲙ [ⲡⲓ-]

12 ⲛⲟϭ ⲃ̄ⲁⲣⲫⲁⲣⲁⲅⲅⲏⲥ· ⲁⲩⲱ ⲁⲩ[ⲟⲩⲟⲛϩ-]
ⲟⲩ ⲛⲁⲓ̈ ⲁⲩⲥⲁϩⲧ ϩⲙ ⲡⲉⲟⲟⲩ· [ⲁⲩⲣ-]

14 ⲥⲫⲣⲁⲅⲓⲍⲉ ⲙⲙⲟⲉⲓ ⲉⲃⲟⲗ ϩⲓⲧⲟⲟⲧ[ⲟⲩ]
ⲛ̄ ⲛ̄ⲏ̄ ⲉⲧϣⲟⲟⲡ ϩⲓⲍⲛ ⲛⲉⲓ̈ϭⲟⲙ [ⲙ̄ⲓ̄ⲭ̄ⲁ̄ⲣ̄ ⟨ⲙⲛ⟩]

5,18   For etheral earth as the lowest level of the heavenly world, see 9,2-6; cf. *Gos.Eg.*
         III 50,10; Plot. *Enn.* 2.9.5,23ff; Orig. *de Princ.*

5,23   [ϯⲛⲁⲩ] requires a slight crowding of letters (for restoration of ⲛⲁⲩ, cf.
         6,3); or possibly [ϯϩⲉ].

5,24-25   παροίκησις, a temporary residence, probably here the place of the soul's
         repose; see also 12,9-17; cf. Plot. *Enn.* II.9.6; Baynes, *Coptic Gnostic Treatise,*
         183 n.

5,26   Before [ⲕⲟ]ⲙⲟⲥ, an indistinct trace, perhaps from the upper left of ⲉ, ⲑ,
         ⲟ, or ⲥ.

5,29   The following text was read solely from blotting on the facing page (p. 4):
         ]ⲟⲟⲩ ⲛ ⲥ.

I received the image of the glories
16   there. I became like
one of them. I left the
18   ethereal (ἀήρ) [earth] and passed by the
aeon (αἰών) copies (ἀντίτυπος) after
20   washing [there] seven times
[in] living [water], once (+κατά) for each
22   [of the] aeons. I did not cease until
[I saw] absolutely all the waters.
24   I ascended to the exile (παροίκησις)
which [really (ὄντως)] exists. [I] was baptized and
26   [   ] world (κόσμος). I ascended to the
repentance (μετάνοια) which really (ὄντως) exists
28   [and was] baptized there
four times. I passed by the

6

sixth [aeon (αἰών)
2   I ascended to the [
I stood there after having seen a light
4   of the truth that really (ὄντως) exists from
its self-begotten (αὐτογενής) root [with]
6   great angels (ἄγγελος) and glories, [
number. I was baptized in the [name of]
8   the divine Autogenes (αὐτογενής)
[by] those powers which are [upon]
10   living waters, Michar and Mi[cheus.]
I was purified by [the] great
12   Barpharanges. Then they [revealed]
themselves to me (and) wrote me in glory.
14   I was sealed (σφραγίζειν) by
those who are over these powers, [Michar,]

6,1   ⲍ̣., or else ⲇ.
6,5   Root, i.e., source or origin; cf. 6,18.
6,6   E.g., ⲅⲉⲛⲉⲟⲟ[ⲩ ⲉⲛⲉⲩ; cf. 63,21-22.
6,9   ⲡ, the flag does not survive.
6,10-16   Cf. *Gos.Eg.* III 64,15-20; *Trim.Prot.* XIII 48,18-21; Baynes, *Coptic Gnostic
          Treatise*, 180-182.
6,10   For ⲙ̄ⲥⲭⲉⲩⲥ, cf. *Gos. Eg.* III 64,15 = IV 76,4.
6,11   A short line.
6,13   Cf. Ps 39:8; 138:16; Rev 14:1; 17:8.
6,15-16   Possibly ⲅⲟⲙ [ⲩⲩ]/ⲙ̄ⲥ[ⲭ]ⲉⲩⲥ ‹ⲙⲛ ⲙ̄ⲥⲭⲁⲣ›·
          ⲙⲛ; cf. *Gos.Eg.* III 64,20=IV 76,9-10.

16 ⲙ̄ⲓ[ⲭⲉⲩⲥ· ⲙⲛ ⲥⲉⲗⲗⲁⲱ ⲙⲛ ⲉⲗⲉ[ⲛⲟⲥ]
   ⲙⲛ ⲍⲱⲧⲉⲛⲉⲑⲗⲟⲥ· ⲁⲩⲱ ⲁⲉⲓϣ[ⲱⲡⲉ]
18 ⲛ ⲟⲩⲁⲅⲅⲉⲗⲟⲥ ⲛ ⲣⲉϥⲛⲁⲩ ⲉ ⲛⲟⲩ[ⲛⲉ]
   ⲁⲩⲱ ⲁⲓ̈ⲁϩⲉⲣⲁⲧ̈ ϩⲓϫⲛ ⲡⲓϩⲟⲩⲉ[ⲓⲧ]
20 ⲉⲧⲉ ⲡⲓⲙⲉϩϥⲧⲟⲟⲩ ⲛⲛ ⲉⲱⲛ ⲡ[ⲉ]
   ⲙⲛ ⲛⲓⲯⲩⲭⲏ ⲁⲉⲓⲥⲙ[ⲟ]ⲩ ⲉ ⲡⲓ[ⲁⲩⲧⲟ-]
22 ⲅⲉⲛⲏⲥ ⲛ ⲛⲟⲩⲧⲉ· ⲙⲛ ⲡⲓϣⲟⲣⲡ ⲛ]
   ⲉⲓⲱⲧ· ⲡⲓⲅⲉⲣⲁⲇⲁⲙⲁ ⲉ[
24 ⲡⲓⲁⲩⲧⲟⲅⲉⲛⲏⲥ ⲡⲓϣⲟⲣ[ⲡ ⲛ ⲣⲱⲙⲉ]
   ⲛ ⲧⲉⲗⲓⲟⲥ ⲙⲛ ⲥⲏⲑ ⲉⲙⲙ[ⲁⲭⲁ ⲥⲏⲑ]
26 ⲡϣⲏⲣⲉ [ⲛ]ⲧⲉ [ⲁ]ⲇⲁⲙⲁⲥ ⲡ[
   ⲧ̄ⲅⲉ[ⲛⲉⲁ ⲛ]ⲛ̣ [ⲁⲧ]ⲕⲓⲙ ⲙⲛ ⲛ[ⲓϥⲧⲟ-]
28 ⲟⲩ ⲛ [ⲫⲱⲥⲧⲏⲣ] ·ⲥ ·ⲏ·.[. . . . . .
   ⲙ̣ [. . . . .]ⲉ̣ⲙ̣[.] .[
30 ⲙⲛ ⲙⲓⲣⲟⲑⲉⲁ ⲧⲙⲁⲁ̣[ⲩ . . . .
   ⲧⲉ̣· ⲙⲛ ⲡⲣⲟⲫⲁⲛⲓⲁ [. . . . .
32 ⲛⲧⲉ ⲛⲓⲟⲩⲟⲉⲓⲛ ⲙⲛ ⲡⲁ̣ϩ[. . . . . . .

‾3

·ⲏ̣ ·[. . . . . .]ⲱ ·ⲁ̣[. . .]ⲟⲥ· ⲁⲩⲱ ⲁⲉⲓ-
2 [ϫⲓ] ⲱ[ⲙⲥ ⲙ̄ ⲡⲓ]ⲙⲉϩⲥⲟ[ⲡ̄ ⲥ]ⲛⲁⲩ ⲉ ⲡⲣⲁⲛ
   [ⲛ]ⲧⲉ̣ ⲡⲓⲁⲩⲧⲟⲅⲉⲛ[ⲏ]ⲥ ⲛ ⲛⲟⲩⲧⲉ ⲉⲃⲟⲗ
4 ϩⲓⲧⲟⲟⲧⲟⲩ ⲛ ⲛⲉⲓ̈ϭⲟⲙ ⲛ ⲟⲩⲱⲧ ⲁⲉⲓϣⲱⲡⲉ ⲛ ⲟⲩⲁⲅⲅⲉⲗⲟⲥ ⲛ ⲅⲉⲛⲟⲥ [ⲛ ⲅⲉ-]
6 [ⲛⲟⲥ] ⲛ ϩⲟⲟⲩⲧ· ⲁⲩ[ⲱ] ⲁⲉⲓⲁϩⲉⲣⲁⲧ̈ ϩⲓϫⲛ ⲡⲓⲙⲉϩⲥⲛⲁⲩ ⲛⲛ ⲉⲱⲛ ⲉⲧⲉ ⲡⲓ-
8 ⲙ̣[ⲉϩ]ϣⲟⲙⲧ̈ ⲡⲉ ⲙⲛ ⲛϣⲏⲣⲉ ⲛⲧⲉ
   [ⲥ]ⲏⲑ ⲁⲉⲓⲥⲙⲟⲩ ⲉ ⲛⲁⲓ̈ ⲛⲁⲓ̈ ⲁⲩⲱ ⲁⲉⲓ-

6,16 Or else, ⲉⲗⲉ[, but cf. ⲉⲗⲉⲛⲟⲥ at *Gos.Eg.* IV 76,11, and ⲉⲗⲁⲓ̈ⲛⲟⲥ at *Gos.Eg.* III 64,21.

6,17 For the restoration, cf. 5,16; 7,4-5.

6,19 Or, stand at rest. Williams, *Immovable Race*, 70-102, connects this "standing" with the achievement of immovability by the visionary in his ascent, and perhaps also with the practice of contemplative standing in meditation.

6,20ff The aeons are numbered both from the top and from the bottom.

6,22 For ϣ[ⲟⲣⲡ ⲛ], cf. 20,8.

6,23 The supralinear stroke begins over ligature of ⲡ into ⲓ; or possibly read ⲡⲓⲅⲉⲣⲁⲇⲁⲙⲁⲥ; (for Geradamas or Pigeradamas, see 13,6; 30,5-6 *passim*; cf. *Gos.Eg.* IV 61,10; *Steles Seth* VII 118,26; see also Schenke, "Sethianism," 594).

6,25 For Seth Emmacha-Seth, see 51,14-15; cf. *Steles Seth* VII 118,28.

6,26 E.g., ⲡ[ⲓⲉⲓⲱⲧ ⲛⲧⲉ]; cf. *Steles Seth* VII 118,28.

6,28 ç, after sigma a supralinear stroke survives I ⲏ·, the trace edited here as punctuation might be from a letter.

16   Mi[ch]eus, Seldao, Ele[nos]
      and Zogenethlos. I [became]
18   a [root-seeing] angel (ἄγγελος)
      and stood upon the first
20   aeon (αἰών) that is, the fourth,
      with the souls (ψυχή). I blessed the
22   divine Autogenes (αὐτογενής) and the
      forefather Geradama, [
24   the Autogenes (αὐτογενής), the first perfect (τέλειος)
      [human], and Seth Emm[acha Seth],
26   the son of [A]damas, the [
      the [immovable race (γενέα)], and the [four]
28   [lights
      [
30   Mirothea, the mother [
      [   ] and Prophania (προφανεία)[
32   of the lights and De-[

                                        7

      [   ] I was
2   [baptized for the] second time in the name
      of the divine Autogenes (αὐτογενής)
4   by these same powers. I
      became an angel (ἄγγελος) of the
6   male race (γένος). I stood upon
      the second aeon (αἰών), that is, the
8   third, with the children of
      Seth. I blessed each of them and

6,29   ϻ at the beginning of this line is best documented in an early photo; cf. Emmel,
        "Photograph Evidence," 189; the papyrus was subsequently damaged.
6,30   E.g., [ⲚⲦⲈ ⲀⲆⲀⲘⲀⲤ; in *Gos.Eg.* III 49,1-7, Mirothea (the light-cloud) is
        Adam's mother and thus the mother of the holy race.
6,31   There is an extraneous ink trace after ⲦⲈ, blotted from the facing page.
6,32   ⲆⲎ, part of a *nomen sacrum*.
7   The ink on this page is faded, but can be read under ultraviolet light. The
        following text was read with UV light from blotting on the facing page (p. 6),
        line 30, Ⲛ̄ⲤϬⲰ.
7,1   Perhaps with slight crowding, Ⲁ[ⲄⲄⲈⲖ]ⲞⲤ.
7,2   Not ⲤⲈ[Ⲡ.
7,7   Or, ⲌⲘ.
7,8-9   Lit., sons, the heavenly counterparts of the group that called itself "the sons
        of Seth."

10   [ⲁⲓ] ⲱⲙⲥ ⲙ̄ ⲡⲓⲙⲉϩϣⲟⲙⲧ̇ ⲛ̄ ⲥⲟⲡ ⲉ
     ⲡⲣⲁⲛ ⲙ̄ ⲡⲓⲁⲩⲧⲟⲅⲉⲛⲏⲥ ⲛ̄ ⲛⲟⲩⲧⲉ

12   ⲉⲃⲟⲗ ϩⲓⲧⲟⲟⲧⲟⲩ ⲛ̄ ⲛⲉⲓ̈ϭⲟⲙ ⲛⲉⲓ̈ϭⲟⲙ
     [ⲁⲓ̈]ϣⲱⲡⲉ ⲛ̄ ⲟⲩⲁⲅⲅⲉⲗⲟⲥ ⲉϥⲟⲩⲁⲁⲃ

14   [ⲁ]ⲉⲓ[ⲁ]ϩⲉⲣⲁⲧ̇ ϩⲓϫⲛ ⲡⲓⲙⲉϩ ⲅ̅ (ⲥⲛⲁⲩ) ⲛ̄
     [ⲛ̄ ⲉⲱ]ⲛ· ⲉ[ⲧ]ⲉ ⲡⲓⲙⲉϩⲥⲛⲁⲩ ⲡⲉ ⲁⲉⲓ-

16   [ⲥⲙⲟ]ⲩ ⲉ [ⲛ̄]ⲁ̈ⲓ ⲛⲁⲓ̈· ⲁⲩⲱ ⲁⲉⲓϫⲓ ⲱⲙⲥ
     [ⲙ̄ ⲡⲓⲙⲉϩ]ⲅ̅ ⲛ̄ ⲥⲟⲡ̇ ⲉⲃⲟⲗ ϩⲓⲧⲟⲟⲧⲟⲩ

18   [ⲛ̄ ⲛⲉⲓ̈ϭⲟⲙ ⲛ]ⲉ̈ⲓ[ϭ]ⲟⲙ ⲁⲓ̈ϣⲱⲡⲉ ⲛ̄
     [ⲟⲩⲁⲅⲅⲉⲗⲟ]ⲥ̇ ⲛ̄ ⲧⲉⲗⲓⲟⲥ· ⲁⲩⲱ

20   [ⲁⲓ̈ⲁϩⲉⲣⲁⲧ̇ ϩⲓϫⲙ̄] ⲡⲓⲙⲉϩϥⲧⲟⲟⲩ ⲉ-
     [ⲧⲉ ⲡⲓϩⲟⲩⲉⲓⲧ ⲡⲉ ⲛ̄]ⲛ̄ ⲉⲱⲛ ⲁⲩⲱ ⲁⲉⲓ-

22   [ⲥⲙⲟⲩ ⲉ ⲛⲁⲓ̈ ⲛⲁⲓ̈· ⲧ]ⲟⲧⲉ ⲁⲉⲓϣⲓⲛⲉ
     [. . . . .]ⲉϥⲏ[. . . .] . ⲁⲉⲓϫⲉ

24   [———   ]ⲉ ⲁⲛⲟⲕ
     [———   [.ⲛ̄ⲧⲉ

26   [———   ]ⲁ̄ⲛⲟⲕ
     [. . . . .]ⲉ̄ ⲙⲙⲟⲩ [. . . . .]ⲧⲉⲡ̄ⲥ

28   [. . . . .] ⲉⲧⲃⲉ ⲟⲩ [. . . .]ⲛⲉ ϩⲉⲛ-
     [. . . .]ⲣ̄[. .] .ϩⲛ ϯϭⲟⲙ [. . . . . .]ⲧⲙ

30   ⲉⲣⲟⲟⲩ ⲛ̄ ⲕⲉⲣⲏⲧⲉ ϩⲛ ⲛⲓⲥⲱⲧⲙ.
     ⲏ̅

     ⲛ̄ⲧⲉ ⲛⲓⲣⲱⲙ[ⲉ] ⲁⲩⲱ [ⲉⲛⲉ ⲛ̄]ⲁ̈ⲓ ⲛⲉ [ⲛⲉ]ⲩ-

2   ϭⲟⲙ· ⲏ ⲛⲁⲓ̈ ⲣ̄[ⲱ] ⲛⲉ ⲛⲉⲩⲣⲁⲛ ⲇⲉ ⲥⲉϣⲉ-
     ⲃⲓⲏⲟⲩⲧ̇ ⲉ ⲛⲉⲧⲉⲣⲏⲩ· ⲁⲩⲱ ⲉϣϫⲉ ⲟⲩ

4   ⲛ̄ ⲯⲩⲭⲏ ϣⲉⲃⲓⲏⲟⲩⲧ ⲉ ⲯⲩⲭⲏ· ⲁⲩⲱ
     ⲉⲧⲃⲉ ⲟⲩ ⲉⲣⲉⲛⲓⲣⲱⲙⲉ ϣⲉⲃⲓⲏⲟⲩⲧ̇

6   ⲉ ⲛⲉⲧⲉⲣⲏⲩ ϩⲛ ⲟⲩ ⲏ ⲟⲩⲏⲣ ⲣⲱ ⲛ̄ ⲣⲱ-
     ⲙⲉ ⲛⲉ· ⲁⲩⲱ ⲡⲉϫⲁϥ ⲛⲁⲓ̈ ⲛ̄[ϭⲓ] ⲡⲓⲛⲟϭ

8   ⲉⲧⲁⲙⲁϩⲧⲉ ⲙ̄ ⲡϫⲓⲥⲉ ⲁⲑ̄ⲣⲟⲩⲛⲓⲟⲥ
     ϫⲉ ⲉϣϫⲉ ⲉⲕⲕⲱⲧⲉ ⲙⲉⲛ ⲛ̄ⲥⲁ ⲛⲏ

10   ⲉⲧⲁⲕⲥⲓⲛⲉ ⲉⲃⲟⲗ ⲛ̄ϩⲏⲧⲟⲩ· ⲏ ⲉ̄-
     ⲧⲃⲉ ⲡⲉⲓ̈ⲕⲁϩ ⲛⲛ ⲁⲏⲣ ϫⲉ ⲉⲧⲃⲉ ⲟⲩ ⲟⲩⲛ-

7,14   {ⲥⲛⲁⲩ}, scribal cancellation (scored out with two horizontal lines), with ⲅ̅
         (= ϣⲟⲙⲧ) written above it.

7,19   ⲛ̣, only a trace of the supralinear stroke remains | As an initiate into the
         mystery religions was often called "perfect," Zostrianos is probably being
         portrayed as one ready to receive the secret knowledge of the cult;
         cf. 1 Cor 2:6; *Did.* 1. 4.

7,22-13,6   *The Revelations from Authrounios.*

7,23   ] ., read ϩ, ⲛ, or ϫ.

7,25   ] ., a trace of a supralinear stroke | ⲛ̣, only a trace of a supralinear stroke.

10 was baptized for the third time
    in the name of the divine Autogenes (αὐτογενής)
12 by each of these powers.
    [I] became a holy angel (ἄγγελος) and
14 stood upon the third
    [aeon (αἰών)], that is, the second. I
16 [blessed] each of them and was baptized
    for the fourth time by
18 [each of] these powers. I became
    [a] perfect (τέλειος) [angel (ἄγγελος)]
20 [and stood upon] the fourth aeon (αἰών)
    [that is, the first], and
22 [I blessed each of them.] Then (τότε) I sought
    [   ] I said
24 [   ] I
    [   ] of
26 [   ] I
    [
28 [   ] why [
    [   ] with power [
30 them in another way in the reports
    8
    of men? [Are these] their
2   powers? Or (ἤ) are these the (same) but (δέ)
    their names differ from one another? Are
4   there souls (ψυχή) different from souls (ψυχή)
    Why are there different
6   kinds of human beings? What and (ἤ) in what way
    are they human?" The great ruler
8   on high Authrounios said to me,
    "Are you asking about those (places) through
10 which you have passed? Or (ἤ)
    about this ethereal (ἀήρ) earth, why

7,27   ]ε, or else] ⲑ.
7,29   E.g., [ⲉⲁ ⲧⲥⲱ]ⲧⲙ.
8,3-4   The mystery is anthropological (why there are types of people who cannot
        be saved).
8,4   Supralinear stroke above ⲛ.
8,7-8   Lit., the great one who presides on high.
8,8   For Authrounios as the Light Harmozel, see 127,22.

ⲧⲁϥ ⲡⲉϊⲧⲩⲡⲟⲥ ⲛ ⲕⲟⲥ̣ⲙⲓⲕⲟⲛ· ⲏ [ⲉ–]
ⲧⲃⲉ ⲛⲓⲁⲛⲧⲓⲧⲩⲡⲟⲥ ⲛⲛ ⲉⲱⲛ ϫⲉ [ⲟⲩ–]
ⲏⲣ ⲡ̣ⲉ· ⲏ ⲉⲧⲃⲉ ⲟⲩ ⲛⲥⲉⲙⲟⲕϩ [ⲁⲛ]
ⲏ ⲉⲧⲃⲉ ϯⲡⲁⲣⲟⲓⲕⲏⲥ[ⲓ]ⲥ ⲙⲛ [ϯⲙⲉⲧⲁ–]
ⲛⲟⲓⲁ ⲙⲛ ⲉⲧⲃⲉ ϯⲕⲧ[ⲓⲥ]ⲓ̣ⲥ ⲛⲛ̣ [
ⲙⲛ ⲡⲓⲕⲟⲥⲙⲟⲥ ⲉⲧⲉ ⲛ[ⲓ]ⲣ̣[. . . . . . .
ⲟⲛⲧⲱⲥ· ϩⲛ ‹ⲟⲩ›ⲟⲩⲱⲛϩ ⲉ̣ⲃ̣[ⲟⲗ . . . . .
ⲙⲟⲕ· ⲩ̲ ⲉⲧⲃⲉ ⲛ[
ⲙⲙⲟϊ ⲉⲣⲟⲟ[ⲩ
ⲟⲩⲧⲉ ⲟⲩⲉϩ[
ⲛⲁⲕ ⲉⲃⲟⲗ· ⲁ[––– ⲡ̅ⲛ̅ⲁ̅ ⲛ]
ⲛ ⲁⲧⲛⲁ̣ⲩ ⲉⲣ[ⲟϥ
ⲙⲛ ϯ[. . .]ⲱⲉ̣[
ⲛⲧⲉ [
ⲙⲟⲥ̣ [
ⲏ [
ⲉⲧ[. . . .]ⲗⲡ ⲛ[. .]ⲕ [. . . . .
ⲁⲩⲱ̣ [. .]ⲙⲁϊ ϩⲱ· [. . . . .
ⲛⲉ[. . . .]ⲏ ⲉⲧⲁϊⲥ .[. . . . .

ⲑ̅

ⲡⲉϫ[ⲁϥ ⲛⲁϊ ⲛ]ϭⲓ ⲡⲓⲛ[ⲟϭ] ⲉⲧⲁⲙⲁϩⲧⲉ
ⲙ ⲡ[ϫⲓ]ⲥ̣ⲉ ⲁⲩⲑⲟⲣⲟⲩⲛ̣ⲓⲟⲥ ϫⲉ ⲡⲕⲁϩ
ⲙⲉⲛ ⲛⲛ ⲁⲏⲣ ⲁϥϩϣⲱⲡⲉ ϩⲛ ⲟ̣ⲩ–
ϣⲁϫⲉ· ⲛⲓϫⲡⲟ ⲇⲉ ⲙⲛ ⲛⲏ ⲉⲧⲧⲁ–
ⲕⲏⲟⲩⲧ̀ ⲉϥⲟⲩⲱⲛϩ ⲙⲙⲟⲟⲩ ⲉⲃⲟⲗ
ϩⲛ ⲟⲩⲙⲛⲧ̀ⲁⲧ̀ⲧⲁⲕⲟ[·] ⲉⲧⲃⲉ ⲡⲓ ⲉϩⲣⲁϊ
ⲛⲧⲉ ⲛⲓⲛⲟϭ ⲛ ⲕⲣⲓⲧⲏⲥ· ϩⲓⲛⲁ ϫⲉ ⲛⲛⲟⲩ–
ϫⲓ ϯⲡⲉ ⲛⲛ ⲉⲥⲑⲏⲥⲓⲥ ⲁⲩⲱ ⲛⲥⲉⲧⲙ–
ⲱⲣⲃ [ϩ]ⲛ ϯⲕⲧⲓⲥⲓⲥ· ⲉⲧⲁⲩⲉⲓ ⲇⲉ ⲉϩⲣⲁϊ
ⲉϫⲙ ⲡⲁϊ· ⲁⲩⲱ ⲉⲧⲁⲩⲛⲁⲩ ⲉⲃⲟⲗ ϩⲓⲧⲙ
ⲡⲁϊ ⲉ ⲛⲓϩⲃⲏⲩⲉ ⲛⲧⲉ ⲡⲓⲕⲟⲥⲙⲟⲥ ⲉⲩ–
ϯ ϩⲁⲡ̀ ⲉ ⲡⲉϥⲁⲣⲭⲱⲛ ⲉϩⲣⲁϊ ⲉⲩⲧⲁⲕⲟ
ⲉ̣ⲩⲧⲩⲡⲟ̣ⲥ ⲡⲉ ⲛⲧⲉ ⲡⲕⲟⲥⲙⲟ̣ⲥ ⲉⲩ
[. . .] .ⲁⲧⲉ̣ ⲙⲛ ⲟⲩⲁⲣⲭⲏ ⲛⲧⲉ ϯϩⲩⲗⲏ

8,16 ⲛ̣, or else ⲏ̣, ⲓ̣, or ⲕ̣; e.g., ⲛⲛ̣[ⲉⲱⲛ].
8,17 ⲣ̣[, or else ϥ̣[.
8,18-19 ⲙ]/ⲙⲟⲕ.
8,29 E.g., [ⲛⲙ]ⲙⲁϊ.
8,30 .[, bottom of a vertical stroke.
9,2 Supralinear stroke missing above ⲁ̅ and ⲩ̅ⲛ̅ⲓ̅ⲟ̅ (lacuna).
9,3-4 Creation by a word is a Jewish motif; cf. Plot. *Enn.* II.9.5.25f where *λόγος* is

12   it has a worldly (κοσμικόν) model (τύπος)? Or (ἤ)
      about the aeon (αἰών) copies (ἀντίτυπος), how
14   many there are? Or (ἤ) why they are [not] in pain?
      Or (ἤ) about the exile (παροίκησις) and
16   repentance (μετάνοια) and about the creation (κτίσις) of
      [   ] and the world (κόσμος) which the [
18   really (ὄντως) [
      you, about [
20   me, them [
      nor (οὐτέ) [
22   you [
      invisible [spirit (πνεῦμα)
24   and the [
      of [
26   [
      [
28   [
      and [
30   [   ] when I [

                                              9

      The [great] ruler on high
2   Authrounios said [to me], "The
      ethereal (ἀήρ) earth came into being by a
4   word, yet (δέ) it is the begotten
      and perishable things that it reveals
6   by its indestructibility. With regard to the coming
      of the great judges (κριτής), (they came) not
8   to (ἵνα) taste perception (αἴσθησις) and to
      be enclosed in creation (κτίσις). But (δέ) when
10   they came upon it and saw through
      it the works of the world (κόσμος),
12   they condemned its ruler (ἄρχων) to death
      because he was a model (τύπος) for the world (κόσμος),
14   a [   ] and an origin (ἀρχή) of matter (ὕλη)

---

        used to designate the plan for the physical world.
9,6-9   The judges belong to the tradition of the watchers in Jubilees 4:15; cf.
        1 Enoch 6. Klijin, Seth, 14-15, 51-52, argues that they are related to traditions
        about Seth as the mediator of knowledge from the antediluvian period.
9,6   Sahidic π–ει εϩραϊ.
9,14   ] .ατε, ink trace is a vertical stroke (e.g., from ν); ε, or ϑ, ϙ, or ç (there
        was no supralinear stroke between τ and this letter).

[ⲉⲧⲁ]ⲡⲟ ⲛ ⲕⲁⲕⲉ ⲉⲧⲧⲁⲕⲏⲟⲩⲧ·
16　　[. . .] ⲛⲁⲓ̈ ⲁ[ⲉ] ⲧⲥⲟⲫⲓⲁ ⲉⲧⲁⲥϭⲱϣⲧ
　　　[ⲉⲣⲟⲟⲩ] ⲁⲥⲧⲁϭⲉ ⲡⲓⲕⲁⲕⲉ ⲉⲥ–
18　　[. . . . .] . . . .ⲕⲏ ϩⲁⲧⲟⲟⲧϥ ⲙ ⲡⲓ–
　　　[. . . . . .ⲟⲩⲧ]ⲧⲡⲟⲥ ⲡⲉ ⲛⲛⲁ–
20　　[　　 ——— 　　] ⲛⲧⲉ ⲧⲟⲩⲥⲓⲁ ⲛ
　　　[　　 ——— 　　]ⲙⲟⲣⲫⲏ ⲛⲛ ⲁⲧ–
22　　[　　 ——— 　　] .ⲉⲩⲉⲓⲇⲟⲥ ⲛ
　　　[　　 ——— 　　]ⲁⲓⲉⲕⲟ
24　　[　　 ——— 　　] ⲡⲧⲏⲣϥ
　　　[　　 ——— 　　]ⲟⲉⲧ
26　　[　　 ——— 　　] .[. . . . .]ϭⲉ
　　　[. . . . .] .[.]ⲕⲁⲕⲉ· [. . . .]ⲟ ⲉⲃⲟⲗ
28　　[. . . . . .]ϣⲁϫⲉ ⲉⲙ[. . .]ⲓϭⲟⲙ
　　　[. . . . .ⲉ]ⲱⲛ ⲛⲧⲉ [ⲧⲕⲧⲓ]ⲥⲓⲥ ⲉ–
30　　ⲛⲁⲩ ⲉⲩⲗⲁⲁⲩ ⲛⲧⲉ ⲛⲓ[ϣⲁ] ⲉⲛⲉϩ
　　　ⲓ̄

　　　ⲁϥⲛⲁⲩ ⲉⲩ[ⲉⲓ]ⲇⲱⲗ[ⲟⲛ ⲁⲩ]ⲱ ⲡⲣⲟⲥ
2　　ⲡⲓⲉⲓⲇⲱⲗ[ⲟⲛ] ⲉⲧⲁϥ[ⲛⲁⲩ ⲉⲣⲟ]ϥ ⲉⲧⲛ–
　　　ϩⲣⲁⲓ̈ ⲛϩⲏⲧϥ [ⲁϥ]ⲧⲁⲙⲓⲟ ⲙ ⲡⲕⲟⲥⲙⲟⲥ·
4　　ⲁⲩⲱ ϩⲛ ⲟⲩⲉⲓⲇⲱⲗⲟⲛ ⲛⲧⲉ ⲟⲩⲉⲓ–
　　　ⲇⲱⲗⲟⲛ ⲁϥⲣ ϩⲱⲃ ⲉ ⲡⲕⲟⲥⲙⲟⲥ·
6　　ⲁⲩⲱ ⲡⲓⲕⲉⲉⲓⲇⲱⲗⲟⲛ ⲛⲧⲉ ⲡⲟⲩ–
　　　ⲱⲛϩ ⲉⲃⲟⲗ ⲁⲩϥⲓⲧϥ ⲛⲧⲟⲟⲧϥ· ⲉⲧⲁⲩ–
8　　ⲧ ⲇⲉ ⲛ ⲟⲩⲙⲁ ⲛ ⲙⲧⲟⲛ ⲛ ⲧⲥⲟⲫⲓⲁ
　　　ⲛ ⲧϣⲉⲃⲓⲱ ⲛ ⲧⲉⲥⲙⲉⲧⲁⲛⲟⲓⲁ· ⲉⲃⲟⲗ
10　　ⲇⲉ ϩⲙ ⲡⲁⲓ ⲉⲙⲛ ⲗⲁⲁⲩ ϩⲣⲁⲓ̈ ⲛϩⲏⲧⲥ ⲛ
　　　ϣⲟⲣⲡ̄ ⲛ ⲉⲓⲇⲱⲗⲟⲛ ⲉϥⲧⲃⲃⲏⲟⲧ
12　　ⲛϩⲣⲁⲓ̈ ⲛϩⲏⲧϥ ⲡⲣ[ⲟ]ⲟⲛ ⲏ ϩⲏⲗⲏ ⲉⲧⲁⲩ–
　　　ϣⲱⲡⲉ ⲉⲃⲟⲗ ϩⲓⲧⲟⲟⲧϥ· ⲁϥⲣ ⲫⲁⲛ–
14　　ⲧⲁⲍⲉⲥⲑⲁⲓ ⲁϥⲣ ϩⲱⲃ ⲉ ⲛ[ⲓ]ⲕⲉ[ϣ]ⲱϫⲛ̄
　　　ⲛ ⲟ[ⲩ]ⲟⲉⲓϣ ⲅⲁⲣ ⲛⲓⲙ ⲉⲥⲧⲁ[ⲕⲏⲟⲩ]ⲧ
16　　ⲛϭⲓ ⲧϩⲓⲕⲱⲛ ⲛⲧⲉ [ⲧ]ⲥⲟⲫⲓⲁ
　　　ⲉⲥⲉ ⲛ ϩⲁⲗϩⲟ· ⲡ[ⲓ]ⲁⲣⲭ[ⲱ]ⲛ ⲇⲉ[

9,15　ⲕⲁⲕⲉ, first ink trace is the top of a vertical stroke; second trace, a lower
　　　right-hand tail; e.g., ⲁ or ⲙ.
9,16ff　The lower Sophia creates the world by looking down; an image perhaps
　　　derived from the Canaanite tradition of the woman in the window.
　　　See also 10,1ff.
9,16　E.g., [ⲛⲁ] ⲛⲁⲓ̈ ⲁⲉ, or [ϩⲛ] ⲛⲁⲓ̈.
9,18　] . . ., tops of three lunate letters (e.g.,. ⲉϭ).
9,19　Cod. ⲛⲛⲁ´.

[begotten] of lost darkness.

16 When [(+δέ)] Sophia (σοφία) looked [at them]
she produced the darkness, as she

18 [   ] is beside the
[   ] is [a model (τύπος)]

20 [   ] of essence (οὐσία)
[   ] form (μορφή)

22 [   ] an image (εἶδος)
[   ] I

24 [   ] the All
[

26 [
[   ] darkness [

28 [   ] word [   ] power
[aeon (αἰών)] of [creation (κτίσις)] to

30 see any of the eternal ones.

10

He saw a reflection (εἴδωλον), and by means of (πρός)

2 the reflection (εἴδωλον) which he [saw]
in it, he created the world (κόσμος).

4 With a reflection (εἴδωλον) of a reflection (εἴδωλον)
he worked at (producing) the world (κόσμος),

6 and then even the reflection (εἴδωλον) belonging to
visible reality was taken from him. But (δέ) to

8 Sophia (σοφία)was given a place of rest
in exchange for her repentance (μετάνοια).

10 In consequence (+δέ), because she had within her no
pure, first reflection (εἴδωλον), (nothing)

12 preexisting (πρῷον) in it or (ἤ) things that had
already (ἤ ἤδη) come into being through it, he

14 used his imagination (φαντάζεσθαι) (and) produced the
remainder; for (γάρ) the image (εἰκών) of Sophia (σοφία)

16 was always being lost,
her countenance deceiving. But (δέ) the Archon (ἄρχων)

9,26   Or,]ₗ̣ͅϩ̣ε.
9,28   E.g., ε𝔐[πεчⳉ]ϥ̣ ϭⲟ𝔐.
9,29   Or, ε]ⲱ ⲛ ⲛ ⲧε[ⲥ ⲑ ⲏ]ⲥ ⳓⲥ; not room for [ϯⲉ ⲥ ⲑ ⲏ]ⲥ ⳓⲥ or [ⲧⲉ ⲥ ⲑ ⲏ]ⲥ ⳓⲥ.
10,1   He, i.e., the ruler or creator of the physical world.
10,5   ⲣ̄ ϩⲱⲃ = ἐργάζεσθαι.
10,12-13   The text is obscure.
10,12   ⲛ̄ⲡ̄ⲣⲱⲛ is expected | that place, lit., him.
10,17-18   E.g., ⲁⲉ [εчεⳉ]ⲓ/ⲛε.

18 ⲛⲉ ⲁⲩⲱ `ⲉϥⲣ ⲥⲱⲙ[ⲁ]´ ⲉϥⲡⲓ[.] .ⲛⲟ̣[
ⲉⲧⲃⲉ ⲡⲓϩⲟⲩⲉ . . .[
20 ⲉⲡⲉⲥⲏⲧ· ⲉ .[
ⲧⲁⲉⲓⲛⲁⲩ ⲉ[
22 ⲉⲫⲏⲧ̀ ⲛ ⲧⲉ[
ⲍⲛ ⲛⲉⲧⲉⲛϩ̣[
24 ⲉⲁϥⲕ .[
ⲛⲉⲱ[
26 ⲛϩⲟⲩ[
ⲛ ⲛ[
28 ⲁⲩ[. . . .] . . .[
ⲧⲉⲗ[ⲓⲟ]ⲥ ⲉⲃⲟⲗ ϩⲓⲧ[. . . . . .
30 ⲡⲓⲣ .[. . . .]ⲍ ⲡⲁⲓ̈ ⲉ[. . . . .
ⲏⲣ .[. . . .] ⲉⲃⲟⲗ ϩⲓⲧⲟ[ⲟ]ⲧϥ· ⲉⲁϥ[ⲟⲩ]
ⲓ̅ⲁ̅
ⲱⲛ[ϩ ⲉⲃⲟⲗ ⲙ] ⲡⲓⲧⲁ[ⲕ]ⲟ ⲛⲧⲉ ⲡⲕⲟⲥⲙⲟⲥ
2 ϩⲛ ⲟ̣[ⲩⲙⲛⲧ]ⲁ̣ⲧ̣[ⲟⲩ[ⲱ]ⲧⲃ ⲉⲃⲟⲗ· ⲛⲓⲁⲛ-
[ⲧⲓⲧⲩ]ⲡⲟⲥ ⲇⲉ ⲛⲛ ⲉⲱⲛ ⲉⲩϣⲟⲟⲡ
4 ⲙ ⲡⲉ[ⲓ̈]ⲣⲏⲧⲉ· ⲛⲧⲟⲟⲩ ⲙⲉⲛ ⲙ̅ⲡⲟⲩ-
ϣⲁϣⲛⲓ ⲉⲩⲉⲓⲇⲉⲁ ⲛⲧⲉ ⲟⲩϭⲟⲙ ⲛ
6 ⲟⲩⲱⲧ· ϩⲉⲛⲉⲟⲟⲩ [ⲛ]ⲉ ⲛ ϣⲁ ⲉⲛⲉϩ
ⲉⲧⲛⲧⲁⲩ ⲙⲙⲁⲩ· ⲁⲩⲱ ⲥⲉϣⲟⲟⲛ̄
8 ⲛ ϩⲉⲛⲙⲁ ⲛ ϯ ϩⲁⲡ ⲛⲧⲉ ⲧⲟⲩⲉⲓ ⲧⲟⲩⲉⲓ ⲛⲧⲉ ⲛⲓϭⲟⲙ· ⲉϣⲱⲡⲉ ⲇⲉ ⲉⲩϣⲁ̄-
10 ⲍⲓ ⲟⲩϧⲉⲓⲛ ⲛϭⲓ ⲛⲓⲯⲩⲭⲏ ⲉⲃⲟⲗ ϩⲓⲧⲛ
ⲡⲟⲩⲟⲉ[ⲓ]ⲛ ⲉⲧϣⲟⲟⲛ̄ ⲛϩⲏⲧⲟⲩ ⲙⲛ
12 ⲡⲓⲧⲩⲡ[ⲟⲥ] ⲉⲧⲉ ϣⲁϥϣⲱⲡⲉ ⲛϩⲏⲧⲟⲩ ⲛ [ⲟⲩ]ⲙⲏⲏϣⲉ ⲛ ⲥⲟⲡ ϩⲛ ⲟⲩⲙⲛⲧ-
14 [ⲁ]ⲧ̄ⲍ[ⲓ] ⲙⲕ[ⲁ]ϩ ⲙⲁⲥⲙⲉⲉⲧⲉ ⲍⲉ ⲉⲥⲛⲁⲩ
[ⲉ .]ⲓⲧⲁ[. . . .]ⲙⲉ ⲁⲩⲱ ⲡⲓϣⲁ ⲉⲛⲉϩ
16 [.] . .[. . . .] ϩ[ⲙ] ⲡⲓⲙⲁⲕⲁⲣⲓⲟⲥ ⲛ ⲉⲓ-
[. . . . .] ⲛ ϯⲟⲩⲉⲓ ⲛ ⲟⲩⲱⲧ
18 [———] ⲧⲟⲩⲉⲓ ⲧⲟⲩⲉⲓ ⲛⲧⲉ
[———] .ⲛ ⲟⲩⲟⲉⲓⲛ ⲉⲧ-
20 [———]ⲣⲟⲩ· ⲙⲛ ⲧⲏ ⲙⲉⲛ
[———]ⲛ ⲧⲏⲣⲥ ⲙⲛ ⲧⲏ

10,18 ⲉϥⲣ ⲥⲱⲙ[, written above the line in smaller letters (same script) |
] ., probably ⲁ, ⲗ, ⲡ, ⲧ, or ϩ.
10,20-21 E.g., ⲉⲓ/ⲧⲁⲉⲓ´, or ⲛⲓ/ⲧⲁⲉⲓ´.
10,31 .[, probably ⲱ, ⲑ, or ϣ.
11,1 Or, [appeared] as the destruction.
11,2 ⲟⲩ[ⲱ Ⲩ]ⲧⲃ.

18   [   ] and made a body (σῶμα) which [
      concerning the greater [
20   down [
      I saw [
22   to the heart [
      [
24   he having [
      [
26   [
      [
28   [
      perfect (τέλειος) through [
30   [
      [   ] through it, as it
                                                        11
      [revealed] the destruction of the world (κόσμος)
2   by its [immutability]. It is (+δέ) in the
      following way that the aeon (αἰών) copies (ἀντίτυπος)
4   exist: they have not (+μέν)
      obtained a form (εἰδέα) from a single power;
6   they do possess eternal glories,
      and they dwell
8   in the judgment seats of each of
      the powers. But (δέ) when
10   souls (ψυχή) are enlightened by
      the light in these (powers) and
12   (by) the model (τύπος) which often comes
      into being in them [without]
14   suffering, she did not think that she saw
      [   ] and the eternal
16   [   ] in the blessed (μακάριος)
      [   ] each single one
18   [   ] each of
      [   ] light
20   [   ], and she (+μέν)
      [   ] whole, and she

11,6   [N]ε; for the plural copula, cf. 113,15.
11,9   I.e., ετⲩⲁⲛ´.
11,14   Perhaps Sophia.
11,15   ⲁ, or else ⲏ, ⲥ, ⲕ, ⲙ, ⲛ, ⲱ, ⲩ, or ϥ.
11,18   Circumflex omitted over the first group ⲉⲥ.

22 [———   ] . ⲁⲩⲱ ⲟⲩ–
    [———   ] ⲙⲛ ⲧⲏ
24 [———   ] ⲧ̣ⲏ ⲉⲧⲉ
    [———   ] ⲧⲏ
26 [———   ] .
    [. . . . .]ⲩⲛ .[. . . . . .]ⲏⲧⲉ
28 [. . . . . . .]ⲏ̣ⲥ̣ⲓ̣ⲥ· [. . . . . . .] .ⲉ
ⲛⲧⲉ ⲧⲙⲉⲧⲁⲛⲟⲓⲁ· ⲟ̣[ⲉⲛⲯ]ⲩ̣ⲭⲏ
ⲓ̅ⲃ̅
ⲕⲁⲧⲁ ϯⲅⲟⲙ ⲉⲧⲛ[ⲧⲁⲩ ⲛ̣ϩ̣ⲏⲧ]ⲟⲩ ⲛ̄–
2 ⲥⲉⲁϩⲉⲣⲁ[ⲧⲟ]ⲩ̣· ⲁ̣ⲩ̣[. .] .[. . . . .] .[. .]
ⲑⲉⲃⲓⲏⲟⲩ ϣⲁⲣ ⲅⲩ̣ⲙⲛⲁ[ⲍⲉ] ⲙ̣[ⲙ̣]ⲟⲟⲩ
4 ⲉⲃⲟ̣[ⲗ] ϩ̣ⲓⲧⲟⲟⲧⲟⲩ ⲛ̄ ⲛ̣ⲓⲁⲛⲧ[ⲓ]ⲧⲩⲡⲟⲥ
ⲛⲏ ⲉⲧⲉ ϣⲁⲩ⳹ⲓ ⲛ̄ ⲟⲩⲧⲩⲡⲟⲥ ⲛⲧⲉ
6 ⲛⲉⲩⲯⲩⲭⲏ ⲉⲧⲓ ⲉⲩϣⲟⲟⲡ̄ ϩⲙ̄ ⲡⲕⲟ–
ⲥⲙⲟⲥ ⲙⲛ̄ⲛⲥⲁ ϯⲟⲓⲏ ⲛ̄ ⲉⲓ ⲉⲃⲟⲗ ⲕⲁ–
8 ⲧⲁ ⲡⲟⲩⲁ ⲡⲟⲩⲁ ⲛⲧⲉ ⲛⲓⲉⲱⲛ ϣⲁⲩ–
ϣⲱⲡⲉ ⲁⲩⲱ ϣⲁⲩⲟⲩⲟⲧ[ⲃ̄]ⲟⲩ ⲉⲃⲟⲗ
10 ⲕⲁⲧⲁ ⲡⲟⲩⲁ ⲡⲟⲩⲁ ⲉⲃⲟⲗ ⲙ̣[ⲉ]ⲛ ϩⲙ̄ ⲡⲓⲁⲛ–
ⲧⲓⲧⲩⲡⲟⲛ ⲛⲧⲉ ϯⲡⲁⲣⲟⲓⲕ[ⲏ]ⲥⲓⲥ ⲉϩⲣⲁⲓ̈
12 ⲉ ϯⲟⲛⲧⲱⲥ ⲉⲧϣ̣[ⲟⲟⲡ̄ ⲙ̄] ⲡⲁⲣⲟⲓⲕⲏ–
ⲥⲓⲥ· ⲉⲃⲟⲗ ⲙⲉⲛ ϩⲙ̄ ⲡⲓⲁ[ⲛ]ⲧⲓⲧⲩⲡⲟⲛ ⲙ̄
14 ⲙⲉⲧⲁⲛⲟⲓⲁ ⲉϩⲣⲁⲓ̈ ⲉ ϯⲟⲛⲧⲱⲥ ⲉ[ⲧ̄]ϣⲟ–
ⲟⲡ̄ ⲙ̄ ⲙⲉⲧⲁⲛⲟⲓⲁ [ⲁⲩⲱ ⲉ]ⲃⲟ̣[ⲗ] ϩ̣[ⲙ ⲡⲓ]ⲁ̣ⲛ–
16 ⲧⲓⲧⲩⲡⲟⲥ ⲛ̄ ⲁⲩⲧⲟ[ⲅⲉⲛⲏⲥ] ⲉ̣ϩⲣⲁⲓ̈ ⲉ ⲡⲓ–]
ⲟⲛⲧⲱⲥ ⲉ̄ⲧϣⲟ[ⲟ]ⲡ̄̄ [ⲛ̄ ⲁⲩⲧ]ⲟ̣ⲩ̣[ⲅⲉⲛⲏⲥ]
18 ⲙⲛ ⲛⲓⲕⲉϣⲱ⳹ⲛ̄[
ⲛⲓⲯⲩⲭⲏ ⲙⲉⲛ ⲛ .[
20 ϣⲟⲟⲡ̄ ϩⲛ ⲟⲩ .[
ⲟⲩ ⲧⲏⲣⲟⲩ ϩⲓ̣[———   ⲛⲓⲁⲛⲧⲓ]
22 ⲧⲩⲡⲟⲥ ⲛⲛ ⲉⲱ[ⲛ
ⲛⲁⲩ ⲙⲉⲛ ϩⲟⲧ[
24 ⲁⲩⲱ ϩⲩ[
ⲉⲃⲟⲗ ϩⲓ[
26 ⲡⲓϣⲁⲩ[
ⲥⲁⲃⲟⲗ̣[
28 ⲟⲉ .[

11,27   Or, ⲛⲧⲉ.
11,28   ⲏ, the trace is a vertical stroke.
12,2   ⲁϩⲉ ⲣⲁⲧ = παρριστῆναι | they, perhaps souls; cf. 11,30.

22 [   ] and a
    [   ] and she
24 [   ] she who
    [
26 [
    [
28 [
    of repentance (μετάνοια), [souls (ψυχή)]
    12
    stand according to (κατά) the power
2   [they have in] themselves. [
    lower, they are trained (γυμνάζειν)
4   by the copies (ἀντίτυπος)
    which receive a model (τύπος)
6   of their souls (ψυχή) while still in the
    world (κόσμος). They came into being
8   after the departure of the aeons (αἰών),
    one by one (+κατά), and they are removed
10 one by one (+κατά) from (+μέν) the
    copy (ἀντίτυπον) of exile (παροίκησις)
12 to the exile (παροίκησις) that really (ὄντως)
    exists, from (+μέν) the copy (ἀντίτυπον) of
14 repentance (μετάνοια) to the repentance (μετάνοια)
    that really (ὄντως) exists, [and from the]
16 copy (ἀντίτυπον) of Autogenes (αὐτογενής)
    [to the Autogenes (αὐτογενής)] that really (ὄντως)
18 exists, and so on. [
    The (+μέν) souls (ψυχή) [
20 exist in a [
    all[copies (ἀντίτυπος)]
22 of aeons (αἰών) [
    (μέν) [
24 and [
    [
26 the [
    [
28 [

_____

12,12-13 †ONTⲱC ... ⲘⲠⲀⲢОⲤKHCⲤC, a literal translation from Greek
         (e.g., τὴν ὄντως ... παροίκησιν).
12,18   ⲛ̅, or else ⲡ.
12,21   Circumflex over the group ⲟⲩ.

ⲛⲁⲉ[. . . . .] ⲉⲃ[
30 ⲛⲧⲉ[. . . . . . .] ⲛ ⲱⲱ[. . . . .
ⲛⲁ̈ⲓ [———]ⲟⲛⲉ[.
ⲥⲧ̄
ⲥⲙ[ⲟⲩ ⲉ ⲡⲛ]ⲟⲩⲧⲉ ⲉⲧⲥⲁϩⲣⲁ̈ⲓ ⲛ
2 ⲛⲓⲛ[ⲟϭ ⲛⲛ] ⲉⲱⲛ ⲙⲛ ⲡⲓⲕⲗⲁ̄ⲥ̄ ⲛⲛ ⲁ-
[ⲧ]ⲙ[ⲓⲥⲉ] ⲙⲛ ⲡⲓⲡⲣⲱⲧⲟⲫⲁ[ⲛ]ⲏⲥ
4 ⲛ ⲛⲟ[ϭ ⲛ] ϩⲟⲟⲩⲧ̄ ⲙⲛ ⲡⲓⲧⲉⲗⲓⲟⲥ
ⲛ ⲁ[ⲗⲟ]ⲩ ⲡⲏ ⲉⲧϫⲟⲥⲉ ⲉ ⲛⲟⲩⲧⲉ
6 ⲙⲛ ⲡⲓⲃⲁⲗ ⲛⲧⲁϥ ⲡ̄ⲓ̄ⲧ̄ⲉⲣⲁⲁⲙⲁ
ⲁⲩⲱ ⲁⲉⲓⲙⲟⲩⲧⲉ ⲉϩⲣⲁ̈ⲓ ⲟⲩⲉ ⲡⲁ-
8 ⲗⲟⲩ ⲛⲧⲉ ⲡⲁⲗⲟⲩ ⲛⲫⲏⲥⲏⲕ ⲁϥⲁϩⲉ-
ⲣⲁⲧϥ ⲛⲁ̈ⲓ ⲁⲩⲱ ⲡⲉϫⲁϥ ϫⲉ ⲡⲁⲅⲅⲉ-
10 ⲗⲟⲥ ⲛⲧⲉ ⲡⲛⲟⲩⲧⲉ ⲡⲓϣⲏⲣⲉ ⲛⲧⲉ
ⲡⲓⲱⲧ̄ [ⲡⲉ ⲁⲛⲟ]ⲕ ⲡⲓⲧⲉⲗⲓⲟⲥ ⲛ ⲣⲱ-
12 ⲙⲉ ⲉⲧⲃ[ⲉ ⲟⲩ] ⲕⲙⲟⲩⲧⲉ ⲉⲣⲟⲉⲓ ⲁⲩⲱ
ⲕⲕⲱ[ⲧⲉ ⲛⲥ]ⲁ ⲛⲏ ⲉⲧⲕⲉⲓⲙ[ⲉ] ⲉⲣⲟⲟⲩ
14 ⲉⲕ[ⲉ] ⲛ [ⲛ ⲁⲧⲙⲙ]ⲉ ⲉⲣⲟⲟⲩ· ⲁⲛⲟⲕ
[ⲁⲉ] ⲡⲉ[ϫⲁ̈ⲓ ϫⲉ] ⲁ̈ⲓⲕⲱⲧⲉ ⲛⲥⲁ ⲡⲓⲙⲟ-
16 [ⲟⲩ]ϫϭ̄ [. . . . . . .] ϥϫⲱⲕ ⲁⲩⲱ ϥϯ
[———]ϫⲉ ⲟⲩⲛ ϭⲟⲙ ⲉⲧⲛ-
18 [ⲧⲁ' ———]ⲉⲧⲛϫⲓ ϫⲱⲕⲙ ⲉⲣⲟ-
[——— ⲛ]ⲉ̈ⲓⲣⲁⲛ ⲥⲉϣⲉ-
20 [ⲃⲓⲏⲟⲩⲧ̄ ———] ⲁⲩⲱ ⲉⲧⲃⲉ ⲟⲩ
[———] .ⲟⲩⲧ̄ ⲉ ⲛⲉⲩ-
22 [———]ⲟϭ[. .]ⲛⲉ ϩⲛ ϯ-
[. . . . . ⲉ]ⲃⲟⲗ [ϩⲛ ϩⲉ]ⲛⲕⲟⲟⲩⲉ
24 [———] ⲛⲓⲣⲱⲙⲉ·
[——— ϣ]ⲉⲃⲓ-
26 [ⲏⲟⲩⲧ̄ ———]ⲩ·
[———]ⲉ
28 [———]ⲣ

12,31   End of line; e.g., ⲁ̈ⲓ].
13,4-5   See 2,7n I eye of God, an ancient Egyptian motif.
13,6   Supralinear stroke above ⲡⲓⲧ missing (in lacuna); ⲡ is certain; letters ⲓⲧ read from ambiguous traces.
13,7-44,31   *The Revelations from Ephesech* (Part One)
    The revelation from Authrounios ends. That the fifth baptism does not occur until 53,15 suggests that the intervening materials were derived from other sources.
13,7   ⲟⲩⲉ, i.e., ⲟⲩⲃⲉ.
13,8   For Ephesech, or Ephesek, see 45,2.11; cf. ⲏⲥⲏⲫⲏⲭ, *Gos.Eg.* III 50,2; 53,25.

```
      [
30    of[
      these [
```
                                              13

```
      [bless the god] above
2     the [great] aeons (αἰών), the
      [unborn] Kalyptos (καλυπτός), the great
4     male Protophanes (πρωτοφανής), the perfect (τέλειος)
      [child] who is higher than god
6     and his eye, Pigeradama.
      I called upon the
8     child of the child Ephesech.  He
      stood before me and said,
10    "O messenger (ἄγγελος) of god, son of the
      father, [I am] the perfect (τέλειος) human.
12    [Why] are you calling on me and
      asking about those things which you know, as
14    though you were [ignorant] of them?" [But (δέ)]
      [I said,] "I have asked about the
16    mixture [        ] it is perfect and gives
      [            ] there is power which
18    [has          ] in which we receive baptism
      [                         ] these names are
20    [different                ] and why
      [
22    [                         ] in the
      [                   from] others
24    [                         ] humans
      [                                different]
26    [
      [
28    [
```

13,11   Or, [ⲚⲦⲞ]Ⲕ | Colpe, "Heidenische, jüdische und Christliche Überlieferung VI," 151, equates the child of the child with the perfect child and argues that Ephesech or Zostrianos is being presented as the *Urmensch* | For the perfect man as Adam, cf. 6,22ff; 30,4-5.

13,14   Cf. 3,32.

13,15   I.e., ⲘⲞⲨⲌⲈ.

13,17   Cod. ⲞⲨⲚ̄.

13,19ff   Repetition for liturgical and/or didactic functions, perhaps resulting from the conflation of sources; cf. 8,1-7.

13,21-22 E.g., ϢⲈⲂⲤ]ⲎⲞⲨⲦ Ⲉ ⲚⲈ[Ⲩ/ⲈⲢⲎⲨ; cf. 8,2-3,5-6.

ιͅΔ̄

ΕϤϪⲱ ⲙⲙⲟⲥ Ϫⲉ [Ϫⲱⲥⲧ]ⲣⲓⲁⲛⲉ

2 ⲥⲱⲧⲙ ⲉⲧⲃⲉ ⲛⲁⲓ̈ [. . . . . .] ϣⲟ-

ⲙⲧ̇ ⲅⲁⲣ ⲛⲉ ⲛϣⲟⲣⲡ̇ [. . . . . . .]ⲙ

4 ⲛ̇ ⲁ.[ⲣ]ⲭⲏ· ⲉⲁⲩⲟⲩⲱⲛ[ⲅ ⲉ]ⲃⲟⲗ ⲅⲛ

ⲟⲩⲁⲣⲭⲏ ⲛ ⲟⲩⲱⲧ ⲛⲧ[. . .] ⲡⲓⲉ-

6 ⲱⲛ ⲛ ⲃ̅ⲁⲣⲃ̣ⲏⲗⲱ̅ ⲙ ⲡⲣⲏⲧⲉ ⲛ ⲅⲉⲛ-

ⲁⲣⲭⲏ ⲁⲛ ⲙⲛ ⲅⲉⲛϭⲟⲙ ⲟⲩⲁⲉ ⲙ

8 ⲡⲣⲏⲧⲉ ⲁⲛ ⲉⲃⲟⲗ ⲅⲛ ⲟⲩⲁⲣⲭⲏ ⲙⲛ

ⲟⲩϭⲟⲙ· ⲉⲁⲩⲟⲩⲱⲛⲅ ⲉ[ⲃ]ⲟⲗ ⲛ ⲁⲣ-

10 ⲭⲏ ⲛⲓⲙ ⲁⲩⲱ ⲁⲩⲧ̇ ϭⲟⲙ ⲛ ϭⲟⲙ ⲛⲓⲙ

ⲁⲩⲱ ⲉⲁⲩⲟⲩⲱⲛ[ⲅ ⲉⲃⲟⲗ ⲅ]ⲙ ⲡⲏ ⲉⲧ̇-

12 ⲥⲟⲧⲛ̇ ⲉⲣⲟⲟⲩ ⲛⲅ[ⲟⲩⲟ] ⲉⲧⲉ ⲛⲁⲓ̈ ⲛⲉ

ⲧⲅⲩⲡⲁⲣⲝⲓⲥ ⲙⲛ [ⲧⲙⲛ]ⲧⲙⲁⲕ[ⲁⲣ]ⲓⲟⲥ

14 ⲁⲩⲱ ⲡⲓⲱⲛⲅ· ⲛⲓ[. . . .]ⲟⲩ[. . .

ⲃⲟⲗ ⲙⲛ ⲛⲉⲩⲉ[ⲣⲏⲩ . . . .]ⲩⲱ[. .

16 ⲉⲃⲟⲗ ⲅⲛ ⲟⲩⲁ .[

ⲁⲩⲱ ⲉⲧⲃⲉ ⲡ[

18 ⲉⲁⲩⲧ̇ ⲣⲁⲛ ⲉ .[

ⲅⲟⲩⲟ ⲛ ⲧⲁ[

20 ⲱⲧ̇ ⲁⲩⲱ ⲅⲉ[

ⲟⲩⲧⲉⲗⲓⲟⲥ [

22 ⲉⲃⲟⲗ ⲅ[ⲛ ⲟ]ⲩⲁ[

ⲉⲟⲩ[. . .] . .[

24 ⲟⲩⲁⲉ̣[

ⲧ .[

26 ⲉ[

ϭ[

28 ⲛ[

ιͅⲉ̄

ⲁⲩⲱ [. . . . .] ⲛϭⲓ ⲟⲩⲙⲟⲟⲩ ⲛⲧⲉ

2 ⲧⲟⲩ[ⲉⲓ ⲧⲟⲩ]ⲉⲓ ⲙⲙⲟⲟⲩ ⲉⲧⲃⲉ ⲡⲁⲓ̈

ⲅ[. . . . .] ⲙⲙⲟⲟⲩ ⲛⲉ ⲛ ⲧⲉⲗⲓⲟⲥ ⲛⲉ·

14,1   Or, saying. A new set of revelations begins.

14,2   E.g., [ⲧⲏⲣⲟⲩ].

14,3   ⲛ̇, or else ⲡ̣.

14,4ff   The discussion turns on the categories of the One and the Three known
        primarily from neo-Platonic thought. See the introduction for the triad of
        Existence, Life, and Blessedness (Mind).

14,5   E.g., ⲛⲧ[ⲁϥ].

14,6   Stroke begins between ⲃ and ⲁ.

14,14   ⲟ <u>ⲩ</u> ⲩ owing to an imperfection in the surface.

14
saying, "[Zost]trianos,
2   listen about these things[
for (γάρ) the first [
4   origins (ἀρχή) are three because they have
appeared from a single origin (ἀρχή) [   ], the
6   Barbelo aeon (αἰών), not as some
origins (ἀρχή) and powers nor (οὐδέ)
8   as from an origin (ἀρχή) and a
power. It is every origin (ἀρχή) that they
10   have revealed; every power that they have strengthened,
and they have appeared from that which
12   is far better than them, that is, (from)
existence (ὕπαρξις), blessedness (μακάριος)
14   and life. [
[   ] their companions [
16   from a [
and concerning the [
18   having named [
more than [
20   and [
a perfect(τέλειος) [
22   from a [
[
24   [
[
26   [
[
28   [

15
And a water of each one of
2   them [   ]; therefore
[   ] are waters (and) perfect (τέλειος).

14,15   ⳣ, or else ⳡ; e.g., ο]ⳡⳣ[ⲛⳠ].
15,1ff   The baptismal waters may be compared to the primeval waters, see 48,3-10;
         55,13-24; 113,1-14. Here each Barbelo aeon is identified with a baptismal
         water and with a member of the philosophical triad of Life, Mind, and
         Existence.
15,1   E.g., [ⲁ ⳟ ⳤ ⳣ Ⲕ].
15,2   Circumflex over the group ⲉⳋ.
15,3   Not ⲡⲉ.

4 ΠΙΜ[ΟΟ]Ϯ ΝΤΕ ΠⲰΝϨ ΕΤΕ ΠΑϮ-
   ΜΝ̇ΤⲰΝϨ ΠΕ· ΠΗ ϮΝΟϮ ΕΤΑΚ-
6 ϪΙ ϪⲰΚΜ ΕΡΟϤ ϨΜ ΠΙΑϮΤΟΓΕΝΗΣ·
   Π[ΙΜΟΟϮ ΔΕ Ν]ΤΕ ϮΜΝ̇ΤΜΑΚΑΡΙ-
8 ΟΣ ΕΤ[Ε ΠΑ]ΠΣΟΟϮΝ ΠΕ· ΠΗ ΕΤΚ-
   ΝΑϪ[Ι ϪⲰ]ΚΜ ΕΡΟϤ ϨΜ ΠΙΠΡⲰΤΟ-
10 ΦΑΝ[ΗΣ·] ΠΙΜΟΟϮ ΔΕ ΝΤΕ ϮϨϒ-
   ΠΑΡϪ[ΙΣ ΠΕΤ]Ε ΠΑϮΜΝ̇ΤΝΟϒΤΕ
12 ΠΕ ΕΤ[Ε Π]ΑΠΙΚΑⲗϒΠΤΟΣ ΠΕ·
   ΑϒⲰ Ϥ[ϢΟΟⲚ] ⲚϬΙ ΠΙΜΟΟϮ ΝΤΕ
14 [ΠΙ]ⲰΝ[Ϩ ΚΑΤΑ] ΟϒϬΟΜ· ΠΑϮΜΝ̇Τ-
   [ΜΑ]ΚΑ[ΡΙΟΣ] Κ]ΑΤΑ ΟϒΣΙΑ· ΠΑ-
16 [ϮΜΝ̇ΤΝΟϒΤΕ] ΔΕ ΚΑΤΑ ΟϒϨϒ-
   [ΠΑΡϪΙΣ ΝΑ]Ϊ Τ]ΗΡΟϒ ΔΕ ϨΕΝΕΙ-
18 [---   Μ]ΝΤϬΟΜ ΜΝ ϨΕ-
   [---   ]ϒ ΝΕΤΕ ϢΑϒ-
20 [---   ]ΜΟΟϒ ΕΤΤΒ-
   [ΒΟ   ---   ]ϒ ·[· ·] ΠΕ ϨⲰ
22 [---   ] · ·[· · · · ·] ΚΑΤΑ
   [Ε]ΤΑϒΒⲰΚ
24 [---   ]ϒϮ·
   [---   ] ΜΜΑϒ
26 [---   ]Ⲱ
   [---   ]ΜΗ
28 [
   ⲒϚ̄
   ϨϒΠΑΡϪΙ[Σ] Μ ΠΡ[ΗΤΕ ΕΤϤ]ϢΟΟⲚ
2 ΜΜΟΣ· ΟϒΜΟΝΟ[Ν ΑϤΟϒ]ⲰϨ ϨΝ
   ΟϒΕΝΝΟΙΑ· ΑⲗⲗΑ ΑϤ ·[· · · · ·]Ν Ε-
4 ΡΟΟϒ ϪΕ ΝΤΟϤ ΠΕ ΠϢ[Ⲱ]ΠΕ Μ ΠΕ-
   ΕΙΡΗΤΕ· ΕΑϤΚⲰ Ν Οϒ[· ·] · Ϥ ϨΙϪΝ
6 ΠΕΤϢΟΟⲚ· ϨΙΝΑ ϪΕ ΝΝΕϤϢⲰΠΕ
   ΝΝ ΑΤΝ ΑΡΗϪϤ Αϒ[Ⲱ] Ν [Α]Ϯ̇ΜΟΡΦΗ·
8 ΑⲗⲗΑ ΕΑϒϪΙΟΟΡ Μ[ΜΟϤ] ΝΑΜΕ
   ΕϒΒΡΡΕ ΠΕ Ε ΠΤΡΕ[ϤϢ]ⲰΠΕ

15,10   ]ΠΙΜΟΟϮ, or possibly, Ο]ϒΜΟΟϮ.
15,12   The identification of the abbreviation Κ̄Λ̄Σ̄ as καλυπτός is based on this
        reference.
15,15   <Οϒ>ΟϒΣΙΑ ?; cf. lines 16-17, ΟϒϨϒ[ΠΑΡϪΙΣ.
15,18   I.e., ϨΕΝ'.
15,22   ] ., trace of a supralinear stroke.
16,1ff The sense is obscure I he, antecedent is unclear.

4   It is the water of life that
       belongs to vitality in which you now
6   have been baptized in the Autogenes (αὐτογενής).
       It is (+δέ) the [water] of blessedness (μακάριος)
8   which [belongs] to knowledge in which you
       will be [baptized] in the Protophanes (πρωτοφανής).
10   It is (+δέ) the water of existence (ὕπαρξις)
       [which] belongs to divinity, that is, to
12   the Kalyptos (καλυπτός).
       Now the water of life
14   [exists in relation to (κατά)] a power, that belonging
       to [blessedness (μακάριος)] in relation to (κατά)
16   essence (οὐσία), and (δέ) that belonging to [Divinity] in
       relation to (κατά) [existence (ὕπαρξις)]. But (δέ) all [these]
18   [   ] authority and
       [   ] those who
20   [   ] water which
       [becomes pure
22   [   ] according to (κατά)
       [when they] depart
24   [
       [
26   [
       [
28   [
       16
       existence (ὕπαρξις) [as he] is
2   in it. [He] not only (οὐ μόνον) [was dwelling]
       in Thought (ἔννοια), but (δέ) he [   ]
4   them that he is one that is [Being] in the following
       way: in order that (ἵνα) what is
6   might not be endless and formless (-μορφή),
       he placed a [   ] over it;
8   but (ἀλλά) in order that [he] might become
       something, the truly new crossed over

16,2   ϩ, only a trace of the connective supralinear stroke survives (nothing from
        ϩ) | lit., in her.
16,3   .ι, either ϥ or ⲡ; probably the latter | ιⲛ, lacuna where a supralinear stroke
        might have stood.
16,4-5 I.e., ⲡⲉ ϊ΄.
16,4   Lacuna above ⲙ | for the restoration, see 17,3.

10 ⲚⲚ ⲞⲨⲀⲀⲨ· ⲈⲨⲚ[ⲦⲀ .] ⲘⲘⲀⲨ
Ⲙ ⲠⲈⲦⲈ ⲠⲰϤ Ⲙ [. . . . .] ⲠⲈ ⲐⲨ-
12 ⲠⲀⲢⲜⲓⲤ ⲘⲚ ⲠϢ[ⲎⲢ]Ⲉ ⲈϤⲀϨⲈⲢⲀ-
ⲦϤ ⲚⲘⲘⲀϤ ⲈϤϢ[ⲓ]Ⲛ[Ⲉ Ⲛ]ⲘⲘⲀϤ [Ⲉ]Ϥ-
14 ⲔⲰⲦⲈ ⲈⲢⲞϤ ⲀⲨ[. . . . .]ⲚⲈ Ⲙ [.] .
ⲚⲤⲀ ⲤⲀ ⲚⲓⲘ· Ⲉ[. . . . .]ⲱ[. .
16 ⲈⲂⲞⲖ ϨⲘ ⲠⲓⲘⲈ[
Ⲭⲓ Ⲙ ⲠⲎ ⲈⲦⲦ .[
18 Ⲛ ϢⲞⲞⲚ Ⲛ Ⲧ[
ⲞⲨⲈⲚⲈⲢⲄⲓⲀ [
20 ⲞⲨⲞⲚϨ· ⲈⲨⲚ[
ⲠⲈϤⲔⲈϢⲀⲬⲈ
22 ⲚⲈ ⲚⲀÏ ⲚϨⲀ .[
ⲀⲨϢ[ⲰⲠ]Ⲉ Ⲙ [
24 Ⲣⲓ Ⲛ̅ⲈⲨ[
Ⲛ .[
26 Ⲉ[
Ⲡ[
28 .[
Ϩ[

$\overline{ⲓⲅ}$

ⲀⲨⲰ ⲤϢⲞⲞⲚ ⲚϬⲓ ϮϬⲞⲘ ⲘⲚ Ϯ-
2 ⲞⲨⲤ[ⲓⲀ] ⲘⲚ ϮⲞⲨⲠⲀⲢⲜⲓⲤ ⲚⲦⲈ
ⲠϢⲰ[Ⲡ]Ⲉ ⲈϤϢⲞⲞⲚ ⲚϬⲓ ⲠⲓⲘⲞ[Ⲟ]Ⲩ·
4 ⲠⲢⲀⲚ [Ⲇ]Ⲉ ⲈⲦⲈⲨⲬⲰⲔⲘ ⲈⲢⲟϤ ⲞⲨ-
ϢⲀⲬⲈ ⲠⲈ ⲚⲦⲈ ⲠⲓⲘⲞⲞⲨ· ⲠϢⲞ-
6 Ⲣ̅Ⲛ ⲞⲨⲚ Ⲙ ⲘⲞⲞⲨ Ⲛ ⲦⲈⲖⲓⲞⲤ ⲚⲦⲈ
ⲠⲓϢⲘ̅Ⲧ̄[ϬⲞ]Ⲙ [Ⲙ] ⲠⲓⲀⲨⲦⲞⲄⲈⲚⲎⲤ
8 ⲞⲨⲰⲚϨ [ⲠⲈ] ⲚⲦⲈ ⲚⲓⲮⲨⲬⲎ Ⲛ ⲦⲈ-
ⲖⲓⲞⲤ· Ⲟ[Ⲩ]ϢⲀⲬⲈ ⲄⲀⲢ ⲠⲈ ⲚⲦⲈ
10 ⲠⲓⲚⲞⲨ[ⲦⲈ Ⲛ] ⲦⲈⲖⲓⲞⲤ Ⲙ ⲠⲦⲢⲈϤϢⲰ-
ⲠⲈ Ⲁ .[. . . . Ⲉ]ⲦⲘⲘⲀⲨ· ⲞⲨⲠⲎⲤⲎ
12 ⲄⲀⲢ ⲚⲦⲈ [ⲚⲀ]Ï ⲦⲎⲢⲞⲨ ⲠⲈ ⲠⲓⲀϨⲞⲢⲀ-
ⲦⲞⲚ Ⲙ Ⲡ̅[Ⲛ]Ⲁ̅ <ⲈⲓⲈ> ⲚⲓⲔⲞⲞⲨⲈ ϨⲈⲚ-

16,14   Ⲛ, without supralinear stroke | Ⲉ, trace of a round letter |] ., top of a
             vertical stroke.
16,17-18   E.g., Ⲣ ϢⲞⲢⲠ]/Ⲛ ϢⲞⲞⲚ.
16,20   E.g., ⲈⲨⲚ[ⲦⲀ´.
16,29   Below the beginning of this line and somewhat to the left the papyrus has
             been patched; written upon the material used as a patch are the letters ϤⲀ,
             in a different script; these bear no relation to the text of *Zostrianos.*
17,1   Ⲥ̅ϢⲞⲞⲚ, supralinear stroke above Ⲥ.

10   it with what
     is his own, [
12   existence (ὕπαρξις) and the [son].
     He is located with him, with him he seeks, with him
14   he surrounds [
     everywhere [
16   from the truth [
     takes him who [
18   exists [
     activity (ἐνέργεια) [
20   life [
     his word also [
22   are these after [
     they became [
24   [
     [
26   [
     [
28   [
     [

                                          17

     And the power exists together with the
2   essence (οὐσία) and the existence (ὕπαρξις)
     of Being, when the water exists.
4   But (δέ) the name in which they wash
     is a word of the water. Then (οὖν)
6   the first perfect (τέλειος) water of
     the three-powered one [of] the Autogenes (αὐτογενής)
8   [is] the perfect (τέλειος) soul's (ψυχή)
     life; for (γάρ) it is a word of
10   the perfect (τέλειος) god while coming into
     being [
12   for (γάρ) the Invisible (ἀόρατον) Spirit (πνεῦμα)
     is a fountain (πηγή) of [them] all. <Thus,>

17,3   Ọ, ink trace from a round letter.
17,4   I.e., ϵτοȣ̄.
17,6   Cf. *Allogenes* XI 45,13,; 47,8-11 *et al.*
17,7   Or, the three-powered Autogenes.
17,12-13 As the ultimate source, the Invisible Spirit is the high god.
17,13   ā̄, only a trace of the supralinear stroke survives | emend ϵτϵ to ϵϳϵ
          ΝϳΚΟΟϨϵ.

14 ЄΒΟλ [Ϩⲛ ϯⲧⲛ]ⲱⲥⲓⲥ ⲛⲉ ⲉϩⲉⲛⲉⲓⲛⲉ
    ⲛⲧⲁϥ [ⲛⲉ· ⲁⲗⲗ]ⲁ ⲡⲏ ⲉⲧⲙⲙⲉ ⲉⲣⲟϥ
16 ⲝⲉ [.] .[. . . . .] ⲁϣ ⲛ ⲣⲏⲧⲉ ⲛ ⲁϣ
    [——   ]ⲟⲛϩ ϩⲓ ⲟⲩⲥⲟⲡ
18 [——   ]ⲱⲛϩ ϩⲣⲁⲓ̈ ϩⲛ ⲟⲩ-
    [——   ]ⲟⲩⲛ ⲡⲉ ⲡⲓⲙⲟ-
20 [——   ]ⲱⲛϩ· ϩⲙ ⲡϣⲱ-
    [——   ϣ]ⲱⲡⲉ ⲛⲛ ⲁⲧⲛ ⲁ-
22 [ⲣⲏⲁϥ   ——   ] ⲡⲉϥ[. . . .]ⲉ ⲙⲙⲓⲛ
    [ⲙⲙⲟϥ   ——   ]ⲱ ⲡⲣⲁⲛ
24 [——   ]ⲩⲧⲉ
    [——   ]ⲉⲉ
26 [——   ] ⲛ
    [_   ——   ]ϥ
ⲓ̅ⲏ̅
    ⲉϥϣⲟⲟⲛ ⲟⲛⲧⲱⲥ· ⲡⲏ ⲡⲉ ⲉϣⲁϥ-
2 ϯ ⲧⲟϣ ⲉⲣⲟϥ· ⲁⲩⲱ ⲛⲏ ⲉⲩ[ⲛ]ⲛⲏⲩ
    ⲉϩⲣⲁⲓ̈ ⲉ ⲡⲓⲙⲟⲟⲩ ⲕⲁⲧⲁ ⲧⲉ[ⲓ̈]ϭⲟⲙ ⲛ
4 ⲟ[ⲩ]ⲱⲧ ⲙⲛ ⲡⲓⲉⲓⲛⲉ ⲛⲧ[ⲉ] ϯⲧⲁⲝⲓⲥ·
    ⲁⲩⲱ ⲡⲓⲡⲣⲱⲧⲟⲫⲁⲛⲏ[ⲥ] ⲛ ⲛⲟϭ ⲛ
6 ϩⲟⲟⲩⲧ ⲛⲛ ⲁⲧⲛⲁⲩ ⲉⲣⲟϥ ⲛ ⲧⲉⲗⲓⲟⲥ ⲛ
    ⲛⲟⲩⲥ· ⲟⲩⲛⲧⲁϥ ⲙ ⲡⲉϥⲙⲟⲟⲩ ⲙⲙⲓⲛ
8 ⲙⲙⲟϥ· ϩⲱⲥ ⲉϣⲱⲡ[ⲉ ⲉ]ⲕϣⲁⲛⲉⲓ ⲉ-
    ⲝⲛ ⲡⲉϥⲧⲟⲡⲟⲥ ⲉⲕ[ⲛⲁⲛⲁ]ⲩ ⲉⲣⲟϥ ⲙ ⲡⲉⲓ̈-
10 ⲣⲏⲧⲉ ⲟⲛ ⲡⲉ ⲡⲉⲓ̈ⲕⲁ̅ⲥ̅ [ⲛⲛ] ⲁⲧⲙⲓⲥⲉ·
    ⲕⲁⲧⲁ ⲡⲟⲩⲁ ⲡⲟⲩⲁ ⲝⲉ ϥϣⲟⲟⲛ ⲛϭⲓ
12 ⲟⲩⲙⲉⲣⲓⲕⲟⲛ ⲙⲛ [ⲟⲩϣⲟ]ⲣⲛ ⲛ ⲉⲓⲇⲟⲥ
    ϩⲓⲛⲁ ⲝⲉ ⲉⲩⲉⲝⲱⲕ ⲙ [ⲡ]ⲉⲓ̈ⲣⲏⲧⲉ· ⲛⲓ-
14 ⲁⲩⲧⲟⲅⲉⲛⲓⲟⲛ ⲅⲁⲣ [ⲛⲛ] ⲉⲱⲛ ϥⲧⲟ-
    ⲟⲩ ⲛⲉ ⲛ ⲧⲉⲗⲓⲟ[ⲥ ⲛⲓ]ⲕⲁⲧⲁ ⲟⲩ[ⲁ] ⲛ-
16 ⲧⲉ ⲛⲓⲡⲁⲛⲧⲉⲗⲓⲟ̅ⲥ̅ [. . ϣⲟ]ⲟⲛ [. .
    ⲛⲁⲓ̈ ⲛ ⲛⲓⲕⲁⲧⲁ ⲟ[ⲩⲁ ⲛ ⲧⲉ]ⲗⲁⲓ̈ⲟⲥ· ⲡ[
18 ϯⲟⲩ ⲝⲉ ⲛⲛ ⲉⲱ[ⲛ . . . . . .] ⲙⲙ[

17,15   I.e., ⲉⲧⲉⲓⲙⲉ | or, himself (or perhaps it).
17,16ff   These lines evidently contained questions.
17,19-20   E.g., ⲙⲟ/[ⲟⲩ].
17,20-21   E.g., ϣⲱ/[ⲡⲉ].
17,21   ⲛ, only a trace of the supralinear stroke survives.
18,1f   Lit., he; Invisible Spirit? | evidently a response to the questions begun
        at 17,16.
18,2ff   Cf. *Apoc.Adam* V 78,5.

14 the rest come from [knowledge (γνῶσις)] as
  his likenesses. [But (ἀλλά)] he who knows himself
16 [   ] what kind and (ἤ) what
  [   ] alive at one time
18 [   ] live with a
  [   ] he is the
20 [   ] life, in the
  [   ] become
22 [limitless   ] his [his]
  [own   ] the name
24 [
  [
26 [
  [

18

  he really (ὄντως) exists-it is so because he
2 limits himself. They [approach]
  the water according to (κατά) this
4 single power and the likeness of order (τάξις).
  The Protophanes (πρωτοφανής), the great male
6 invisible perfect (τέλειος) mind (νοῦς),
  has his own water
8 as (ὡς) you [will see]
  when you arrive at his place (τόπος). This
10 is also the case with the unborn Kalyptos (καλυπτός).
  In (+δέ) relation to (κατά) each one a
12 partial (μερικόν) exists together with a first form (εἶδος),
  so that (ἵνα) they might become perfect in this way;
14 for (γάρ) the self-begotten (αὐτογενιόν) aeons (αἰών)
  are four perfect (τέλειος) (entities). [The] individuals
16 (+κατά) of the all-perfect ones (παντέλειος)[exist
  them as [perfect (τέλειος) individuals (κατά)].
18 And (δέ) the [ ] aeon (αἰών) [

18,11-12 See also 22,1 above; cf. Plot. *Enn.* II 1.31-40.
18,13 ϊ, or ϳ.
18,15 ΝΤΕ, Ν has a supralinear stroke | ΝϳΚΑΤΑ ΟϮΑ, those who exist by
    themselves, i.e., solitaries or individuals; cf. 19,11.16 *passim.*
18,16 ῆ, only the flag is in lacuna; e.g., [ΣΕϢΟ]Οῆ [ϨΝ].
18,17-18 E.g., Π[ϳ]ϮΟϮ, or Π[ϳΜΕϨ]ϮΟϮ; cf. 19,11-14; 53,15-25.
18,18 ΜΜ, a trace of the supralinear stroke over the first Μ also survives.

```
       ⲙ ⲡⲓⲁⲩⲧⲟⲅⲉⲛ[ⲏⲥ
20     ⲧⲏⲣⲟⲩ ⲅⲁⲣ ϩⲉⲛ[
       ϩⲟⲟⲩⲧ ⲛ ⲧ .[
22     ⲛⲓⲡⲧⲏⲣϥ ⲅⲁ[ⲣ                          ⲧⲉ-]
       ⲗⲓⲟⲥ ⲛ ⲛⲟⲩ[ⲧⲉ                          ⲡⲓϣⲟ-]
24     ⲙⲧ̇ ⲛ [ϩⲟⲟ]ⲩⲧ̇ [
       ⲕⲁⲧⲁ [ⲟⲩ]ⲁ̣ ⲛ [ⲧⲉⲗⲓⲟⲥ
26     ϩⲙ ⲡ[
       ⲫ[
28     ⲉ[
        .[
30      .[
        .[
```

```
                                            ⲓ̄[ⲑ̄]
       ⲧⲉⲗⲓⲟⲥ· ⲛⲏ ⲉⲧϣⲟⲟⲛ̇ ⲕⲁⲧ[ⲁ ⲟ]ⲩ-
2      ⲉⲓⲇⲟⲥ̣ ⲙⲛ ⲟⲩⲅⲉⲛⲟⲥ· ⲁⲩ[ⲱ] ⲟⲩ-
       ⲧⲏⲣϥ ⲙⲛ ⲟⲩⲇⲓⲁⲫⲟⲣⲁ [ⲙ ⲙ]ⲉⲣⲓ-
4      ⲕⲟⲛ[·] ⲧ̇ϩⲓⲏ ⲛ ⲃ̄ⲱ̄ⲕ ⲉϩⲣⲁ̈ⲓ ⲉⲧϫⲟⲥⲉ
       ⲉ ⲧⲉⲗⲓⲟⲥ ⲙⲛ ⲡⲓⲕ̄ⲁ̄ⲥ ⲟⲛ ⲙ ⲡⲉⲓ̈ⲣⲏ-
6      ⲧⲉ· ⲡⲓⲁⲩⲧⲟⲅⲉⲛⲏⲥ ⲇⲉ ⲛ ⲛⲟⲩⲧⲉ
       ⲟⲩϣⲟⲣⲛ̇ ⲛ ⲁⲣⲭⲱⲛ ⲡⲉ ⲛⲧⲉ ⲛⲉ-
8      ⲧⲉ ⲛⲟⲩⲩ ⲛⲛ ⲉⲱⲛ ⲙⲛ ⲛⲓⲁⲅⲅⲉⲗⲟⲥ
       ⲙ ⲡⲣⲏⲧⲉ ⲛ ϩⲉⲛⲙⲉⲣⲟⲥ ⲛⲧⲁϥ· ⲛⲏ ⲅⲁⲣ
10     ⲉⲧⲉ ⲡⲓϥⲧⲟⲟⲩ ϣⲟⲟⲛ̇ ⲙⲙⲟϥ ⲕⲁ-
       ⲧⲁ ⲟⲩⲁ ⲥⲉⲛⲧⲉ ⲡⲉⲙⲉϩⲧⲟⲩ ⲛⲛ ⲉ-
12     ⲱⲛ ⲙⲙⲁⲩ ϩⲓ ⲟⲩⲥⲟⲛ· ⲁⲩⲱ ϥϣⲟ-
       ⲟⲛ̇ ⲛϭⲓ ⲡⲓⲙⲉϩⲧⲟⲩ ϩⲛ ⲟⲩⲁ· ⲡⲓ-
14     ϥⲧⲟⲟⲩ [ⲡⲉ ⲕ]ⲁⲧⲁ ⲙⲉⲣⲟⲥ ⲡⲓⲙⲉϩ-
       ⲧⲟⲩ· ⲛ̣ .[ . . .]ⲟⲩ ⲇⲉ ⲥⲉϫⲏⲕ ⲉⲃⲟⲗ
16     ⲕⲁⲧⲁ ⲟⲩⲁ [ⲉⲩ]ⲛⲧⲁⲩ ⲙⲙⲁⲩ ⲛ ⲟⲩ-
       [ . . . . ] ⲙ̣ [ . . . . . ]ⲧⲉ ⲟⲛ ϥϣⲟⲟⲛ̇ ⲛ
18     [ . . . . . . . . ϩⲟ]ⲟⲩⲧ̇ ⲛ ⲕⲁⲧⲁ ⲟⲩⲁ
       [        ———         ]ⲙ ⲅⲁⲣ ⲡⲉ ⲛⲧⲉ
20     [        ———         ] ⲛ ⲛⲟⲩⲧⲉ·  ⲡⲓ-
       [        ———         ] ⲇⲉ ⲛⲛ ⲁⲧⲛⲁⲩ
22     [ⲉⲣⲟ  ———      ] ⲛ ϩⲟ[ⲟⲩⲧ̇] ⲛ ⲛⲟⲩⲥ
```

18,21	E.g., ⲧⲉ[ⲗⲓⲟⲥ]; elsewhere Protophanes is called the perfect male; cf. 19,21f.
18,24	ⲧ̇, only the flag is in lacuna.
19,2-3	Not ⲟⲩⲡⲧⲏⲣϥ; cf. 23,14; 33,9.
19,6ff	Cf. 127,15-128,7.
19,11	Cod. ⲥⲉⲛ̄ⲧⲉ.

of the Autogenes (αὐτογενής) [
20   for (γάρ) all[
      male [
22   for (γάρ) the alls [
      [perfect (τέλειος) god   the triple-]
24   [male
      [perfect (τέλειος)] individual (+κατά) [
26   in the [
      [
28   [
      [
30   [
      [
                                        1[9]
      perfect (τέλειος), those who exist according to (κατά)
2   a form (εἶδος), a race (γένος), an
      all and a partial (μερικόν) difference (διαφορά).
4   This is also the case for the highway of ascent that is
      higher than perfect (τέλειος) and Kalyptos (καλυπτός).
6   The (+δέ) divine Autogenes (αὐτογενής) is
      chief archon (ἀρχών) of his
8   own aeons (αἰών) and angels (ἄγγελος)
      as his parts (μέρος): for (γάρ) those
10   who are the four individually (+κατά)
      belong to him; they belong to the fifth
12   aeon (αἰών) together, and the
      fifth exists in one. The four
14   [are] the fifth, part by part (κατὰ μέρος).
      But (δέ) [   ] (they) are
16   perfect individually (κατά) [because they] have a
      [   ] he is also [   ] with
18   [male] individually (+κατά)
      [   ] for (γάρ) he is a [   ] of
20   [   ]divine [   ]; the
      and (δέ) [   ] invisible
22   [   ] male mind (νοῦς)

19,15   Ⲛ, or Ⲏ.
19,17-18 Probably Ⲛ/[Ⲅ]Ⲥ.
19,17   E.g., Ⲙ[ⲡⲉⲓ̈ⲣⲏ]ⲧⲉ; cf. 19,4.
19,19   E.g., ⲟⲩⲅⲟ]ⲙ.

```
     [        ———        ]  ṇ  τε̣[ . . . ε]τ̄ϣοοπ
24   [        ———           ] . .[ . . .] .ṇ· ο⳨
     [        ———                                      ]⳨
26   [        ———                                      ]⳨
     [        ———                                      ]ε
28   [
     [̲        ———                                      ]ε
     κ̄
```

ṇ ϩεṇμερος ετοṇϩ ⲁ⳨ⲱ ṇ τελιος
2 π[ιⲡ]τηρ[ϥ] ⲇε ⲁ⳨ⲱ πιϭεⲛ[ο]ⲥ μ̄ ⲡⲁⲛ–
   τε̣λιος μ̄ⲛ πη ετⲝⲟⲥε̣ ε τελιⲟⲥ
4 ⲁ⳨ⲱ μ̄ μⲁⲕⲁⲣιⲟⲥ· πιⲕⲁ̣λ⳨ⲡⲧⲟⲥ
   ⲇε ⲛ ⲝⲡⲟ ⲉⲃⲟⲗ μ̄μⲟϥ μⲁ⳨ⲁⲁϥ·
6 ⲉ⳨ⲁⲣⲭη ⲡⲉ ⲉϥⲣ ϣⲣⲡ̄ ⲛ ϣⲟⲟⲡ̄ ⲛⲧⲉ
   ⲡⲓⲁ⳨ⲧⲟⲅⲉⲛⲏⲥ ⲉ⳨ⲛⲟ⳨ⲧⲉ ⲡⲉ ⲁ⳨ⲱ
8 ⲛ ϣⲟⲣⲡ̄ ⲛ ⲉⲓⲱⲧ· ⲉ⳨ⲗⲟⲉⲓϭⲉ ⲡⲉ ⲛ–
   ⲧⲉ ⲡⲓⲡⲣⲱⲧⲟⲫⲁⲛⲏⲥ· ⲉ⳨ⲉⲓⲱⲧ
10 ⲡⲉ ⲛⲧⲉ ⲛⲉⲧⲉ ⲛⲟ⳨ϥ μ̄ μⲉⲣⲟⲥ·
   ⲉ⳨ⲛⲟ⳨ⲧⲉ ⲛ ⲉⲓⲱⲧ ⲡⲉ ⲉ⳨ⲣ ϣⲣⲡ̄
12 ⲛ ⲉⲓμⲉ ⲉⲣⲟϥ· ⲁ⳨ⲱ ⲛⲉⲧⲉⲓμⲉ ⲉⲣⲟϥ
   ⲁⲛ· ⲟ⳨ϭⲟμ ⲅⲁⲣ ⲉⲃⲟⲗ μ̄μⲟϥ ⲡⲉ μ̄ⲛ
14 ⲟ⳨ϩ[ⲓ]ⲱⲧ̄ ⲉⲃⲟⲗ μ̄[μⲟ]ϥ μⲁ⳨ⲁⲁϥ·
   ⲉⲧⲃⲉ ⲡⲁⲓ̈ ⲟ⳨ⲁⲧⲉ̣[ⲓⲱ]ⲧ̄ ⲡⲉ· ⲡⲓⲁⲧ–
16 ⲛⲁ⳨ ⲇⲉ ⲉⲣⲟϥ ⲛ [ϣ]μ̄ϭⲟμ· ⲧ̄ϣⲟ–
   ⲣⲡ̄ ⲛ ⲉⲛⲛⲟⲓⲁ̄ ⲛ[ⲧⲉ ⲛⲁⲓ̈] ⲧⲏⲣⲟ[⳨] ⲡⲓ[ⲁϩⲟ–]
18 ⲣⲁⲧⲟⲛ μ̄ ⲡⲛⲁ̄· ⲟ̣[. . . .]ⲏ ṇ [. . .
   ⲣⲟ⳨ ⲡⲉ· ⲁ⳨ⲱ [
20 ⲟ⳨ⲥⲓⲁ ⲉⲥϩⲁ[
   μ̄ⲛ ⲟ⳨ϩ⳨ⲡⲁⲣ[ⲝⲓⲥ
22 ⲟ⳨ⲛ ϩⲉⲛϩ⳨[ⲡⲁⲣⲝⲓⲥ
   ⲟ⳨ⲱⲛ[ϩ .]ⲧⲁ[
24 μⲁⲕⲁ[ⲣⲓⲟ]ⲥ· ⲁ[
   ⲛ ⲧ̄μⲛ[ⲧ .]ⲟ[
26 ⲛⲁⲓ̈ ⲧ[ⲏⲣⲟ⳨
   ⲡⲓ[
28 ⲛ [
   ⲛ [

20,5   ⲛⲝⲡⲟ ... translate αὐτογενής; see also 15,12.
20,11-13 Kalyptos, the hidden aeon, cannot be seen from the lower aeons.
20,11   Or, a father-god.
20,15   ⲁⲧ̄, or ⲁⲧ̣ | cf. Heb 7:3.

```
       [              ] which exists
24     [
       [
26     [
       [
28     [
       [
       20
```
living and perfect (τέλειος) parts (μέρος).
2   (About) the All (+δέ) and the all-perfect (παντέλειος)
       race (γένος) and one who is higher than perfect (τέλειος)
4   and blessed (μακάριος). The (+δέ)
       self-begotten Kalyptos (καλυπτός)
6.   is a preexisting origin (ἀρχή) of
       the Autogenes (αὐτογενής), a god and
8   a forefather, a cause of the
       Protophanes (πρωτοφανής), a father
10   of the parts (μέρος) that are his.
       As a divine father, he is
12   foreknown, but he is
       unknown; for (γάρ) he is a power and
14   a father from himself.
       Therefore, he is [fatherless].
16   The (+δέ) invisible three-powered, the
       first thought (ἔννοια) [of] all [these], the
18   Invisible (ἀόρατον) Spirit (πνεῦμα) [
       is [   ], and [
20   essence (οὐσία) which [
       and existence (ὕπαρξις) [
22   there are [existences (ὕπαρξις)
       [life
24   blessed (μακάριος) [
       the [
26   all [these
       the [
28   [
       [

────────────

20,16   Or, triple-power; though often applied to intermediate beings in related
         documents, Zost uses this term of the Spirit; see Pearson, "Marsenes,"
         245-46.
20,18-19 E.g., ο[ⲩⲡⲏⲧ]ⲏ ⲛ[ⲧⲉ ⲛⲁ]ⲓ̈ ⲧⲏ]/ⲣⲟⲩ ⲡⲉ.
```
```

30 ⲧⲉ[

ⲕⲁ

ⲟⲛ̄ ⲛ̄ϩⲣⲁⲓ̈ ⲛ̄ϩⲏⲧⲟⲩ· ⲁ[. . . . . .] .

2 ϩⲛ ϩⲉ[ⲛ]ⲕⲟⲟⲧⲉ ⲛ̄ⲧⲟⲩ ⲧ[. . . .
ⲉⲃⲟⲗ ϩⲓⲧⲟⲟⲧⲟⲩ ⲧⲏⲣⲟⲩ ⲛ̄[ϩⲣ]ⲁ̣ⲓ̈

4 ϩⲛ ⲟⲩⲙⲏⲏϣⲉ ⲙ̄ ⲙⲁ· ⲡⲓⲙⲁ ⲉⲧⲁⲩ-
ⲟⲩⲁϣϥ ⲁⲩⲱ ⲡⲓⲙⲁ ⲉⲧⲉ ϩⲛⲁϥ

6 ⲉⲩⲛ̄ϩⲣⲁⲓ̈ ϩⲙ ⲙⲁ ⲛⲓⲙ· ⲁⲩⲱ ⲉⲛ-
ⲥⲉ ⲛ̄ϩⲣⲁⲓ̈ ϩⲛ ⲗⲁⲁⲩ ⲙ̄ ⲙⲁ ⲁⲛ· ⲁⲩⲱ

8 ⲉⲩⲣ ⲭⲱⲣⲓⲛ ⲉⲩⲡ̄ⲛⲁ· ϩⲉⲛⲁⲧⲥⲱ-
ⲙⲁ ⲅⲁⲣ ⲛⲉ ⲁⲩⲱ ⲥⲉⲥⲟⲧⲡ̄ ⲉ ϩⲉⲛ-

10 ⲁⲧⲥⲱⲙⲁ· ϩⲉⲛⲁⲧⲡⲱϣ ⲛⲉ ⲙⲛ
ϩⲉⲛⲙⲉⲉⲧⲉ ⲉⲧⲟⲛϩ· ⲁⲩⲱ ⲟⲩϭⲟⲙ

12 ⲛ̄ⲧⲉ ⲧⲙⲉ ⲙⲛ ⲛⲏ ⲉⲧⲧⲟⲩⲃⲏⲟⲩⲧ̇
ⲛ̄ⲧⲉ ⲛⲁⲓ̈ ⲛ̄[ϩⲟ]ⲩⲟ· ⲉⲩϣⲟⲟⲡ̄ ⲡⲣⲟⲥ

14 ⲡⲁⲓ̈ ⲛ̄ϩⲟ[ⲩⲟ] ⲉⲩⲧⲟⲩⲃⲏⲟⲩⲧ· ⲁⲩⲱ
ⲙ̄ ⲡⲣⲏⲧⲉ ⲛ [ⲛ̄ⲥ]ⲱⲙⲁ ⲁⲛ ⲉⲧϣⲟ-

16 ⲟⲛ̄ ϩⲛ ⲟⲩ[ⲧⲟ]ⲡⲟⲥ ⲛ ⲟⲩⲱⲧ̇
ⲡⲁⲛⲧⲱ[ⲥ ⲟⲩ]ⲛⲧⲁⲩ ⲙ̄ⲙⲁⲩ ⲛ

18 [ⲟ]ⲩⲁⲛⲁⲅⲕⲏ ⲏ [ⲕ]ⲁⲧⲁ ⲡⲧⲏⲣϥ· ⲏ ⲕⲁ-
[ⲧ]ⲁ ⲟⲩⲙⲉⲣⲟⲥ[· ϯ]ϩⲓⲏ ⲟⲩⲛ ⲛ ⲃⲱⲕ

20 [ⲉ]ϩⲣⲁⲓ̈ ⲉ̣ .[. .] . .[. .] ⲟⲩⲧⲃ̄ⲃⲟ ⲡⲉ
[. .]ⲧ̣[. . . . .] ⲧⲟⲩⲉⲓ ⲧⲟⲩⲉⲓ

22 [———   ]ⲥ ⲕϣ[. . .] ⲉϩⲣⲁⲓ̈
[———   ⲙ]ⲙⲓⲛ̣ [ⲙ̄]ⲙⲟⲥ ⲁⲩⲱ

24 [———   ]ⲟ̣[. . . . .] ⲙ̄ⲙⲟⲟⲩ·
[———   ]ϣⲟ

26 [ⲟ. ———   ]ⲧ̣ⲉ
[———   ]ⲱ

28 [———   ⲡⲁⲛ]ⲧ̣ⲱⲥ
[_   ———   ]ⲟⲩϥ

ⲕⲃ

ⲙ̄ ⲙ̄[ⲉ]ⲣⲓⲕⲟⲛ ⲛ̄ⲛ ⲉⲱⲛ· ⲁⲩⲱ

2 [ⲁϥϣⲁ]ϫ̣ⲉ ϫⲉ ⲡⲱⲥ ⲟⲩⲛ ϣϭⲟⲙ
[ⲙ̄]ⲙⲟϥ ⲛ ϣⲱⲡ̄ ⲉⲣⲟϥ ⲛ ⲟⲩⲧⲩ-

4 ⲡⲟⲥ ⲛ ϣⲁ ⲉⲛⲉϩ· ⲁⲩⲱ ϣⲁϥⲕⲟⲓ-
ⲛⲱⲛⲓ ⲛ̄ϭⲓ ⲡⲛⲟⲉⲣⲟⲥ ⲛ ⲕⲁⲑⲟⲗⲓ-

21,1   Or, dwell in them (assumes [ϣⲟ] on p. 20).
21,4   They, evidently the constituent members of an aeon, probably Protophanes;
           see 22,10.
21,17   Or, certainly.
21,20   E.g., [ⲉ]ϩⲣⲁⲓ̈ ⲉ̣ ⲡ[ⲓⲙ]ⲁ̣ ⲡ[ⲁⲓ̈].

30   [

21

[exist] in them, [
2   in others, they [
by them all
4   in many places. (They are) in
every place that he
6   loves and desires, yet
they are not in any place.
8 ┃ They contain (χωρεῖν) spirit (πνεῦμα);
for (γάρ) they are incorporeal (-σῶμα) yet are better
10   than incorporeal (-σῶμα). They are undivided with
living thoughts and a power
12   of truth with those purer
than these since with respect to (πρός)
14   him they are purer and
are not like bodies (σῶμα) which
16   are in one place (τόπος).
Above all (πάντως), they have necessity
18   (ἀναγκή) either (ἤ) in relation to (κατά) the All
or (ἤ) to (κατά) a part (μέρος). Therefore (οὖν),
20   [the] way of ascent [   ] is pure
[   ] each (fem.)
22   [
[   ] herself and
24   [   ]them
[
26   [
[
28   [above all (πάντως)]
[
22
partial (μεπικόν) aeons (αἰών). Then
2   [he said], "How (πῶς) then (οὖν) can he
contain an
4   eternal model (τύπος)? The
general (καθολικόν) intellect (νοερός) shares (κοινωνεῖν)

22,2   Cod. ογ N̄ ┃ or, [ⲁ ï ϣ ⲁ] ⳅ ⲉ ┃ restoration assumes question is being
repeated.
22,4-5   Or, Can the intellect share . . .?
22,5-6   –ⲣⲟⲥ . . .–ⲕⲟ ⲛ, sic; cf. 23,19-20.
22,5   Cf. 23, 19,22.

6 ΚΟΝ· ΕϢΑϥϪⲰΚ ⲈⲂⲞⲖ ⲚϬⲒ ⲠⲒ-
ⲘⲞⲞⲨ Ⲛ ⲀⲨⲦⲞⲄⲈⲚⲎⲤ· ⲈϢⲰ-

8 ⲠⲈ ⲆⲈ ⲈϥϢⲀⲚⲈⲒⲘⲈ ⲈⲢⲞϥ ⲘⲚ
ⲚⲀï ⲦⲎⲢⲞⲨ· ⲠⲒⲘⲞⲞⲨ Ⲙ ⲠⲢⲰ-

10 ⲦⲞⲪⲀⲚⲎⲤ ⲠⲈ· ⲈϢⲰⲠⲈ ⲆⲈ
ⲈϥϢⲀⲚϨⲰⲦⲚ ⲚⲘⲘⲀϥ ⲘⲚ ⲚⲀï

12 ⲦⲎⲢⲞⲨ· ⲠⲀⲠⲒⲔⲀⲖⲨⲠ⟨Ⲧ⟩ⲞⲤ ⲠⲈ·
ⲠⲈïⲈⲒⲚⲈ ⲞⲚ ⲈⲦϢⲞⲞⲠ ϨⲚ ⲚⲒ-

14 ⲈⲰⲚ· ⲈⲈⲒⲘⲈ Ⲉ [ⲚⲀ]ï ⲔⲀⲦⲀ ⲞⲨⲀ
ⲘⲚ ⲚⲒⲘⲈⲢⲞⲤ Ⲛ [. . . .]ⲞⲤ ⲚⲈ· ⲚⲎ

16 ⲚⲦⲈ ⲠⲦⲎⲢϥ [Ⲙ Ⲡ]ⲘⲀ ⲈⲦⲈ ⲠⲤⲞ-
ⲞⲨⲚ ⲘⲘⲀⲨ [ⲀⲨⲰ] ⲠⲎ ⲈⲦⲞⲨⲈⲒ-

18 ⲘⲈ ⲈⲢⲞϥ ⲀⲨⲠ[Ⲱ]ⲢϪ [Ⲉ]ⲂⲞⲖ· Ⲁ[ⲨⲰ]
ⲞⲨⲘⲚⲦϢ[ⲂⲎⲢ] ⲈⲦⲚⲦⲀⲨ [ⲚϨⲢⲀï]

20 ϨⲚ ⲚⲈⲨⲈⲢⲎ[Ⲩ]· Ⲡ[Ⲧ]ⲎⲢϥ ⲀⲨ[Ⲱ ⲚⲀï]
ⲦⲎⲢⲞⲨ ⲈⲨ .[. . . . . . .] .[.]ⲞⲨ[. . .

22 ϪⲰΚⲘ Ⲉ ⲠⲒ[ϪⲰΚⲘ Ⲛ ⲀⲨⲦⲞⲄⲈ-]
ⲚⲎⲤ [. .] ϢⲀϥ[

24 Ⲛ ⲦⲈ[. .] . .[
Ⲙ[

26 Ⲙ[
 .[

28 .[
 .[

ΚⲤ̄

ⲘⲘⲀⲨ ⲈϥⲞⲨⲰⲚϨ ⲘⲘⲞ[ϥ ⲈⲂ]ⲞⲖ

2 ⲈⲦⲈ ⲠⲀï ⲠⲈ ⲈⲦⲀϥⲈⲒⲘⲈ [Ϫⲉ Ⲡ]ⲰⲤ
ϥϢⲞⲞⲠ ⲚⲀϥ· ⲀⲨⲰ ⲞⲨⲚⲦⲀ]ϥ Ⲛ-

4 Ⲛ ⲞⲨⲘⲚⲦϢⲂⲎⲢ ϨⲀ ⲚⲈⲨⲈⲢⲎⲨ
ⲀϥϪⲰΚⲘ Ⲉ ⲠⲒϪⲰΚⲘ Ⲙ ⲠⲢⲰⲦⲞ-

6 ⲪⲀⲚⲎⲤ· ϯⲀⲢⲬⲎ ⲆⲈ ⲚⲦⲈ ⲚⲀï Ⲉ-
ϢⲰⲠⲈ ⲈϢⲀϥⲈⲒⲘⲈ ⲈⲢⲞⲤ Ϫⲉ

8 ⲠⲰⲤ ⲤⲈⲞⲨⲞⲚϨ ⲈⲂⲞⲖ ⲦⲎⲢⲞⲨ ϨⲚ
ⲞⲨⲀⲠⲈ Ⲛ ⲞⲨⲰⲦ· ⲀⲨⲰ ⲠⲰⲤ

10 ⲈⲨϨⲞⲦⲠ ⲚϬⲒ ⲚⲀï ⲦⲎⲢⲞⲨ ϢⲀⲨ-
ⲠⲰⲢϪ ⲈⲂⲞⲖ· ⲀⲨⲰ ⲠⲰⲤ ϢⲀⲨ-

22,11   Or, when he is reconciled with all of them.
22,12   ⟨Ⲧ⟩, omitted in text.
22,14-16   Text is obscure.
22,15   Ⲛ, only the supralinear stroke survives.
22,17   -ⲈⲒ, Ⲓ, ink trace of the bottom of a vertical stroke.

6   when the self-begotten (αὐτογενής)
     water becomes perfect.

8   When (+δέ) one knows it and
     all these, he is the

10   first-visible (πρωτοφανής) water. When (+δέ)
     one joins oneself with all these, one is

12   that water which belongs to Kalyptos (καλυπτός),
     whose image is still in the

14   aeons (αἰών). To understand individually (+κατά)
     with their parts (μέρος), they are [   ], those

16   of the All where
     knowledge is. They have

18   [separated] from him whom they knew and
     (from) fellowship

20   with one another. The All and all
     [these

22   wash in the [washing of]
     [Autogenes (αὐτογενής)] he [

24   of [
     [

26   [
     [

28   [
     [

                                   23

     he appears to [him],

2   that is, when one knows how (πῶς)
     he exists for him and (how) he has

4   fellowship with their companions, one has
     washed in the washing of Protophanes (πρωτοφανής).

6   And (δέ) if in understanding the
     origin (ἀρχή) of these,

8   how (πῶς) they all appear from
     a single origin, how (πῶς)

10   all who are joined come to
     be divided, how (πῶς) those

22,19-20   For fellowship, see also 23,3-6.
22,22   For the restoration, see 23,5.17.
23,3   Cod. Ⲛⲓ, a vertical stroke and a trace of the supralinear stroke survive.
23,9   Lit., a single head.
23,10-11   Or, how can (they) be divided?

12 ϩⲱⲧⲛ̄ ⲟⲛ ⲛϭⲓ ⲛⲏ ⲉⲧⲁⲩⲡⲱⲣ︥ϫ
ⲉⲃⲟⲗ· ⲁⲩⲱ ⲡⲱⲥ ϣⲁⲣⲉⲛⲥⲙⲉ-

14 ⲣⲟⲥ ϩⲱ[ⲧⲛ̄ ⲙ]ⲛ̣ ⲛⲓⲧⲏⲣϥ ⲁⲩⲱ ⲛⲓⲉⲓⲇⲟⲥ ⲙⲛ ⲛ[ⲓⲅⲉ]ⲛⲟⲥ· ⲉϣⲱⲡⲉ

16 ⲉⲣϣⲁ ⲟⲩ[ⲁ ⲉⲓ]ⲙ̣ⲉ̣ ⲉ ⲛⲁⲓ̈ ⲁϥϫⲱⲕⲙ
ⲉ ⲡⲓϫⲱ[ⲕⲙ ⲛ̄] ⲕ̄ⲁⲥ ⲁⲩⲱ ⲕⲁⲧⲁ

18 ⲡⲟⲩⲁ ⲡⲟⲩⲁ [ⲛ ⲛⲓ]ⲧⲟⲡⲟⲥ· ⲟⲩⲛⲧⲁϥ ⲙⲙⲁⲩ ⲛ ⲟ[ⲩ]ⲙⲉⲣⲓⲕⲟⲛ ⲛⲧⲉ

20 ⲛⲓϣ̣ⲁ̣ ⲉⲛⲉ[ϩ ⲁⲩ]ⲱ ϣⲁϥⲃⲱⲕ
ⲉϩ[ⲣⲁⲓ̈ . . . ⲙ]ⲡ̣ⲣ̣ⲏ̣[ⲧⲉ] ⲉϣⲁϥ-

22 [. . . . . . ⲧⲟⲩ]ⲃⲏⲟ[ⲩ ⲛ ϩ]ⲁ̣ⲡⲗⲟⲩⲛ
ⲛ ⲟⲩⲟⲉⲓϣ ⲛ[ⲓⲙ] ⲉϥ[. .] ̣.ⲩ̣ ⲉϩⲣⲁⲓ̈

24 ⲉ ⲟⲩⲁ ⲙ̣ ⲡ[——]ϣ̣
ⲛⲓⲙ ⲉϥⲧⲟⲩⲃ̣[ⲏⲟⲩⲧ̈ ⲛ ϩⲁⲡ]ⲗⲟⲩ̈·

26 ϣⲁϥⲙⲟⲩϩ ⲉⲃⲟ[ⲗ . . . .]ⲙ̣ⲉ
ϩⲛ ⲟⲩϩⲩⲡⲁⲣϫⲓⲥ ⲙ̣ [. . . . .]ⲁ̣

28 ⲁⲩⲱ ⲟⲩⲡ̄ⲛ̄ⲁ ⲉϥⲟⲩ[ⲁⲁⲃ] ⲙ̣ⲛ

ⲕ̄ⲇ

ⲗⲁⲁⲩ ⲛ̄ⲧⲁϥ ⲛ̄ⲥⲁⲃⲟⲗ ⲙ̄ⲙⲟϥ· ϣⲁϥ-

2 ⲛ̣[ⲁⲩ ⲙ̣]ⲉ̣ⲛ ϩⲛ ⲟⲩⲯⲩⲭⲏ ⲇⲉ ⲛ ⲧⲉⲗⲓ-
ⲟ[ⲥ ⲉ ⲛ]ⲁⲛⲓ̣ⲁⲩⲧⲟⲅⲉⲛⲏⲥ· ϩⲛ ⲟⲩⲛⲟⲩⲥ

4 ⲇ[ⲉ ⲉ] ⲛⲁⲡⲓϣⲙⲛ̄ⲧϩ̣ⲟⲟⲩⲧ̈· ϩⲛ ⲟⲩ-
ⲡ̄ⲛ̄ⲁ ⲇⲉ ⲉϥⲟⲩⲁⲁⲃ ⲛⲁⲛⲓⲡⲣⲱⲧⲟⲫⲁ-

6 ⲛⲏⲥ· ϣⲁϥⲥⲱⲧⲙ ⲇⲉ ⲉⲧⲃⲉ ⲡⲓⲕ̄ⲁ̄ⲥ
ⲉⲃⲟⲗ ϩⲓⲧⲛ ⲛⲓϭⲟⲙ ⲛⲧⲉ ⲡⲓⲡ̄ⲛ̄ⲁ ⲉⲧⲁⲩ-

8 ⲉⲓ ⲉⲃⲟⲗ ⲙⲙⲟϥ ϩⲛ ⟨ⲟⲩ⟩ⲟⲩⲱⲛϩ ⲉⲃⲟⲗ ⲉϥ-
ⲥⲟⲧⲡ ⲛ̄ϩⲟⲩⲟ ⲛⲧⲉ ⲡⲓⲁϩⲟⲣⲁⲧⲟⲛ ⲙ̄

10 ⲡ̄ⲛ̄ⲁ· ϩ̄ⲣⲁⲓ̈ ⲇⲉ ϩⲛ ϯⲉⲛⲛⲟⲓⲁ ⲧⲁⲓ̈ ⲉⲧ-
ϣⲟⲟⲡ̄ ϯⲛⲟⲩ ϩⲛ ⲟⲩⲥⲓⲥⲏ· ⲛ̄ϩⲣⲁⲓ̈ ⲇⲉ

12 ϩⲛ ϯϣⲟⲣⲡ̄ ⲛ ⲉⲛⲛⲟⲓⲁ· ⲉⲧⲃⲉ ⲡⲓϣⲙⲧ̄-
ϭⲟⲙ ⲛ ⲁϩⲟⲣⲁⲧⲟⲛ ⲙ̄ ⲡ̄ⲛ̄ⲁ ⲉⲩⲥⲱⲧⲙ

14 ϭⲉ ⲡⲉ ⲙ̄ⲛ ⲟⲩϭⲟⲙ ⲛ̄ⲧⲉ ⲟⲩⲥⲓⲥⲏ ⲉⲥ-
ⲧⲟⲩⲃⲏⲟⲩⲧ̈ ϩⲛ ⲟⲩ[ⲡ̄]ⲛ̣ⲁ ⲉϥⲧⲁⲛϩⲟ

16 ϯⲧⲉⲗⲓⲟⲥ ⲁⲩⲱ ⲛ .[.] .[.] ⲛ ⲧⲉⲗⲓⲟⲥ
ⲁⲩⲱ ⲙ̄ ⲡⲁⲛⲧⲉ[ⲗⲓⲟ]ⲥ̣· ⲥⲉϣⲟⲟⲡ̄

23,14 ⲛⲓⲧ̄ⲏ̄ⲣ̄ϥ, sic; cf. 19,3; 33,9.
23,15 Cf. *Marsanes* X 42,24-25.
23,18 Lacuna is too small for [ⲛⲧⲉ ⲛⲓ].
23,22 –ⲃ̣ⲏⲟ[ⲩ⟨ⲧ⟩?
23,24 E.g., ⲟⲩⲟⲉⲓ]ϣ.
23,25 Or, ⲧⲟⲩⲃ[ⲏⲩ | i.e., ϩⲁⲡⲗⲟⲩⲛ.
24,2 ⲙ̣]ⲉⲛ ... ⲇⲉ, sic (corrupt text?).

12 who are divided join
again, and how (πῶς) the parts (μέρος)
14 [join with] the alls and the
species (εἶδος) and [races (γένος)]—when
16 one understands these things, one has washed
in the washing of Kalyptos (καλυπτός). According
18 to (κατά) each of [the] places (τόπος) one has
a portion (μερικόν) of the
20 eternal ones [and] one ascends
[as] he
22 [pure] and simple (ἁπλοῦν),
he is always [
24 one of the [
[   ] he is pure [for] simpleness (-απλοῦν).
26 He is filled [
in [   ] existence (ὕπαρξις)
28 and a holy spirit (πνεῦμα). There is
24
nothing of his outside of him. He can [see]
2 (+μέν) with his perfect (τέλειος) soul (ψυχή) those (+δέ)
who belong to autogenic ones (αὐτογενής); with his mind (νοῦς)
4 (+δέ), those who belong to the triple-male; (+δέ) with
his holy spirit (πνεῦμα), those who belong to Protophanic
6 (πρωτοφανής) ones. He (+δέ) can learn of Kalyptos (καλυπτός)
through the powers of the Spirit (πνεῦμα) from whom they
8 have come forth in a far better
revelation of the Invisible (ἀόρατον)
10 Spirit (πνεῦμα). And (δέ) by means of thought (ἔννοια)
which now is in silence (σιγή) and (δέ)
12 by first thought (ἔννοια) (he learns) of the three-
powered Invisible (ἀόρατον) Spirit (πνεῦμα), since there
14 is then a report and a silent (σιγή) power
purified by a life-giving spirit (πνεῦμα).
16 (It is) perfect (τέλειος) and perfect (τέλειος) [   ]
and all-perfect (παντέλειος).

24,4–5 The Triple-male is here distinguished as an entity separate from Protophanes;
cf. 44,27-30.
24,12 Barbelo is the first thought of Spirit.
24,14 Silence is a typical characteristic of the upper realms of the heavenly world;
cf. Ign. Eph. 19.
24,16 E.g., Ϣ[Ο]Ρ[Π]; cf. 17,5f.

18 ογΝ ΝϭΙ ϩΕΝΕΟ[Ογ Ε]ΥΤΗϢ ΕϩΡΑΪ
   ΕϪΝ ΝΑΪ Ν ΡΕϤΤ[ΑΝϩΟ] ΝΗ ΕΤΑΥϪΙ

20 ωΜC Ν ΤΑΠΜΕ [Μ]Ν ΟγΓΝωCΙC·
   Αγω ΝΗ ΜΕ[Ν Ε]ΤΜΠϢΑ ϢΑγΑΡ[Εϩ]

22 ΕΡΟΟγ· ΝΗ Δ[Ε] ΕΤΕ ϩΕΝΕΒΟλ ϩΜ
   ΠΕΪΓΕΝΟC ΑΝ [ΝΕ .] . .[. .]Αγ[

24 Αγω Ϣ[Α]γΒωϢ[Κ. . . . . .] . ΑΪ Ε-
   ΤΕγΝΤ[.]ΝΕ Μ[

26 ΕΒΟλ [. . ϩ]Μ Π[ΙΜ]ΕϩϯΟγ ΕϢΑϤ- [
   ω[———   ]ΑΝΤΙΤγΠΟC

28 Κ[———   ]Α ΝΤΕ ΝΙΑΙωΝ
   Ο[———   ] ΝϭΙ ΟγϪωΚΜ

30 [———   ]Ε· ΕϢωΠΕ ΔΕ ΕΡ-
   [ϢΑ ΟγΑ] ΚΑΚϤ ΑϩΝΟγ Μ ΠΚΟC-
                                  KE
   ΜΟC Αγω ΝϤΚω ΕϩΡΑΪ [Ν ϯΓΝωC]ΙC·

2 Αγω ΠΗ ΜΕΝ ΕΤΕ ΜΜΝ[ΤΑϤ Ν Ο]γ-
   ΜΑ Ν ϢωΠΕ ΜΝ ΟγϬΟΜ· Α[γω] ΕϤ-

4 ΟγΗϩ ΝCΑ ϩΕΝϩΗΒΤΕ ΝΤΕ ϩΕΝ-
   ΚΟΟγΕ ϤϬΑλΗΟγϯ· ΠΗ ΔΕ ΕΤΕ

6 ΜΠϤΕΙΡΕ Ν λΑΑγ Ν ΝΟΒΕ ΕCΡω-
   ϢΕ ΝΑϤ ΝϬΙ ΟγΓΝωCΙC· ΕϤϤΙ Μ

8 ΠΡΟΟγϢ Ν λΑΑγ ΑΝ ΕϤΡ ΜΕΤΑ-
   ΝΟΕΙ· ΟγΝ ϩΕΝϪωΚΜ ΔΕ ΤΗϢ

10 ϩΝ ΝΑΪ Ν ΤΟγϩΕ· ϯΙΗ ΔΕ Ε-
   ϩΟγΝ Ε ΝΙΑγΤΟΓΕΝΗC· ΠΗ ϯ-

12 ΝΟγ ΕΤΑΚϪΙ ωΜC ΝϩΗΤϤ Ν CΟΠ
   ΝΙΜ ΕΤCΜ[Π]ϢΑ Ε ΝΑγ Ε ΝΙΚΑΤΑ

14 ΟγΑ Ν [ΤΕλΙΟ]C· ΕγΓΝωCΙC ΠΕ
   ΝΤΕ ΠΤΗΡϤ [ΕΤ]ΑCϢωΠΕ ΕΒΟλ

16 ϩΝ ΝΙϬΟΜ Ν[ΤΕ] ΝΙΑγΤΟΓΕΝΗC
   ΠΗ ΕΤΚΝΑΑ[Ϥ] ΕΚϢΑΝΟγω-

18 ΤΒ Ν ΝΙΕωΝ Μ [ΠΑ]ΝΤΕλΙΟC· ΠΙ-
   ΜΕϩϢΟΜϯ ΔΕ [Ν] ϪωΚΜ ΕΚϢΑΝ-

24,19-20   Or, glories are [life-givers] set over those who have been baptized.
24,20   Bohairic, ΤΑϕΜΗΙ.
24,24   ΝΑΪ and ΤΑΪ are possible.
24,25   Cod. M̄.
24,26   E.g., [ΔΕ ϩ]Μ.
24,31   Cf. 23,15-16.
25,2-3   Or, then he has no dwelling place or power.

18   Glories, then (οὖν), which are set
       over these are [life-givers] who have
20   been baptized in truth and knowledge (γνῶσις).
       Those (+δέ) who are worthy are guarded,
22   but (δέ) those who [are] not
       from this race (γένος) [
24   and they go [
       [
26   [in] the fifth, he being [
       [   ] copy (ἀντίτυπον)
28   [   ] of the aeons (αἰών)
       [   ] namely a washing
30   [   ] but (δέ) if
       [one] strips off the world (κόσμος)

                                      25

       and lays aside [knowledge (γνῶσις)],
2   then he (+δέ) is one who has no
       dwelling place and power, [and]
4   because he follows the ways of the others,
       he is also a sojourner; but (δέ) the one
6   who has committed no sin because
       knowledge (γνῶσις) was sufficient for him
8   is not anxious when he repents (μετάνοια),
       and (δέ) then (οὖν) washings are appointed
10   in these in addition. (Concerning) the path (+δέ)
       to the self-begotten ones (αὐτογενής), the one
12   in which you have now been baptized each
       time, (a path) worthy of seeing the [perfect (τέλειος)]
14   individuals (+κατά): it serves as knowledge (γνῶσις)
       of the All since it came into being
16   from the powers of the self-begotten ones (αὐτογενής),
       the one you acquire when you pass
18   through the all-perfect (παντέλειος) aeons (αἰών).
       When you receive the third

25,4   I.e., because he does not exercise this knowledge; cf. 1,22-25; 27,17-19.
25,5   Status as a sojourner was perhaps related to the region called Exile, lit., a
          temporary residence.
25,7   Emend to ⲚⲀϤ.
25,10   ⲚⲦⲞⲨϨⲈ for ⲚⲦⲞⲨⲞ | ⲆⲈ, i.e., ⲦⲈ ?
25,11-17 ⲠⲎ is taken as a collective reference to Autogenes.

20 ⲀⲰⲔⲘ Ⲉ . .[. . . .]ⲦⲈ ⲈⲔⲈⲤⲰⲦⲘ
Ⲉ Ⲛⲥ[. . . . .] ⲞⲚ[Ⲧ]ⲰⲤ Ⲙ ⲠⲒⲘⲀ
22 Ⲉ[. . . . . Ⲉ]ⲦⲂⲈ [ⲚⲈ]Ⲓ̈ⲢⲀⲚ ⲆⲈ
ⲈⲨϢⲞⲞⲚ̇ Ⲙ [Ⲡ]ⲈⲒ̈Ⲣ[ⲎⲦ]Ⲉ ⲈⲞⲨⲀ
24 ⲆⲈ ⲠⲈ ⲀⲨ[　　—　　　　　　]Ⲧ̇
ⲠⲈ Ⲙ ⲠⲢⲎⲦ[Ⲉ　—　　　　　]Ⲕ
26 ϨⲘ ⲠⲦⲢⲈⲨϢⲰ[. . . . .]
ϢⲞⲞⲚ̇ ⲀⲨⲰ ⲈⲀ[. . . . .]
28 ⲞⲨϢⲀⲀⲈ ⲚⲦⲀⲨⲠⲞ[. . . . .]
ⲔⲊ̅
ⲠⲀⲒ̈ ⲠⲈ ⲞⲨⲢⲀⲚ ⲈⲨϢⲞⲞⲚ̇ ⲞⲚⲦⲰⲤ
2 Ⲙ[Ⲛ . . .] ⲈⲦⲈⲨ ⲘⲘⲞⲤ· ⲀⲨⲰ
Ⲥ[ⲈϢⲞ]ⲞⲚ̇ ⲚϬⲒ ⲚⲈⲦϢⲞⲞⲚ̇ ϨⲚ ⲞⲨ—
4 ⲚⲞ[ⲨϨ]Ⲙ ⲈⲚⲈⲦⲈ ⲈⲨⲈⲒⲚⲈ· ⲀⲨⲰ ⲠⲈⲨ—
ⲈⲒⲚⲈ ϨⲘ ⲠⲦⲈⲚⲞⲤ ⲚϨⲢⲀⲒ̈ ϨⲘ ⲠⲈⲦⲈ
6 ⲠⲰϤ· ϢⲀⲨⲚⲀⲨ ⲆⲈ ⲀⲨⲰ ϢⲀⲨⲘⲘⲈ
ⲀⲨⲰ ϢⲀⲨⲂⲰⲔ ⲈϨⲞⲨⲚ ⲈⲢⲞϤ ⲀⲨⲰ
8 ϢⲀⲨⲀⲒ ⲈⲒⲚⲈ ⲘⲘⲞϤ· ϨⲚ ⲞⲨⲤⲘⲎ ⲆⲈ
Ⲉ ⲀⲞⲞⲨ ⲀⲨⲰ Ⲉ ⲤⲰⲦⲘ· ϨⲚ ⲞⲨⲤⲰⲦⲘ
10 ⲆⲈ ⲤⲈⲈ Ⲛ ⲀⲦϬⲞⲘ ⲈϨⲈⲚⲈⲤⲐⲎⲦⲞⲚ
ⲚⲈ ⲀⲨⲰ Ⲛ ⲤⲰⲘⲀⲦⲒⲔⲞⲚ· Ⲙ ⲠⲢⲎⲦⲈ
12 ⲞⲨⲚ ⲈϢⲀⲨϬⲘϬⲞⲘ Ⲉ ϢⲰⲠ̇ ⲈⲢⲞⲞ—
ⲞⲨ· ⲈϢⲀⲨϢⲰⲠ̇ ⲈⲢⲞⲞⲨ Ⲙ ⲠⲈⲒ̈ⲢⲎ—
14 ⲦⲈ ⲀⲨⲰ ⲞⲨⲈⲒⲆⲰ[ⲖⲞ]Ⲛ̇ ⲠⲈ ⲈϤⲀⲞⲀ[Ϩ]
Ⲙ ⲠⲈⲒ̈ⲢⲎⲦⲈ ⲈϢ[ⲀϤ]ϢⲰⲠⲈ ⲈⲂⲞⲖ
16 ϨⲚ ⲞⲨⲀⲒⲤⲐⲎⲤⲒ[Ⲥ Ϩ]Ⲛ ⲞⲨϢⲀⲀⲈ
ⲈϤⲤⲞⲦ̇Ⲡ ⲘⲈⲚ Ⲉ [Ⲧϯⲫ]ⲨⲤⲒⲤ Ⲛ ϨⲨⲖ—
18 ⲔⲞⲚ· ⲈϤⲐⲈⲂⲒⲎ[Ⲩ] ⲆⲈ [Ⲩ̅] Ⲉ ϯ̇ⲞⲨⲤⲒⲀ
Ⲛ ⲚⲞⲈⲢⲞⲚ· [Ⲩ̅ Ⲉ]ⲦⲂⲈ ⲦⲀⲒⲀⲪⲞⲢⲀ ⲆⲈ
20 ⲚⲦⲈ ⲚⲒⲮⲨⲬⲎ [Ⲙ]ⲠⲢⲢ ϢⲠⲎⲢⲈ· ϨⲘ
ⲠⲦⲢⲈⲨⲘⲈⲈⲨⲈ ⲆⲈ ⲀⲈ ⲤⲈϢⲈⲂⲒⲎ—
22 ⲞⲨ̇Ⲧ ⲚⲤⲈⲈⲒⲚ[Ⲉ ⲀⲚ . . . Ϣ]ⲀⲢⲞⲚ
ⲚⲈ ⲚⲦⲈ Ⲛ[Ⲏ] ⲈⲦⲘ[. . . . .] ⲘⲚ
24 ⲠⲎ ⲘⲞ .[.] ϢⲀϤ[. . . ⲱ[. .] ⲈⲂⲞⲖ

25,20　　ⲉ̣. ., first ink trace is fromⲉ, ⲑ, ⲟ, orⲥ; second, fromⲚ, Ⲏ, ⲓ, orⲩ; third,
　　　　　from eitherⲟ, orⲥ;ⲉ ⲛⲟ[ⲩ is possible.
25,21-22　E.g.,ⲉ ⲛⲓ[ⲉⲱⲛ ⲉⲧϢⲟⲟⲡ]ⲟⲛ[ⲧ]ⲱⲥ Ⲙ ⲡⲓⲙⲁ/ⲉ[ⲧⲙⲙⲁⲩ.
25,23　　ⲛ̇, orⲡ.
25,28-26,1　Probablyⲉⲧⲉ]/ⲡⲁⲓ̈ ⲡⲉ.
26,2-4　　Text is corrupt.
26,2　　　Ⲙ[Ⲛ, a supralinear stroke connectedⲘ with the following letter (in lacuna)
　　　　　Ⅰ her, i.e., Barbelo?

20 washing [   ], you will learn
    about the [   ] really (ὄντως)[
22 in [   ] place. About [these] names (+δέ),
    they are as follows: because
24 he (+δέ) is one, [
    is like [
26 while he [
    exists and [
28 a word they [
    26
    This is a name which really (ὄντως) exists
2   [with   ] within her.
    These who exist do so in
4   [safety] . . . resembles. His
    resemblance in race (γένος) (is) within what is
6   his own. He (+δέ) can see (it), understand (it),
    enter it and
8   take a resemblance from it. They (+δέ)
    (can) speak aloud and hear sounds, but (δέ)
10 they are unable to obey because they
    are perceptible (αἰσθητόν) and somatic (σωματικόν).
12 Therefore (οὖν), just as they are able to contain
    them by containing them thus,
14 so is he a reflection (εἴδωλον) [in anguish]
    in this way, having come into existence
16 in perception (αἴσθησις) [by] a word which
    is (+μέν) better than material (ὑλικόν) [nature (φύσις)]
18 but (δέ) lower than intellectual (νοερόν)
    essence (οὐσία). Do not be amazed about the
20 differences (διαφορά) among souls (ψυχή).
    When (+δέ) it is thought that they are
22 different and do [not resemble
    [   ] of those who [   ] and
24 that [

_____

26,4   ⲚⲞ, the ink trace is from Ο, Ⲉ, Θ, or Ⲥ.
26,6-8 Cf. Isa 6:9-10.
26,6   I.e., ⲉⲥⲙⲉ.
26,16   Or, ⲙⲓⲚ ?
26,18   –ⲕⲟⲚ, sic | Ⲁⲉ [Ⲩ], uncertain.
26,23   Either ⲙ̄ⲓ or ⲙⲓ, (lacuna above the letter).
26,24   Possibly ⲡ ⲏ ⲙⲉⲚ[.

```
      ϩΝ ΟΥ[ϹΜ]Η .[ . . .] ΕϥΤΑΚΗΟΥⲦ
26    ΕΠ[   ———        ]ΧΗ ΝΤΑΥΝ
      Ϲ[    ———        ]ΥϹⲰΜΑ· ΠΗ ΔΕ
28    Ε[ . . . . . . . . ]ΕϥΧΡΟΝΟϹ ΕϢΑϥ-
      Ç[ . . . . . . . ]Λ Ν ΟΥΟΕΙϢ ΕΡΕ-
                                    ⎯⎯
                                    ΚⳊ
```

```
      ΤΕΥⲮΧΗ ϢΟΟⲚ Ν [ . . . . . . . ]
2     ΠΟΥϹⲰΜΑ· ΝΗ ΜΕΝ ΕΤ[ΤΟΥΒΗ-]
      ΟΥⲦ Ε ΠΤΗΡϤ ϤΤΟΟΥ Ν [ΕΙΔΟ]Ϲ
4     ΕΤΝΤΑΥ· ΝΗ ΔΕ ΕΤΕ Ν[ϩΡΑΪ ϨΝ Ο]Υ-
      ΧΡΟΝΟϹ ΠϹΕΙΤ ΝΕ· ΤΟΥΕΙ ΤΟΥΕΙ
6     ΜΜΟΟΥ· ΟΥΝΤΑϤ Μ ΠΕϹΕΙΔΟϹ
      ΜΝ ΠΕϹΤⲰⲚ ΑΥⲰ <Ν>ΕΥΕΙΝΕ ϹΕ-
8     ϢΕΒΙΗΟΥⲦ ΕΥΠⲰΡϪ ΕΒΟΛ· ΑΥⲰ
      ϹΕΑϨΕΡΑΤΟ· ΑΥⲰ ΕΥΡ ϢΒΗΡ
10    Ν ϢⲰΠΕ ΜΝ ΝΑΪⲮΧΗ ΤΗΡΟΥ
      ΝϬΙ ϨΕΝΚΕΑΤΜΟΥ Μ ⲮΧΗ ΕΤΒΕ
12    Ⳁ[ϹΟ]ΦΙΑ ΕΤΑϹϬⲰϢⲦ Ε ΠΕϹΗⲦ
      ϢΟΜΤ ΓΑΡ Ν ΕΙΔΟϹ ΝΕ ΝΤ[Ε] ΝΙⲮΥ-
14    Χ[Η] ΝΝ ΑΤ[ΜΟ]Υ· ΜΝ ΝΗ ΜΕΝ ΕΤΑΥ-
      ϪΙ ΝΟΥΝΕ [ΕΒ]ΟΛ ϨΙϪΝ ⳀΠΑΡΟΙΚΗ-
16    ϹΙϹ ΕΜΝ[ΤΑΥ] ΜΜΑΥ Ν ΟΥϬΟΜ
      Ν ϪΠΟ Ε[ϹΝΜ]ΜΑΥ ΜΑΥΑ[Α]Υ
18    ΕΥΟΥΗϨ Ν[ϹΑ Ϩ]ΕΝϨΒΗΤΕ ΝΤΕ
      ϨΕΝΚΟΟΥΕ· Π[Η] ΔΕ ΕΥΕΙΔΟϹ Ν
20    ΟΥⲰⲦ ΠΕ ΕⲚΤΟϤ ΠΕΤΟΥΡ
      . Α[ . . . . . . . .]ϥ· ΝΗ ΔΕ ΕΤΑϨΕ-
22    ΡΑ[ΤΟΥ ϨΙϪΝ ⳀΜΕ[Τ]ΑΝΟΙΑ ΕΤΕ
      Μ[ . .]ϥΡ[ . .] . .Α .[ . . ]ΝΟΒΕ·
24    ΕϹΡⲰϢΕ [ . .] ϨΙ[ . . . ]ⳀΝⲰϹΙϹ
      ΕΥΒΡΡΕ Π[ . . . . . . . . .] ΟΥΝ-
26    ΤΑϤ ΔΕ ΜΜ[ΑΥ . . . . . ΔΙ]Α-
```

26,25   .[, trace from ⲁ, ⲗ, or ⲇ.
27,1   E.g., ϢΟΟⲚ Ν[ϢΒΗΡ ΝΤΕ].
27,3   Ν, a trace from Ν, ⲃ, Τ, Η, Ι, Κ, or ⲣ; possibly there was a supralinear stroke above the letter.
27,5   ΠϹΕΙΤ for ⲮΙⲦ.
27,6   Emend to ΟΥΝΤΑϹ ?
27,10   I.e., ΝΕΪⲮΥΧΗ.
27,13-18   Cf. 5,24-6,10; 11,15-17.
27,14   Ν, only the supralinear stroke survives.

aloud [   ] he being lost
26   [
     [   ] body (σῶμα), and (δέ) that
28   [   ] time (χρόνος), he
     [   ] a desire

27

their souls (ψυχή) exist as [
2   their body (σῶμα). As (+μέν) for those who are
     totally [pure], what they possess are four
4   [species (εἶδος)], but (δέ) those [in]
     time (χρόνος) are nine. Each one
6   of them has its species (εἶδος)
     and custom. Their likenesses
8   differ, being distinct, and
     they stand. Other immortal souls (ψυχή)
10   associate with all
     these souls (ψυχή) because of
12   the Sophia (σοφία) who looked down.
     For (γάρ) there are three species (εἶδος) of
14   immortal souls : first (+μέν), those that have
     taken root upon the exile (παροίκησις)
16   because they have no ability
     to beget, (something) that only those
18   who follow the ways of
     the others have. As for (+δέ) the one that is a
20   single species (εἶδος) which
     [   ]. Second (δέ), those that stand
22   [upon the] repentance (μετάνοια) which
     [   ] sin,
24   (it) being sufficient [   ] knowledge (γνῶσις)
     being new [
26   and (δέ) he has [

27,17   Or, to be begotten.
27,18   Cf. 25,4.
27,21   . ⲁ, the trace is possibly from ⲁ, ⲇ, ⲗ, or ⲕ; possibly a Greek verb beginning ⲕⲁ– | ⲙⲙⲟⲓϥ, or ⲉⲣⲟⲓϥ.
27,23   Read either ⲙ̄, or ⲙ (lacuna); e.g., ⲙ[ⲡ]ϥ (with broad spacing of letters) | . .ⲁ[, before ⲁ read ⲏ, or else ⲥ, preceded by a descending ligature as from ⲁ, ⲗ, ⲙ, etc.; e.g., ⲏⲁ, or ⲁ̄ⲥⲁ.
27,24   ⲟⲥ (with characteristic supralinear stroke) almost certain; e.g., [ⲁⲉ] ⲟⲥ]ⲧⲛ ⲟⲩ]ⲧⲛⲱⲥⲥ.

ⲫⲟⲣⲁ· ⲟⲩⲁⲛⲛ[. . . . . . .]ⲁⲩⲣ
28 ⲛⲟⲃⲉ ⲙⲛ ϩⲉⲛⲕⲟⲟ[ⲩⲉ. . .]
────
ⲕⲏ
ⲁⲩ[ⲣ ⲙⲉ]ⲧⲁⲛⲟⲉⲓ ⲙⲛ ϩⲉⲛⲕⲟⲟⲩⲉ
2 [. . . . .]ⲥ ⲉⲃⲟⲗ ⲙⲙⲟⲟⲩ ⲙⲁⲩⲁⲁⲩ
.[. . . . .] ⲅⲁⲣ ⲛ ⲉⲓⲇⲟⲥ ⲉⲧϣⲟⲟⲛ̄ ⲛ-
4 ⲧⲟ[. . .] ⲙⲛ ⲛⲏ ⲙⲉⲛ ⲉⲧⲁⲩⲉⲓⲣⲉ ⲛ̄
ⲛ[ⲓ]ⲛⲟⲃⲉ ⲧⲏⲣⲟⲩ ⲁⲩⲱ ⲁⲩⲣ ⲙⲉⲧⲁ-
6 ⲛⲟⲉⲓ· ⲏ ϩⲉⲛⲙⲉⲣⲟⲥ ⲛⲉ ⲏ ⲛ̄ⲧⲟⲟⲩ
ⲉⲁⲩⲱϣ ⲉⲃⲟⲗ ⲙⲙⲟⲟⲩ ⲙⲁⲩⲁⲁⲩ
8 ⲉⲧⲃⲉ ⲡⲁⲓ̈ ⲛⲉⲩⲕⲉⲉⲱⲛ ⲥⲟⲟⲩ ⲛⲉ
ⲕⲁⲧⲁ ⲡⲓⲧⲟⲡⲟⲥ ⲉⲧⲡⲏϩ ⲉⲣⲟⲟⲩ
10 ϩⲛ ϯⲟⲩⲉⲓ ⲧⲟⲩⲉⲓ ⲙⲙⲟⲟⲩ· ⲡⲓⲙⲉϩ-
ϣⲟⲙⲧ̄ ⲇⲉ ⲡⲉ ⲡⲁⲛⲓⲯⲩⲭⲏ ⲛ̄ⲧⲉ
12 ⲛⲓⲁⲩⲧⲟⲅⲉⲛⲓⲟⲛ ⲉⲩⲛⲧⲁⲩ ⲙⲙⲁⲩ
ⲛ ⲟⲩϣⲁϫⲉ ⲛ̄ⲧⲉ ϯⲙⲛⲧⲙⲉ ⲛ̄ ⲁⲧ-
14 ϣⲁϫⲉ ⲙⲙⲟⲩ ⲉϥϣⲟ[ⲟ]ⲛ̄ ϩⲛ ⲟⲩ-
ⲅⲛⲱⲥⲓⲥ ⲙⲛ ⲟⲩϭⲟ[ⲙ ⲉⲃ]ⲟⲗ ⲙⲙ[ⲟ-]
16 ⲟⲩ ⲙⲁⲩⲁⲁⲩ ⲙⲛ [. . . .]ϩ ⲛ̄ ϣ[ⲁ] ⲉ-
ⲛⲉϩ· ⲉⲩⲛⲧⲁⲩ [ⲇⲉ] ⲙⲙⲁⲩ ⲛ̄ ϥⲧⲟⲟⲩ
18 ⲛ̄ ⲇⲓⲁⲫⲟⲣⲁ ⲙ̄ ⲡⲣ[ⲏⲧⲉ] ⲟⲛ ⲉ[ⲧⲟ]ⲩϣⲟ-
ⲟⲛ̄ ⲛϭⲓ ⲛⲓⲉⲓⲇⲟ[ⲥ] ⲛ̄ⲧⲉ̣ ⲛⲓⲁⲅⲅⲉⲗⲟⲥ
20 ⲁⲩⲱ ⲙⲛ ⲛⲏ [ⲉⲧ]ⲣ ⲁⲅⲁⲡⲁ ⲛ̄ ϯⲙⲛⲧⲙⲉ
ⲙⲛ ⲛⲏ ⲉⲧⲣ ϩⲉ[ⲗ]ⲡⲓⲥ ⲙⲛ ⲛⲏ ⲉⲧⲛⲁϩ-
22 ⲧⲉ ⲉⲩⲛⲧⲁⲩ [. . .]ⲛ ⲛⲏ [ⲉ]ⲧϩⲟ[.]ⲧ̄
ⲁⲩⲱ ⲥⲉϣⲟⲟ[ⲛ̄ . . . . . .]ⲏⲧ[.
24 ⲥⲉϣⲟⲟ[ⲛ̄] ⲉϥⲧ[. . . . .] . .[
ⲛⲓⲁⲩⲧ[ⲟⲅⲉ]ⲛⲏⲥ [. . .]ϣ̣[. .] . ⲙⲉ
26 ⲡⲁⲟⲩ[ⲱⲛ]ϩ ⲛ̄ [ⲧⲉⲗ]ⲓⲟⲥ ⲡⲉ· ⲡⲓⲙ[ⲉϩ-]
ⲥⲛ[ⲁⲩ . . . .]ⲙⲉ ⲡⲉ· ⲡⲓ-

────────────

27,27   ⲛⲛ[, no supralinear stroke over the first ⲛ, but possibly over the second one (lacuna).

28,3-4 E.g., ⲛ/ⲧⲟ[ⲟⲧϥ].

28,7   I.e., ⲉⲁⲩⲟⲩⲱϣ?

28,10   I.e., ⲧⲟⲩⲉⲓ ⲧⲟⲩⲉⲓ.

28,16   E.g., [ⲟⲩⲱ]ⲛϩ, (with a slight crowding of letters).

28,17   ⲙⲙⲁⲩ, ⲩ read in 1971, now best attested in photo A; papyrus subsequently damaged.

28,18-19 ϣⲟ/ⲟⲡ, first ⲟ read in 1971, now best attested in photo A; papyrus subsequently damaged.

28,20-22 Love, hope, believe may be an allusion to faith, hope, and love in 1 Cor 13. Here love is understood as love for truth rather than love of

difference (διαφορά) [   ] they have

28   sinned with the others [

28

they repented (μετανοεῖν) with others

2   [   ] from them alone.

For (γάρ) [ ] (are) species (εἶδος) which exist

4   [   ] with those (+μέν) who committed

all sins, and they repented (μετανοεῖν).

6   Either (ἤ) they are parts (μέρος), or (ἤ) they

desired of their own accord.

8   Therefore, their aeons (αἰών) also are six

according to (κατά) the place (τόπος) which has come

10 to each (fem.) of them. The third

(+δέ) (species) is that of the souls (ψυχή) of

12 the self-begotten ones (αὐτογενιόν) because they

have a word of the ineffable

14 truth, one which exists in

knowledge (γνῶσις) and [power] from

16 themselves alone and eternal [

They have [(+δέ)] four differentiations

18 (διαφορά) just as the species (εἶδος)

of angels (ἄγγελος) [who] exist:

20 those who love (ἀγαπᾶν) the truth;

those who hope (ἐλπίς); those who

22 believe having [ ]; those who are [

They exist [

24 they exist, he being [

the self-begotten ones (αὐτογενής) [

26 he is the one belonging to [perfect (τέλειος) life];

the [second] is [   ] the

---

       neighbor as in Paul. A fourth verb in the series cannot be read. The extant
letters do not lend support to Reizenstein's thesis of a Gnostic list that adds
knowledge to the Pauline triad (see Bultmann, ἐλπίς, p. 532);
cf. 31,18-19.

28,22 ⲓⲛ, no supralinear stroke | ⲛ̣, or ⲏ̣ | [.]ⲧ̇, ⲧ̇ connected to the preceding
       letter (in lacuna) by a supralinear stroke; e.g., ⲅⲟ[ⲡ]ⲧ̇.

28,23 E.g., ⲥⲉϣⲟⲟ[ⲛ̄ ⲛ̄ϩⲣⲁⲓ̈ ϩⲛ̄]ⲏⲧ[ϥ].

28,24] . . ., first trace is from ⲥ or ⲛ; second trace, from ⲃ,ⲧ,ⲏ,ⲋ,ⲕ, or ⲛ.

28,25] ., read either ⲙ̣ or ⲁ̣.

28,27 E.g., ⲥⲛ[ⲁⲩ ⲡⲗⲟⲩⲱⲛϩ ⲙ]ⲉ.

28 ⲙ[. . . . .]ⲁⲟⲩⲧⲛⲱⲥ[ⲓⲥ] .[
    ⲩ̣[. . . . .] ⲡ̣ⲓⲙⲉϩϥⲧⲟⲟⲩ̣
30 ⲡ̣[ⲁⲛⲓⲯⲩ]ⲭⲏ ⲛⲛ ⲁⲧⲙⲟⲩ ⲡⲉ
                                    ⲕ̄ⲑ̄
    ⲙ ⲡⲉⲓ̈ⲣⲏⲧⲉ ⲟⲛ ⲥⲉⲩⲟⲟ[ⲛ̄ ⲙⲙⲁ]ⲩ
2   ⲛ̄ϭⲓ [ϥ]ⲧⲟⲟⲩ ⲙ̄ ⲫⲱⲥⲧⲏⲣ [ϥⲕⲏ ⲙ̄]ⲉⲛ
    ϩⲓⲁ̄ⲛ ⲡⲓϣⲟⲣⲡ̄ ⲛⲛ ⲉⲱⲛ ⲛ[ϭⲓ ⲁⲣⲙ]ⲟ̄ⲍⲏ̄ⲁ̄ . .
4   [ⲟ]ⲩⲱϣ ⲛⲧⲉ ⲡⲛⲟⲩⲧ[ⲉ . .] .[. .] ⲛ̄
    ⲧⲙⲉ ⲙⲛ ⲟⲩϩⲱⲧⲡ̄ ⲛⲧⲉ ⲟⲩⲯⲩⲭⲏ·
6   ϥⲕⲏ ⲇⲉ ϩⲓ[ⲁ̄]ⲛ ⲡⲓⲙⲉϩⲥⲛⲁⲩ ⲛϭⲓ ⲱ̄ⲣⲟ‐
    ⲓ̈ⲁ̄ⲏ̄ⲁ̄ ⲟⲩϭⲟⲙ ⲛ̄ ⲣⲉϥⲉ[ⲥⲱ]ⲣ̣ϩ ⲛ̄ⲧⲉ
8   ⲧ̄ⲙⲛ̄ⲧⲙⲉ[·] ϥⲕⲏ ⲇⲉ ϩⲓⲁ̄ⲛ ⲡⲓⲙⲉϩ‐
    ϣⲟⲙⲧ̄ ⲛϭⲓ ⲇⲁⲩⲉⲓⲑⲉ ⲟⲩⲉⲓⲱⲣϩ ⲛ̄‐
10 ⲧⲉ ⲟⲩⲧⲛⲱⲥ[ⲓ]ⲥ̄· ϥⲕⲏ ⲇⲉ ϩⲓⲁ̄ⲛ ⲡⲓ‐
    ⲙⲉ[ϩ̄]ϥⲧⲟⲟⲩ ⲛϭⲓ ⲏ̄ⲗⲏ̄ⲗⲏ̄ⲑ̄ ⲟⲩϩⲟⲣ‐
12 ⲙ̣[ⲏ] ⲙⲛ ⲟⲩϭⲱⲣϭ ϩⲁ ⲧ̄ⲙⲛ̄ⲧⲙⲉ·
    ⲡⲓ[ϥ]ⲧⲟⲟⲩ ⲇⲉ ⲥⲉϣⲟⲟⲡ̄ ⲉϩⲉⲛ‐
14 ϣ̣[ⲁ]ⲍ̣ⲉ ⲛⲓⲉ ⲛ̄ⲧⲉ ⲧ̄ⲙⲛ̄ⲧⲙⲉ ⲙⲛ ⲟⲩ‐
    ⲧ̄[ⲛ]ⲱⲥⲓ[ⲥ] ⲥⲉⲩ̣[ϣ]ⲟⲟⲛ̄ ⲇⲉ ⲉⲛⲛⲁⲡⲓ‐
16 ⲡⲣ[ⲱ]ⲧⲟⲫⲁⲛⲏⲥ ⲁⲛ ⲛⲉ· ⲁⲗⲗⲁ ⲛⲁ‐
    ⲧ̄ⲙⲁⲁⲩ [ⲛⲉ ⲉⲓ]ⲩⲙⲉⲉⲩⲉ ⲇⲉ ⲛⲧⲉ
18 ⲡⲓⲛⲟⲩⲥ ⲛ̄ ⲧ[ⲉⲗⲓ]ⲟⲥ ⲛⲧⲉ ⲡⲟⲩⲟ‐
    ⲉⲓⲛ ⲉ ⲧⲣⲉⲛⲓⲯⲩ̄ⲩ̣[ⲭ]ⲏ ⲛⲛ ⲁⲧⲙⲟⲩ
20 ϣⲱⲡ̄ ⲉⲣⲟⲟⲩ [ⲛ] ⲟⲩⲧⲛⲱⲥⲓⲥ·
    [.]ⲛ .[.]ⲩ̣[. . . . . .]ⲉ ⲛⲁⲓ̈ ⲡⲓⲁⲩⲧⲟⲧⲉ‐
22 [ⲛⲏⲥ . . . .]ⲟ̣ⲣⲥⲉ[.]ⲟ̣ⲁⲥ ⲟⲩⲱ‐
    ⲛ̣ϩ [. . . .] .[. . . .]ⲟ̣ⲙ ⲡ̣[. .] . ⲧⲏⲣⲟⲩ
24 ⲟⲩϣⲁⲍⲉ ⲡⲓⲉ .]ⲉ ⲛ [. . .]ⲣ̣ⲟⲥ ⲛ̄‐
    ⲛ ⲁⲧϣⲁⲍⲉ̣ [. . . . . ⲧ̄ⲙ]ⲛ̄ⲧⲙⲉ·
26 ⲡⲏ ⲉⲧϣⲁⲍⲉ̣[. . . . . ⲟⲩⲱ]ⲛϩ

28,28-29 E.g., ⲛ̄/ϣ[ⲁ ⲉⲛⲉϩ ⲡⲉ·].
28,28   E.g., ⲙ[ⲙⲉϩϣⲟⲙⲧ ⲡ]ⲁ.
28,29   ϣ, or else ϥ or ⲱ.
28,30   For the restoration, see 28,11.
29,1-20   The four lights relate to the four types of souls. According to 127,15ff they
          are the lights of the Autogenes aeon; here they belong to the mother (15-17)
          who may be the Mirothea of 30,14.
29,4   E.g., ⲡⲛⲟⲩⲧ̣[ⲉ ⲡⲉ] |] .[, trace from ⲣ, ϥ, ⲯ, ⲧ̄, or ⲫ | final ⲛ, read
          either ⲛ or ⲛ̄ (lacuna) | promise of God, lit., will; cf. Luke 24:49.
29,5   ⲛⲧⲉ, ⲧ (certain); read in 1971, now best attested in photo A; papyrus
          subsequently damaged | or, a reconciliation of soul.

28 [   ] knowledge (γνῶσις)
    [   ] the fourth is
30 that one [belonging to the] immortal [souls (ψυχή).]

                                                 29

    The four lights (φωστήρ) exist
2   [there] in this way. [Arm]ozel [is]
    [set] (+μέν) over the first aeon (αἰών).
4   [   ] a promise of god [   ] of
    truth and a joining of soul (ψυχή);
6   Oroiael (+δέ) a powerful seer
    of truth is set over the
8   the second; Daveithe (+δέ) a vision
    of knowledge (γνῶσις) is set over
10 the third. Eleleth (+δέ) an eager impulse
    and preparation for truth
12 is set over the fourth.
    The four (+δέ) exist as
14 expressions of truth and
    knowledge (γνῶσις). They (+δέ) exist, although they
16 do not belong to Protophanes (πρωτοφανής) but (ἀλλά)
    to the mother, a thought of
18 the perfect (τέλειος) mind (νοῦς) of the
    light so that immortal souls (ψυχή)
20 might receive knowledge (γνῶσις) for themselves.
    [   ] these, the Autogenes (αὐτογενής)
22 [   ]–orse–[ ]–oas, a
    life [   ] all,
24 he is a word [
    ineffable [the] truth
26 he who says [revelation]

    ─────────────────

29,6-7   Lit., a power belonging to the class "seer of truth."
29,7   Supralinear stroke also covers ï.
29,16   π ρ[ω], ρ attested in photo A; papyrus subsequenly damaged.
29,17   ᴀε, i.e., τε.
29,18   Perfect mind, i.e., the Protophanes aeon.
29,21   The first ɴ had no supralinear stroke | ⲧ, or perhaps ε.
29,22   ọ, or else ⲑ; read in 1971; now best attested in photo A; papyrus
         subsequently damaged | ε̄, or else ⲑ, ọ, or ç.
29,23   ]ọ, read ọ, ⲑ, ⲟ, or perhaps ρ |ⲙ had no supralinear stroke | π[, read ß,
         ⲧ, ⲏ, ʃ, ⲕ, ⲛ, or π |] ., ligature from ⲧ, π, τ, or ⲧ.
29,24   π̣, or else ʃⲧ | e.g., ⲟⲩ ⲱ ⲁ ϫ ⲉ π[ⲉ ⲕ]ⲉ ⲛ[ⲛⲟⲉⲣⲟⲥ.

ⲈⲂⲞⲖ ⲈⲦⲂⲈ Ⲛ .[. . . . .] .ⳞⲤ
28 ⲀⲈ ⲈϤϢⲞⲞⲚ̄ Ⲛ [. . . . .]ϢⲞ–
ⲞⲚ̄ ⲚⲤⲀ ⲠϢⲰÏ ϨⲚ [. . . . . .] ⲀⲦ̄–
ⲇ̄
ⲠⲞ[. . . . .]ⲞⲦⲚ̄ ϨⲚ ⲞⲨⲚⲞⲨϨⲂ ⲚⲦⲞϹ
2 Ⲛ [. . . . .] . .Ϲ· ⲚϨⲢⲀÏ ϨⲚ ⲞⲨ‹ⲞⲨ›Ⲟ[Ⲉ]ⲓⲚ Ⲛ̄
Ⲛ[. . . .]Ⲛ ⲘⲚ ⲞⲨⲘⲈⲈⲦⲈ ⲚϨⲢⲀ̣Ï ϨⲚ
4 Ⲟ[Ⲩ . . . Ⲛ]ⲦⲀϤ· ⲀⲆⲀⲘⲀⲤ ⲀⲈ Ⲡ[ⲓ]ⲦⲈ[Ⲗⲓ–]
Ⲟ[Ϲ] Ⲛ ⲢⲰⲘⲈ ⲈⲨ̄ⲂⲀⲖ ⲠⲈ ⲚⲦⲈ ⲠⲓⲀⲨ[Ⲧ]Ⲟ–
6 ⲦⲈⲚⲎⲤ· ⲞⲨⲦⲚⲰⲤⲓⲤ ⲚⲦⲀϤ ⲠⲈ ⲈϤⲈⲖϤ
ⲀⲈ ⲠⲓⲀⲨⲦⲞⲦ[Ⲉ]ⲚⲎⲤ Ⲛ ⲚⲞⲨⲦⲈ ⲞⲨ–
8 ϢⲀⲀⲈ ⲠⲈ ⲚⲦⲈ [Ⲡ]ⲓⲚⲞⲨⲤ Ⲛ ⲦⲈ[Ⲗ]ⲓⲞⲤ
ⲚⲦⲈ ⳨ⲘⲚⲦⲘⲈ· ⲠⲓϢⲎⲢⲈ ⲀⲈ ⲚⲦⲈ
10 ⲀⲆⲀⲘⲀⲚ ⲤⲎⲐ ⲈϤⲚⲚⲎⲨ̄ ⲈϨⲢⲀÏ Ⲉ ⲦⲞⲨ–
Ⲉⲓ ⲦⲞⲨ̄Ⲉⲓ ⲚⲦⲈ ⲚⲓⲮⲨⲬⲎ· ⲈⲨ̄[Ⲧ]ⲚⲰⲤⲓⲤ
12 ⲠⲈ ⲈϤⲢⲰϢⲈ Ⲉ ⲚⲀÏ· ⲀⲨⲰ ⲈⲦⲂⲈ ⲠⲀÏ
ⲀⲤϢⲰⲠⲈ ⲈⲂⲞⲖ ⲘⲘⲞϤ ⲚϬⲓ [⳨ⲤⲠ]ⲞⲢⲀ
14 ⲈⲦⲞⲚϨ: ‾v‾‾v‾ ⲘⲓⲢⲞⲐⲈⲀ Ⲁ[Ⲉ] ⲦⲈ [. . .] Ⲧ[
ⲠⲓⲀⲨⲦⲞⲦⲈⲚⲎⲤ Ⲛ [ⲚⲞ]ⲨⲦⲈ Ⲟ[Ⲩ . .
16 ⲈⲂⲞⲖ ⲚϨⲎⲦⲤ ⲘⲚ . . [. . . . .] ⲈⲨ̄[Ⲙ]ⲈⲈⲨ̄[Ⲉ]
ⲀⲈ ⲚⲦⲈ ⲠⲓⲚⲞⲨ[Ϲ Ⲛ] ⲦⲈⲖⲓⲞⲤ ⲈⲦⲂⲈ
18 ⲦⲈⲦⲈ ⲦⲰⲤ Ⲛ ϨⲨ[ⲠⲀⲢⲜ]ⲓⲤ Ⲁ[Ⲉ] ⲞⲨ ⲦⲈ
Ⲏ ⲀⲈ ⲚⲈⲤϢⲞⲞⲚ̄ [. . Ⲛ Ⲁ]Ϣ Ⲛ ⲢⲎⲦⲈ
20 ⲀⲨⲰ ⲀⲈ ⲤϢⲞ̣[ⲞⲚ̄] ⲈⲦⲂⲈ ⲠⲀÏ ⲘⲈⲚ
ⲠⲓⲀⲨⲦⲞⲦⲈⲚ[Ⲏ]Ϲ Ⲛ ⲚⲞⲨⲦⲈ ⲞⲨϢⲀ–
22 ⲀⲈ ⲠⲈ ⲘⲚ ⲞⲨ[Ⲧ]ⲚⲰⲤⲓⲤ· ⲀⲨⲰ ⳨–
ⲦⲚⲰⲤⲓⲤ ⲘⲈⲚ [—— ϢⲀ̣–]
24 ⲀⲈ· ⲈⲦⲂ[Ⲉ] ⲠⲀÏ .[. . . . .
ⲀⲆⲀⲘⲀ[. . .]ⲠⲀ[. . . .] .[. . .]ⲘⲀ̣[
26 ⲦⲈ Ⲛⲓ[ϨⲀ]ⲠⲖⲞ[ⲨⲚ] ⲈⲦⲀⲤⲞⲨⲰⲚ[Ϩ
ⲈⲂⲞ̣[Ⲗ . . . . ⲞⲨ]ϢⲓⲂⲈ ⲚⲦⲈ Ⲛ[ⲓ–]

30,1   Ⲟ[, or else Ⲉ,Ⲑ, or Ϭ | e.g., Ϩ]ⲞⲦⲠ.
30,2   ] . .Ϲ, each trace is the bottom of a vertical stroke; the spacing suggests]
       . ⲓϹ | Ⲛ̄, only the supralinear stroke survives.
30,3   Ⲛ[ⲞⲈⲢⲞ]Ⲛ?
30,4-5 The heavenly Adam belongs to the Autogenes system.
30,6   ⲞⲨⲦⲚⲰⲤⲓⲤ, Ⲩ read in 1977; now best attested in photo A; papyrus
       subsequently damaged | Ⲛ̄ⲦⲀϤ, supralinear stroke above Ⲛ read in 1971;
       now best attested in photo A; papyrus subsequently damaged | no supralinear
       stroke over ⲖϤ | comprehends, lit., receives.
30,7   Ⲛ ⲚⲞⲨⲦⲈ, first Ⲛ (with supralinear stroke) read in 1978; papyrus
       subsequently damaged, now best attested in photo A.

concerning the [
28 that it exists as [
exists above in [
30
[   ] in a yoking of it
2 [   ] in [   ] light
and thought within his
4 [   ]. Since Adam (+δέ), the perfect (τέλειος)
man, is an eye of Autogenes (αὐτογενής),
6 it is his knowledge (γνῶσις) which comprehends
that the divine Autogenes (αὐτογενής)
8 is a word of [the] perfect (τέλειος) mind (νοῦς)
of truth. The son (+δέ) of
10 Adam, Seth, comes to
each of the souls (ψυχή) as knowledge (γνῶσις)
12 sufficient for them. Therefore,
[the] living [seed (σπορά)] came into existence
14 from him. Mirothea (+δέ) is [
the divine Autogenes (αὐτογενής), [a
16 from her and [   ], since she is a thought
of the perfect (τέλειος) mind (νοῦς), because of
18 that existence (ὕπαρξις) of hers. What is she?
Or (ἤ) did she exist? [   ] in what way?
20 Does she exist? Therefore (+μέν),
the divine Autogenes (αὐτογενής)
22 is word and knowledge (γνῶσις), and the
knowledge (γνῶσις) (+μέν) [word]
24 therefore [
Adama[
26 the [simple ones (ἁπλοῦν)], when she appeared
[   ] a change of [the]

30,9   ΝΤΕ, supralinear stroke omitted above Ν (error).
30,10-12   The heavenly Seth is the primary revealer.
30,10   ⲁⲇⲁⲙⲁⲛ, sic (from Greek genitive).
30,17   ⲉⲧⲃⲉ, read in 1971; now letters ⲉⲧ only attested in photo A; papyrus
           subsequently damaged | ⲇⲉ, i.e., ⲧⲉ.
30,20   Cod. has supralinear stroke over ⲥ | ⲙⲉⲛ, ⲉ written upon the false
           start of another letter | or, because of him.
30,24   ⲡⲁ⳾, ⲡ more fully preserved in 1971; now best attested in photo A;
           papyrus subsequently damaged.
30,25   Possibly ⲁⲇⲁⲙⲁⲓⲥ | ϩⲁ]ⲡⲗⲓⲟⲩⲥ?
30,26   Or [ⲩⲥ]?

28 ⲯⲩ[ⲭⲏ . . . .]ⲉ ϩⲱⲱⲥ ⲧⲉ[.] .[

ⲧⲉ[. . . . . . . .ⲧ]ⲉⲗⲓⲟⲥ· ⲉⲧⲃⲉ ⲛ[ⲓ—]

30 ⲧⲉ[ⲗⲓⲟⲥ . . .] ⲛⲓⲙⲛ̄ⲧⲁⲅⲅⲉⲗⲟⲥ

[ⲗⲁ]

[. . . .]ϣⲉⲛⲥⲟ[. . . . .

2 [. . .]ⲱⲡⲉ ⲟⲩⲛ[. . . . .

[. ⲯ]ⲩⲭⲏ ⲛ̄ⲛ[. . . . .

4 [. . . .]ⲙⲟⲩ ⲁⲩ[. . . . .

[. . . . .] . ⲡⲓ[. .]ⲙⲟⲥ ⲛⲛ

6 [. . . . .]ⲛ .[ⲛⲓⲁⲛ]ⲧⲓⲧⲩⲡⲟⲥ

[——— ⲟ]ⲛ̄ⲧⲱⲥ

8 [. . . . .]ⲟⲛ[. .]ⲥ̣ⲓⲥ ⲉⲧ̄ϣⲟ—

[. . . . .]ⲛ ϯⲙⲉⲧⲁⲛⲟⲓⲁ

10 [. . . . . .]ⲁ̈ⲓ ⲉ ⲡⲉⲓ̈ⲙⲁ ⲉϩⲣⲁⲓ̈

[. . . . . .] . ⲉⲧϣⲟⲟⲛ̄ ⲛ ⲁⲩ—

12 [. . . . . .] ⲛⲛ ⲉⲱⲛ· ⲉϣⲱⲡⲉ

[. . . . . .]ⲛⲉ ⲁⲩⲱ ⲉⲥⲣ ⲁ̣ⲅ̣[ⲁ]ⲡⲁⲛ

14 [. . . . . . .] ⲉ̣ⲥ̣ⲁϩⲉⲣⲁⲧⲥ ϩⲓⲁ̄ⲛ

[.]ⲙⲉ [. . . . .] ⲛ̄ⲛ ⲉⲱⲛ ⲉⲩⲛ—

16 [ⲧⲁⲥ] ⲙⲙ[ⲁⲩ ⲙ] ⲡⲓⲫⲱⲥⲧⲏⲣ ⲏ

[ⲗⲏ]ⲗⲏⲑ [. . . .]ϣⲱⲡⲉ ⲛ ⲟⲩⲁⲛ

18 [. . .]ⲣⲉϥⲛⲁ[ⲩ ⲉ ⲛ]ⲟⲩⲧⲉ· ⲉϣⲱ—

[ⲡⲉ ⲇⲉ ⲉⲥⲣ ϩⲉⲗ[ⲡⲓ]ⲥ ⲁⲩⲱ ⲉ̄ⲥⲉ—

20 ⲱⲣϩ· ⲟⲩⲁ[. . . . .]ⲥ ⲇⲉ ⲛ ⲅⲉⲛⲟⲥ

[——— ⲁϩ]ⲉⲣⲁⲧⲥ ϩⲓⲁ̄ⲛ

22 [———]ⲧⲁⲥ ⲙⲙⲁⲩ

[———]ⲑ̄· ⲉϣⲱ

24 [ⲡⲉ ———]ⲟⲥ ϩⲱ

[———]ϣⲁⲥ

26 [———]ⲟⲩ

[———] .

28 [———] .

[———]ⲁⲩ

[ⲗⲃ]

[. . . . .]ⲥ̣ϩⲟⲧⲛ̄ ⲙ[. . . .

30,28] .[, apparently a supralinear stroke connected this letter to the preceding ones (in lacuna).

31 Evidently the discussion of Mirothea and the Autogenes system continued for several more pages.

31,1 ⲛ may have a supralinear stroke (lacuna).

31,6 .[, read ⲃ, ⲧ, ⲏ, ⲓ, ⲕ, ⲛ, or ⲣ.

31,9 .]ⲛ, a supralinear stroke connected these two letters; e.g., ⲙ]ⲛ.

28 souls (ψυχή) [   ] she herself is [
    [   ]perfect (τέλειος). Concerning [the]
30 [perfect (τέλειος) . . .] the angelic beings (ἄγγελος)
                                              [31]

    [
2   [   ] then (οὖν)[
    [soul (ψυχή)
4   [die
    [
6   [   ] the copies (ἀντίτυπος)
    [   ] really (ὄντως)
8   [   ] which [
    [   ] repentance (μετάνοια)
10 [   ] to this place
    [   ] which exists as
12 [   ] aeons (αἰών), if
    [   ] and she loves (ἀγαπᾶν)
14 [   ] she stands upon
    [   ] aeon (αἰών)
16 [having] the light (φωστήρ)
    E[le]lleth [   ] become a
18 [   ] god-seer.
    [But (δέ) if] she hopes (ἐλπίς), then she
20 perceives. And (δέ) a [   ] race (γένος)
    [   ] she stands upon
22 [
    [
24 [
    [
26 [
    [
28 [
    [
    [32]
    [   ] she is chosen

31,15   Perhaps [ⲡⲓ]ⲙⲉ[ⲅ ⲩⲧⲟⲟⲩ]; cf. 29,10-11.
31,16   ⲏ (last letter of the line) has an apostrophe directly above it.
31,17   ⲟⲩⲁⲛ, no supralinear stroke over the letter ⲛ.
31,19   Then, ⲁⲩⲱ to introduce an apodosis.
31,20   E.g., ⲟⲩⲁ[ⲅⲅⲉⲗⲟ]ⲥ.
31,23   ]ⲑ, or else ⲉ̄ or ⲥ̄; ⲥ̄ⲏ̄]ⲑ ?

2   [. . . . .]ẹⲥⲁϩⲉⲣⲁⲧ[ⲥ . .
    [⸺   ]ⲣⲛ̄ ⲚⲚ [. . .
4   [. . . . .]ⲁⲩ ⲙ ⲡⲓⲫ[ⲱⲥ−]
    ⲦⲎⲢ ⲀⲢ[ⲘⲞⲌⲎⲀ]
6   ⲡⲉ ⲛ ⲟⲩⲁ[
    ⲤⲘⲞ[.] .[
8   ⲉϩⲣⲁï ⲉϫ[ⲛ] ϯϭⲟⲙ . . . .
    ⲀϩⲈⲢⲀⲦⲕ ϩⲓϫ[ⲛ
10 ⲡⲓⲞⲩⲞⲈⲓⲚ ⲈⲦ[. . . . .
    Ⲁⲩⲱ Ⲛ ⲀⲦϯ ⲱ[ⲓ] ⲈⲢ[Ⲟ . . . . .
12 ⲚⲞϭ ⲡⲉ ⲡⲓⲀⲓⲱⲚ· Ⲁ[. . . . . .
    ⲦⲀ[. .] Ⲛ ⲚⲎ ⲘⲀⲩⲀⲀⲩ [. . . . . . .
14 ⲂⲞⲗ ϩⲘ ⲡⲓⲦⲈⲗⲓⲞ[Ⲥ . . . .
    ϭⲞⲘ ⲈⲦⲘⲘⲀⲩ [. . . .]ⲦⲈ.[. . .
16 ⲱϭⲞⲘ· Ⲏ ⲘⲘ[. . .]ⲱⲱ[. . .
    ⲱϭⲞⲘ ⲚⲦⲈ Ⲟⲩ[. . . .]ⲞⲚ[. . .
18 Ⲛ[ⲓ]Ⲙ ⲚⲦⲈ ⲦⲈⲯ̇[ⲩ]ⲬⲎ .Ⲛ Ⲁ[. . . .
    [Ⲉ]ⲥⲐ̇ⲎⲦⲞⲚ [. . .]ⲀⲀ̇ⲩ ⲀⲚ ⲘⲚ [. . .
20 ⲐⲘⲓⲔⲞⲚ· Ⲁⲗ[ⲀⲀ .]ⲔⲈⲀⲦ̇ ϫⲞ[. .
    Ⲛ ⲔⲀⲦⲀ ⲞⲩⲀ̇ [. . . . .] . Ⲥ[. .]Ⲁ .[. .
22 ⲈⲘⲚ ⲀⲀⲀⲩ [. . . . .] .[. .
    ⲘⲘⲞⲩ· [
24 ⲈⲦⲩ[
    Ⲙ ⲞⲚ[
26 Ⲁⲩ[
    Ⲥ[
28 ϩ[Ⲛ
    [

                                    ⲁⲩ̄
    Ⲁⲩⲱ ⲚⲚ ⲀⲦⲤⲱ[. . . . . . .]ϩ[ⲓ−
2   [ϫ]Ⲛ ⲞⲩⲞⲚ ⲚⲓⲘ [⸺]Ⲛ
    [. . .]Ⲛ ⲚⲓⲘ [.]Ⲁ[⸺]Ⲥⲡⲉ
4   [. . . .]ⲦⲘⲞⲢⲪⲎ[. . . . .] . .[.]Ⲙ
    [. . . . .]ⲚⲚ Ⲁ[. . . .]ⲓⲞ ⲘⲚ ⲡⲀï
6   [. . . . .]Ⲧ̇[. . . .]Ⲁ ⲘⲚ ⲡⲈïⲦⲩ−
    [ⲡⲞⲤ. ⸺   Ⲙ]Ⲛ ⲀⲀⲀⲩ Ⲛ

32,3-4   E.g., [. . .ⲱⲟ]ⲣⲡ ⲚⲚ[ⲉⲱⲚ/ⲉⲩⲚⲦⲀ*ⲩ* ⲚⲘ]Ⲁⲩ.
32,6-7   The *paragraphos* and the second person singular subject in l.9 indicate that
          there was a break at this point.
32,11-12 Probably Ⲟⲩ]/ⲚⲞϭ; cf. 4,18; 131,21.
32,11   E.g., ⲈⲢ[Ⲟⲩ.

2   [   ] she stands [
      [
4   [   ] the light (φωστήρ)
      Ar[mozel
6   [
      [
8   upon the [power
      you stand upon [
10   the light which [
      and measureless [
12   the aeon (αἰών) is great [
      [   ] those alone [
14   [   ] the perfect (τέλειος) [
      that power [
16   be able, and (ἤ) [
      be able [   ] every [
18   of his soul (ψυχή) [
      perceptible (αἰσθητόν) [   ] not with [
20   [but (ἀλλά)] you are [
      individually (+κατά) [
22   there being nothing [
      him [
24   which he [
      [
26   [
      [
28   [in
      [

                                            33
      and [
2   upon every one [
      every [
4   [ ] form (μορφή) [
      [   ] and this one
6   [   ] and this [model (τύπος)]
      [   ] and something

_____

32,13-14   Probably ϵ]/ʙολ.
32,16   ⳉ, probably this (or else ϥ,†,ψ, or ф).
32,18   .ɴ, possibly ɴ̄ɴ.
32,20   Room for [λλ ϵ], or [λλ ɴʃ] | ọ[, or else ҫ, ѳ, or ҫ.
33,1   E.g., ⲁⲧⲥⳉ[ⲙⲁ | ҙ]ʃ, connected (as usual) by a circumflex.

8   [----   ϢⲀ Ⲉ]ⲚⲈϨ· ⲞⲨⲦⲈ
    [----   ]ⲈⲦⲈ ⲞⲨⲦⲎⲢϤ Ⲉ
10   [----   ] . ⲀⲦⲰⲀⲚ Ⲙ ⲠⲈⲈⲓ–
    [----   ]Ⲙ ⲈϤⲀⲤⲓⲎⲞⲨⲦ
12   [----   ] ⲈⲀϤϢⲰⲦ ⲈⲢⲞϤ
    [----   ]ⲠⲓⲦⲈⲖⲓⲞ[Ⲥ] Ⲛ ⲚⲞⲨⲤ·
14   [----   ]Ⲉ ⲚⲚ ⲀⲦⲠⲰϢ
    [----   ⲞⲨ]ⲞⲈⲓⲚ Ⲛ ⲦⲈⲖⲞⲤ Ⲛ
16   [----   ]ϤϢⲞⲞⲚ̀ ⲆⲈ ϨⲘ
    [----   Ⲁ]ⲆⲀⲘⲀⲤ· ⲀⲨⲰ
18   [----   Ⲡ]ⲓⲀⲨⲦⲞⲄⲈ–
[ⲚⲎⲤ   ----   Ⲁ]ⲨⲰ ϢⲀϤⲂⲰⲔ
20   [---   ]ⲞⲤ Ⲛ ⲚⲞⲨⲤ
    [---   ] ⲠⲓⲔⲀⲤ Ⲛ ⲚⲞⲨ–
22   [---   ]Ⲛ̀ Ⲛ ⲈⲓⲘⲈ
    [---   ]Ⲙ· ⲀⲖⲖⲀ
24   [---   Ψ]Ⲩ]ⲬⲎ Ⲉ
    [---   ]ⲘⲀⲨ
26   [---   ]Ⲱ
    [---   ]ⲚϨ
28   [
    [---   ]Ⲥ
[ⲖⲆ]
    .[. . . . .] Ⲛ ϨⲨⲠⲀⲢⲌⲓⲤ
2   [. . . . . Ⲉ]ⲂⲞⲖ ⲈⲤⲚⲦⲀⲨ
    [. . . . .] .[.]ⲨⲚⲈ[. . .
4   .[. . . . .] ϨⲈⲚⲘⲈϨⲂ̄ [Ⲛ]
[ⲄⲞ]Ⲙ ⲘⲚ [. . .] Ⲡⲁ[
6   ⲘⲈϨⲦ̄ ⲆⲈ [. .]ⲈⲚ[
ⲰⲚϨ ⲈⲂⲞⲖ [
8   ⲈⲦⲈ Ⲛ[
ⲞⲨ Ⲛ ⲞⲨ[
10   ϨⲈ Ⲛ ΨⲨⲬⲎ· Ⲁ[. . . . .
ϬⲈ ⲚⲓⲀⲓⲰⲚ ⲆⲈ [. . . . .
12   ⲘⲀ Ⲛ ϢⲰⲠⲈ .[. . . . .

33,9   ⲦⲎⲢϤ, sic; cf. 19,3; 23,14.
33,11   I.e., not heavy.
33,12   Not room for ϢⲰⲰⲦ.
33,18-22   Note the progression Autogenes to Protophanes to Kalyptos; perhaps
          Barbelo was named here also.
33,20   E.g., ⲦⲈⲖⲓⲞⲤ.

8   [   ] eternal, nor (οὔτε)
    [   ] an all
10 [   ] increasing from this
    [   ] he is light
12 [   ] because he lacked
    [   ]the perfect (τέλειος) mind (νοῦς)
14 [   ] undivided
    [   ] perfect (τέλειος) light
16 [   ] and (δέ) he is in
    [   ] Adam, and
18 [the] Autoge[nes] (αὐτογενής)
    [   ] and he goes
20 [   ] mind (νοῦς)
    [   ] the divine Kalyptos (καλυπτός)
22 [   ] knowledge
    [   ] but (ἀλλά)
24 [   ] soul (ψυχή)
    [
26 [
    [
28 [
    [
    [34]
    [   ] existence (ὕπαρξις)
2   [   ] she having
    [
4   [   ] some second
    powers and [
6   and (δέ) third [
    [
8   which [
    [
10 soul (ψυχή), [
    And (δέ) the aeons (αἰών) [
12 dwelling place [

33,21-22   E.g., ΝΟⲨ/[ΤⲈ.
33,22   E.g., ϢΟⲢ]Ⲛ̄.
34,1   Kalyptos?; cf. 15,10-12.
34,4   Ⲃ̄, uncertain (supralinear stroke in lacuna); cf. 34,6.
34,6-7   ΟⲨ]/ⲰⲚⲈ?
34,12   I.e., a heavenly home | cf. the vocabulary here with that of pp. 55 and 113.

```
     ⲯⲩⲭⲏ ⲙⲛ ϩⲉⲛ[ . . . . . . . . .
14   ϩ[ⲉ]ⲛ̅[ⲛ]ⲟⲩⲧⲉ ⲛ[ . . . . . . . . .
     ⳓⲟⲥⲉ ⲉ ⲛⲟⲩⲧⲉ [ . . . . . . . .
16   ⲛⲧⲉ ⲛⲓⲁⲩⲧⲟ[ⲅⲉⲛⲏⲥ . . . .
     ⲙⲙⲁⲩ ⲙ̅ ⲡⲓⲁⲩ[ⲧⲟⲅⲉⲛⲏⲥ . .
18   ⲛ ϣⲟⲣⲡ̅ ⲛ ⲛⲟⲩ[ . . . . . . . . .
     ⲛ ⲁⲅⲅⲉⲗ[ⲟ]ⲥ [
20   ⲛ̅ ⲁϩⲟⲣⲁⲧⲟ[ⲛ
     ⲉⲃⲟⲗ ⲛ ϩⲉⲛ[
22   ⲯⲩⲭⲏ ⲙⲛ [
     ⲛⲛ ⲉⲱⲛ .[
24   ⳓⲉ ⲉ ϯⲯ[ⲩⲭⲏ
     ⲁⲅⲅⲉⲗⲟⲥ
26   ⲭⲏ ⲙ̅[
     ⲅⲉ[
28   ⲱ̣[
     ⳓ[
30   ⲉ̣[
                                              ⲗⲉ̄
     ⲧⲁ̣ⲥ ⲙⲙⲁⲩ ⲛ [ ——        ] .ⲉ
2    [ . ]ⲁ̈ⲓ ϣⲁ ⲉⲛ[ⲉϩ . . . . . . .]ⲉ ⲛ
     [.]ⲟⲡ· ͮͮ ⲁⲩⲱ [ ——        ]ⲁⲏⲏ
4    [ . .]ⲉ [ . . . . . .]ϣⲁ̣[ . . . .]ⲁⲧⲥ· ⲉϣⲱ-
     ⲡⲉ ⳓ[ⲉ. . . .]ⲁⲛ .[ . . .]ⲛⳓⲓ ⲟⲩⲯⲩⲭⲏ
6    ⲡⲁ .[ . . . . . . . .]ϣ̣ⲱⲡⲉ ⲛ ⲟⲩ-
     ⲁⲅ[ⲅⲉⲗⲟⲥ —— ]ⲉ̣ ⳓⲉ ⲛ ⲕⲟⲥ-
8    ⲙⲟ̣ⲥ[ . . . . ⲛⲓⲁⲧ]ⲅⲉⲗⲟⲥ ⲁⲩⲱ ⲛⲓ-
     [              ——         ⲧ]ⲏ ⲉⲧⲟⲩⲁⲁⲃ ⲥⲥⲟ-
10   [              ——        ]ⲁ̣ⲓⲱⲛ ⳓⲉ ⲉⲧⲥⲁ
     [              ——        ⲁⲩⲧⲟⲅ]ⲉⲛⲏⲥ ⲟⲩⲛⲧⲉ
12   [              ——        ]ⲙⲟⲟⲩ ⲡ[ . . . . .]ⲩ
     [              ——        ]ⲧⲉ ⲛ ⲁⲣⲭⲱⲛ·
14   [              ——        ] ⲉⲩⲛⲧⲁⲩ ⲙⲙⲁⲩ
     [              ——        ⳓⲓⲁ]ⲫⲟⲣⲁ· ⲉⲧⲉ ⲉⲧⲃⲏ
16   [ⲏⲧ ——        ]ⲧⲁ̈ⲓ ⲁⲛ ⲧⲉ ⲉϣⲁⳓⲉ
     [        ——        ] .ⲛ̣ϩⲟⲟⲩ[ .] .ⲉ
```

34,15   See 2,7n.
34,18   E.g., ⲛⲟⲩ[ⲥ, or ⲛⲟⲩ[ⲧⲉ, or ⲛⲟⲉ[ⲣⲟⲛ.
34,19-20   E.g., ⲡ̄ⲛⲁ̄]/ⲛ̅ ⲁϩⲟⲣⲁⲧⲟⲛ.
35,1   E.g., ⲟⲩⲛ]/ⲧⲁⲥ.
35,2-3   E.g., ⲙⲏⲏϣ]ⲉ ⲛ/[ⲥ]ⲟⲡ.

soul (ψυχή) and [
14 gods [
    higher than god [
16 of the [self-begotten ones (αὐτογενής)
    Autogenes (αὐτογενής) [
18 first [
    angel (ἄγγελος) [
20 invisible (ἀόρατον) [
    some [
22 soul (ψυχή) and [
    aeons (αἰών) [
24 and (δέ) to the [soul (ψυχή)
    angel (ἄγγελος) [
26 [
    [
28 [
    [
30 [

                                      35

    [
2   [   ] eternal[
    [   ]. And [
4   [
    and (δέ) if [   ] namely a soul (ψυχή)
6   [becomes] an
    [angel (ἄγγελος)...], and (δέ) [
8   world (κόσμος) [   ] angels (ἄγγελος) and
    [   ] that holy one (fem.)
10 [   ] and (δέ) aeon (αἰών) which
    [Autog]enes (αὐτογενής) has
12 [   ] them, the [
    [   ] archon (ἄρχων)
14 [   ] they have
    [difference (διαφορά)] which
16 [   ] she is not, to speak
    [

35,4   E.g., ϣⲁ[ⲥⲁϩⲉⲣ]ⲁⲧ꞊ⳓ.
35,6   Or, ϣⲓϯⲡⲉ.
35,9   ⲥⲥⲟ′, supralinear stroke over the first ⲥ.
35,12 Or, water.
35,17 ϩⲟⲟⳓ[ⲧ]?

```
18  [      ----                    ]ⲣⲁϥ· ⲙⲛ
    [      ----       ⲁⲩⲧⲟⲅⲉⲛ]ⲏⲥ ⲛ ⲛⲟⲩⲧⲉ
20  [      ----                    ]ⲉⲧϣⲟⲟⲛ̀
    [      ----                    ]ⲥⲱⲧⲙ
22  [      ----        ⲁ]ⲩ[ⲧ]ⲟⲅⲉⲛⲏⲥ
    [      ----                    ]ⲉ ⲛⲧⲉ
24  [      ----                    ]ⲟⲥ
    [      ----                    ]ⲛ
26  [      ----                    ]ⲛ̀
    [
28  [
    ̄ⲁ̄[ⲉ̄]
    ⲛ ⲧ.[ . . . . . . .]ⲱⲥ ᵛᵛ ⲟⲩⲛⲧ[ⲁ˙.]
2   [ⲙ]ⲙ[ⲁⲩ. . . . ] .ⲛ ϯⲅ̄ⲩⲡ[ⲁ]ⲣⲝ̄[ⲥⲥ]
    .[ . . . . . . . . .] ⲛⲛ ⲟⲩⲱⲛϩ [ .
4   ⲧ[ . . . . . . . ]ϣⲟ[ⲟ]ⲛ̀ ⲉⲧⲃⲉ [ . .
    ϣⲁⲍⲉ ⲛ[ . . . .]ⲥ ⲛ [ . . . . . .] . .[
6   ⲡⲥⲁⲗⲟⲩ .[ . .]ⲟⲟ[ . . . . . ]ϩⲟⲟ[ⲩⲧ̄]
    ⲉⲩⲅⲟ̣ⲧ ⲛ̄[   ----        ] ⲛⲏ[ .
8   ⲛ ⲛⲟⲩ[ ___   ----       ⲁ]ϩⲟⲣⲁ-
    ⲧⲟⲛ ⲙ ⲡ̄ⲛ̄ⲁ̄ ⲁ[ . . . . . . . .] .[ . .
10  ϩⲙ ⲡⲥⲧⲉⲗⲥⲟ[ⲥ
    ⲙⲉⲧⲉⲙⲉⲛ ⲛ̣ .[
12  ⲙⲛ ⲟⲩⲁⲣⲭⲏ· .[
    ⲛ ⲁ[ⲅⲁ]ⲡ̄ⲏ ⲙⲛ ⲟ[ⲩ
14  ⲛⲧⲉ ϯⲃⲁⲣⲃⲏⲗⲱ[
    ⲉⲃⲟⲗ ⲙⲛ ⲟⲩⲙ[
16  ⲡⲥⲛⲟⲩⲥ ⲛⲧⲉ [
    ⲥⲛⲧⲉ ⲛⲉ ⲛⲁ̈ⲓ ⲛ [
18  ⲡ[ⲥ]ⲙⲉⲉⲩⲉ .[
    ⲃⲟ̣ⲗ ϩⲙ ⲡⲥⲟ[ ___
20  ϩⲛ ϯⲃⲁⲣ̄ⲃⲏⲗⲱ[
    ⲡⲥⲕⲁ̄ⲥ ⲇⲉ .[
22  ⲛⲁ̈ⲓ ⲧⲏⲣⲟ[ⲩ
    ⲙ ⲡⲁⲣⲑⲉ[ⲛⲟⲥ
24  ⲁⲥⲟⲩⲉ̣[
```

---

36   Pagination, only a trace of the supralinear stroke survives; the numerals do not survive.

36,5   E.g., ϣⲁⲍⲉ ⲛ[ⲧⲉⲗⲥⲟⲥ; cf. 35,10.

36,6   ⲟ̣[, or else ⲥ̣[.

36,9   ⲡ̄ⲛ̄ⲁ̄, nothing of the supralinear stroke survives.

18   [   ] and

      [   ] divine [Autogen]es (αὐτογενής)

20   [   ] which exists

      [   ] hear

22   [A]u[t]ogenes (αὐτογενής)

      [   ] of

24   [

      [

26   [

      [

28   [

      3[6]

      [   ] has

2   [   ] existence (ὕπαρξις)

      [   ] life

4   [   ] exist, concerning [

      word [

6   the child [   ] male

      for a generation [

8   [

      invisible (ἀόρατον) spirit (πνεῦμα) [

10   in the perfect (τέλειος) [

      [

12   and an origin (ἀρχή) [

      love (ἀγάπη) and [

14   of Barbel[o

      and a [

16   the mind of [   ] mind (νοῦς) [

      these are two [

18   thought [

      in the [

20   in Barbel[o

      and (δέ) the Kalyptos (καλυπτός) [

22   all these [   ] the

      virgin (παρθένος) [

24   she [

36,16-17   A *paragraphos* appears here.

36,17   ⲥ ⲛ, oblique mark above ⲛ is not ink.

36,22-23   E.g., ⲧⲃⲁⲣⲃ ⲏ ⲗ ⲱ]/ⲙ ⲡⲁⲣⲑⲉ[ⲛⲟⲥ.

36,24   ⲉ[, not ⲱ[; e.g., ⲟ ⲩ ⲉ[ⲛ ⳉ.

```
     ϨΝ ΟⲨ[
26   ⲘΝ[
     ϪΠ[
28   ⲦⲀ[
     Ⲙ[
                                    ⲗ̄ⲍ̄
     ϨⲘ ⲠⲎ ⲈⲦⲘⲘⲀ[Ⲩ . . . . . .] .ⲦϬΟⲘ
2    [ .]ⲉ̣ .[ .]ⲦⲈ ⲠⲎ Ⲉ[ . . . . . . . . .] ΝΟⲨ-
     ⲈⲂΟⲀ̣ ϨⲘ Π[ .]ⲉ̣[ . . . . . .] ⲀⲀ]ⲀⲀ
4    ΟⲨⲈϨ̣ΟⲀ̣ [Ϩ]Ν ⲦϬΟ[Ⲙ Ν]ⲦⲈ ⲠⲎ [Ⲉ]ⲦⲘ-
     ⲘⲀ[Ⲩ . . . ϢΟ[ΟⲠ̀ ΟΝ]ⲦⲰⲤ ⲈⲤ-
6    ϢΟ̣[ . . . . . . . . .] ΝⲦⲀϤ ⲦⲈ·
     Π[ . . . . . . . . Ⲉ]ⲨⲢ ϢΟⲢⲠ̀
8    Ṇ Ο̣[ . . . . . . . .] . . Ⲉ ΝⲦⲈ ⲠⲎ Ⲉ-
     [Ⲧ]Ⲙ̣[ⲘⲀⲨ . . . .]ϥ̇· ΝⲦΟϤ ϪⲈ ΠⲓⲀⲦ̇
10   [      ----          ]Ⲁ̇· ΝⲦΟϤ ⲘⲀⲨⲀⲀϤ
     [      ----          ] .ϯ̇ ΝⲀϤ Ⲙ ΠⲢⲰϢⲈ
12   [      ----          ] .Ⲁ̇ⲦϢϢ̣[ . .] ΝⲀϤ
     [      ----          ]ϥ̇ ⲦⲎⲢΟⲨ[·] Ⲉϥϯ
14   [      ----          ]ⲩ̇ ⲈⲂΟⲀ ϨⲓⲦΝ ΝⲈ
     [      ----          ]Ⲉ Πⲁⲓ ⲄⲀⲢ ϨⲈΝⲘⲈ
16   [      ----          ]Ⲥ ϨⲓΝⲀ ϪⲈ ⲈϤⲈϢⲰ-
     [      ----          ] .̇ ⲀⲨⲰ Π[Ⲉ]Ⲧ̣Ⲉ
18   [      ----          ]ⲦⲈ ⲘⲘΟϤ Ν
     [      ----          ]Ⲁ̇Ⲧ̇ⲠⲰⲢϪ Ⲉⲣ̇ΟϤ·
20   [      ----          ϨⲀ]ⲣϬΗⲀⲰ· ⲀϤⲦΟ-
     [      ----          Ϩⲓ]ΝⲀ ϪⲈ ⲈϤⲈϢⲰ-
22   [      ----          ]Ⲙ̄Ⲛ̇ⲘⲀⲔⲀ
     [ⲣⲓΟⲤ     ----        ]ⲤⲓⲤ Ν ΟⲨ-
24   [                     ] ⲦΗⲣΟⲨ:
     [                     ].ϥⲉⲓ
26   [                     ] .ⲁ̣
     [                     ]ⲁ̣
28   [                     ]ⲣ
     [                     ]ⲁ̣ⲓΟ[
```

37,1   ] ., connected to preceding letter by a supralinear stroke; e.g., Ⲙ]Ṇ.

37,2   .[, read Ⲧ, Ⲏ, ϥ,Ⲕ, Ⲛ, or Ⲛ̄ | ΝΟⲨ´, lacuna above Ⲛ where a supralinear
        stroke may have stood.

37,6   Ọ, or else ϛ or ⲉ̣.

37,7   A supralinear stroke enters from left and terminates above the first letter of

in a [
26   and [
    [
28   [
    [

37

in that [   ] power
2   [
    from [   ] but (ἀλλά)
4   (is) from the power of that one
    [...   really (ὄντως) exists], she
6   [   ] is his
    [   ] they [being] first
8   [   ] of that one
    [   ] and (δέ) he is the
10   [   ] he alone
           ] give him enough
12   [   ] to him
    [   ] all, he gives
14   [   ] through the
    [   ] for (γάρ) [ ] some
16   [   ] in order that (ἵνα) he might
    [   ] and that one which
18   [   ] him
    [   ] undivided
20   [Ba]rbelo; he
    [in order that (ἵνα)] he might
22   [blessedness (-μακάριος)]
    [
24   [   ] all
    [   ] he comes
26   [
    [
28   [
    [

---

the line; perhaps from a *paragraphos* as at 36,16-17.
37,8   ] . .ⲉ, possibly ⲯⲧ̄]ⲭⲏ̄ [ⲧ]ⲉ (with small or crowded letters).
37,16-17   E.g., ⲉϥⲉ ϣⲱ[ⲡⲉ; cf. 37,21-22.
37,25   ⲉⲥ, with circumflex.
37,29   E.g., ⲧⲉ]ⲗ̣ⲥ̣ⲟ̣[ⲥ.

[ⲗⲏ]

ⲟⲩ[. . . . . . .] ⲛ̄ⲧⲉ ⲡ︦ⲓⲧⲉⲗⲓⲟ[ⲥ] ⲛ̄

2 ⲛⲟ[ⲩⲥ . . . . . .]ⲥ̄ⲧⲡ ⲁⲩⲱ ⲉϥ[. .

   ⲛ̣ [. . . . .] ⲛ̄ ⲧⲉⲗⲓⲟⲥ ⲙ̄ ⲡ̄ⲛ̣[ⲁ̄]

4 ⲉ̣[. . . . . ⲧ]ⲉⲗⲓⲟ̣ⲥ ⲉ̄ϥ̄ⲟⲛ̄ϩ ⲛ̄

   ϣⲁ ⲉⲛⲉ[ϩ . . .]ⲩⲧ[. . . . .] .ⲛ̣[.

6 ⲉⲣⲟϥ· ⲁⲩⲱ[. .]ⲟ̣ⲟ̣[. . . ⲡ]ⲁ̈ ⲉϥ-

   ϣⲟⲟⲛ̣[――   ]ⲡⲉ ⲛ̄-

8 ⲧⲉ ⲡ︦ⲓⲧ[――   ϣ]ⲁⲭⲉ

   ⲡⲉ ⲉⲃⲟⲗ ϩ︦ⲛ [. . . . .] .[.

10 ⲉⲧ̄ϣⲟⲟⲛ̣ ϩ︦ⲙ̣ [

   ⲛ̄ⲧⲁⲩ ⲛ̄ ⲛⲁ̈ ⲧ̣ⲏ[ⲣⲟⲩ

12 ϣⲁ ⲉⲛⲉϩ· ⲉ̄ .[

   ⲟⲡ [ϩ]ⲙ̄ ⲡⲓ̄ϣⲙ̣[ⲧ̄ϭ̄ⲟⲙ

14 ϣ[ⲟⲟ]ⲛ̣ ϩ︦ⲙ̄ ⲡⲓ̄[

   ⲛⲉ ⲛ̄ ⲛⲏ ⲉ̄ⲧ̄ϣⲟ̣[ⲟⲛ̣

16 ⲛ̄ ⲧⲉⲗⲓⲟⲥ· ⲛ̄ ⲧ̄[

   ⲡ︦ⲓⲡⲣⲱⲧⲟⲫⲁ̣[ⲛⲏⲥ

18 ⲛⲟⲩⲥ· ⲁⲗⲗⲁ .[

   ⲧⲟ̣ⲩ̄ⲃⲏⲟ̣[ⲩⲧ̄

20 ⲁⲩⲱ ⲡⲏ ⲙ̣[

   ⲛ̄ⲧⲉ ⲟⲩⲉⲓⲛⲉ̣ [

22 ⲟⲩⲱⲛ̄ϩ ⲉⲃⲟ̣[ⲗ

   ⲁⲩⲱ ⲡⲓⲁ̣[ⲧ̄

24 ⲡⲉ ⲛ̄ ⲧ̄[

   ⲙ̄ⲙⲟϥ [

26 ⲛ̄ ⲧ̄.[

   ⲡ̄[

28 ⲙ̄[

   ϩ .[

30   .[

                                   [ⲗ︦ⲑ]

   [―――   ] .ⲥ·

2 [.]ⲙ̣ⲉϥ̄ .[―――   ] ⲛ̄ϭⲓ

   [. .]ⲟ̄ⲩ[―――   ] .ϥⲉ

4 [―――   ]ⲛ̣̄

   [―――   ⲉ]ⲧ̄ⲃ̄ⲏⲏⲧ̄ϥ ⲉⲩ-

6 [―――   ] . .ϯ ϣⲱⲗϩ ⲉⲣⲟϥ·

38,1   ⲛ̄, only the supralinear stroke survives.
38,1-2 I.e., Protophanes, see 18,5-7; cf. 38,17.
38,5-6 E.g., ⲁ̣]ⲧ̄ⲛ[ⲁⲩ]/ⲉⲣⲟϥ.

[38]
a [　　　　] of the perfect (τέλειος)
2　[mind (νοῦς)　　　] and he [
　　[　　　　　] perfect (τέλειος) spirit (πνεῦμα)
4　[　　　　] perfect (τέλειος), he lives
　　forever [
6　him, and [　　　　　　] he
　　exists [
8　of the [
　　he is [a word] from[
10　which is in [
　　of them all[
12　eternal [
　　[　　] in the three-[powered
14　is in the [
　　[　　　　　] those which [are
16　perfect (τέλειος) [
　　the Protopha[nes (πρωτοφανής)
18　mind (νοῦς), but (ἀλλά) [
　　pure [
20　and he [
　　of an image [
22　appear [
　　and the [
24　[
　　him[
26　[
　　[
28　[
　　[
30　[

　　　　　　　　　　　　　　　　[39]

　　[
2　[　　　　　　　　　　　　] namely
　　[
4　[
　　[　　　　　　　　　] because of him they
6　[　　　　　　　　　] I mark it

_____

38,13　　**оп**, flag in lacuna.
38,19　　Or, **ТОΥΒ ΗΟ[Υ**.
39　　　The topic may still be the Protophanes.

	[	----	ϩⲁ]ⲡⲗⲟⲩⲥ ⲡⲉ
8	[	----	ⲧ]ⲁⲣ ⲡⲉ ⲛ
	[	----	ⲙ .ϥ ϩⲱⲥ ⲉϥϣⲟ-
10	[ⲟⲡ	----	]ⲱ ϩⲱⲥ ⲉⲕⲉⲟⲩⲁ
	[	----	] .ⲟ[.]ⲉⲧⲉ ⲡⲁⲓ̈ ⲡⲉ
12	[	----	]ϣⲱⲱⲧ̇· ⲉⲧⲃⲉ
	[	----	]ϣⲙ̇ⲧϩⲟ[ⲟⲩⲧ] ⲛ̣
14	[	----	ϣⲟⲟ]ⲛ̣ ⲟⲛⲧⲱ[ⲥ] ⲛⲧⲉ
	[	----	ⲛⲟ]ⲩⲥ ⲛⲧⲉ ⲧⲅ̄ⲛⲱ-
16	[ⲥⲓⲥ	----	]ⲉ ⲛⲏ ⲉⲧϣⲟⲟⲛ̇
	[	----	]ⲧⲉ ⲉⲧⲉ ⲟⲩⲛⲧⲁϥ
18	[	----	]ϣⲟⲟⲛ̇ ⲟⲛⲧⲱⲥ·
	[	----	] .ⲁⲩⲱ ⲟⲩ .[.]ⲱ
20	[	----	ⲉ]ⲃⲟⲗ· ⲁⲩⲱ ⲁ̣ⲥ-
	[	----	]ⲩ ⲙ ⲙⲉϩⲥⲛⲁⲩ
22	[	----	ⲧ]ⲉⲗⲓⲟⲥ· ⲉⲧⲉ
	[	----	ⲟ]ⲩⲱⲛϩ ⲉⲃⲟⲗ
24	[	----	]ϩⲏⲧϥ ⲉⲩ-
	[	----	]ⲡⲓⲕⲁ̄ⲥ·
26	[	----	] ⲛ ⲁⲧ̇-
	[	----	] ⲛ ⲟⲩ-
28	[	----	] ⲛ ⲁⲧ̇-
	[	----	ⲉⲓ]ⲇⲟⲥ
30	[	----	]ⲉ
	[_	----	] ⲛ ⲛⲁⲓ̈
	[ⲙ̄]		
	ⲗⲟ [	----	]ⲁ̣ϩ̣ⲡ[. . .]
2	ⲡ[	----	]ⲣⲟ̣ⲩ[
	ⲧ[	----	]ⲩ .[
4	ⲟ[		
	ⲉⲓⲇⲟⲥ ⲃ̄ [		
6	ⲉⲩⲧⲛⲱϭⲓⲥ	----	ⲡⲓⲡⲣⲱ-]
	ⲧⲟⲫⲁ[ⲛⲏⲥ	----	ϩⲟ-]
8	ⲟⲩⲧ ⲛ [	----	-ⲩⲛ-]
	ⲧⲁϥ ⲙⲙⲁⲩ ⲛ [	----	ϩⲩⲡⲁⲣ-]
10	ⳉⲓⲥ ⲛϩⲣⲁⲓ̈ [		
	ⲁ̇ⲧⲙⲓⲥⲉ· ⲉⲩ[		
12	ⲙⲉϩϣⲟⲙⲧ̇ ⲛ̣ [		

40,1   Possibly another line of text above what we have called line 1.
40,5-6   A *paragraphos* appears here.
40,5   ⲃ̄, i.e., ⲥⲛⲁⲩ.

```
      [                              ] he is simple (ἁπλοῦς)
 8    [                              ] for (γάρ) he is
      [                              ] as (ὧς) he exists
10    [                              ] as (ὧς) to another
      [                              ] that is,
12    [                              ] need.  Concerning
      [                              ] triple-male
14    [                              ] really (ὄντως) [exists] as
      [                    mind (νοῦς)] of knowledge (γνῶσις)
16    [                              ] those who exist
      [                              ] which he has
18    [                              ] really (ὄντως) exist
      [                              ] and a [
20    [                              ] and she
      [                              ] second
22    [                              ] perfect (τέλειος) which
      [                              ] appear
24    [                              ] in him they
      [                              ] Kalyptos (καλυπτός)
26    [
      [
28    [
      [                    species (εἶδος)]
30    [
      [                              ]these
    [40]
      [
 2    [
      [
 4    [
      second species (εἶδος) [
 6    a knowledge (γνῶσις) [
      [Protophanes (πρωτοφανής)
 8    [male
      he has [
10    existence (ὕπαρξις) [
      unborn, they [
12    third [
```

40,8   E.g., ΝΙΝΟ**ⲧ**C.
40,11-12 E.g., [ⲠⲒ]/ⲘⲈ**Ⲣ**ϢⲞⲘⲦ Ⲛ[ⲚⲈⲰⲚ.

```
       [ . . .] .ⲉⲩⲛⲧ[ⲁϥ ⲙⲙⲁⲩ
14     ⲉⲓⲙⲉ· ⲁⲩⲱ ⲉ.[
       ϣⲟⲟⲡ̄ ϩⲓ ⲟⲩⲙ[ⲁ
16     ⲡⲉ ⲙ ⲡⲁⲛⲧⲉⲗ[ⲓⲟⲥ    ———    ⲙⲁⲕⲁ-]
       ⲣⲓⲟⲥ ⲉⲙⲛ ⲗ[ⲁⲁⲩ
18     ⲙⲙⲁⲩ· ⲁ[
       ⲉⲃⲟⲗ· ⲉⲃⲟⲗ [
20     ⲛⲟⲩⲧⲉ ⲡ.[
       ⲧⲩ ⲛⲙⲙⲁϥ [
22     ⲛ ⲟⲩⲱ.[
       ⲛ ⲧⲉⲗ[ⲓⲟⲥ
24     ⲛⲧⲉ ⲡ[
       ⲕⲁⲥ̄ [
26     ⲃⲁ[
       ⲁ[
28     ⲱ[
       ⲁ[
                                    ⲙⲁ̄
       [ .] . ⲕⲁ[     ———        ]ⲓⲉⲓⲙⲉ
2      [ . .]ⲛⲱ[      ———         ] ⲛⲧⲉ
       [ . . .] .[     ———         ⲡⲣ]ⲱⲧⲟ-
4      [ⲫⲁ]ⲛⲏⲥ  ———     ⲡ]ⲓⲛⲟⲩ[ⲥ] ⲛⲧⲉ
       [              ———         ]ⲁⲩ ⲛ ⲛⲓⲅⲟⲙ
6      [              ———        ] ⲡⲧⲏⲣϥ ⲛϩⲣⲁⲓ̈
       [              ———         ] ⲁⲩⲱ ϥϣⲟ-
8      [ⲟⲡ           ———        ] ⲧⲉⲓ̈ⲅⲛⲱⲥⲓⲥ ⲛ
       [              ———        ]ⲛⲟⲩⲧⲉ ⲡⲓⲁⲩⲧⲟ-
10     [ⲅⲉⲛⲏⲥ·    ⲡⲓⲁⲩⲧⲟ]ⲅⲉⲛⲏⲥ ⲇⲉ ⲛ ⲛⲟⲩ-
       [ⲧⲉ          ] ⲛⲧⲉ ⲡⲓⲁⲗⲟⲩ ⲛⲧⲉ
12     [ . . . . . ϩ ⲟ ⲟ ⲩ ⲧ ·]ϣⲙⲧ̄[ϩ]ⲟⲟⲩⲧ̄· ⲡⲉ̣ⲓ̈ϩⲟⲟⲩⲧ̄
       [ . . . . . . . .]ⲡⲟ[ .] ⲡⲉ ⲙⲛ ⲟⲩ[ⲉⲓ]ⲇⲟⲥ
14     [ . . . . . . . .] ⲛ ⲧⲉⲗⲓⲟⲥ ⲉⲙⲙⲛⲧⲁϥ
       [ . . . .]ⲡ[ . . . . .] ⲛ̣ϩⲣⲁⲓ̈ ϩⲛ ⲟⲩⲧⲛⲱⲥⲓⲥ
16     [ . . . .]ⲱⲧ̄ ⲙ [ⲡ]ⲣⲏⲧⲉ ⲙ ⲡⲏ ⲉⲧⲙⲙⲁⲩ·
       [ . . . .] ⲟⲩϣ[ⲱ]ⲡⲉ ⲛⲧⲉ ⲛⲓⲕⲁⲧⲁ ⲟⲩⲁ
18     [ⲙⲛ] ⲟⲩⲧⲛⲱ[ⲥ]ⲓ̣[ⲥ] ⲛ ⲟⲩⲱⲧ̄ ⲛⲧⲉ ⲛⲓ-
       [ⲕ]ⲁ̣ⲧ̣ⲁ̣ ⲟⲩⲁ [ .]ⲟ̣[ . . . .] ⲕⲁⲧⲁ ⲡⲧⲣϥ
```

40,15-16   E.g., [ϣⲱ]/ⲡⲉ ⲙ ⲡⲁⲛⲧⲉⲗ[ⲓⲟⲥ.

40,19   Cod. ⲉⲃⲟⲗ 'ⲉⲃⲟⲗ.

40,25   ⲥ̄, only the supralinear stroke survives.

41   Pagination, only traces of the ornamental bar below the number survive; the

[he] has [

14 knowledge and [

exist together [

16 all-perfect (παντέλειος) [

[blessed (μακάριος)], since there is not [

18 [

[

20 god [

with him [

22 [

[perfect (τέλειος)

24 of the [

Kalyptos (καλυπτός) [

26 [

[

28 [

[

41

[   ] know

2 [   ] of

[Pr]oto[phanes (πρωτοφανής)]

4 [   ] the mind (νοῦς)

[   ] the powers

6 [   ] the all

[   ] and he [exists]

8 [   ] this knowledge (γνῶσις)

[   ] divine, the Auto[genes (αὐτογενής)]

10 and (δέ) [the] divine Auto[genes (αὐτογενής)]

[   ] of the child of

12 [   ] triple-male, this male

[   ] is [   ] and a species (εἶδος)

14 [   ] perfect (τέλειος) because it does not have

[   ] in a knowledge (γνῶσις)

16 [   ] like that one

[   ] a being of the individuals (+κατά)

18 [and] a single knowledge (γνῶσις) of the

individuals (+κατά) [   ] according to (κατά) the all

---

numerals do not survive.

41,11-12   The expression ⲡϨⲁⲗⲟⲩ ⲚⲦⲉ/ⲡϨⲁⲗⲟⲩ probably occurred.

41,14   ⲉⲘⲘ´, sic.

41,16   E.g., [Ⲛ ⲞⲨ]ⲱⲦ.

```
20  [ . . .]ⲱⲕ[ . . . . . .] ⲛ̄ ⲧⲉⲗⲓⲟⲥ· ⲡⲓϩⲟ-
    [ⲟ]ⲩⲧ̀ ⲇⲉ [ . . . . . . .] ⲛ̄ ⲛⲟⲩⲧⲉ ⲟⲩ-
22  [ . .] ⲱ . .[ . . . . .]ⲉ ⲡⲓⲕⲗ̄ⲥ· ⲡⲓⲕⲗ̄ⲥ
    [ⲇⲉ] ⲛ̄ ⲛ[ . . . . . .] ⲛ̄ ⲛⲟⲩⲧⲉ· ⲟⲩⲁⲣ-
24  [ⲭⲏ      ———        ]ⲉⲓϭ . ⲁⲩⲱ ⲟⲩϭⲟⲙ
    [         ———        ]ⲥ ⲛ̄ⲧ[ⲉ] ⲛⲁⲓ̈ ⲧⲏⲣⲟⲩ:
26  [         ———                 ⲟⲛ]ⲧⲱⲥ
    [         ———                       ]ⲉ
28  [         ———                       ]ⲙⲉ
    [         ———                       ]ⲓ-
30  [         ———                 ⲡⲣⲱ]ⲧⲟ-
    [ⲫⲁⲛⲏⲥ   ———                 ]ⲡ̄ⲣⲱ-
    [ⲙ̄ⲃ]
    ⲧⲟ[ⲫⲁⲛⲏⲥ   ———            ]ⲩⲉⲣ[ . .
2   ⲟⲩ[            ———          ]ⲛ̣ⲟⲩⲥ [ . . . .
    ⲙ[ . . .         ———          ]ⲉⲩ[ . . . .
4   ⲉⲓ[
    ⲧⲁⲡⲧⲏ[ⲣϥ
6   ⲛ̄ⲛ ⲁⲧⲙⲓⲥ[ⲉ
    ⲛ̄ ⲣⲱⲙⲉ ⲛ̄[
8   ⲇⲉ ⲥⲉⲏ[
    ϩⲙ ⲙⲛ ⲡⲏ̣ ⲉ[ⲧ
10  ⲁⲩⲱ ⲡⲏ ⲉⲧⲣ [
    ⲡⲏ ⲉⲧϭⲁⲗⲏⲟ̣[ⲩⲧ̀ . . . . . .
12  ⲟⲛ̄ ϩⲙ ⲡⲓⲉⲥⲑⲏ[ⲧ]ⲟⲛ [ⲛ̄ ⲕⲟⲥⲙⲟⲥ]
    ⲉϥ[ⲟ]ⲛ̣ϩ ⲙⲛ ⲡⲏ [ⲉ]ⲧ̄ⲙⲟⲟ[ⲩⲧ̀ . . .
14  . .[ .] ⲉ ⲧⲏⲣⲟⲩ ⲉⲩ[ . . . . . . .
    ϣⲁϣⲛⲓ ⲉⲩⲟⲩϫⲁⲓ̈ [ . .]ⲁ .[ . . .
16  ⲡⲏ ⲉⲧ̄ⲙⲟⲟⲩⲧ̀ ⲛⲁⲓ̈ ⲇ[ⲉ] ⲧⲏ[ⲣⲟⲩ]
    ⲉⲙⲡⲟⲩⲣ ϩⲁⲉ ⲛ̄ ⲟ[ⲩⲟ]ⲩϫⲁⲓ̈ [ . . .
18  ϣⲟⲣⲡ̄· ⲁⲗⲗⲁ ⲉⲩ[ⲛⲟ]ⲩϩⲙ ⲛ̄ϩ[ⲟⲩ-]
    ⲟ [ⲇ]ⲉ ⲉⲩϣⲟⲟⲡ̄ ⲉⲧⲑⲉⲃⲓⲏⲟ [ⲩ  ͞ⲩ ]
20  ⲁⲩⲱ ⲡⲓⲣⲱ[ⲙⲉ ⲛ̄ⲧⲉ] ⲛⲉⲧ̄ⲙⲟ[ⲟⲩⲧ̀]
    ⲧⲉϥⲯⲩⲭⲏ ⲙ[ⲛ ⲡⲉϥⲛⲟ]ⲩⲥ ⲁⲩ[ⲱ]
22  ⲡⲉϥⲥⲱⲙⲁ [ⲥⲉⲙⲟⲟⲩ]ⲧ̀ ⲧⲏⲣ[ⲟⲩ]
```

41,21   E.g., [ⲛ̄ ⲧⲉⲗⲓⲟⲥ].
41,22   . .[, first trace is from ⲉ, ⲑ, ⲟ, or ⲥ; second trace from ⲁ, ⲙ, ⲩ, ⲱ, or ϣ.
41,23-24 E.g., [ⲇⲉ] ⲛ̄ ⲛ[ⲁⲧⲙⲓⲥⲉ] ⲛ̄ ⲛⲟⲩⲧⲉ· ⲟⲩⲁⲣ/[ⲭⲏ ⲡⲉ.
42,8-9   E.g., ⲛⲟⲩ]/ϩⲙ.
42,11-12 E.g., ϣⲟ]/ⲟⲡ.
42,14   . .[, first trace is from ⲉ or ⲑ.

20 [   ] perfect (τέλειος)
    But (δέ) the male [   ] mind (νοῦς)
22 [   ] the Kalyptos (καλυπτός),
    [but (δέ)] the divine [   ] Kalyptos (καλυπτός) [
24 [   ] and a power
    [   ] of all these
26 [really (ὄντως)]
    [
28 [
    [
30 [...Pro]to[phanes (πρωτοφανής)
    [
    [42]
    [Pro]to[phanes (πρωτοφανής)
2   [   ] mind (νοῦς) [
    [
4   [
    she who belongs to the [All
6   unborn [
    man [
8   they [
    with that one who [
10 and he who[
    he who dwells [
12 in the perceptible (αἰσθητόν) [world (κόσμος)]
    living with that dead one [
14 [   ] all [
    obtain salvation [
16 that dead one. Yet (δέ) [all] of them
    did not need salvation [
18 first, but (ἀλλά) they are safe
    and (δέ) exist very humbly.
20 (About) the mortal (type of) humanity:
    its soul (ψυχή), [its mind (νοῦς)] and
22 its body (σῶμα) all [are] all [dead].

42,20   Restore ⲚⲦⲈ or else simply Ⲛ | humanity, lit., man; in this Gnostic anthro-
        pology of souls the mortal type comes first, followed by that with immortal
        soul (43,1-3), that in the Exile (43,13-18), that in the Repentance (43,19ff), and
        finally the one that can be saved (44,1ff).
42,22   Or [ⲈⲦⲘⲞⲞⲨ]Ⲧ̄ ⲦⲎⲢ[Ϥ].

ϩ€ΝΆΙ ϻΚΆC Ν[. . . . . .]ϩϙ[. . .
24 ϩ€Ν€ΙΟΤ[€] ΝΤ€ [——— ϩϫ-]
ΆΙΚΟΝ· ϩ€Ν .[
26 ΠΙΚϢϙΤ Οϫ[
ΚΟ[
28 Ο .[
Κ .[
30 €[

$$\overline{ΜΓ}$$

€ϤΟϫΟΤΒ €ΒΟᾺ: ⱽ Π[Ι]ϻ€ϩCΝΆϫ Δ€
2 Ν ρϢϻ€ Π€ ϯΨϫΧΗ ΝΝ ΆΤϻΟϫ
€Τ[Ϣ]ΟΟῙ ϩΝ ΝΗ €ΤϻΟΟϫΤ
4 €CϤ[Ι Ν] ΟϫρϙΟϫϢ ΝΆC· ΤΟΤ€
[ΤΆ]ρ ϢΆC€Ι[ρ]€ Ν ΟϫϢΙΝ€ Ν Ν€-
6 Τρ ΝΆϤρ€ [ΚΆΤΆ ΠΟ]ϫΆ ΠΟϫΆ ϻ-
ϻϙϙϫ· Ά[ϫϢ ϢΆCρ] €ϩθΆΝ€Cθ€
8 € Π[Ι]ϻΚΆϩ Ν [Cϖ]ϻΆΤΙΚΟΝ ϢΆϫ-
[. . . . .]ϫϖC ΆϫϢ ϢΆCρ
10 [. . . . . . .-ϫ]ΝΤΆC ϻϻΆϫ Ν-
[Ν Οϫ]ΝΟϫΤ€ Ν ϢΆ €Ν€ϩ· ϢΆCρ
12 ϢΒΗρ Ν ϢϖΠ[€] ϻΝ ϩ€ΝΔ[€ϻϖ]Ν:
[ΠΙ]ρϢϻ€ Δ€ €ΤϢΟΟῙ ϩΝ ϯ-
14 [Π]ΆρΟΙΚΗ[C]ΙC· €ϢϖΠ€ Δ€ €-
[ΟϫΝ]ΤΆϤ ϻϻΆϫ Ν ΟϫϬΙΝ€ ΝΤ€ ϯ-
16 [ϻΝ]Τϻ€ Ν[ϩ]ρΆϊ ΝϩΗΤϤ €ϤΟϫΗ[€-]
[Οϫ] Ά ΝΙϩΒΗϫ€ ΝΤ€ ϩ€ΝΚΟΟϫ€
18 €ϫϢΟΟῙ Κ[ΆΚ]ϖC ΝΆϊ €ϫϪ[ϖ-]
[ρ]ῆ: ⱽⱽ ΠΙρϖ[ϻ€] €Τρ ϻ€ΤΆ-
20 [ΝΟΙ] €ϢϖΠ€ €[Ϥ]ϢΆΝΚϖϤ ΝCϖϤ
[Ν] Ν€Τϻ[ΟΟϫΤ] ΝϤρ €ΠΙθϫϻΙ

42,23 ϻΚΆC, error for ϻΚΆϩ (or alternate form with the same meaning) |
suffering results from being trapped in the material world; cf. 43,7-8; 46,2-6.
42,25 .[, read Χ or Δ ; e.g., Δ[€ϻϖΝ; cf. 43,12.
43,1 Lit., he | ΟϫΟΤΒ €ΒΟᾺ, a reference to the transmigration of souls; cf.
Apoc.Pet. VII 83,31ff.
43,4 Cf. 25,5-8; a sinless one does not have to be anxious.
43,5 [ΤΆρ] ϢΆC€Ι[ρ]€, first ink trace is from ρ, Ϥ or possibly ϯ or Ψ; second
trace, like the ligature of Ά into C ; €, or else θ ; last trace is ambiguous (at
upper right of the square) | for ΤΟΤ€ ΤΆρ, cf. 44,13 | for €Ιρ€ Ν
ΟϫϢΙΝ€, cf. 43,25.
43,6-7 Or, each other.
43,12 Daimons could be either good or evil. Three types of daimons were

Sufferings [
24 fathers of [
[material (ὑλικόν)
26 the fire [
[
28 [
[
30 [

43

it transforms. The (+δέ) second (type of
2 humanity is the immortal soul (ψυχή)
in those who die,
4 anxious over itself; [for (γάρ)] then (τότε)
[it seeks] those things
6 which are profitable [according to (κατά)] each
of them [and] experiences (αἰσθάνεσθαι)
8 bodily (σωματικόν) suffering. They
[   ] and it
10 [having]
an eternal god, it
12 associates with daimons (δαίμων).
Now (δέ) about the (type of) humanity in the
14 exile (παροίκησις): when (+δέ)
it discovers the
16 truth in itself, it is far
from the deeds of others
18 who live [wrongly (κακῶς)] (and) stumble.
(About) the (type of) humanity that repents (μετανοεῖν):
20 when it renounces
dead things and desires (ἐπιθυμεῖν)

---

recognized by some Middle Platonic writers: incarnate souls, souls of the
dead, and disincarnate souls; see also 27,9-20.

43,14   For exile as the heavenly level above the airy-earth, see 5,18-25; the next
higher level is the repentance (43,19; cf. 5,29).

43,16   ͡ιε͡ι, either obliterated by the scribe or ruined by an imperfection in the
papyrus and left for cancelled.

43,17   ⲁ, the verb takes ⲛ′ or ⲉ′ with its object, but the present ink trace resembles
on ⲁ, ⲕ, ⲗ, ⲙ, ⲭ, or ϩ; the AA² form ⲁ′ does not occur elsewhere in this
text | see 25,5n.

43,20   Written ⲉ͡ⲱ ͣ ⲱⲡⲉ because of imperfection in the papyrus | lit., leave
behind oneself.

43,21   Written ⲛⲉⲧ ͣ ⲙ (imperfection in papyrus).

22 [ε] ΝΗ ετ[ϣ]ο[οπ]· πιΝΟΥϲ ΝΝ ᴀ-
    [τ]ΜΟΥ ΜΝ †ΨΥΧΗ ΝΝ ᴀτΜΟΥ

24 [.] Ν̣ [. . .]ε̣Ч6επΗ ετΒΗΗτΟΥ Ν
    ϣΟΡπ εЧειΡε Ν ΟΥϣιΝε

26 ετΒΗτЧ Ντε †πΡᴀ̣ϫ̣ι[ϲ ᴀ]Ν
    ᴀλλᴀ Ντε Νι̣ϩΒΗΥ ε[Βο]λ̣

28 ϭᴀρ ϩΜ πᴀϊ ϣᴀЧ[.]ϲ̣ ΝΟ[. . .
    εΝΝ[. . . . .]ο[. . . . .] ᴀΥω

30 ϣᴀϣΝ[ϲ ——   ] .
    [Μᴀ]

    πιΡωΜε Δε ετε ϣᴀΥΝᴀϩΜεЧ

2   πε πΗ ετκωτε ΝϲωЧ ΜΝ πεЧ-
    ΝΟΥϲ ᴀΥω ΝЧ6ιΝε Μ πο[Υ]ᴀ πΟΥᴀ

4   ΜΜΟΟΥ· ᴀΥω ϫε ΟΥΝτ[ᴀ]Ч Μ[ΜᴀΥ Ν]
    ΟΥΗΡ Ν 6ΟΜ: <u>vv</u> πι[Ρ]ωΜ[ε Δε Ν-]

6   τᴀЧΝΟΥϩΜ πε̣ πΗ [ε]τε̣ Μπε̣Че̣ι-
    Με ε Νᴀϊ Μ[. . . . . Μ] πΡΗτε ε-

8   τΟΥϣΟΟπ̄ Μ[ΜΟϲ] ᴀλλᴀ ΝτΟЧ
    ϩωωЧ Νϩρᴀϊ ϩΜ [πι]ϣᴀϫε Μ [πρ]Η̣-

10 τε ετЧϣΟΟπ̄ Μ̣ΜΟϲ . . . . .
    ᴀЧϫι Μ ΠΟΥεϲ [

12 ϩΜ Μᴀ Νιμ εᴀ[Ч]ϣ[ω]πε Ν̣ [ϩᴀ-]
    πλΟΥΝ ᴀΥω Ν̄ ΟΥᴀ τΟτε ϭᴀ[Ρ]

14 ᴀ̣[ЧΝ]ΟΥϩΜ Ν6ι [π]ᴀ̣ϊ ετΝ ϣϭ[ΟΜ]
    ΜΜΟЧ ε Ρ ΧωΡιΝ εΒΟλ ϩιτΝ [Νᴀϊ]

16 τΗΡΟΥ· ϣᴀЧϣωπε εΝτ[. .
    Νᴀϊ τΗΡΟΥ· εϣωπ̄ εЧϣᴀ[ΝΟΥ]

18 ωϣ πᴀλιΝ ΟΝ ε[ϲ]ε̣ ЧπωΡ[ϫ Ν-]
    ϲ[ᴀ]ΒΟλ Ν Νᴀϊ τΗΡΟΥ· ᴀΥω Ν[τΟЧ]

20 ΝЧρ ᴀΝᴀΧωρι[Ν ε]ΡΟЧ ΜᴀΥᴀ[ᴀЧ]
    πᴀϊ ϭᴀρ ϣᴀ[Чϣ]ωπε [Ν] ΝΟΥ[τ-]

43,23   Written ΜΟΥ <u>Υ</u>ΜΝ (imperfection in papyrus).

43,24   ]Ν̣ [. . .]ε̣, no supralinear stroke above Ν̣ (possibly read πι̣ϲ instead); ε̣,
        or else ϲ | or 6ε πΗ?

43,27   λ, or else ᴀ.

43,28-29 E.g., ϣᴀЧ[ϫ]ϲ ΝΟ[ΥΝΟ6Ν]/εΝΝΟϲᴀ.

43,29   Neither Ν had a supralinear stroke | ᴀΥω *vacat* .

43,30   Or possibly [π]ϣᴀϣΝ[ϲ; second ϣ and Ν read with ultraviolet in 1971,
        papyrus subsequently damaged; now best attested (though imperfectly) in
        photo A.

44,2   Lit., himself; cf. the admonition of 130,18ff to awaken the god within
        oneself.

22   those things which exist, because the immortal
mind ($\nu o\hat{\upsilon}\varsigma$) and immortal soul ($\psi\upsilon\chi\acute{\eta}$),
24   [   ] . . . about them
making an inquiry about it first,
26   not about conduct ($\pi\rho\tilde{a}\xi\iota\varsigma$)
but ($\dot{a}\lambda\lambda\dot{a}$) about their deeds.
28   For ($\gamma\acute{a}\rho$) from him he [
[   ] and
30   [   ] obtain [
[44]
The ($+\delta\acute{\epsilon}$) (type of) humanity that can be saved
2   is the one that seeks itself and
its mind ($\nu o\hat{\upsilon}\varsigma$) and finds each one
4   of them. Oh how much power
this (type) has! The humanity [$(+\delta\acute{\epsilon})$]
6   that has been saved is that which has not known
how these [
8   as they exist, but ($\dot{a}\lambda\lambda\dot{a}$) it is
itself within [the] word
10   as it exists [in it
received each [
12   in every place, having become
simple ($\dot{a}\pi\lambda o\hat{\upsilon}\nu$) and one; for ($\gamma\acute{a}\rho$) then ($\tau\acute{o}\tau\epsilon$)
14   this (type) is saved because it can
pass ($\chi\omega\rho\epsilon\hat{\iota}\nu$) through [them]
16   all and can become [
them all. If it
18   [wishes], then it again ($\pi\acute{a}\lambda\iota\nu$) parts
from them all and
20   withdraws ($\dot{a}\nu a\chi\omega\rho\epsilon\hat{\iota}\nu$) into itself [alone];
for ($\gamma\acute{a}\rho$) it can become divine

44,3-4   Or, each water.
44,6   Or, the humanity that saves.
44,7-8   For ⲙ ⲡⲣ ⲏ ⲧ ⲉ. . .ⲙ ⲙ ⲟ ⲥ; cf. 16,1-2; 44,9-10; and 129,7-8; see Crum,
              305a and compare ⲛ ⲑⲉ. . .ⲙ ⲙ ⲟ ⲥ.
44,7   E.g., ⲙ[ⲙ ⲟ ⲟ ⲧ]; or ⲙ[ⲙ ⲁ ⲁ ⲧ].
44,15   I.e., ⲭ ⲱ ⲣ ⲥ.
44,16   E.g., ⲉ ⲛ [ⲧ ⲙ ⲉ ⲉ].
44,17   Elided form of ⲉ ⲩ ⲱ ⲡ ⲉ.
44,20 & 22 ⲁ ⲛ ⲁ ⲭ ⲱ ⲡ ⲥ ⲛ, the length of the lacuna demands restoration of −ⲡ ⲥ ⲛ.
44,20-22 Cf. 45,12-15.
44,20   ⲛ̣, the left vertical stroke and part of the supralinear stroke survive.

22 ε αϥρ αναχω[ρ]ɴ ε πⲛⲟⲩⲧⲉ
ⲡⲁï ⲁⲛⲟⲕ ⲉⲧ[ⲁɪⲥ]ⲱⲧⲙ ⲉⲣⲟϥ

24 ⲁïⲉɪⲛⲉ ⲉ̣ⲣⲁï ⲛ ⲟ̣ⲩⲥⲙ[ⲟ]ⲩ ⲙ ⲡ[ⲛⲟⲩ–]
ⲧⲉ ⲉⲧⲟⲛ̣ⲅ ⲁⲩⲱ ⲛⲛ ⲁⲧⲙɪⲥⲉ [ⲉⲧⲛ–]

26 ⲅ̣ⲣⲁï ⲅⲛ ⲟⲩⲙⲛ̄ⲧⲙⲉ ⲙⲛ ⲡɪⲕ[ⲁ̄ⲥ]
ⲛⲛ ⲁⲧⲙɪⲥⲉ ⲙⲛ ⲡɪⲡⲣⲱⲧⲟⲫⲁ̣[ⲛ]

28 ⲛⲛ [ⲁ]ⲧⲛⲁⲩ ⲉⲣⲟϥ ⲛ ⲅ̣ⲟⲟⲩⲧ̄ ⲛ̣ ⲧ[ⲉ–]
ⲗ̣ɪⲟⲥ ⲛ ⲛⲟⲩⲥ ⲙⲛ ⲡɪⲁⲧⲛⲁⲩ ⲉ–

30 ⲣⲟϥ ⲛ̣ ⲁⲗⲟⲩ ⲛ ⲱ̄ⲙ̄ⲧ̄ⲅ̣ⲟ[ⲟ]ⲩⲧ̄
ⲙ[ⲛ ⲡɪⲁ]ⲩ̄ⲧⲟⲅ̣[ⲉⲛ]ⲏⲥ ⲛ [ⲛⲟ]ⲩ̣ⲧ̣ⲉ̣

[ⲙ̄]ⲉ̣

ⲁⲩⲱ ⲡⲉⲝⲁï ⲙ̄ ⲡⲁⲗⲟⲩ ⲛⲧⲉ ⲡⲁⲗⲟⲩ

2 ⲉⲧⲕⲏ ⲛⲙⲙⲁï ⲛ̄ⲫⲏⲥⲏⲕ ⲝⲉⲩ–
ⲛ ϭⲟⲙ ⲛ ⲧⲉⲕⲥⲟⲫɪⲁ ⲉ ⲧⲁⲙⲟⲉɪ ⲉ

4 ⲡɪⲝⲱⲱⲣⲉ ⲉⲃⲟⲗ ⲛⲧⲉ ⲡⲣⲱⲙⲉ
[ⲉ]ⲧⲟⲩⲛⲟ[ⲩ]ⲅ̣ⲙ ⲙⲙⲟϥ· ⲁⲩⲱ ⲝⲉ

6 ⲛ[ɪ]ⲙ ⲛ[ⲉ] ⲛⲏ [ⲉ]ⲧ̄[ⲧ]ⲉ̣ⲅ ⲉⲣⲟϥ· ⲁⲩⲱ
ⲝⲉ ⲛɪⲙ ⲛⲉ̣ [ⲛⲏ ⲉ]ⲧⲡⲱⲱ ⲙⲙⲟϥ

8 ⲝ[ⲉ]ⲕⲁⲁⲥ ⲉ[ⲩⲛ]ⲁⲉɪⲙⲉ ⲛϭɪ ⲛɪⲥⲱ–
ⲧ[ⲛ̄] ⲉⲧⲟⲛⲅ̣ [ⲁ]ⲩⲱ ⲧⲟⲧⲉ ⲁϥⲝⲟⲟⲥ

10 ⲛⲁ[ï . . . .] .ⲁ̣ ⲅⲛ ⲟⲩ‹ⲟⲩ›ⲱⲛ̣ⲅ ⲉⲃⲟⲗ
ⲛϭɪ ⲡⲁⲗⲟ̣ⲩ ⲛⲧⲉ ⲡⲁⲗⲟⲩ ⲛ̄ⲫⲏⲥⲏⲕ

12 ⲝⲉ ⲉⲱⲱⲡⲉ ⲉϥⲅ̣ⲱⲁⲛⲣ ⲁ[ⲛⲁⲭ]ⲱ–
ⲣ[ɪ] ⲉⲣⲟϥ ⲙⲁⲩⲁⲁϥ ⲛ ⲟⲩⲙⲏⲏⲱⲉ

14 ⲛ ⲥⲟⲡ ⲁⲩⲱ ⲛϥⲱⲱⲡⲉ ⲙ ⲡⲕⲱ–
[ⲧ]ⲉ ⲛ ⲧ̄ⲛⲱⲥɪⲥ ⲛⲧⲉ ⲅⲉⲛⲕⲟⲟⲩⲉ

16 [ⲙ]ⲁϥⲉɪⲙⲉ ⲛϭɪ ⲡɪⲛⲟⲩⲥ ⲙⲛ ⲧ̄–
[ⲁⲣ]ⲭⲏ ⲛⲛ ⲁⲧⲙⲟⲩ· ⲧⲟⲧⲉ ⲟⲩⲛ–

18 [ⲧ]ⲁϥ ⲙⲙⲁⲩ ⲛ ⲟⲩⲱⲱⲧ̄ ⲱ[ⲁ]ϥ–
ⲕⲱⲧⲉ ⲅⲁⲣ ⲅⲱⲱ[ϥ] ⲙ̄ⲛⲧⲁϥ ⲁⲩⲱ

20 [ⲱ]ⲁϥⲡⲱⲣⲝ ⲛⲥ[ⲁ]ⲃⲟⲗ ⲙⲙⲟϥ ⲛϥ–
[ⲁ]ⲅⲉⲣⲁⲧϥ ⲛ .[. . . .] ⲛϥⲱⲱⲡⲉ ⲛ–

44,23-31 The doxology marks the end of the audition. Here the Spirit is named as the living, unborn God.

44,25 ⲁⲧ′, ⲧ more fully preserved in 1972; now best attested in photo A; papyrus subsequently damaged.

44,30 ⲱⲙ̄ⲧ′, ⲧ more fully preserved in 1980; now best attested in photo A; papyrus subsequently damaged.

45 Pagination; only a trace of the ornamental bar below the second numeral survives; the numerals do not survive.

45,1-57,12 *The Revelations from Ephesech* (part 2)

45,1 A new set of revelations from Ephesech begins, but the anthropological

22   by having taken refuge in god."
      When [I] heard this,
24   I brought a blessing to the truly living
      and unborn God [who is]
26   in truth, (to) the unborn Kalyptos (καλυπτός),
      (to) the Protophanes (πρωτοφανής),
28   the invisible male perfect (τέλειος)
      mind (νοῦς), (to) the invisible
30   thrice-male Child
      [and (to) the] divine Autogenes (αὐτογενής)

                                           [4]5

      I said to the child of the child
2   Ephesech who was with me, "Can
      your wisdom (σοφία) instruct me about
4   the scattering of the (type of) humanity
      that is saved, and (about) who
6   those are that are mixed with it and
      who those are that divide it,
8   in order that the living elect
      might know?" Then (τότε) the
10   child of the child
      Ephesek told [me   ] openly,
12   "When (this type) withdraws (ἀναχωρεῖν)
      into itself alone many
14   times and and is close to
      the knowledge (γνῶσις) of others,
16   mind (νοῦς) and immortal [origin (ἀρχή)] will [not]
      understand. Then (τότε)
18   (this type) has a shortage,
      for (γάρ) it turns, has nothing and
20   separates from it and
      stands [   ] and exists

---

          concerns about who can and cannot be saved continue; see 13,8n.
45,2-3   I.e., ⲍⲉ ⲟⲩⲛ ⲅⲟⲙ | cf. Wis. 9:9-11.
45,10   ⲛⲁ[ⲓ̈, lines 11-13 have an uninscribed space in this position owing to an
          imperfection in the papyrus | ⲏⲛ, or possibly ⲙⲛ.
45,11   –ⲥⲏⲕ , sic; cf. –ⲥⲏⲭ in line 2.
45,13   —ⲣ[ⲥ], no room for –ⲣ[ⲥⲛ].
45,14-15 For ⲙⲡⲕⲱⲧⲉ as πρός +acc, see Crum, 126b.
45,16   [ⲙ]ⲁϥ´, also possible is [ϣ]ⲁϥ´.
45,18   Lit., he. Shortage denotes the loss suffered by the heavenly world.

22 [ϩ]ⲣⲁⲓ̈ ϩⲛ ⲟⲩ[ϩⲟⲣ]ⲙ̄ⲏ ⲛ ϣⲙ̄ⲙⲟ·
 [ⲉ] ⲡⲙⲁ ⲛⲩϣⲱⲡⲉ ⲛ ⲟⲩⲁ ϣⲁⲩ—
24 ⲉⲓⲛ[ⲉ] ϭⲉ ⲛ ⲟⲩⲙⲏⲏϣⲉ ⲙ̄ ⲙⲟⲣ—
 [ⲫ]ⲏ[·] ⲁⲩⲱ ⲉⲩϣⲁⲛⲣⲓⲕⲉ ϣⲁⲩ—
26 [ϣ]ⲱⲡⲉ ⲉⲩϣⲓⲛⲉ ⲛⲥⲁ ⲛⲏ ⲉⲧⲉ
 [ⲛ]ⲥⲉϣⲟⲟⲡ̄ ⲁⲛ· ⲁⲩⲱ ⲉⲩϣⲁⲛ—
28 ϩⲉ ⲉϩⲣⲁⲓ̈ ⲉ ⲛⲁⲓ̈ ϩⲛ ⲟⲩⲛⲟⲏⲙⲁ
 ⲁⲩⲱ ⲉⲙ̄ⲛ ϭ[ⲟ]ⲙ ⲛⲩⲉⲓ[ᵛ]ⲙⲉ ⲉ—
30 ⲣⲟⲟⲩ ⲛ ⲕⲉ[ⲣ]ⲏⲧⲉ· ⲉ[ⲓ ᵛ ⲙ]ⲏⲧⲓ
 ⲙ̅ⲋ̅
 ⲛⲩⲁⲓ ⲙ̄ ⲡⲟⲩⲟⲉⲓⲛ ϣⲁⲩϣⲱⲡⲉ ⲛ
2 ⲟⲩⲫⲩⲥⲓⲥ· ⲁⲩⲱ ⲙ̄ ⲡⲉⲓ̈ⲣⲏⲧⲉ
 ϣⲁⲩⲉⲓ ⲉϩⲣⲁⲓ̈ ⲉⲩⲁⲡⲟ ⲉⲧⲃⲏⲏⲧϥ
4 ⲁⲩⲱ ϣⲁⲩⲣ ⲁⲧϣⲁⲝⲉ ⲉⲧⲃⲉ ⲛ[ⲓ—]
 ⲙ̄ⲕⲟⲟϩ· ⲙⲛ ϯⲙⲛ[ⲧ]ⲁⲧⲛ [ⲁ]ⲣⲏ[ⲝϥ]
6 ⲛ̄ⲧⲉ ϯⲅⲩⲗⲏ· ⲉⲩ[ⲛⲧ]ⲁϥ [ⲛ] ⲟⲩϭⲟⲙ
 ⲛ ϣⲁ ⲉⲛⲉϩ ⲙ̄[ⲙⲁⲩ ⲛ] ⲁⲧⲙⲟⲩ
8 ϣⲁⲩⲥⲟⲛϩϥ ⲛ̄ϩ[ⲣⲁⲓ̈ ϩⲓ]ⲙ ⲡⲓⲉⲓ ⲉ [ⲑⲏ] ⲛ—
 ⲧⲉ ⲡⲥⲱⲙⲁ· ϣⲁ[ⲩⲁⲓ]ⲧϥ ⲉⲩⲟⲛ[ϩ]
10 ⲁⲩⲱ ϣⲁⲩⲥⲟⲛϩ[ϥ ⲛ ⲟⲩⲟⲉⲓ]ϣ
 ⲛⲓⲙ ⲛ̄ϩⲣⲁⲓ̈ ϩⲛ ϩⲉⲛⲥⲛⲁⲩϩ ⲉⲧⲛⲁ—
12 ϣⲧ ⲉⲩϭⲱⲝⲉ ᵛᵛᵛ ⲙ̄ⲙⲟϥ ⲉⲃⲟⲗ
 ϩⲓ[ⲧⲛ] ⲛⲓϣⲉ ⲛⲓⲙ ⲉⲧϩⲟⲟⲩ· ϣⲁⲛ—
14 ⲧϥⲁ[ⲓ]ⲧϥ ⲟⲛ ⲁⲩⲱ ⲛ̄ϥⲣ ⲁⲣⲝⲓ ⲟⲛ
 ⲉϣⲱⲡⲉ ϩⲣⲁⲓ̈ ⲛ̄ϩⲏⲧϥ· ⲉⲧⲃⲉ ⲡ[ⲁⲓ̈]
16 ⲥⲉⲧⲏϣ ⲉϩⲣⲁⲓ̈ ⲉⲝ̄ⲛ ⲡⲓⲟⲩⲝⲁⲓ̈ ⲛ̄[ⲧⲉ]
 ⲛⲁⲓ̈· ⲁⲩⲱ ⲛⲁⲓ̈ϭⲟⲙ ⲛⲁⲓ̈ ⲥⲉϣⲟ[ⲟⲡ̄]
18 ϩⲙ ⲡⲓⲙⲁ· ⲁⲩⲱ ⲛ̄ϩⲣⲁⲓ̈ ϩⲛ ⲛⲓⲁⲩ[ⲧⲟ—]
 ⲅⲉⲛⲏⲥ ⲕⲁⲧⲁ ⲡⲟⲩⲁ ⲡⲟⲩⲁ ⲛ̄ⲧⲉ ⲛ[ⲓⲉ—]
20 ⲱⲛ ⲥⲉⲁϩⲉⲣⲁ[ⲧⲟ]ⲩ ⲛ̄ϭⲓ ϩⲉⲛⲉⲟⲟⲩ
 ϩⲓⲛⲁ ⲝⲉ ⲉϥⲉⲛⲟ[ⲩ]ϩⲙ ⲛⲥⲁⲥⲡⲓⲣ ⲛⲁ[ⲓ̈]

45,22 For ϩⲟⲣⲙⲏ in a positive sense, see 29,11 | or, within.
45,25 ⲣⲓⲕⲉ = κλίνειν.
45,28 Or, in perception.
45,29 & 30 An uninscribed space was probably left in each of the lacunas because of an imperfection in the papyrus (visible in *Facsimile Edition: Codex VIII*, 45, lines 24-28).
46,1-2 Lit., he becomes nature.
46,3 Lit., comes down to a birth.
46,5 Lit., infinity; cf. 1,15f.
46,7 Not room for ⲛⲛ].
46,8 No circumflex over the group ⲉⲓ, and no abnormal writing of this verb |

22 by means of an alien [impulse (ὁρμή)].
    Instead of becoming one,
24 therefore, it takes many forms (μορφή).
    When it turns aside, it
26 comes into being seeking those things that
    do not exist. When it
28 falls down to them in thought (νόημα),
    then it cannot understand them
30 in another way, unless perhaps (εἰ μήτι)
    46
    it is enlightened, and it will become
2   (a part of) nature (φύσις). Thus
    (this type) comes down to birth because of it
4   and is speechless because of the pains
    and the infiniteness
6   of matter (ὕλη). Although it possesses an
    eternal and immortal power,
8   (this type) is bound within the [movement]
    of the body (σῶμα). It is [made] alive
10 and is bound [always]
    within cruel,
12 cutting bonds
    by every evil spirit, until
14 it [acts] again and begins (ἄρχειν) again
    to come to its senses. Therefore,
16 (powers) are appointed for their salvation,
    and each of the powers resides
18 in this world. Within the self-begotten
    ones (αὐτογενής) corresponding to (κατά) each of
20 the [aeons (αἰών)] stand glories
    so that (ἵνα) one who is in the [world]

---

        lit., [advance].
46,12   ⲩⲩⲩ, space left uninscribed because of an imperfection in the papyrus.
46,14   Written ⲁ[ⲥ]ⲩ̅ⲧϥ owing to an imperfection in the papyrus I ⲁⲣⲝⲥ,
        common miswriting of ⲁⲣⲭⲥ.
46,15   I.e., to recognize one's true spiritual self. Cf. *Apoc.Pet.* VII 84,12-13; Luke
        15:17.
46,17   I.e., ⲛⲉⲓ̈ϭⲟⲙ ⲛⲁⲓ̈.
46,18-31 I.e., the self-begotten aeons contain the saving thoughts.
46,18   Lit., in this place.
46,21   I.e., ⲛⲥⲁⲥⲡⲓⲣ ⟨ⲛ⟩ ⲛⲁⲓ̈ I As glories are hypostasized thoughts, one's
        thoughts become the means of attaining salvation.

22 ⲚϬⲒ ⲠⲎ ⲈⲦⲘ Ⲡ[ⲤⲘⲀ Ⲛ]ⲤⲈⲞⲞⲨ ⲆⲈ Ϩ[ⲈⲚ–]
    ⲚⲞⲎⲘⲀ ⲚⲈ Ⲛ ⲦⲈⲖ[Ⲥ]ⲞⲤ ⲈⲨⲞⲚϨ Ⲉ Ⲛ[Ⲥ–]
24 ϬⲞⲘ ⲚⲤⲈⲦⲀⲔⲞ ⟨ⲀⲚ⟩ ⲆⲈ ϨⲈⲚⲦⲨⲠⲞⲤ [ⲚⲈ]
    ⲚⲦⲈ ⲞⲨⲞⲨⳆⲀⲒ· ⲈⲦⲈ ⲈϢⲀⲢ[Ⲉ]Ⲡ[ⲞⲨⲀ]
26 ⲠⲞⲨⲀ ⳆⲒⲦⲞⲨ ⲈⲨⲈⲚⲞⲨϨⲘ ⲈϨⲢ[ⲀⲒ Ⲉ–]
    ⲢⲞⲞⲨ· ⲀⲨⲰ ⲈϤⳆⲤ ⲦⲨⲠⲞⲤ· ⲈϤ–
28 ⳆⲤ ϬⲞⲘ ⲈⲂⲞⲖ ϨⲒⲦⲚ ⲠⲀⲒ ⲠⲀⲒ· ⲀⲨ[Ⲱ]
    ⲈⲨⲚⲦⲀϤ Ⲙ ⲠⲤⲈⲞⲞⲨ Ⲛ ⲞⲨⲂⲞⲎⲐⲞ[Ⲥ]
30 Ⲙ ⲠⲤⲢ[Ⲏ]ⲦⲈ ϢⲀϤⲤ[Ⲥ]ⲚⲈ Ⲙ ⲠⲤⲔⲞⲤⲘⲞⲤ
    ⲀⲨ[Ⲱ ⲚⲤ]Ⲉ[Ⲱ]Ⲛ [. . .]Ⲙ· ⲀⲨⲰ ⲤⲈϢⲞ–
                                            Ⲙ̄[Ϩ]

    ⲞⲠ ⲚϬⲒ ⲚⲤⲢⲈϤⲀⲢⲈϨ ⲚⲦⲈ ϮⲮⲨⲬⲎ
2   ⲚⲚ ⲀⲨⲘⲞⲨ ̄ⲄⲀⲘⲀⲖ̄Ⲓ̄Ⲏ̄Ⲗ ̄Ⲙ̄Ⲛ̄
    ⲤⲦⲢⲈⲘⲮⲞⲨⲬⲞⲤ· ⲀⲨⲰ ̄Ⲁ̄Ⲕ̄Ⲣ̄Ⲁ̄Ⲙ̄Ⲁ̄Ⲥ̄
4   [Ⲙ]Ⲛ ̄Ⲗ̄Ⲱ̄Ⲏ̄Ⲗ̄· ⲀⲨⲰ ̄Ⲙ̄Ⲛ̄Ⲏ̄Ⲥ̄Ⲓ̄Ⲛ̄Ⲟ̄Ⲩ̄Ⲥ̄·
    [Ⲡ]ⲀⲒ Ⲡ[Ⲥ]Ⲡ̄Ⲛ̄Ⲁ̄ [Ⲡ]Ⲉ ⲚⲚ ⲀⲨⲘⲞⲨ ̄Ⲓ̄Ⲉ̄Ⲥ̄Ⲥ̄Ⲉ̄Ⲩ̄Ⲥ̄
6   [Ⲙ]Ⲁ̄Ϫ̄Ⲁ̄Ⲣ̄Ⲉ̄Ⲩ̄[Ⲥ̄] ̄Ⲓ̄Ⲉ̄[Ⲥ̄]Ⲥ̄Ⲉ̄Ⲇ̄Ⲉ̄Ⲕ̄Ⲉ̄Ⲩ̄Ⲥ̄:
    [.] ⲀϮⲦⲞⲨ [. . .] ̄Ⲛ̄ⲦⲈ ⲠⲤⲀⲖⲞⲨ ⲠⲈ
8   [. .]Ⲱ̄Ⲣ̄ ⲠⲀⲖ[Ⲟ]Ⲩ ⲚⲦⲈ ⲠⲀⲖⲞⲨ· ⲀⲨⲰ
    .[. .] . .[. . . .]ⲞⲔ· ⲞⲢⲘⲞⲤ ⲆⲈ
10 ⲠⲈ[. . . . . .]Ϣ̄ Ⲉ̄ⳆⲚ ϮⲤⲠⲞⲢⲀ ⲈⲦⲞ–
    ̄Ⲛ̄Ϩ· ⲔⲀⲘ[. .]Ⲏ̄Ⲗ̄ ⲆⲈ ⲠⲈ ⲠⲤⲢⲈϤϮ ̄Ⲡ̄Ⲛ̄Ⲁ̄
12 ⲚⲎ ⲆⲈ Ϭ[Ⲉ]ⲀϨⲈⲢⲀⲦⲞⲨ ⲚⲚⲀϨⲢ[ⲀⲨ·] Ϭⲉ–

46,24   ⟨ⲀⲚ⟩, carelessly omitted by a copyist.
46,25   ⲈϢⲀ̄Ⲣ[Ⲉ], ⲁ read from ambiguous trace; Ⲣ, or else ϥ, ϯ, or ⲯ; not
         ⲈϢⲰⲠ̄[Ⲉ].
46,30   I.e., ⲠⲈⲒⲢⲎⲦⲈ | cf. 4,13-28.
46,31   ]Ⲙ, connected to the preceding letter by a supralinear stroke; possibly
         [ⲤⲰⲦ]Ⲙ.
47,1ff   Many of the heavenly beings named on this page are well known from other
         NHC sources; for the Autogenes aeons, see especially *Gos. Eg.* III 52-53;
         62-65.
47,2   Gamaliel is known in the O.T., see Num 1:10 and 2:20. According to *Gos.Eg.*
         III 52,19-21; 64,24-27, he is one of the ministers of the First Light Harmozel
         of the Autogenes; cf. *Apoc.Adam* V 75,22-26; *Melch.* IX 5,17-20; *Marsanes* X
         64,19-20; *Trim. Prot.* XIII 48,25-30.
47,3   For Akrames and Strompsouchos, see *Gos.Eg.* III 65,6-8.
47,4   [Ⲙ]Ⲛ, part of the supralinear stroke connecting these letters survives along
         with the letter Ⲛ | Ⲱ, or else ⲁ, Ⲙ, or Ϣ; ⲖⲀ[ⲢⲤ]ⲎⲖ is also possible
         with crowding (but not ⲀⲢⲒ̈ⲎⲖ or Ⲓ̈ⲰⲎⲖ) | Ⲏ̄, supralinear stroke is not
         preserved above this letter (in lacuna) | Loel, *hapax leg.* in NHC. David-
         son, *Angels*, 175, so names an angel of the south wind. Mnesinous is
         connected at 6,10 with baptismal waters as a companion of Micheus and

22   might be saved beside them. The glories (+δέ) are
      perfect (τέλειος) thoughts (νόημα) appearing in powers.
24   They are imperishable because [they are] models (τύπος)
      of salvation which each
26   saved one receives.
      One receives a model (τύπος) (and)
28   strength from each of them, and
      with the glory as a helper (βοηθός)
30   one will thus pass out from the world (κόσμος)
      [and the aeons (αἰών)   ]. These

                                              4[7]

      are the guardians of the immortal
2   soul (ψυχή): Gamaliel and
      Strempsouchos, Akramas
4   and Loel, and Mnesinous.
      [This is the] immortal spirit (πνεῦμα), Yesseus-
6   [M]azareu[s]-Ye[s]sedekeus.
      (He) is [   ] of the child
8   [   ]–or, the child of the child, and
      [   ] But (δέ) Ormos
10   is [   ] over the living seed (σπορά)
      and Kam-[ ]el is the spirit-giver (-πνεῦμα).
12   There (+δέ) stand before [them] the following:

      Michar; cf. *Gos.Eg.* III 64,15-16; *Apoc.Adam* V 84,5-8; *Trim. Prot.* XIII 48,19-20.
47,5-6   Yesseus-Mazareus-Yessedekeus may be a corruption of the name Jesus.
         He is the great attendant of the living water in *Gos.Eg.* III 66,10-15 where
         he is also called the child of the child. In *Apoc.Adam* V 85,29-31, he is the
         holy seed, the living water. Schenke, "Gnostic Sethianism," 603, identi
         fies him as the personification of the celestial baptismal water.
47,5   Or [ⲚⲀⲒ ⲚⲤ]ⲠⲚⲀ [Ⲛ]Ⲉ | ⲓ̈, the supralinear stroke begins over this
         letter.
47,6   ⲓ̈, the supralinear stroke begins over this letter.
47,7   [.], trace of ⲃ, ⲑ, ⲟ, ⲣ, or ⲅ (not ⲫ) | ϯ., or else ⲯ; there was no supralinear
         stroke above this group of letters.
47,8-10 At 13,8 Ephesech is called the child of the child; elsewhere the phrase refers
         to the heavenly Adam; cf. Schenke, "Das Sethianische Systems," 170.
47,8   ]ⲱⲡ̄, or else]ⲱ̄ⲃ̄; the supralinear stroke began earlier in the word
         (where there is now a lacuna).
47,9   For Ormos, cf. Hormos in *Gos.Eg.* III 60,2. Davidson, *Angels*, 215, lists an
         Ormos as the "angel of the tenth hour of the day, serving under Uriel."
47,11   E.g., ⲔⲀⲘ[ⲀⲀⲤ]ⲎⲀ; perhaps as a variant for Gamalial; cf. *Trim. Prot.* XIII
         48,19-20. At 58,21-22 Gabriel is called a spirit-giver.
47,12   ϭⲉ–, there was no stroke above these letters | ϭ, or else ⲟⲩ.

ïⲥⲁⲩⲏⲗ ⲙⲛ ⲁⲩⲇⲁⲏⲗ ⲁⲩⲱ [ⲁ]ⲃⲣⲁⲥⲁⲝ
14 ⲛ︦ⲥⲁⲛⲧⲃⲁ ⲫⲁⲗⲉⲣⲓⲥ ⲛⲙ ⲫⲁⲗⲥⲏⲥ
[ⲁⲩ]ⲱ ⲉⲩⲣⲓⲟⲥ· ⲛⲥⲣⲉⲩⲁⲣⲉϩ ⲛ︦ⲧⲉ
16 [ⲡⲓ]ⲉⲟⲟⲩ ⲥⲧⲏⲑⲉⲩⲥ ⲙⲛ ⲑⲉⲟ—
[ⲡⲉ]ⲙⲡⲧⲟⲥ ⲙⲛ ⲉⲩⲣⲩⲙⲉⲛⲉⲩⲥ
18 ⲙⲛ ⲟⲁⲥⲏⲛ· ⲛⲓⲃⲟⲏⲑⲟⲥ ⲇⲉ ϩ[ⲛ]
[ϩ]ⲱⲃ ⲛⲓⲙ ⲡⲉ ⲃⲁ[. . .]ⲙⲟⲥ· ⲙⲛ
20 [.]ⲥⲱⲛ ⲙⲛ ⲉⲓⲣ[.]ⲛ· ⲙⲛ ⲗⲁⲗⲁⲙⲉⲩⲥ
ⲙⲛ ⲉⲓⲇⲟⲙⲉⲛⲉⲩⲥ· ⲙⲛ ⲁⲩⲑⲣⲟⲩ—
22 [ⲛ]ⲓⲟⲥ· ⲛⲥⲣⲉⲩϯ ϩⲁⲡ︦ ⲡⲉ ⲥⲩⲙⲫⲑⲁⲣ
[ⲁ]ⲩⲱ ⲉⲩⲕⲣⲉⲃⲱⲥ ⲙⲛ ⲕⲉⲓⲗⲁⲣ:
24 [ⲡ]ⲓ[ⲡⲁ]ⲣⲁⲗⲏⲙⲡⲧⲱⲣ ⲥⲁⲙⲃⲗⲱ· ⲛⲓ—
[ⲁⲩ]ⲅⲉⲗⲟⲥ ⲛ ⲣⲉⲩϫⲓ ⲙⲟⲉⲓⲧ ϩⲏⲧⲟⲩ
26 [ⲛ] ⲛⲓⲅⲏⲡⲉ ⲛ ⲕⲗⲟⲟⲗⲉ ⲥⲁⲫⲫⲱ
ⲙⲛ ⲑⲟⲩⲣⲱ: ⲁⲩ︦ ⲛⲁ ï ⲉⲧⲁ ⲩ ϫ ⲟ—
28 ⲟ ⲩ ⲁ ⲩⲧⲁⲙⲟ ï ⲉ ⲛⲁ ï ⲧⲏⲣⲟⲩ ⲉⲧ—
ϣⲟⲟⲡ︦ ϩⲛ ⲛⲓⲁⲩⲧⲟⲅⲉⲛⲏⲥ ⲛ—
30 ⲛ ⲉⲱⲛ ⲁⲩⲱ ⲛⲉⲧⲉ ⲛ [ⲟⲩ]ⲟⲉⲓⲛ
ⲙ︦ⲏ
ⲧⲏⲣⲟⲩ ⲛ ϣ ⲁ ⲉⲛⲉϩ· ⲁⲩⲱ ⲛ ⲧⲉⲗⲓⲟⲥ
2 ⲉⲩϫⲏⲕ ⲉⲃⲟⲗ ⲛ ⲕⲁⲧⲁ ⲟⲩⲁ· ⲁⲩⲱ
ⲁ ï ⲛⲁⲩ ⲕⲁⲧⲁ ⲡⲟⲩⲁ ⲡ[ⲟ]ⲩⲁ ⲛⲧⲉ
4 ⲛⲓⲉⲱⲛ ⲉⲩⲕⲁϩ ⲉϥⲟ[ⲛ]ϩ ⲙⲛ [ⲟⲩ—]
ⲙⲟⲟⲩ ⲉϥⲟⲛϩ· ⲙ[ⲛ] ⲟⲩ[ⲁⲏ]ⲣ [ⲉϥⲉ]
6 ⲛ ⲟⲩⲟⲉⲓⲛ· ⲁⲩⲱ [ⲟ]ⲩⲕⲱϩ[ⲧ ⲉⲧⲉ—]
ⲙⲉϥⲣⲱⲕ[ϩ ⲛⲁ ï ⲧ]ⲏⲣⲟⲩ ⲉϩ[ⲉⲛ—]
8 ϩⲁⲡⲗⲟⲩⲛ ⲛⲉ [ⲁⲩ]ⲱ ⲛⲛ ⲁⲧ[ⲟⲩⲱ—]
ⲧⲃ ⲉⲃⲟⲗ· ⲙⲛ ϩ[ⲉⲛϫⲱⲟⲛ ⲛϩ]ⲁ—

47,13   Supralinear stroke above ⲃⲣⲁ is in lacuna | Isauel (Seisauel?) and Audael
           are *hapax leg.* in NHC. Abrasax appears in *Gos.Eg.* III 52,26-53,1 as a
           minister of the Light Eleleth; in *Apoc.Adam* V 75,22-26 he, Gamaliel and
           Sablo (the inheritors) descend to lead the elect from the world. The
           haeresiologists place him in the system of Basilides as the archon who
           mediates between men and animals (Iren. *Adv.Haer.* I.9.4).
47,14   ⲛⲥⲁⲛ, characteristic top traces | ⲛⲙ, i.e. ⲙⲛ.
47,16-18   In *Gos.Eg.* III 64,13 Theopemptos is a great general. In *Gos.Eg.* III 65,1-5, an
           Olses and Hereumaios preside over the rising sun.
47,20   For Lalameus, see 88,13 and *Allogenes* XI 54,20.
47,21   For Authrounios, see 8-9 above and 127,22ff.
47,22   ⲡⲉ, sic | for the great judges, see also 9,6-9.
47,24   Also Sablo and Samlo; see 47,13n.

Seisauel and Audael and [A]brasax;
14 the myriads Phaleris, Phalses,
[and] Eurios; the guardians of
16 glory, Stetheus,
Theo[pe]mptos, Eurumeneus
18 and Olsen; their (+δέ) assistants (βοηθός) [in]
everything are Ba–[　]–mos,
20 [　]–son, Eir–[　]n, Lalameus,
Eidomeneus and Authrou[n]ios;
22 the judges are Sumphthar,
Eukrebos and Keilar;
24 the inheritor (παραλήμπτωρ) (is) Samblo;
the angels (ἄγγελος) who guide
26 the misty clouds are Sappho
and Thouro." When he had said
28 these things, he told me about all of those
in the self-begotten (αὐτογενής)
30 aeons (αἰών). They were all
48
eternal lights, perfect
2 as perfect individuals (+κατά).
In relation to (κατά) each one of the
4 aeons (αἰών) I saw a living earth, a
living water, [air (ἀήρ) made]
6 of light and a fire [that]
cannot consume. All of [these] are
8 simple (ἀπλοῦν) and immutable:
simple (ἀπλοῦν) and

47,27ff　The topic reverts to that of eternal models.
47,30　I.e., ΝΕΤΟ.
48,3-7　See also 55,15-18; 113,9-14. The search for imperishable elements was one of
the concerns in middle Platonism and of late antiquity in general. This list
of earth, water, air, and fire may ultimately be Persian in origin; see Zaehner,
Zurvan, 67,72ff, 222f; cf. Schweizer, "Slaves of the Elements."
48,5-7　For the restorations, cf. 55,16-19.
48,6　[Ο]ΤΚΩϩ[Τ, first trace is from Β, Τ, Η, Ϛ, Κ, or else Ν; second, from
Θ,Ο,Ρ,Ω, or else Ш | ϩ[Τ., these two letters were connected by a
supralinear stroke.
48,9　τὸ ζῷον represents for Plotinus a mixture of soul and body to form a living
being; see Plot. *Enn.* I.1.2-3,7.

10 ⲡⲗⲟⲩⲛ ⲁⲩⲱ [ⲛ ϣⲁ ⲉⲛ]ⲉϩ
    ⲉⲩⲛⲧⲁⲩ ⲛ ⲟⲩⲥ .[. . .] ⲛ ⲟⲩⲙⲏ–
12 ⲏϣⲉ ⲛ ⲣⲏⲧⲉ· ⲙⲛ ϩ[ⲉ]ⲛϣⲏⲛ
    [ⲉ]ⲙⲁⲩⲧⲁⲕⲟ ⲛ ⲟⲩⲙⲏⲏϣⲉ
14 ⲛ ⲣⲏⲧⲉ· ⲙⲛ ϩⲉⲛⲛⲧⲏⲅ ⲟ[ⲛ] ⲙ̄
    ⲡⲉⲓⲣⲏⲧⲉ ⲙⲛ ⲛⲁⲓ ⲧⲏⲣⲟⲩ ⲙ[ⲛ]
16 ⲟⲩⲕⲁⲣⲡⲟⲥ ⲉⲙⲁϥⲧⲁⲕⲟ ⲙ[ⲛ]
    ϩⲉⲛⲣⲱⲙⲉ ⲉⲧⲟⲛϩ ⲙⲛ ⲉⲓⲇ[ⲟⲥ]
18 ⲛⲓⲙ· ⲙⲛ ϩⲉⲛⲯⲩⲭⲏ ⲛⲛ ⲁⲧⲙ[ⲟⲩ]
    ⲁⲩⲱ ⲙⲟⲣ[ⲫ]ⲏ ⲛⲓⲙ ⲙⲛ ⲉⲓⲇⲟ[ⲥ]
20 ⲛⲓⲙ ⲛⲧⲉ ⲟⲩⲛⲟⲩⲥ· ⲙⲛ ϩⲉⲛ–
    ⲛⲟⲩⲧⲉ ⲛ ⲧⲁⲡⲙⲁⲙⲉ· ⲙⲛ
22 ϩⲉⲛⲁⲅⲅⲉⲗⲟⲥ ⲉⲩϣⲟⲟⲡ̄ ϩ[ⲛ]
    ⲟⲩⲛⲟϭ ⲛⲛ ⲉⲟⲟⲩ· ⲙⲛ ⲟⲩ–
24 ⲥⲱⲙⲁ ⲉⲙⲁⲩⲃⲱⲗ ⲉⲃⲟⲗ [ⲙⲛ]
    ⲟⲩϫⲡⲟ ⲛⲛ ⲁⲧⲙⲓⲥⲉ ⲙⲛ ⲟⲩ–
26 ⲉⲥⲑⲏⲥⲓⲥ ⲛⲛ ⲁⲧⲕⲓⲙ· ⲁⲩⲱ
    ⲛⲉϥⲙⲙⲁⲩ ⲟⲛ ⲡⲉ ⲛϭⲓ ⲡⲏ ⲉⲧ–
28 ϫⲓ ⲙⲕⲁϩ ⲉϥⲉ ⲛ ⲁⲧϫⲓ ⲙⲕⲁϩ·
    ⲛⲉⲩϭⲟⲙ ⲧⲁ[ⲣ] ⲡⲉ ⲛⲧⲉ ⲟⲩϭⲟⲙ· ‾‾‾‾

                          [ⲙⲑ]
   [——   ] .ⲁ. .
2 [. . . . . .] ⲁ[. . . . . . .]ϣⲓⲃⲉ·
   [. . . .] .ⲟⲩ[. . . . . .]ⲁⲧⲃⲱⲗ
4 [. . . .]ⲁ· ⲁ[. . . . . . .]ⲱⲥ ⲛⲁⲓ
   [. . . .]ⲩ[. . . . . .] .ⲩ ⲧⲏⲣⲟⲩ
6 [——   ] .ⲛ̄ⲉ· ⲛⲧⲟⲟⲩ
   [——   ]ⲧⲟⲟⲧⲟⲩ ⲧⲏ–
8 [——   ] .ⲡ ⲛϩⲣⲁⲓ ⲛ
   [——   ]ⲁ· ⲉⲩϣⲟ .[
10 [——   ]ϣⲱⲡⲉ [.] .[
   [——   ]ⲉ̄ ⲛ ⲛⲉ[

Lines 12 and following do not survive.

48,10   ⲓⲉ, a horizontal ligature into the next letter remains; from ⲁ, ⲉ, ⲗ, ⲙ, etc.
48,11   E.g., ⲥⲱ[ⲙⲁ.
48,14   ⲙ̄, only the supralinear stroke survives.
48,19   ⲉⲓⲇⲉ[ⲁ is also possible.
48,24   ⲉⲱⲙⲁⲩ´, sic.
48,25   Or, an origin without birth.
48,27-29 Colpe, "Heidnische, jüdische und Christliche Uberlieferung VI" 153,
           considers this passage a puzzling pagan reference to aphthartodocetic
           Christology. It is more likely a reference to some heavenly power;
           cf. 42,23n.

10   [eternal living animals (ζῷον)],
     having [   ] of
12   many kinds; trees
     of many kinds that do not
14   perish, [also] plants
     of this sort; and all of these:
16   imperishable fruit (καρπός),
     living human beings and every species (εἶδος),
18   immortal souls (ψυχή),
     every form (μορφή) and
20   species (εἶδος) of mind (νοῦς);
     gods of truth,
22   angels (ἄγγελος) existing in
     great glory, an
24   indissoluble body (σῶμα),
     an unborn issue and
26   an immovable perception (αἴσθησις).
     Also there was that which
28   suffers, although it is unable to suffer,
     for (γάρ) it was a power of a power.

                                              [49]
2   [   ] change
     [   ] indissoluble
4   [   ] these
     [   ] all
6   [   ] they are [   ] they
     [
8   [
     [
10   [   ] come into being [
     [
     Lines 12 and following do not survive.

48,28-29   A *paragraphos* is visible under ultraviolet light.
48,29   Or possibly ΝΕ[Ο]ⲩ.
49-58   The line numbers on these pages are only approximate, having been ascer-
           tained by comparison with the remains of page 59, where line 1 can be
           identified with certainty.
49   Line numbers on this page are only approximate I the context and the
           vocabulary suggest that pages 49 and 50 were concerned with the Autogenes
           aeon; cf. pp. 5 and 52.
49,3   Length of the second lacuna attested in photo A.

[ⲛ̄]

ⲛⲧⲉ[

2 ⲣⲟⲩ.[. . . .]ⲛ ϩⲁⲡⲁ[ⲟⲩⲛ

ⲛ ⲧⲉⲗⲓ[ⲟⲥ . . . .]ⲉ .[

4 ⲛ ϣⲁ ⲉⲛ[ⲉϩ . . . . .]ⲟ .[

ⲛ ⲉⲱⲛ ⲛ[

6 ⲡⲉ ⲁⲩⲱ ⲡ[

ⲍⲓ ϭⲟⲙ ⲉⲃ[ⲟⲗ

8 ⲁⲩⲱ ⲛⲉⲩ[

[ϩ]ⲛ ⲟⲩⲙⲛ̄ⲧ̄[

10 [.]ⲣ[.] ϭⲁⲣ ϣ[

[. .] .ⲩ ⲁⲛ· [

Lines 12 and following do not survive.

[ⲛ̄ⲁ]

[——   ]ⲟⲩ ϩⲛ

2 [——   ]ⲑⲟⲣϭⲟ . .ⲥ̄

[——   ]ⲛⲟⲩϭⲓⲧⲏ

4 [——   ]ⲙ̄ⲟⲩ ⲡⲉ

[——   ] .ⲡⲉ ⲡⲉ ⲡⲛⲟⲩ-

6 [ⲧⲉ ——   ] .ⲛⲉⲛⲥⲙⲟⲩ

[——   ]ⲛ ⲡⲓϭⲉⲣⲁⲇⲁⲙⲁ[

8 [——   ] . . ⲁⲁⲩ ⲛⲧⲉ ⲛ[.

[——   ]ⲧⲛ ⲧⲉ ϯⲉⲟ[ⲟⲩ]

10 [——   ]ⲡⲉⲛⲟ[

[——   ]ⲙⲁⲁⲩ[

12 [. . . . .] ⲙⲛ ⲡ̄ⲁ̄ⲏ̄ⲥ̄ⲓ̄ⲑ̄ⲉ̄ⲁ̄

[ϯⲙⲁⲁⲩ] ⲛⲧⲉ ⲛⲓⲁⲅⲅⲉⲗⲟⲥ ⲙⲛ

14 [ⲡⲓϣⲏⲣ]ⲉ ⲛⲧⲉ ⲁ̄ⲇ̄ⲁ̄ⲙ̄ⲁ̄ⲥ̄ ⲥⲏ[   ]

[ⲉⲙⲙⲁ]ⲭⲁ ⲥⲏⲑ ⲡⲓⲱⲧ ⲛⲧ[ⲉ]

16 [ϯϭⲉⲛ]ⲉⲁ̇ ⲛⲛ ⲁⲧⲕⲓⲙ ⲙⲛ[. .

[ⲡⲓϥⲧ]ⲟⲟⲩ ⲙ̄ ⲫ[ⲱ]ⲥⲧⲏⲣ ⲁ̄ⲣ̄ⲙ̄[ⲟ̄ⲍ̄ⲏ̄ⲗ̄]

---

50   Line numbers on this page are only approximate.

50,2   ⲛ ϩⲁⲡⲁ[, ⲛ and ϩ only attested by photo A; papyrus now incomplete.

50,4-5   Probably ⲛ]/ⲛ ⲉⲱⲛ.

51   Line numbers on this page are only approximate.

51,2   Or]ⲑⲟⲣⲟ . .ⲥ̄; the supralinear stroke began earlier in this word
            (where now there is a lacuna).

51,6   Or, our blessings; cf. 6,21-32.

51,7   Supralinear stroke begins over ⲓ; possibly ⲡⲓϭⲉⲣⲁⲇⲁⲙⲁ[ⲥ̄.

51,8   E.g.,] .ⲁⲁⲩ, or]ⲟⲩⲁⲁⲩ.

51,11   E.g., ⲙ]ⲙⲁⲁⲩ.

[50]
of[

2   [   ] simple (ἁπλοῦν) [
       perfect (τέλειος)[
4   eternal [
       aeon (αἰών) [
6   and [
       receive power [
8   and their [
       in a [
10   for (γάρ) [
       [   ] not [
       Lines 12 and following do not survive.

                                                    [51]

       [   ] in
2   [   ]–thorso–. .–s
       [   ] silence (σιγή)
4   [   ] he is [
       [   ] he is [god]
6   [   ] we were blessing
       [   ] Pigeradama[
8   [   ] of [
       [   ] she is the glory
10   [   ] our [
       [   ] mother [
12   [   ] and Pleistha
       [the mother] of the angels (ἄγγελος) with
14   [the son] of Adam, Se[th]
       [Emma]cha Seth, the father of
16   [the] immovable [race (γενέα)] and [
       [the] four lights (φωστήρ), Arm[mozel],

51,12   Supralinear stroke begins over ϩ | for Pleisthea, cf. *Gos.Eg.* III 56,4–13, where
          she is a great Light, the mother of angels and lights, who comes forth from
          Seth along with Daveithe.
51,13   [ϯⲘⲀⲀⲩ]; cf. *Gos.Eg.* III 56,6.
51,14-15 See 6,25n.
51,14   [ⲡϣⲱ Ⲏ ⲣ]ⲉ; cf. 30,9.
51,15   ]x̄, or else]k̄ or]c̄; the supralinear stroke began earlier in this word (where
          now there is a lacuna).
51,16   Perhaps no text is missing as at 6,27.
51,17   The name ⲀⲣⲘ[ⲟϫ Ⲏ ⲗ] extended far into the right margin; supralinear
          stroke preserved only over Ⲁⲣ (lacuna).

18   [ⲱⲡⲟⲓ̈ⲁ̅]ⲏ̅ⲗ̅ ⲛ̅ⲁ̅ⲧⲉⲓⲑⲉ· ⲏ̅ⲗ̅ⲏ̅ⲗ̅ⲑ̅·
     [. . . . . .] ⲁⲛⲥⲙⲟⲩ ⲕⲁⲧⲁ ⲣⲁⲛ·
20   [. . . . .] ⲛⲁⲩ ⲉⲣⲟϥ ⲡⲓⲣⲉϥⲁⲙⲁϩ–
     [ⲧⲉ ⲙ ⲡⲉ]ⲟⲟⲩ ⲡⲁⲗⲟⲩ ⲛ ϣⲙ̅ⲧ̅–
22   [. . . . .] ⲛ ϣⲙ̅ⲧ̅ϩⲟⲟⲩⲧ ⲛ
     [. . . .]ⲟⲩⲙⲛ̅ⲧⲛⲟϭ ⲉⲛϫ̅ⲱ
24   [ⲙⲙⲟ]ⲥ̣ ϫⲉ ⲛ̅ⲧⲕⲟⲩⲁ ⲛ̅ⲧⲕ
     [ⲟⲩⲁ ⲛ̅]ⲧⲕⲟⲩⲁ ⲡⲓⲁⲗⲟⲩ
     [ⲛ̅ⲃ̅]

     ⲛ̅ⲧ[ⲉ ⲡⲓⲁⲗⲟⲩ
2   ⲓ̈ⲁ̅ⲧⲟ[
     ϣⲟⲟ[ⲛ̅
4   ⲉⲁⲥ ⲉ̅ .[
     ⲙ ⲙⲟⲏ[---   ⲛ–]
6   ⲧⲕⲟⲩⲁ ⲛ̣ⲧ[ⲕⲟⲩⲁ
     ϛⲉⲙⲉⲗⲉⲗ̅ [
8   ⲧⲉⲗⲙⲁⲭⲏ̅ [
     ⲱⲙⲱⲑⲉⲙ[
10   [ϩ̣]ⲟ̣[ⲟ̣]ⲩ̅ⲧ̅ ⲡ[
     [. .]ⲉϥϫⲡ[ⲟ   ---   ⲡⲓⲣⲉϥⲁ–]
12   ⲙⲁϩⲧⲉ ⲙ ⲡⲉ̣[ⲟⲟⲩ
     ϣ ⲟⲩⲁϣϥ ⲡⲏ ⲉⲧⲛ[
14   ⲡⲁⲛⲧⲉⲗⲓⲟⲥ ⲡⲁⲛ[
     ⲧⲏⲣⲟⲩ: ⲭ̅ ⲁ̅ⲕⲣⲱⲛ [
16   ⲡⲓϣⲙ̅ⲧ̅ϩⲟⲟⲩⲧ ⲁⲗ[
     ⲱⲱⲱⲱⲱⲃ ⲧ̅ⲣⲉⲓⲥ̣ⲉ[
18   ⲛ̅ⲧⲕⲟⲩⲡⲛ̅ⲁ̅ ⲉⲃⲟⲗ ϩⲛ [ⲟⲩ–]
     ⲡ̅ⲛ̅ⲁ̅· ⲛ̅ⲧⲕ‹ⲟⲩ›ⲟⲩⲟⲉⲓⲛ ⲉ̣[ⲃⲟⲗ]
20   ϩⲛ ‹ⲟⲩ›ⲟⲩⲟⲉⲓⲛ· ⲛ̅ⲧⲕ[ⲟⲩⲥⲓⲧⲏ]

51,18   [ⲱⲡⲟⲓ̈ⲁ̅], a slightly crowded restoration | ⲛ is written separate from the
           letters ⲁ̅ⲁ̅ⲧⲉⲓⲑⲉ and with its own supralinear stroke.
51,20-21   Cf. 54,15-16.
51,20   E.g., ⲁⲩⲱ ⲁⲛ]ⲛⲁⲩ.
51,23   Lit., greatness.
51,24-25   One, i.e., not divided; cf. 52,5-6; 88,16-17; *Steles Seth* VII 125,23-25;
           Allogenes XI 54,22-23.
52   Line numbers on this page are only approximate.
52,2   Or else ⲓ̈ⲁ̅ⲧϛ; the supralinear stroke begins over ⲁ; e.g., ⲓ̈ⲁ̅ⲧⲟ[ⲙⲉⲛⲏⲥ;
           cf. *Allogenes* XI 54,35.
52,4   No supralinear stroke over ⲉⲁⲥ.
52,5-6   ⲛ]/ⲧⲕⲟⲩⲁ; another statement of this phrase should be restored in
           either 5 or 6.

18   [Oroia]el, Daveithe, Eleleth.
    [   ] we blessed by (+κατά) name.
20   [ ] saw the self-controlled
    [glory], the thrice-[   ] child,
22   [   ] thrice-male
    [   ] majesty, as we said
24   "You are one, you are
    [one], you are one, o child
    [52]
    of [the child
2   Yato-[
    exist [
4   [
    [you are]
6   one, you [are one
    Semelel [
8   Telmache[
    Omothem[
10   male [
    [ ] he begets [the]
12   self-controlled [glory
    desire him who [
14   all-perfect (παντέλειος) [
    all. Akron [
16   thrice-male, aa[
    ooooob†treise[
18   you are spirit (πνεῦμα) from
    spirit (πνεῦμα); you are light
20   from light; you are [silence (σιγή)]

52,5   Ⲙ̄ ⲘⲞ Ⲏ, sic.
52,7   Ⲥ, or else ⲉ̣, ⲑ, or ⲟ̣.
52,8   Ⲧ, or else Ⲧ̣ | for a Telmachel, see *Gos.Eg.* IV 59,19ff.
52,14   E.g., ⲠⲀⲚ[ⲦⲰⲤ.
52,16-17 ⲁⲁ...ⲱⲱ, magical *stoicheia*; see also 118,18.21; 127,1-3; cf. *Gos.Eg.* III 44,3-9; 66,8-22; 67,17.
52,17   Between ⲃ and Ⲧ, apparently a cryptic character (ϛ with a short horizontal bar intersecting it near the top); possibly the copyist meant to write only ϛ.
52,18ff See 51,24n; cf. Nicene Creed Art. 2.
52,19-20 ⟨ⲟⲩ⟩...⟨ⲟⲩ⟩..., carelessly omitted by a copyist.
52,20   [ⲟⲩⲥ ϛ Ⲧ Ⲏ] extended far into the right margin.

ⲉⲃⲟⲗ ϩⲛ ⲟⲩⲥⲓⲧⲏ· ⲛ̅[ⲧⲕ ⲟⲩ−]
22 ⲉⲛⲛⲟⲓⲁ ⲉⲃⲟⲗ ϩⲛ ⲟ̣[ⲩⲉⲛ−]
ⲛⲟⲓⲁ ⲡϣⲏⲣⲉ ⲛ̅ⲧ̣[ⲉ ⲡⲛⲟⲩ−]
24 ⲧⲉ ⲡⲛⲟⲩⲧⲉ ⲅ̅ ⲡ̅ⲩ̅ [. .
ⲩ̅ⲱⲁ̣ ⲙⲁⲣⲛ̅ϫⲟⲟⲩ [

[ⲛⲅ̅]

[——   ]ϥ·
2 [——   ]ⲟⲩ
[——   ]ⲛϫⲟ
4 [. . . . .]ϣⲁϫⲉ
[. . . . .]ⲛⲉ ⲧ̅ⲛⲟⲩ̣[
6 [. . . . .] ⲙⲛ ⲧ̅ⲛⲟ̣[
[. . . . . . .]ⲟ̣ⲩⲧⲉ ⲉⲃⲟ[ⲗ
8 [. . . . . . .]ⲩ̣ⲥⲟⲡ̅ ⲁⲛ ⲥⲙ[
[. . . . . .]ⲓ̣ⲁⲧⲛⲁⲩ ⲉⲣⲟ̣[ⲓ
10 [. . . . . .ⲃ̣]ⲁ̣ⲣ̅ⲃⲏⲗ[ⲱ
[. . . . . . .] ⲡ̣ⲓⲁⲧ̣[
12 [. . . . .] ⲡⲓⲡⲣⲱⲛⲏⲥ ⲛ
[ϣⲙ̅ⲧ]ϩⲟⲟⲩⲧ̣ ⲙⲛ ⲧⲁ ⲛⲓⲉⲟ−
14 [ⲟⲩ ⲧⲏ]ⲣⲟⲩ ⲓ̈ⲟⲩⲏⲗ: ⲁⲩⲱ
[ⲉⲧⲁⲓ̈]ϫⲱⲕⲙ ⲙ̅ ⲡⲙⲉϩϥ̅ⲟⲩ
16 [ⲛ ⲥⲟ]ⲡ̅ ⲉ ⲡⲣⲁⲛ ⲛⲧⲉ ⲡⲓⲁⲩ−
[ⲧⲟ]ⲅ̣ⲉⲛⲏⲥ ⲉⲃⲟⲗ ϩⲓⲧⲟⲟⲧ̣[ⲟⲩ]
18 ⲛ ⲛ]ⲉⲓ̈ϭⲟⲙ ⲛⲉⲓ̈ϭⲟⲙ ⲁⲉⲓ−
[ϣ]ⲱⲡⲉ ⲛⲛ ⲟⲩⲛⲟⲩⲧⲉ
20 [ⲁⲓ̈ⲁϩⲉ]ⲣⲁⲧ̅ ϩⲓϫⲛ ⲡⲓⲙⲉϩϥ̅−
[ⲟⲩ ⲛⲛ] ⲉⲱⲛ ⲛ ϭⲱⲣⲅ ⲛⲧⲉ
22 [ⲛⲁⲓ̈ ⲧⲏ]ⲣ̣ⲟⲩ· ⲁⲉⲓⲛⲁⲩ ⲉ ⲛⲁ−
[ⲡⲓⲁⲩ]ⲧⲟ̄ⲅⲉⲛⲏⲥ ⲧⲏⲣⲟⲩ
24 [ⲛⲏ ⲉ]ⲧ̣ϣⲟ̣[ⲟ]ⲡ̅ ⲟⲛⲧⲱⲥ
[ⲁⲩ]ⲱ [ⲁ]ⲉⲓϫⲱⲕⲙ ⲛ ⲧ̅ⲟⲩ

52,24   Last letter, a cryptic character (ⲩ with a long horizontal bar through its vertical stroke, and a supralinear stroke above the character).

52,25   First and third letters are cryptic characters; first, as in 24 but without the supralinear stroke; third, ⲗ with a short vertical stroke inside the angle of its two legs, not touching the intersection (there is a supralinear stroke above the character).

53   Line numbers on this page are only approximate.

53,5   E.g., ⲧⲛⲟⲩ[ⲛⲉ].

from silence (σιγή); [you are]
22 thought (ἔννοια) from thought (ἔννοια),
O son of [god],
24 the god . . .[
. . . let us speak [

[53]

[
2   [
[
4   [   ] word
[   ] the [
6   [   ] and the [
[
8   [   ] not a time
[   ] invisible [
10 [B]arbelo
[   ] the
12 [   ] the [thrice-] male
Prones, and she who belongs to
14 all the glories, Youel.
[When I was] baptized the fifth
16 [time] in the name of the
Autogenes (αὐτογενής) by
18 each of these powers, I
became divine.
20 [I] stood at rest upon the [fifth]
aeon (αἰών), a combination of
22 all [of them]; I saw all those
belonging to [the] Autogenes (αὐτογενής)
24 who really (ὄντως) exist.
I was baptized five

53,9   E.g., ΠⲒϤ´...ⲉ ⲡ ⲟ[ϥ, or ⲚⲒϤ´...ⲉ ⲡ ⲟ]ⲟⲩ; the trace is not from ✝.
53,14 For Youel, also Yoel, see 54,17; 57,15; 125,14.; cf. *Gos.Eg.* III 44,27;
Allogenes XI, 50,20.
53,15 Or [ⲁⲉⲥ] (very widely spaced) | for the fourth baptism in the Autogenes,
see 7,16.
53,25 Lit., I washed.

```
        [ⲚⲆ]
        Ⲛ ⲤⲞ[Ⲡ
2       ⲘⲚ Ï[
        ⲚⲦⲈ Ⲡ[
4       ⳜⲀⲢⲈⲨ[
        ⲈⲂⲞⲖ Ϩ[Ⲛ    ———           Ⲉ—]
6       ⲦⲘⲘⲀⲨ[
        Ⲛ ⲦⲈⲖⲒⲞⲤ [
8       ⲘⲚ ϮⲚⲞϬ Ⲙ [
        [Ⲉ]ⲞⲞⲨ ⲦⲀⲚ[
10      [ . . . ]ⲚⲞⲤ Ⲛ [
        [ⲚⲞ]ⲨⲦⲈ· Ϯ[
12      ⲞⲨⲰⲚϨ ⲈⲂⲞⲖ . .[
        ⲦⲈⲖⲒⲞⲤ ⲈⲦⲔⲎⲂ ⲦⲎ[Ⲣ'
14      ⲦⲀⲚⲒⲈⳁⲆⲞⲤ ⲦⲎⲢⲞⲨ [
        Ⲛ ϨⲞⲞⲨⲦ· ϮⲢⲈⳟⲀ[ⲘⲀϨⲦⲈ]
16      Ⲙ ⲠⲈⲞⲞⲨ· ⲦⲘⲀⲀⲨ [
        [Ⲛ]ⳁⲈⲞⲞⲨ ÏⲞⲨⲎⲖ ⲘⲚ Ⲡ[ⳁⳝⲦⲞ—]
18      ⲞⲨ Ⲙ ⲪⲰⲤⲦⲎⲢ ⲚⲦⲈ [Ⲡⳁ—]
        ⲠⲢⲰⲦⲞⲪⲀⲚⲎⲤ Ⲛ [ⲚⲞϬ]
20      Ⲛ ⲚⲞⲨⲤ ⲤⲈⲖⲘⲈⲚ Ⲙ[Ⲛ ⲚⲎ ⲈⲦ—]
        ⲔⲎ ⲚⲘⲘⲀⳟ ⲚⳁⲢⲈⳟ[ⲞⲨⲈⲚϨ]
22      ⲚⲞⲨⲦⲈ ⲈⲂⲞⲖ· ⳜⲀⲬⲐ[ⲞⲤ]
        ⲘⲚ ÏⲀⲬⲐⲞⲤ· ⲤⲎⲐⲈ[ⲨⲤ]
24      ⲘⲚ ⲀⲚⲦⳁⲪⲀⲚ[ⲦⲎ]Ⲥ· [ⲤⲈⲖ—]
        ⲆⲀⲰ· ⲘⲚ ⲈⲖⲈ[Ⲛ]ⲞⲤ [
                                        [ⲚⲈ]
        [    ———              ] .ⲦⲞ
2       [    ———              ]Ⲛ Ⲉⳁ
        [    ———              ] Ⲉ ⲠⳁⲀ—
4       [    ———              ]ⲰⲚⲈⲨ
        [    ———              ]ⲈⳁⲚⲈ
6       [    ———              ]ⲞⲞⲚ Ⲛ
```

---

54   Line numbers on this page are only approximate.
54,2-3   E.g., ⲠⲀⲖⲞⲨ]/ⲚⲦⲈ Ⲡ[ⲀⲖⲞⲨ.
54,2   A supralinear stroke may have begun over Ï (lacuna).
54,3-4   E.g., ⳁⲈⲤⲤⲈⲨⲤ ⲘⲀ]/ⳜⲀⲢⲈⲨⲤ [ⳁⲈⲤⲤⲈⲆⲈⲔⲈⲨⲤ; see 47,5-6n.
54,8   E.g., Ⲙ [ⲠⲀⲢⲐⲈⲚⳁⲔⲞⲚ ⲚⲚ]; cf. 125,14-15.
54,9   E.g., ⲦⲀⲚ[ⳁⲈⲞⲞⲨ ⲦⲎⲢⲞⲨ]; cf. 57,13-15.
54,16   E.g., [ⲚⲦⲈ], or [ⲦⲀ].
54,22-23   For ⳜⲀⲬⲐ[ⲞⲤ], cf. 126,12.

[54]
    times[
2   and [
    of the [
4   -zareu-[
    from [
6   that [
    perfect (τέλειος) [
8   and the great [
    glory, she who belongs to [
10   [
    god, the [
12   appear [
    perfect (τέλειος) which is doubled [
14   she who belongs to all species (εἶδος)[
    -male, the [self-controlled]
16   glory, the mother [
    [the] glories, Youel, and the
18   [four] lights (φωστήρ) of [the]
    [great] mind (νοῦς)
20   Protophanes (πρωτοφανής): Selmen [and those]
    with him, the
22   god-[revealers] Zachth[os]
    and Yachthos, Sethe[us]
24   and Antiphan[te]s, [Sel-]
    dao and Ele[n]nos [

                               [55]
    [
2   [   ] go
    [   ] the
4   [
    [   ] likeness
6   [   ] as

54,23-24   For C̄ H Θ Є[ϒC]/ⲙ ⲛ ⲁ̄ⲛⲧⲓϛ⳽ⲫⲁⲛⲧⲏⲥ, cf. 126,16-17.
54,24-25   For the restoration, cf. *Gos. Eg.* III 64,21.
54,25   No trace of a supralinear stroke over Є ⲁ Є[.]ọ̣ç̣ | cf. Schmidt-McDermott,
            Jehu and the Untitled Text, where Sellao and Eleinos are aeons of Sophia
            (U264) and a Setheus is lord of the pleroma (U234).
55   Line numbers on this page are only approximate.
55,2   Circumflex over the group Є ſ.

```
        [      ---           ]ΝΤΕ ΝΙΑⲨ-
8       [      ---           ]ΝΑⲨ ΓΑΡ Ε
        [      ---           ]ⲈⲰΝ ⲈⲨⲈⲤ-
10      [      ---           ]ⲈⲰⲦⲞ
        [      ---           Ⲫ]ⲰⲤⲦⲎ[Ⲣ
12      [ . . . . . . . . .]Ⲛ Ⲛ[Ⲥ]ⲈⲞⲞⲨ ⲚⲈⲰⲦⲞ
        [ . . . . . ] ⲚⲀⲒ̈ ⲚⲈ ⲔⲀⲦⲀ ⲠⲞⲨⲀ
14      [ⲠⲞⲨⲀ] ⲚⲦⲈ ⲚⲤⲈⲰⲚ· ⲞⲨ-
        [ⲔⲀⲈ Ⲉ]ⲨⲞⲚⲈ ⲘⲚ ⲞⲨⲘⲞⲞⲨ
16      [ⲈⲨⲞⲚ]Ⲉ ⲘⲚ ⲞⲨⲀⲎⲢ ⲈⲨⲈ Ⲛ
        [ⲞⲨ]ⲞⲈⲓⲚ ⲘⲚ ⲞⲨⲔⲰⲈ̇
18      [ⲈⲨⲠ]ⲢⲢⲒⲰⲞⲨ ⲈⲂⲞⲖ ⲈⲘⲀⲨ-
        [ⲢⲰ]ⲔⲈ ⲘⲚ ⲈⲚⲌⲰⲞⲚ ⲀⲨⲰ
20      [ⲈⲚⲰ]ⲎⲚ· ⲀⲨⲰ ⲈⲚⲮⲨⲬⲎ
        [ⲘⲚ Ⲉ]ⲈⲚⲚⲞⲨⲤ ⲘⲚ ⲈⲚⲢⲰⲘⲈ
22      [ⲘⲚ Ⲛ]Ⲏ ⲦⲎⲢⲞⲨ ⲈⲦⲰ̅Ⲟ̅Ⲡ̅
        [ⲚⲘⲘⲀ]Ⲩ· ⲈⲚⲚⲞⲨⲦⲈ ⲆⲈ
24      [ⲘⲚ] ⲈⲚⲄⲞ[Ⲙ] ⲀⲨⲰ ⲈⲚⲀⲨ-
        [ⲄⲈ]ⲖⲞⲤ ⲀⲚ· ⲚⲀⲒ̈ ⲦⲎⲢⲞⲨ ΓΑⲢ
        [Ⲛ̅Ⲋ̅]
        ⲚⲈⲈ[
2       ⲀⲨⲰ [
        ⲀⲨⲰ Ⲛ[
4       ⲰⲞⲞⲠ̅ [
        ⲦⲎⲢⲞⲨ [
6       ⲦⲎⲢⲞⲨ Ⲉ[
        [ .]Ⲩ ⲦⲎⲢⲞⲨ [
8       ⲚⲈ· ⲈⲨⲈ Ⲛ .[
        [Ⲁ]ⲨⲰ ⲈⲨⲈ[
10      [ . .]Ⲁ ⲀⲨⲰ [
        [ⲀⲨ]Ⲱ ⲚⲎ Ⲉ[ .] .[
12      ⲞⲨⲨ Ⲙ ⲠⲒⲀⲨⲦⲞⲄⲈⲚ[ⲎⲤ ⲀⲨⲰ ⲀⲒ̈-]
        ⲌⲒ ⲈⲒⲚⲈ ⲈⲂⲞⲖ ⲈⲚ ⲚⲀⲒ̈ [ⲦⲎⲢⲞⲨ . .
14      ⲞⲨⲰⲚ ⲚⲄⲒ ⲚⲤⲈⲰⲚ Ⲛ[ⲦⲈ ⲠⲒ]
        ⲀⲨⲦⲞⲄⲈⲚⲎⲤ ⲞⲨⲚⲞ[Ϭ Ⲛ ⲞⲨⲞ-]
16      ⲈⲒⲚ ⲰⲀⲨⲠⲒⲢⲈ ⲈⲈⲢⲀⲒ̈ Ⲉ[
        ⲈⲂⲞⲖ ⲈⲚ ⲚⲤⲈⲰⲚ ⲚⲦⲈ Ⲡ[ⲒⲰⲘ̅Ⲧ̅-]
```

55,9   No circumflex over the group ⲈⲒ.
55,13-19   Cf. 48,3-7 and 113,9-14.
56   Line numbers on this page are only approximate.
56,4   Flag of Ⲡ not preserved.

```
        [                              ] of the [
8       [                                  ], for (γάρ) [   ] see
        [                              ] aeon (αἰών) [
10      [                              ] more
        [                              ] light (φωστήρ)
12      [                              ] more glories
        [     ] these are in relation (κατά) to
14      [each] of the aeons (αἰών): a
        living [earth] and a
16      [living] water, and air (ἀήρ) made of
        light and a blazing
18      fire which cannot
        [consume], and living animals (ζῷον) and
20      [trees]; souls (ψυχή)
        [and] minds (νοῦς) and human beings
22      [and] all those who dwell
        [with them]; but (δέ) (there are) no gods
24      [or] powers or
        angels (ἄγγελος); for (γάρ) all these
        [56]
        [
2       and [
        and [
4       exist [
        all [
6       all [
        [    ] all [
8       [    ] they being [
        and they being [
10      [    ] and [
        [and] those [
12      the Autogen[es (αὐτογενής). I]
        received a likeness from [all] these [
14      The aeons (αἰών) [of the] Autogenes (αὐτογενής)
        [        ]; a [great light]
16      came forth [
        from the aeons (αἰών) of the [thrice]
```

56,13   Or, [ⲉⲩⲁ̅ⲩ=].
56,14   Cf. 129,23–24.
56,15-16   Cf. Acts 9:3; 22:6; 26:13.
56,17-18   Thrice male, i.e., the Protophanes aeon.

18 ϩⲟⲟⲩⲧ̅ ⲁⲩⲱ ⲛⲉⲩϯ [ⲉⲟⲟⲩ]
ⲛⲁⲩ· ⲛⲉⲣⲉ ⲡⲓϥⲧⲟ[ⲟⲩ]
20 ⲛ̅ⲛ ⲉⲱⲛ ⲛⲉⲧⲟⲩⲱϣ[ⲥ ⲉⲃⲟⲗ]
ⲛ̅ϩⲣⲁⲓ̈ ϧⲛ ⲟⲩⲉⲱⲛ ⲛ̅ ⲟⲩ[
22 ⲙ̅ ⲡⲥⲙⲟⲧ̅ ⲛ̅ⲛ ⲟⲩⲉ[
ⲟⲩⲱⲧ̅ ⲉϥϣⲟⲟⲛ̅ ⲙ̅ .[
24 ⲁⲩⲱ ⲧⲟⲧⲉ ⲁϥ[. .]ⲧ ⲛϭⲓ ⲏ̅[
ⲡⲁⲗⲟⲩ ⲛ̅ⲧⲉ ⲡⲁ[ⲗ]ⲟⲩ ⲁ[

[ⲛ̅ⲍ̅]

[———] .ⲁ
2 [———]ⲉⲩ
[———]ⲟⲩⲥ
4 [———]ⲁ̣ⲧⲟⲩ
[——— ï ⲉ̈ⲥⲥⲉⲩⲥ] ⲙⲁⲍⲁ–
6 [ⲣⲉⲩⲥ ï ⲉ̈ⲥⲥⲉⲗⲉ]ⲕⲉⲩⲥ [.] .
[———]ⲟⲙ ⲛ̅ⲧⲉ[
8 [. . . . . . ⲥⲫⲣ]ⲁⲅⲓⲥ ϩⲓⲱⲱϥ
[. . . . . . .] .[. . .] ⲙ̅ⲛ ⲅⲁⲃⲣⲓⲏ[ⲗ]
10 [. . . . . . .] ⲛ [. . .] ⲛ ⲟⲩ[.
[. . . . . . .] .ⲩ .[.]ⲉⲛⲥⲫⲣⲁⲅⲓ[ⲥ]
12 [. . . .] .ⲛ ϥⲧⲟⲟⲩ ⲛ̅ ⲅⲉⲛⲟⲥ
[ⲁⲩⲱ] ⲁ̣ⲥⲉⲓ ⲛ̅ⲛⲁϩⲣⲁⲓ̈ ⲛ̅ϭⲓ ⲧⲁ–
14 [ⲛⲥⲉⲟ]ⲟⲩ ⲛ̅ ϩⲟⲟⲩⲧ̅ ⲁⲩⲱ ⲙ̅
[ⲡⲁⲣⲑⲉ]ⲛⲓⲕⲟⲛ ï ⲱ̅ⲏ̅ⲗ̅· ⲁⲩ[ⲱ]
16 [ⲁⲉⲓ]ϣⲟϫⲛⲉ ⲉⲧⲃⲉ ⲛⲓⲕⲗⲟⲟ[ⲙ]
[ⲡⲉϫ]ⲁⲥ ⲛⲁⲓ̈ ϫⲉ ⲉⲧⲃⲉ ⲟⲩ
18 [ⲁϥϣ]ⲟϫⲛⲉ ⲛ̅ϭⲓ ⲡⲉⲕ̅ⲡ̅ⲛ̅ⲁ̅
[ⲉⲧⲃ]ⲉ ⲛⲓⲕⲗⲟⲟⲙ ⲙ̅ⲛ ⲛⲓ–
20 [ⲥⲫⲣ]ⲁⲅⲓⲥ ⲉⲧⲕⲏ ϩⲓⲱⲟⲩ
[. . .] ⲛⲉ ⲛⲓⲕⲗⲟⲟⲙ ⲉⲧϯ ϭⲟⲙ
22 [ⲙ̅ ⲡ̅ⲛ̅]ⲁ̅ ⲛⲓⲙ ⲙ̅ⲛ ⲯⲩⲭⲏ ⲛⲓⲙ
[ⲛⲓⲥⲫ]ⲣⲁⲅⲓⲥ ⲗⲉ ⲉⲧϣⲟⲟⲡ

56,20 ϣ was connected to the following letter (now in lacuna) by a supralinear
stroke; for the restoration, cf. 81,13.
56,21 E.g., ⲟ̣ⲩ̣[ⲟⲉⲛ].
56,24 ⲏ̣[, ambiguous trace; nothing of the supralinear stroke survives;
ⲏ̣[ⲫⲏⲥⲏⲭ] would extend unusually far into the margin.
57 Line numbers on this page are only approximate.
57,5-6 For the restorations, see 47,5-6.
57,5 No supralinear stroke over ⲙ.
57,7 E.g., ⲕⲗⲟ]ⲟⲙ.

18 male, and they [glorified]
    them. The four
20 aeons (αἰών) were desiring
    within a [   ] aeon (αἰών)
22 the [   ] pattern [
    single one existing [
24 Then (τότε) E-[   ], the
    child of the child [

                                                [57]

    [
2   [
    [
4   [
    [Yesseus] Maza-
6   [reus Yessede]keus [
    [   ] of
8   [seal (σφραγίς)] upon him
    [   ] and Gabrie[l]
10 [
    [   ] seal (σφραγίς)
12 [   ] four races (γένος)
    There came before me she who belongs to
14 [the glories], the male and
    [virginal (παρθενικόν)] Yoel.
16 [I] wondered about the crowns,
    (and) she [said] to me, "Why
18 [has] your spirit (πνεῦμα) been wondering
    [about] the crowns and the
20 [seals (σφραγίς)] on them?
    [   ] (they) are the crowns which strengthen
22 every [spirit (πνεῦμα)] and every soul (ψυχή);
    and (δέ) [the] seals (σφραγίς) which are

57,9   See 47,11n. Gabriel appears in both the O.T. and N.T.; in *Gos.Eg.* III
           52,19ff, he is a minister of Oroiael in Autogenes.
57,12   Supralinear stroke not preserved over first N.
57,13-63,17 *The Revelations from Yoel*
57,15   See 53,14n. The new revelations evidently served as a summary of the
           gnosis of the Barbelo aeons.
57,16   ⲔⲀⲞⲞ[Ⲙ; cf. lines 19 and 21.
57,18-22   The seals and crowns serve as guardians.
57,21   E.g., [ⲚⲀⲒ̈].

24 [ϩⲓⲱ]ⲟⲩ ⲛⲓⲙⲛ̄ⲧ̄ⲅⲉⲛⲟⲥ ⲙⲛ̄
[. .] ⲡⲓⲁϩⲟⲣⲁⲧⲟⲛ ⲙ ⲡⲛ̄ⲁ
[ⲛ̄ⲏ̄]
ⲛⲉ ⲙ[
2 ⲑⲉⲛ[
ⲛⲏ [
4 ⲙⲉⲛ [
ⲇⲉ ⲛ ⲱ[
6 ⲡⲁⲣⲑⲉ[ⲛⲟⲥ
. .ⲥ ⲇⲉ ⲛ [
8 [.]ϣⲣ ⲁⲓⲧⲓ [
.ⲣⲟ ϩⲛ ⲛⲓ[
10 [ϩ]ⲏⲧⲟⲩ ⲛ[
[. . .] . ⲁⲩⲱ [. .]ⲡ[
12 [. . .] ⲭ̅ ⲁϥϯ [ⲅⲟ]ⲙ ⲛ[
ⲛⲓⲥⲫⲣⲁⲅⲓⲥ ⲇⲉ ⲛ̄[
14 ⲅⲉⲛⲟⲥ ⲛⲁⲡⲓⲁⲩⲧⲟ[ⲅⲉⲛⲏⲥ]
ⲛⲉ ⲙⲛ̄ ⲡⲓⲡⲣⲱⲧⲟⲫⲁ[ⲛⲏⲥ]
16 ⲙⲛ ⲡⲓⲕ̄ⲗ̄ⲥ̄· ⲁⲩⲱ ⲡⲓⲁ[ϩⲟⲣⲁ-]
ⲧⲟⲛ ⲙ ⲡⲛ̄ⲁ ⲟⲩⲅⲟⲙ [ⲙ ⲯⲩ-]
18 ⲭⲓⲕⲟⲛ ⲁⲩⲱ ⲛ ⲛⲟⲉⲣ[ⲟⲛ ⲡⲉ]
ⲟⲩⲣⲉϥⲉⲓⲙⲉ ⲁⲩⲱ ⲛ [ⲣⲉϥ-]
20 ⲣ ϣⲟⲣⲡ̄ ⲛ ⲉⲓⲙⲉ· ⲁⲩ[ⲱ ⲉ-]
ⲧⲃⲉ ⲡⲁⲓ̈ ⲉϥⲛ̄ⲧⲟⲟⲧ[ϥ ⲛ ⲅⲁ-]
22 ⲃⲣⲓⲏⲗ ⲡⲓⲣⲉϥϯ ⲡⲛ̄ⲁ· ϩⲓ[ⲛⲁ]
ⲉϣⲱⲡⲉ ⲉϥϣⲁⲛϯ ⲛ [ⲟⲩ-]
24 ⲡⲛ̄ⲁ ⲉϥⲟⲩⲁⲁⲃ ⲛϥⲣ ⲥⲫ[ⲣⲁ-]
ⲅⲓⲍⲉ ⲙⲙⲟϥ ϩⲙ ⲡⲓⲕⲗ[ⲟⲙ]
26 ⲁⲩⲱ ⲛϥϯ ⲕⲗⲟⲙ ⲛⲁϥ ⲉ[ⲩ-]
ⲛⲧⲁϥ ⲛ ϩⲉⲛⲛⲟⲩⲧⲉ [

ⲛ̄[ⲑ]
[----   ⲟ]ⲩⲅⲟⲙ
2 [----   ] ⲡⲓⲥⲁ
[----   ]ⲟⲃ
4 [----   ]ⲩ.
[----   ]ⲡⲓ .
6 [----   ]ⲧⲏⲣ ⲛⲁ[

57,25   E.g., [ⲛⲁ].
58   Line numbers on this page are only approximate.
58,1-2   E.g., [ⲡⲁⲣ]/ⲑⲉⲛⲓⲟⲥ.
58,13-14 E.g., ⲛ[ⲧⲉ ⲛⲓϣⲱⲙⲧ]/ⲅⲉⲛⲟⲥ.

24   [upon] the triple-races (-γένος) and
[   ] the Invisible (ἀόρατον) Spirit (πνεῦμα)
[58]
[
2   [
[
4   [
and (δέ) [
6   [virgin (παρθένος)
[   ] and (δέ) [
8   [   ] seek (αἰτεῖν)[
[   ] in the [
10   [in] them[
[   ] and [
12   [   ] he [strengthened
and (δέ) the seals (σφραγίς) [   ] race
14   (γένος), those belonging to the [Autogenes (αὐτογενής)]
and the Protophanes (πρωτοφανής) and
16   the Kalyptos (καλυπτός). The [Invisible (ἀόρατον)]
Spirit (πνεῦμα) [is] a psychic (ψυχικόν)
18   and intellectual (νοερόν) power,
a knower and
20   a fore-knower. Therefore
it (Spirit?) is with [Ga]briel
22   the spirit-giver (-πνεῦμα) [so that (ἵνα)]
when he gives [a]
24   holy spirit (πνεῦμα), he might
seal (σφραγίζειν) him with the crown
26   and crown him,
[having] gods [

                                   5[9]
[   ] power
2   [   ] the
[
4   [
[   ] the
6   [

58,22-23   For the restoration, cf. 123,3.
58,22   No supralinear stroke over ⲃⲣⲓⲏⲗ.
58,24-26   Him, probably a type of humanity.

```
     [      ---           ]ⲛ ⲉⲩⲱ[
 8   [      ---           ]ⲛⲡⲛⲁ .
     [      ---         ]ⲱ ⲉⲧⲟⲩⲉ[
10   [ . . . . . . . .] ⲟⲩ [ . . .]ⲉⲉⲩ
     [ . . . . . . .]ⲥⲟ .[ .]ⲉⲩϣⲟ[ⲟⲛ̄]
12   [ . . . . . .]ⲁⲩ ⲁⲩⲱ ⲛⲉⲩⲛϩⲣⲁⲓ̈
     [ⲛϩⲏⲧ]ⲟⲩ ⲁⲛ ϩⲓⲛⲁ ϫⲉ ⲉⲩⲉ—
14   [ϣⲱ]ⲡⲉ ⲛ ϩⲁⲡⲗⲟⲩⲛ· ⲁⲩⲱ
     [ⲛⲥⲉ]ϣⲧⲙϣⲱⲡⲉ ⲉⲩⲕⲏⲃ
16   [ⲕⲁⲧ]ⲁ̣ ⲗⲁⲁⲩ ⲛ ⲥⲙⲟⲧ· ⲁⲩⲱ
     [ⲛⲁⲓ̈] ⲙⲉⲛ ⲛⲉ ⲛⲓⲕⲁⲧⲁ ⲟⲩⲁ ⲛ
18   [ϩⲁⲡ]ⲗⲟⲩⲛ ⲁⲩⲱ ⲛ ⲧⲉⲗⲓⲟⲥ·
     [ . . . .]ⲣϥ ⲁⲩⲱ ⲛⲁⲓ̈ ⲧⲏⲣⲟⲩ
20   [ . . .]ⲱⲛ ⲛⲧⲉ ⲛⲓⲉⲱⲛ ⲉⲩ—
     [ . . .]ⲕ ⲙⲙⲟϥ· ⲛⲁⲓ̈ ⲧⲏⲣⲟⲩ
22   [ . . ⲉ]ⲧϣⲟⲟⲛ̄ ϩⲓ ⲟⲩⲙⲁ
     [ . . ⲡ]ⲁⲛⲧⲉⲗⲓⲟⲛ· ⲡⲁⲟⲩⲛⲟϭ
24   [ . . .]ⲙ ⲡⲉ ⲉ ⲛⲁⲩ ⲉⲣⲟⲟⲩ
     [ . . .]ⲧⲛⲁⲩ ⲅⲁⲣ ⲉⲣⲟϥ ⲙ
     ⲝ̄
     ⲡⲣ[
 2   ⲟⲩ[
     ⲙⲟ[
 4   ⲧⲉⲗⲓⲟ̣[ⲥ
     [ . .]ϯϩ[
 6   [ .] .ⲟⲩⲱ[
     [ . .]ⲙ ⲛⲓⲙ [
 8   ϣⲟⲟⲛ̄ ⲟ[
     ⲁⲣ ⲡⲉ ⲉⲛϩ[
10   [ . .ⲥ]ⲱⲧⲙ [ⲉⲣ]ⲟϥ ϩⲓ[
     [ . . .]ⲁ ⲁⲩⲱ [ .] .ⲩ[
12   ⲛϩⲣⲁⲓ̈ ϩⲛ ⲟⲩⲉⲛⲛⲟ[ⲓⲁ
     ⲟⲩϣⲟⲣⲛ̄ ⲛ ⲉⲛⲛⲟⲓ[ⲁ
14   ⲉⲡⲓⲇⲏ ϩⲛ ⲟⲩϭⲟⲙ ⲁⲩ[
     ⲛⲟⲩⲧⲉⲗⲓⲟⲥ ⲧⲉ· ⲁ[
16   ϣϣⲉ ⲉⲣⲟⲕ ⲉ ⲧⲁϣ[
```

59,10-25   Location of the left margin is hypothetical.
59,10   Circumflex over the group ϩⲓ.
59,15   Cf. 82,22.
59,16   ]ⲁ̣, a trace from ⲁ or ⲙ.
59,20   E.g., [ⲛⲓⲉ]ⲱⲛ, or [ⲟⲩϩⲓⲕ]ⲱⲛ.

[

8   [   ] spirit (πνεῦμα)

       [   ] to one (fem.)

10   [

       [   ] they exist

12   [   ] and they were

       not [in] them in order that (ἵνα) they might

14   [become] simple (ἁπλοῦν)

       and [might not] be doubled

16   [according to (κατά)] any pattern.

       [These] (+μέν) are the simple

18   (ἁπλοῦν), perfect (τέλειος) individuals (+κατά):

       [   ] and all these

20   [   ] of the aeons (αἰών)

       [   ] him, all these

22   [   ] who reside in a place

       [   ] all-perfect (παντέλειος); it (took) a great

24   [   ] to see them,

       for (γάρ) [ ] see [

       60

       [

2   [

       [

4   perfect (τέλειος) [

       [

6   [

       [   ] every [

8   exist [

       he is [

10   [hear] him [

       [   ] and [

12   in thought (ἔννοια) [

       a first thought (ἔννοια) [

14   since (ἐπειδή) [   ] with power [

       she was perfect (τέλειος), [

16   it is fitting for you to [

59,24   E.g., [N ϬO]м.

59,25   E.g., [OⲩⲀ]TNⲀⲩ.

60,8   E.g., O[NTⲱC.

60,15   No supralinear stroke over N.

60,16   Supralinear stroke over first ϣ; e.g., TⲀϣ[ⲉ Oⲉⲋϣ].

ⲉⲧⲃⲉ ϩⲱⲃ ⲛⲓⲙ· ⲁⲩⲱ[

18   ⲛⲏ ⲉⲧⲕⲛⲁⲥⲱⲧⲙ ⲉ[ⲣⲟⲟⲩ]
ⲉⲃⲟⲗ ϩⲓⲧⲛ ⲟⲩⲉⲛⲛ̣[ⲟⲓⲁ]

20   ⲛⲧⲉ ⲛⲏ ⲉⲧ̇ϫⲟⲥⲉ ⲉ ⲧ̣[ⲉⲗⲓ−]
ⲟⲥ ⲁⲩⲱ ⲙⲛ ⲛⲉⲧⲕⲛ̣[ⲁⲥⲟⲩ−]

22   ⲱⲛⲟⲩ ϩⲛ ⲟⲩⲯⲩⲭⲏ [ⲛⲧⲉ]
ⲛⲓⲧⲉⲗⲓⲟⲥ· ⲅⲅ ⲁⲩⲱ [ⲉ−]

24   ⲧⲁⲥ ϫⲉ ⲛⲁⲓ̈ ⲁⲥϯ ⲱⲙ[ⲥ
                                     [ⲝⲁ]

[−−−   ]ⲛ̣ϩ

2   [−−−   ] ⲙ

[−−−   ] ·ⲧⲉ

4   [−−−   ] ⲛ ⲛ[

[. . . . .]ⲱ ⲛ ⲛ [

6   [. . . . .]ⲟⲥ ⲛ ⲛ̣[

[. . . . . .] ·[. . .] ⲡⲓϣⲟⲣⲡ̇

8   [. . . . . . .]ⲩ̣ⲱ ⲁⲉⲓϫⲓ ϭⲟⲙ

[. . . .]ⲩ̣ⲱ ⲁ̣[ ]ⲟⲩⲱ[. .]

10   [. . . .]ⲱ ⲁ[ⲉⲓ]ϫⲓ ⲙⲟⲣⲫⲏ

[. . .] ·ⲉ· ⲁⲩⲱ ⲁⲉⲓϫⲓ ⲟⲩⲟ−

12   [. . ·]ϥϣⲟⲟⲡ̇ ϩⲓϫⲙ ⲡⲁϣⲁ−
[. . ·]ϫⲓ ⲟⲩⲡ̅ⲛ̅ⲁ ⲉϥⲧⲟⲩⲃⲏ[ⲩ]

14   [ⲁⲉⲓ]ϣⲱⲡⲉ ⲉⲓ̈ϣⲟⲟⲡ̇ ⲟⲛ−
[ⲧⲱⲥ]˙ ⲁⲩⲱ ⲧⲟⲧⲉ ⲁⲥⲛ̇ⲧ

16   [ⲉϩ]ⲟⲩⲛ ⲉ ⲡⲓⲛⲟϭ ⲛⲛ ⲉ−
[ⲱⲛ] ⲡⲓⲙⲁ ⲉⲧⲉ ⲡⲓϣⲙ̇ⲧ̇

18   [ϩⲟⲟ]ⲩ̇ⲧ̇ ⲛ ⲧⲉⲗⲓⲟⲥ ⲙ−
[ⲙⲁⲩ]· ⲁⲩⲱ ⲁⲉⲓⲛⲁⲩ ⲉ

20   [ⲡⲁ]ⲗⲟⲩ ⲛⲛ ⲁⲧⲛⲁⲩ ⲉⲣⲟϥ
[ϩⲣⲁ]ⲓ̈ ϩⲛ ⲟⲩ‹ⲟⲩ›ⲟⲉⲓⲛ ⲛⲛ ⲁⲧ−

22   [ⲛⲁ]ⲩ ⲉⲣⲟϥ· ⲅⲅ ⲧⲟⲧⲉ ⲟⲛ
[ⲁⲥ]ϯ ⲱⲙⲥ ⲛⲁⲓ̈ ⲛϩⲣⲁⲓ̈ ϩⲛ
[ⲝⲃ]
ⲉⲩ[
2   ⲉⲧ̣[
ϫⲟⲟ[

60,22   I.e., in the souls.
60,24   After ⲱⲙ[ⲥ (here or next line) ⲛⲁⲓ̈ is to be restored.
61,9   Written ⲁⲩ̣.]ⲟⲩ because of an imperfection in the papyrus.
61,11-12   E.g., ⲟⲩⲟ[ⲉⲓⲛ ⲉ]ϥ.
61,11   ] ·ⲉ, e.g.,]ⲁ̣ⲉ, or]ⲙⲉ.

about everything, and [
18 those to whom you will listen,
through a thought (ἔννοια)
20 of those higher than perfect (τέλειος)
and also those whom you will [know]
22 in the souls (ψυχή) [of]
the perfect ones (τέλειος)."
24 [When] she had said this, she [baptized me]

                                                    [61]

[
2   [
[
4   [
[
6   [
[   ] the first
8   [   ] I received power
[
10 [I] received form (μορφή)
[   ] I received [
12 [   ] existing over my
[   ] receive a holy spirit (πνεῦμα).
14 [I] came into being [really (ὄντως)] existing.
Then (τότε), she brought me
16 into the great [aeon (αἰών)]
where the perfect (τέλειος)
18 thrice-male (is).
I saw
20 [the] invisible child
within an invisible
22 light. Then (τότε)
[she] baptized me again in
                                                    [62]
[
2   [
[

61,12-13   E.g., ⲡⲁϣⲁ[ⲝⲉ ⲁ̈]ⲝ ̣ⲋ.
61,16-18   I.e., Protophanes.
61,20   Cf. 44,27-30.
61,22   Written ⲉⲣⲟ̄ϥ· ⲧⲟⲧⲉ because of an imperfection in the papyrus.
62,1   Or, ⲉ̄ⲟ̈[.

4   [. .]ϭⲟ[
     [. .] ⲡⲉⲥⲥ .[
6   [ⲙ]ⲙⲟϥ ⲡⲉ[
     [ⲁⲩ]ⲱ ⲁⲉⲓ .[
8   [ⲁ]ⲉⲓϭⲙ ϭⲟⲙ ⲉ ⲛ[
     [. .] .ⲛⲓⲛⲟϭ ⲛⲛ ⲁ .[
10   [. . ⲁ]ⲩⲱ ⲛ [ⲧ]ⲉⲗⲟ[ⲥ
     ⲡⲉⲙⲁⲥ ⲛⲁⲓ̈ ⲛϭⲓ ⲧⲁⲛ[ⲓⲉⲟⲟⲩ]
12   ⲧⲏⲣⲟⲩ ⲓ̈ⲱ̅ⲏ̅ⲗ ⲙⲉ ⲛⲓⲙ[ⲱⲕⲙ]
     ⲧⲏⲣⲟⲩ ⲉⲧⲥⲙⲡϣⲁ ⲛ̣ [ⲙⲓ]
14   ⲱⲙⲥ ⲛ̅ⲏ̅ⲧⲟⲩ ⲁⲕⲙ[ⲓⲧⲟⲩ]
     [ⲁ]ⲩⲱ ⲁⲕϣⲱⲡⲉ ⲛ ⲧⲉ[ⲗⲓⲟⲥ
16   [.] .ⲟⲥ ⲡⲓⲥⲱⲧⲙ ⲛ̅ⲧⲉ[
     ⲧⲏⲣⲟⲩ· ϯⲛⲟⲩ ϭⲉ ⲙⲟ[ⲩⲧⲉ]
18   ⲟⲩⲉ ⲥ̅ⲁ̅ⲗ̅ⲁ̅ⲙ̅ⲉ̅ⲝ̅ ⲙⲛ .[
     ⲙⲛ ϯⲡⲁⲛⲧⲉⲗⲓⲟⲥ ⲁ̅ⲣ̅ .[
20   ⲛⲓⲫⲱⲥⲧⲏⲣ ⲛ̅ⲧⲉ ⲡⲓⲁⲓ[ⲱⲛ]
     ⲛ̅ ⲃ̅ⲁ̅ⲣ̅ⲃ̅ⲏ̅ⲗ̅ⲱ̅ ⲙⲛ ϯⲧⲛⲱ[ⲥⲓⲥ]
22   ⲛ̅ ⲁⲧϯ ϣⲓ ⲉⲣⲟⲥ· ⲁⲩⲱ [ⲛⲏ]
     ⲉⲧⲙⲙⲁⲩ ⲥⲉⲛⲁϭⲱⲗⲡ [ⲉⲃⲟⲗ]
                                   [ϩ̅ⲅ̅]

     [----   ]ⲁ̣ⲧⲛⲁⲩ
2   [----   ] .ⲏⲥⲡ[
     [----   ]ⲟⲩ[
4   [----   ]ⲉⲁⲩ[
     [----   ] .ⲉⲧ .[
6   [. . . . . ⲃ]ⲁⲣⲃⲏⲗⲱ ⲙ ⲡⲁⲣ[ⲑⲉ-]
     [ⲛⲟⲥ ⲁⲩⲱ] ⲡⲓⲁⲧⲛⲁⲩ ⲉⲣⲟϥ
8   [ⲛ̅ ϣⲙⲧϭ]ⲟ̣ⲙ ⲙ̅ ⲡ̅ⲛ̅ⲁ̅· ⲛ̣[ⲁⲓ̈]
     [ⲉⲧⲁⲥⲙⲟ]ⲟ̣ⲩ ⲛⲁⲓ̈ ⲛϭⲓ ⲧⲁ [ⲛⲓⲉ-]
10   [ⲟⲟⲩ] ⲧ̣ⲏⲣⲟⲩ ⲓ̈ⲟⲩⲏ̅ⲗ ⲁⲥⲕⲁ-
     [ⲁⲧ̀ ⲁ]ⲩⲱ ⲁⲥⲃⲱⲕ ⲁⲥⲁϩⲉⲣⲁ-
12   [ⲧⲥ ⲛ̅]ⲛⲁϩⲣⲁϥ ⲙ̅ ⲡⲓⲡⲣⲱⲧⲟ-
     [ⲫⲁⲛ]ⲏⲥ· ⲧⲟⲧⲉ ⲁⲛⲟⲕ ⲛⲉⲓ-
14   [ⲁϩⲉⲣ]ⲁ̀ⲧ̀ ⲛ̅ϩⲣⲁⲓ̈ ϩⲓⲙⲙ ⲡⲁⲡ̅ⲛ̅[ⲁ̅]
     [ⲉⲉⲓ]ⲧⲱⲃϩ ⲉⲙⲁⲧⲉ ⲛ̅ ⲛⲓⲛⲟϭ

62,9   Or, ⲛ ⲛⲁ | .[, e.g., ϯ̣[.
62,13   Lit., washings | ⲉⲧⲥⲙⲡϣⲁ, as in Bohairic.
62,17-19   See 63,18-21 and 64,8.
62,18   I.e., ⲟⲩⲃⲉ | .[, e.g., ϭ̣[.
62,19   ⲁ̅ⲣ̅.[, traces of a nomen sacrum with supralinear stroke (beginning

4   [
     [
6   [
     [and] I [
8   I was able to [
     [   ] the great ones [
10   [   ] and perfect (τέλειος) [
     Yoel who belongs to all [the glories]
12   said to me,
     "You have [received] all the [baptisms]
14   in which it is fitting to [be] baptized,
     and you have become [perfect (τέλειος)
16   [   ] the hearing of [
     all. Now [call] again
18   upon Salamex and [
     and the all-perfect (παντέλειος) Ar-[
20   the lights (φωστήρ) of the [aeon (αἰών)]
     Barbelo and immeasurable
22   knowledge (γνῶσις). [They]
     will reveal

                                   [63]
    [   ] invisible
2   [
     [
4   [
     [   ] which [
6   [virgin (παρθένος)] Barbelo
     [and] the invisible
8   [three-] powered Spirit (πνεῦμα). [When]
     Youel who belongs to all [the glories]
10   [had said this] to me, she
     [put me down] and went (and) stood
12   before the Proto[phan]es (πρωτοφανής).
     Then (τότε) I
14   [stood, presiding] over my spirit (πνεῦμα),
     [while] praying fervently to the great

---

       over **p**; there is a lacuna over the following trace).
63,6   Supralinear stroke not preserved over -**pβ** -.
63,9-10   Cf. 125,13-14; 53,13-14.
63,13-17 Cf. 3,14-19.

16 [ⲙ ⲫ]ⲱⲥⲧⲏⲣ ⲛ̅ϩⲣⲁⲓ̈ ϩⲛ ⲟⲩ–
    [ⲉⲛⲛ]ⲟⲓ̈ⲁ· ⲛⲉⲉⲓ̈ⲙⲟⲩⲧⲉ

18 [ⲟⲩ]ⲃⲉ ⲥⲁ̅ⲗ̅ⲁ̅ⲙ̅ⲉ̅ⲝ̅ ⲙⲛ ⲥⲉ–
    [. .]ⲉⲛ ⲙⲛ ϯⲡⲁⲛⲧⲉⲗⲓⲟⲥ

20 [. .] ⲧ̅ⲏ̅· ⲁⲩⲱ ⲁⲓ̈ⲛⲁⲩ ⲉ ϩⲉⲛ–
    [ⲉⲟ]ⲟⲩ ⲉⲛⲉⲁⲩ ⲉ ϩⲉⲛϭⲟⲙ

22 [ⲁⲩ]ⲱ ⲁⲩⲭⲱϩ ⲉⲣⲟⲉⲓ· ⲁⲓ̈ϭⲙ ϭⲟⲙ
    [ⲝ̅ⲇ̅]
    ⲁ .[

2 ϩⲙ ⲡⲁ[
    [ⲁ]ⲩⲱ .[

4 [.]ϯⲡⲁ .[
    [.]ⲟⲟⲩⲧ[. . .] .[

6 [ⲁ]ⲥϩⲱⲃⲥ ⲉⲃⲟⲗ [
    [ⲟⲩ] ⲧⲏⲣⲟⲩ· [

8 [.]ⲥ̅ⲁ̅ⲗ̅ⲁ̅ⲙ̅ⲉ̅ⲝ̅ ⲙ[ⲛ
    [ⲛ]ⲏ ⲉⲧⲁⲩϭⲱⲗ̅ⲛ̅ [ⲛⲁⲓ̈ ⲉⲃⲟⲗ]

10 ⲛ ϩⲱⲃ ⲛⲓⲙ ⲉⲩϫⲱ ⲙ[ⲙⲟⲥ]
    ϫⲉ ⲍ̅ⲱⲥⲧⲣⲓⲁⲛⲉ ⲥ̅[ⲱⲧⲙ]

12 ⲉⲧⲃⲉ ⲛⲏ ⲉⲧⲕⲕⲱⲧ̅[ⲉ ⲛ̅–]
    ⲥⲱⲟⲩ· v v v ⲛⲉ ⲟⲩ[

14 ⲁⲩⲱ ⲟⲩⲁ ⲟⲩⲱⲧ ⲡ̅[ⲉ ⲉⲧ–]
    ϣⲟⲟⲛ̅ ϩⲁⲑⲏ ⲛ ⲛⲁⲓ̈ ⲧ[ⲏⲣⲟⲩ]

16 ⲉⲧ̅ϣⲟⲟⲛ̅ ⲟⲛⲧⲱⲥ [ϩⲙ ⲡⲓ–]
    ⲡⲛ̅ⲁ̅ ⲛ ⲁⲧ̅ϣⲓ ⲉⲣ[ⲟϥ]

18 ⲁⲩⲱ ⲛ ⲁⲧ̅ⲡⲱⲣϫ ⲛ [. . .]
    ⲟⲩⲁ ⲙ ⲡ[ⲏ]ⲧⲏⲣϥ ⲉⲧ[ϣⲟ–]

20 ⲟⲛ̅ ⲛϩⲏⲧϥ ⲙⲛ ⲡⲓ .[. . .]
    ⲙⲙⲟϥ ⲙⲛ ⲡⲏ ⲉⲧ̅ⲙ[

22 ⲛⲥⲱϥ· ⲉⲛⲧⲟϥ ⲙⲁⲩ[ⲁⲁϥ
    ⲉⲧϫⲓⲟⲟⲣ ⲙⲙⲟϥ ⲛ [
                             [ⲝ̅ⲉ̅]

    [. .]ⲧ̅ϥ [. .]ⲁⲧ[. . . . . . .

63,17-?   *The Revelations from Salamex*

63,17   Or, [ⲥⲟ]ⲫⲓⲁ | written ⲛⲉⲉⲓ because of papyrus surface (elsewhere
              ⲛⲉⲓ̈´).

63,18-19   No supralinear stroke over ⲥⲉ; ⲥⲉ [ⲁⲙ]ⲉⲛ, impossible because of word
              division.

63,20   [. .] ⲧ̅ⲏ̅, traces of a nomen sacrum with supralinear stroke; trace
              is probably from ⲙ or ⲁ, but possibly also from ⲍ, ⲗ, ⲕ, ⲥ, ϩ, etc.

63,21   Sahidic, ⲉⲛⲁⲁⲩ.

63,22   Or, and I was anointed.

64,5   E.g., [ϩ]ⲟⲟⲩⲧ.

16 lights (φωστήρ) in
    thought (ἔννοια). I began calling
18 upon Salamex and Se-
    [   ]-en and the (fem.) all-perfect (παντέλειος)
20 [   ]-e. I saw
    [glories] greater than powers,
22 [and] they anointed me. I was able
    [64]
    [
2   in my [
    and [
4   [
    [
6   she covered [
    all [
8   Salamex [and
    [those] who have revealed
10 everything [to me] saying,
    "Zostrianos, [learn]
12 of those things about which you asked.
    [
14 and [he was] a single one [who]
    exists before [all] these
16 who really (ὄντως) exist [in the]
    immeasurable and undivided
18 Spirit (πνεῦμα) [
    . . . of the all which [exists]
20 in it and the [
    . . . and that one which [
22 after it. It is he alone
    who crosses it [

                                          [65]

    [

───────────

64,7   [ΟΥ], scored through by diagonal stroke in codex.
64,9-12   The new revelations begin.
64,11   Cf. 14,1.
64,13   E.g., ΝЄ Ο[ΥⲀ ΠЄ]; cf. 76,15.
64,14-22   Perhaps Kalyptos is the topic.
64,20   E.g., ⲀⲓΤϢⲀϪЄ.
64,21-22   E.g., ЄΤⲘ[Ν]ⲓΝCⲰϤ.
64,22   ЄΝΤΟϤ, no supralinear stroke was possible over Ν because of an im-
           perfection in the papyrus.

2 [. .]ṇ[.]ⲁ ⲛ ⲁⲧ̄[. . . . . .]ⲁⲧ−
   [. . . .] .ⲁ̇ⲧⲟ[. . . .] ⲛ ⲁⲧ̄−
4 [. . . .]ⲏ̄ⲛⲁⲩ̄[. . .]ⲟⲩ̄ .
   [. . . . . . .] .[. . ⲛ]ⲁ̇ⲓ ⲧⲏⲣ[ⲟⲩ]
6 [. . . . .]ⲁⲣ[.]ⲏ ⲡⲉ ṇ [.
   [. . . . . . . ⲟ]ⲩϣⲟⲣⲡ̄ ⲛ .[
8 [. . . . . ⲛ]ⲧⲉ ⲉⲛⲛⲟⲓⲁ ⲛ̣ⲓ[ⲙ]
   [. . . . .]ⲉ ⲛⲧⲉ ϭⲟⲙ ⲛ̣ⲓ[ⲙ]
10 [. . . . .] ⲉϩⲟⲩⲛ ⲉ ⲡⲉ[ⲥⲏⲧ]
   [. . .] ⲉϥⲥⲉⲙⲛⲏⲩ̄ ⲉϩⲟⲩⲛ
12 [. .]ⲥ̣ⲁϩⲉⲣⲁⲧϥ̄· ⲉϥⲟⲩⲟ−
   [ⲧⲃ ⲉ]ϩⲟⲩⲛ ⲉ ⲡⲓⲉⲓ ⲉⲩⲙⲁ
14 [. . .] ⲙⲛ ⲟⲩⲁⲧⲛ ⲁⲣⲏϫϥ̄
   [ⲁⲩ]ⲱ ⲉϥϫⲟⲥⲉ ⲉϩⲟⲧⲉ ⲁ−
16 [ⲧⲛ] ⲣⲁⲧϥ ⲛⲓⲙ· ⲁⲩⲱ ⲉϥϯ
   [. . .] ⲉⲛⲉⲁϥ ⲉ ⲥⲱⲙⲁ ⲛⲓⲙ
18 [ⲉ]ϥⲧⲟⲩⲃⲏⲩ̄ ⲉ ⲁⲧⲥⲱⲙⲁ
   [ⲛⲓ]ⲙ· ⲉϥⲛⲁ ⲉϩⲟⲩⲛ ⲉ ⲉⲛ−
20 [ⲛⲟⲓ]ⲁ ⲛⲓⲙ ⲙⲛ ⲥⲱⲙⲁ ⲛⲓⲙ
   [ⲉϥ]ⲉ ⲛ ϭⲟⲙ ⲉ ⲛⲁⲓ ⲧⲏⲣⲟⲩ
22 [ⲅⲉⲛ]ⲟⲥ ⲛⲓⲙ ⲙⲛ ⲉⲓⲁⲟⲥ
   [ⲛⲓⲙ] ⲉⲩⲡⲧⲏⲣϥ ⲛⲧⲁⲩ ⲡⲉ
   [ⲝ̄ⲉ̄]
   [. . . . .]ϣⲟⲟⲛ̄ [. . .
2 ⲁⲩ[. . . . . .]ⲟⲟⲛ̄ ⲟⲛ[. . .
   ⲛ ⲧ[. . . . . .] .ⲧⲏⲣ[. . . .
4 [.]ⲣ̄ⲁⲣⲉ[. . . .]ⲣϥ̄ ⲡⲓ[. . .
   [. .]ⲕⲟⲛ .[. . .]ⲣⲱ ⲛ ⲛ[. . .
6 ⲁ· ⲉⲩⲙⲉⲣⲓⲕ[ⲟⲛ . . . .
   [. .]ⲙⲉⲣⲟⲥ ⲧⲏⲣ[−−− ϣⲟ]
8 [ⲟ]ⲡ̄ ⲛ̄ϩⲣⲁⲓ̈ ϩⲛ ⲟⲩ[. . . . . .
   ⲥⲟⲩⲱⲛⲥ ⲉⲥ .[. . . . . . .
10 [. .]ⲣⲉ ⲉⲃⲟⲗ ⲙⲙ[ⲟϥ ⲡⲉ]
   [. .] .ⲟⲩ ⲉⲧϣⲟ[ⲟⲛ̄ ⲟⲛ−]
12 ⲧⲱⲥ̄ ⲉⲧⲉ ⲉⲃⲟⲗ ⲙⲙⲟϥ [ⲙ̄]
   ⲡⲓⲡⲛ̄ⲁ̄ ⲉⲧϣⲟⲟⲛ̄ ⲟⲛ[ⲧⲱⲥ]

65,6   E.g., ⲟⲩ]ⲁⲣ[ⲭ]ⲏ ⲡⲉ.
65,11 Qualitative of ⲥⲙⲓⲛⲉ.
65,12 ⲥ̣, or else]ⲉ̣.
65,17 E.g., [ϭⲟⲙ].
66,2   E.g., ϣ[ⲟⲟⲛ ⲟⲛ[ⲧⲱⲥ].

2   [
     [
4   [
     [   ] all these
6   [   ] he is[
     [a] first [
8   [of] every thought (ἔννοια)
     [   ] of every power
10   [downward]
     [   ] he is established
12   [   ] stands, he [passes]
     into the pathway to a place
14   [   ] and infinite.
     He is far higher than
16   any unaccessible one, yet he gives
     [   ] greater than any body (σῶμα)
18   (and) purer than any disembodied one (-σῶμα),
     yet entering into every
20   thought (ἔννοια) and every body (σῶμα),
     [because he] is more powerful than them all,
22   (than) any race (γένος) or species (εἶδος),
     as their All.
     [66]
     [   ] exist [
2   [
     [
4   [
     [
6   to a [partial (μερικόν)
     [   ] part (μέρος) [
8   [exist] in a [
     know her [
10   [he is] from [him]
     [   ] which really (ὄντως) exists,
12   who (is) from
     the Spirit (πνεῦμα) that [really (ὄντως)] exists,

66,4-5   E.g., ⲡϣ[ⲙⲉ]/[ⲣϣ]ⲕⲟⲛ; cf. 66,6.
66,4   ϣ, or else ⲃ, ϥ, ⲏ, ⲕ, or ⲛ.
66,5   ⲱ, or else ⲱ̣ | room for [ϣ] between ⲱ and ⲛ.
66,8   ⲛ̣, or else ⲡ̣.
66,9   .[, bottom of a vertical stroke; probably from ⲧ or ⲩ.

14 ⲡⲓⲟⲩⲁ ⲙⲁⲩⲁⲁϥ ⲛ ϣ[. .
ϭⲟⲙ ⲅⲁⲣ ⲛⲉ ⲛⲧⲉ ϥ[. . . .
16 ⲛⲁⲥ· ϯϩⲩⲡⲁⲣⲝⲓⲥ .[. .
ⲡⲱⲛϩ ⲇⲉ ⲙⲛ ϯⲙⲛⲧ[ⲙⲁ-]
18 ⲕⲁⲣⲓⲟⲥ· ⲁⲩⲱ ⲛϩⲣ[ⲁⲓ ϩⲛ]
ϯϩⲩⲡⲁⲣⲝⲓⲥ ϥϣⲟⲟⲡ[
20 ⲟⲩⲁⲡⲉ ⲛ ϩⲁⲡⲗⲟⲩⲛ ⲟⲩ[ϣⲁ-]
ⲝⲉ ⲛⲧⲁϥ ⲙⲛ ⲟⲩⲉⲓⲁⲟ[ⲥ]
22 ⲁⲩⲱ ⲡⲏ ⲉⲧϥⲛⲁϭⲓⲛ[ⲉ ⲙ-]
ⲙⲁϥ ϣⲁϥⲧⲣⲉϥϣⲱ[ⲡⲉ]
24 ⲉϥϣⲟⲟⲡ ⲛϩⲣⲁⲓ ⲇ[ⲉ ϩⲛ]
ϯⲙⲛⲧⲱⲛϩ ϥⲟⲛϩ ⲁ[

[ⳉ̄ⲅ̄]

[. . . . .] ⲛ[ϩ]ⲣⲁⲓ [
2 [. . . . .]ⲓⲟⲥ ϥϣ .[. .] ⲝⲉⲩⲛ-
[ⲧⲁϥ ⲙⲙ]ⲁⲩ ⲛ ⲟⲩ ⲙ[ⲛ]ⲧ[ⲉⲓⲙⲉ
4 [. . . . .]ⲙⲙⲉ ⲉ ⲛⲁⲓ ⲧⲏⲣⲟ[ⲩ
[. . . .] .ⲡⲉ ⲉⲣⲟϥ ⲙⲁⲩⲁⲁ[ϥ
6 [. . . . . . .] ⲡⲛⲟⲩⲧⲉ ⲅⲁⲣ [
[. . . . . . .]ⲁⲩ ⲉⲓⲙⲏⲧⲓ ⲉ[
8 [. . . . . . ⲙ]ⲁⲩⲁⲁϥ· ⲁⲩⲱ ϥϣ[
[. . . . . . .] ⲛϩⲣⲁⲓ ⲛϩⲏⲧϥ [
10 [. . . . . . .] · ⲡⲓⲟⲩⲱⲧ ⲛ [
[. . . . . . .]ⲁ· ⲉϥϣⲟⲟⲡ ⲅⲁⲣ ⲛ [
12 [ϩⲣⲁⲓ ϩ]ⲙ ⲡⲉⲧⲉ ⲡⲱϥ ⲉⲧϣⲟ-
[ⲟⲡ ⲛ] ⲟⲩⲉⲓⲁⲉⲁ ⲛⲧⲉ ⲟⲩⲉⲓⲁⲉⲁ
14 [ϯⲙⲛ]ⲧⲟⲩⲱⲧ ⲛⲧⲉ ϯϩⲉⲛ-
[ⲛⲁⲥ·] ⲁⲩⲱ ⲉϥϣⲟⲟⲡ ⲙ ⲡ[-
16 [. . . .] ⲉϥⲛϩⲣⲁⲓ ⲛϩⲏⲧϥ ϩⲙ
[ⲡⲓⲛ]ⲟⲩⲥ ⲁⲩⲱ ϥⲛϩⲣⲁⲓ ⲛϩ-
18 [ⲧ]ϥ ⲉϥⲛⲛⲏⲩ ⲉⲃⲟⲗ ⲉ ⲗⲁⲁⲩ
ⲙ ⲙⲁ ⲁⲛ ⲉⲩⲡⲛⲁ̄ ⲛ ⲟⲩⲱⲧ
20 [ⲡ]ⲉ ⲛ ⲧⲉⲗⲓⲟⲥ ⲛ ϩⲁⲡⲗⲟⲩⲛ
[ⲉⲩ]ⲧⲟⲡⲟⲥ ⲛⲧⲁϥ ⲡⲉ ⲙⲛ
22 [. . .] ⲉϥϣⲱⲡⲉ ϩⲣⲁⲓ ⲛϩⲏⲧϥ

66,14   ϣ[, connected to the following letter (in lacuna) by a supralinear stroke.
66,15-18   Cf. 14,9-14.
66,17   ϯ, the flag does not survive.
66,19   Perhaps Kalyptos; cf. 15,10-12; 68,14-26.
66,20   Origin, lit., head.
66,22-23   Sahidic ⲙⲓ/ⲙⲟϥ.

14 the one alone [
    for (γάρ) they are powers of
16 [   ], existence (ΰπαρξις) [
    and (δέ) life and
18 blessedness (μακάριος). In
    existence (ΰπαρξις) he exists [
20 a simple (ἁπλοῦν) origin,
    his [word] and species (εἶδος).
22 Let the one who will find
    him come into existence.
24 Existing [(+δέ) in]
    Life, he is alive [

                                    [67]

    [
2   [
    [he having] knowledge
4   [   ] know all these [
    [   ] him alone [
6   [   ], for (γάρ) god [
    [[unless (εἰ μήτι) [
8   [   ] alone, and he[
    [   ] in him [
10 [   ] the single [
    [   ] for (γάρ) he exists as [
12 [in] that which is his, which [exists]
    [as] a form (ἰδέα) of a form (ἰδέα),
14 [the] unity of the
    [unity (ἑνάς)]. He exists as [the]
16 [   ] since he is in
    [the] mind (νοῦς). He is within
18 it, not coming forth to any
    place, because he [is] a single
20 perfect (τέλειος), simple (ἁπλοῦν) spirit (πνεῦμα).
    [Because] it is his place (τόπος) and
22 [   ], it is within him [and] the Alls

67,5   He, antecedant is not clear.
67,14-15   For ϩ ⲉ ⲛ [ⲛ ⲁ ⲥ], see. 75,20n.
67,14   ⲛ ⲓ ⲧ̄, a trace of the supralinear stroke (above ⲧ) survives; for the restora-
           tion, cf. 68,26; 84,20; 86,22-23.
67,16   E.g., [ⲡ ⲛ ⲁ]; cf. 64,17; or [ⲱ ⲛ ϩ].
67,21   Or, [ⲟ ⲩ].

[ⲁⲩ]ⲱ ⲛⲓⲧⲏⲣⲟⲩ· ⲁⲩⲱ
24 [ⲉϥϣ]ⲟⲟⲛ ⲛⲧⲟϥ ⲛϭⲓ ⲡⲉⲧ-
[ϩⲏ]
[. . . . .] . . .[. .]ⲡ̣[
2 [. . . . .] ⲙⲛ ⲟ̣ⲩ̣ⲱ̣[
ⲁⲩⲱ [ⲟ]ⲩⲣⲉϥϣⲱⲡ [ⲛϩⲣⲁⲓ]
4 ⲛϩⲏⲧ[ϥ ⲩ̄] ⲡⲓⲱⲛϩ ⲇ[ⲉ
[ⲉⲛ]ⲉ̣ⲣⲅⲓⲁ ⲇⲉ ⲛⲧⲉ ϯ[
6 [.]ⲥ ⲛⲛ ⲁⲧⲟⲩⲥⲓⲁ· ⲡ[
[ⲉ]ⲧ̄ϣⲟⲟⲛ ⲛϩ̣ⲏ̣[ⲧϥ
8 [ϣⲟ]ⲟⲛ ⲛϩⲏⲧϥ [
ϣⲟⲟⲛ ⲉⲧⲃⲏⲏⲧ[ϥ
10 ⲙⲁⲕⲁⲣⲓⲟⲥ ⲙⲛ ⲟ[ⲩ
[ⲧ]ⲉⲗⲓⲟⲥ· ⲁⲩⲱ [
12 [ⲉ]ⲧ̄ϣⲟⲟⲛ ϩⲛ [
ⲉⲧϣⲟⲟⲛ ⲟⲛⲧⲱ̣ⲥ [ⲟⲩ-]
14 ⲙⲁⲕⲁⲣⲓⲟⲥ ⲧⲉ ϯⲉⲓⲇ[ⲉⲁ]
ⲛⲧⲉ ϯⲉⲛⲉⲣⲅⲓⲁ ⲉⲧ[ϣⲟ-]
16 ⲟ̄ⲛ ⲉϣⲁϥϫⲓ ⲛ ϯϩⲩⲡ[ⲁⲣ-]
ϩⲓⲥ· ϣⲁϥϫⲓ ϭⲟⲙ ⲡ[
18 ⲟⲩⲙⲛ̄ⲧⲧⲉⲗⲓⲟⲥ ⲉⲙ[
ⲡⲱⲣϫ ⲉⲃⲟⲗ ⲉⲛⲉϩ· ⲧⲟ[ⲧⲉ]
20 ϥϣⲟⲟⲛ ⲛ ⲧⲉⲗⲓⲟⲥ· ⲉⲧⲃ[ⲉ]
ⲡⲁⲓ ϥϣⲟⲟⲛ ⲛ ⲧⲉⲗⲓⲟⲥ
22 ⲉϥⲉ ⲛⲛ ⲁⲧ̄ⲡⲱⲣϫ ⲉⲣⲟϥ
ⲙⲛ ⲡⲉϥⲥⲁ ⲙⲙⲓⲛ ⲙⲙⲟϥ
24 ⲙⲙⲛ ⲗⲁⲁⲩ ⲅⲁⲣ ⲉϥϣ[ⲟ-]
ⲟ̄ⲛ ϩⲁ ⲧⲉϥⲉϩ ⲉⲓⲙⲏ[ⲧⲓ]
26 ϯⲙⲛ̄ⲧⲟⲩⲱⲧ̄ ⲛ ⲧⲉ[ⲗⲓⲟⲥ]

$$[\overline{ϩ\theta}]$$
(Page 69 does not survive. It was probably a blank
   but was counted in the paging.)

$$[\overline{ⲟ}]$$
(Page 70 does not survive. It was probably a blank
   but was counted in the paging.)

67,23   Not ⲛⲓⲡⲧⲏⲣϥ.
68,2   ⲱ, or else ϥ or ϣ.

that he comes into being.
24 [It is] he who exists, he who
    [68]
    [
2   [   ] and a [
    and a [protector]
4   in [him]. Life [(+δέ)
    and (δέ) activity (ἐνέργεια) of the (fem.) [
6   insubstantial (-οὐσία) [   ], the [
    which exists in [him
8   [exists] in him [
    exists because of [him
10 blessed (μακάριος) and [a
    perfect (τέλειος), and [
12 which exists in [
    which really (ὄντως) exists.
14 Blessed (μακάριος) is the [form (ἰδέα)]
    of the activity (ἐνέργεια) that exists.
16 By receiving existence (ὕπαρξις),
    he receives power, the [
18 a perfection (-τέλειος) [
    separate forever. Then (τότε)
20 he exists as perfect (τέλειος). Therefore,
    he exists as perfect (τέλειος)
22 because he is undivided
    with his own region,
24 for (γάρ) nothing exists
    before him except (εἰ μήτι)
26 the [perfect (τέλειος)] unity.

[69]
(Page 69 does not survive. It was probably a blank
   but was counted in the paging.)

[70]
(Page 70 does not survive. It was probably a blank
   but was counted in the paging.)

_____

68,3   ⲣⲉϥϣⲱⲡ = ἀντιλήμπτωρ.
68,6   Or, non-essential; cf. 79,8.

(Page 71 is a blank; it had pagination.)

(Page 72 is a blank; it had pagination.)

```
     [ . . . . . ]Ϩⲩⲡⲁⲣ[ⲝⲓⲥ
 2   [ . . . .] .ⲟ[ⲩ]ⲍⲁⲓ̈ ⲧⲉ ⲛ [
     [ . ⲧⲏ]ⲣⲟⲩ[·] ⲁⲩⲱ ⲡⲏ ⲉ̣[
 4   [ . . .]ϣϭⲟⲙ ⲟⲩⲇⲉ ⲛϥ[
     [ . . .]ⲟⲟϥ· ⲉϣⲱⲡⲉ ⲉϥ[ϣⲁⲛ-]
 6   [ . . .]ⲛ̅ⲧϥ ⲛⲁϥ ⲛⲁⲓ̈ ⲧⲏⲣ[ⲟⲩ]
     [ . . . .] ⲉⲃⲟⲗ· ⲡⲏ ⲅⲁⲣ ⲉⲧ[
 8   [ . . . .] Ϩⲛ ϯϨⲩⲡⲁⲣⲝⲓⲥ
     [ . .] ⲡⲁⲓ̈ ⲡⲁⲛⲧⲱⲥ ϥϣⲟ-
10   [ⲟⲡ̅] ⲙ ⲡⲓⲱⲛϨ· Ϩⲛ ϯⲙⲛ̅ⲧ-
     [ⲙⲁ]ⲕⲁⲣⲓⲟⲥ ⲇⲉ ϥⲓⲙⲉ· ⲁⲩⲱ
12   [ⲉϣ]ⲱⲛ̅ ⲉϥϣⲁⲛⲍⲓ ⲙⲛ ⲛⲓ-
     [ⲉⲟ]ⲟⲩ ⲟⲩⲧⲉⲗⲓⲟⲥ ⲡⲉ·
14   [ⲉϣ]ⲱⲡⲉ ⲇⲉ ⲉϥϣⲁⲛⲍⲓ ⲙⲛ
     [ⲥⲛⲁ]ⲩ ⲏ ⲟⲩⲁ· ⲟⲩϯϨⲉ ⲡⲉ
16   [ⲙ ⲡ]ⲣⲏⲧⲉ ⲉⲧⲁϥⲍⲓ ⲉⲃⲟⲗ
     [ⲙⲙ]ⲟϥ· ⲉⲩϣⲟⲟⲡ̅ ⲉⲧⲃⲉ
18   [ⲡⲁ]ⲓ̈ ⲛϭⲓ ⲛⲏ ⲉⲧⲉ ⲟⲩⲛ ⲯⲩⲭⲏ
     [ⲛϨ]ⲏⲧⲟⲩ ⲙⲛ ⲛⲓⲁⲧ̅ⲯⲩⲭⲏ·
20   [ⲉⲧ]ⲃⲉ ⲡⲁⲓ̈ ⲛⲏ ⲉⲧⲛⲉⲛⲟⲩ-
     [Ϩⲙ] ⲉⲧⲃⲉ ⲡⲁⲓ̈ ⲛⲏ ⲉⲧⲛⲁ-
22   [ⲧⲁ]ⲕⲟ· ⲉϣⲱⲡⲉ ⲉⲙⲡⲟⲩ-
     [ⲍⲓ ⲉ]ⲃⲟⲗ ⲙⲙⲟϥ· ⲉⲧⲃⲉ
24   [ⲡⲁ]ⲓ̈ ⲟⲩϨⲩⲗⲏ ⲧⲉ ⲙⲛ Ϩⲉⲛ-
     [ⲥ]ⲱⲙⲁ· ⲉⲧⲃⲉ ⲡⲁⲓ̈ ⲟⲩⲁⲧ̅-
```

```
     [ . . . . . . ]ⲩⲛⲟⲩⲁ[
 2   [ⲉⲧ]ⲃⲉ ⲡⲁⲓ̈ ⲉⲑ[ .]ⲉ̣[
```

73,9   E.g., [Ϩⲙ] ⲡⲁⲓ̈.

73,12   ⲉϣ]ⲱⲛ̅, elision for ⲉϣⲱⲡⲉ (as at 44,17).

73,17-24   Because the Kalyptos aeon is hidden or veiled, it is imperfectly appre-
hended by the lower aeons. The emanation process, repeated many times
over, explains how an imperfect physical world came into being from a
perfect origin. Those without souls, i.e., those who are entirely material,

[71]
(Page 71 is a blank; it had pagination.)

[72]
(Page 72 is a blank; it had pagination.)

[73]

[   ] existence (ὕπαρξις) [
2   [   ] she is salvation [
[. . .   all] and he [
4   [   ] be able, nor (οὐδέ) does he [
[   ], if he
6   [   ] him to him, all these
[   ], for (γάρ) he [who
8   [   ] in existence (ὕπαρξις)
[   ] this one, he totally (πάντως)
10   [exists] as life, and (δέ) in
blessedness (-μακάριος) he has knowledge.
12   If he apprehends the
[glories], he is perfect (τέλειος);
14   but (δέ) if he apprehends
[two] or (ἤ) one, he is drunk,
16   as having received
[from] him. It is for [this] reason
18   that there are those with souls (ψυχή)
and those without souls (-ψυχή);
20   for this reason (there are) those who will
be saved and those who will
22   [perish], since they have not [received]
from him; for [this] reason
24   (there are) matter (ὕλη) and
bodies (σῶμα); for this reason non-
[74]
[   ] . . . [
2   [for] this reason [

---

have nothing to be redeemed and will perish.
73,20   —Νε′, Sahidic —Να′ (future tense); cf. 96,2.
74   Abraided passage read under ultraviolet light.
74,1   Ν may have had supralinear stroke.
74,2   ϴ, or else ϛ | ϛ, or else ϴ.

[. .]ογ [τ]ηρϥ [.] ετβε[
4 [.] .ρο . παϊ [.]ε̣τρ ϣ[ρ̅ π̅ ν]
[ϣ]οοπ̄· αγω εϥ .[
6 [.]γ̣ε ογαπε ν ϩαπ[λογν
[. .]π̅ν̅α̅ ογω̇τ ε̣[
8 ρ[. .] εροϥ πε· αγω [. . . . ϩγ-]
παρχ̄ιϲ †ειλεα [
10 [.]ε ντаϥ· αγω κα[τα †ε-]
[ν]ερϲια ετε πιωνϩ [
12 πε· αγω κατα †μν̄[ττε-]
λιοϲ ετε †ϭομ τ[ε ν νο-]
14 εροn εγογοειν τ[ε
πιϣομ̄τ εϥαϩερατ[ϥ ϩι ογ-]
16 con̄ εϥκιμ ϩι ογϛ̣[on̄]
nϩραϊ ϩm ma nim aγ[ω ϩραϊ]
18 ϩn λααγ m ma an εϥ[
naγ τηρογ αγω εϥ[ρ ε-]
20 nερϲι πιατϣαχε m[μοϥ]
n ατ† ραn εροϥ· n [
22 ϣοοn̄ εβολ mμοϥ [
me εϥmοτn mμοϥ n̄[
24 ϩn τεϥmn̄ττελιοϛ [——— m-]
πϥχι εβολ ϩm μορφ[η nιm]

$$\overline{[ο̅ε̅]}$$

[ετ]βε παϊ [
2 [.] .ογ .[. . . . .] v̱ [. .
[. . .]τγ[. . . . .] .ογ[. .
4 [. .] n λα[αγ . . .]εnηϛ[.
[. . .]π[. . . . . .]οϛ mn [.
6 [. . .]ο̣[. . .] .απ̣αnι v̱ .[.
[. . . . . .] ϩn †ϩγπαρχ̄[ιϲ
8 [. . . . .] ϣοοn̄ ϩn †mn̄-
[. . .] nτε πιωnϩ· ϩn †-
10 [mn̄]τελιοϛ λε mn †mn̄[τ̄-]
[ειm]ε· †mn̄τmακαριοϛ

74,4   ] ., probably read н, ι, n, or ϥ | o, possibly a trace of a round letter after o.

74,5   .[, read в, τ, н, к, n or ρ.

74,6   Cf. 23,9; *Asclepius* VI 69,14ff; or, ογα πε.

74,7   ε̣, or else θ.

74,12   n, only a trace of the supralinear stroke survives.

... every [   ] because of [

4 this [ ] who [pre-]
   exists, and he [

6 ... a [simple (ἁπλοῦν)] origin, [
   [ ] single spirit (πνεῦμα) [

8 he is [   ], and [
   existence (ὕπαρξις), form (ἰδέα), [

10 [   ] of him. It is [in accordance with (κατά)]
   activity (ἐνέργεια) which [   ] life

12 and in relation to (κατά) perfection (-τέλειος)
   which is intellectual (νοερόν)

14 power that [she is] a [   ] light [
   It is together that the three stand,

16 they move together.
   It is in every place yet

18 not in any place that they [
   them all and produce (ἐνεργεῖν)

20 the ineffable
   unnameable [

22 exist from him[
   resting in him [

24 in her perfection (-τέλειος)[   ] he
   has [not] received from [every] form (μορφή) [
                                          [75]
   because of him [

2 [
   [

4 [anything
   [

6 [
   [   ] in existence (ὕπαρξις)[

8 [   ] exist in the
   [   ] of life. But (δέ) in

10 perfection (-τέλειος) and
   [knowledge] (is) blessedness (-μακάριος).

74,16-18   Lit., he; i.e., the three.
74,17   Ⲛ̄ϩⲣⲁ ⲓ̈...ϩⲣⲁ ⲓ̈; cf. 125,7-8.
74,18   E.g., ⲉϥ[ϯ ϭⲟⲙ].
74,23   Ⲛ̄, or else ⲅ̄, Ⲏ, ϥ, or ⲕ.
75   Location of the left margin is only approximate.
75,11-20   The text is obscure.

12 [ⲚⲀⲒ Ⲧ]ⲎⲢⲞⲨ ⲆⲈ ⲚⲈⲨϢⲞⲟⲡ̇
    [ϨⲚ ϯ]Ⲙ̅ⲚⲦⲀⲦ̇ⲠⲰⲢⲆ ⲚⲦⲈ

14 [ⲠⲒ]ⲠⲚⲀ· ϯⲘ̅ⲚⲦⲈⲒⲘⲈ ⲆⲈ
    [. . . .] ⲈⲦⲂⲎⲎⲦⲤ ⲠⲈ ϯⲘ̅ⲚⲦ-

16 [ⲚⲞ]ⲨⲦⲈ ⲘⲚ ϯⲘ̅ⲚⲦⲀⲦⲞⲨ-
    [. . .]ⲁ· ⲀⲨⲰ ϯⲘ̅ⲚⲦⲘⲀⲔⲀ-

18 [ⲢⲒⲞ]Ⲥ ⲘⲚ ⲠⲒⲰⲚϨ· ⲀⲨⲰ ϯ-
    [ⲘⲚ]ⲦⲈⲒⲘⲈ ⲘⲚ ϯⲘ̅ⲚⲦⲀⲄⲀ-

20 ⲐⲞⲤ· ⲀⲨⲰ ⲞⲨϨⲈⲚⲚⲀⲤ
    Ⲙ[Ⲛ] ⲞⲨⲘ̅ⲚⲦⲞⲨⲰⲦ· ⲀⲨⲰ

22 Ϩ[Ⲁ]ⲠⲖⲰⲤ ⲚⲀⲒ ⲦⲎⲢⲞⲨ ⲠⲒⲦ-
    Ⲧ[Ⲃ]ⲂⲞ ⲚⲦⲈ ϯⲘ̅ⲚⲦⲀⲦⲘⲒⲤⲈ

24 [. .]ⲣ ϢⲞⲢⲡ̇ Ⲛ ϢⲞⲟⲡ̇ ⲚⲀⲨ
    [. .]Ⲓ ⲚⲀⲒ ⲦⲎⲢⲞⲨ ⲘⲚ ⲠⲒ-
    [ⲞϤ]

    [——   ]ⲚⲈϤⲘ[

2   [——   Ϩⲣⲁ]Ⲓ̈ ϨⲚ Ⲛ[
    [. . . .] .[. . . . .]ⲞⲖ .[

4   [. . .]Ⲧⲁ[. . . . . .] Ⲙ Ⲡⲣ[
    [. .]ⲞⲨⲤ ϯ[. . . . .]ⲨⲤ Ⲡ[

6   [. . Ⲟ]ⲨⲞⲈⲒ[Ⲛ] Ⲉ[. . . .]Ⲉⲩ[
    [Ⲟ]ⲨⲀⲒⲰⲚ ⲞⲨⲄ .[

8   Ⲛ̇[Ϩ]ⲣⲁⲒ̈ ϨⲚ ⲞⲨⲘⲈ[
    Ⲙ̅ⲚⲦⲀⲦⲘⲒⲤⲈ· ⲈϤϢ[

10   ⲀⲢ Ⲛ ⲞⲨⲀⲈⲒϢ ⲚⲒⲘ ⲀϤ[
    [Ⲛ]ⲤⲰϤ ⲈϤⲚⲀⲨ ⲈⲢⲞϤ .[

12   ⲀⲨⲰ ⲈϤϢⲞⲟⲡ̇ ⲈⲞⲨ[Ⲁ ⲠⲈ]
    Ⲛ Ϩⲁ̅ⲠⲖⲞⲨⲚ· ⲈⲨⲘⲚ[ⲦⲘⲀ-]

14   ⲔⲀⲢⲒⲞⲤ ⲠⲈ Ⲛ̇ϨⲣⲁⲒ̈ ϨⲚ Ⲟ[Ⲩ-]
    Ⲙ̅ⲚⲦⲦⲈⲖⲒⲞⲤ ⲚⲈⲞⲨⲁ[

16   Ⲛ ⲦⲈⲖⲒⲞⲤ ⲀⲨⲰ Ⲙ̅ ⲘⲀⲔ̇[ⲀⲢⲒⲞⲤ]
    ⲈⲤⲢ Ϩⲁⲉ Ⲙ̅ ⲠⲀⲒ ⲚⲦⲈ ⲠⲎ̅ [Ⲉ-]

18   ⲦⲘⲘⲀⲨ ⲆⲈ ⲚⲀⲤⲢ Ϩⲁⲉ[
    ⲚⲦⲀϤ ⲆⲈ ⲚⲈϤⲞⲨⲎϨ Ⲛ̅Ϥ[ⲰⲤ]

20   ⲠⲈ ⲘⲚ ⲞⲨⲤⲞⲞⲨⲚ· Ⲁ[Ⲩ]Ⲱ
    ⲞⲨⲦⲚⲰⲤⲒⲤ ⲚⲦⲀϤ Ⲉ[Ϥ]ϢⲞ-

75,12   I.e., the Barbelo aeons?
75,15   I.e., the Spirit.
75,17   For ⲁ may be read ϩ, or possibly ⲕ, ⲗ, or ⲙ.
75,20   ϨⲈⲚⲚⲀⲤ = ἑνάς; not ἐννέας.
75,24   [. .]ⲣ, a conjugation.
76,4   ⲣ may have had supralinear stroke.

12   All [these] (+δέ) were
      [in the] indivisibility of
14   [the] Spirit (πνεῦμα). Because of (+δέ)
      [   ] knowledge it is
16   [divinity] and [
      and blessedness (-μακάριος)
18   and life and
      knowledge and goodness (-αγαθός)
20   and unity (ἑνάς)
      and singleness.
22   In short (ἁπλῶς), all these (are) the
      purity of barrenness
24   [ ] pre-exist him
      [ ] all these and the
      [76]
      [   ] his [
2   [   ] in [
      [
4   [
      [
6   [
      aeon (αἰών), a [
8   in a [
      barrenness, he [
10   ... always he [
      after him, seeing him [
12   It is because he [is] one that he is
      simple (ἁπλοῦν). Because he is
14   blessedness (-μακάριος) in
      perfection (-τέλειος) ... [
16   perfect (τέλειος) and [blessed (μακάριος)],
      lacking this (part) of that one
18   because she lacked his [
      because he followed [her]
20   with knowledge.
      It is outside of himself that

76,7   E.g., ⲟⲩⲥⲟ[ⲙ.
76,10   E.g., ⲁϥ[ⲕⲱⲧⲉ]; cf. 44,2 and 64,12.
76,12-20 The text is obscure.
76,16ff   The unnamed female who appears in the next 10 pages is probably
              Barbelo; see 77,13-25n.

22 ⲟⲛ̄ ⲛⲥⲁⲃⲟⲗ ⲙⲙⲟϥ· ⲙⲛ
    ⲡⲏ ⲉⲧⲙⲟⲩϣⲧ̄ ⲙⲙ[ⲟ]ϥ
24 ⲉϥϣⲟⲟⲛ̄ ⲛ̄ϩⲏⲧϥ· ⲟ[ⲩ–]
    ⲉⲓⲇⲱⲗⲟⲛ ⲙⲛ ⲟⲩϩⲓ[

                                    [ⲟ͞ⲍ]

    [. .]ⲣ ϩⲁⲉ ⲙ̄[. . . . .
2   [. . .]ⲙⲁⲩ [. . . . .]ⲉ̣[. . .
    [. . .]ⲙⲁⲩ [. . . . . . ϩⲁ]ⲡ[ⲗⲟ]ⲩ͞
4   [. . .]ⲡⲉϩ̣[. . . . .]ⲉϥⲡ[. .
    [. . .]ⲥⲟ[. . . . . .]ⲛⲁⲩ· ⲁ[ⲩ]ⲱ
6   [. .] .ⲉⲉ[. . .]ⲉⲛ[.]ϥⲛⲁϩⲓ .ⲉ̣
    [. . .]ⲧⲁ̣[. . .] .ⲡⲁⲓ̈ ⲁⲥ̄ϣ̣ⲱ[.]ⲡ̄
8   [. . . . .]ⲗⲁ ⲙ ⲡⲓⲡⲗⲏⲣⲱⲙⲁ
    [. . .] .ⲉⲧⲁⲥⲟⲩⲁϣϥ ϩⲱ–
10 [ⲱⲥ ⲛ]ⲁ̣ⲥ ⲁⲛ· ⲡⲁⲓ̈ ⲛⲧⲁⲥ–
    [. . .]ⲁⲁϥ ⲛⲥⲁⲃⲟⲗ ⲛ ϯⲙⲛ̄ⲧ–
12 [ⲧⲉⲗⲓ]ⲟⲥ· ⲁⲥⲡⲱⲣⲝ ⲉⲃⲟⲗ
    [ϯⲙⲛ̄ⲧ]ⲡⲁⲛⲧⲉⲗⲓⲟⲥ ⲅⲁⲣ ⲧⲉ
14 [ⲛⲧ]ⲉ ⲟⲩⲙⲛ̄ⲧⲧⲉⲗⲓⲟⲥ ⲉⲥ–
    ϣⲟⲟⲛ̄ ⲛ ⲟⲩⲙⲟⲩϣⲧ̄·
16 [ⲁ]ⲩⲱ ⲡⲣⲟⲥ ⲡⲏ ⲉⲧⲙⲙⲁⲩ
    [ⲧⲏ] ⲟⲩⲝⲡⲟ ⲧⲉ ⲉⲥⲟⲩⲏϩ ⲛ–
18 ⲥⲱϥ· ⲁⲩⲱ ϯⲉⲃⲟⲗ ϩⲛ ϯ–
    [ϭ]ⲟⲙ ⲛⲛ ⲁⲧϣⲁⲝⲉ ⲙⲙⲟⲥ
20 [ⲛ]ⲧⲁϥ· ⲉⲥⲛⲧⲁⲥ ⲙⲙⲁⲩ
    ⲛ ⲟⲩϣⲟⲣⲡ̄ ⲛ ϭⲟⲙ· ⲙⲛ
22 ϯϣⲟⲣⲡ̄ ⲙ ⲙⲛ̄ⲧⲁⲧⲙⲓⲥⲉ
    ⲉⲧⲙⲛⲛⲥⲁ ⲡⲏ ⲉⲧⲙⲙⲁⲩ
24 ⲝⲉ ⲡⲣⲟⲥ ⲛⲓⲕⲉϣⲱⲝⲛ̄
    ⲧⲏⲣⲟⲩ ⲟⲩϣⲟⲣⲡ̄ ⲛⲛ ⲉⲱⲛ
    [ⲟ͞ⲏ]

    [––   ]ⲡⲉ ⲛ [. .
2   [. . .] .[. . . . . .]ⲁⲧ̄ [. .
    ⲛ [. .]ⲡ[. . . . . . .]ⲧⲧⲟ[. .
4   [ⲧⲏ]ⲣⲟⲩ [. . . . .]ⲩⲡⲁ[. .
    ⲛ[ⲛ] ⲁⲧⲟⲩ[. . . . . .]ϯ[. .

76,25   ϩⲓ, with circumflex; e.g., ϩⲓ[ⲕⲱⲛ].
77,1   ⲙ̄, or else ⲁ.
77,3   I.e., ϩⲁⲡⲗⲟⲩⲛ.
77,5   ⲱ, or else ϣ.
77,6   E.g., ϥⲛⲁϩ[ⲧ]ⲉ.

22   his knowledge (γνῶσις) dwells;
       it dwells with the one who
24   examines himself, [a]
       reflection (εἴδωλον) and a [

[77]

        [   ] be lacking [
2   [
        [   ] simple (ἁπλοῦν)
4   [
        [   ] and
6   [
        [   ] this, she [
8   [   ] the pleroma (πλήρωμα)
        [   ] which she did not desire
10   for [herself]. She has
        [   ] him outside of the
12   [perfection (-τέλειος)]; she has divided,
       for (γάρ) she is [the] all-perfection (-παντέλειος)
14   [of] perfection (-τέλειος),
       existing as thought.
16   With respect to (πρός) it (Spirit?)
       [she] is a begetting which follows
18   from it, and as one (fem.) from
       its ineffable power
20   she has
       a first power and
22   the first barrenness
       after it,
24   because with respect to (πρός) all the
       rest a first aeon (αἰών)

[78]

        [
2   [
        [
4   [all
        [

77,7   ⲱ, or else ⲩ; ⲩⲱ[.]ⲛ̣ (read with ultraviolet light).
77,9   Or, when she did not desire.
77,13-25   This description of the first emanation from the Spirit best fits Barbelo.
77,13   Not room for [ⲟⲩⲙ̄ⲛ̄ⲧ] in the lacuna; also possible are [ⲝⲉⲩ], i.e.,
                ⲝⲉⲟⲩ, [ⲧⲁⲟⲩ] and [ⲧⲁⲛ].

6 T[.] ⲚⲦⲈ ⲡ[.]ⲉ[. . . .] .ϥⲉ[. .
   ⲙ[. .]ⲉ ⲚⲘ ⲡⲎ .[. . . . . .
8 Ⲛ [ⲉ]ⲓⲙⲉ ⲈⲢⲞϤ ⲈϤϢⲞⲞ[ⲡ ⲞⲚ—]
   ⲦⲰⲤ ⲈⲦⲈⲰⲚ ⲡⲈ Ⲛ ϥ[. . .
10 ⲈⲚ ⲞⲨⲈⲚⲈⲢⲦⲓⲀ ⲆⲈ [. .
   ⲄⲞⲘ ⲀⲨⲰ ⲞⲨⲈⲨ .[.
12 ⲚⲚⲀⲤⲢ ⲀⲢⲬⲒ ⲈⲚ Ⲛ [. .
   ⲬⲢⲞⲚⲞⲤ· ⲀⲖⲖⲀ ⲀⲤ[ⲞⲨⲰ—]
14 ⲚⲈ ⲈⲂⲞⲖ ⲈⲚ ⲞⲨⲘⲚ̄ⲦϢⲀ [ⲉ—]
   ⲚⲈⲈ· ⲈⲀⲤⲀⲈⲢⲀⲦⲤ ⲚⲚ[ⲁ—]
16 ⲈⲢⲀϤ ⲈⲚ ⲞⲨⲘⲚ̄ⲦϢⲀ ⲈⲚ[ⲉⲈ]
   ⲀⲨⲰ ⲀⲤⲢ ⲈⲂⲎ ⲈⲂⲞⲖ ⲈⲒⲦⲚ ϯ—
18 ⲘⲚⲦⲚⲞϬ ⲚⲦⲈ ϮⲘⲚ̄ϯ[. .
   ⲚⲦⲀϤ· ⲀⲤⲀⲈⲢⲀⲦⲤ Ⲉ[ⲥ—]
20 ⲚⲀⲨ ⲈⲢⲞϤ ⲀⲨⲰ ⲈⲤⲦ[ⲉ]ⲖⲎ[ⲗ]
   ⲘⲘⲞⲤ ⲈⲤⲘⲈⲈ ⲈⲂⲞⲖ ⲈⲚ Ⲟ[ⲩ—]
22 ⲘⲚ̄ⲦⲬⲢⲎⲤⲦⲞⲤ ⲘⲘ[Ⲟ]Ⲥ [. .
   ⲢⲊ ⲈⲂⲞⲖ· ⲀⲖⲖⲀ ⲚⲦⲀⲤⲘⲞ[
                              [ⲟ̄ⲑ̄]

a [———   ]ⲥ̄
   [. . . .]ⲚⲞ̣[
2 [. . . .]ϯ̇ .[. . . . . .] .[. . . .]
   [. . . .] .[. . . . . .]ⲚⲦ[. .]
4 [. . . .] .[. . . . . .]ⲦⲈⲚⲊ[. .]Ⲩ
   [———   ]Ⲥ Ⲛ ⲚⲀ.[.]Ⲩ
6 [———   ]ⲉ ⲈⲤϢ[. .]ⲛ̄
   [. . . . . . .]ϢⲞⲢⲡ̄ Ⲛ ⲈⲨⲡⲀⲢ—
8 [ⳅⲓⲥ . . .] ⲀⲦⲞⲨⲤⲓⲀ· ⲘⲚⲚ—
   [ⲤⲀ .]Ⲏ ⲈⲦⲘⲘⲀⲨ· ⲈⲂⲞⲖ
10 [ⲈⲒⲦ]Ⲙ ⲡⲊⲀⲦ̄ⲡⲰⲢⳅ ⲡⲢⲞⲤ
   [ϯⲈ]ⲨⲡⲀⲢⳅⲒⲤ ⲈⲚ ⲞⲨⲈⲚⲈⲢ—
12 [ⲦⲓⲀ ⲘⲚ] ϯⲘⲚ̄ⲦⲦⲈⲖⲒⲞⲤ Ⲛ ⲚⲞ—

78,7-8 E.g., [ϢⲞⲢⲡ̄]/Ⲛ [ⲉ]ⲓⲘⲈ.
78,11 .[, the trace is not compatible with ⲗ (it is a vertical stroke, as in ⲃ, ⲧ, ⲏ, ⲓ, ⲕ, ⲛ, or ⲡ); not room for ⲈⲨⲡ[ⲀⲢⳅⲒⲤ unless this word was crowded far into the margin.
78,12 ⲀⲢⳅⲒ, common miswriting of ⲀⲢⲬⲒ.
78,18 Cf. 51,23n.
78,22-23 E.g., [ⲈⲤⲡⲰ]/Ⲣⳅ, or [Ⲛ ⲀⲦⲡⲰ]Ⲣⳅ.
78,22 Cf. 13,14.
79 Line numbers on this page are only approximate. Somewhat lower than the

6   [   ] of the [
     [   ] with him [
8   know him; he really (ὄντως)
     exists as an aeon (αἰών) [
10   And (δέ) in activity (ἐνέργεια) [
     power and a [
12   she did not begin (ἀρχεῖν) [
     time (χρόνος), but (ἀλλά) she [appeared]
14   from eternity,
     having stood before
16   it (Spirit?) in eternity.
     She was darkened by the
18   majesty of its [
     She stood
20   looking at it and rejoicing
     because she was filled with its
22   kindness (χρηστός), [
     . . . but (ἀλλά) when she had [

                                              [79]

a   [– –
     [
2   [
     [
4   [
     [
6   [   ] she [
     [   ] first [existence (ὕπαρξις)]
8   [   ] insubstantial (-ουσία),
     [after] that [   ]. It is
10   [from] the undivided one toward (πρός)
     existence (ὕπαρξις) by an activity (ἐνέργεια)
12   [intellectual (νοερόν)] perfection (τέλειος)

———————

        place where pagination is expected, there is an ink trace resembling ϲ or
        the right side of π or τ, with an ornamental bar below it (see line a); not
        compatible with ο̄θ and probably neither pagination nor text. Text
        begins at line 1.
79,2   τ̣, connected to the preceding letter (in lacuna) by a supralinear stroke.
79,4   τ̣, or else π̣.
79,6   E.g., ⲉⲥϣ[ⲟⲟ]ⲙ̄, or ⲉⲥϣ[ⲱ]ⲙ̄.
79,9   ]ⲏ̣ can also be read ⲓ̣, ⲛ̣, or ⲱ̣; restore either π]ⲏ̣, or τ]ⲏ̣, or ⲛ]ⲏ̣;
        cf. 77,23.

```
     [ЄРОN] ΜN ΠІⲰNϨ N NOЄРОN
14   [ЄϤ]КІΜ ЄТЄ NЄOⲨΜNϮ-
     [ΜⲀ]КⲀРІОС ПЄ ΜN OⲨΜN-
16   [ТN]OⲨТЄ· ⲀⲨⲰ ΠІΠⲚⲀ
     [ТН]РϤ N ТЄⲖІОС N ϨⲀΠⲖOⲨ
18   [Ⲁ]ⲨⲰ NN ⲀТNⲀⲨ ЄРОϤ
     [ЄⲀ]ϤϢⲰПЄ N OⲨΜNТОⲨ-
20   ⲰϮ ϨN OⲨϨⲨПⲀРⲌІС ΜN
     [OⲨ]ЄNЄРГІⲀ ΜN OⲨϢΜϮ-
22   [ϬOΜ] N ϨⲀΠⲖOⲨN· OⲨ-
     [ΠⲚⲀ] NN ⲀТNⲀⲨ ЄРОϤ OⲨ-
24   [ϨІ]КⲰN NТЄ ПН ЄТ-
     [Ϣ]OOⲡ̄ ОNТⲰС ПІОⲨⲀ
     [Π̄]
     [         ⸺           ] ·[
2    ·[ · ·] ·[ · · · · · · ·] ·Ⲁϥ[
     Ⳉ[ ·] ·ϬΜ[ · · · · · · ·] · ·[
4     ·[ · ·] · · · [
      ·[ ·] ΜⲘN[
6    Μ ПІОN[Т]Ⲱϲ [ЄТϢOOⲡ̄
     Є[Ϥ]ϢOOⲡ̄ ϨN O[Ⲩ
8    ТЄ ТⲀЇ ЄⲨϨІКⲰN ТЄ ·[
     ПЄ ϨN OⲨКⲰТЄ Μ[
10   ϬOΜ Є ϨⲰТⲡ̄ ΜN ПЄϤ ·[
     ЄⲀСNⲀⲨ Є ПІϢⲰϢ[
12   ПН ЄNЄϤϢOOⲡ̄ NⲀ[
     ϮΜNϮПⲀNТЄⲖІОС N [
14   ЄТΜΜⲀⲨ· ⳁЄ ПН ΜЄ[
     ϢOРⲡ̄ N ϢOOⲡ̄ ⲀⲨⲰ [
16   КН ϨІⳁN NⲀЇ ТНРОⲨ ЄϤ[
     ϢOРⲡ̄ N ϢOOⲡ̄ ЄⲨЄІΜ[Є]
18   ЄРОϤ N ϢΜТϬOΜ· ПІ[Ⲁ-]
     ϨOРⲀТОN Μ ПⲚⲀ ЄΜПϤ[Р]
20   ⲀϮЄІΜЄ РⲰ ЄNЄϨ· [NЄϤ-]
     ЄІΜЄ ⲀⲖⲖⲀ NЄϤϢO[Oⲡ̄ N]
22   OⲨΜNϮТЄⲖІОϲ [ΜN OⲨ-]
     ΜNϮΜⲀ[К]ⲀРІОС· Ⲩ    Т[
```

79,17   I.e., ϨⲀΠⲖOⲨN.
79,19   Or possibly just [Ⲁ]ϤϢⲰПЄ.
80   Line numbers on this page are only approximate.
80,7   ⲛ̄, the flag is not preserved.

and intellectual (νοερόν) life
14 that he moves, he who was
blessedness (-μακάριος) and
16 divinity. The [whole] Spirit (πνεῦμα),
perfect (τέλειος), simple (ἁπλοῦν)
18 and invisible,
[has] become a unity
20 in existence (ὕπαρξις) and
activity (ἐνέργεια) and a
22 simple (ἁπλοῦν) three-[powered] one,
an invisible spirit (πνεῦμα), an
24 image (εἰκών) of that which
really (ὄντως) exists, the one
[80]
[
2 [
[
4 [
[
6 of the really (ὄντως) [existing
[he] exists in a [
8 . . . she being an image (εἰκών) [
in a turning [
10 power to join with its [
she having seen the [
12 which was [
the all-perfection (-παντέλειος) [
14 that one, because it [
pre-exists and [
16 rest upon all these, it [
pre-exists being known
18 as three-powered. The
Invisible (ἀόρατον) Spirit (πνεῦμα) has not
20 ever [been] ignorant: [it always]
knew, but (ἀλλά) it was always
22 perfection (-τέλειος) [and]
blessedness (-μακάριος) [

80,11   ⲱ, or else ⲩ; e.g., ⲩⲱⲩ[ⲧ; cf. 39,12; 45,18.
80,14   E.g., ⲙⲉ[ⲛ ⲉϥⲣ].
80,16   E.g., ⲉϥ[ⲣ].

[π̄ᾱ]

[ℵ]ⲧⲁⲥⲣ ⲁⲧⲉⲥⲙⲉ [
2 ⲁⲩⲱ ⲉⲥϣ[⸺]
ϭⲱⲙⲁ ⲙⲛ ℵ[
4 . ⲉⲣⲏⲧ ⲉ[
[.]ⲟⲩⲟⲉⲓℵ [
6 [. .]ⲥϣⲟ[ⲟⲛ̄] ⲉⲕ .[
[.]ⲩ̄ⲗⲟⲉⲥ .[. .]ⲥⲧⲉ π[.]ⲥⲕⲉ· ϩ[ⲥ]ℵⲁ
8 ⲍⲉ ⲛⲛⲉⲥⲉⲥ ⲉⲃⲟⲗ ⲛ̄ϩⲟⲩⲟ
[ⲁ]ⲩⲱ ⲛⲥϣⲱⲡⲉ ϩⲥ ⲡⲟⲩⲉ
10 ⲛ̄ⲧⲉ ⲑⲙ̄ⲛ̄ⲧ̄ⲧⲉⲗ̄ⲥⲟⲥ· ⲁⲥ–
ⲙ̄ⲙⲉ ⲉⲣⲟⲥ ⲙⲛ ⲡⲏ ⲉⲧⲙ–
12 ⲙⲁⲩ· ⲁⲩⲱ ⲁⲥⲁϩⲉⲣⲁⲧⲥ
[ϩⲱ]ⲱⲥ ⲁⲥⲟⲩⲱϣ ⲉⲃⲟⲗ
14 [ⲉⲧ]ⲃⲉ ⲡⲏ ⲉⲧⲙⲙⲁⲩ· ⲁⲩⲱ
[ⲉ]ⲡⲓⲇⲏ ⲛⲉⲥϣⲟⲟⲛ̄ ⲉⲃⲟⲗ
16 [ϩⲙ ⲡ]ⲏ ⲉⲧϣⲟⲟⲛ̄ ⲟⲛⲧⲱⲥ
{[ⲛ]ⲉⲥϣⲟⲟⲛ̄ ⲉⲃⲟⲗ ϩⲙ ⲡⲏ ⲉⲧ
18 ϣⲟⲟⲛ̄ ⲟⲛⲧⲱⲥ} ⲙⲛ ⲛⲏ
[ⲧ]ⲏⲣⲟⲩ ⲉⲥⲟⲩⲱⲛⲥ ⲁⲩⲱ
20 [ⲥ]ⲥⲟⲩⲛ ⲡⲏ ⲉⲧⲣ ϣⲣⲛ̄ ⲛ ϣⲟ–
[ⲟ]ⲛ̄· ⲉⲁⲩⲟⲩⲁϩⲟⲩ ⲛ̄ⲥⲱϥ
22 ⲁⲩϣⲱⲡⲉ ⲉⲩϣⲟⲟⲛ̄ {ⲁⲩ–
ϣⲱ[ⲡ]ⲉ ⲉⲩϣⲟⲟⲛ̄]} ⲁⲩⲱ
24 ⲉⲩⲟⲩⲟⲛϩ ⲉⲃ[ⲟⲗ] ϩⲥⲧⲛ ⲛⲏ

[π̄β̄]

[ⲉⲧⲣ ϣⲟⲣ]ⲛ̄ ⲛ [ϣ]ⲟⲟⲛ̄· ⲁⲩⲱ
2 .[. . . . . ⲉ]ⲃⲟⲗ ϩⲥⲧⲛ ⲛⲥ[
[⸺] ⲉⲁⲩⲟⲩⲱⲛ[ϩ]
4 [ⲉⲃⲟⲗ ⸺] ⲥⲛⲧⲉ ⲙ [
[⸺] ⲁⲩⲟⲩⲱ[ⲛϩ]
6 [ⲉⲃⲟⲗ . . . .] .[. ⲡ]ⲏ ⲉⲧ–
ⲣ ϣⲟⲣⲛ̄ ⲛ ⲉⲥⲙⲉ ⲉⲣⲟϥ ⲉⲩ–
8 ⲭⲱⲣⲏⲙⲁ ⲡⲉ ⲛ ϣⲁ ⲉⲛⲉϩ·
ⲉⲁϥϣⲱⲡⲉ ⲛ ⲟⲩⲙⲉ[ϩ–]
10 ⲥⲛⲧⲉ ⲛ̄ⲧⲉ ⲧⲉϥⲅⲛⲱⲥⲥ

81,7 .[, ⲁ, ⲙ, or ⲇ; apparently not ⲗⲟⲉⲥⲅⲉ (as 20,1) for palaeographic
reasons. | π[.]ⲥ, no trema over ⲥ.
81,8 I.e., emanate from the Spirit; cf. 83,15-19.
81,11 Or, she knew it (perfection) and it (spirit).
81,17-18 {[ⲛ]ⲉⲥ´...ⲟⲛⲧⲱⲥ} carelessly repeated by the scribe or his predecessor.

[81]

she became ignorant [
2   and she [
body (σῶμα) and [
4   promise [
light [
6   [   ] she exists [
...[   ] in order that (ἵνα)
8   she might not come forth anymore
nor come into existence apart
10   from perfection (-τέλειος). She
knew herself and it (Spirit?).
12   She made herself stand,
[as (ὡς)] she was at rest
14   [because of] it.
Since (ἐπειδή) she was
16   [from] that which really (ὄντως) exists
{she was from the one who
18   really (ὄντως) exists} and all
those, she knows herself
20   and the one that pre-exists.
By following it
22   they came into being existing {they
came into being existing} and
24   appearing through those
[82]
[who pre-]exist. And
2   [   ] through the [
[   ] they having appeared
4   [   ] two [
[   ] they appeared
6   [the one] who
knows it beforehand, as
8   an eternal space (χώρημα),
since he had become
10   its second knowledge (γνῶσις),

81,18-19   Perhaps ⲀⲚ ⲚⲎ/[Ⲧ]ⲎⲢⲞⲨ is misplaced and should follow ⸌ⳙⲞ/Oⲛ̄
in 20-21.
81,22-23   {ⲀⲨ´...ⳙOOⲠ} carelessly repeated by the scribe or his predecessor.
82,2   Or, ⲚⲎ̣.
82,7   ⲛ̄, the flag is not preserved.
82,10-13   Since Barbelo is first gnosis, Kalyptos is a second gnosis.

ⲡⲁⲗⲓⲛ ⲟⲛ ⳨ⲧⲅⲛⲱⲥⲓⲥ ⲛⲧ[ⲉ]

12   ⲧⲉϥⲅⲛⲱⲥⲓⲥ ⲉⲧⲉ ⲡⲓⲕⲁ[ⲥ]
ⲡⲉ ⲛⲛ ⲁⲧⲙⲓⲥⲉ· ⲁⲩⲱ [ⲡⲓ–]

14   ⲟⲛⲧⲱⲥ ⲉⲧϣⲟⲟⲡ̇ ⲟ[ⲛ ⲁⲩ–]
ⲁϩⲉⲣⲁⲧⲟⲩ ϩⲓⲍⲙ ⲡⲁⲓ̈· [ⲉ–]

16   ⲧⲃⲉ ⲡⲁⲓ̈ ⲅⲁⲣ ⲁⲥⲥⲟⲩ[ⲱⲛϥ]
ϩⲓⲛⲁ ⲍⲉ ⲉⲣⲉⲛⲏ ⲉⲧⲟⲩⲏ[ϩ]

18   ⲛⲥⲱⲥ ϣⲱⲡⲉ ⲉⲩⲛⲧⲁ[ⲩ]
ⲛ ⲟⲩⲧⲟⲡⲟⲥ ⲁⲩⲱ ⲛⲥⲉ–

20   ϣⲧⲙⲣ ϣⲟⲣⲡ̇ ⲉⲣⲟⲥ ⲛ[ϭⲓ]
ⲛⲏ ⲉⲧⲛⲏⲩ ⲉⲃⲟⲗ [ⲁ]ⲗⲗⲁ

22   ⲛⲥⲉϣⲱⲡⲉ ⲉⲩ[ⲟ]ⲩⲁⲁⲃ
ⲛ ϩⲁⲡⲗⲟⲩⲛ· ⳨ⲕⲁⲧⲁ–

24   ⲛⲟⲏⲥⲓ[ⲥ ⲧ]ⲉ ⲛⲧⲉ ⲡⲛⲟⲩ–

                                    [ⲡⲅ̅]

[ⲧ]ⲉ ⲉⲧⲣ ϣⲣⲡ̇ ⲛ ϣ[ⲟⲟⲡ̇· ⲁⲥ–]

2   ⲟⲩⲱϣⲥ ⲉ[ⲃⲟⲗ
ⲉ ⲡⲓϩⲁⲡⲗⲟⲩ[ⲛ – – –   ] .ⲥ

4   ⲛ̇ ⲟⲩⲟⲩⲍⲁⲓ̈ [
[.] ⲟⲩⲟⲩⲍⲁⲓ̈ [

6   [. .] . . ⲡⲏ ⲙⲉⲛ̇ .[
[. . . ⲟ]ⲩⲟⲉⲓⲛ ⲉⲧ[ⲟ]ⲩⲣ ϣ[ⲣ]ⲡ̇

8   [ⲛ ⲉⲓⲙ]ⲉ ⲉⲣⲟϥ ⲁⲩⲙⲟⲩⲧⲉ ⲉⲣⲟⲥ
[ⲍⲉ] ⳨ⲃⲁⲣⲃⲏⲗⲱ ⲉⲃⲟⲗ ϩⲓⲧⲛ

10   [⳨]ⲉⲛⲛⲟⲓⲁ· ⳨ϣⲙ̇ⲧⲉ–
[ⲛⲟⲥ] ⲛ ϩⲟⲟⲩⲧ̇ ⲙ ⲡⲁⲣⲑⲉⲛⲟⲥ

12   [ⲛ ⲧ]ⲉⲗⲓⲟⲥ· ⳨ⲧⲅⲛⲱⲥⲓⲥ ⲍⲉ
[ⲛⲧⲉ] ⲧⲁⲓ̈ ⲧⲏ ⲉⲧⲁⲥϣⲱⲡⲉ

14   [ⲉⲃⲟ]ⲗ̣ ϩⲓⲧⲟⲟⲧⲥ ⲍⲉ ⲛⲛⲟⲩ–
[.]ⲟⲕⲥ ⲉ ⲡⲉⲥⲏⲧ̇ ⲁⲩⲱ ⲍⲉ

16   [ⲛ]ⲛⲉⲥⲉⲓ ⲉⲃⲟⲗ ⲛϩⲟⲩⲟ ⲉ–
ⲃⲟⲗ ϩⲓⲧⲛ ⲛⲏ ⲉⲧϣⲟⲟⲡ̇

18   [ⲛ]ϩⲏⲧⲥ ⲙⲛ ⲛⲏ ⲉⲧⲟⲩⲏϩ
ⲛⲥⲱⲥ· ⲁⲗⲗⲁ ⲉⲥϣⲟⲟⲡ̇

20   ⲛ ϩⲁⲡⲗⲟⲩⲛ ⲍⲉ ⲉⲥⲉⲃⲙ
[ϭ]ⲟⲙ ⲉ ⲥⲟⲩⲱⲛ ⲡⲛⲟⲩⲧⲉ

22   ⲉⲧ[ⲣ] ϣⲣⲡ̇ ⲛ ϣⲟⲟⲡ̇ ⲍⲉ
ⲁⲥ[ϣ]ⲱⲡⲉ ⲉⲛⲁⲛⲟⲩⲥ ⲛ–

24   ⲧⲉ ⲡⲏ ⲉⲧⲙⲙ[ⲁ]ⲩ ⲉⲁⲥⲟⲩ–

82,14   ⲛ̇, the flag is not preserved.
83,15   ọ, or else ḅ, ⲑ, p̣, or possibly ϩ̣ or ϣ̣.

once again (πάλιν) the knowledge (γνῶσις) of
12   his knowledge (γνῶσις), the unborn
Kalyptos (καλυπτός). [They]
14   stood at rest upon the one
that really (ὄντως) exists;
16   for (γάρ) she knew about it,
in order that (ἵνα) those that follow
18   her might come into being having
a place (τόπος) and that
20   those that come forth (from her)
might not be before her but (ἀλλά)
22   might become holy
(and) simple (ἁπλοῦν). She is the
24   comprehension (κατανόησις) of the god

[83]

who pre-[exists. She]
2   rested [
to the simple (ἁπλοῦν) [
4   salvation [
salvation [
6   [   ] he (+μέν) [
[   ] light which was fore-
8   [known]. She was called
Barbelo by
10   thought (ἔννοια), the thrice-[race (γένος)]
(which is) male, virginal (παρθένος)
12   (and) perfect (τέλειος). And (δέ) through
knowledge (γνῶσις) of her she came
14   into being in order that they might not
[   ] her down and that
16   she might not come forth anymore
through those
18   in her and those that follow
her. Rather (ἀλλά), she is
20   simple (ἁπλοῦν) in order that she might
be able to know the god
22   who pre-exists because
she came into being as a good (product)
24   of it since she

83,24-25   E.g., **ⲟⲩ/[ⲱⲛ̄ϩ ⲛ...] ⲉⲃⲟⲗ.**
83,24   Lit., of that one; probably the Spirit.

[. . . . . . .] . .[. . .] ⲉⲃⲟⲗ ⲛ
[ⲡⲁ]
[. . . . . ⲟ]ⲩⲙⲛ̄ⲧⲁⲧⲙⲓⲥ[ⲉ]
2 [___ ⲙ]ⲉϩϣⲟⲙⲧ̄
.[. . . . .] . ⲥⲛⲁⲩ ⲛ ⲁⲓⲁ-
4 [. . . . .]ⲧ̄ ⲛ ⲧⲉ[ï]ϩⲉ .[
.[. . . . ϩⲟ]ⲟⲩⲧ̄ ⲁⲉ . .[
6 ⲣ̄[. . . . . . .] . ⲉⲛ[
ⲣ̄[. .] ⲛ ⲛⲉ[. .]ⲛ ⲙⲛ ϯⲙ̄[
8 ⲧⲉ ⲙ ⲙ[ⲛ̄]ⲧⲁ̄ⲧⲙⲓⲥ[ⲉ
ⲥⲓⲥ ⲧⲉ ⲟⲩⲙⲉϩⲥⲛⲧⲉ ⲛ[
10 ⲕⲱⲛ̄ . ⲁⲥⲁϩⲉⲣⲁⲧⲥ [
ϣⲟⲣⲡ̄ ⲛ̄ⲧⲉ ⲡⲓⲟⲛⲧⲱ[ⲥ ⲉⲧ-]
12 ϣⲟⲟⲡ̄ ⲟⲛⲧⲱⲥ ⲛ ⲕ[
ⲧⲉ ϯⲙⲛ̄ⲧⲙⲁⲕⲁⲣⲓⲟ[ⲥ ___
14 ⲛ̄ⲧⲉ ⲡⲓⲁϩⲟⲣⲁⲧⲟⲛ ⲙ ⲡ̄ⲛⲁ̄
ϯⲅⲛⲱⲥⲓⲥ ⲛ̄ⲧⲉ ϯϣⲟⲣ[ⲡ̄]
16 ⲛ ϩⲩⲡⲁⲣⲝⲓⲥ ⲛϩⲣⲁï ϩⲛ ϯ-
ⲙⲛ̄ⲧϩⲁⲡⲗⲟⲩⲥ ⲛ̄ⲧⲉ ⲡⲓ[ⲁ-]
18 ⲧⲛⲁⲩ ⲉⲣⲟϥ ⲙ ⲡ̄ⲛⲁ̄ ⲛ ϩⲣⲁï
ϩⲛ ϯϩⲉⲛⲛⲁⲥ ⲉϥⲉⲓⲛⲉ ⲛ̄-
20 ϩⲣⲁï ϩⲛ ϯⲙⲛ̄ⲧⲟⲩⲱⲧ ⲧ[ⲏ]
ⲉⲧⲧⲟⲩⲃⲏⲩ ⲁⲩⲱ [.]ⲁ[
22 ⲉⲓⲁⲟⲥ· [ⲁ]ⲩⲱ ϥϣ[ⲟ]ⲟⲛ̄
ⲛ̄ⲅⲓ ⲡⲏ ⲉⲧ[
[ⲡ̄ⲉ]
[
2 [
[
4 [
[
6 [___] . .[. . .] . ⸱
[___]ⲉⲓⲙⲉ ⲁⲉ
8 [___] ⲙⲛ ϯⲙⲛ̄ⲧ-
[. . . . . ⲁ]ⲩⲱ ϯ[ⲙⲛ̄ⲧⲧⲉ]ⲗⲓⲟⲥ
10 [. . . ⲉ]ⲛⲉⲣⲅⲓ ⲁⲉ [ⲙⲙ]ⲟϥ ⲁⲩⲱ
[. . . .]ⲕϥ ⲡⲓϣⲟⲣⲡ̄ ⲛ ⲕⲁ̄ⲥ

83,25   . .], indistinct traces.
84,3-4   E.g., ⲁ/ⲓⲁ[ⲫⲟⲣⲁ].
84,7-8   E.g., ⲛⲓ/ⲧⲉ.
84,9-10   E.g., ⲛⲓ[ϩⲓ]/ⲕⲱⲛ.

[

[84]

[   ] barrenness

2   [   ] third

[   ]two

4   [   ] of this way[

[   ] and (δέ) [male

6   [

[   ] and the

8   [   ] barrenness [

[. . . she] is a second [

10   . . . she stood [

first of the reality (-ὄντως) [which]

12   really (ὄντως) exists [

. . . the blessedness (-μακάριος) [

14   of the Invisible (ἀόρατον) [Spirit (πνεῦμα)

the knowledge (γνῶσις) of the first

16   existence (ὕπαρξις) in the

simplicity (-ἁπλοῦς) of the

18   Invisible Spirit (πνεῦμα)

in the unity (ἑνάς). It is similar

20   in the singleness that

is pure and [

22   species (εἶδος). And he who [

exists [

                                                 [85]

[

2   [

[

4   [

[

6   [

[   ] and (δέ) knows

8   [   ] and the

[   ] and the [perfection (-τέλειος)]

10   and (δέ) [   ] produces (ἐνεργεῖν) it and

[   ] the first Kalyptos (καλυπτός)

84,10   .ⲁⲥ, possibly ⲉ̣ⲁⲥ.

84,17   -ⲟⲩⲥ, sic.

85   Line numbers on this page are only approximate.

12   [. . . .]ⲧⲉ ⲛⲧⲟⲟⲩ ⲧⲏⲣⲟⲩ ϯ-
      [ϩⲩⲡ]ⲁⲣⲝⲓⲥ ⲙⲛ ϯⲉⲛⲉⲣⲅⲓⲁ
14   ϯ[ⲙ]ⲛⲧⲛⲟⲩⲧⲉ ⲡⲓⲅⲉⲛⲟⲥ
      ⲁⲩⲱ ⲡⲓⲉⲓⲇⲟⲥ· ⲛⲓϭⲟⲙ ⲇⲉ
16   ⲟⲩⲁ ⲛⲉ ⲁⲩⲱ ⲛϩⲣⲁⲓ̈ ϩⲛ ⲟⲩ
      ϫⲉ ⳇⲉ ⲛ ⲟⲩⲁ· ⲉⲧⲉ ⲡⲁⲓ̈ ⲡⲉ
18   ⲛⲟⲩⲙⲉⲣⲓⲕⲟⲛ ⲁⲛ ⲁⲗⲗⲁ
      ⲛⲏ ⲛⲧⲉ ⲡⲧ[ⲏⲣ]ⳇ· ⵣ ϫⲉ ⲟⲩ
20   ⲡⲉ ⲡⲓⲟⲩⲁ ⲉⲧⲉ ϯϩⲉ[ⲛ]ⲛⲁⲥ
      ⲧⲉ ⲁ[ⲩ]ⲱ ⲉⲃⲟⲗ ϩⲓⲧⲛ ϯⲉⲛⲉⲣ-
22   ⲅⲓⲁ [. .]ⲁⲥ[. . . . .]ⲙⲛⲧⲱⲛϩ
      ⲙⲛ[. . . .] .[. . . .] ⲡⲉ ⲛⲧⲉ
24   [___ --- ___   ]ⲧⲏⲣⳇ ⲇⲉ
      [ⲡ̅ⲋ̅]
      [
2   [
      .[
4   ⲡ[
      [
6   ⲃ[
      ⲉ [
8   ϭⲟⲙ ⲁ[
      ⲧⲉ ⲙ ⲡⲣⲏ[ⲧⲉ
10   ⲡⲁⲣ[. . . .]ⲉⲥⲑⲏ[ⲧⲟⲛ
      ⲙⲉⲛ .[. ⲡ]ⲁⲛⲧⲉⲗⲓⲟⲥ
12   ⲙⲁⲩ ⲉⲁ⳽ϫⲟⲟⲥ ⲉⲥⲥ[ⲙⲟⲩ]
      ϫⲉ ⲛⲧⲕⲟⲩⲛⲟⲅ ⲁ̅ϥ̅ⲣ̅[ⲏ̅ⲇ̅ⲱ̅ⲛ̅]
14   ⲛⲧⲕⲟⲩⲧⲉⲗⲓⲟⲥ ⲛⲉ⳽[
      ⲉⲥϫⲱ ⲙⲙⲟⲥ ⲉ ⲧⲉⳇϩⲩⲡ[ⲁ]ⲣ-
16   ⲝⲓⲥ ϫⲉ ⲛⲧⲕⲟⲩⲛⲟⲅ ⲁ̅ⲏ̅ⲓ̅ϥ̅ⲁ̅[
      ϯⲉⲛⲉⲣⲅⲓⲁ ⲛⲧⲁⳇ ⲙⲛ ⲟⲩⲱⲛ[ϩ]
18   ⲁⲩⲱ ⲟⲩⲙⲛⲧⲛⲟⲩⲧⲉ ⲧ̅[ⲉ]
      ⲛⲧⲕⲟⲩⲛⲟⲅ ϩⲁⲣⲙⲏⲇⲱ[ⲛ
20   ⲡⲁⲛⲓⲉⲟⲟⲩ [ⲧ]ⲏ̅[ⲣ]ⲟⲩ ⲉ̅ⲡ̅ⲓ̅ϥ̅[

85,14   Asyndetic lack of conjunctions.
85,15-16   Or, the powers are one, but in what way?
85,17   The letter ⳉ must have protruded into the left margin; ⳉ , or else ⲩ̨ or
             possibly ⲧ or ϭ (not ⲁ and not a mark of punctuation).
85,21-22   E.g., ϯⲉⲛⲉⲣ/ⲅⲓⲁ [ⲛⲧ]ⲁⲥ [ⲙⲛ ϯ]ⲙⲛⲧⲱⲛϩ.
85,23   ] .[, a supralinear stroke.
86   Line numbers on this page are only approximate.
86,12   Cf. 51,6-19.

12   [   ] them all,
      existence (ὕπαρξις) and activity (ἐνέργεια),
14   divinity, race (γένος)
      and species (εἶδος). But (δέ) are the powers
16   one? In what way
      (is it) that he is one, that is,
18   not a partial one (μερικόν), but (ἀλλά)
      (one of) those of the All? What
20   is the unity which is unity (ἑνάς)?
      Is it from
22   activity (ἐνέργεια) [   ] life
      and [   ] of
24   [   ] And (δέ) all [
      [86]
      [
2   [
      [
4   [
      [
6   [
      [
8   power [
      . . . as [
10   . . . [   ] perceptible (αἰσθητόν)[
      [   ] all-perfect (παντέλειος) [
12   she [blessed (them)] saying
      "You are great, Aphr[edon].
14   You are perfect (τέλειος), Neph-[
      To his existence (ὕπαρξις) she says,
16   "You are great, Deipha-[
      She [is] his activity (ἐνέργεια) and life
18   and divinity.
      You are great, Harmedo[n
20   one who belongs to [all] the glories, Epiph-[

86,13   For Aphredon, see also 88,1.18; 122,6-7; cf. *Steles Seth* VII 126,10;
         Allogenes XI 54,23.
86,16   -ï - had the supralinear stroke above it.
86,18   ⳉ [ε] might be expected, but if this is the reading, ⳉ was abnormally
         written so that the trace resembles the left branch of a ⲧ; palaeographically
         the preferable reading of this trace is ⲧ.
86,19   Also Armedon, the first light of Kalyptos according to 120,3; cf. *Steles Seth*
         VII 126,12 and *Allogenes* XI 54,12.

ⲧⲉϥⲙⲛ̄ⲧⲙ̄[ⲁ]ⲕⲁⲣ[ⲟⲥ ⲇⲉ ⲙⲛ̄
22 ϯⲙⲛ̄ⲧⲧⲉⲗ[ⲓⲟ]ⲥ ⲛ̄[ⲧⲉ] ϯⲙⲛ̄ⲧ-
ⲟⲩⲱⲧ̇ .[. . .]ⲁⲟ[. .]ⲟⲩ ⲟ[ⲩ
24 ⲧⲏⲣϥ ϧⲓ ⲟ[

[ⲡⲍ̄]

[
2 [----   ]ⲁ
[
4 [
[
6 [----   ]ⲁ
[----   ] . ⲱ̄ⲁ ⲉⲛⲉϧ
8 [. . . . . . .] .[. . . .] ⲛ̄ ⲛⲟⲉⲣⲟⲛ
[. . . . . .]ⲉϧⲛ̄[. .] .[ⲧⲉⲗ]ⲓⲟⲥ
10 [ϯ ⲃⲁⲣⲃ]ⲏⲗⲱ ⲙ̄ ⲡ[ⲁⲣⲑⲉ]ⲛⲟⲥ
[ⲉⲃⲟⲗ] ϧⲓⲧⲟⲟⲧⲥ ⲛ̄ ϯⲙⲛ̄ⲧϧⲁ-
12 [ⲡⲗⲟ]ⲩⲥ ⲛⲧⲉ ϯⲙⲛ̄ⲧⲙⲁⲕⲁ-
[ⲣⲓⲟⲥ] ⲛ̄ⲧⲉ ⲡⲓϣⲙⲧ̄ϭⲟⲙ ⲛ̄
14 [ⲁϧⲟ]ⲣⲁⲧ[ⲟ]ⲛ ⲙ̄ ⲡⲛ̄ⲁ· ⲧⲏ ⲉ-
ⲧⲁⲥⲉⲓⲙⲉ ⲉ ⲡⲏ ⲉⲧⲙ̄ⲙⲁⲩ
16 ⲁⲥⲉⲓⲙⲉ ⲉⲣⲟⲥ· ⲡⲏ ⲇⲉ ⲉϥⲉ
ⲛ̄ ⲟⲩⲁ ⲛⲥⲁ ⲥⲁ ⲛⲓⲙ ⲉϥⲉ ⲛ̄-
18 ⲛ̄ ⲁⲧ̄ⲡⲱⲣⲝ ⲉⲣⲟϥ ⲉⲁϥⲛ̄
[. .] . ⲁϥϧⲟ[. .]ⲟⲥ ⲛⲥⲉ[ⲓ]ⲙⲉ
20 [ⲉⲣⲟⲥ ⲉ]ⲩⲉⲛⲉⲣⲅⲓⲁ ⲛⲧⲁϥ
[ⲧⲉ . . .]ⲉⲧ[.] ⲛ̄ϥⲉⲓⲙⲉ ⲉ
22 [. . . . .]ⲟ[. . . .] ⲉⲩⲉⲓⲙⲉ
[. . . . .] ⲛ̄ϧⲣⲁⲓ̈ ϧⲛ̄ ⲕⲉ-
[ⲡ̄ⲏ̄]
[
2 [
[
4 ⲁ
.[
6 ϧ[
ⲉ[
8 ⲙ[

And (δέ) his blessedness (-μακάριος) and
22 the perfection (-τέλειος) [of] the
    unity [
24 all[

                                        [87]
    [
2   [
    [
4   [
    [
6   [
    [   ] forever
8   [   ] intellectual (νοερόν)
    [perfect (τέλειος)]
10 [the virgin (παρθένος) Barb]elo
    through the simplicity (-ἀπλοῦς)
12 of the blessedness (-μακάριος)
    of the three-powered
14 Invisible (ἀόρατον) Spirit (πνεῦμα). She
    who has known it
16 has known herself. And (δέ) that one, being
    one everywhere, being
18 undivided, having
    [   ] has [   ] and she has known
20 [herself as] its activity (ἐνέργεια)
    [   ] and he has known
22 [   ] knowledge
    [   ] within . . .
    [88]
    [
2   [
    [
4   [
    [
6   [
    [
8   [

87,14-15   Or, after she has known it.
87,16   ⲁ, not ⲉ.
87,18   ⲉⲁ ⳏ ⲛ, supralinear stroke over ⲛ.
88   Line numbers on this page are only approximate.

```
     ⲥⲙⲟⲩ ⲉ[
10   ⲍⲉ .[ .] . ⲃ̄ⲏ[ⲣ]ⲥ̄[ⲑⲉⲩ ⲉⲣⲥⲧⲉⲛⲁⲟⲣ]
     ⲱⲣ[ⲥⲙⲉⲛⲥ]ⲉ· ⲁⲣ[ⲁⲙⲉⲛ]
12   ⲁⲗⲫⲁ[ⲉⲧ]ⲉ̄· ⲏⲗⲁⲥⲟ[ⲩⲫⲉⲩ]
     ⲁⲁⲗⲁⲙⲉⲩ· ⲛⲟⲏⲑⲉⲩ[
14   ⲟⲩⲛⲟϭ ⲡⲉ ⲡⲉⲕⲣⲁⲛ ⲁ[
     ϥⲍⲟⲟⲣ· ⲡⲏ ⲉⲧ[ⲉ]ⲥⲙⲉ̣ [ⲉ-]
16   ϥⲥⲙⲉ ⲉ ⲛⲁⲓ̈ ⲧⲏⲣⲟⲩ· ⲛⲧ[ⲕ-]
     ⲟⲩⲁ ⲛⲧⲕⲟⲩⲁ ϭⲥⲟⲩ ⲉ .[
18   ⲁⲫⲣⲏⲇⲱⲛ̄ ⲛⲧⲟⲕ ⲡⲉ ⲡ[ⲥⲉ-]
     ⲱⲛ ⲛⲧⲉ ⲛⲥⲉⲱⲛ ⲛⲧⲉ ⲡ[ⲥ-]
20   ⲛⲟϭ ⲛ̄ ⲧⲉⲗ[ⲥⲟ]ϭ ⲡⲥ̄ϣ[ⲟⲣ]ⲡ̄
     ⲛ̄ ⲕⲗ̄ϭ ⲛⲧⲉ ϯ[ⲙ]ⲉϩ .[
22   ⲛⲛ ⲉⲛⲉⲣⲧⲥⲁ̣ [ⲁ]ⲩϣ [
     ⲧⲁⲛ ⲡⲉ ⲛ ⲁ̣[ . .]ⲁ[
24   ⲡⲉϥⲉⲥⲛ̣ⲉ̣ [
     ⲛⲧⲁϥ ⲉϥ .[
                                        [ⲡ̄ⲑ]
     [
2    [
     [
4    [   ----                            ]ⲙ
     [   ----                            ]ϣⲟ
6    [
     [
8    [   ----                          ] .
     [   ----              ϩⲩⲡⲁⲣ]ⲝⲥ[ⲥ
10   [   ----            ] ⲁⲩϣ ⲉϥ-
     [   ----                      ]ⲩⲧⲉ
12   [   ----                      ]ϣⲱ
     [   ----                      ]ⲡⲉ ϩⲛ
14   [   ----                   ⲡ ]ⲥⲉⲟ-
     [ⲟⲩ   ----              ϩ ]ⲉⲛⲉⲟⲟⲩ
16   [      ----              ]ⲡⲟⲥ· ⲟⲩ-
     [      ----              ] ϩⲛ
18   [      ----              ]ⲧⲏ
```

88,10   The final trace is of a vertical stroke, as from ⲃ, ⲧ, ⲏ, ⲥ, ⲕ, or ⲛ | for the restoration, cf. *Allogenes* XI 54,17-20.

88,11   Possibly the supralinear stroke ended over ⲉ, now in lacuna.

88,12   ⲉ̣, or else ⲧ or ϯ (other alternatives are probably excluded) | ⲟ̣, or else ϭ.

bless [
10   [   ]O Be[ritheu, Erigenaor],
Or[imeni]os, Ar[amen],
12   Alphl[eg], Elilio[upheus],
Lalamenus, Noetheus[
14   great is your name [
it is strong. He who knows (it)
16   knows everything. You are
one, you are one, Sious, E-[
18   Aphredon, you are the [aeon (αἰών)]
of the aeons (αἰών) of the
20   perfect (τέλειος) great one, the first
Kalyptos (καλυπτός) of the [
22   activity (ἐνέργεια), and [
. . . he is [
24   his image [
of his, he [

                                                      [89]

      [
2   [
      [
4   [
      [
6   [
      [
8   [
      [existence (ὕπαρξις)]
10   [   ] and he
      [
12   [
      [   ] in
14   [the glory]
      [   ] glories
16   [   ] a
      [   ] in
18   [

_____

88,14   E.g., ⲁ[ⲧⲱ].
88,21   .[, compatible with the first letter of all cardinal numbers from one to ten.
89   Line numbers on this page are only approximate | very little text survives
         through p. 108.

```
     [
20   [        ---                    ] .ⲛ
     [        ---                   ]ⲉⲱⲛ
22   [        ---                   ]ⲟⲥⲁ
     [        ---                   ]ⲏⲟⲩ
24   [_       ---                   ]ⲟⲩⲧⲉ
     [ϥ̄]
     [
2    [
     [
4    [
     [
6    [
     [
8    [
     ϣⲟⲟ̣[ⲡ
10   ⲡⲉ̣ ⲛ ⲁ̣[
     ⲛ [
12   ⲙ[ⲛ
     ⲕⲁ[
14   ⲛⲉ̣[
     ⲙⲛ̀ .[
16   ⲙⲁⲕ[ⲁⲣⲓⲟⲥ
     ⲛ ⲛ[
18   ⲁⲥ[
     ⲣ[
20   ⲧ[
     ⲉⲛⲁ[
22   ⲛⲧⲉ[
     ⲉⲟ̣[
24   ⲱⲛⲅ̣ [
     ⲉϣ .[
                                      ϥ̄[ⲁ̄]
     [
2    [
     [
4    [
     [
6    [
     [
```

90   Line numbers on this page are only approximate.

```
      [
20    [
      [                   ] aeon (αἰών)
22    [
      [
24    [
      [90]
      [
2     [
      [
4     [
      [
6     [
      [
8     [
      exist [
10    [
      [
12    [and
      [
14    [
      [
16    [blessed (μακάριος)
      [
18    [
      [
20    [
      [
22    [
      [
24    [
      [
                                              [91]
      [
2     [
      [
4     [
      [
6     [
      [
```

---

8   [———   ]ⲉ

    [———   ]ⲛ ⲛⲟⲩⲧⲉ

10 [———   ] .ⲧⲉ ⲉⲃⲟⲗ·

    [. . . . . . .] . .[. . . . . .] .[.]ⲱϥ

12 [. . . . .]ⲙⲡⲓⲙ[. . . . .]ⲧⲉ

    [. . . . .]ⲩⲉⲉⲧ[. . .] ϣⲟⲣⲡ̄

14 [. . .]ⲙⲉⲉⲣ[. .] ⲙⲛ ϩⲉⲛϭⲟⲙ

    [. .]ⲣⲉϥ[. . . .]ⲛ̄ ⲉⲣⲟϥ ⲙ̄ ⲡⲁⲛ-

16 [ⲧⲉⲗ]ⲟⲥ [. . . .]ⲥⲙ ⲛⲉ ⲛⲧⲉ

    [ⲛ]ⲁ̈ⲓ ⲧⲏⲣ[ⲟⲩ] ⲁⲩⲱ ⲟⲩⲗⲟ̈ⲓ-

18 [ϭ]ⲉ ⲛⲧⲁ[. ⲧ]ⲏⲣⲟⲩ ⲉⲩⲙⲛⲧ-

    [.] .[. .]ⲟⲥ[. . .] .[. .]ⲃ̄ⲁⲣⲃⲏⲗⲱ‾

20 [. . .]ϥⲱⲡ[. . .] . ⲉ[ⲣ]ⲟϥ ⲁⲩⲱ

    [. . . .] .ⲁϥ[.] ⲛⲁ̈ⲓ ⲧⲏⲣⲟⲩ ⲛ

22 [. . . . .]ⲏⲧ̣[.] ⲉⲙ̄ⲡϥ̄ⲕⲁⲗⲁ

    [. . . . .] ⲙⲛ ⲧⲉϥⲙⲛⲧ̇-

24 [———   ]ⲩ̄ⲱⲡⲉ

    [. . . . .]ⲡ̣· ⲁⲗⲗⲁ

    [ϥ̄ⲃ̄]

    [

2   [

    [

4   [

    [

6   [

    [

8   .[

    [

10 ⲛⲧⲉ ⲛ[

    ⲉⲃⲟ[ⲗ] . .[

12 ⲁⲩ[ⲱ . . .]ϣⲱ .[

    ⲛⲧⲁⲥ[. . .]ⲩ ⲛ ⲥ .[

14 ⲟⲩⲱⲧ̇ [. . . .]ⲏⲉⲧ[

    ⲙⲛ ⲟⲩⲙ[. . . . .] .ⲙ[

16 ⲛϩⲣⲁ̈ⲓ ϩⲛ ⲟ[ⲩ. . .]ϩⲁ[

    ⲕⲁⲧⲁ ⲡⲓⲛⲟⲏ[ⲙⲁ] ⲉⲧϣ[ⲟⲟⲡ]

18 ⲟⲛⲧⲱ[ⲥ .] ⲉⲧ̣[ϣⲟ]ⲟⲛ̄ ⲛ [

91,12   Lacunas over both ⲙ s.

91,18   E.g., ⲛⲧⲁ[ⲩ.

91,19   [.] .[, the trace consists solely of a supralinear stroke |] .[. . .]ⲃ̄, a
           supralinear stroke connected this letter with the following one.

8   [
    [
    [   ] divine
10 [
    [
12 [   ] ... [
    [   ] ... [   ] first
14 [   ] ... [   ] and powers
    [   ] ... [all-perfect ($\pi\alpha\nu\tau\acute{\epsilon}\lambda\epsilon\iota\sigma$)]
16 they are [   ] of
    all these and a
18 cause of all [   ], a
    [   ] Barbelo
20 [   ] ... [   ] him an
    [   ] all these
22 [   ] he not having
    [   ] and his
24 [   ] become
    [   ] but ($\dot{\alpha}\lambda\lambda\acute{\alpha}$)
    [92]
    [
2   [
    [
4   [
    [
6   [
    [
8   [
    [
10 of [
    ... [
12 [and
    [
14 single [
    and a [
16 in [a
    according to ($\kappa\alpha\tau\acute{\alpha}$) the [thought ($\nu\acute{o}\eta\mu\alpha$)] which
18 really ($\acute{o}\nu\tau\omega\varsigma$) [exists   ] which exists as [

91,20   ⲡ may have had a flag.
91,22-23   E.g., ⲕⲁⲗⲁ/[ⲧⲁⲩ.
92   Line numbers on this page are only approximate.
92,18-19   E.g., ⲛ[ⲟⲩⲁⲧ]/ϯ ⲡⲁⲛ, or ⲛ[ⲁⲧ]/ϯ ⲡⲁⲛ; cf. 74,21.

ϯⲣⲁⲛ ⲉ[. . . . . .] ⲛ [. .]ⲁ̣ⲧ̣[
20 ⲥⲟⲩ[. . . . . .]ⲡ̣ⲓⲛ[
ⲕⲗ̅ⲥ̅ ⲛ [. . . . . .]ⲟ[
22 ⲡ ⲛ̅ⲟ̣[. . . . . .]ⲛⲧ[
ϣⲙ̅ⲧ̣[.]ⲥ̣[
24 ⲛⲉ ⲛ [
ⲁⲗⲗⲁ [

[ϥ̅ⲧ̅]

ϯ ⲣⲁⲛ ⲉⲣⲟϥ ⲛⲁ̈ⲓ ⲧⲏⲣⲟⲩ ϣⲁⲩ-
2 ⲣ ⲡⲣⲏⲧⲉ ⲉⲩⲛⲛⲏⲩ ⲉⲃⲟ̣ⲗ
ⲟ̣ⲙ ⲡⲏ ⲉⲧⲑⲉⲃ[ⲓⲏ]ⲟ̣ⲩ̣ⲧ ⲉ-
4 ϣ[ⲱ]ⲡⲉ ⲇⲉ ⲉⲕϣⲁⲛϯ ⲉⲟ̣ⲟⲩ
ⲉⲧ[ⲃⲏ]ⲛ̣ⲧϥ· ⲉϣⲱ[ⲡⲉ] ⲇⲉ ⲉⲕ-
6 ϣⲁ[ⲛ] .ⲉⲉⲩⲧ[. . ⲟ̣]ⲩ̣ⲡⲁⲣ-
ϫ̅[ⲓⲥ . . .]ⲡϣ .[. . . . . .]ⲡⲉϥ-
8 ⲟ̣ .[. . . . . .]ⲥ[. . . . . .]ⲛⲁ ⲛ ⲟⲩ-
ⲟ̣[⸻   ]ⲛ̣ ϩⲁⲡⲗⲟⲩⲛ
10 .[⸻   ]ⲛ̣
[⸻   ]ϥ·
12 [⸻   ]ⲉϥⲛⲁ
[⸻   ] .ϥ·
14 [⸻   ] .ⲡⲏ ⲉ
[⸻   ⲥⲟⲩ]ⲱⲛϥ
16 [⸻   ]ⲩⲧⲛ· ⲛ
ϩⲣⲁ[⸻   ] ⲛ ⲧⲉⲗⲓⲟⲥ
18 ⲉϥⲉ[⸻   ⲧⲉⲗ]ⲓⲟⲥ
ⲁⲩⲱ[⸻   ]ⲁⲉ
20 ⲧⲛ̣ [⸻   ]ϫⲱⲕ
ⲉ[⸻   ]ⲛⲙⲉ
22 [⸻   ]ⲡⲉϥ-
[⸻   ]ⲧⲁⲩ
24 [⸻   ]ⲁϥ·
[⸻] .ⲁ̣ⲩ ⲉϯⲙⲛ
26 [⸻   ]ⲛⲉⲧⲙ[.

[ϥ̅ⲇ̅]
[ⲉ]ⲙ̅ⲡϥ̅ϭⲙ ϭⲟⲙ ⲉ ⲛⲁⲩ ⲉⲣⲟⲥ
2 ⲉⲧⲃⲉ ⲡⲁ̈ⲓ ⲙⲙⲛ ϣϭⲟⲙ ⲉ ϫⲓ-
ⲧϥ ⲙ ⲡⲉ̈ⲓⲣⲏⲧⲉ ⲛ̅ϩⲣⲁ̈ⲓ ϩⲛ

92,23   ϯ̣, or else ⲧ̣.
93,6-7   ⲙ̣ⲉⲉⲩ̣ⲉ [ⲉⲧϩ]ⲩⲡⲁⲣϫ̅/ⲓⲥ might be expected.

name [

20   [

Kalyptos (καλυπτός) [

22   No-[

thrice-[

24   [

but (ἀλλά) [

                                            [93]

name him. All these come,

2   as it were,

from him who is pure.

4   If (+δέ) you give glory

because of him, and (δέ) if you

6   [   ] existence (ὕπαρξις)

[   ] his

8   [   ] a

[   ] simple (ἁπλοῦν)

10   [

[

12   [   ] he will

[

14   [   ] that one

know] him

16   [   ] . . .

[   ] perfect (τέλειος)

18   he being [perfect (τέλειος)]

and [

20   [   ] perfect

[

22   [   ] his

[

24   [   ] him

[   ] . . . to the

26   [

[94]

he was not able to see her.

2   Therefore, it is impossible to receive

him in this way in

93,6   ] ., the trace is compatible with e.g., ⲙ | ⲧ, the trace is probably not
compatible with ⲉ, although this is uncertain.

4 ογββ[ο] ντε †ϻντνοϭ
   εογⲁ πε ν τεⲗ[ⲓο]ⲥ ντε
6 π[ⲏ ε]ⲧϩ̅ν ογεν[. . .]ⲥντε
   π[. . . . . .] .εε[. . .] .ⳅ̅ ετε
8 ν ο[. . . . . . .]ⲁⲛ̣ [. .ⲥⲟⲩ]ⲱⲛϥ
   ετβε[. . . .]ⳅ̅[. . . . .]ϣⲁⲝε
10 ϻ[ϻ]ⲟ̣ϥ [———   ] .ⲉ
   τε̣[
12 ⲱⲛ[
   ετ .[
14 ϩⲓⲟ[
   ϻ πε[———   ] .ⲥ[
16 εⲧⲕⲱ[———   ]ⲧⲁⲣ[
   ⲛⲁⲛ ⲛ[———   ]ⲩ ⲉⲣⲟϥ[
18 τ[——— ϣⲟⲟ]ⲛ̅ ϩⲓ ογⲙⲁ[
   τ[———   ] ⲇⲉ ϻⲙⲟ[
20 ⲕⲁ .[———   ]ⲛ ϩⲓ . .[
   ⲕⲁ[
22 ⲕⲁ[
   ⲛ τ[
24 τⲁϥ[
   . . ογτε̣[———   ⲇⲓⲁ-]
                             [ϥ]ⲉ

   ϕⲟⲣⲁ ντε ⲛⲁⲓ̈ ϻⲛ ϩⲉⲛⲁⲅ-
2 ⲅⲉⲗⲟⲥ· ⲁⲩⲱ ϩⲉⲛⲇⲓⲁϕⲟ-
   ⲣⲁ ντε ⲛⲁⲓ̈ ϻⲛ ϩⲉⲛⲣⲱⲙⲉ
4 ⲁⲩⲱ [ϩⲉ]ⲛⲇⲓⲁϕⲟⲣⲁ ⲛⲧⲉ
   ⲛⲁⲓ̈ [ϻⲛ] ογϩⲩⲡ[ⲁⲣ]ⳅⲓⲥ·
6 ⲁⲩⲱ [ϩⲉ]ⲛⲟ .[. . . . . .]ⲟⲩ
   ⲥⲓ[. . . . . .]ⲟ .[. . . . . . .]ⲛⲟⲩ
8 ⲏ[. . . . . .] ϻⲛ [ⲟⲩⲉⲥ]ⲑ̅ⲏⲥⲓⲥ
   [———   ]ⲧⲱⲥ
10 [———   ]ⲛⲛⲏ
   [———   ]ⲟ̣ⲛⲧⲱⲥ
12 [———   ]ⲟⲩ·
   ⲕ̣ⲁⲓⳅ[ⲁⲣ . . . . .] ⲡⲓⲕⲟⲥⲙⲟⲥ

94,4   ϻⲛ, only the supralinear stroke that connected these letters now survives | cf. 51,23; 78,18.
94,6   ογⲉⲛ, or else ογⲉ | ⲥⲛⲧⲉ, supralinear stroke over ⲛ | perhaps ογⲉⲛ[ⲛⲁ]ⲥ ⲛⲧⲉ, but elsewhere spelled ϩⲉⲛⲛⲁⲥ.
94,14   The group ϩⲓ has no circumflex.

4   majestic purity,
as a perfect (τέλειος) one of
6   [him who] is in [
[   ] which
8   [know] him
concerning [   ] say
10   it [
[
12   [
which [
14   [
[
16   which [   ] for (γάρ)
[   ] him
18   [exist] together
[   ] and (δέ) [
20   [
[
22   [
[
24   [
. . . nor (οὔτε) [

                                         [9]5
[differences (διαφορά)] between these and
2   angels (ἄγγελος), and differences (διαφορά)
between these and human beings,
4   and differences (διαφορά) between
these [and] existence (ὕπαρξις).
6   And [
[
8   [   ] and [perception (αἴσθησις)]
[
10 [
[   ] really (ὄντως)
12 [
[for truly (καὶ γάρ)   ] the [perceptible (αἰσθητόν)]

95,6   .[, perhaps ⲟⲩ[.
95,7   .[, a round letter.
95,9   E.g., ⲟ ⲛ]ⲧⲱⲥ.
95,13 ⲧ, a tiny, ambiguous trace.

14 ⲛ ⲉⲥ[ⲑ ⲏ ⲧ ⲟⲛ . . ⲙ] ⲡ̣[ⲣ]ⲏⲧⲉ
  ⲉ[——   ]ⲛⲟⲩ
16 ⲉ̣ⲩ̣ⲡ̣[ⲁⲣϩ̣ⲓⲥ   ——   ]ⲩ̣
  ⲅⲁⲣ ⲉ̣ⲩ[
18 ⲁⲩⲱ[——   ] .ⲁ̣
  ⲛ .[——   ]ⲉ̣

Lines 20 and following (ca. 4 lines) do not survive.

[ϥ̅ⲋ̅]

 [ⲛ̄]ⲁ̣ϩⲱⲛ ⲉⲣⲟϥ ϩⲛ ⲟⲩⲥ̣ⲟⲟⲩⲛ
2 ϣⲁϥϫⲓ ϭⲟⲙ· ⲁⲩⲱ ⲡⲏ ⲉⲧⲛⲉ—
 ⲟⲩⲉ ⲙⲙⲟϥ· ϣⲁϥⲑⲃⲃⲓⲟ·
4 ⲁⲛⲟⲕ ⲇⲉ ⲡⲉϫⲁⲉ̣ⲓ [ϫⲉ] ⲉⲧⲃⲉ ⲟ[ⲩ]
 ⲟⲩ̣ⲛ ⲁⲩⲱⲱⲡ[ⲉ ⲛϭⲓ] ⲛⲓⲣⲉϥϯ
6 ϩⲁⲡ [ⲏ] ⲟⲩ ⲡⲉ ⲡϫ̣[ⲓ ⲙ]ⲕⲁϩ ⲛ̄ⲧⲉ
 ⲡⲓ̣[. . . . .] ⲛ ⲛⲉ̣[. . . . .] .ⲉ ⲅⲁⲣ
8 ⲛⲁ[.]ⲁ̣ [. . . .]ϯ ⲙ̣[. . . . . . .] .ⲙⲉ
 ⲁⲩⲱ [. . . . .] .ⲟ[. . . . .] .ⲡⲉ
10 ϫⲓ[
 ϣⲱ[
12 ⲁⲗⲗ[ⲁ
 ⲛⲥⲉ[——   ]ϯ̄ .[. .
14 ⲉⲃⲟⲗ ϩⲓ̣[ⲧⲛ   ——   ] ⲉⲧϩⲉ̣[
 ⲡⲓϫⲓ ⲙ̄ⲕ̣[ⲁϩ . . . . . .] ϩⲓⲧⲙ [
16 ⲡⲥⲟ[——   ]ϥ̣ϯⲟ[
 ⲛ .[——   ]ϣⲟⲟⲛ̣
18 ⲛ ϭ̣[——   ] .ⲉⲥⲟⲩ—
 ⲏϩ [——   ]ⲱⲣϫ:
20 [——   ]ⲛ̄ [
 [——   ] .ⲡ[

Lines 22 and following (ca. 4 lines) do not survive.

[ϥ̅ⲍ̅]

 [ϩ]ⲟⲟⲩⲧ̄ ⲉⲩⲧⲛⲱ[ⲥⲓ]ⲥ ⲧ[ⲉ ⲛⲧ]ⲉ
2 ⲡⲓϣⲙ̅ⲧϭⲟⲙ ⲛⲛ ⲁⲧⲛⲁⲩ ⲉⲣⲟϥ
 [ⲛ] ⲛⲟϭ ⲙ ⲡ̅ⲛ̅ⲁ̅· ϯϩⲓⲕⲱⲛ ⲛⲧⲉ
4 [ⲡⲓϣⲟⲣ]ⲡ̄ ⲛ ⲕ̅ⲁ̅ⲥ̅· ϯⲙⲛ̄ⲧⲙⲁ—
 [ⲕⲁⲣⲓⲟⲥ ⲉⲧ]ϣⲟⲟⲛ̄ ϩⲙ ⲡⲓⲁϩⲟ—
6 [ⲣⲁⲧⲟⲛ ⲙ] ⲡ̅ⲛ̅ⲁ̅· ⲭⲱ[. . .] ϯⲁ̇ⲧ

96,2   I.e., ⲉⲧⲛⲁ´; cf. 71,20.
96,5   ⲛϭⲓ], must have been written small.
96,6   ϫ̣[ⲓ ⲙ]ⲕⲁϩ; cf. 96,15.
96,8   ⲁ̣, or else ϩ.
96,14   ⲉ̣[, or else ⲑ, ⲟ, or ϭ. | e.g., ϩⲉ[ⲉ].

14   world (κόσμος) [   ] like
      [
16   [existence (ὕπαρξις)
      for (γάρ) [
18   and [
      [
      Lines 20 and following (ca. 4 lines) do not survive.
      [96]
      will approach him in knowledge,
2   he receives power, but he who is
      far from him is humbled."
4   And (δέ) I said, "Why
      then (οὖν) have the judges come
6   into being? What [(+ἤ)] is the [suffering] of
      the [   ] for (γάρ)
8   . . . [
      and [
10   [
      [
12   but (ἀλλά) [
      [
14   through [   ] who [
      suffering [   ] through [
16   the [   ] . . .
      [   ] exists
18   [   ] she
      dwells [
20   [
      [
      Lines 22 and following (ca. 4 lines) do not survive.
                                              [97]
      male, since she is knowledge (γνῶσις) [of]
2   the three-powered invisible
      great Spirit (πνεῦμα), the image (εἰκών) of
4   [the first] Kalyptos (καλυπτός), the
      [blessedness (-μακάριος)] in the
6   [Invisible (ἀόρατον)] Spirit (πνεῦμα), [   ] the

96,17   ṇ̄, the flag is not preserved.
96,21   π̣[, connected to the following letter (in lacuna) by a supralinear stroke.
97,4   Cf. 85,11.
97,6   ѡ̣, or else ⱳ̣.

```
     [ . . . . . . . . .] .[ . . . . . .]ⲁⲧ
8    [ . . . . . . . .]ⲅⲱ[ . . . . . .] ⲅⲁⲣ
     [ . . . . . . .]ⲃ .[ . . . . . .] ⲉϥⲉⲥⲙⲉ
10   [        ───                    ]·
     [        ───                    ]ⲅⲉⲥⲧ̇
12   [        ───                    ]ⲛ ⲁ̇ⲧ
     [        ───                    ]ⲙⲟⲩⲃ
14   [ . .]ⲛⲟ̣[    ───                ] ⲉⲥⲟⲩ–
     ⲱⲛⲃ ⲉ[ⲃⲟⲗ    ───               ]ⲅⲛⲱ–
16   ⲥⲥⲥ ⲙ [        ───              ]ⲥⲁⲃⲉ–
     ⲣⲁ[ⲧ]ⲥ[        ───              ] .ⲥ
18   ⲛ ⲛ[            ───              ⲃ]ⲙ
     [                ───            ]·
20   [                ───            ] .ⲙ
```

Lines 21 and following (ca. 6 lines) do not survive.

```
[ϥ̄ⲏ̄]
     [ . .] ⲟⲩ[ⲃⲉ]ⲛⲛⲁⲥ ⲛ ⲧⲉⲗⲥⲟⲥ ⲛ–
2    ⲧⲉ ⲟⲩⲃⲉⲛⲛⲁⲥ ⲉⲥⲁ̇ⲏⲕ· ⲁ[ⲩⲱ]
     [ⲉ]ⲧⲁⲥⲡⲱⲩ ⲉ ⲡⲧⲏⲣϥ ⲉⲃ[ⲟⲗ]
4    ⲃⲥⲧⲛ [ⲡ]ⲧⲏⲣϥ· ⲉ[
     ⲃⲩⲡⲁⲣⲝⲥⲥ ⲙⲛ̣ [
6    ⲧⲉ [ . . .] ⲛⲥⲙⲉⲉⲩⲉ [
     ⲡ[ . . . . . . .] . .[
8    ⲟ[ . . . . . . .] .ⲥ̣[
     ⲉⲥⲑ[ⲏⲥⲥⲥ .ⲡⲥⲛ[
10   ⲣ[
     ⲙ [
12   ⲃⲥ[
     ⲛ .[
14   ⲟⲥ̣[     ───                    ]ⲣⲟ
     ⲉⲥ[     ───                    ]ⲧⲙⲙ[
16   ⲁ[      ───                    ] .ⲥ . ⲉ
     ⲉⲗ[     ───                    ]ⲉ ⲛ
18   ⲃ[      ───                    ] .
     ⲡ[
20    .[
      .[
```

Lines 22 and following (ca. 5 lines) do not survive.

98,9   ⲑ, or else ⲥ̣.

```
    [
8   [                          ] for (γάρ)
    [                          ] he knows
10  [
    [                          ] . . .
12  [                          ] . . .
    [                          ] fill
14  [                          ] she
    appears [
16  knowledge (γνῶσις) [       ] she
    stands [
18  [                          ]
    [
20  [
```

Lines 21 and following (ca. 6 lines) do not survive.

[98]

```
    [    ] a perfect (τέλειος) unity (ἐνάς) of
2   a complete unity (ἐνάς). [And]
    when she divided the All [
4   from the All [
    existence (ὕπαρξις) and [
6   [        ] the thoughts [
    [
8   [
    [perception (αἴσθησις)
10  [
    [
12  [
    [
14  [
    [
16  [
    [
18  [
    [
20  [
    [
```

Lines 22 and following (ca. 5 lines) do not survive.

[ϥ̅ⲑ̅]

[. . . . . .]ⲥⲉⲥⲁ .[
2   [. ϩⲩⲡⲁ]ⲣⲝ̅ⲓⲥ ⲙ̅[. . . . .]ⲧ̇
     [. . . . . . .] ϩⲙ [.]ⲉ̣[———   ]ⲉⲧ̇
4   [———   ]ⲩⲧ̇
     [———   ⲉ]ⲥⲙⲉ
6   [———   ]ⲟϥ·
     [———   ]ⲟⲛ
8   [———   ]ⲁⲣ
     [———   ]ⲥ̣ⲥⲙⲟⲩ
10   [———   ]ⲁ
     [———   ] .ⲛ̅ ⲛ
12   [———   ]ⲝ̅ⲛ
     [———   ] .ⲁ̅ ⲛ
14   [———   ]ⲉⲧ̇
     [———   ] . ⲟⲩ
16   [———   ] ⲁ̅ⲩⲱ
     [———   ]ⲁ
18   [———   ]ⲉ
     [———   ]ⲧ̇
20   [———   ]ⲟ

Lines 21 and following (ca. 6 lines) do not survive.

[ⲣ̅]
     ⲧ[. . . . .]ϣⲟⲙ[. . . . .
2   ⲟ̣[. . . . . . .]ⲉⲧⲉ[. . . . . .
     .[. . . . .]ⲙ[.]ⲥ[. . . .
4   ⲧⲉ .[
     ⲛ ⲧ[
6   ⲁⲣⲙ[ⲟⲍⲏⲁ
     ⲛⲥ̣[
8   ⲥⲥ̣ⲥ[
     ⲡⲉ ϯⲃ̅[
10   ϩⲥ̣ⲧ[ⲛ
     ⲅⲟⲙ [
12   ⲣⲛ̅ .[
     ⲛ ⲥⲉ̣[

99,3   ⲉ̣, or else ⲑ, ϩ, or ⲥ.
99,11   ] .ⲛ̅, connected to the letter (in lacuna) by a supralinear stroke; e.g., ϣ]ⲣⲛ̅.
99,13   ⲁ̅, connected to the preceding letter by a supralinear stroke; probably ⲡ]ⲛⲁ̅.

[99]

```
[          ] . . . [
2    [existence (ὕπαρξις)
     [    ] in [                    ] which
4    [
     [                             ] knowledge
6    [
     [
8    [
     [                             ] she blesses
10   [
     [
12   [
     [
14   [                             ] which
     [
16   [                             ] and
     [
18   [
     [
20   [
```

Lines 21 and following (ca. 6 lines) do not survive.

[100]
```
     [
2    [
     [
4    [
     [
6    Arm[ozel
     [
8    [
     is the [
10   [through
     power [
12   [
     [
```

99,19   Iᴛ̄, connected to the preceding letter (in lacuna) by a supralinear stroke;
        e.g., ϢⲘIᴛ′.

100,9   ⲃ̄I, connected to the following letter (in lacuna) by a supralinear stroke;
        probably ⲃ̄Iⲁⲣⲃⲃⲏⲗⲱ.

14 ϣⲱ[
   ⲉⲧ[
16 ⲉⲃⲟ̣[ⲗ
   ⲉ[
18 ⲧⲟ̣[
   ⲡⲛ̄ [
20 ⲛ [
   .[

Lines 22 and following (ca. 4 lines) do not survive.

[ⲡⲁ̄]

  [. . . . .] .ⲁⲧⲛⲁⲩ ⲉ[ⲣⲟϥ . . . .
2 [. . . . . .] .ⲅⲉ ⲡ ⲏ ⲉ̣[. . . . .
  [. . . . ⲡ]ⲁ̈ⲓ ⲡⲉ ⲡⲉⲥⲉ̣[. . . . .]ⲧ̇
4 [---   ]ⲁ ⲛ [. . . .]ⲛⲱ—
  [---   ]ⲙⲟⲟ̣[. . .]ⲉⲥⲁⲟⲥ
6 [---   ]ⲟⲛ
  [---   ]ⲉⲥϩⲩ—
8 [---   ] .ⲛ̄ ⲟⲩ—
  [---   ]ⲁⲧ̇—
10 [---   ]ⲥ ⲛ
  [---   ]ϣⲉ‾
12 [---   ]ⲡⲥⲕⲁⲥ
  [---   ⲁ]ⲧ̇ⲡ ⲱ ϣ
14 [---   ]ⲟϥ
  [---   ] .ⲉⲥ
16 [---   ] .ⲉ
  [---   ⲉⲛ]ⲛⲟ̣ⲥⲁ
18 [---   ]ⲉ
  [---   ]ⲟⲉ

Lines 20 and following (ca. 4 lines) do not survive.

[ⲡ̄ⲃ̄]

  ⲡ[. . . . . ⲉ]ⲧ̇ϣⲟⲟⲛ̇ [. . . . .
2 ⲡ[. . . . .] ⲡⲥⲕⲉⲟ .[. . . . .
  ⲟ[. . . . .]ⲥⲱⲧ ⲟ̣ⲩ̄ϩ̣[. . . . .
4 ⲙⲛ [. . .]ⲛ̣ⲧ̣[
  ⲡϥ ⲛ [. . .]ⲁⲟ[
6 ⲛ ⲟ[. . . . .] .[
  ⲟⲩ̣ϩ̣[

101,1   ] ., possibly ⲛ]ⲛ̣.
101,3   ⲡ̣, or else ⲧ̣ | ⲉ̣, or else ⲑ.
101,5   ⲙ̣, a trace from the bottom right of the letter | ⲟ̣, or else ⲥ̣.

14   [
      which[
16   [
      [
18   [
      [
20   [
      [
Lines 22 and following (ca. 4 lines) do not survive.
                                              [101]
      [   ] invisible [
2   [   ] that one [
      [this] is the [
4   [
      [   ] species (εἶδος)
6   [
      [
8   [   ] of a
      [
10   [
      [
12   [   ] Kalyptos (καλυπτός)
      [   ] undivided
14   [
      [
16   [
      [thought (ἔννοια)]
18   [
      [
Lines 20 and following (ca. 4 lines) do not survive.
      [102]
      [   ] which exist [
2   [   ] the [
      [
4   and [
      [
6   [
      [

102,2   E.g., Π𝒥ΚΕΟ𝒰[ⲁ.
102,3   ⳉ, or else ⲁ.
102,4   Possibly ⲙ]ⲛ⳨[.

8   oⲩⲱ[
     ⲉϥ[.]ⲧ̣[
10   ⲥⲉ[
     ⲛⲁ[
12   ⲛⲱ[
     ⲁⲩⲱ̣ [
14   ⲛⲏ[
     oⲩ[
16   ⲙ ⲙ[
     ⲱ[
18   ⲉ[
     ⳤⲉⲛ̣[
20   ⲡ̣[
     ⲙ [

Lines 22 and following (ca. 4 lines) do not survive.

                                           [ⲣ̅ⲅ̅]
     [.]ⲉⲛⲁⲣⲭⲏ ⲛ ⲧ̣[. . . . .]
2   [. .]ⲧ̣ϣ̣ọọⲛ̣ oⲛ[ⲧⲱⲥ . . .] .ⲉ
     [.]ⲧ̣ϣ̣ọọⲛ̣ [. . . . . . oⲩ]ⲥ̣ⲓⲁ
4   [---   ]ⲁ̈ⲓ ⳤⲙ
     [---   ⲡⲁ]ⲓ̈ ⲡⲉ·
6   [---   ] ϯⲙⲛ̣ⲧ̄–
     [---   ]ⲉoⲩ–
8   [---   ]ọoⲩ
     [---   ]ⲁⲥ
10   [---   ]ⲧoⲩ
     [---   ⲉⲃ]oⲗ
12   [---   ] ϣⲁⲩ–
     [---   ]ⲁ̈ⲓ ⲁⲛ
14   [---   ]ⲉⲧoⲩ
     [---   ] ⲡⲁ̈ⲓ
16   [---   ]ⲣ
     [---   ]ⲗ
18   [
     [---   ] ⲙⲛ

Lines 20 and following (ca. 6 lines) do not survive.
     [ⲣ̅ⲇ̅]
     ⲙ [. . . . .] ⲉⲥoⲩⲱⳤ ⲉ̣[ⲃoⲗ]
2   ⲙ [. . . . .] ⲛⲧⲉ ⲛⲏ ⲉⲧọ[. . .
     ⲏⲉ̣[. . . . . . .] .ⲁ̈ⲓ [.]ⲏ ⲛ̣ⲧⲉ ⲡⲓ[. . . .

103,1   E.g., [ⳤ]ⲉⲛⲁⲣⲭⲏ.

8   [
     he [
10   [
     [
12   [
     and [
14   those [
     a [
16   [
     [
18   [
     some [
20   [
     [

Lines 22 and following (ca. 4 lines) do not survive.

                                        [103]

     [   ] origin (ἀρχή) [
2   [. . . really (ὄντως)] exist [
     [   ] exist [essence (οὐσία)]
4   [   ] in
     [this] is
6   [   ] the
     [
8   [
     [
10   [
     [   ] . . .
12   [   ] they
     [   ] not
14   [
     [   ] this
16   [
     [
18   [
     [   ] and

Lines 20 and following (ca. 6 lines) do not survive.
     [104]
     [   ] she appears
2   [   ] of those who [
     [   ] . . . of the [

4 ⲁⲩⲱ [
ⲡⲁⲓ̈ ⲁ .[
6 ⲡⲓ̇ⲛⲟ .[
ⲉⲧⲟ̣[
8 ⲛⲁⲩ[
ⲛⲉ ⲡⲁ.[
10 ⲏ ⲣ[
ⲁⲧ̄ .[
12 ⲃⲟⲗ ⲙ [
ⲙ̇ⲙⲟ[
14 ⲁϥ̇ϣ[
ⲟⲛⲧⲱ[ⲥ
16 ϣ ⲏ[
ⲡ ⲏ ⲉ[
18 ⲇⲉ [
ⲧ .[
20 ⲛ̇ϩ̇ⲣ[ⲁ̇ⲓ̈
ⲡ̇ⲓ̇.[
22 ⲣ[
ⲡ[

Lines 24 and following (ca. 4 lines) do not survive.

[ⲣ̄ⲉ̄]
ⲛⲉ ⲛⲏ ⲉⲧⲁϩⲉ̣[ⲣⲁⲧⲟⲩ. . . .] ⲙ
2 ⲡⲓ̇ⲉⲱⲛ ⲙ ⲙ[. . . . .] ⲛ̄-
ⲛⲏⲩ ⲉϩⲣⲁⲓ̈ ⲛ ⲟ̣[. . . . .]ⲉ
4 [. . .]ⲱⲧⲡ [. . . . .] ⲉⲧ̇
ϣⲟⲟⲛ̇ ϩⲙ [. . . . .] .ⲡ ⲏ
6 ⲙⲉⲛ ⲉ̣[——] .ⲏ ⲣ
[——] ⲡ ⲏ
8 [——]ⲉ ⲟⲩⲁ
[—— ⲟ]ⲩⲁ ⲣⲭ ⲏ
10 [——]ⲟⲩⲧ̇
[——] ⲙ ⲛ
12 [——]ⲁ̇· ⲡⲁⲓ̈
[—— ϩ]ⲩⲗⲏ
14 [——]ⲟ̣ⲩⲱ̇ⲧ̇
[——]ⲟⲩ ⲛ
16 [ϣ]ⲟ]ⲡ̄

104,22 ⲣ̄[, connected to the following letter (in lacuna) by a supralinear stroke.
105,3 ⲟ̣, or else ⲉ̣, ⲑ, or ⲥ̣.

4   and [
     this [
6   the [
     [
8   see [
     [
10   [
     [
12   [
     [
14   he [
     really (ὄντως) [
16   [
     that [
18   and (δέ) [
     [
20   [
     [
22   [
     [

Lines 24 and following (ca. 4 lines) do not survive.

                                          [105]

     are those who [stand
2   the aeon (αἰών) of [
     come up to [
4   . . . [   ] which
     exist in [   ] that one
6   on the one hand (μέν) [
     [   ] that one
8   [   ] one
     [an] origin (ἀρχή)
10   [
     [   ] and
12   [   ] this one
     [   ] matter (ὕλη)
14   [   ] single
     [
16   [exist]

105,4   Probably]ⲱⲧⲛ̄ (flag in lacuna).
105,9   Possibly ⲁⲡⲝⲏ.

```
      [        ----                  ]ⲁ
18    [        ----                  ]ⲩ
      [        ----                  ]ⲉⲧ̇
20    [        ----                  ] ⲙⲛ
      [        ----                  ]ⲁ̣
```

Lines 22 and following (ca. 4 lines) do not survive.

[ⲣ̅ⲋ̅]

```
      ⲡ[ . . . . . . . . .] ⲁⲩⲱ ⲉϥϣⲟⲟ[ⲛ̅
2     ⲉ[ . . . . . . . . . .] ⲡⲉ ⲁⲩⲱ ⲛ ⲁ[
      ⲡ[ . . . . . . . . . .] ϣⲱⲁϩ ⲛⲧⲉ ⲟⲩ[
4     ⲧⲛⲟ[ . . . . . . . . .] ⲛ ⲟⲩⲁⲣ[
      ⲁⲩ[ . . . . . . . ⲟ]ⲩⲁⲉ ⲛⲧⲉ ⲛ[
6     ⲙⲉϩ[          ----          ]ⲉ ⲡⲏ ⲡ[
      ⲉⲧⲟ̣[          ----          ] .[
8     ⲕⲟⲟ[
      ⲡⲟⲩⲉ[
10    ⲙⲛ [
      ⲧⲉ .[
12    ⲏⲡⲉ̣[
      ⲱⲛϩ [
14    ⲕⲁⲧ[ⲁ
      ⲉⲧⲉ[
16    ⲣⲟⲩ[
      ⲁⲩ[
18    ⲡⲁ[
      ⲉⲁ[
20    ⲉⲧ[
      ⲁ[
22    ⲩ̣[
```

Lines 23 and following (ca. 4 lines) do not survive.

[ⲣ̅ⲍ̅]

```
      ⲙⲙⲟⲩ ⲛϩⲣ[ⲁⲓ̈ . . . . . .]ⲥ̣
2     [ .]ⲁ̣ⲥⲓⲥ· ⲁⲩⲱ .[ . . . . . . . .]ⲉ̣
      [ϩ]ⲩⲡⲁⲣⲝⲓⲥ [ . . . . . . . .] .ⲥⲥ
4      .[ .]ⲱ ⲙⲛ ⲡ[ . . . . . ϣ]ⲟⲟⲛ̅
      ⲙ ⲡⲣⲏⲧⲉ̣ [ . . . . . . . .]ⲟⲩ
6     ⲉⲓⲁ[ⲱⲗⲟⲛ          ----          ϣ]ⲟⲣⲡ̅
      [          ----          ]ⲙ
```

105,20-21   Extra space was left between these lines because of an imperfection in the
surface of the papyrus.

```
     [
18   [
     [                    ] which
20   [                    ] and
     [
```

Lines 22 and following (ca. 4 lines) do not survive.

[106]

```
     [                        ] and he exists
2    [                          ] he is [   ] and [
     [                        ] mark of a [
4    [                        ] an
     [                        ] nor (οὐδέ) of [
6    [                        ] that one [
     [
8    [
     [
10   and [
     [
12   number [
     [
14   [according to (κατά) [
     which [
16   [
     [
18   [
     [
20   [
     [
22   [
```

Lines 23 and following (ca. 4 lines) do not survive.

[107]

```
     them [
2    . . . and [
     existence (ὕπαρξις) [
4    [   ] and the [              ] exist
     as [
6    reflection (εἴδωλον) [        ] first
     [
```

106,7   ] .[, top of a round letter, read in 1972, now best attested in photo A; papyrus subsequently damaged.

107,1   Or, waters.

8   [——   ϣ]ⲟⲣⲡ̄

     [——   ] ⲚⲦⲈ ⲚⲤ—

10 [——   ]ⲁ

     [——   ]Ⲛ Ⲛ

12 [——   ] ⲡⲁⲓ̈

     [——   ] .ⲁ

14 [——   ] ϢⲞⲘ—

     [——   ]ⲞⲨ

16 [

     [——   ]ⲁ̣ Ⲛ

18 [——   ]ⲁ̣ⲓ̈

     [——   ]ⲉ̣ⲓ̈

20 [——   ] .

     [——   ⲟ]Ⲩⲁ·

Lines 22 and following (ca. 6 lines) do not survive.

[ⲣ̄ⲏ̄]

ⲁ[. . . . .]ⲚⲈ ⲀⲚ ⲈⲨϮ ⲚⲀ̣[.

2 ⲈⲘ [. . . . . . .] ⲠⲎ ⲈⲦϢⲞⲞⲚ̄ [

ⲈⲂ[ⲞⲖ . . . . . .] ⲦⲎⲢⲞⲨ ⲘⲚ̣

4 ⲠⲎ Ⲉ[. . . . .] ⲞⲨⲘⲎϢ[Ⲉ

Ⲛ ⲤⲬⲎ̣[. . . . .]ⲦⲀⲘ̣Ⲟ Ⲏ [.

6 ⲦⲀⲠ[——   ] .[. .

ⲀⲨⲰ [

8 ⲈⲂⲞⲖ [

ⲦⲀϪⲤ Ⲙ̣[

10 ⲠⲤⲀ[Ϯ

ϢⲞⲘ[

12 ⲈⲘ ⲠⲤ[

ⲚⲀⲒ̈· .[

14 ⲚⲤϢⲞ[

ⲚⲦⲈ̣ [

16 ⲞⲚⲈ̣ .[

ⲈⲠ[

18 ⲞⲞ[

ⲞⲨ[

20 ⲈⲨ[

ⲈⲚ̣ [

22 Ⲧ[

Lines 23 and following (ca. 3 lines) do not survive.

107,11   ]Ⲛ, connected to the preceding letter (in lacuna) by a supralinear stroke.

108,3   Ⲛ̣, only the supralinear stroke survives.

8   [   ] first
     [   ] of the
10 [
     [
12 [   ] this one
     [
14 [
     [
16 [
     [
18 [
     [
20 [one]
     [

Lines 22 and following (ca. 6 lines) do not survive.

[108]
     [   ] not, they giving [
2   [   ] he who exists [
     [   ] all and
4   he [   ] a multitude
    ... [   ] creation
6   [
    and [
8   [
    ... [
10 the [
     [
12 in the [
    these [
14 the [
    of [
16 [
     [
18 [
     [
20 [
    in [
22 [

Lines 23 and following (ca. 3 lines) do not survive.

108,5   E.g., ⲤⲬⲎⲘⲀ.

Pages 109-112 do not survive.

[ρϳⲅ̄]

ⲙ̄ⲛ ϩⲉⲛⲁⲅⲅⲉⲗⲟⲥ ⲙ̄ⲛ ϩⲉⲛⲇⲉ-
2 ⲙⲱⲛ ⲁⲩⲱ ϩⲉⲛⲛⲟⲩⲥ ⲙ[ⲛ] ϩⲉⲛ-
ⲯⲩⲭⲏ· ⲁⲩⲱ ϩⲉⲛⲍⲱⲟⲛ [ⲙ]ⲛ
4 ϩⲉⲛϣⲏⲛ ⲙ̄ⲛ ϩⲉⲛⲥⲱⲙⲁ ⲙ̄ⲛ
ⲛⲏ ⲉⲧϣⲟⲟⲡ̄ ϩⲁⲑⲏ ⲛ̄ ⲛⲁⲓ̈· ⲛⲏ
6 ⲛ̄ⲧⲉ ⲛⲓϩⲁⲡⲗⲟⲩⲛ ⲛ̄ ϛⲧⲟⲓⲭⲓⲱⲛ
ⲛ̄ⲧⲉ ⲛⲓⲁⲣⲭⲏ ⲛ̄ ϩⲁⲡⲗ[ⲟ]ⲩ[ⲛ]· ⲙ̄ⲛ
8 ⲛ[ⲏ ⲉ]ⲧϣⲟⲟⲡ̄ ϩⲛ̄ [ⲟⲩ]ⲁ̄ⲱϣ
ⲉ[. . .] ⲁⲩⲱ ⲛ̄ ⲁⲧⲙⲟⲩⲁϭ ⲟⲩⲁⲏⲣ
10 [ⲙ̄ⲛ ⲟ]ⲩⲙⲟⲟⲩ ⲁⲩⲱ ⲟⲩⲕⲁϩ
[ⲙ]ⲛ̄ ⲟⲩⲏⲡⲉ ⲁⲩⲱ ⲟⲩⲛ̄[ⲟ]ⲩⲧ̄ⲃ
12 ⲙ̄ⲛ ⲟⲩⲕⲓⲙ ⲁⲩⲱ ⲟ[ⲩ . . .]ⲟⲱ ⲙ̄ⲛ
[ⲟ]ⲩⲧⲁⲝⲓⲥ ⲁⲩⲱ ⲟⲩⲛⲓϥⲉ ⲙ̄ⲛ
14 [ⲛⲓⲕ]ⲉϣⲱⲁ̄ⲛ̄ ⲧⲏⲣⲟⲩ· ϩⲉⲛⲙⲉϩ
[ϥⲧ]ⲟⲟⲩ ⲇⲉ ⲛ̄ ϭⲟⲙ ⲛⲉ ⲉⲧϣⲟⲟⲡ̄
16 [ϩⲙ̄] ⲡⲓⲙ[ⲉϩ]ϥⲧⲟⲟⲩ ⲛ̄ⲛ ⲉⲱⲛ· ⲛⲏ
[ⲉⲧ]ϣ[ⲟ]ⲟⲡ̄ ϩⲛ̄ ⲛⲓⲡ[.] .[.] ⲁⲩⲱ
18 [.]ϫⲱⲕ ⲉⲃⲟⲗ ⲛ̄ⲧⲉ [. . .] ⲛⲓϭⲟⲙ
[. . .] ϩⲉⲛϭⲟⲙ ϩⲉⲛ[. . .]ⲥ ⲛ̄ⲧⲉ
20 [. . .]ⲟⲩ· ϩⲉⲛⲧ̄[. . . .] ⲛ̄ⲧⲉ
[. . . . .] ϩⲉⲛ[ⲁⲅⲅⲉⲗ]ⲟⲥ ⲛ̄
22 [ⲧⲉ ⲛⲓⲁ]ⲅⲅⲉⲗⲟⲥ [ϩⲉⲛ]ⲯⲩⲭⲏ
[ⲛ̄ⲧⲉ ⲛⲓ]ⲯⲩⲭⲏ· ϩⲉ[ⲛ]ⲍⲱⲟⲛ [ⲛ̄]
24 [ⲧⲉ ⲛⲓⲍ]ⲱⲟⲛ ϩⲉⲛϣⲏⲛ ⲛ̄[ⲧⲉ]
[ⲛⲓϣⲏⲛ]· ϩⲉⲛⲥⲩ[.] .[. . . .
26 [. . . . .] ⲁⲩⲱ ϩ[ⲉⲛ . . . . . .
[. . . .]ⲁⲧⲁ̄ⲩ[. . . . .
28 [. . . . . .] .[

[ρϳ]ⲇ

ⲙ̄ⲙⲓⲛ ⲙ̄ⲙⲟϥ· ⲁⲩⲱ ⲟⲩⲟⲛ ⲛ[ⲏ]
2 ⲙⲉⲛ ϩⲱⲥ ⲉϩⲉⲛϫⲡⲟ ⲛⲉ· ⲙ̄ⲛ
ⲛ[ⲏ] ⲙⲉⲛ ⲉⲧϣⲟⲟⲡ̄ ϩⲛ̄ ⲟⲩϫⲡⲟ
4 ⲛ̄ⲛ ⲁⲧⲙⲓⲥⲉ· ⲁⲩⲱ ⲟⲩⲟⲛ ⲛⲏ ⲙ̄[ⲉⲛ]
ⲉⲧⲟⲩⲁⲁⲃ· ⲁⲩⲱ ⲉϩⲉⲛϣⲁ ⲉ[ⲛⲉϩ]

113,1-14   See 48,3-7n.
113,6   ϛⲧⲟⲓⲭⲓⲱⲛ, sic.
113,15   Or ⲉⲩϣⲟⲟⲡ̄.
113,17-18   See *Facsimile Edition: Introduction*, pl. 13*.

Pages 109-112 do not survive.

[113]

and angels (ἄγγελος),
2 daimons (δαίμων), minds (νοῦς),
souls (ψυχή), living animals (ζῷον),
4 trees and bodies (σῶμα),
those which are prior to them: those
6 of the simple (ἁπλοῦν) elements (στοιχεῖον)
of simple (ἁπλοῦν) origins (ἀρχή), and
8 those which are in a
[   ] and unmixed confusion: air (ἀήρ)
10 [and] water, earth
number, connection,
12 motion, [   ] and
order (τάξις), breath and
14 all the rest. There are (+δέ)
fourth powers which are
16 [in] the fourth aeon (αἰών), those
[which] are in the [   ] and
18 [ ] perfect of [   ] powers
[   ] powers [   ] of
20 [   ] of
[angels (ἄγγελος)]
22 [of the] angels (ἄγγελος), souls (ψυχή)
[of the] souls (ψυχή), living animals (ζῷον)
24 [of the] living animals (ζῷον), trees [of]
[the trees
26 [   ] and [
[   ] . . . [
28 [

[114]

his own. There are [those]
2 (+μέν) (that exist) as (ὡς) begotten ones, and
those that are in an unborn
4 begetting; and there are those (+μέν)
that are holy and eternal,

113,20   ϛ, or else ⲡ.
113,22-24   For the restoration, cf. 48,12-18; 55,19-23.
113,27   ⲁ, or else ⲗ | ϛ, or else ⲟ.

6   ne· ⲙ̄ⲛ ⲛ̄ⲁⲧⲟⲩⲱⲧⲃ ⲉⲃⲟⲗ ⲛ̄-
     ⲅⲣⲁⲓ̈ [ϩⲛ ⲟ]ⲩ<ⲟⲩ>ⲱⲧⲃ ⲉⲃⲟⲗ· ⲙ̄ⲛ ⲟⲩ-
8   ⲧⲁⲕⲟ [ⲛ̄ϩⲣ]ⲁⲓ̈ ϩⲛ ⲟⲩⲙ̄ⲛⲧⲁ[ⲧ]ⲧⲁⲕⲟ·
     ⲁⲩⲱ ⲟⲩⲟⲛ ⲛ̄ⲏ ⲙⲉⲛ ϩⲱ[ⲥ] ⲉϩⲉⲛ-
10   ⲧⲏⲣⲟⲩ ⲛⲉ· ⲟⲩⲟⲛ ⲛ̄ⲏ ⲉ[ϩⲉⲛ ⲅⲉ-]
     ⲛⲟⲥ ⲛⲉ ⲙ̄ⲛ ⲛ̄ⲏ ⲉⲧϣⲟⲟⲡ̄ [ϩⲛ ⲟ]ⲩ-
12   ⲕⲟⲥ[ⲙⲟ]ⲥ ⲙ̄ⲛ ⲟⲩⲧⲁⲝⲓⲥ· ⲟⲩ[ⲟⲛ]
     ⲛ̄ⲏ ⲙⲉⲛ ϩⲛ ⲟⲩⲙ̄ⲛⲧⲁⲧ̄ⲧ[ⲁⲕⲟ]
14   ⲁⲩⲱ ⲟⲩⲟⲛ ⲛ̄ϣⲟⲣⲡ̄ ⲉ[ⲧⲁϩⲉ-]
     ⲣⲁⲧⲟⲩ ⲙ̄ⲛ ⲛ̄ⲓⲙⲉϩⲥ̄ⲛⲁⲩ [ϩⲛ]
16   ⲛ̄ⲁⲓ̈ ⲧⲏⲣⲟⲩ· ⲛ̄ⲏ ⲧ[ⲏⲣ]ⲟⲩ [ⲉⲧϣⲟ-]
     ⲟⲡ̄ [ⲉⲃ]ⲟ[ⲗ ϩ]ⲛ ⲛ̄ⲁⲓ̈· ⲁⲩⲱ ⲛ̄ⲏ [ⲉⲧ-]
18   ϣⲟⲟⲡ̄ [ϩⲛ] ⲛ̄ⲁⲓ̈· ⲁⲩⲱ ⲉⲃⲟⲗ
     ⲛ̄ⲁⲓ̈ ⲉⲧ[ⲟⲩ]ⲏϩ ⲛ̄ⲥⲁ ⲛ̄ⲁⲓ̈· .[. . . .]
20   ⲃⲟⲗ ⲙ̄[. . . .]ⲩ ⲉ[. . . . .]
     ⲛ̄ⲁⲓ̈ [. . . . .] ⲉⲧⲟⲩ[. . . . . .]
22   ⲁⲩⲱ ⲁ[ⲩⲁ]ϩⲉⲣⲁⲧⲟ[ⲩ ⲛ̄ϭⲓ ⲛ̄ⲓ-]
     [ⲙ̄]ⲉϩϥⲧⲟⲟⲩ ⲛ̄ⲛ ⲉⲱ[ⲛ . . . .]
24   [. . . . .] ⲉⲩϣⲟⲟⲡ̄ [. . . . . .]
     [. . . . .]ⲉ ⲉⲧϣⲟ[. . . .]
26   [. . . . .] . ⲧⲏⲣ .[. . . . .]
                              [ⲣ̄ⲓ]ⲉ̄
     ⲛ̄ϩⲏⲧⲟⲩ ⲉϥⲝⲟⲟⲣ ⲉⲃⲟⲗ· ⲁⲩⲱ
2   ⲉⲛⲥⲉϩⲟⲝϩⲉⲝ ⲛ̄ ⲛⲉⲧⲉⲣⲏⲩ [ⲁ]ⲛ
     ⲁⲗⲗⲁ ⲛ̄ⲧⲟⲟⲩ ϩⲱⲟⲩ ⲉⲧⲟⲛϩ ⲛ̄-
4   [ϩ]ⲣⲁⲓ̈ ⲛ̄ϩⲏⲧⲟⲩ ⲉⲩϣⲟⲟⲡ̄ ⲁⲩⲱ
     ⲉⲩϯ ⲙⲁⲧⲉ ⲙ̄ⲛ ⲛⲉⲧⲉⲣⲏⲩ ϩⲱⲥ
6   [ⲉ]ⲩϣⲟⲟⲡ̄ ⲉⲃⲟⲗ ϩⲛ ⲟⲩⲁⲣⲭⲏ ⲛ̄
     ⲟⲩⲱⲧ· ⲁⲩⲱ ⲥⲉϣⲟ[ⲟⲡ̄] ⲉⲩϩⲟ-
8   ⲧⲛ̄ [ⲝ]ⲉ ⲥⲉϣⲟⲟⲡ̄ ⲧⲏⲣⲟⲩ ⲛ̄ϩⲣⲁⲓ̈
     ϩⲛ ⲟ[ⲩ]ⲉⲱⲛ ⲛ̄ ⲟⲩⲱⲧ ⲛ̄ⲧⲉ ⲡⲓⲕⲁ̄ⲥ
10   [. . .] .ⲉ ϩⲛ ⲟⲩϭⲟⲙ ⲉⲩⲡⲟⲣⲝ ⲉⲃⲟⲗ·
     [ⲕ]ⲁⲧⲁ ⲅⲁⲣ ⲡⲟⲩⲁ ⲡⲟⲩⲁ ⲛ̄ⲧⲉ ⲛ̄ⲓⲉ-
12   [ⲱ]ⲛ ⲥⲉϣⲟⲟⲡ̄ ⲉⲩⲁϩⲉⲣⲁⲧⲟⲩ
     [ⲕⲁ]ⲧⲁ ⲡⲏ ⲉⲧⲡⲏϩ ⲉⲣⲟⲟⲩ· ⲡⲓⲕⲁ̄ⲥ
14   [ⲇⲉ ⲟ]ⲩⲉⲱⲛ ⲛ̄ ⲟⲩⲱⲧ ⲡⲉ ⲟⲩⲛ-

114,17-19   See *Facsimile Edition: Introduction*, pl. 14*.
114,17   ⲛ̄, or else ⲡ.
114,18   ⲡ, or else ⲗ I e.g., ⲉⲃⲟ[ⲗ ϩⲛ].
114,19-20   E.g., ⲉ]/ⲃⲟⲗ.
114,20   E.g., ⲙ[ⲙⲟⲟ]ⲩ.

6   those unchanged
    by death and
8   perishable by indestructibility.
    And there are those (+μέν) that exist as (ὡς)
10 alls; there are those [that are]
    [races (γένος)] and those that are [in a]
12 world (κόσμος) with order (τάξις); there are
    those (+μέν) in [in destructibility],
14 and there are the first ones [that stand]
    and the second ones [in]
16 all of them, [all] those [that]
    derive from them and [those that]
18 are [in] them. And [
    these that [follow] them [
20 [
    these [
22 and [the] fourth aeons (αἰών)
    stood [
24 [   ] they existing [
    [   ] . . . [
26 [

                                              [11]5
    in them, he being scattered abroad.
2   They do not restrict one another,
    but (ἀλλά) they are alive in them
4   dwelling among themselves and
    agreeing with one another, as (ὡς)
6   those who come from a single
    origin (ἀρχή). They are joined together
8   because they are all
    in a single aeon (αἰών) of Kalyptos (καλυπτός),
10 [   ] being divided in power.
    For (γάρ) they exist in relation to (κατά) each
12 of the aeons (αἰών), standing in
    relation to (κατά) the one which has reached them.
14 [But (δέ)] Kalyptos (καλυπτός) is [a] single aeon (αἰών);

114,22   Cf. 114,14-15; 116,15-16.
114,26   ⲡ ., after ⲡ only a supralinear stroke (beginning over ⲡ) survives;
         e.g., ⲦⲎⲣⳠ.
115,8   ⲛ̄, or else ⲛ.

[ⲧⲁϥ] ⲙ̅ⲙⲁⲩ ⲛ ϥⲧⲟⲟⲩ ⲛ ⲇⲓⲁⲫⲟ-
16 [ⲣⲁ ⲛ]ⲧⲉ ϩⲉⲛⲉⲱⲛ· ⲁⲩⲱ ⲕⲁⲧⲁ
[ⲡⲟ]ⲩⲁ ⲡⲟⲩⲁ ⲛ̅ⲧⲉ ⲛⲓⲉⲱⲛ ⲟⲩⲛ-
18 [ⲧⲁ]ⲩ̅ ⲙ̅ⲙⲁⲩ ⲛ ϩⲉⲛ[ⲅⲟ]ⲙ̅ ⲙ̅ ⲡⲣⲏ-
[ⲧⲉ ⲛ] ϩⲉⲛϣⲟⲣⲡ̅ ⲁⲛ ⲙⲛ ϩⲉⲛⲙⲉϩ-
20 [ⲥⲛⲁ]ⲩ̅ ⲛ̣ⲁⲓ̈ ⲧⲏⲣⲟⲩ ⲅⲁⲣ ϩⲉⲛϣⲁ ⲉ-
[ⲛⲉϩ ⲛⲉ ⲁⲩ]ⲱ [ⲥ]ⲉϣ[ⲉ]ⲃ̣ⲓ̈ⲏⲟⲩⲧ
22 [. . . . . ⲟ]ⲩⲧⲁⲝⲓⲥ ⲙ[ⲛ] ⲟⲩⲉⲟⲟⲩ
[. . . . . . .] .ⲉ ⲉⲧϣⲟ[ⲟ]ⲛ̅ ⲛ̣ϩ̣[ⲣⲁ]ⲓ̈
24 [ϩⲛ . . . .]ϥⲧⲟⲟⲩ ⲛⲛ ⲉⲱⲛ [ⲙ]ⲛ̣
[. . . . . ⲉ]ⲧⲣ ϣⲟⲣⲡ ⲛ ϣ̣[ⲟⲟⲛ̅]
26 [. . . . . . .]ⲛⲟⲩⲧ[ⲉ
[. . . . . .]ⲥ ⲛⲉ ⲙ[
28 [. . . . .] . .[
[ⲣⲓ̅ⲋ̅]
ⲛⲁⲓ̈ ⲧⲏⲣⲟⲩ ⲇⲉ ⲥⲉϣⲟⲟⲛ̅ ⲛ̅-
2 ϩⲣⲁ̣ⲓ̈ ϩⲛ ⲟⲩⲁ ⲉⲩϣⲟⲟⲛ ϩⲓ ⲟⲩⲙⲁ
ⲁⲩⲱ ⲕⲁⲧⲁ ⲟⲩⲁ ⲉⲩϫⲏⲕ ⲉⲃⲟⲗ
4 ⲛ̅ϩⲣⲁⲓ̈ ϩⲛ ⲟⲩⲙⲛ̅ⲧϣⲃⲏⲣ ⲁⲩ[ⲱ]
ⲉⲁⲩⲙⲟⲩϩ ⲉⲃⲟⲗ ⲙ̅ ⲡⲓⲉⲱⲛ ⲉ[ⲧ̄-]
6 ϣⲟⲟⲛ̅ [ⲟ]ⲛⲧⲱⲥ· ⲁⲩⲱ ⲟⲩⲟⲛ
ⲛⲏ ⲙⲉ[ⲛ] ⲛ̣ϩⲏⲧⲟⲩ ⲉⲧⲁϩⲉⲣⲁⲧⲟⲩ
8 ϩⲱⲥ ⲉⲩϣⲟⲟⲛ̅ ϩⲛ ⲟⲩⲟ[ⲩ]ⲥⲓⲁ
ⲙⲛ ⲛⲏ ⲙⲉⲛ ⲙ̅ ⲡⲣⲏⲧⲉ ⲛ̅ [ⲟⲩⲟⲩⲥ]ⲓⲁ
10 ϩⲛ ⲟⲩⲡⲣⲁⲝⲓⲥ ⲏ ⲟⲩⲝⲓ ⲙ̅ⲕ[ⲁϩ ⲉ]ⲩ̅-
ϣⲟⲟⲛ̅ ϩⲛ ⲟⲩⲙⲉϩⲥⲛⲁⲩ· ⲉ[ⲥϣⲟ-]
12 ⲟⲛ̅ ⲅⲁⲣ ⲛ̅ϩⲏⲧⲟⲩ ⲛ̅ϭⲓ ϯⲙⲛ̅ⲧ[ⲁⲧⲙⲓ-]
ⲥⲉ ⲛ̅ⲧⲉ ⲛⲓⲙⲛ̅ⲧⲁⲧⲙⲓⲥⲉ [ⲉⲧϣⲟ-]
14 ⲟⲛ̅ ⲟⲛⲧⲱⲥ· ⲁⲩⲱ ⲛⲓⲁ[ⲧⲙⲓⲥⲉ]
ⲉⲧⲁⲩϣⲱⲡⲉ ⲉⲥⲁϩⲉⲣⲁ[ⲧⲥ ⲛ̅-]
16 ϭⲓ ⲧⲉⲩϭⲟⲙ· ⲉⲥⲙ̅ⲙⲁⲩ ⲛ̅ϭ[ⲓ ⲟⲩ-]
ⲟⲩⲥⲓ[ⲁ ⲛ]ⲛ ⲁⲧⲥⲱⲙⲁ ⲙⲛ [ⲟⲩⲥⲱ]
18 ⲙⲁ ⲉⲧⲉ ⲙⲁⲥⲧⲉⲕⲟ· ⲉⲩⲙ̅[ⲡⲓⲙⲁ]
ⲉⲧⲙ̅ⲙⲁⲩ ⲛ̅ϭⲓ ⲡⲓⲁⲧⲟ̣[ⲩⲱⲧⲃ ⲉ-]
20 ⲃⲟⲗ ⲉⲧϣⲟⲟⲛ̅ ⲟ̣[ⲛⲧⲱⲥ ⲁⲩⲱ]
ⲡⲏ ⲉϣ[ⲁ]ϥⲟⲩⲱⲧⲃ [ⲉⲃⲟⲗ ϩⲛ ⲟⲩ-]
22 ϣ[ⲓ]ⲃⲉ ⲉϥⲁϩⲉⲣⲁⲧϥ ⲙⲛ ⲛⲁⲓ̈ ⲧⲏ-]
ⲣ̣[ⲟ]ⲩ ⲛ̅ϭⲓ [ⲡⲓ]ⲕⲱϩⲧ̅ ⲛ[
24 [. . . . . . .]ⲁ̣[ⲧ̅]ⲧⲁⲕⲟ· ⲁ[

115,24   E.g., [ϩⲛ ⲡⲓⲙⲉϩ]ϥⲧⲟⲟⲩ.
116,12   ⲙⲛ̣ⲧ̣, or else ⲙⲛⲧ̣.

[he] has four different (διαφορά)

16   aeons (αἰών). In relation to (κατά)
    each of the aeons (αἰών)

18   they have powers, not
    like first and second (powers),

20   for (γάρ) all these [are]
    eternals, [but] they are different

22   [   ] order (τάξις) and glory
    [   ] which exists

24   [in   ] four aeons (αἰών) and
    [   ] that preexists

26   [   ] god [
    [   ] they are [

28   [

[116]

All (+δέ) of them exist

2   in one, dwelling together,
    yet perfected individually (+κατά)

4   in fellowship and
    filled with the aeon (αἰών) which

6   really (ὄντως) exists. There are
    those among them (+μέν) that stand

8   as (ὡς) dwelling in essence (οὐσία) and
    those (+μέν) (that stand) as [essence (οὐσια)]

10   in conduct (πρᾶξις) or (ἤ) [suffering because]
    they are in a second; for (γάρ)

12   the unengenderedness of the ungenerated
    ones that really (ὄντως) exist is among

14   them. When the ungenerated
    have come into being, their power

16   stands; there is there an
    incorporeal (-σῶμα) essence (οὐσία) with [an]

18   imperishable [body (σῶμα)]; the
    [immutable one] is [there]

20   that [really (ὄντως)] exists.
    Because it transforms [through]

22   change, [the] fire stands
    [with all of them]

24   [indestructible

116,21   Transforms, lit., crosses over.

[· . . . .] .ογⲁ ⲛ̣[

<u>ⲣ[ⲓ]ⲍ</u>

ⲉϥⲁϩⲉⲣⲁⲧϥ· ⲉⲧⲙⲡⲙⲁ ⲉⲧⲙ—

2   ⲙⲁⲩ ⲛ̄ϭⲓ ⲛⲓⲍⲱⲟⲛ ⲧⲏⲣⲟⲩ ⲉⲧ—

     ϣⲟⲟⲡ̄ ⲛ ⲕⲁⲧⲁ ⲟⲩⲁ ⲉⲩϩⲟⲧⲡ̄

4   [ϩ]ⲓ ⲟ[ⲩ]ⲙⲁ ⲧⲏⲣⲟⲩ· ⲉⲥⲙⲙⲁⲩ ⲛ̄—

     ϭⲓ ϯⲅ̣ⲛⲱⲥⲓⲥ ⲛⲧⲉ ϯⲅ̣ⲛⲱⲥⲓⲥ

6   ⲙⲛ ⲟⲩⲧⲁϩⲟ ⲛⲧⲉ ϯ[ⲙ]ⲛ̄ⲧⲁⲧ—

     ⲉⲓⲙⲉ· ⲉϥⲙⲙⲁⲩ ⲛ̄ϭⲓ ⲟⲩⲭⲁⲟⲥ

8   ⲙⲛ [ⲟⲩⲧⲟ]ⲡⲟⲥ ⲛⲧⲁⲩ ⲧⲏⲣⲟⲩ

     ⲉϥ[ϫⲏⲕ] ⲉⲃⲟⲗ ⲁⲩⲱ ⲉⲧⲉ ⲛ ⲃⲣⲣⲉ·

10 [ⲟ]ⲩ<ⲟⲩ>ⲟⲉⲓⲛ ⲇⲉ ⲛ ⲧⲁⲡⲙⲉ ⲁⲩⲱ ⲟⲩ—

     [ⲕ]ⲁⲕⲉ ⲉⲁⲩϫⲓ ⲟⲩⲟⲉⲓⲛ ⲙⲛ ⲡⲏ

12 [ⲉ]ⲧⲉ ⲛϥϣⲟⲟⲡ̄ ⲁⲛ ⲟⲛⲧⲱⲥ·

     [ⲡⲏ ⲛ]ⲉϥϣⲟⲟⲡ̄ ⲁⲛ ⲟⲛⲧⲱⲥ·

14 [· . . ⲡ]ⲓⲁⲧϣⲱⲡⲉ ⲉⲧⲉ ⲛϥϣⲟ—

     [ⲟⲡ̄] ⲁⲛ ⲉ ⲡⲧⲏⲣϥ· ⲛⲧⲟϥ ⲇⲉ ⲡⲓ—

16 [ⲁⲅⲁ]ⲑⲟⲛ ⲉⲧⲉ ⲉⲃⲟⲗ ⲙⲙⲟϥ ⲡⲉ

     [ⲡⲓ]ⲁⲅⲁⲑⲟⲛ ⲙⲛ ⲡⲏ [ⲉⲧ]ⲛⲁⲛⲟⲩ

18 [ⲁⲩ]ⲱ ⲡⲛⲟⲩⲧⲉ ⲉⲧⲉ ⲉⲃⲟⲗ ⲙ—

     [ⲙⲟϥ] ⲡ[ⲉ] ⲡⲛⲟⲩⲧⲉ ⲙⲛ ⲡⲏ ⲉⲧ—

20 [· . . . .]ⲧⲉ· ⲡⲏ ⲉⲧⲛⲉⲁϥ·

     [· . . . . . .]ⲩ ⲅⲁⲣ ϩⲛ ⲟⲩⲙⲉⲣⲟⲥ

22 [· . . . . .]ⲉⲓⲇⲟⲥ ⲙⲛ ⲡⲛⲟⲩ[ⲧ]ⲉ

     [· . . . . .] ⲉⲧⲙⲙⲁⲩ ⲙⲛ ⲡⲏ [. .]

24 [· . . . . ⲟ]ⲩⲛⲟⲩⲧⲉ [

     [· . . . . .]ⲉ ⲛⲁⲓ̈ ⲧⲏ[ⲣⲟⲩ]

26 [· . . . . .]ϯ̄ ⲕⲁⲕ[ⲉ

     [· . . · . . . .]ϥ[

<u>ⲣ[ⲓ]ⲏ</u>

     ⲁⲩⲱ ⲟⲩⲅⲉⲛⲟⲥ· ⲁⲩⲱ ⲉⲙⲡϥ—

2   ⲧⲱϩ ⲙⲛ ⲗⲁⲁⲩ· ⲁⲗⲗⲁ ⲉϥϭⲉⲉⲧ

     ⲙⲁⲩⲁⲁϥ ⲛ̄ϩⲣⲁⲓ̈ ⲛ̄ϩⲏⲧϥ ⲁⲩⲱ

4   ⲉϥⲙⲟⲧⲛ ⲙⲙⲟϥ ⲛ̄ϩⲣⲁⲓ̈ ϩⲙ ⲡⲓ[ⲁ—]

     ⲣⲏϫϥ ⲛⲧⲁϥ ⲛⲛ ⲁⲧⲛ ⲁⲣⲏϫϥ· ⲡⲁⲓ̈

6   ⲇⲉ ⲡⲉ [ⲡ]ⲛⲟⲩⲧⲉ ⲛⲧⲉ ⲛⲏ ⲉⲧϣⲟ—

     ⲟⲡ̄ ⲟⲛⲧⲱⲥ· ⲟⲩⲣ[ⲉϥ]ⲛ[ⲁⲩ] ⲉⲣⲟϥ

117,4-5   I.e., Kalyptos; cf. 118,10.

117,10   Cf. Bohairic ⲧⲁϥⲙⲏⲓ.

117,20   Sahidic ⲉⲧ—ⲛⲁⲁϥ.

118,1   ⲉⲙⲡϥ, ⲡϥ (connected by supralinear stroke) read in 1972; papyrus

[   ] one [

    he stands. It is there that
2   all living animals (ζῷον) are,
    existing individually (+κατά), (yet) all
4   joined together. The knowledge (γνῶσις)
    of the knowledge (γνῶσις) is there
6   together with a setting up of ignorance.
    Chaos (χάος) is there
8   and (also) a [perfect place (τόπος)]
    for all of them, and they are new.
10   True (+δέ) light (is there),
    also enlightened darkness together with the one
12   that does not really (ὄντως) exist–
    [it] does not really (ὄντως) exist.
14   [   ] the non-being that does
    not exist at all. But (δέ) as for him, he (is)
16   [Good (ἀγαθόν)] from which derives
    the good (ἀγαθόν) and what is pleasant,
18   and he (is) the god from
    [whom] comes god and he who
20   [   ], he who is great.
    For (γάρ) [   ] in part (μέρος)
22   [   ] form (εἶδος) and god
    that [   ] and the one [
24   [   ] a god [
    [   ] all these [
26   [   ] darkness [
    [

    and race (γένος). He has not
2   mixed with anything, but (ἀλλά) he remains
    alone in himself and
4   rests himself on his
    limitless limit.
6   He (+δέ) is [the] god of those that
    really (ὄντως) exist, a [seer]

---

    subsequently damaged; now best attested in photo A.

118,5   The scribe first wrote ⲁⲧⲁⲣ ⲏ ⲁ ϥ, then added ⲛ̄ above the line after ⲧ.
118,6-7   ⲱ ⲟ /ⲟ ⲛ̄, first ⲟ read in 1972; papyrus subsequently damaged;
    now best attested in photo A.

8 ⲙⲛ ⲟⲩⲣⲉϥⲟⲩⲉⲛϩ ⲛⲟ[ⲩⲧⲉ ⲉⲃ]ⲟⲗ·
   ⲉⲁⲥϯ ϭⲟⲙ ⲙ ⲡⲏ ⲉⲧⲥⲟ[ⲩⲱⲛⲥ]
10 ⲛϭⲓ ϯⲃⲁⲣⲃⲏⲗⲱ ⲡⲓⲁⲓⲱⲛ ϯ[ⲧⲛⲱ–]
   ⲥⲓⲥ ⲛⲧⲉ ⲡⲓⲁϩⲟⲣⲁⲧⲟⲛ ⲛ̅ ϣⲙ[ⲧ̅–]
12 ϭⲟⲙ ⲛ ⲧⲉⲗⲓⲟⲥ ⲙ ⲡ̅ⲛ̅ⲁ̅ ⲁϯ[
   ⲛⲁⲥ ⲉⲥϫⲱ ⲙⲙⲟⲥ ϫⲉ ϥ[
14 ⲟⲩⲱⲛϩ ϯⲟⲛϩ ⲛϩⲣⲁ ̈ⲓ ϧⲛ ⲟ[
   ⲕⲟⲛϩ ⲡⲓⲟⲩⲁ· ϥⲟⲛϩ ⲛϭ[ⲓ ⲡⲏ]
16 ⲉⲧⲉ ⲛ [ϣ]ⲟⲙⲧ̅ ⲛⲧⲟⲕ ⲡⲉ [ⲡϣⲟ–]
   ⲙⲧ̀ ⲉⲧⲉ ⲛ ϣⲟⲙⲧ̅ ⲛ ⲕⲱ[ⲃ . . .]
18 ⲉⲉⲉ· ⲡⲓϣⲟⲣⲡ̅ ⲛ ⲍ̅ ⲛ̣ [
   ϯⲙⲉϩϣⲟⲙⲧⲉ [
20 ⲡⲓⲙⲉϩⲥⲛⲁⲩ ⲛ ⲥ ·[
   ⲉⲉⲉⲉ ⲁⲁⲁⲁⲁⲁ[
22 [.] ϭ̣ⲛⲧⲉ ⲡⲁ ̈ⲓ ⲇⲉ ϥⲧ[ⲟⲟⲩ
   [. . . .] . . ϯⲧⲛⲱ[ⲥⲓⲥ
24 [. . . . .]ⲧϥ· ⲧⲏ[
   [–––   ]ⲉ ̣ⲓ[

                              [ⲣ̣ⲓ̣]ⲑ̄
   ⲟⲩⲙⲉⲣⲟⲥ· ⲁϣ ⲛ ⲛⲟⲩⲥ ⲁⲩⲱ
2 ⲁϣ ⲛ ⲥⲟⲫⲓⲁ· ⲁⲩⲱ ⲁϣ ⲛⲛ ⲉⲡⲓⲥ–
   ⲧⲏⲙⲏ ⲏ ⲁϣ ⲛ ⲥⲃⲱ· ϣⲁⲩϯ ⲣⲁⲛ
4 [ⲁ]ⲉ ⲉ̱ [ⲛ]ⲉϥⲫⲱⲥⲧⲏⲣ ⲡⲓϣⲟⲣⲡ̅ ⲙⲉⲛ
   [ⲡⲉ ⲁⲣⲙⲏ]ⲇⲱⲛ ⲙⲛ ⲧⲏ ⲉⲧⲛⲙⲙⲁϥ
6 . .[. . . ⲡ]ⲓⲙⲉϩⲥⲛⲁⲩ ⲡⲉ ⲇⲓⲫⲁ–
   ⲛⲉ[. . ⲙⲛ ⲧ]ⲏ ⲉⲧⲛⲙ[ⲙ]ⲁϥ ⲇⲏ ̈ⲓ
8 ⲫ̅[. . . ⲡ]ⲓⲙⲉϩϣⲟⲙⲧ̀ ⲡⲉ
   [ⲙⲁⲗⲥⲏⲇ]ⲱⲛ ⲙⲛ ⲧⲏ ⲉⲧⲛⲙⲙⲁϥ
10 [. . . . .] ⲡⲓⲙⲉϩϥⲧⲟⲟⲩ ⲡⲉ
   [. . . .]ⲥ ⲙⲛ ⲧⲏ ⲉⲧⲛⲙⲙⲁϥ ⲟⲗⲙⲓⲥ
12 [ⲁⲩⲱ] ϥϣⲟⲟⲡ̅ ⲛϭⲓ ⲡⲓⲕⲁ̅ⲥ̅ ⲉⲁϥ–
   [. . . .] .ⲙⲛ ⲧⲉϥⲓⲇⲉⲁ· ⲁⲩⲱ
14 [ϥϣⲟⲟ]ⲡ̅ ⲛⲛ ⲁⲧⲟⲩⲱⲛϩ ⲛ ⲛⲁ ̈ⲓ
   [ⲧⲏⲣ]ⲟⲩ ϩⲓⲛⲁ ϫⲉ ⲉⲧⲉϫⲓ ϭⲟⲙ
16 [ⲉⲃⲟ]ⲗ ϩⲓ[ⲧ]ⲟⲟⲧϥ ⲧⲏⲣⲟⲩ ⲉⲩ–

118,13   E.g., ϥ[ⲟⲛϩ ϩ̄ⲛ]; cf. 3,10–11.
118,14   E.g., ϩ̄ⲛ ⲟ[ⲩⲁ].
118,17   Probably magical *stoicheia* begin at the end of this line.
118,18   ⲉⲉⲉ, magical *stoicheia*.
118,22   Possibly [ⲟ]ⲩⲛⲧⲉ.
119,5   Cf. 127,9 (not room for ϩⲁⲣⲙⲏⲇⲱⲛ).

8   and a revealer of god.
      When she had strengthened him who [knew her],
10   the aeon (αἰών) Barbelo, the knowledge
      (γνῶσις) of the invisible (ἀόρατον) three-
12   powered perfect (τέλειος) Spirit (πνεῦμα) [
      her, saying, "He [
14   life. I am alive in [
      You, the One, are alive. He is alive, [he]
16   who is three. It is you who are [the]
      [three] who [   ] three [doubled
18   e e e. The first of seven [
      the third [
20   the second [
      e e e e a a a a a a a[
22   [ ] two, but (δέ) he [four]
      [   ] knowledge (γνῶσις) [
24   [   ] . . . [
      [

                                        [11]9
      part (μέρος)? What kind of mind (νοῦς)?
2   What kind of wisdom (σοφία)? What kind of under-
      standing (ἐπιστήμη), what kind of teaching? His (+δέ)
4   lights (φωστήρ) are given names: the first (+δέ)
      [is Arme]don and his consort (is)
6   [   ]; the second (+δέ) is Dipha-
      ne-[and] his consort (is) Dei-
8   ph-[   ]; the third is
      [Malsed]on and his consort (is)
10 [   ]; the fourth is
      [   ]-s and his consort (is) Olmis.
12 Kalyptos (καλυπτός) exists having
      [   ] and his Idea (ἰδέα).
14 [He is] invisible to all
      these so that (ἵνα) they all might be
16 strengthened by him

119,5-10   The names of the consorts are mostly in lacunae; cf. *Steles Seth* VII
              126,10-12; *Allogenes* XI 54,6-13.
119,6   No supralinear stroke over ΔΙΦΑ.
119,9   No supralinear stroke over]ΩΝ.
119,11   E.g., [COΛ.ΜΙC; cf. 122,12 and 126,4; *Allogenes* XI, 54,7; Schmidt-
              McDermott, *Untitled Text*, 252,21f, has a Solmistes.

[. .]ⲥⲧⲉ ⲉϥϣⲟⲟⲛ̄ [ⲛ̄]ϩⲣⲁⲓ̈ ϩⲙ
18   [. . .]ⲱ . ⲙ ⲡⲁⲛⲧⲉⲗⲓⲟⲥ ⲉⲧⲛ̄‐
[ⲧⲁϥ ⲙ ⲡⲓ]ϥⲧⲟⲟⲩ ⲉⲩϣⲟⲟⲛ̄
20   [. . . . . ⲁ]ⲩⲱ ⲡⲓϣⲟⲣⲛ̄ ⲛⲓ‐
[. . . . . ⲟ]ⲩⲇⲉ ⲕⲁⲧⲁ ⲟⲩϩⲱ‐
22   [. . . . . .]ⲏϩ ⲉⲣⲟϥ ⲙⲁⲩⲁⲁ[ϥ]
[. . . . . ⲃ]ⲁⲣⲃⲏⲗⲱ [. . . .]ⲏ ⲁ̣[. .] .
24   [. . . . . . .]ⲛ̄ⲧ[. . . . .
[. . . . . .]ϥⲱ[. . . . .

ⲣ̄[ⲕ]
ⲉⲓⲙⲉ ⲉⲣⲟϥ ⲙⲛ ⲡⲏ ⲉⲧⲕⲏ ⲉ‐
2   ϩⲣⲁⲓ̈ ⲉⲩⲙⲉϩⲥⲛⲁⲩ· ⲡⲓϣⲟⲣⲛ̄
ⲇⲉ ⲛⲧⲉ ⲛⲓⲉⲱⲛ ⲡⲉ ϩⲁⲣⲙⲏⲇⲱⲛ
4   ⲡⲓⲉⲟⲟⲩ ⲛ ⲉⲓⲱⲧ̄ ⲡⲓⲙⲉ[ϩ]ⲥⲛⲁⲩ
ⲇⲉ ⲙ ⲫⲱⲥⲧⲏⲣ ⲡⲏ ⲉⲧ[ⲉ ⲛ̄ϥⲉⲓⲙⲉ]
6   ⲉⲣⲟϥ ⲁⲛ· ⲁⲗⲗⲁ ⲛⲓⲕⲁ̣ⲧ̣[ⲁ ⲟⲩⲁ ⲧⲏ‐]
ⲣⲟⲩ ⲟⲩⲥⲟⲫⲓⲁ ⲛ [. . . . . . .]ϣⲟ‐
8   ⲟⲛ̄ ϩⲙ ⲡⲓⲙⲉϩϥⲧⲟ[ⲟⲩ ⲛⲛ ⲉⲱ]ⲛ·
ⲡⲏ ⲉⲧⲁϥⲟⲩⲱⲛϩ ⲉⲃ[ⲟⲗ ⲙⲙⲟϥ]
10   ⲙⲛ ⲛⲓⲉⲟⲟⲩ ⲧⲏⲣⲟⲩ [ⲡⲓⲙⲉϩϣⲟ‐]
ⲙ̄ⲧ ⲇⲉ ⲙ ⲫⲱⲥⲧⲏⲣ ⲡⲏ ⲉ̣[. . . . .]
12   ⲉⲣⲟϥ ⲁⲛ· ⲉⲡⲓϣⲁϫⲉ ⲛⲧ[ⲉ ⲛⲓⲉⲓ‐]
ⲇⲟⲥ ⲧⲏⲣⲟⲩ ⲙⲛ ⲡⲓⲕⲉⲉ[ⲟⲟⲩ]
14   ⲉⲧⲙⲙⲁⲩ ϯⲉⲡⲓⲥⲧⲏⲙ[ⲏ ⲧⲏ ⲉⲧ‐]
ⲛ̄ϩⲣⲁⲓ̈ ϩⲙ ⲡⲓⲙⲉϩϣⲟⲙⲧ̄ ⲛ̄[ⲛ ⲉⲱⲛ]
16   ⲟⲩⲛ ϥⲧⲟⲟⲩ ϣⲟⲟⲛ̄ ⲛ̄ϩⲣ[ⲁⲓ̈ ⲛ‐]
ϩⲏⲧϥ· ⲙⲁⲗⲥⲏⲇⲱⲛ[·] ⲙⲛ ⲙ̣[. .
18   ⲛⲓⲟⲥ· ⲡ[ⲓ]ⲙⲉϩϥⲧⲟⲟⲩ ⲇⲉ ⲙ ⲫⲱ‐]
ⲥⲧⲏⲣ ⲡⲉ ⲡⲏ ⲉⲧⲛⲁⲩ [ⲉ]ⲣ̣ⲟ . .
20   ⲛⲧⲉ ⲛⲓⲉⲓⲇⲟⲥ ⲧⲏⲣⲟ̣[ⲩ . . . .
ϩⲓ ⲟⲩⲙⲁ ⲉⲩϣⲟ̣[ⲟⲛ̄ . . . . .
22   ⲟⲩⲥⲃⲱ ⲙⲛ ⲟⲩⲉⲟⲟ̣[ⲩ . . . .
ⲙⲛ ⲧⲙⲉ ⲛⲧⲉ ⲡⲓϥⲧ[ⲟⲟⲩ ⲛⲛ ⲉⲱⲛ]
24   ⲟ̣[ⲗ̣]ⲙ̣ⲓⲥ [. . .] ⲙⲛ ⲡⲓⲁ[. . . . .
[———   ] ϩⲓ [. . . . . .
26   [———   ]ⲟⲱ[. . . . . .

119,18   E.g., [ⲡ ⲓⲉ]ⲱⲛ̣; final trace not compatible with ⲧ.
120,11   Cod. [. . .] <u>vacat</u>
120,16-17 Or, there are four in Malcedon and ...
120,16   Cod. ⲟⲩⲛ̄.

[   ] he exists in
18 [   ] all-perfect (παντέλειος) because
[he has] four existing
20 [   ] and the first, the
[   ] nor (οὐδέ) according to (κατά) a
22 [   ] alone
[B]arbelo [
24 [
[
1[20]
know him and the one who is set
2   over a second. The first
(+δέ) of the aeons (αἰών) is Harmedon,
4   the father-glory. The second
(+δέ) light (φωστήρ) (is) one whom [he does] not [know],
6   but (ἀλλά) all the [individuals (+κατά)],
wisdom (σοφία) [   ], reside
8   in the fourth [aeon (αἰών),]
who has revealed [himself]
10 and all the glories. [The third]
(+δέ) light (φωστήρ) (is) he [
12 not . . . as the expression of all
[the species (εἶδος)] and that other
14 [glory], understanding (ἐπιστήμη), [who is]
in the third [aeon (αἰών)].
16 There are four in him:
Malsedon and [
18 -nios. The fourth [(+δέ)]
light (φωστήρ) is the one who sees [
20 of all the forms (εἶδος)
existing together[
22 a teaching and glory [
and the truth of the [four aeons (αἰών)],
24 O[l]mis, [   ] and the [
[
26 [

120,17-18   ϻ[———]/ⲛⲓⲟⲥ, a proper name, no supralinear stroke.
120,19   Probably [ⲉ]ⲡ[ⲟⲟⲩ], or [ⲉ]ⲡ[ⲟⲩ].
120,21   E.g., [ⲟⲛ ⲕⲁⲧⲁ ⲟⲩⲁ ⲛ].
120,24   ọ, or else ç.

[ρκα]

ⲙⲉϩϯⲟⲩ· ⲁⲩⲱ ⲡϣⲟⲣⲡ ⲉ-
2 ⲧⲉ ⲡⲓⲙⲉϩⲥⲛⲁⲩ <u>ⲡⲉ</u> ⲉⲧⲉ ⲡⲁⲓ
ⲡⲉ ⲛⲧⲟϥ ⲡⲉ ⲡⲓⲕⲁⲥ ⲙ ⲡⲁⲛⲧⲉⲗⲓⲟⲥ
4 ⲥⲉϣⲟⲟⲛ̄ ⲅⲁⲣ <u>ⲛ̄ϭⲓ</u> ⲡⲓϥⲧⲟⲟⲩ ⲙ
ⲫⲱⲥⲧ[ⲏ]ⲣ· ⲡⲓⲕⲁⲥ ⲇⲉ ⲉⲧⲁϥⲡⲱϣ
6 ⲟⲛ· ⲁⲩⲱ ⲛⲁ̣ⲓ̈ ⲉⲩϣⲟⲟⲛ̄ ϩⲓ ⲟⲩ-
ⲙⲁ· ⲁⲩⲱ [ⲛ̄]ⲁ̣ⲓ̈ ⲉⲧⲥⲟⲟⲩⲛ ⲛⲉⲧ-
8 ϣⲟⲟⲛ̄ ⲛ [ⲉ]ⲟⲟⲩ ⲧⲏⲣⲟⲩ· ⲛ̄ⲧⲟ-
ⲟ[ⲩ ⲧⲏⲣⲟ]ⲩ ⲉⲧⲉ ⲛ ⲧⲉⲗⲓⲟⲥ· ⲡⲁⲓ
10 [. . . .]ⲥ̣ⲟⲟⲩⲛ ⲛ ϩⲱⲃ ⲛⲓⲙ ⲛ̄-
ⲧⲁⲩ ⲧⲏⲣⲟⲩ ⲉⲧⲡⲁⲛⲧⲉⲗⲓⲟⲥ
12 ⲡⲉ· ⲉⲧⲉ ⲉⲃⲟⲗ ⲙⲙⲟϥ ⲡⲉ ϭⲟⲙ
[ⲛ̄]ⲓ̈ⲙ· ⲁⲩⲱ ⲟⲩⲟⲛ ⲛⲓⲙ ⲙⲛ ⲡⲓ-
14 ⲉⲱⲛ̄ ⲧⲏⲣϥ ⲛ̄ⲧⲁⲩ· ⲡⲏ ⲉϣⲁⲩ-
[ⲉ]ⲓ̣ ⲉϩⲣⲁ̈ⲓ ⲉⲣⲟϥ ⲧⲏⲣⲟⲩ· ⲁⲩⲱ
16 ϣⲁⲩⲉⲓ ⲉⲃⲟⲗ ⲙ̄ⲙⲟϥ ⲛ̄ϭⲓ ⲛⲁⲓ
[ⲧⲏⲣ]ⲟⲩ· ϯϭⲟⲙ ⲛ̄ⲧⲉ̣ ⲛⲁⲓ ⲧⲏ-
18 [ⲣⲟ]ⲩ· ⲧⲁⲣⲭⲏ ⲛ̄ⲧⲉ ⲛⲁⲓ ⲧⲏ-
[ⲣⲟⲩ· ⲉ]ϣⲱⲡⲉ ⲉϥϣⲁⲛⲉⲓⲙⲉ
20 [ⲙ̄ⲙⲟⲟⲩ] ⲁϥϣⲱⲡⲉ ⲛ ⲟⲩⲙⲉϩ-
[. . . . . . .]ⲉⲱⲛ· ⲙⲛ ⲟⲩⲙⲉϩ-
22 [. . . . . .]ⲙ̄ⲛ̄ⲧⲁⲧⲙⲓⲥⲉ· ⲉⲩ-
[. . . . .] ϩⲉⲛⲕⲉⲉⲱⲛ ϩⲣⲁ[ⲓ̈]
24 [ϩⲛ . . .]ⲟⲩ .[. . . . .
[. . . . . .]ⲟ[
26 [. . . . .] .ⲁ .[. . . . .
ⲣ[ⲕ]ⲃ
ϣⲱⲡⲉ ⲛⲛ ⲟⲩⲃⲁⲣⲃⲏⲗⲱ ϣⲁϥ-
2 ϣⲱⲡⲉ ⲛⲛ ⲟⲩϣⲟⲣⲡ ⲛⲛ ⲉⲱⲛ
ⲉⲧⲃⲉ ϯⲙⲛ̄ⲧϣⲁ ⲉⲛⲉϩ ⲛⲧⲉ ⲡⲓ-
4 ⲁϩⲟⲣⲁⲧⲟⲛ ⲙ ⲡ̄ⲛ̄ⲁ· ϯⲙⲉϩⲥⲛⲧⲉ
ⲙ ⲙⲛ̄ⲧⲁⲧⲙⲓⲥⲉ· ⲛⲓ[ⲉ]ⲟⲟⲩ ⲇⲉ
6 ⲧⲏⲣⲟⲩ ⲛⲁⲓ ⲛⲉ ⲛⲓⲁϥⲣⲏⲇⲱⲛ
ⲛⲛ ⲁⲧⲛ ⲁⲣⲏⲝⲛⲟⲩ [. ⲛ]ⲓⲁ̈ⲧϣⲁ-
8 ⲝⲉ ⲙ̄ⲙⲟⲟⲩ ⲛⲓⲣⲉϥⲟ[ⲩ]ⲱⲛϩ ⲉⲃⲟⲗ·
ⲛⲓⲁⲧⲟⲩⲱⲧⲃ ⲉⲃⲟⲗ ⲛ[ⲓ . . . . .]
10 ⲧⲏⲣⲟⲩ· ⲛⲓⲣⲉϥⲟⲩⲉⲛϩ ⲉⲟⲟⲩ ⲉⲃⲟⲗ
ⲛⲓⲙⲁⲣⲝ̄ⲏⲇⲱⲛ· ⲛⲏ ⲉⲧⲟⲩⲟⲛϩ ⲉ-
12 ⲃⲟⲗ ⲉⲩⲕⲏⲃ· ⲛⲓⲥⲟⲗⲙⲓⲥ ⲛⲓⲁⲧ[ⲛ]

122,5   For glories, see 46,22-26.

[121]

fifth. The first (is the one)

2 who is the second, that is, it is
the all-perfect (παντέλειος) Kalyptos (καλυπτός),

4 for (γάρ) there are four lights
(φωστήρ). It (+δέ) is Kalyptos (καλυπτός) who has

6 divided again. They dwell together, and
these who know all those that

8 exist as glories, all of them
perfect (τέλειος). This one

10 [   ] knows everything about
them all, since he is all-perfect (παντέλειος).

12 From him is every
power, every one and

14 their entire aeon (αἰών), because they all
come to him.

16 They all come from him,
the power of them

18 all (and) the origin (ἀρχή) of them all.
When he learned

20 [of them], he became a
[   ] aeon (αἰών) and a

22 [   ] ingenerateness.
[   ] other aeons (αἰών)

24 [in   ] a [
[

26 [

1[2]2

become a Barbelo, he

2 becomes a first aeon (αἰών)
because of the eternity of the

4 Invisible (ἀόρατον) Spirit (πνεῦμα), the second
ingenerateness (fem.). These (+δέ) are all

6 the glories: the limitless
Aphredons, [the]

8 ineffables, the revealers,
all the [   ] immutables,

10 the glory-revealers;
the twice-revealed

12 Marsedons, the limitless Solmises

ⲁⲣⲏⲝⲛⲟⲩ· ⲛⲓⲟⲩⲱⲛϩ ⲉⲃⲟⲗ ⲙ-

14 ⲙⲟⲟⲩ ⲙⲁⲩⲁⲁⲩ· ⲛⲏ ⲉⲧⲙⲉ[ϩ]

ⲉⲃⲟⲗ ⲛⲛ ⲉⲟⲟⲩ· ⲛⲏ ⲉⲧⲟϩ[ⲉ ⲉ]

16 ⲉⲟⲟⲩ[· ⲛ]ⲣ̅ⲉ̅ⲩⲥⲙⲟⲩ ⲛⲓⲙ[ⲁⲣⲭ ⲏ-]

ⲇⲱⲛ· ⲛⲓⲕⲁ̅ⲥ̅ ⲛⲏ ⲉⲧ[. . . . .]

18 ⲉⲃⲟⲗ· ⲛⲓⲁⲣⲏⲝⲛⲟⲩ ⲛ[ⲏ ⲉⲧⲕⲏ]

ϩⲓⲝⲛ ⲛⲓⲁⲣⲏⲝⲛⲟⲩ [. . . . .

20 ⲉⲧⲉ ⲛⲏ ⲉⲧϣⲟⲟⲡ ϩ[ⲛ . . . .

ⲉ̅ⲧⲉ· . . . . . ⲧⲁϩ .[. . . . . .

22 [—] .[. . . . . .

[—]ⲙ .[. . . . . .

Lines 24 and following (ca. 1 or 2 lines) do not survive.

[ⲣ̅ⲕ̅ⲅ̅]

ⲙⲙⲁⲩ ⲛ ϩⲉⲛⲁⲛⲧⲃⲁ ⲛⲛ ⲉⲟⲟⲩ

2 ⲛϩⲣⲁ̈ⲓ ⲛϩⲏⲧⲟⲩ· ⲉⲧⲃⲉ ⲡⲁ̈ⲓ ⲟⲩ-

ⲉⲟⲟⲩ ⲉⲩⲝⲏⲕ ⲡⲉ ϩⲓⲛⲁ ⲉϣⲱⲡⲉ

4 ⲉⲩϣⲁⲛϭⲙ ϭⲟⲙ ⲉ ⲛⲟⲩϩⲃ ⲁⲩⲱ

ⲛϥⲁⲙⲁϩⲧⲉ ⲛϥϣⲱⲡⲉ ⲛ ⲧⲉⲗⲓⲟⲥ

6 ⲉⲧⲃⲉ ⲡⲁ̈ⲓ ⲕⲁⲛ ⲉⲩϣⲁⲛⲉⲓ ⲉϩⲣⲁ̈ⲓ

ⲉⲩⲥⲱⲙⲁ ⲙⲛ ⲟⲩ⟨ⲟⲩ⟩ⲱⲧⲃ ⲉⲃⲟⲗ ⲛ-

8 ⲧⲉ ⲟⲩϩⲩⲗⲏ ⲉⲧⲃⲉ ⲧⲟⲩⲙⲛ̅ⲧ-

ⲡⲁⲛ[ⲧ]ⲉ̅[ⲗⲓ]ⲟⲥ ⲙⲁⲩⲝⲓ ⲛ ⲟⲩⲧⲁⲉⲓⲟ

10 ⲛϩⲟⲩⲟ· ⲉⲧⲉ ⲉⲃⲟⲗ ⲙⲙⲟϥ ⲡⲉ

ⲛⲁ̈ⲓ ⲧⲏⲣⲟⲩ ⲉⲩⲝⲏⲕ ⲉⲃⲟⲗ ⲙⲛ

12 [ⲛ]ⲏ ⲉⲧⲛⲙⲙⲁϥ· ⲕⲁⲓⲅⲁⲣ ⲡⲟⲩⲁ

ⲡⲟⲩⲁ ⲛⲧⲉ ⲛⲓⲉⲱⲛ ⲟⲩⲛⲧⲁϥ ⲙ-

14 [ⲙ]ⲁⲩ ⲛ ϩⲉⲛⲁⲛⲧⲃⲁ ⲛⲛ ⲉⲱⲛ ⲛ-

ϩⲣⲁ̈ⲓ ⲛϩⲏⲧϥ ϩⲓⲛⲁ ⲉϥϣⲟⲟⲡ ϩⲓ ⲟⲩ-

16 ⲙⲁ ⲝⲉ ⲉϥϣⲱⲡⲉ ⲛⲛ ⲟⲩⲉⲱⲛ

ⲛ ⲧⲉⲗⲓⲟⲥ· ⲉϥϣⲟⲟⲡ ⲝⲉ ϩⲛ ϯ-

18 [ⲙⲛ̅ⲧⲙ]ⲁ̈[ⲕ]ⲁⲣⲓⲟⲥ ⲛⲧⲉ ⲡϣⲙⲧ-

[ϭⲟⲙ ⲛ ⲧⲉ]ⲗⲓⲟⲥ ⲛ ⲁϩⲟⲣⲁⲧⲟⲛ

20 [ⲙ ⲡ̅ⲛ̅ⲁ̅ . .]ⲱϥ ⲙ ⲡⲓⲕⲁ ⲣⲱϥ ⲛ

[. . . . .]ⲧⲉ ⲉⲧⲟⲩⲣ ϣⲟⲣⲡ̅

22 [. . . . . . .]ⲟⲩ· ⲙⲛ ϯ[ⲅ]ⲛⲱⲥⲓⲥ

[. . . . . .]ⲡ .[

24 [. . . . .]ⲙ[

[. . . . .] .[

122,19-20   E.g., ⲙⲉ]/ⲉⲩⲉ.
122,20-21   E.g., ϩⲛ ⲛⲓⲙⲉ]ⲉⲩⲉ.
123   Pagination; only a trace of the lower ornamental bar survives.
123,1   Cf. 123,12-14.

the self-revealers
14 who are [full]
of glory, those who [wait for]
16 glory, the blessers, the M[arse-]
dons; the Kalyptoi (καλυπτός) who [
18 the limits [those who are]
upon the limits [
20 ... those that dwell [in
[
22 [
[
Lines 24 and following (ca. 1 or 2 lines) do not survive.

[123]

ten thousand glories
2 in them. Therefore, it is
a perfect glory so that (ἵνα) whenever
4 it can join (another) and
prevail, it becomes perfect (τέλειος).
6 Thus, even if (κἄν) it enters
into a body (σῶμα) and a death (coming) from
8 matter (ὕλη), they do not
receive greater honor because of
10 their all-perfectness (-παντέλειος)from which
all these come, being perfect, together with
12 those that are with him. Indeed (καὶ γάρ) each
of the aeons (αἰών) has
14 ten thousand aeons (αἰών)
in himself, so that (ἵνα) by existing together
16 he may become a perfect (τέλειος)
aeon (αἰών). There is (+δέ) in the
18 [Blessedness (-μακάριος)] of the three-
[powered] perfect (τέλειος) Invisible (ἀόρατον)
20 [Spirit (πνεῦμα)   ] silence
[   ] who became first
22 [   ] and the knowledge (γνῶσις)
[
24 [|
[

123,3   ϩⲓⲚⲀ for ϩⲱⲤⲦⲈ.
123,14   I.e., countless aeons.
123,17-18 I.e., Protophanes.

ρκ̅[δ̅]

ΤΗΡϤ ΟⲨϹⲒϹΗ ΝΤΕ ϮⲄΝⲰϹⲒϹ Μ̄

2 ΜΕϩϹΝΤΕ· ΠϢΟΡⲠ̄ Μ̄ ΜΕΕⲨΕ

ΝϩⲢⲀΪ ϩΝ ΟⲨϮ ΜΕΤΕ ΝΤΕ ΠϢΜⲦ-

4 ϬΟΜ ϫΕ ⲀϤΟⲨΕϩ ϹⲀϩΝΕ ΝⲀϹ Ε ΤΡΕϹ-

ΕⲒΜΕ ΕΡΟϤ· ϩⲒΝⲀ ϫΕ ΕϤΕϢⲰΠΕ

6 Μ̄ ΠⲀΝΤΕⲖⲒΟϹ· ⲀⲨⲰ ΕϤΕ Ν ΤΕⲖⲒΟϹ

ΝϩⲢⲀⲒ Ν̄ϩΗΤϤ· ΕⲨΕⲒΜΕ ΕΡΟϤ ΕΒΟⲖ

8 ϩⲒΤΟΟΤϹ Ν ΟⲨΜ̄ΝⲦϩⲀⲠⲖΟⲨϹ Μ̄Ν

ΟⲨΜ̄ΝΤΜⲀΚⲀΡⲒΟϹ· ⲁ[ϊϫⲒ] Ν̄ ΟⲨΜ̄ⲚⲦ-

10 ⲀⲄⲀⲐΟϹ ΕΒΟⲖ ϩⲒΤΟΟⲦϤ Μ̄ ΠΗ ΕΤΟⲨ-

Ηϩ Ν̄ϹⲰϤ ΝΤΕ ΠⲒΕⲰΝ Ν ΒⲀⲢⲂΗⲖⲰ

12 ΠΗ ΕⲦϮ Μ̄ ΠϢⲰΠΕ ΝⲀϤ· ΝΕ .[

ΤⲰϤ ⲀΝ ΤΕ ϮϬΟΜ ⲀⲖⲖⲀ ΤⲀ ΠΗ ΕΤΜ̄-

14 ΜⲀⲨ ΤΕ· ΝⲒΕⲰΝ ΔΕ ΕⲦϢΟΟⲠ̄

ΟΝΤⲰϹ ΕⲨϢΟΟⲠ̄ ϩΝ ΟⲨϹⲒϹΗ

16 ΝΕΟⲨⲀΤΕΝΕΡⲄⲒⲀ ΤΕ Ϯϩ̄ⲨⲠⲀⲢϪⲒϹ

ⲀⲨⲰ ΝΕΟⲨⲀⲦϢⲀϪΕ Μ̄ΜΟϹ ΤΕ

18 ϮⲄΝⲰϹⲒϹ ΝΤΕ ΠⲒΚⲀⲒ̅Ϲ ΕΤⲦⲀ-]

ϩⲞ Μ̄ΜΟϤ· ΕⲀϤΕⲒ Ε[ΒΟⲖ ϩΜ ΠⲒ-]

20 ΜΕϩϤΤΟΟⲨ ΠⲒΜΟ[. . . . . . .

ΜΕΕⲨΕ ΠⲒⲠⲢⲰΤΟ[ΦⲀΝΗϹ Ν̄]

22 ϩΟ[Ο]ⲨⲦ Ν̄ ΤΕⲖⲒΟϹ Ν [ΝΟⲨϹ . .

[—   ]Δⲱ[. . . . . . .

24 [—   ] .Ν[. . . . .

[ρ̅]κⲉ̅

ϩⲒΚⲰΝ ΝΤⲀϤ ΠΕ ΕϤϢΗϢ Ν̄Μ-

2 ΜⲀϤ ϩΜ ΠⲒΕΟΟⲨ Μ̄Ν ϮϬΟΜ· ϩΝ

ΟⲨΤⲀϪⲒϹ ΔΕ ΕϤϪΟϹΕ ΕΡΟϤ

4 ⲀⲨⲰ ΝϩⲢⲀϊ ϩΝ ΟⲨΕⲰΝ ⲀΝ·

ΕⲨΝΤⲀϤ Ν ΝⲀϊ ΤΗΡΟⲨ Μ̄ ⲠⲢΗΤΕ

6 Μ̄ ΠΗ ΕⲨΟΝϩ ΕⲨϢΟΟⲠ̄ ϩⲒ ΟⲨΜⲀ

ΝϩⲢⲀϊ ϩΝ ΟⲨⲀ· Μ̄Ν ΠⲒΕⲰΝ ΕⲦ-

8 ϩⲢⲀϊ ϩ[Ν ΝΝ] ΕⲰΝ ΕⲨΝΤⲀϤ Μ̄ΜⲀⲨ

Ν ΟⲨΔⲒ[Ⲁ]ΦΟΡⲀ ΕϹΕ Ν ϤΤΟΟⲨ

10 Μ̄Ν Ν[Ⲓ]ΚΕϢⲰϪⲠ̄ ΤΗΡΟⲨ ΕⲦ-

ϢΟΟⲠ̄ ϩΜ ΠⲒΜⲀ ΕⲦΜ̄ΜⲀⲨ· ΠⲒ-

124,12 ΝⲈ .[, the trace can be read Ν, ⲧ, Η, ϫ, or Ϗ | perhaps the Autogenes.

124,13 Ink trace (resembling ϫ) visible after Μ at the end of this line is not part of the text.

124,14 ϢΟΟⲠ̄, Ⲡ̄ more fully preserved in 1972 (read Ⲡ̄ or Π); now best attested

12[4]

whole, a silence (σιγή) of the second

2   knowledge (γνῶσις), the first thought
in the will of the Three-

4   Powered, because he commanded her
to know him so that (ἵνα) he might become

6   all-perfect (παντέλειος) and perfect (τέλειος)
in himself. By simplicity (-ἁπλοῦς)

8   and blessedness (-μακάριος) he is
recognized. [I received]

10   goodness (-ἀγαθός) through that
follower of the Barbelo aeon (αἰών),

12   the one who gives being to himself . . . [
(she) is not the power, but (ἀλλά) she belongs to

14   him. The (+δέ) aeons (αἰών) which really (ὄντως)
exist do so in silence (σιγή).

16   Existence (ὕπαρξις) was inactivity (-ἐνέργεια),
and knowledge (γνῶσις) of the self-established

18   Kalyptos (καλυπτός) was ineffable.
Having come [from the]

20   fourth, the [
thought, the Proto[phanes (πρωτοφανής)],

22   as (the) perfect (τέλειος) male [Mind (νοῦς)
[

24   [

                                                    [1]25

it is his image (εἰκών), equal to

2   him in power and glory, but (δέ)
with respect to order (τάξις) higher than

4   him, not (higher) in aeon (αἰών).
Like him has all

6   these (entities) living (and) dwelling together
in one. Together with the aeon (αἰών)

8   in the aeons (αἰών) has
a fourfold difference (διαφορά)

10   with all the rest that
are there. But (δέ)

---

in photo A; papyrus subsequently damaged.
124,22   [ΝΟⲨⲤ; cf. 44,29; 124,6.
125,1-11   Probably the Protophanes.

12 ⲕⲁⲥ ⲇⲉ ⲉϥϣⲟⲟⲡ ⲟⲛⲧⲱⲥ ⲉⲥ-
ⲕⲏ ⲇⲉ ⲛⲙⲙⲁϥ ⲛϭⲓ ⲧⲁ ⲛⲓⲉⲟⲟⲩ

14 ⲧⲏⲣⲟⲩ ⲓ̈ⲟⲩⲏⲗ · ⲡⲓⲉⲟⲟⲩ ⲛ ϩⲟⲟⲩⲧ ⲙ ⲡⲁⲣⲑⲉⲛⲟⲥ· ⲉⲧⲉ ⲉ-

16 ⲃⲟⲗ ϩⲓⲧⲟⲟⲧⲥ ⲁⲩⲛⲁⲩ ⲉ ⲛⲓⲡⲁⲛ-
ⲧⲉⲗⲓⲟⲛ ⲧⲏⲣⲟⲩ· ⲛⲉⲧⲁϩⲉ ⲇⲉ

18 [ⲉⲣ]ⲁⲧⲟⲩ ⲛⲛⲁϩⲣⲁϥ ⲡⲉ ⲡⲓϣⲟⲙⲧ̇-
[. . . . .] .[.] .ⲛ ⲁⲗⲟⲩ· ⲡⲓϣⲙⲧ̇-

20 [. . . . . . .]ⲥ ⲡⲓⲁⲩⲧⲟⲅⲉⲛⲏⲥ ⲛ
[. . . . .] ⲉⲩⲛⲧⲁϥ ⲇⲉ ⲙⲙⲁⲩ

22 [. . . . .] ⲛϩⲣⲁⲓ̈ ϩⲛ ⲟⲩⲁ ⲉⲩⲧⲟ-
[. . . . ⲡ]ⲏ ⲟⲛ ⲉⲧⲁⲙⲁϩⲧⲉ ⲉ ⲡⲓ-

24 [. . . . . . .] ⲉϥϣⲟⲟⲡ̇ ϩⲛ̣ [
[. . . . . . .]ϭⲁ[

ⲣ̅ⲕ̅[ⲋ̅]

ⲡⲉ ⲛⲧⲉ ϩⲉⲛⲁⲛⲧⲃⲁ ⲛ ⲕⲱⲃ· ⲡⲓ-

2 ϣⲟⲣⲡ̇ ⲇⲉ ⲛⲛ ⲉⲱⲛ ⲉⲧϣⲟⲟⲡ
ⲛϩⲏⲧϥ ⲉⲧⲉ ⲉⲃⲟⲗ ⲙⲙⲟϥ ⲡⲉ

4 ⲡϣⲟⲣⲡ̇ ⲙ ⲫⲱⲥⲧⲏⲣ· ⲥⲟⲗⲙⲓⲥ
ⲙⲛ ⲡⲓⲣⲉϥⲟⲩⲉⲛϩ ⲛⲟⲩⲧⲉ ⲉⲃⲟⲗ

6 ⲉⲩⲁⲧⲛ ⲁⲣⲏϫϥ ⲡⲉ ⲕⲁⲧⲁ ⲡⲓⲧⲩ-
ⲡⲟⲥ ⲉⲧϣⲟⲟⲡ̇ ⲛϩⲣⲁⲓ̈ ϩⲙ ⲡⲓⲕⲁⲥ

8 ⲛⲛ ⲉⲱⲛ ⲙⲛ ⲇⲟϩⲟⲙ[ⲉⲇ]ⲱⲛ·
ⲡⲓⲙⲉϩⲥⲛⲁⲩ ⲛⲛ ⲉⲱ[ⲛ] ⲁⲕⲣⲉⲙⲱⲛ

10 ⲡⲓⲁⲧϣⲁϫⲉ ⲙⲙⲟϥ ⲉⲩⲛⲧⲁϥ
ⲙⲙⲁⲩ ⲙ ⲡⲓⲙⲉϩⲥⲛⲁⲩ ⲙ ⲫⲱⲥ-

12 ⲧⲏⲣ· ⲍⲁⲭⲑⲟⲥ ⲙⲛ ⲓ̈ⲁⲭⲑⲟⲥ· ⲡⲓ-
ⲙⲉϩϣⲟⲙⲧ̇ ⲇⲉ ⲛⲛ ⲉⲱⲛ ⲡⲉ ⲁⲙ-

14 ⲃⲣⲟⲥⲓⲟⲥ ⲡⲓⲡⲁⲣⲑⲉⲛⲟⲥ ⲉⲩⲛⲧⲁ[ϥ]
ⲙⲙⲁⲩ ⲙ ⲡⲓⲙⲉϩϣⲟⲙⲧ̇ ⲙ ⲫⲱ-

16 ⲥⲧⲏⲣ ⲥⲏⲑⲉⲩⲥ ⲙⲛ ⲁⲛⲧⲓⲫⲁ̣ⲛ̣-
ⲧⲏⲥ· ⲡⲓⲙⲉϩϥⲧⲟⲟⲩ ⲇ[ⲉ] ⲛ[ⲛ ⲉ-]

18 ⲱⲛ ⲡⲉ ⲡⲓⲣⲉϥⲥⲙⲟⲩ [. . . . .
ⲅⲉⲛⲟⲥ ⲉⲩⲛⲧⲁϥ ⲙⲙ[ⲁⲩ ⲙ ⲡⲓⲙⲉϩ-]

20 ϥⲧⲟⲟⲩ ⲙ ⲫⲱⲥⲧⲏ[ⲣ ⲥⲉⲗⲇⲁⲱ]

125,17 −ⲥⲟⲛ, sic.

125,19] .[.] ., first trace is the top of a knobbed letter (ⲁ, ⲗ, ⲙ, ⲱ, ⲩ) or of a
vertical stroke, or a punctuation mark; second trace is a high, straight
ligature into the following letter, viz. from ⲧ, ⲧ̄, ⲉ, ⲡ, or ϯ, but probably
not from ⲩ.

125,24 ϩⲛ̣, or ϩⲓ.

126,4 See 119,11n.

12   Kalyptos (καλυπτός) really (ὄντως) exists,
and (δέ) with him is located she who belongs to
14   all the glories, Youel, the male
virgin (παρθένος) glory, through
16   whom are seen all the
all-perfect ones (παντέλειον): those (+δέ)
18   that stand before him are the thrice
[   ] child, the thrice
20   [   ], the Autogenes (αὐτογενής)
[   ]. He (+δέ) has
22   [   ] in one ...
[the one] again who prevails over the
24   [   ] existing in [
[
12[6]
of ten thousand-fold. The
2   first (+δέ) aeon (αἰών)
in him, from whom is
4   the first light (φωστήρ), (is) Solmis
and the god revealer,
6   being infinite according to (κατά) the
type (τύπος) in the Kalyptos (καλυπτός)
8   aeon (αἰών) and Doxomedon.
The second aeon (αἰών) (is) Akremon
10   the ineffable with
the second light (φωστήρ)
12   Zachthos and Yachtos. The
third (+δέ) aeon (αἰών) is Am-
14   brosios the virgin (παρθένος) with
the third light (φωστήρ)
16   Setheus and Antiphantes.
The [(+δέ)] fourth aeon (αἰών)
18   is the blesser [
race (γένος) with [the]
20   fourth light (φωστήρ) [Seldao]

126,8   For Doxomedon as another name for Kalyptos, see *Gos.Eg.*III 41,13-16;
              *Melch.*IX 6,1; 16,30.
126,12   Supralinear stroke begins over ï.
126,13-14 ⲁⲙⲃⲣⲟⲥⲓⲟⲥ, without supralinear stroke.
126,16-17 ⲁⲛⲧⲓфⲁ̣ⲛ̣ⲧĤⲥ, without supralinear stroke.
126,17   ⲛ̣, only the supralinear stroke survives.

ⲘⲚ ⲈⲖⲈⲚⲞⲤ· ϢⲀⲨ[. . . . .
22 ⲘⲈⲚ Ⲉ[ⲣ]ⲞϤ ⲈⲂⲞⲖ ϨⲒⲦ[. . . . . .
[———   ]ⲀⲣⲘ[ⲎⲆⲰⲚ
24 [———   ] .[. . . . . .
[ⲣ]Ⲕ︦Ⲅ︦

ⲪⲞⲎ ⳾ⲞⲎ ⳾ⲎⲞⲎ ⳾Ⲏ[. .] ⳾ⲰⲤ⳾
2   ⳾ⲰⲤ⳾ ⳾ⲀⲰ ⳾ⲎⲞⲞⲞ ⳾ⲎⲤⲈⲚ ⳾ⲎⲤ-
ⲈⲚ· ⲤⲈⲞⲚϨ ⲚϬⲒ ⲚⲒⲔⲀⲦⲀ ⲞⲨⲀ ⲀⲨⲰ
4   ⲠⲒϤⲦⲞⲞⲨ ⲈⲦⲈ Ⲛ ϢⲘⲞⲨⲚ Ⲛ ⲔⲰⲂ
ⲎⲞⲞⲞⲞⲎⲀⲎϢ ⲚⲦⲞⲔ ⲈⲦϨⲀ ⲦⲈⲨ-
6   ⲈϨⲎ ⲀⲨⲰ ⲚⲦⲞⲔ ⲈⲦϨⲚ ⲚⲀⲒ̈ ⲦⲎ-
ⲣⲞⲨ· ⲀⲨⲰ ⲚⲀⲒ̈ ⲘⲈⲚ ⲈⲦⲚϨⲣⲀⲒ̈ ϨⲘ
8   ⲠⲒⲠⲣⲰⲦⲞⲪⲀⲚⲎⲤ Ⲛ ⲦⲈⲖⲒⲞⲤ Ⲛ
ⲀⲣⲘⲎⲆⲰⲚ Ⲛ ϨⲞⲞⲨⲦ· ϮⲈⲚⲈⲣⳬⲒⲀ
10 ⲚⲦⲈ ⲚⲀ[Ⲓ̈] ⲦⲎⲣⲞⲨ ⲈⲦϢⲞⲞⲠ ϨⲒ ⲞⲨ-
ⲘⲀ· ⲈⲠⲒⲆⲎ ⲚⲈⲨϢⲞⲞⲠ ⲚϬⲒ ⲚⲒ-
12 ⲔⲀⲦⲀ ⲞⲨⲀ ⲦⲎⲣⲞⲨ Ⲛ ⲦⲈⲖⲒⲞⲤ
ⲀⲤⲞⲨⲰⲚϨ ⲈⲂⲞⲖ ⲞⲚ ⲚϬⲒ ϮⲈⲚⲈⲣ-
14 ⳬⲒⲀ ⲚⲦⲈ ⲚⲒⲔⲀⲦⲀ ⲞⲨⲀ ⲦⲎⲣⲞⲨ· ⲠⲒ-
ⲀⲨⲦⲞⲄⲈⲚⲎⲤ Ⲛ ⲚⲞⲨⲦⲈ· ⲚⲦⲞϤ
16 ⲘⲈⲚ ⲈϤⲀϨⲈⲣⲀⲦϤ ⲚϨⲣⲀⲒ̈ ϨⲚ ⲞⲨ-
ⲈⲰⲚ· ⲈⲦⲚ ϤⲦⲞⲞⲨ Ⲛ ⲆⲒⲀⲪⲞⲣⲀ
18 ⲚⲦⲈ ϨⲈⲚⲈⲰⲚ ⲚϨⲣⲀⲒ̈ ⲚϨⲎⲦϤ Ⲛ-
[Ⲧ]Ⲉ ⲚⲒⲀⲨⲦⲞⲄⲈⲚⲎⲤ· ⲠϢⲞⲣⲠ̄
20 ⲆⲈ ⲚⲚ [Ⲉ]ⲰⲚ ⲈⲦϢⲞⲞⲠ̄ ⲚϨⲎⲦϤ
[Ⲛ]ⲦⲈ Ⲡ[ⲒϢ]ⲞⲣⲠ̄ Ⲙ ⲪⲰⲤⲦⲎⲣ
22 [ⲀⲣⲘⲞⳅⲎ]Ⲗ· ⲞⲣⲚⲈⲞⲤ ⲈⲨⲐⲢⲞⲨ
ⲚⲒⲞⲤ [ⲠⲎ] ⲀⲨⲘⲞⲨⲦⲈ ⲈⲣⲞϤ
24 [ⳅⲈ . . . . .]Ⲁ .[. . . . .
[. . ⲠⲒⲘⲈϨ]ⲤⲚⲀⲨ ⳅ[Ⲉ ⲚⲚ ⲈⲰⲚ ⲚⲦⲈ]
26 [ⲠⲒⲘⲈϨⲤⲚ]ⲀⲨ Ⲙ [ⲪⲰⲤⲦⲎⲣ Ⲱ-]
[ⲣⲞⲒ̈ⲀⲎⲖ . .]ⲨⲆⲀϬ[.]ⲞⲤ· ⲀⲠ[. .

126,22   Ⲙ, or else Ⲱ, Ϣ, or possibly Ϥ | Ⲉ, or else Ⲟ or Ϭ (not Ⲩ).
126,23   Or, Ϩ]ⲀⲣⲘ.
127,1-3   The arrangement of these *stoicheia* into patterns is the work of the modern
          editors.
127,7-9   Or, they are within the first-appearing, perfect, male Armedon.
127,18   Different, lit., differences.
127,20   ⳅⲈ, ⳅ more fully attested (but still uncertain) in photo D; cf. *Facsimile
          Edition: Codex VIII*, pl.4.

and Elenos. They [
22 him (+μέν) . . . [
    [   ] Arm[edon
24 [

                                                    [1]27
    phoe zoe zeoe ze[ ] zosi
2   zosi zao zeooo zesen zes-
    en - the individuals (+κατά) and the four
4   who are eight-fold are alive.
    eooooeaeo - you who are before
6   them, you who are in them
    all. They (+μέν) are within
8   the perfect (τέλειος) male Armedon
    Protophanes (πρωτοφανής), the activity (ἐνέργεια)
10 of all those that dwell together.
    Since (ἐπειδή) all the individuals (+κατά) were
12 existing as perfect ones (τέλειος),
    the activity (ἐνέργεια) of all the
14 individuals (+κατά) appeared again. As for
    the divine Autogenes (αὐτογενής), he
16 stands (+μέν) within an
    aeon (αἰών), having within himself
18 four different (διαφορά)
    self-begotten (αὐτογενής) aeons (αἰών). The
20 first (+δέ) aeon (αἰών) in him
    of the first light (φωστήρ)
22 is [Harmoze]l-Orneos-Euthrou-
    nios, also called
24 [
    [The] second (+δέ) [aeon (αἰών) of]
26 [the second light (φωστήρ) is]
    [Oraiael   ]-udas-[.]-osAp[

127,21ff The names of these four lights were well-used in antiquity; cf. *Ap.John* II,
          Gos. Eg. III, *Melch.* IX, *Trim. Prot.* XIII, and Iren. *Adv.Haer.* I. 27. With
          variations they appear as archangels in intertestamental Jewish literature
          such as I and II Enoch.
127,22   Ⲓⲁ̄, the supralinear stroke does not survive.
127,23   ] ⲁⲩ, there was no ligature into ⲁ, thus ⲉⲧ]ⲁⲩ′ probably cannot be read.
127,25   ⳝⲓⲉ ⲛⲛ ⲉⲱⲛ ⲛⲧⲉ], this restoration makes a long line of text.
127,27   ç, or else ọ.

р̄[кн]

  ⲁⲣⲣⲟⲥ[. . .] ⲡⲓⲙⲉϩϣⲟⲙⲧ̄ ⲇⲉ ⲛ-
2 ⲧⲉ ⲡⲓⲙⲉϩϣⲟⲙⲧ̄ ⲙ̄ ⲫⲱⲥⲧⲏⲣ
  ⲇⲁⲩⲉⲓⲑⲉ· ⲗⲁⲣⲁⲛⲉⲩⲥ· ⲉⲡⲓⲫⲁ-
4 ⲛⲓⲟⲥ· ⲉⲓⲇⲉⲟⲥ· ⲡⲓⲙⲉϩϥⲧⲟⲟⲩ
  ⲇⲉ ⲛ̄ⲧⲉ ⲡⲓⲙⲉϩϥⲧⲟⲟⲩ ⲙ̄ ⲫⲱ-
6 ⲥⲧⲏⲣ ⲏ̄ⲗ̄ⲏ̄ⲗ̄ⲏ̄ⲑ· ⲕⲟⲇⲏⲣⲏ· ⲉⲡⲓ-
  ⲫⲁⲛⲓⲟⲥ· ⲁⲗⲗⲟⲩⲉⲛⲓⲟⲥ[·] ⲛⲓⲕⲟ-
8 ⲟⲩⲉ ⲇⲉ ⲧⲏⲣⲟⲩ ⲉⲧϣⲟ[ⲟ]ⲡ̄ ϩⲛ̄ ϯ-
  ϩⲩⲗⲏ ⲛ̄ⲧⲟⲟⲩ ⲧⲏⲣⲟⲩ ⲛ̄[ⲉⲩ]ⲑⲉⲉⲧ̄
10 ⲡⲉ· ⲁⲩⲱ ⲉⲧⲃⲉ ⲟⲩⲥⲛⲱ[ⲥ]ⲓⲥ ⲛ̄ⲧⲉ
  ⲟⲩⲙⲛ̄ⲧⲛⲟϭ ⲙⲛ̄ ⲟⲩⲧⲟⲗⲙⲏ ⲁⲩⲱ
12 ⲟⲩϭⲟⲙ ⲉⲁⲩϣⲱⲡⲉ ⲁⲩⲱ ⲁⲩ-
  ⲥⲉⲗⲥⲱⲗⲟⲩ· ⲉⲁⲩⲣ ⲁⲧⲉⲓⲙⲉ ⲉ ⲡ-
14 ⲛⲟⲩⲧⲉ ⲥⲉⲛⲁⲃⲱⲗ ⲉⲃⲟⲗ· ⲉⲓⲥ ϩⲏ-
  ⲏⲧⲉ ϫ︦ⲱⲥⲧⲣⲓⲁⲛⲉ ⲁⲕⲥⲱⲧⲙ̄
16 ⲉⲣⲟⲟⲩ ⲧⲏⲣⲟⲩ ⲛⲁⲓ̈ ⲉⲧⲉ ⲛⲓⲛⲟⲩⲧⲉ
  ⲉ ⲛ ⲁ̄ⲧⲉⲓⲙⲉ ⲉⲣⲟⲟⲩ· ⲁⲩⲱ ⲉⲩⲉ ⲛ-
18 ⲛ ⲁⲧⲛ ⲁⲣⲏϫⲛⲟⲩ ⲛ̄ ϩⲉⲛⲁⲅⲅⲉⲗⲟⲥ
  ⲁⲛⲟⲕ ⲇⲉ ⲁⲓ̈ⲧⲟⲗⲙⲁ ⲡⲉ[ϫ]ⲁⲓ̈ ϫⲉ ⲉ[ⲧⲓ]
20 ⲟⲛ ϯⲕⲱⲧⲉ ⲉⲧⲃⲉ ⲡⲓϣⲙ̄ⲧϭⲟⲙ [ⲛ-]
  ⲛ ⲁⲧⲛⲁⲩ ⲉⲣⲟϥ ⲛ̄ ⲧⲉⲗⲓ[ⲟⲥ] ⲙ̄ ⲡ̄ⲛ̄[ⲁ]
22 ⲡⲱⲥ ϥϣⲟⲟⲡ̄ ⲛⲁϥ ⲁⲩ[. .] . . . .[.
  ⲉⲓϭⲉ ⲉ ⲛⲁⲓ̈ ⲧⲏⲣⲟⲩ· ⲙ̄[. . .]ⲏ ⲉⲧ̄
24 ϣ[ⲟ]ⲟⲡ̄ ⲟⲛⲧⲱⲥ ⲉⲙ[. . . .]ⲧⲉⲥ
  [. . . . .]ⲉ[.]ϫ[. .] ⲁϣ ⲡⲉ ⲡ[. . . . . .
26 [. . . . . . .]ⲙⲁ[. .]ⲩ ⲏ ⲟ[. . . . . .
  [. . . . . .] . ⲛ̄ⲧⲉ[.]ϫⲟ̄ⲟ̄[. . . . . .

[р̄к]ⲑ

  ⲟⲩ ⲉⲙⲁⲧⲉ ⲁⲩⲕⲁⲁ[ⲧ ⲁ]ⲩⲃⲱⲕ·
2 ⲁⲩⲱ ⲁϥⲉⲓ ⲛ̄ⲛⲁϩⲣⲁⲓ̈ ⲛ̄ϭⲓ ⲁⲡⲟⲫⲁⲛⲧⲏⲥ·
  ⲙⲛ̄ ⲁⲫⲣⲟⲡⲁⲓⲥ· ⲡⲁⲣⲑⲉⲛⲱⲫⲱⲧⲟⲥ·
4 ⲁⲩⲱ ⲁϥⲛ̄ⲧ̄ ⲉϩⲟⲩⲛ ⲉ ⲡⲓⲡⲣⲱⲧⲟⲫⲁⲛⲏⲥ ⲛ̄ ⲛⲟϭ ⲛ̄ ϩⲟⲟⲩⲧ̄ ⲛ̄ ⲧⲉⲗⲓⲟⲥ ⲛ̄
6 ⲛⲟⲩⲥ· ⲁⲩⲱ ⲁⲓ̈ⲛⲁⲩ ⲉ ⲛⲁⲓ̈ ⲧⲏⲣⲟⲩ

128,7   No supralinear stroke over ⲁⲗⲗⲟⲩⲉⲛⲓⲟⲥ.
128,10-18 The final set of revelations end.
128,15-17 Cf. *Allogenes* XI 52,13-33; I Enoch 80. Widengren, "Iran," pp. 95-115,
           argues for the Iranian origin of this motif.
128,18   Cf. 1 Peter 1:12.
128,22   ] . . .[, first trace is from ⲏ, ⲓ, ⲛ, ⲡ, or ⲧ; second, from ⲉ, ⲑ, ⲟ, ⲥ, or ⲫ;
           third is top stroke of ⲧ, or a supralinear stroke.

1[28]

Arros-[   ]. The (+δέ) third (aeon)

2   of the third light (φωστήρ) (is)

Daveithe-Laraneus-Epipha-

4   nios-Eideos. The (+δέ) fourth

(aeon) of the fourth light (φωστήρ)

6   is Eleleth-Kodere-Epi-

phanios-Allogenios. But (δέ) as

8   for all the rest that reside in

matter (ὕλη), [they] were all left (there).

10   It was because of their knowledge (γνῶσις) of

majesty, their audacity (τόλμιν) and power that

12   they came into existence and

adorned themselves. Because they did not

14   know god, they shall pass away.

Behold, Zostrianos, you have heard

16   all these things of which the gods

are ignorant and (which) seem

18   infinite to angels (ἄγγελος)."

I (+δέ) on my part became bold and said,

20   "I am [still (ἔτι)] wondering about the three-

powered invisible perfect (τέλειος) Spirit (πνεῦμα)-

22   how (πῶς) it exists for itself, [

. . . everything [   ] which

24   really (ὄντως) exist [

[   ] what is the [

26   [   ] and (ἤ) [

[   ] of [

[12]9

very, they set [me] (down and) left.

2   Apophantes with Aphropais the

Virgin-light (παρθενωφωτός) came before me

4   and brought me into Protophanes (πρωτοφανής),

(the) great male perfect (τέλειος)

6   Mind (νοῦς). There I saw all of them

128,23   ϭ, or else ϛ or ϵ | .]ⲏ; e.g., ⲡ]ⲏ, ⲧ]ⲏ, or ⲛ]ⲏ.

128,26   ⲙ, or else ⲁ or ⲁ̣ | ⲁ, or else ⲙ | ⲩ, or else ϛ | ọ, or else ϛ.

128,27   ] ., bottom of a vertical stroke, e.g., ϵ, or else ϛ | ọ, or else ϛ.

129   The surface of the papyrus is badly deteriorated; ink traces read under ultraviolet light.

129,1-132,5   *The Descent of Zostrianos to Record and Teach.*

ⲉⲧⲙⲙⲁⲩ ⲙ̄ ⲡⲣⲏⲧⲉ ⲉⲧⲟⲩϣⲟⲟⲡ̄
8 ⲙⲙⲟⲥ ⲛ̄ϩⲣⲁⲓ̈ ϩⲛ ⲟⲩⲁ· ⲁⲩⲱ ⲁⲉⲓϩⲱ-
ⲧⲡ̄ ⲛ̄ⲙ̄ⲙⲁⲩ ⲧⲏⲣⲟⲩ ⲁⲉⲓⲥⲙⲟⲩ
10 ⲉ ⲡⲓⲉⲱⲛ ⲛ̄ ⲕ̄ⲁ̄ⲥ̄ ⲙⲛ ⳁⲃⲁⲣⲃⲏⲗⲱ
ⲙ̄ ⲡⲁⲣⲑⲉⲛⲟⲥ ⲙⲛ ⲡⲓⲁϩⲟⲣⲁⲧⲟⲛ
12 ⲙ̄ ⲡ̄ⲛ̄ⲁ̄· ⲁⲩⲱ ⲁⲉⲓϣⲱⲡⲉ ⲙ̄ ⲡⲁⲛⲧⲉⲗⲓⲟⲥ ⲁⲉⲓϫⲓ ϭⲟⲙ ⲁⲩⲥⲁϩⲧ̄
14 ϩⲙ ⲡⲉⲟⲟⲩ ⲁⲩⲣ ⲥⲫⲣⲁⲅⲓϫⲉ ⲙ̄-
ⲙⲟⲉⲓ· ⲁⲉⲓϫⲓ ⲛ̄ ⲟⲩⲕⲗⲟⲙ ⲛ̄ ⲧⲉ-
16 ⲗⲓⲟⲥ ⲙ̄ ⲡⲓⲙⲁ ⲉⲧⲙⲙⲁⲩ ⲁⲓ̈ⲉⲓ
ⲉⲃⲟⲗ ⲉ ⲛⲓⲕⲁⲧⲁ ⲟⲩⲁ ⲛ̄ ⲧⲉⲗⲓⲟⲥ
18 ⲁⲩⲱ ⲛⲁⲩϣⲓⲛⲉ ⲙ̄ⲙⲟⲉⲓ ⲧⲏ-
ⲣⲟⲩ ⲡⲉ· ⲛⲉⲩⲥⲱⲧⲙ ⲉ ⲛⲓⲙⲛ̄-
20 ⲧⲛⲟϭ ⲛ̄ⲧⲉ ⳁⲅⲛⲱⲥⲓⲥ ⲛⲉⲩⲧⲉ-
ⲗⲏⲗ ⲙ̄[ⲙⲟ]ⲟⲩ ⲡⲉ· ⲁⲩⲱ ⲛⲉⲩ-
22 ϫⲓ ϭⲟⲙ[·] ⲁⲩⲱ ⲁⲛⲟⲕ ⲟⲛ ⲉⲧⲁⲓ̈-
ⲉⲓ ⲉϩⲣ[ⲁⲓ̈] ⲉ ⲛⲓⲉⲱⲛ ⲛ̄ⲧⲉ ⲛⲓⲁⲩ-
24 ⲧⲟⲅⲉ[ⲛ]ⲏⲥ ⲁⲉⲓϫⲓ ⲛⲛ ⲟⲩⲉⲓⲛ[ⲉ ⲙ—]
ⲙⲉ ⲉ[ϥⲧ]ⲟⲩⲃⲏⲩ ⲉϥⲙ̄ⲡϣⲁ
26 ⲛ̄ ⲧⲁⲓ̈[ⲥⲑ]ⲏⲥⲓⲥ· ⲁⲓ̈ⲉⲓ ⲉϩⲣⲁⲓ̈ ⲉ
ⲛⲓⲁⲛⲧⲓⲧⲩⲡⲟⲥ ⲛⲛ ⲉⲱⲛ̄
28 ⲁⲩⲱ ⲁ̣[ⲓ̈]ⲉⲓ ⲉⲃⲟⲗ ⲙ̄ⲙⲁⲩ ⲉϩ[ⲣⲁⲓ̈]
ⲣ̄ⲗ̄

ⲉ ⲡⲕ[ⲁϩ ⲛ̄]ⲛ ⲁⲏⲣ· ⲁⲩⲱ ⲁⲓ̈ⲥϩⲁⲓ̈ ⲛ̄
2 ϣⲟⲙⲧ̄ ⲙ̄ ⲡⲩϩⲟⲥ ⲁⲉⲓⲕⲁⲁⲩ
ⲉⲩⲧⲛⲱⲥⲓⲥ ⲛ̄ ⲛⲏ ⲉⲧⲛⲏⲩ ⲙⲛ̄-
4 ⲥⲱⲉⲓ ⲛⲓⲥⲱⲧⲡ̄ ⲉⲧⲟⲛϩ· ⲁⲩⲱ ⲁ-
ⲛⲟⲕ ⲁⲓ̈ⲉⲓ ⲉϩⲣⲁⲓ̈ ⲉ ⲡⲕⲟⲥⲙⲟⲥ ⲛ̄-
6 ⲛ ⲉⲥⲑⲏⲧⲟⲛ ⲁⲩⲱ ⲁⲓ̈ⳁ ⲙ̄ ⲡⲁⲧⲟⲩ-
ⲱⳁ ϩⲓⲱⲱⲧ ⲉϥⲉ ⲛⲛ ⲁⲧⲥⲃⲱ·
8 ⲁⲉⲓⳁ ϭⲟⲙ ⲛⲁϥ ⲁⲉⲓⲙⲟⲟϣⲉ ⲉⲉⲓⲧⲁ-
ϣⲉ ⲟⲉⲓϣ ⲛⲁⲩ ⲧⲏⲣⲟ[ⲩ ⲛ̄] ⳁⲙⲛⲧⲙⲉ·
10 ⲟⲩⲧⲉ ⲛⲓⲙⲛⲧⲁⲅⲅⲉⲗⲟⲥ ⲛ̄ⲧⲉ ⲡⲕⲟⲥⲙⲟⲥ ⲟⲩⲧⲉ ⲛⲓⲁⲣⲭⲱⲛ ⲙ̄ⲡⲟⲩ-
12 ⲛⲁⲩ ⲉⲣⲟⲉⲓ· ⲟⲩⲙⲏⲏϣⲉ ⲅⲁⲣ ⲛ̄ ⲧ[ϭⲁ—]
ⲉⲓⲟ ⲛ̄ⲧⲁⲩⲛⲧ ⲉ ⲡⲙⲟⲩ ⲁⲉⲓⲃⲟⲗⲟ̣[ⲩ]

129,7-8   ⲡⲣⲏⲧⲉ . . . ⲙ̄ⲙⲟⲥ, sic.
129,18   I.e., ⲛⲉⲩ·.
129,19-20   Lit., greatness.
130,1   See 4,20 and 5,18 for his ascent.
130,2   πύξος, for πυξίον, a writing tablet made of box-wood; cf. *Steles Seth* VII

as they exist
8   in one. I united
with them all (and) blessed the
10   Kalyptos (καλυπτός) aeon (αἰών), the
virgin (παρθένος) Barbelo and the Invisible(ἀόρατον)
12   Spirit (πνεῦμα). I became all-perfect (παντέλειος)
and received power. I was written
14   in glory and sealed.
I received there
16   a perfect (τέλειος) crown. I came
forth to the perfect (τέλειος) individuals (+κατά).
18   All of them began questioning
me, listening to the
20   magnitude of my knowledge (γνῶσις),
rejoicing and
22   receiving power. When I again
came down to the aeons (αἰών) of
24   Autogenes (αὐτογενής), I received a true
image, pure (yet) suitable for
26   the perceptible (αἴσθησις) (world). I came
down to the aeon (αἰών) copies (ἀντίτυπος)
28   and came down here
130
to the ethereal (ἀήρ) [earth] . I wrote
2   three wooden tablets (πύξος) (and) left them
as knowledge (γνῶσις) for those who would
4   come after me, the living elect.
Then I came down to the perceptible (αἴσθησις)
6   world (κόσμος) and put on
my image. Because it was ignorant,
8   I strengthened it (and) went about
preaching the truth to everyone.
10   Neither (οὔτε) the angelic beings (-ἄγγελος) of
the world (κόσμος) nor (οὔτε) the archons (ἄρχων)
12   saw me, for (γάρ) I evaded a multitude
of [judgments] that brought me near death.

118,10-11. By delivering the gnosis to others Zostrianos becomes a
          redeemed redeemer; cf. 1 Enoch 82:1, and 2 Enoch 33:47.54.
130,6-7   See 4,23-25 where he leaves his body on earth; cf. 2 Cor 5:1-5.
130,12   Ⲧ, or else ⲡ̄.

14 ⲉⲃⲟⲗ· ⲟⲩⲙⲏⲏϣⲉ ⲇⲉ ⲉⲧⲥⲟⲣⲙ
ⲁⲉⲓⲧⲟⲩⲛⲟⲥⲟⲩ ⲉⲓϫⲱ ⲙⲙⲟⲥ

16 ϫⲉ ⲉⲓⲙⲉ ⲛⲏ ⲉⲧⲟⲛ2 ⲙⲛ ϯⲥⲡⲟⲣ[ⲁ]
ⲉⲧⲟⲩⲁⲁⲃ ⲛⲧⲉ ⲥ̄ⲏ̄ⲑ̄ ⲩ̅ ⲙⲡⲣⲧⲟⲩ[ⲟ ⲛ-]

18 ⲁ̀ⲧⲥⲱⲧⲙ ⲛⲥⲱⲉⲓ· ⲙⲁⲧⲟⲩ ⲛ[ⲉⲥ]
ⲡⲉⲧⲛⲛⲟⲩⲧⲉ 2ⲁ ⲡⲛⲟⲩⲧⲉ· ⲁ[ⲩⲱ]

20 ϯⲯⲩⲭⲏ ⲛ ⲁ̀ⲧⲕⲁ2[ⲓ]ⲁ̀ ⲉ̀ⲧⲥⲟ[ⲧⲡ̄]
ϯ ϭⲟⲙ ⲛⲁⲥ ⲁⲩⲱ ⲁⲛ[ⲁⲩ] ⲉ ⲡⲓⲟⲩ-

22 ⲱⲧⲃ ⲉⲃⲟⲗ ⲉⲧⲙ ⲡⲓⲙ[ⲁ] ⲁⲩⲱ
ⲕⲱⲧⲉ ⲛⲥⲁ ϯⲙⲛⲧⲁ[ⲧ]ⲙⲓⲥⲉ ⲛ̄-

24 ⲛ ⲁⲧⲟⲩⲱⲧⲃ ⲉⲃⲟⲗ [ⲡⲉⲓ]ⲱ̀ⲧ ⲛⲧⲉ
ⲛⲁⲓ̈ ⲧⲏⲣⲟⲩ ϥⲧⲱ2ⲙ [ⲙ̄]ⲙⲱⲧⲛ

26 ⲉ̣[ⲩⲥ]ⲟ2ⲉ ⲛⲏⲧⲛ ⲁⲩⲱ ⲉⲩϫⲓ ⲙⲙⲱ-
　　　　　　　　　　　　　[ⲣ̄ⲁ̄]ⲁ̄

ⲧⲛ ⲛ ϭⲟⲛⲥ ϥⲛⲁⲕⲁ ⲧⲏ̄[ⲛ]ⲉ̣ ⲛⲥⲱϥ ⲁⲛ·

2 ⲙⲡⲣϫⲱⲕⲙ ⲙⲙⲱⲧⲛ 2ⲛ ⲟⲩⲙⲟⲩ·
ⲟⲩⲧⲉ ⲙⲡⲣϯ ⲧⲏⲛⲉ ⲛⲧⲟⲟⲧⲟⲩ ⲛ

4 ⲛⲏ ⲉ̀ⲧⲟ̀ⲉⲃⲓⲏⲩ ⲉⲣⲱⲧⲛ 2ⲁ ⲛⲏ ⲉⲧ-
ⲥⲟⲧⲡ̄· ⲡⲱ̀ⲧ ⲛⲧⲟⲟⲧϥ ⲙ̄ ⲡⲓϫⲓⲃⲉ

6 ⲙⲛ ⲡⲓⲥⲛⲁ2 ⲛⲧⲉ ϯⲙⲛⲧⲥⲓⲙⲉ·
ⲁⲩⲱ ⲥⲱⲧⲡ̄ ⲛⲏⲧⲛ ⲙ̄ ⲡⲓⲟⲩϫⲁⲉⲓ

8 ⲛⲧⲉ ϯⲙ̄ⲛⲧ2ⲟⲟⲩⲧ· ⲛⲧⲁⲧⲉⲧⲛ-
ⲉⲓ ⲁⲛ [ⲉ] ϫ̣[ⲓ] ⲙ̄ⲕⲁ2· ⲁⲗⲗⲁ ⲛⲧⲁⲧⲉⲧⲛ-

10 ⲉⲓ ⲉ ⲃⲱⲗ ⲙ ⲡⲉⲧⲛⲥⲛⲁ2 ⲉⲃⲟⲗ· ⲃⲁⲗ
ⲧⲏⲛⲉ ⲉⲃⲟⲗ· ⲁⲩⲱ ⲡⲏ ⲉⲧⲁϥⲙⲟⲩⲣ

12 ⲙ̄ⲙⲱⲧⲛ ⲉϥⲉⲃⲱⲗ ⲉⲃⲟⲗ· ⲛⲁ2ⲙ
ⲧⲏⲛⲉ 2ⲓⲛⲉ ϫⲉ ⲉⲣⲉⲧⲏ ⲉⲧⲙⲙⲁⲩ

14 ⲉⲥⲉⲛⲟⲩ2ⲙ· ⲡⲓⲭ̄ⲣ̄ⲥ̄ ⲛ ⲉⲓⲱⲧ ⲁϥ-
ⲧⲛⲛⲟⲟⲩ ⲛⲏⲧⲛ ⲙ̄ ⲡⲓⲥⲱⲧⲏⲣ

16 ⲁⲩⲱ ⲁϥϯ ⲛⲏⲧⲛ ⲛ ϯϭⲟⲙ· ⲉⲧⲃⲉ
ⲟⲩ ⲧⲉⲧⲛⲁ2ⲉ· ⲕⲱⲧⲉ ⲉⲩⲕⲱⲧⲉ

18 ⲛⲥⲁ ⲧⲏⲩⲧⲛ· ⲉⲩⲧⲱ2ⲙ ⲙⲙⲱ-
ⲧⲛ ⲥⲱⲧⲙ· ⲟⲩⲕⲟⲩⲉⲓ ⲅⲁⲣ ⲡⲉ

20 [ⲡⲓ]ⲭⲣⲟ̣[ⲛⲟ]ⲥ ⲙⲡⲣⲧⲣⲉⲩ2 2ⲁⲗ ⲙ-
ⲙⲱⲧ[ⲛ] ⲟⲩⲛⲟϭ ⲡⲉ ⲡⲓⲁⲓⲱⲛ

22 ⲛⲧⲉ ⲡ[ⲓⲁ]ⲓⲱⲛ ⲛⲧⲉ ⲛⲉⲧⲟⲛ2·

130,16ff　The concluding homily does not refer in specific terms to the gnosis
　　　　　revealed to Zostrianos earlier in the tractate.
130,19　　I.e., discover the divine part in yourself.
130,20　　I.e., ⲕⲁⲕⲓⲁ.
130,22　　Lit., the crossing over.
130,23　　ⲛ̄, only the supralinear stroke survives.

14   But (δέ) an erring multitude
      I awakened saying,

16   "Understand, you who are alive, the holy
      seed (σπορά) of Seth. Do not [be]

18   disobedient to me. [Awaken]
      your divine part to god, and

20   as for your sinless elect soul (ψυχή),
      strengthen it. Note the

22   dissolution of this world and
      seek the immutable

24   ingenerateness. The [Father] of
      all these invites you.

26   Although (others) reprove you (and) ill-treat

                                        131

      you, he will not abandon you.

2   Do not baptize yourselves with death
      nor (οὐτέ) entrust yourselves to those

4   who are inferior to you as if to
      those who are better. Flee from the madness

6   and the bondage of femaleness,
      and choose for yourselves the salvation

8   of maleness. You have
      not come to suffer; rather (ἀλλά), you have

10   come to escape your bondage. Release
      yourselves, and that which has bound

12   you will be dissolved. Save
      yourselves so that (ἵνα) your soul

14   may be saved. The kind (χρηστός) Father
      has sent you the Savior (σωτήρ)

16   and given you strength. Why
      are you hesitating? Seek when you are

18   sought; when you are invited,
      listen. For (γάρ) the time (χρόνος) is

20   short. Do not be led
      astray. Great is the aeon (αἰών)

22   of the aeons (αἰών) of the living ones,

131,9   Circumflex has been abnormally omitted above the group ες.
131,13   Soul, lit., that (fem.) one there.
131,14   x̄p̄c̄ for χρηστός; cf. 78,22.
131,17-18 Cf. 3,18f.
131,21-22 Cf. 2 Enoch 65:8.

ⲙⲛ ⲧ[ⲕⲟ]ⲗⲁⲥⲓⲥ ⲛⲧⲉ ⲛⲏ ⲉⲧ̣ⲟ̣ [ⲛ]
24 ⲁ̇ⲧⲧⲱ̇ⲧ ⲛ ⲣ̣ⲏ̇ⲧ· ⲟⲩ̇ⲛ ⲟⲩ̇ⲙⲏ—
ⲏⲩⲉ ⲛ [ⲥ]ⲛⲁ̣ⲣ̣ ⲕⲱⲧⲉ ⲉⲣ̇ⲱⲧⲛ
26 ⲙⲛ ⲣ̣ⲉⲛⲣⲉϥⲧ ⲕⲟⲗⲁⲥⲓⲥ· ⱽⱽⱽ
ⲣ̣[ⲗ]ⲃ̣
ⲡⲱ̣ⲣ̣ ⲛ̣[ⲣ̣ⲣ]ⲁ̣ⲓ̈ ⲣⲛ ⲟⲩⲕⲟⲩⲉⲓ ⲛ ⲥⲏⲟ[ⲩ]
2 ⲉⲙⲡⲁⲧϥⲧⲁⲣ̣ⲱⲧⲛ ⲛ̣ϭ̣ⲓ ⲡ̣ⲓⲧⲁⲕⲟ·
ⲁⲛⲁ̣ⲩ ⲉ ⲡⲓⲟⲩⲟⲉⲓⲛ ⲡⲱ̇ⲧ ⲛⲥⲁ—
4 ⲃ̣ⲟⲗ ⲙ ⲡⲓⲕⲁⲕⲉ· ⲙⲡⲣⲧⲣ̇ⲉⲩⲣ ⲣ̣ⲁ̣ⲗ̣
ⲙ̣ⲙ̣ⲱⲧⲛ ⲡⲣⲟⲥ ⲟⲩⲧⲁⲕⲟ:
6   ⲍⲱⲥⲧⲣⲓⲁⲛⲟⲥ
          ⲟ̅ⲗ̅ⲍ̅ ⲗ̅ϥ̅ ⲑ̅ⲟ̅ⲃ̅ ⲗ̅ⲉ̅ϥ̅ ⲑ̅ⲱ̅ⲩ̅ ⲥ̅ⲱ̅ⲧ̅
8   ⲩ̅ⲣ̅ϥ̅ⲑ̅ ⲛ̅ⲗ̅ⲭ̅ ⲗ̅ⲉ̅ⲗ̅ⲱ̅ⲑ̅ⲟ̅ⲃ̅ⲗ̅ⲉ̅ϥ̅·
          ⲑ̅ⲱ̅ ⲟ̅ⲗ̅ⲍ̅ ⲧ̅ⲥ̅ⲗ̅ⲑ̅ⲱ̅ⲯ̅ [ⲗ̅ⲭ̅]

132,2   Death, lit., destruction.
132,6-9 These lines are set off in the manuscript by rows of ornaments and rules.
         To solve the cryptogram, divide the Greek alphabet into three sets of eight
         letters (ασθ, ι-π, ρω), then reverse the letter values of each set, except for

yet (so also is) the [punishment (κόλασις)]
24 of those who are unconvinced.
Many bonds and chastisers (+κόλασις)
26 surround you.
1[3]2
Flee quickly
2 before death reaches you.
Look at the light. Flee
4 the darkness. Do not be led
astray to your destruction."
6   Zostrianos
Oracles of Truth of
8 Zostrianos. God of Truth.
Teachings of Zoroaster.

ι (=ϥ) and ρ (=υρ), so that a=θ΄, κ=π, σ=ω, etc. (See Doresse, "Les apocalypses de Zoroastre.")

132,7 c̄ω†, i.e., c̄ωⲯ.
132,8 ⲁⲉⲗⲱ, or else ⲁⲉⲗⳡ
132,9 ⲧⲣ, written both times with ⲣ nestled under right stroke of ⲧ.

NHC VIII, 2: THE LETTER OF PETER TO PHILIP
INTRODUCTION
Marvin W. Meyer

Bibliography:
Bethge, "Brief des Petrus an Philippus"; Bethge, "Der sogennante Brief"; Koschorke, "Eine gnostische Paraphrase"; Koschorke, "Eine gnostische Pfingstpredigt"; Koschorke, *Die Polemik der Gnostiker*; Luttikhuizen, "The Letter of Peter to Philip"; Ménard, *La Lettre de Pierre à Philippe*; Ménard, "La Lettre de Pierre à Philippe"; Ménard, "Pierre à Philippe: sa structure"; Meyer, *The Letter of Peter to Philip*; Meyer, "The Light and Voice on the Damascus Road"; Parrott, "Gnostic and Orthodox Disciples"; Tröger, "Doketistische Christologie in Nag-Hammadi-Texten"; Wisse-Meyer, "The Letter of Peter to Philip."

The *Letter of Peter to Philip* fills most of the concluding nine pages of Codex VIII. Situated immediately after the long tractate *Zostrianos*, the *Letter of Peter to Philip* bears little literary or theological relationship to the tractate that precedes it. Rather, the *Letter of Peter to Philip* most likely was included in Codex VIII because, of the tractates the scribe was commissioned to copy, it was an appropriate length to fill the pages at the end of the codex.

The *Letter of Peter to Philip* opens with a superscribed title derived from the letter which forms the first part of the tractate: ⲦⲈⲠⲒⲤⲦⲟⲖ̣Ⲏ ⲘⲠⲈⲦⲢⲞⲤ ⲈⲦⲀϤϪⲞⲞⲨⳓ ⲘⲪⲒⲖⲒⲠ̅ⲠⲞⲤ, "The letter of Peter which he sent to Philip" (132,10-11). Like several other tractates in the Nag Hammadi library (*Apocryphon of James* [NHC I,2], *Treatise on Resurrection* [NHC I,4], *Eugnostos* [NHC III,3]), the *Letter of Peter to Philip* is presented, in part, as a letter or epistle. In addition to these letters in the Nag Hammadi library, other letters were also in use among the Gnostics (for example, Ptolemy's *Letter to Flora*; and letters of Valentinus, Monoimus the Arabian, and perhaps Marcion; cf. in Foerster, *Gnosis*). Furthermore, just as a magnificent epistolary tradition developed around Paul and the Pauline school, so also a more modest collection of letters came to be ascribed to Peter. These Petrine or pseudo-Petrine letters include, in addition to the *Letter of Peter to Philip*, the catholic letters of Peter in the NT, the *Epistula Petri* at the opening of the Pseudo-Clementines, and perhaps another letter of Peter known only from a brief quotation in Optatus of Milevis (Puech, "Les nouveaux écrits gnostiques," 117,n.4). Of these letters the Ps.-Clem. *Epistula Petri* is of special interest since it shares a number of features with the *Letter of Peter to Philip*. Not only is it prefixed to a collection of materials relating to Peter; it also seeks to attest the authority of Peter, and as it concludes, the *Contestatio* begins by referring to the recipient (James the Just) reading and responding to the letter in a manner reminiscent of Philip in the *Letter of Peter to Philip* (133,8-11). After the closing of the *Epistula Petri*, the *Contestatio* opens as follows: Ἀναγνοὺς οὖν ὁ Ἰάκωβος τὴν ἐπιστολὴν μετεκαλέσατο τοὺς πρεσβυτέρους καὶ αὐτοῖς ἀναγνούς, "he spoke to the assembled group about the kerygmatic materials of Peter." The *Letter of Peter to Philip*, however, is not to be identified with any of these letters attributed to Peter and must represent a newly-discovered work in the Petrine corpus.

The body of the *Letter of Peter to Philip* may be divided into two major sections: the letter itself (132,12-133,8) and the account of the meetings of the apostles (133,8-140,27). The letter of Peter opens in typical Greek epistolary fashion (132,12-15) and proceeds to describe the separation of Philip (here apparently a composite of Philip the apostle and Philip the evangelist–see the note to 132,14-15) and the need for a meeting of all the apostles. At 133,8 the letter concludes somewhat abruptly, and after the reference to the willing response of Philip to Peter; at 133,8-11, Philip disappears from the scene and is only implicitly present as an anonymous member of the apostolic group.

The balance of the *Letter of Peter to Philip* provides an account of the apostolic gatherings, often in the form of a "dialogue" between the resurrected Christ and the apostles. After Peter and the apostles come together for the first meeting on the Mount of Olives (133,12-17), they offer two prayers, one directed to the Father (133,17-134,1) and the other to the Son (134,2-9). Following their prayers the risen Christ appears to the apostles as a light and a voice (134,9-18). The apostles raise a two-part indirect question (134,18-23) and five direct questions (134,23-135,2). The voice from the light (135,3-8) provides revelatory answers to several of these questions by discoursing on the deficiency of the aeons (135,8-136,15) and the fullness (136,16-137,4), and the detainment (137,4-9) and the struggle of the apostles (137,10-13). After an additional question of the apostles and the revealer's answer (137,13-138,3), the revelation concludes (138,3-7) and the apostles journey to Jerusalem (138,7-10).

As they go up to Jerusalem, their discussion about the problem of suffering (138,10-16) prompts a response by Peter (138,17-20) as well as by a revelatory voice (138,21-139,4 [?]). The contents of the disclosure suggest that the revelatory voice is that of Christ. When the apostles reach Jerusalem, they teach and heal (139,4-9). Peter delivers a paradigmatic sermon (139,9-140,1[?]) with three central parts: the citation of a traditional credo (139,15-21), the interpretation of that credo (139,21-28), and a concluding exhortation (139,28-140,1[?]). After a prayer offered by Peter, the apostles are filled with holy spirit and part in order to preach (140,1[?]-13). Finally, at a last gathering of the apostles, Jesus appears again to commission them (140,13-23), and the tractate closes with the apostles departing once more to preach (140,23-27).

In its present form the *Letter of Peter to Philip* is clearly a Christian Gnostic tractate. Taken as a whole, the tractate is to be seen as a part of the Petrine tradition (against Bethge, who suggests in "Der sogennante Brief" that the tractate may be part of a Gnostic *Acts of Philip*): Peter is the leader, the spokesman, the preacher among the apostles, and appears to be described as having his own disciples (ΝΕϤΜΑΘΗΤΗϹ, 139,10). The only other apostle mentioned by name is Philip, who is submissive to the authority of Peter and whose place in the tractate seems intended to highlight the preeminent authority of Peter. With their leader, Peter, the apostles gather at Olivet and are taught by the risen Savior; upon returning to Jerusalem they teach in the temple and perform healings; and eventually they go forth to preach, filled with holy spirit. In other words, not only the place of Peter but also the scenario of the narrative would suggest that the *Letter of Peter to Philip* shares important features with part of the first (Petrine) section of the NT Acts of the Apostles (chapters 1-12).

That the author of the *Letter of Peter to Philip* makes use of Christian traditions cannot be doubted. In particular, numerous parallels between this tractate and the first half of the NT Acts may be noted, including scenes, themes, and terms which are similar in these two documents (see the notes). Even the genre of literature they represent—a narrative on Peter and the apostles within which are included revelatory, liturgical, and edificatory materials—is similar, although in the case of the *Letter of Peter to Philip* the narrative has been prefixed with a letter of Peter. Furthermore, the author of the *Letter of Peter to Philip* is familiar with other Christian traditions besides Lukan materials. The Savior's second revelatory answer (136,16-137,4) resembles the Johannine Logos hymn (see Koschorke, "Eine gnostische Paraphrase"), though the similarities must not be overdrawn (cf. Meyer, *The Letter of Peter to Philip*, 131-33; 177-78). Again, the traditional kerygmatic formulae in the credo (139,15-21) show affinities with similar formulae to be found throughout early Christian literature (see the note to 139,15-21, as well as Meyer, *The Letter of Peter to Philip*, 152-53; the parallels in John 19 are particularly close to the credo in the *Letter of Peter to Philip*), and the little "Pentecost" of the *Letter of Peter to Philip* (140,1[?]-13) shares features with the Johannine "Pentecost" account (20:19-23). The author of this tractate also mentions previous revelatory utterances of the Savior (135,5-6; 138,2-3.22-24;

139,11-12), utterances frequently said to have been given while Jesus was embodied. Presumably these revelations of the embodied Savior could refer to such teachings as are presented in the canonical gospels; and ΠϤΤΟΟⲨ ΝϢⲀϪⲈ of 140,25 could have been understood as the four gospels to be sent to the four directions; see Meyer, *The Letter of Peter to Philip*, 160-61. (Bethge, "Brief des Petrus an Philippus," 175, and "Der sogennante Brief," 168-70, suggests that originally the text may have read ⲈΠϤΤΟΟⲨ ΝⲤⲀ ϪⲈ, "to the four directions, so that," which through dittography became ⲈΠϤΤΟΟⲨ ΝⲤⲀ ϪⲈ {ϪⲈ}; this text then could have been modified to ⲈΠϤΤΟΟⲨ ΝϢⲀϪⲈ ϪⲈ, "eine Verschlimmbesserung zum normalen Sahidisch.") Hence, it is clear that the author of the *Letter of Peter to Philip* is conversant with early Christian materials and desires to establish continuity with these earlier traditions. The author's understanding of the Christian message, it is maintained, is legitimate and authentic: Jesus communicated all these truths before, but because of unbelief the message must now be proclaimed again (135,3-8).

Within the narrative framework of the *Letter of Peter to Philip* are included materials in which Gnostic emphases can be seen with clarity. In particular this observation applies to the Gnostic "dialogue," the revelatory discourse of the Savior uttered in answer to the questions of the apostles. The first four revelatory answers (135,8-137,13) are at most marginally Christian, though here they have been legitimated as revelations of the risen Lord. The first answer (135,8-136,15), which provides an abbreviated version of the myth of the mother, illustrates no overtly Christian features at all. It reflects a rather simple version of the myth and is similar to the Sophia myth of the *Apocryphon of John* (NHC II 9,25ff; III 14,9ff; IV 15,1ff; BG 36,16ff) and the Barbelognostics of Irenaeus (*Adv. Haer.* 1.29.1-4) in terminology (ⲦⲘⲀⲀⲨ, *mater*; ⲠⲀⲨⲐⲀⲆⲎⲤ, *Authadia*) and general presentation. This set of four revelatory answers furnishes a Gnostic perspective on the fall into deficiency and the attainment of fullness (the first two answers: 135,8-136,15; 136,16-137,4), and on the imprisonment and the struggle of Gnostics in the world (the last two answers: 137,4-13). To this set of answers has been appended an additional question and answer (137,13-138,3) which utilizes different terms and focuses upon the life and mission of the apostles. Gnostic in perspective like the other answers, this additional answer does show Christian concerns and illustrates a dominant issue of the *Letter of Peter to Philip*, the suffering of the believer.

In addition to the questions and answers in the Gnostic "dialogue," other materials similarly used in the tractate may also show Gnostic proclivities. The two prayers of the gathered apostles (133,17-134,9) contain traditional terms and themes commonly found in early Christian prayers, but they also proclaim a luminosity and glory which make them especially appropriate as the prayers of Gnostic Christians. Again, the description of the resurrected Christ as a light and a voice (134,9-14; 135,3-4; 137,17-19; 138,11-13. 21-22) represents a primitive way of depicting the appearances of the risen Lord, but among Gnostic Christians such theophanic descriptions are particularly appreciated (Meyer, "The Light and Voice on the Damascus Road," 30-34). Again, in the discussion of the sufferings of the Lord and the apostles, a motif occurs which is prevalent in Gnostic sources: human "smallness" (ΤΕΝΜΝΤΚΟΟⲧ[ΕⲤ], 138,20). Yet again, the reception of "a spirit of understanding" (ΟⲩΠΝⲀ ΝΤΕ ΟⲩΕΠⲤ[Ⲥ]ΤΗΜΗ, 140,5-6) and spiritual power (ΟⲩϬⲀΜ/ΟⲩϬΟΜ, 140,21. 27) from Christ are especially important for Gnostic Christians.

In the brief sermon of Peter (139,9-140,1[?]) Gnostic tendencies are even more clearly seen. A traditional Christian credo constitutes the first part of the sermon (139,15-21), and traditional terms are applied to Jesus (ΠⲀΟΕⲤⲤ ⲤⲤ, 139,25-26; ΠⲰΗΡΕ, 139,26; ΠⲤⲀΡⲬΗⲤΟⲤ ΝΤΕ ΠΕΝⲰΝⲈ, 139,27-28), but the credo is interpreted according to the Gnostic Christian theology of the author of the *Letter of Peter to Philip*. From the time of his incarnation Jesus suffered, but he suffered as one who is "a stranger to this suffering" (ΟⲩⲰΜΜΟ Μ/ΠΕЇⲀⲤ ΜΚⲀⲈ, 139,21-22). A Christological tension remains as the sermon stresses both the reality of Jesus' sufferings and the glory of his divinity. In contrast to the suffering illuminator Jesus (139,15), the sermon continues, the followers of Jesus suffer because of "the transgression of the mother" (ΤΠⲀΡⲀϬⲀⲤⲤ ΝΤΜⲀⲀⲧ, 139,23). This phrase is reminiscent of references to the fall of mother Eve and refers, for the Gnostic Christian author, to the mother often named Sophia in other versions of the myth. She is also called ΤΜⲀⲀⲧ at 135,12, and her tragic fall is seen as the source of human sufferings. This reference to "the transgression of the mother" thus may provide another point of contact between the figures of Eve and Sophia in Gnostic literature.

It is possible, then, to suggest a general outline for the literary history of the *Letter of Peter to Philip*. On the basis of the parallels with the *Apocryphon of John* and Irenaeus (see above), we may suggest that the *Letter of Peter to Philip* was written around the end of the second century C.E. or into the third. The author of the text presumably wrote in Greek: such may be intimated by the presence of Greek loan words (including technical terms, particles, prepositions, and conjunctions) and Greek idioms (e.g., ⲈΝ ⲤⲰΜⲀ/ⲈΜ ΠⲤⲰΜⲀ for ἐν (τῷ) σώματι). The author apparently was a Christian Gnostic who was well versed in the Christian tradition, and who used and interpreted that tradition in a Christian

Gnostic fashion. A Gnostic "dialogue" has been constructed, though it is less a true dialogue than a revelatory discourse of Christ in answer to questions raised by the apostles. Within this "dialogue" are included Gnostic materials which are non-Christian or only marginally Christian; these materials have been adopted as revelatory disclosures of the risen Christ. On the basis of the Christian and Gnostic traditions with which the author was familiar, the author compiled a narrative document with a revelatory focus. The letter itself was added at the beginning of this narrative in order to stress the authoritative place of Peter, and the *Letter of Peter to Philip* subsequently received its present title. Finally, the Greek tractate was translated into Coptic and found its way into Codex VIII of the Nag Hammadi library.

Like other tractates within the Nag Hammadi library, the *Letter of Peter to Philip* appears to be a Coptic translation of a Greek text. The dialect represented by the Coptic of the tractate is Sahidic, although dialectical peculiarities, including forms traditionally called Bohairic, may be recognized (see Meyer, *The Letter of Peter to Philip*, 69-90, esp. 79-83). The text has survived in a relatively intact condition. Besides the minor lacunae, which can be restored with considerable confidence, the *Letter of Peter to Philip* has only three major lacunae, all at the top of the latter pages of the codex: 137,1-2; 139,1-4; 140,1-2.

According to the reports of James M. Robinson and Stephen Emmel, a somewhat divergent Coptic text of the *Letter of Peter to Philip* is to be found in a papyrus codex which at the present time is neither published nor available for study. Emmel has indicated that it bears the title ⲦⲈⲠⲒⲤⲦⲟⲖⲎ ⲚⲦⲈ ⲠⲈⲦⲢⲞⲤ ϢⲀ ⲪⲒⲖⲒⲠⲠⲞⲤ (see Bethge, "Der Brief des Petrus an Philippus," 5-6; Robinson, "Introduction," *Facsimile Edition: Introduction*, 21; Schneemelcher, *Neutestamentliche Apokryphen I*, 255 and 276). A March, 1991, memo from Robinson reads: "In 1991 an out-of-focus photograph of nine lines at the top of a page permitted the following collation:

At 135,25, read ⲈⲚⲀⲤⲰⲚ, for ⲈⲚⲤⲈⲱⲚ.
At 135,26-27, read ⲀⲩⲢⲀϢⲈ ⲦⲎⲢⲟⲩ, for ⲀⲩⲢⲀϢⲈⲒⲚⲞⲤ
    ⲚⲤⲦⲞⲘ ⲦⲎⲢⲟⲩ.
At 135,28, read ⲀⲩϢⲱ[ⲠⲈ], for ⲀⲩⲀⲠⲞⲟⲩ.
At 136,1 read ⲚⲤⲈⲤⲞⲟⲩⲚⲈ, for ⲚⲤ[Ⲉ]Ⲥ[Ⲟ]ⲟⲩⲚ.
At 136,1-2, read Ⲙ[/]ϢⲞⲞⲠ ⳨Ⲛ ⲚϢⲞⲢ[, for Ⲙⲡ[ ]/
    ϢⲢⲠ ⲚϢⲞⲞⲠ· ⲈⲠⲤ⳨Ⲏ."

10   ⲧⲉⲡⲓⲥⲧⲟⲗⲏ ⲙ̄ⲡⲉⲧⲣⲟⲥ ⲉⲧⲁϥ—
        ⲍⲟⲟⲩⲥ ⲙ̄ⲫⲓⲗⲓⲡ̄ⲡⲟⲥ·:

12   ⲡⲉⲧⲣⲟⲥ ⲡⲁⲡⲟⲥⲧⲟⲗⲟⲥ ⲛⲧⲉ ⲓ̄[ⲥ̄]
        ⲡⲉⲭ̄ⲥ̄ ⲙ̄ⲫⲓⲗⲓⲡ̄ⲡⲟⲥ ⲡⲉⲛⲥⲟⲛ ⲙ̄

14   ⲙⲉⲣⲓⲧ ⲙⲛ ⲡⲉⲛϣⲃⲏⲣⲁⲡⲟⲥⲧⲟ—
        ⲗⲟⲥ ⲙⲛ ⲛⲥⲛⲏⲩ ⲉⲧⲛ̄ⲙ̄ⲙⲁⲕ ⲭⲉ[ⲣⲉ]

16   ϯⲟⲩⲱϣ ⲇⲉ ⲛⲕⲓⲙⲉ ⲡⲉⲛⲥⲟⲛ [ⲍⲉ]
        ⲁⲛⲍⲓ ⲛϩⲉⲛⲉⲛⲧⲟⲗⲏ ⲛ̄[ⲧ]ⲟⲟⲧϥ [ⲙ̄]

18   ⲡⲉⲛⲍⲟⲉⲓⲥ ⲙⲛ ⲡⲥⲱ[ⲧ]ⲏⲣ ⲛ̄[ⲧⲉ]
        ⲡⲕⲟⲥⲙⲟⲥ ⲧⲏⲣϥ ⲍⲉ [ⲉⲛ]ⲗⲁⲉⲓ ⲉ[ⲩ—]

20   [ⲙ̄]ⲁ ⲍⲉ ⲉⲛⲁϯ ⲥⲃⲱ ⲁⲩ[ⲱ] ⲛⲧ̄ⲛⲧⲁ—
        ϣⲉ ⲟⲉⲓϣ ϩⲣⲁⲓ̈ ϩⲙ ⲡⲓ[ⲟ]ⲩⲍⲁⲓ̈ ⲉ—

22   ⲧⲁⲩⲉⲣⲏⲧ ⲙ̄ⲙⲟϥ ⲛⲁⲛ ⲉⲃⲟⲗ ϩⲓ—
                                        [ⲣ]ⲁⲩ̣

[ⲧ]ⲛ ⲡⲉⲛⲍⲟⲉⲓⲥ ⲓ̄ⲥ̄ ⲡⲉⲭ̄[ⲥ̄·] ⲛ̄ⲧⲟⲕ ⲇⲉ

2   [ⲛ̄]ⲉϣⲁⲕⲡⲱⲣⲍ ⲉⲃⲟⲗ ⲙ̄ⲙⲟⲛ· ⲁⲩⲱ
        ⲙ̄ⲡⲉⲕⲙⲉⲣⲉ ⲡⲓⲧⲣⲉⲛⲉⲓ ⲉⲩⲙⲁ

4   ⲁⲩⲱ ⲛⲧⲛⲉⲓⲙⲉ ⲍⲉ ⲉⲛⲁⲧⲟϣⲛ ⲛ
        ⲁϣ ⲛ ϩⲉ ⲍⲉ ⲉⲛⲁϩⲓ ϣⲙ̄ⲛⲟⲩϥⲉ·

6   ⲉϣⲍⲉ ⲟⲩⲛ ⲁⲥⲣ ⲁⲛⲁⲕ ⲡⲉⲛⲥⲟⲛ ⲍⲉ
        ⲉⲕⲉⲉⲓ ⲕⲁⲧⲁ ⲛⲉⲛⲧⲟⲗⲏ ⲛⲧⲉ ⲡⲉⲛ—

8   ⲛⲟⲩⲧⲉ̣ ⲓ̄ⲥ̄· ⲛⲁⲓ̈ ⲛ̄ⲧⲉⲣⲉϥⲍⲓⲧⲟⲩ
        ⲛϭⲓ ⲫ[ⲓⲗⲓ]ⲡ̄ⲡⲟⲥ ⲁⲩⲱ ⲛ̄ⲧⲉⲣⲉϥⲟ—

10   ϣⲟⲩ ⲁϥⲃⲱⲕ ⲉⲣⲁⲧϥ ⲙ̄ⲡⲉⲧⲣⲟⲥ
        ϩⲛ ⲟⲩⲣⲁϣⲉ ⲉϥⲧⲉⲗⲏⲗ ⲙ̄ⲙⲟϥ·

12   ⲧⲟⲧⲉ ⲁⲡⲉⲧⲣⲟⲥ ⲁϥⲥⲱⲟⲩϩ

NOTES TO TEXT
Frederik Wisse

132,10-11   Indented and spaced off in the codex. The phrase is not a descriptive
            title for the whole tractate but only the caption of the letter
            (132, 12-133, 8).

132,15   The epistolary χαίρειν (in Coptic ⲭⲁⲓⲣⲉ) can be abbreviated at the end
            of a line to ⲭⲁ, ⲭⲁⲓ, or ⲭⲁⲓⲣ, according to usage in Greek papyri.
            Here the average length of the lines would suggest an abbreviation. The
            ⲉ is an itacistic spelling for ⲁⲓ.

133,8   At the end of the letter there is a blank space of about one letter in the
            manuscript; viz., ⲓ̄ⲥ̄· ⊻ ⲛⲁⲓ̈.

132

10   The letter (ἐπιστολή) of Peter which he
            sent to Philip:
12   "Peter, the apostle (ἀπόστολος) of Jesus
      Christ, to Philip our beloved
14   brother and our fellow apostle (-ἀπόστολος)
      and the brethren who are with you: greetings (χαίρειν)!
16   Now (δέ) I want you to know, our brother, [that]
      we received orders (ἐντολή) from
18   our Lord and the Savior (σωτήρ) of
      the whole world (κόσμος) that [we] should come [together]
20   to give instruction and
      preach in the salvation
22   which was promised us by

                                        [1]33
      our Lord Jesus Christ. But (δέ) as for you,
2   you were separate from us, and
      you did not desire us to come together
4   and to know how we should organize
      ourselves in order that we might tell the good news.
6   Therefore (οὖν) would it be agreeable to you, our brother, to
      come according to (κατά) the orders (ἐντολή) of our
8   God Jesus?" When Philip had received these,
      and when he had read
10   them, he went to Peter
      rejoicing with gladness.
12   Then (τότε) Peter gathered

COMMENTARY
Marvin W. Meyer

132,13-14   ΠΕΝCΟΝ ⲘⲘⲈⲣⲓ⳦; cf. esp. *Pistis Sophia* 44; also Acts 15:23; Rom
              1:7; 2 Cor 1:1; etc.
132,14-15   Philip the apostle; cf. Mark 3:18 par.; John 1:43-48; 6:5-7; 12:21-22;
              14:8-9; Acts 1:13; Philip the evangelist; cf. Acts 6:5,8:4-40; 21:8-9. The
              two figures named Philip were often conflated in early Christian
              literature (cf. Meyer, *The Letter of Peter to Philip*, 93-94).
132,16-133,1 Cf. Luke 24:44-49; Acts 1:1-8.
133,1-5   Cf. Acts 8:4-40, esp. 8:4-25.
133,8   ΝΟ⳦⳦Ε as a christological title; cf. John 20:28; Ign. *Rom.* 3.3;
              Smyrn. 1.1; apocryphal Acts of the Apostles.

     ⲙ ⲡⲕⲉⲥⲉⲉⲡⲉ ⲁⲩⲃⲱⲕ ⲉϫⲙ

14 ⲡⲧⲟⲟⲩ ⲉⲧⲉ ϣⲁⲩⲙⲟⲩⲧⲉ ⲉⲣⲟϥ

     ϫⲉ ⲡⲁⲛⲓϫⲟⲉⲓⲧ ⲡⲙⲁ ⲉⲧⲉ ϣⲁⲩ—

16 ⲥⲱⲟⲩϩ ⲉⲙⲁⲩ ⲙⲛ ⲡⲙⲁⲕⲁⲣⲓⲟⲥ

     ⲛⲭ̅ⲥ̅ ϩⲟⲧⲁⲛ ⲉϥϩⲛ ⲥⲱⲙⲁ· ⲧⲟ—

18 ⲧⲉ ⲛⲧⲉⲣⲟⲩⲉⲓ ⲉⲩⲙⲁ ⲛϭⲓ ⲛⲁⲡⲟⲥ—

     ⲧⲟⲗⲟⲥ ⲁⲩⲱ ⲁⲩⲛⲟϫⲟⲩ ⲉϫⲛ

20 ⲛⲉⲩⲡⲁⲧ̇ ⲁⲩϣⲗⲏⲗ ⲛϯϩⲉ ⲉⲩ—

     ϫⲱ ⲙ[ⲙⲟ]ⲥ ϫⲉ ⲡⲓⲱⲧ̇ ⲡⲓⲱⲧ̇

22 ⲡ̣ⲓ̣ⲱⲧ̇ ⲛⲧⲉ ⲡⲟⲩⲟⲉⲓⲛ ⲡⲁⲓ̈ ⲉ—

     ⲧⲉⲩⲛⲧⲁϥ ⲛⲛⲓⲁⲫⲑⲁⲣⲥⲓⲁ

24 ⲥⲱⲧ[ⲙ] ⲉⲣⲟⲛ ⲕⲁⲧⲁ ⲑⲉ ⲉⲧⲁ[ⲕ]

     ⲙ̇ⲧⲱ[ⲟ]ⲩ ϩⲙ ⲡⲉⲕⲁⲗⲟⲩ ⲉⲧ—

26 ⲟⲩⲁⲁⲃ̣ [ⲓ]̅ⲥ̅ ⲡⲉⲭ̅ⲥ̅· ⲛⲧⲟϥ ⲅⲁⲣ

     ⲁϥϣⲱⲡⲉ ⲛⲁⲛ ⲛⲟⲩⲫⲱⲥⲧⲏⲣ

     ⲣ̅[ⲗ̅ⲁ̅]

     ϩⲙ ⲡⲕⲁ̣ⲕⲉ ⲁⲉⲓⲟ ⲥⲱⲧⲙ ⲉⲣⲟⲛ̣·

2   ⲁⲩⲱ ⲁⲩⲕⲟⲧⲟⲩ ⲛⲕⲉⲥⲟⲡ̣ ⲁⲩ—

     ϣⲗⲏⲗ ⲉⲩϫⲱ ⲙⲙⲟⲥ ϫⲉ ⲡϣⲏ—

4   ⲣⲉ ⲛⲧⲉ ⲡⲱⲛϩ ⲡϣⲏⲣⲉ ⲛⲧⲉ ϯ—

     ⲙⲛ̇ⲧⲁⲧⲙⲟⲩ· ⲡⲁⲓ̈ ⲉⲧϣ̣ⲟⲟⲡ̣ ϩⲙ

6   ⲡⲟⲩⲟⲉⲓⲛ· ⲡϣⲏⲣⲉ ⲡⲉⲭ̅ⲥ̅ ⲛⲧⲉ

     ϯⲙⲛ̇ⲧⲁⲧⲙⲟⲩ· ⲡⲉⲛⲣⲉ̣ϥⲥⲱⲧⲉ

8   ⲙⲁϯ ⲛⲁⲛ ⲛⲛⲟⲩϭⲁⲙ· ⲉⲡⲓⲇⲏ ⲥⲉ—

     ⲕⲱⲧⲉ ⲛⲥⲱⲛ ⲉϩⲟⲧⲃⲛ [ⲧ]ⲟ̣ⲧⲉ ⲁϥ—

10 ⲟⲩⲱⲛϩ ⲉⲃⲟⲗ ⲛϭⲓ ⲟⲩⲛⲟϭ ⲛ ⲟⲩⲟⲉⲓ[ⲛ]

133,22   ⲧ̇, flag is uncertain on papyrus.

133,25   H.-M. Schenke has argued that ⲙ̇ⲧⲱⲟⲩ can be a form of the infinitive
           of ⲙⲁⲧⲉ ("Middle Egyptian Dialect," (104)58*). ⲁⲗⲟⲩ could also
           mean servant.

the others also. They went upon
14 the mountain which is called
"the (mount) of olives," the place where they used
16 to gather with the blessed (μακάριος)
Christ when (ὅταν) he was in the body (σῶμα). Then (τότε),
18 when the apostles (ἀπόστολος) had come together,
and had thrown themselves upon
20 their knees, they prayed thus
saying, "Father, Father,
22 Father of the Light, who
possesses the incorruptions (ἀφθαρσία),
24 hear us just as (κατά) [thou hast]
[taken pleasure] in thy holy
26 child Jesus Christ. For (γάρ) he
became for us an illuminator (φωστήρ)
1[34]
in the darkness. Yea hear us."
2 And they prayed again another time
saying, "Son
4 of Life, Son of
Immortality, who is in
6 the light, Son, Christ of
Immortality, our Redeemer,
8 give us power, for (ἐπειδή) they
seek to kill us." Then (τότε)
10 a great Light appeared

133,13-17 ΠΑΝΙϪΟΕΙ⳦; cf. esp. Luke 19:29; 21:37; Acts 1:12; also Luke 22:39;
Pistis Sophia 6; 8; 77; Soph. Jes. Chr. III 90,14-91,20; Apoc. Paul
V 19,8-13. ΠϪΑΚΑΡΙΟⲤ Ν̄Χ̄Ⲥ; cf. Gos. Mary BG 8,12.
133,19-20 Genuflection; cf. Luke 22:41; Acts 7:60; 9:40; 20:36; 21:5.
133,21-22 ΠΙⲰ⳦ Ν̄ΤΕ ΠΟⲩΟΕΙΝ; cf. 1 John 1:5; John 1:1-18.
133,24-134,1 Petition; cf. Dial. Sav. III 121,5-9. ΚΑΤΑ ⲐΕ ΕΤΑ[Κ]/ϪΤⲰ[Ο]ⲩ; cf.
Mark 1:11 par.; Matt 12:18-21 (Isa 42:1-4); 17:5; 2 Pet 1:17; Gos. Eb. frg.
4; also Acts 9:22 (Oxyrhynchite; Old Latin). ΠΕΚΑΛΟⲩ Ε⳦/ΟⲩΑΑΒ
[Ⲓ̄Ⲥ̄ ΠΕΧ̄Ⲥ; cf. esp. Acts 4:27,30; Did. 9.2,3; 10.2,3; also Acts 3:13,
26; 1 Clem. 59. 2-4; Mart. Pol. 14.1-3; 20.2; Diog. Laert. VIII.9-11; IX.1.
133,27 ΦⲰⲤΤΗΡ; cf. Acts of Philip 21; Apoc. Adam V 85,28-31; Kephalaia,
passim; Lampe, Lexicon, s.v. φωστήρ.
134,9-14 Light and voice of the risen Christ; cf. Mark 9:2-8 par.; 2 Pet 1:16-19;
Acts 9:1-9; 22:4-11; 26:9-18; 1 Cor 15; Rev 1:12-16; Gos. Truth I
31,13-16; Ap. John II 2,1-9; 30,33-35; Soph. Jes. Chr. III 91,10-13; Apoc.
Pet . VII 71,32-72,2; 83,6-15; Trim. Prot. XIII 47,28-29; Pistis Sophia 2-5;
Acts of Thomas 80; 111; etc.

ϨⲰⲤⲦⲈ ⲚⲦⲈⲠⲒⲦⲞⲞⲨ Ⲣ ⲞⲨⲞⲈⲒⲚ

12 ⲈⲂⲞⲖ ϨⲘ ⲠⲒⲰⲢϨ ⲚⲦⲈ ⲠⲎ ⲈⲦⲀϤⲞⲨ-
ⲰⲚϨ ⲈⲂⲞⲖ· ⲀⲨⲰ ⲀⲨⲤⲘⲎ ⲀⲤⲰϢ

14 ⲈⲂⲞⲖ ϢⲀⲢⲞⲞⲨ ⲈⲤϪⲰ ⲘⲘⲞⲤ ϪⲈ
ϪⲒ ⲤⲘⲎ ⲈⲚⲀϢⲀϪⲈ ϪⲈ ⲈⲈⲒⲈϪⲞ[Ⲥ]

16 ⲚⲎⲦⲚ· ⲈⲦⲂⲈ ⲞⲨ ⲦⲈⲦⲚϢⲒⲚⲈ Ⲙ-
ⲘⲞⲈⲒ ⲀⲚⲞⲔ ⲠⲈ Ⲓ̄Ⲥ̄ ⲠⲈⲬⲤ ⲈⲦϢ[Ⲟ-]

18 Ⲟⲡ̄ ⲘⲚ ⲦⲎⲨⲦⲚ ϢⲀ ⲈⲚⲈϨ· ⲦⲞⲦ[Ⲉ]
ⲀⲚⲀⲠⲞⲤⲦⲞⲖⲞⲤ ⲀⲨⲞⲨⲰϢ[Ⲃ]

20 ⲀⲨⲰ ⲚⲀⲨϪⲰ ⲘⲘⲞⲤ ϪⲈ ⲠϪⲞ-
ⲈⲒⲤ ⲦⲚⲞⲨⲰϢ ⲈⲈⲒⲘⲈ Ⲉ ⲠϢⲱ-

22 ⲰⲦ̄ ⲚⲦⲈ ⲚⲈⲰⲚ ⲘⲚ ⲠⲈ[Ⲩ]ⲠⲖⲎ-
ⲢⲰⲘⲀ· ⲀⲨⲰ ϪⲈ ⲠⲰ[Ⲥ] ⲤⲈⲀⲘⲀ[Ϩ-]

24 ⲦⲈ ⲘⲘⲞⲚ ϨⲘ ⲠⲒⲘⲀ ⲚϢⲰⲠⲈ·
Ⲏ ⲠⲰⲤ ⲀⲚⲈⲒ ⲈⲠⲒⲘⲀ Ⲏ ⲈⲚⲀⲂⲰⲔ

26 ⲚⲀϢ ⲚⲢⲎⲦⲈ· Ⲏ ⲠⲰⲤ ⲞⲨⲚⲦⲀⲚ
                                        [Ⲣ̄Ⲗ̄Ⲉ]

[Ⲛ̄ⲦⲈϨⲞ]ⲨⲤⲒⲀ ⲚⲦⲈ ϮⲠⲀⲢϨⲎⲤⲒⲀ·

2 [Ⲏ] ⲈⲦⲂ̄Ⲉ ⲞⲨ ⲚⲒϬⲞⲘ ⲤⲈϮ ⲚⲘⲘⲀⲚ·
ⲦⲞⲦⲈ ⲀⲨⲤⲘⲎ ϢⲰⲠⲈ ⲚⲀⲨ ⲈⲂⲞⲖ

4 ϨⲘ ⲠⲞⲨⲞⲈⲒⲚ ⲈⲤϪⲰ ⲘⲘⲞⲤ ϪⲈ Ⲛ-
ⲦⲰⲦⲚ ⲞⲨⲀⲦ̇ⲦⲎⲨⲦⲚ ⲈⲦⲢ ⲘⲚ-

6 ⲦⲢⲈ ϪⲈ ⲀⲈⲒϪⲈ ⲚⲀⲒ̈ ⲦⲎⲢⲞⲨ ⲚⲎⲦⲚ
ⲀⲖ[Ⲗ]Ⲁ [Ⲉ]ⲦⲂ̄Ⲉ ⲦⲈⲦⲚⲘⲚⲦⲀⲦⲚⲀϨⲦⲈ

8 Ϯ[Ⲛ]ⲀϢⲀϪⲈ ⲚⲔⲈⲤⲞⲠ· ⲈⲦⲂⲈ
[ⲠϢⲰ]Ⲱ̄Ⲧ ⲘⲈⲚ ⲚⲦⲈ ⲚⲈⲰⲚ ⲠⲀⲒ̈

10 [ⲠⲈ] ⲠⲒϢⲰⲰⲦ ⲈⲦ<Ⲁ>ϮⲘⲚⲦⲀⲦ-
ϬⲰⲦⲘ ϪⲈ ⲘⲚ ϮⲘⲚⲦⲀⲦϢⲞϪⲚⲈ

12 ⲚⲦⲈ ⲦⲘⲀⲀⲨ ⲈⲦⲀⲤⲞⲨⲰⲚϨ ⲈⲂⲞⲖ
ⲈϪⲘ ⲠⲞⲨⲀϨ ⲤⲀϨⲚⲈ ⲚⲦⲈ ϮⲘⲚⲦ-

134,22   The Ⲕ in ⲠⲈⲔ ("thy") has been corrected to an upsilon ⲠⲈⲨ
          ("their"). In terms of the answer to this question in 136,16-137,4 the
          uncorrected reading fits better.
135,10   Ms. reads ⲈⲦⲈϮ.

so that (ὥστε) the mountain shone
12 from the sight of him who had
appeared. And a voice called
14 out to them saying,
"Listen to my words that I may speak
16 to you. Why are you asking
me? I am Jesus Christ who
18 am with you forever." Then (τότε)
the apostles (ἀπόστολος) answered
20 and said, "Lord,
we would like to know the deficiency
22 of the aeons (αἰών) and their pleroma (πλήρωμα)."
And: "How (πῶς) are
24 we detained in this dwelling place?" Further (ἤ):
"How (πῶς) did we come to this place?" And (ἤ): "In what
26 manner shall we depart?" Again (ἤ): "How (πῶς) do we have

[135]

[the] authority (ἐξουσία) of boldness (παρρησία)?"
2   [And (ἤ)]: "Why do the powers fight against us?"
Then (τότε) a voice came to them out
4   of the light saying,
"It is you yourselves who are witnesses
6   that I spoke all these things to you.
But (ἀλλά) because of your unbelief
8   I shall speak again. First
of all (μέν) concerning [the deficiency] of the Aeons (αἰών), this
10 [is] the deficiency, when (+δέ)
the disobedience and the foolishness
12 of the mother appeared
without the commandment of the majesty

134,17-18   Cf. Matt 28:20; *Ap. John* II 2,12-13.
134,18-23   Two-part indirect question; cf. *Dial. Sav.* III 139,13-15. Series of
            questions; cf. *Ap. John* II 1,17-29; *Hyp. Arch.* II 93,32-94,2; *Soph. Jes.
            Chr.* III 91,2-9; *Zost.* VIII 2,24-3,13; *Excerpta ex Theodoto* 78.2.
135,1   [ⲉϩⲟ]ⲧ̄ⲥⲓⲁ ⲛⲧⲉ ⲧⲡⲁⲣϩⲏⲥⲓⲁ; cf. Acts 4:29,31; *Acts of Philip* 97.
135,10-15   ⲧⲙⲛ̄ⲧⲁⲧ/ⲥⲱⲧⲙ ⲇⲉ ⲙⲛ ⲧⲙⲛ̄ⲧⲁⲧϣⲟϫⲛⲉ; cf. *Ap. John* II 9,25-
            35; Gen 3; 1 Tim 2:14; *Barn.* 12.5; Iren., *Adv. Haer.* I.2.2; *Excerpta ex
            Theodoto* 23.2. ⲧⲙⲁⲁⲩ; cf. *Ap. John* II 10,6-7.18.21; 11,9-10; 12,8;
            13,4.14.28.30.32; Iren., *Adv.Haer.* I. 29.4; also *Soph. Jes. Chr.* III 114,14-15;
            104,17-18 par. *Eugnostos* V 9,4-5; Hipp., *Ref.* VI.34.8; etc. ⲧⲙⲛ̄ⲧ/ⲛⲟⲅ;
            cf. *Ap.John* II 4,1-2; 6,15; Iren., *Adv. Haer.* I.2.1-2; etc.

14 ⲛⲟϭ ⲛⲧⲉ ⲡⲓⲱⲧ· ⲁⲥⲟⲩⲱϣ ⲉ
ⲧⲟⲩⲛⲟⲥ ⲛϩⲉⲛⲉⲱⲛ ⲁⲩⲱ ⲉⲧⲁⲥ—

16 ϣⲁϫⲉ ⲁϥⲟⲩⲱϩ ⲉⲃⲟⲗ ⲛϭⲓ ⲡⲓⲁⲩ—
ⲑⲁⲇⲏⲥ· ⲉⲧⲁⲥϣⲱϫⲛ̅ ⲇⲉ ⲛⲟⲩ—

18 ⲙⲉⲣⲟⲥ ⲁϥⲁⲙⲁϩⲧⲉ ⲙⲙⲟϥ ⲛϭⲓ ⲡⲓ—
ⲁⲩⲑⲁⲇⲏⲥ· ⲁⲩⲱ ⲁϥϣⲱⲡⲉ ⲛ—

20 ⲟⲩϣⲱⲱⲧ̇ ⲡⲁⲓ ⲡⲉ ⲡϣⲱⲧ̇
[ⲛ]ⲧⲉ ⲛⲓⲉⲱⲛ· ⲉⲧⲁⲡⲓⲁⲩⲑⲁⲇⲏⲥ

22 ϭⲉ ⲉⲧⲁϥϫⲓ ⲛⲟⲩⲙⲉⲣⲟⲥ ⲁϥϫⲟϥ
ⲁⲩⲱ ⲁϥⲕⲱ ⲛϩⲉⲛϭⲟⲙ ⲉϩⲣⲁⲓ

24 ⲉϫⲱϥ ⲙⲛ ϩⲉⲛⲉⲝⲟⲩⲥⲓⲁ·
ⲁⲩⲱ [ⲁ]ϥⲟⲗϥ ⲉϩⲟⲩⲛ ⲉⲛⲓⲉⲱⲛ

26 ⲉⲧⲙⲟ[ⲟ]ⲩⲧ̇· ⲁⲩⲱ ⲁⲩⲣⲁϣⲉ
ⲛϭⲓ ⲛⲓϭⲟⲙ ⲧⲏⲣⲟⲩ ⲛⲧⲉ ⲡⲕⲟⲥ—

28 ⲙⲟⲥ ϫⲉ ⲁⲩϫⲡⲟⲟⲩ· ⲛⲧⲟⲟⲩ
ⲣ̅[ⲗⲋ̅]
ⲇⲉ ⲛⲥⲉϭⲟⲟⲩⲛ ⲁⲛ ⲙⲡⲓ[ⲱⲧ ⲉⲧⲣ]

2 ϣⲣⲡ̅ ⲛϣⲟⲟⲡ̅· ⲉⲡⲓⲇⲏ ϩⲉ[ⲛ]ϣⲙ̅—
ⲙⲟ ⲙⲙⲟϥ ⲛⲉ· ⲁⲗⲗⲁ ⲡⲁⲓ ⲡ[ⲉ]ⲧⲁ[ⲩ—]

4 ϯ ϭⲟⲙ ⲛⲁϥ ⲁⲩⲱ ⲁⲩϣⲙϣⲉ ⲙⲙⲟϥ
ⲉⲁⲩⲥⲙⲟⲩ ⲉⲣⲟϥ· ⲛⲧⲟϥ ⲇⲉ ⲡⲓⲁⲩ—

6 ⲑⲁⲇⲏⲥ ⲁϥϫⲓⲥⲉ ⲛϩⲏⲧ̇ ⲉϩⲣⲁⲓ ⲉϫⲙ
ⲡⲓⲥⲙⲟⲩ ⲛⲧⲉ ⲛⲓϭⲟⲙ· ⲁϥ[ϣ]ⲱⲡ[ⲉ] ⲛ—

8 ⲟⲩⲣⲉϥⲕⲱϩ· ⲁⲩⲱ ⲁϥⲟ[ⲩ]ⲱϣ [ⲉ]ⲧⲁ—
ⲙⲓⲟ ⲛⲛⲟⲩϩⲓⲕⲱⲛ ⲉⲡⲙ[ⲁ ⲛⲛⲟⲩϩⲓⲕⲱⲛ]

10 ⲙⲛ ⲟⲩⲙⲟⲣⲫⲏ ⲉⲡⲙⲁ ⲛⲛⲟⲩⲙ[ⲟⲣ—]
ⲫⲏ· ⲁϥⲧⲱϣ ⲇⲉ ⲛⲛⲓϭⲟⲙ ϩⲣⲁⲓ ϩⲛ

12 ⲧⲉϥⲉⲝⲟⲩⲥⲓⲁ ϫⲉ ⲉⲧⲉⲡⲗⲁⲥⲥⲁ ⲛϩⲉ[ⲛ—]
ⲥⲱⲙⲁ ⲉⲩⲙⲟⲟⲩⲧ̇· ⲁⲩⲱ ⲁⲩϣⲱ—

14 ⲡⲉ ⲉⲃⲟⲗ ϩⲛ ⲟⲩⲙⲛ̅ⲧⲁⲧⲉⲓⲛⲉ ⲉⲃⲟⲗ
ϩⲛ ϯⲓⲇⲉⲁ ⲉⲧⲉⲁⲥϣⲱⲡⲉ·   ⳝⳝⳝⳝ

135,16   Perhaps to be emended to ⲟⲩⲱ‹ⲛ›ϩ, "appeared."

136,9   The reconstruction ⲛⲛⲟⲩϩⲓⲕⲱⲛ requires an unusually long line but
          is suggested by the phrase that follows and the parallel in *Gos. Thom.* II
          37, 34. The meaning is that the Archons created the human form or
          image according to the heavenly image which appeared to them (cf.
          Ap. John II 14,24-15,13).

14 of the Father. She wanted
    to raise up aeons (αἰών). And when she
16 spoke, the Arrogant One (αὐθάδης) followed.
    And (δέ) when she left behind a
18 part (μέρος), the Arrogant One (αὐθάδης)
    laid hold of it, and it became a
20 deficiency. This is the deficiency
    of the aeons (αἰών). Now when the Arrogant One (αὐθάδης)
22 had taken a part (μέρος), he sowed it.
    And he placed powers over
24 it and authorities (ἐξουσία)
    And [he] enclosed it in the aeons (αἰών)
26 which are dead. And all the
    powers of the world (κόσμος) rejoiced
28 that they had been begotten.
    1[36]
    But (δέ) they do not know the
2   pre-existent [Father], since (ἐπειδή) they are
    strangers to him. But (ἀλλά) this is the one to whom
4   they gave power and whom they served
    by praising him. But (δέ) he, the Arrogant One (αὐθάδης),
6   became proud on account of
    the praise of the powers. He became
8   an envier, and he wanted to
    make an image (εἰκών) in the place [of an image (εἰκών)]
10 and a form (μορφή) in the place of a form (μορφή).
    And (δέ) he commissioned the powers within
12 his authority (ἐξουσία) to mold (πλάσσειν)
    mortal bodies (σῶμα). And they came
14 to be from a misrepresentation, from
    the semblance (ἰδέα) which had emerged.

135,15-16   ⲉⲧⲁⲥ/ϣⲁⲝⲉ; cf. Ap. John II 10,19; Orig. World II 100,10-19.
135,16-17   ⲡⲓⲁⲧ/ⲑⲁⲁⲏⲥ; cf. Ap. John II 13,27; IV 21,16; BG 46,1;
            Iren., Adv. Haer. I.29.4; also Hyp. Arch. II 90,29; 92,27; 94,17.
135,21-24   Arrogant One takes a portion; cf. Ap. John II 10,19-28; 13,22-23;
            Iren., Adv. Haer. I.29.4; also Hyp. Arch. II 87,12.21; 94,14.32 (on
            ⲙⲉⲣⲟⲥ).
136,9-11   Cf. Gos. Thom. II 37,31-35; 1 Cor 15:49.
136,12-13   ⲉⲧⲉⲡⲗⲁⲥⲥⲁ ⲛⲟⲉ/[ⲛ]/ⲥⲱⲙⲁ ⲉⲧⲙⲟⲟⲩⲧ̇; cf. Ap. John II 15,1-
            19,15; Orig. World II 114,15-115,3; etc.
136,14-15   ⲟⲩⲙⲛⲧⲁⲧⲉⲓⲛⲉ; cf. Hyp. Arch. II 87,15-20.

16 ετβε πιπληρωμα δε ανοκ πετε
αυτννοουτ εϩραϊ ϩμ πϲωμα ε-
18 τβε πιϲπερμα ετεαϥϩε εβολ
αυω αϊει εϩραϊ επευπλαϲμα ετ-
20 μοουτ· ντοου δε μπουϲ[ου-]
ωντ νευμεευε εροει δε αν[οκ]
22 ουρωμε εϥμοουτ· αυω αϊϣ[α-]
δε μν πετε πωϊ ντου δε αϥϲω-
24 τμ ναϊ κατα τετνϩ[ε] ϩωτ
τηυτν ναϊ εταυϲω[τ]μ μποου
26 αυω αϊϯ ναυ ννουεϩουϲια δε·
εϥεει εϩουν ε ϯκληρονομια
28 ντε τεϥμντειωτ· αυω αϊϥι

[ρμζ]

[---   α]υμοуϩ εβολ
2 [. . . . .] .κ ϩραϊ ϩμ πεϥουδαϊ· επιδη
[δε] δε ν[ε]ουϣωτ πε ετβε παϊ αϥ-
4 ϣωπε [ν]ουπληρωμα· ετβε πη
πε δε ϲεαμαϩτε μμωτν δε ντωτν
6 νετε νουει· εϣωπε ετετνακακ
τηνε καϩηυ μπαϊ εττακηουτ· το-
8 τε ετετναϣωπε νϩενφωϲτηρ
ϩν τμητε νϩενρωμε ευμοουτ
10 πη δ[ε] δε ντωτν ετναϯ μν νιϭομ
δε ν[τ]οου μμντау νουμτον κα-
12 [τα] τετνϩε· επιδη νϲεουωϣ αν
[ϩι]να ντετννουϩμ· τοτε αναπος-
14 [τ]ολος ουωϣτ ν κεϲοπ ευδω μ-
μοϲ δε πδοειϲ ματαμον δε αϣ
16 [τ]ε θε ετνναϯ μν νιαρχων· επιδη
[νια]ρχων ϲεντπε μμον· τοτε

16   Next (δέ) concerning the pleroma (πλήρωμα): I am the one who
     was sent down in the body (σῶμα)
18   because of the seed (σπέρμα) which had fallen away.
     And I came down into their mortal mold (πλάσμα).
20   But (δέ) they did not
     recognize me; they were thinking of me that I
22   was a mortal man. And I
     spoke with him who belongs to me, and (δέ) he
24   harkened to me just as (κατά) you too
     who harkened today.
26   And I gave him authority (ἐξουσία) in order that
     he might enter into the inheritance (κληρονομία)
28   of his fatherhood. And I took

                                                      [137]
     [   ] they were filled
2   [   ] in his salvation. [And (δέ)]
     since (ἐπειδή) he was a deficiency, for this reason he
4   became a pleroma (πλήρωμα). It is because of this
     that you are being detained because you
6   belong to me. When you strip off
     from yourselves what is corrupted, then (τότε)
8   you will become illuminators (φωστήρ)
     in the midst of mortal men.
10   And (δέ), this (is the reason) that you will fight against the
     powers, because [they] do not have rest like (κατά)
12   you, since (ἐπειδή) they do not wish
     that (ἵνα) you be saved." Then (τότε) the apostles (ἀπόστολος)
14   worshipped again, saying,
     "Lord, tell us: In what
16   way shall we fight against the archons (ἄρχων), since (ἐπειδή)
     [the] archons (ἄρχων) are above us?" Then (τότε)

136,16-137,4   Cf. John 1:1-18. ⲀⲠⲞⲨⳠ[ⲞⲨ]/ⲰⲚⲦ̇; cf. John 1:10; Ap. John II 30,20-
               21; Treat. Seth VII 52,8-10. ⲠⲈⲦⲈ ⲠⲰ[ï]; cf. John 1:11; 2 Apoc. Jas.
               V 55,15-20; Treat. Seth VII 59,9-11. ⲀⲒ† ⲚⲀϤ ⲚⲚⲞⲨⲈϪⲞⲨⲤⲒⲀ;
               cf. John 1:12. Deficiency to fullness; cf. Ap. John II 25,11-16.
137,4-9   Cf. Dial. Sav. III 140,14-19, and the direct questions (above) at VIII
               134,23-26. ⲈⲦⲈⲦⲚⲀⲔⲀⲔ/ⲦⲎⲚⲈ ⲔⲀϨ ⲎⲨ; cf. Ap. Jas. I 14,35-36;
               Gos. Thom. II 37,4-6; Dial. Sav. III 132,11-12; 2 Ap. Jas. V 56,7-14;
               Acts of Thomas 111; Poimandres 24-26; Hipp, Ref. V.8.44; contrast
               2 Cor 5:2-3. ϨⲈⲚⲪⲰⲤⲦⲎⲢ; cf. Phil 2:15; Gos. Phil. II 61,29-32 (on
               becoming ϨⲈⲚⲪⲰⲤⲦⲎⲢ, like Christ).
137,16-17   Cf. Dial. Sav. III 138,11-14.

18 [ⲁⲩⲥ]ⲙⲏ ⲁⲥⲱϣ ⲉⲃⲟⲗ ϣⲁⲣⲟⲟⲩ ⲉⲃⲟⲗ
   [ϩ]ⲙ ⲡⲏ ⲉⲧⲉ ⲛⲉϥⲟⲩⲟⲛϩ ⲉⲃⲟⲗ ⲉⲥϫⲱ
20 [ⲙ]ⲙⲟⲥ ϫⲉ ⲛⲧⲱⲧⲛ ⲇⲉ ⲉⲧⲉⲧⲛⲁϯ
   [ⲛ]ⲙⲙⲁⲩ ⲛϯϩⲉ· ⲛⲓⲁⲣⲭⲱⲛ ⲅⲁⲣ ⲉⲧϯ
22 ⲙⲛ ⲡⲓⲣⲱⲙⲉ ⲉⲧⲥⲁϩⲟⲩⲛ· ⲛⲧⲱⲧⲛ
   [ⲇ]ⲉ ⲉⲧⲉⲧⲛⲉϯ ⲛⲙⲙⲁⲩ ⲛϯϩⲉ· ⲁⲙⲏ—
24 ⲉⲓⲧⲛ ⲉⲩⲙⲁ ⲁⲩⲱ ϯ ⲥⲃⲱ ϩⲙ ⲡⲕⲟⲥ—
   ⲙⲟⲥ ⲙⲡⲓⲟⲩϫⲁⲓ ϩⲛ ⲟⲩⲉⲣⲏⲧ· ⲁⲩⲱ
26 ⲛⲧⲱⲧⲛ ϩⲱⲕⲧⲏⲩⲧⲛ ⲛϩⲣⲁⲓ ϩⲛ ϯϭⲟⲙ
   ⲛⲧⲉ ⲡⲁ[ⲉ]ⲓⲱⲧ· ⲁⲩⲱ ⲟⲩⲱⲛϩ ⲙ—
28 ⲡⲉⲧⲛⲧⲱⲃ ⲉⲃⲟⲗ· ⲁⲩⲱ ⲛⲧⲟϥ ⲡⲓ—
   ⲱⲧ ϥⲛⲁⲣⲃⲟⲏⲑⲓ ⲉⲣⲱⲧⲛ· ϩⲱⲥ ⲉⲁϥ—
30 ⲣⲃⲟⲏⲑⲓ ⲉⲣⲱⲧⲛ ⲉⲁϥⲧⲁⲩⲟⲉⲓ·
   [ⲣⲗⲏ]
   ⲙⲡⲣ[ⲣϭ]ⲁⲃϩ[ⲏⲧ ϯⲛⲉⲙⲏⲧⲛ ϣⲁ ⲉⲛⲉϩ]
2 ⲕⲁⲧⲁ ⲑⲉ ⲉⲧⲁⲓⲣ ϣⲣⲛ̄ ⲛϫⲟ[ⲟ]ⲥ [ⲛⲏ—]
   ⲧⲛ ϩⲟⲧⲁⲛ ⲉⲉⲓϩⲙ ⲡ[ⲥ]ⲱⲙⲁ· [ⲧ]ⲟⲧⲉ
4 ⲁⲥϣⲱⲡⲉ ⲛϭⲓ ⲟⲩⲉⲃⲣⲏϭⲉⲥ ⲙⲛ ⲟⲩ—
   ϩⲣⲟⲩⲙⲡⲉ ⲉⲃⲟⲗ ϩⲛ ⲧⲡⲉ· ⲁⲩⲱ ⲁⲩ—
6 ⲧⲱⲣⲛ̄ ⲙⲡⲉⲧⲁϥⲟⲩⲱⲛϩ ⲛⲁⲩ ⲉⲃⲟⲗ
   ⲙⲡⲓⲙⲁ ⲉⲧⲙⲙⲁⲩ ⲉϩⲣⲁⲓ ⲉⲧⲡⲉ· ⲧⲟⲧⲉ
8 ⲁⲛⲁⲡⲟⲥⲧⲟⲗⲟⲥ ⲁⲩϣⲛ̄ ϩⲙⲟⲧ ⲛⲧⲙ
   ⲡϫⲟⲉⲓⲥ ϩⲣⲁⲓ ϩⲛ ⲥⲙⲟⲩ ⲛⲓⲙ ⲁⲩⲱ
10 ⲁⲩⲕⲟⲧⲟⲩ ⲉϩⲣⲁⲓ ⲉⲑ̄ⲓ̄ⲗ̄ⲏ̄ⲙ̄ ⲉ[ⲩ]ⲛ—
   ⲛⲏⲩ ⲇⲉ ⲉϩⲣⲁⲓ ⲛⲁⲩϣⲁϫⲉ ⲙⲛ ⲛⲉ[ⲩ—]
12 ⲉⲣⲏⲩ ϩⲓⲧⲉϩⲓⲏ· ⲉⲧⲃⲉ ⲡⲓⲟⲩⲟⲉⲓⲛ [ⲉ—]
   ⲧⲉⲁϥϣⲱⲡⲉ· ⲁⲩⲱ ⲁϥϣⲱⲡⲉ ⲛ—
14 ϭⲓ ⲟⲩϣⲁϫⲉ ⲉⲧⲃⲉ ⲡϫⲟⲉⲓⲥ ⲉ[ⲩ]ϫⲱ
   ⲙⲙⲟⲥ ϫⲉ ⲉϣϫⲉ ⲛⲧⲟϥ ⲡⲉⲛϫⲟⲉ[ⲓⲥ]
16 ⲁϥϫⲓ ⲙⲕⲁϩ ϩⲓⲉ ⲁⲟⲩⲏⲣ ⲅⲉ ⲁⲛⲟⲛ[:]
   ⲁϥⲟⲩⲱϣⲃ ⲛϭⲓ ⲡⲉⲧⲣⲟⲥ ⲉϥϫⲱ
18 ⲙⲙⲟⲥ ϫⲉ ⲁϥϫⲓ ⲙⲕⲁϩ ⲉⲧⲃⲏⲏⲧ[ⲛ]
   ⲁⲩⲱ ϩⲁⲡⲥ ⲉⲣⲟⲛ ϩⲱⲱⲛ ⲉⲧⲣⲉ[ⲛ—]
20 ϫⲓ ⲙⲕⲁϩ ⲉⲧⲃⲉ ⲧⲉⲛⲙⲛⲧⲕⲟⲩ[ⲉⲓ]

138,1   It is possible (so also Layton, for 138 and 139) that there was one line
         yet higher which is now completely lost.
138,14   The original fai was corrected to upsilon.

18 [a] voice called out to them from
    the appearance, saying,
20 "Now (δέ) you will fight
    against them in this way, for (γάρ) the archons (ἄρχων) are
22 fighting against the inner man. And (δέ) you
    are to fight against them in this way: Come
24 together and teach in the world (κόσμος)
    the salvation with a promise. And
26 you, gird yourselves with the power
    of my Father, and let
28 your prayer be known. And he, the
    Father, will help (βοηθεῖν) you as (ὡς) he has
30 helped (βοηθεῖν) you by sending me.
    [138]
    Be not afraid, [I am with you forever,]
2   as (κατά) I previously [said to]
    you when (ὅταν) I was in the body (σῶμα)." Then (τότε)
4   there came lightning and
    thunder from heaven, and
6   what appeared to them in that place was taken
    up to heaven. Then (τότε)
8   the apostles (ἀπόστολος) gave thanks to
    the Lord with every blessing. And
10 they returned to Jerusalem.
    And (δέ) while coming up they spoke with
12 each other on the road concerning the light
    which had come. And a remark was made
14 concerning the Lord. It was
    said, "If he, our Lord,
16 suffered, then how much (must) we (suffer)?"
    Peter answered saying,
18 "He suffered on [our] behalf
    and it is necessary for us too
20 to suffer because of our smallness.

137,22   ΠΙΡΩΜΕ ΕΤϹΑϩΟⲨΝ; cf. Eph. 6:10-20; Iren., Adv. Haer. I.21.4;
          Hipp., Ref. VII.27.6.
137,30   ΕⲀϤΤⲀⲨΟΕϤ; cf. John 7:33; 16:5, etc.
138,5-7   Cf. Luke 24:51; Acts 1:9, also 10:16.
138,7-10 Cf. Luke 24:52-53; Acts 1:12.
138,20   ΤΕΝⲘΝΤⲔΟⲨ[ΕϤ]; cf. Treat. Res. I 46,34-38; Tri. Trac. I 115,3-11;
          Treat. Seth VII 54,4.10; 69,11-12; contrast Mark 10:13-16 par.; Gos.
          Thom. II 37,20-23; 41,10-12.

ⲧⲟⲧⲉ ⲁⲩⲥⲙⲏ ϣⲱⲡⲉ ϣⲁⲣⲟⲟⲩ
22 ⲉⲥϫⲱ ⲙⲙⲟⲥ ϫⲉ ⲁⲓϫⲟⲥ ⲛⲏⲧⲛ
ⲛϩⲁϩ ⲛⲥⲟⲛ̄ ϫⲉ ϩⲁⲡⲥ ⲉⲣⲱⲧⲛ
24 ⲉⲧⲣⲉⲧⲛϫⲓ ⲙⲕⲁϩ· ϩⲁ-
ⲡⲥ ⲉⲧⲣⲉⲩⲛⲧⲏⲩⲧⲛ ⲉϩⲉⲛⲥⲩ-
26 ⲛⲁⲅⲱⲅⲏ ⲙⲛ ϩⲉⲛϩⲩⲧⲉⲙⲱⲛ
ϩⲱⲥⲧⲉ ⲛⲧⲉⲧⲛϫⲓ ⲙⲕⲁϩ· ⲡⲏ ⲇⲉ
28 ⲉⲧⲉ ⲛϥⲛⲁϫⲓ ⲙⲕⲁϩ ⲁⲛ ⲟⲩⲇⲉ
                                    [ⲣ̄ⲗ̄ⲑ̄]

[
2 [---   ] .[.ⲡ]ⲓ̈ⲱⲧ̣
[---   ]ⲙ ϫⲉⲕⲁⲁⲥ ⲉϥ-
4 [. .]ⲉ̣ⲣⲉ̣[. . . . . .ⲁ]ⲛⲁⲡⲟⲥⲧⲟⲗⲟⲥ ⲇⲉ
[ⲁⲩ]ⲣ̣ⲁ̣ϣ̣[ⲉ] ⲉ̣[ⲙⲁ]ⲧ̣ⲉ ⲁⲩⲱ ⲁⲩⲉⲓ ⲉϩⲣⲁⲓ̈
6 [ⲉⲟⲓ]ⲏⲙ ⲁⲩⲱ ⲁⲩⲉⲓ ⲉϩⲣⲁⲓ̈ ⲉⲡⲣⲡⲉ ⲁⲩϯ
[ⲥⲃ]ⲱ ϩⲛ ⲟⲩⲟⲩ͞ϫⲁⲓ̈ ϩⲣⲁⲓ̈ ϩⲙ ⲡⲣⲁⲛ ⲛⲧⲉ
8 [ⲡϫ]ⲟⲉⲓⲥ ⲓ͞ⲥ ⲡⲉ͞ⲭ͞ⲥ· ⲁⲩⲱ ⲁⲩⲣ ⲡⲁϩⲣⲉ
[ⲉⲩ]ⲙⲏⲏϣⲉ· ⲁⲩⲟⲩⲱⲛ ⲇⲉ ⲉⲣⲱϥ ⲛϭⲓ
10 [ⲡⲉ]ⲧⲣⲟⲥ ⲡ[ⲉ]ϫⲁϥ̣ ⲛⲛⲉϥⲙⲁⲑⲏⲧⲏⲥ ϫⲉ
[ⲙⲏ] ⲡⲉⲛϫⲟⲉⲓⲥ ⲓ͞ⲥ ϩⲟⲧⲁⲛ ⲉϥϩⲛ ⲥⲱⲙⲁ
12 [ⲉϥ]ϯ ⲙⲁⲉⲓⲛ ⲛⲁⲛ ⲉϩⲱⲃ ⲛⲓⲙ ⲛⲧⲟϥ ⲅⲁⲣ
[ⲁϥ]ⲉⲓ ⲉϩⲣⲁⲓ̈· ⲛⲁⲥⲛⲏⲩ ϫⲓ ⲥⲙⲏ ⲉⲧⲁⲥⲙⲏ
14 [ⲁⲩ]ⲱ ⲁϥⲙⲟⲩϩ ⲉⲃⲟⲗ ϩⲛ ⲟⲩⲡ͞ⲛ͞ⲁ ⲉϥⲟⲩⲁⲁⲃ
[ⲡⲉ]ϫⲁϥ ⲛϯϩⲉ ϫⲉ ⲡⲉⲛⲫⲱⲥⲧⲏⲣ ⲓ͞ⲥ
16 [ⲁϥⲉⲓ] ⲉϩⲣⲁⲓ̈ ⲁⲩⲱ ⲁⲩⲁϣⲧϥ· ⲁⲩⲱ ⲁϥⲣ̄ⲫⲟ-
[ⲣⲓ ⲛⲟ]ⲩⲕⲗⲟⲙ ⲛϣⲟ‹ⲛ›ⲧⲉ· ⲁⲩⲱ ⲁϥϯ ϩⲓ-
18 [ⲱⲱϥ] ⲛⲛⲟⲩⲥⲧⲟⲗⲏ ⲛϫⲏϭⲉ ⲁⲩⲱ ⲁⲩ-
[ⲁϣ]ⲧϥ ⲉϫⲛ ⲟⲩϣⲉ ⲁⲩⲱ ⲁⲩⲧⲟⲙⲥϥ ϩⲛ

138,22   Some ink, possibly a high stop, is visible at the end of the line, although no punctuation mark is expected at this point.

139,1   The first, lost line is a conjecture on the basis of the height of the writing of the column in the previous pages.

139,17   Ms reads ϣⲟⲙⲧⲉ, "three (fem.)" which makes little sense and does not fit the gender of ⲕⲗⲟⲙ.

Then (τότε) a voice came to them,

22 saying, "I have told you
many times: It is necessary for you

24 to suffer. It is
necessary that they bring you to synagogues (συναγωγή)

26 and governors (ἡγεμών),
so that (ὥστε) you will suffer. But (δέ) he

28 who does not suffer and does not (οὐδε)

[139]

[

2 [the] Father
[   ] in order that he may

4 [.] And (δέ) the apostles (ἀπόστολος)
rejoiced [greatly] and came up

6 to Jerusalem. And they came up to the temple and gave
instruction in salvation in the name of

8 [the] Lord Jesus Christ. And they healed
[a] multitude. And (δέ) Peter opened his mouth,

10 he said to his (fellow) disciples (μαθητής),
["Did (μή)] our Lord Jesus, when (ὅταν) he was in the

12 body (σῶμα), show us everything? For (γάρ) he
came down. My brothers, listen to my voice."

14 And he was filled with a holy spirit (πνεῦμα).
He spoke thus: "Our illuminator (φωστήρ), Jesus,

16 [came] down and was crucified. And he bore (φορεῖν)
a crown of thorns. And he put on

18 a purple garment (στολή). And he was
[crucified] on a tree and he was buried in

138,22-24   Cf. Luke 24:26; Acts 14:22; also 1 Thess 3:3-4; 2 Thess 1:5-8; 2 Tim
3:12-13; esp. *Ap. Jas.* I 6,15-17 (4,37-6,21).

138,24-27   Cf. Matt 10:17-18; Luke 21:12; perhaps also Mark 13:9.

139,4-9   Cf. Luke 24:52-53; Acts 1:12; 2:42-47; 5:12-16,42. Teaching in the
name of Christ; cf. Luke 24:47; Acts 2:38; 3:6; 4:10; etc.

139,10   ΝΕϥΜΑΘΗΤΗС; cf. shorter ending of Mark; Ign. *Smyrn* 3.2.

139,14   ΑϥΜΟΥϩ ΕΒΟΛ ϩΝ ΟΥΠΝΑ ΕϥΟΥΑΑΒ; cf. Acts 4:8,31; 7:55;
13:9,52.

139,15-140,1 Cf. Acts 2:14-40; also other Petrine speeches in Acts. Credo: note the
details in Matt 27, Mark 15, Luke 23, esp. John 19 (e.g., 19:5: φορῶν
τὸν ἀκάνθινον στέφανον καὶ τὸ πορφυροῦν ἱμάτιον); Acts 5:30; 10:39-
41; 13:29-30; 1 Cor 15:3-5; etc. ΟΥϢΜΜΟ: perhaps cf. *Gos. Truth* I 31,
1-4; *Apoc. Adam* V 69,17-18; *Acts Pet. 12 Apost.* VI 3,4-11; *Acts of
Thomas* 109; etc. ΠϪΑΡΧΗΤΟС; cf. Acts 3:15; 5:31; also Heb 2:10;
12:2; 2 *Clem.* 20. 5.

20 ο[ⲩ]ⲙϩⲁⲟⲩ ⲁⲩⲱ ⲁϥⲧⲱⲛϥ ⲉⲃⲟⲗ ϩⲛ ⲛⲉⲧ-
ⲙ[ⲟⲟ]ⲩⲧ: <u>ⲩⲩⲩ</u> ⲛⲁⲥⲛⲏⲩ ⲟⲩϣⲙⲙⲟ ⲙ-

22 ⲡⲉⲓϫⲓ ⲙⲕⲁϩ ⲡⲉ ⲓ̅ⲥ̅· ⲁⲗⲗⲁ ⲁⲛⲟⲛ ⲡⲉⲧⲉ-
ⲁⲛϫⲓ ⲙⲕⲁϩ ϩⲛ ⲧⲡⲁⲣⲁⲃⲁⲥⲓⲥ ⲛⲧⲙⲁⲁⲩ

24 ⲁⲩⲱ ⲉⲧⲃⲉ ⲡⲁⲓ̈ ⲁϥⲉⲣⲉ ⲛϩⲱⲃ ⲛⲓⲙ
ⲕⲁⲧⲁ ⲟⲩⲉⲓⲛⲉ ϩⲣⲁⲓ̈ ⲛϩⲏⲧⲛ· ⲡϫⲟⲉⲓⲥ

26 ⲅⲁⲣ ⲓ̅ⲥ̅ ⲡϣⲏⲣⲉ ⲛⲧⲉ ⲡⲉⲟⲟⲩ ⲙⲡⲓⲱⲧ
ⲛⲁⲧϯ ϣⲓ ⲉⲣⲟϥ ⲡⲁⲓ̈ ⲡⲉ ⲡⲓⲁⲣⲭⲏⲅⲟⲥ

28 ⲛⲧⲉ ⲡⲉⲛⲱⲛϩ· <u>ⲩⲩ</u> ⲛⲁⲥⲛⲏⲩ ⲙⲡⲣ-
ⲧⲣⲉⲛⲥⲱⲧⲙ ⲟⲩⲛ ⲛⲥⲁ ⲛⲉⲓ̈ⲁⲛⲟ-

30 ⲙⲟⲥ ⲁⲩⲱ ⲛⲧⲛⲙⲟⲟϣⲉ ϩⲣⲁⲓ̈ ϩⲛ
[ⲣ̅ⲙ̅]

[— ⲧⲟⲧⲉ ⲁⲡⲉ-]

2 ⲧⲣⲟⲥ ⲁϥ[ⲥ]ⲱⲟ[ⲩϩ ⲉϩⲟⲩⲛ ⲙⲡⲕⲉⲥⲉ-]
[ⲉ]ⲡⲉ ⲉϥϫⲱ [ⲙⲙⲟⲥ ϫⲉ ⲡⲉⲛϫⲟⲉ]ⲓⲥ ⲓ̅[ⲥ̅]

4 ⲡⲉⲭ̅ⲥ̅ ⲡⲁⲣⲭⲏⲅⲟⲥ ⲛ̅[ⲧⲉ ⲡⲉ]ⲛⲙ̅ⲧⲟ[ⲛ]
ⲙⲁϯ ⲛⲁⲛ ⲛⲟⲩⲡⲛⲁ ⲛⲧⲉ ⲟⲩⲉⲡⲓ[ⲥ-]

6 ⲧⲏⲙⲏ ϩⲓⲛⲁ ⲁⲛⲟⲛ ϩⲱⲱⲛ ϫⲉ ⲉⲛⲉ-
ⲉⲓⲣⲉ ⲛϩⲉⲛϭⲟⲙ· ⲧⲟⲧⲉ ⲁⲡⲉⲧ[ⲣⲟⲥ]

8 ⲙⲛ ⲛⲓⲕⲉⲁⲡⲟⲥⲧⲟⲗⲟⲥ ⲁⲩⲛⲁⲩ ⲉ[ⲣⲟϥ]
ⲁⲩⲱ ⲁⲩⲙⲟⲩϩ ⲉⲃⲟⲗ [ϩⲛ] ⲟⲩⲡⲛ[ⲁ]

10 ⲉϥⲟⲩⲁⲁⲃ· ⲁⲩⲱ ⲁⲡⲟⲩⲁ ⲡⲟⲩⲁ
ⲉⲓⲣⲉ ⲛϩⲉⲛⲧⲁⲗϭⲟ· ⲁⲩⲱ ⲁⲩⲡⲱⲣϫ

12 ⲉⲃⲟⲗ ϫⲉ ⲉⲩⲉⲧⲁϣⲉ ⲟⲉⲓϣ ⲙⲡϫⲟ-
ⲉⲓⲥ ⲓ̅ⲥ̅ ⲁⲩⲱ ⲁⲩⲥⲱⲟⲩϩ ϣⲁ ⲛⲉ[ⲩ-]

14 ⲉⲣⲏⲩ ⲁⲩⲣⲁⲥⲡⲁⲍⲉ ⲙⲙⲟⲟⲩ [ⲉⲩ-]
ϫⲱ ⲙⲙⲟⲥ ϫⲉ ϩⲁⲙⲏⲛ: <u>ⲩⲩ</u> ⲧⲟ[ⲧⲉ]

16 ⲁϥⲟⲩⲱⲛϩ ⲉⲃⲟⲗ ⲛϭⲓ ⲓ̅ⲥ̅ ⲉϥϫⲱ [ⲙ-]
ⲙⲟⲥ ⲛⲁⲩ ϫⲉ ϯⲣⲏⲛⲏ ⲛⲏⲧⲛ [ⲧⲏⲣ-]

18 ⲧⲛ ⲙⲛ ⲟⲩⲟⲛ ⲛⲓⲙ ⲉⲧⲛⲁϩⲧⲉ ⲉ-
ⲡⲁⲣⲁⲛ· ⲉⲧⲉⲧⲛⲁⲃⲱⲕ ⲇⲉ ⲉϥⲉ-

20 ϣⲱⲡⲉ ⲛⲏⲧⲛ ⲛϭⲓ ⲟⲩⲣⲁϣⲉ ⲙⲛ
ⲟⲩϩⲙⲟⲧ ⲙⲛ ⲟⲩϭⲁⲙ· ⲙⲡⲣⲣ

22 ϭⲁⲃϩⲏⲧ ⲇⲉ ⲉⲓⲥ ϩⲏⲧⲉ ϯⲛⲉⲙⲏⲧⲛ

139,25   Lit., "according to a likeness in us."
139,26   Or, "the Son of the glory of the Immeasurable Father."
140,1   See note to 139,1.

20   a tomb. And he rose from the
     dead. My brothers, Jesus is a stranger
22   to this suffering. But (ἀλλά) we are the ones who have
     suffered through the transgression (παράβασις) of the mother.
24   And because of this, he did everything
     like (κατά) us.
26   For (γάρ) the Lord Jesus, the Son of the immeasurable glory of
     the Father, he is the author (ἀρχηγός)
28   of our life. My brothers, let
     us therefore (οὖν) not obey these lawless ones (ἄνομος)
30   and walk in
     [140]
     [. Then (τότε) Pe-]
2   ter [gathered together the others also,]
     saying, ["O, Lord Jesus]
4   Christ, author (ἀρχηγός) [of our] rest,
     give us a spirit (πνεῦμα) of understanding (ἐπιστήμη)
6   in order that (ἵνα) we also may
     perform wonders." Then (τότε) Peter
8   and the other apostles (ἀπόστολος) saw [him]
     and they were filled with a holy spirit (πνεῦμα).
10   And each one
     performed healings. And they parted
12   in order to preach the Lord
     Jesus. And they came together
14   and greeted (ἀσπάζεσθαι) each other
     saying, "Amen" (ἀμήν). Then (τότε)
16   Jesus appeared, saying
     to them, "Peace (εἰρήνη) to you [all]
18   and everyone who believes in
     my name. And (δέ) when you depart,
20   joy be to you and
     grace and power. And (δέ) be not
22   afraid; behold, I am with you

140,7-10   Cf. John 20:19-23 ("Pentecost" is accompanied by an appearance of the
               resurrected Christ; the disciples are happy, ἰδόντες τὸν κύριον, who
               greets them with a greeting of peace, commissions them, and imparts
               πνεῦμα ἅγιον; also Acts 2:1-4.
140,14   ⲁⲩⲣⲁⲥⲡⲁϫⲉ ⲙ̄ⲙⲟⲟⲩ; cf. Rom 16:16; 1 Cor 16:20; 2 Cor 13:12;
               etc.
140,17-23   Commission; cf. Matt 28:18-20; Luke 24:44-49; John 20:19-23; Acts
               1:8; also Mark 16:15-18; *Soph. Jes. Chr.* III 119,1-8.

ϢΑ ЄΝЄϨ· <u>Ⴝ</u> ΤΟΤЄ ΑΝ‹Α›ΠΟϹΤΟ—
24 λΟϹ ΑΥΠΩΡⳆ ΜΜΟΟΥ ЄΒΟλ
ЄϨΡΑϊ ЄΠІϤΤΟΟΥ ΝϢΑⳆЄ ⳆЄ ЄΥ—
26 ЄΤΑϢЄ ΟЄІϢ ΑΥΩ ΑΥΒΩΚ
ϨΝ ΟΥϬΟΜ ΝΤЄ Ι͞Ϲ ϨΝ ΟΥЄІΡΗΝ̣[Η]:

140,23   Ms. reads ΟΠΟϹΤΟλΟϹ.
140,25   One expects the text to read: ЄΠІϤΤΟΟΥ Ν̄‹ΚΑІΜΑ›, "into the four
           regions (of the earth)"; perhaps some text was accidentally omitted.

forever." Then (τότε) the apostles (ἀπόστολος)
24 parted from each other
into four words in order to
26 preach. And they went
by a power of Jesus, in peace (εἰρήνη).

140,25   ΕΠΙϤΤΟΟⲨ ΝϢⲀϪⲈ; cf. Iren., *Adv. Haer.* III.11.8 (four gospels for
the τέσσαρα κλίματα τοῦ κόσμου). On four directions, see *Acts of
Thomas* 28, conclusion to *Pistis Sophia*, *Epistula Apostolorum* 30, etc.

INDICES

WORD INDICES

Coptic, Greek, and Proper Name indices are provided for each tractate. Words in the Coptic indices are listed according to Crum's Coptic Dictionary, with a few exceptions. If the Crum spelling is not actually represented in the text, it is placed in parentheses. In general the abbreviations used are those in Crum; e.g., nouns are cited by nn, by gender m. or f. where possible and verbs are cited as vb. Some very common words such as ⲁⲩⲱ are not indexed. Greek nouns and adjectives are cited in the nominative case, verbs in the infinitive. Unless the Coptic spelling of Greek words is significantly different, it is not given. A few proper names which are also Greek words are cited in both the Greek and Proper Name indices.

COPTIC WORDS: VIII: *I*

ⲁⲗⲉ (4a) vb. 4,22.

ⲁⲗⲟⲩ (5a) nn m.,f. 2,9; 13,5; 36,6; 41,11; 44,30; 47,7; 51,21; 61,20; 125,19.
ⲡⲁⲗⲟⲩ ⲛⲧⲉ ⲡⲁⲗⲟⲩ 13, 7-8; 45,1.11; 47,8; 51,25-52,[1]; 56,25.

ⲁⲙⲟⲩ (7b) vb. 4,13.

ⲁⲙⲁϩⲧⲉ (9a) vb. 2,17-18.18; 8,8; 9,1; 52,[11-12]; 123,5; 125,23.
ⲣⲉϥⲁⲙⲁϩⲧⲉ 51,20-21; 54,[15].

ⲁⲛ (10b) neg part. 3,12; ; 5,8; 8,14; 14,7.8; 20,13; 21,15; 24,21;25,8; 26,22;
29,16; 32,19; 35,16; 43,[26]; 45,27; 46,24; 53,8; 55,25; 59,13; 67,19; 74,18;
77,10; 85,18; 103,13; 108,1; 115,2.9; 117,12.13.15; 120,6.12; 124,4; 125,23;
131,1.9.

ⲁⲛⲟⲕ (11b) pron. 1,2.9; 3,20; 4,21; 7,24.26; 13,11.14; 44,23; 63,13; 96,4;
128,19; 129,22; 130,4-5. ⲛⲧⲟⲕ (ⲛⲧⲕ) 4,9; 51,24.24.[25]; 52,[5-
6].[6].18.19.20.21; 86,13.14.16.19; 88,[16],.17.18; 118,16; 127,5.6. ⲛⲧⲟϥ
2,10; 16,4; 27,20; 37,9.10; 44,8.19; 64,22; 67,24; 117,15; 121,13; 127,15.
ⲛⲧⲟⲥ 30,1. ⲛⲧⲟⲟⲩ 11,4; 21,2; 28,6; 49,6; 85,12; 115,3; 121,8-9; 128,9.

ⲁⲛⲧⲃⲁ, see ⲧⲃⲁ.

ⲁⲡⲉ (13b) nn f. 23,9; 66,20; 74,6.

(ⲁⲣⲏϫ') nn m. ⲡⲓⲁⲣⲏϫϥ ⲛⲧⲁϥ 118,4-5, ⲛⲁⲧⲛⲁⲣⲏϫⲛ',15;
16,7; 17,[21-22]; 65,14; 118,5; 122,7; 126,6; 128,18. ⲛⲓⲁⲧ[ⲛ]ⲁⲣⲏϫⲛ'
122.12-13. ⲛⲓⲁⲣⲏϫⲛⲟⲩ 122,18.19. ⲙⲛⲧⲛⲁⲣⲏϫϥ 46,[5].

ⲁⲣⲉϩ, see ϩⲁⲣⲉϥ.

(ⲁⲥⲁⲓ) (17b) vb. ⲁⲥⲓⲏⲟⲩⲧ † 33.11.

ⲁⲧⲟ (19a) nn m. 2,11.

ⲁⲩⲱ (19b) conj. *passim*.

ⲁϣ interog pron. 3,3; 17,16; 119,2.3; 128,25. ⲉϣ 8,3.

(ⲃ̄) (27a) ⲙⲉϩⲃ 19,4.

ⲃⲱⲕ (29a) vb. 15,23; 21,19; 23,20; 24,[24]; 26,7; 33,19; 63,11; 129,1.

ⲃⲁⲗ (31b) nn f. 13,6; 30,5.

ⲃⲱⲗ (32a) vb. 48,24; 128,14; 131,10.12. ⲃⲁⲗ 131.13. ⲃⲟⲗ' 130,13.
ϩⲉⲛⲉⲃⲟⲗ nn m. 24,22. ⲁⲧⲃⲱⲗ adj. 49,3. ⲉⲃⲟⲗ *passim*. ⲛⲥⲁⲃⲟⲗ
prep. 1,27; 24,1; 44,18-19; 45,20; 76,22; 77,11; 132,3-4.

ⲃⲣⲣⲉ (43a) adj. 16,9; 27,25; 117,9.

(ⲅ̄) (49a) ⲙⲉϩⲅ̄ 7,17.

ⲉⲛⲉϩ (57a) nn m. ⲣⲱ ⲉⲛⲉϩ 1,26; 4,5; 80,20. ϣⲁ ⲉⲛⲉϩ 1,[2.][9-10];
3,30.32; 9,30; 11,6.15; 22,4; 23,20; 28,16-17; 33,[8]; 35,2; 38,5.12; 43,11;
46,7; 48,1.[10]; 50,4; 82,8; 87,7; 114,[5]; 115,[20-21]. ⲙⲛⲧϣⲁⲉⲛⲉϩ
78,14-15.16; 122,3. ⲛⲓϣⲁⲉⲛⲉϩ 23,20.

ⲉⲣⲏⲧ (58a) vb. 81,4.

ⲉⲣⲏⲩ (59a) nn m, f. 8,3.6; 14,15; 22,20; 23,4; 115,2.5.

(ЄСНТ) (60a) nn m. ЄΠЄСНТ 10,20; 27,12; 65,[10]; 83,15.

ЄТ, ЄТЄ, ЄѲ passim.

ЄТВЄ (61a) prep. 3,24.31; 4,[3]; 7,28; 8,5.10-11.11.[12-13].14.15.16.19; 9,6;
   10,19; 13,[12].20; 14,2.17; 15,2; 20,15; 24,6.12; 25, [22]; 26,19; 27,11; 28,8;
   29,27; 30,12.17.20.24.29; 36,4; 39,12; 46,4.15; 57,16.17.[19]; 58,20-21;
   60,17; 64,12; 68,20; 73,17.[20].21.23.25; 74,[2].3; 75,[1]; 81,[14]; 82,15-
   16; 94,2.9; 96,4; 122,3; 123,2.6.8; 128,10.20; 131,16. ЄТВ ННТ' 35,[15-
   16]; 39,5; 43,24.26; 46,3; 75,15; 93,5. ЄТВЄ ΠΑΪ 20,15; 28,8; 30,12.20.24;
   46,[15]; 94,2; 123,2.6.

ЄООⲨ (62a) nn m. 4,25; 5,15; 6,6.13; 11,6; 24,[18]; 46,20.22.29; 47,16; 48,23;
   51,[9].[21]; 52,[12]; 53,[13-14]; 54,9.16.17; 55,12; 56,[18]; 57,[14]; 62,[11];
   63,[9-10].[21]; 73,[13]; 86,20; 89,[14-15].15; 93,4; 115,22; 120,4.10.[13].22;
   121,[8]; 122.5.10.15.16; 123.1.3; 125.2.13.14; 129.14.

ЄШ ⲌЄ (63b) conjunct. 8,9.

ЄⲤ (70a) vb. 37,25; 55,2; 131,9.10. ЄⲤ ЄⲌ N 18,8. ЄⲤ(N)NAⲈ ⲢАЇ 57,13;
   129,2. ЄⲤ ЄВОⲖ 12.7; 24.8; 81.8; 83,16; 121,16; 124,[19]; 129.16-17.28.
   ЄⲤ ЄⲈⲢАЇ, ЄⲤ ЄⲈАⲢЇ Є' 5,24.26; 6,2; 129,23.26; 130,5. ΠⲤЄⲤ (ΠⲤ)
   9,6; 46.8; 65.13.

ЄⲤЄ (74a) conjunct. 44,[18].

ЄⲤ ⲘЄ (77b) vb. 3,14; 13,13; 20,12.12; 22,8.14.17-18; 23.2.7.16; 40,14; 41.1;
   44.6-7; 45.8.16.29; 58,20; 78.8; 80,17.21; 82.7; 83.8; 85,7; 87.15.16.19.21.22;
   88.15; 97.9; 99,5; 120,1.5; 121.19; 124.5.7; 130,16. ⲘⲘЄ 17,15; 26.6; 67.4;
   81.11. ⲘЄ 73,11; 88,16; 120,23; 129,25. ЄⲤ ⲘЄ nn m. 33,22. ⲘNTЄⲤ ⲘЄ
   (ⲘNTⲘЄ) nn f. 29,25; 30,9; 43,16; 44,26; 67.3; 75.[10-11].14.19. АТЄⲤ ⲘЄ
   (АТⲘⲘЄ) 3,32; 80,20; 81,1; 128,13.17. ⲘNTАТЄⲤ ⲘЄ 117,6-7.
   ⲢЄⲨЄⲤ ⲘЄ 58,19.

ЄⲤNЄ (78b) vb. ЄⲤNЄ ЄⲈⲢАЇ 3,15; 44,24. NT' 1,24; 130,13. NT ЄⲈОⲨN
   129,4.

ЄⲤNЄ (80b) vb. 26,4.22; 45,24; 84,19. nn m. 2,[28-29]; 17,14; 18,4; 22,13;
   26.5.8; 27.7; 38,21; 55.5; 56.13; 88,24; 129.24. ⲤNЄ 5,15.

(ЄⲤООⲢ) (82a) ⲌⲤООⲢ nn m. 16,8; 43,5.25; 61,15; 64,23.

ЄⲤⲢЄ (83a) vb. 3,26; 25,6; 28,4; 43,5.25. Ⲣ +nn, adj. 1,14; 2,5.31; 3,20.25;
   10,5.14; 27,9.27; 42,10.17; 43,6.11; 46,4; 58.20; 75,24; 76,17.18; 78,17;
   80,[19]; 81,1.20; 82,[1].7.20; 83,1.1.[22]; 93,2; 115,25; 123,21; 128,13;
   131,20; 132,4. Ⲣ + Greek 6,13; 10,13.18; 12,3.; 21,8; 28,[1].5.20.21; 25,9;
   31,13.19; 43.[7].9.19.21; 44,15.20.22; 45.12; 46.14; 58.8.24; 74,14; 78.12;
   129.14. Є† 10,17; 26,10; 47,30; 48,28; 56,8.9; 130,7. О† 130,17; 131,23.
   ⲀⲤТ' 46,9.14.

ЄⲤⲰⲢⲈ (84b) vb. 31,19-20. nn m. 29,[7].9.

(ЄⲤС) (85a) interject. ЄⲤСⲈ ННТЄ 128,14-15.

(ЇⲰС) (86a) nn m. ЇНС 4,31.

ЄＩШＴ (86b) nn m. 2,14; 4,10; 6,23; 20,8.9.11.14.[15]; 120,4; 130,[24]; 131,14. ＳШＴ 4,8.9; 13,11; 51,15. ЄＩＯＴЄ pl. 3,17.18.19; 42,24. ШＯＰП ＮЄＳШＴ 6,22-23; 20,8.

КЄ (90b) nn m, f. 7,30; 28,8; 39,10; 45,30; 113,14; 120,13; 121,23; 125,10. ＮＳＫＯＯＴＥ 17,13; 128,7-8. ０ЄＮКＯＯＴＥ 4,7; 13,23; 21,2; 25,4-5; 27,19.28; 28,1; 43,27; 45,15. Adv. 10,6; 12,18.

КＯＴＳ (92b) nn m,f. 1,23; 4,19; 131,19; 132,1. ＡＮＴＫＯＴＥＳ 3,24-25.

КШ (94b) vb. 4,[23]; 16,5; 43,20. КＡ´ 3,20; 5,[22]; 123,20; 131,1. КＡＡ´ 63,10-11; 129,1; 130,2. КН† ＮＡＡＡ´ 45,2; 54,21; 125,13. КН† ０ＩＡ Ｎ 5,2; 29,[2-3.6.8.10; 80,16; 122,[18-19]. КШ, КН† Є０ＰＡＩ 25,1; 120,1-2. КШ ０ＳШ´ 57,20.

КШＢ (98b) vb. 118.[17]; 126,1; 127,4. КНＢ† 54,13; 59.15; 122,12.

(КШК) (100b) vb. КАК´ Ａ０ＮＯＴ 24,31.

КＡКЄ (101b) nn m. 1,11.14; 5,12; 9,15.17.27; 117,[11].[26]; 132,4.

КＡＯＯＡЄ (104a) nn f. 4,23; 47,26.

КＡＯＡ (104b) nn m. 58,[25].26; 129,15. КＡＯＯＡ 57,16.19.21.

КＳＡ (108a) vb. 74,16; 79,14. nn m. 113,12. ＡＴКＳＡ 6,[27]; 48,26; 51,16.

КШＴЄ (124a) vb. 2,13; 3,19.25; 8,9; 13,15; 16,14; 45,14-15.19; 80,9; 128,20; 130,23; 131,17.25. КＯＴ´ 4,14. КШＴ ＮＣＡ, ＮＣШ´ 13,[13]; 44,2; 64,12-13; 131,17-18.

КＡ０ (131a) nn m. 4,24; 5,[18]; 8,11; 9,2; 43,8; 48,4; 55,[15]; 96,6.[15]; 113,10; 116,[10]; 130,[1].

КШ０Ｔ (133b) nn m. 42,26; 48,6; 55,17; 116,23.

ＡＳＢЄ (136b) vb. 3,31; 131,5.

ＡＡＡＴ (146a) nn used a pron. 3,[26]; 9,30; 16,10; 21,7; 24,1; 25,6.8; 59,16; 67,18; 74,18; 75,[4]; 118,2. ＡＮＡＡＡＴ 10,10; 32,22; 33,7; 40,[17]; 68,24.

(ＡШＡ０) (151a) vb. ＡＯＡК† 26,[14].

ＡＯＳＧЄ (151b) nn f. 3,[2-3]; 20,8; 91,17-18.

ＡＡ (153a) nn m. 3,21; 5,14.15.[20].28; 10,8; 11,8; 21,4.4.5.6.7; 22,16; 25,3.21; 44,12; 45,23; 46,18.22; 61,17; 65,13; 67,19; 74,17.18; 130,22. ПЄＩＡＡ (ПＳＡＡ) 4,20; 31,10 116,18. ＡＡ ＮШШПЄ 34,12. ０Ｓ ＯＴＡＡ 40,15; 59,22; 94,18; 116,2; 117,[4]; 120,21; 121,6-7; 123,15-16; 125,6; 127,10-11. (Ａ)ПＡＡ ЄＴＡＡＡＴ 117,1-2; 125,11; 129,16.

ＡЄ (156b) nn f. 1,8; 6,4; 16,16; 21,12; 29,5; 120,23. ＡＮＴＡЄ 1,8; 28,13.20; 29,8.12.14; 30,9; 43,16; 44,26; 130,9. ＮＡＡЄ 16,8. ＴＡПＡЄ, ＴＡПＡＡЄ 1,8; 24,20; 48,21; 117,10.

(ＡＯＴ) (159a) vb. ＡＯＴＴＴ† 1,17; 42,13.16.[20].[22]; 43,3.[21]. nn m. 130,13; 131,2. ＡＴＡＯＴ 27,11.[14]; 28,30; 29,19; 43,2.22-23.23; 45,17; 46,7; 47,2.5; 48,18.

ＡКＡ０ (163a) ＡＯК０† 3,23; 8,14. ＡＳ ＡКＡ０ 11,14; 48,28; 131,9. ＡＴＡＳ ＡКＡ０ 48,28.

ⲘⲘⲚ´,ⲘⲚ´(166b) vb. 33,7;40,17; 45,29; 68,24; 94,2. ⲘⲚⲧⲁˊ 25,2; 27,16; 41,14; 45,19.

ⲘⲘⲒⲚ (168b) particle+ⲘⲘⲟˊ

ⲘⲚ (169b) prep. *passim.*

ⲘⲚ (170a) conjunct. *passim.*

ⲘⲎⲚⲈ (172a) adv. 3,15.

ⲘⲡϢⲁ (179a) vb. 3,21; 4,[16-17]; 24,21; 25,13; 62,13; 129,25.

Ⲙⲟⲩⲣ (180a) vb. 131,11.

ⲘⲒⲤⲈ (184b)ⲁⲧⲘⲒⲤⲈ 2,23.29; 13,[2-3]; 18,10; 40,11; 42,6; 44,25.27; 48,25; 82,13; 114,4; 116,[14]. ⲘⲚⲧⲁⲧⲘⲒⲤⲈ 75,23; 76,9; 77,22; 84,1.8; 116,[12-13].13; 121,22; 122,5; 130,23.

ⲘⲟⲈⲒⲧ (188a) nn m. 5,[4-5]. ⲣⲉⲩϪⲒ ⲘⲟⲈⲒⲧ 47,25.

ⲘⲁⲧⲈ (189a) vb. ✝ ⲘⲁⲧⲈ 115,5. ✝ ⲘⲈⲧⲈ 124,3.

(ⲘⲁⲧⲈ) (190a) adv. ⲈⲘⲁⲧⲈ, ⲘⲘⲁⲧⲈ 3,24; 63,15; 129,1.

ⲘⲟⲩⲧⲈ (191b) vb. 13,12; 62,[17]; 83,8; 127,23. ⲘⲟⲩⲧⲈ ⲟⲩⲂⲈ 63,17-18. ⲘⲟⲩⲧⲈ ⲈϨⲣⲁⲓ 13,7.

(ⲘⲧⲟⲚ) (193b) vb. ⲘⲟⲧⲚ✝ 74,23; 118,4. nn m. 3,21; 10,8.

Ⲙⲁⲩ, ⲘⲘⲁⲩ (196b) adv. *passim.*

Ⲙⲁⲁⲩ (197a) nn f. 6,30; 29,17; 51,11.[13]; 54,16.

Ⲙⲟⲟⲩ (197b) nn m. 5,[21].23; 6,10; 15,1.3.[4].[7].10.13.20; 17,3.5.6; 18,3.7; 22,7.9; 48,5; 55,15; 113,10.

Ⲙⲁⲩⲁⲁˊ, Ⲙⲁⲩⲁⲧˊ (198b) adj. 2,8; 3,8; 20,5.14; 27,17; 28,2.7.16; 32,13; 37,10; 44,20; 45,13; 66,14; 67,5.8; 118,3; 119,22; 122,14.

ⲘⲈⲈⲩⲈ (199a) vb. 4,[8-9]; 11,14. ⲡⲧⲣⲉⲩⲘⲈⲈⲩⲈ 26,21. nn m. 21,11; 29,17; 30,3.[16]; 36,18; 98,6; 124,2.21.

ⲘⲎⲎϢⲈ (202a) nn m. 2,11; 11,13; 21,4; 45,13.24; 48,11-12.13; 108,4; 130,12.14; 131,24-25.

ⲘⲟⲟϢⲈ (203b) vb. 4,31; 130,8.

ⲘⲟⲩϢⲧ (206b) vb. 76,23; 77,15.

ⲘⲟⲩϨ (208a)vb. 97,13. ⲘⲈϨ ⲈⲂⲟⲗ,ⲘⲟⲩϨ ⲈⲂⲟⲗ (ϨⲚ)23,26; 78,21; 116,5; 122,14-15.

(ⲘⲟⲩϪϬ) (214a) vb. ⲘⲟϪϬ✝ 1,29. ⲘⲟϪⲕ✝ 2,22. ⲡⲒⲘⲟⲟⲩϪϬ 13,[15-16]. ⲁⲧⲘⲟⲩϪϬ 113,9.

Ⲛ´, ⲘⲘⲟˊ (215a) *passim.*

Ⲛ´, Ⲛⲁˊ (216a) prep. 1,2; 2,12; 3,6.29; 4,12.20; 6,13; 8,7.22; 23,3; 25,7; 37,11.12; 56,19; 57,17; 58,26; 73,6; 75,24; 124,4; 130,8.26.

Ⲛⲁ (217b) vb. 65,19.

(Ⲛⲁⲁ) (218b) vb. Ⲛⲁⲁˊ 25,18. ⲈⲚⲈⲁˊ 63,21; 65,17; 117,20.

Ⲛⲟⲩ (219b) vb. Ⲛⲟⲩ ⲈⲂⲟⲗ 37,2-3. ⲚⲎⲩ✝ ⲈⲂⲟⲗ 67,18; 93,2. ⲚⲎⲩ✝ ⲈϨⲣⲁⲓ 18,2-3; 30,10; 130,3.

ⲚⲟⲂⲈ (222a) nn m. 25,6; 27,23.28; 28,5.

ⲛⲓⲙ (225b) adj. 1,26; 5,[2]; 10,15; 14,10.10; 16,15; 21,6; 23,[23].25; 25,13; 32,[18]; 33,2.3; 44,12; 45,[6].7; 46,11.13; 47,19; 48,18.19.20; 57,22.22; 60,7.17; 64,10; 65,[8].[9].16.17.[19].20.20.22.[23]; 74,17.[25]; 76,10; 87,17; 121,10.13.13.

ⲛⲁⲛⲟⲩ' (227a) vb. 3,[1]. ⲉⲛⲁⲛⲟⲩ' 83,23. ⲉⲧⲛⲁⲛⲟⲩ' 117,7.

ⲛⲟⲩⲛⲉ (227b) nn f. 6,5.[18]; 27,15.

ⲛⲧⲉ (230a) *passim.*

ⲛⲟⲩⲧⲉ (230b) nn m. 1,7.18; 2,4.[7].22; 3,16; 4,11; 6,8.22; 7,3.11; 13,[1].5.10; 17,10; 18,[23]; 19,6.20; 20,7.11; 29,4; 30,7.[15].21; 31,[18]; 34,14.15; 35,19; 40,20; 41,9.[10-11].23; 43,11; 44,21-22.22.[24-25].31; 48,21; 51,[5-6]; 52,[23-24].24; 53,19; 54,[11].22; 55,23; 58,27; 67,6; 82,24-83,1; 83,21; 91,9; 115,26; 117,18.19.22.24; 118,6.[8]; 126,5; 127,15; 128,14.16; 130,19.19. ⲙⲛⲧⲛⲟⲩⲧⲉ 15,11.[16]; 75,15-16; 79,[15-16]; 85,14; 86,18.

ⲛⲁⲩ (233b) vb. 2,9; 4,29; 5,[23]; 6,3; 9,10.30; 10,1.[2].21; 11,14; 18,[9]; 24,2; 25,13; 26,6; 48,3; 51,20; 53,22; 55,8; 59,24.25; 61,19; 63,20; 76,11; 78,20; 80,11; 94,1; 104,8; 125,16; 129,6; 130,12. ⲁⲛⲁⲩ 130,[21]; 132,3. ⲣⲉ ⲛⲁⲩ 6,18; 31,18; 118,[7]. ⲁⲧⲛⲁⲩ 2,27; 8,23; 18,6; 19,21; 20,15-16; 44,28.29; 53,9; 61,20.[21-22]; 63,1.7; 79,18.23; 84,17-18; 97,2; 101,1; 128,21.

ⲛⲁⲩ (234b) nn m. 1,23.

ⲛϣⲟⲧ (237a) vb. ⲛⲁϣⲧ' 3,28; 46,11-12.

ⲛⲓϥⲉ (238a) nn m. 46,13; 113,13.

(ⲛⲟⲩϥⲣ) (239b) ⲛⲁϥⲣⲉ ⲛⲛ ⲙ. 43,6.

ⲛⲟⲩϩⲃ (243a) nn m. 30,11; 113,[11]; 123,4.

ⲛⲟⲩϩⲙ (243b) vb. 4,[4].7.16; 26,4; 42.18; 44.6.[14]; 45.5; 46,21.26; 73,[20-21]; 131,14. ⲛⲁϩⲙ' 131,12. ⲛⲁϩⲙⲉ' 44,1. ⲛⲟⲩϩⲙ ⲉⲃⲟⲗ ϩⲛ 4,26.

ⲛⲁϩⲧⲉ (246a) vb. 28,21-22.

ⲛⲟϭ (250a) adj. 3,32; 4,18.21.21.23; 6,6.9.12; 8,7; 9,1.7; 13,[2].4; 18,5; 32,12; 48.23; 54.8; 56.15; 56,15; 59,23; 61,16; 62,9; 63,15; 86,13.16.19; 88,14.20; 97,3; 129,5; 131,21. ⲙⲛⲧⲛⲟϭ 51,23; 78,18; 94,4; 128,11; 129,19-20.

ⲛϭⲓ (252a) *passim*

ⲟⲛ (255b) adj. 4,9.14; 18,10; 19,5.17; 22,13; 23,12; 29,1; 44,18; 46,14.14; 48,[14].27; 61,22; 82,11.[14]; 121,6; 128,20; 129,22.

ⲟⲉⲓϣ (257b) nn. ⲧⲁϣⲉ ⲟⲉⲓϣ 4,15; 130,8-9.

ⲡⲁⲓ (259a) pron. *passim.*

ⲡⲏ (260b) pron. *passim.*

ⲡⲱ' (260b) pron. 16,11; 19,8; 20,10; 26,6; 30,18; 67,12; 128,22.

(ⲡⲉⲓⲣⲉ) (267a) vb. ⲡⲓⲣⲉ ⲉϩⲣⲁⲓ 56,16. ⲡⲣⲣⲓⲟⲩ 55,18.

ⲡⲱⲣⲝ (271b) vb. 1,10. ⲡⲱⲣⲝ ⲉⲃⲟⲗ 22,18; 23,11.12-13; 68,19; 77,12. ⲡⲟⲣⲝ† ⲉⲃⲟⲗ 27,8; 115,10. ⲡⲱⲣⲝ ⲛⲥⲁⲃⲟⲗ 1,27; 44,18-19;

45,20. ⲁⲧⲡⲱⲣⲝ 37,19; 64,18; 68,22; 79,10; 87,18. ⲙⲛⲧⲁⲧⲡⲱⲣⲝ 75,13.

(ⲯⲓⲥ) (273b) nn m. ⲡⲥⲥⲉⲓⲧ 27,5.

ⲡⲱⲧ (274a) vb. 131,5; 132,3.

ⲡⲱϣ (277a) vb. 45,7; 98,3; 121,5. ⲁⲧⲡⲱϣⲉ 2,27-28; 21,10; 33,14; 101,13.

ⲡⲱϩ (280a) vb. 132,1. ⲡⲏϩ† ⲉ′ 28,9; 115,13.

(ⲡⲉⲝⲉ) (285a) vb. ⲡⲉⲝⲁ′ 3,30; 8,7; 9,1; 13,9.[15]; 45,1; 57,[17]; 62,11; 96,4; 128,19.

(ⲣⲟ) (288b) nn m. ⲕⲁⲣⲱϥ 123,20.

ⲣⲱ (290a) particle 1,25; 4,5; 8,[2].6; 80,20.

ⲣⲓⲕⲉ (291b) vb. 45,25.

ⲣⲱⲕϩ (293a) vb. 48,7; 55,19.

ⲣⲱⲙⲉ (294b) nn m. 4,12; 6,[24]; 8,[1].5.6-7; 13,11-12.24; 30,5; 42,7.20; 43,2.13.[19]; 44,1.[5]; 45,4; 48,17; 55,21; 95,3.

ⲣⲁⲛ (297b) nn m. 6,[7]; 7,2.11; 8,2; 13,19; 17,4.23; 25,22; 26,1; 51,19; 53,16; 88,14. † ⲣⲁⲛ 14,18; 92,19; 93,1; 119,3. ⲁⲧ†ⲣⲁⲛ 74,21.

ⲣⲁⲧ′ (302b) nn m. ⲁⲧⲛ ⲣⲁⲧ′ 65,15-16. ⲁϩⲉⲣⲁⲧ see ⲱϩⲉ.

ⲣⲏⲧⲉ (304b) nn m. 2,11; 7,30; 48,12.14; 93,2. ⲡⲉⲓⲣⲏⲧⲉ 2,12; 11,4; 16,4-5; 18,9-10.13; 19,5-6; 25,[23]; 26,13-14.15; 29,1; 46,2; 48,15; 94,3. ⲙⲡⲣⲏⲧⲉ 1,23; 5,7.16; 14,6.7-8; 16,[1]; 19,9; 21,15; 23,[21]; 25,25; 26,11; 28,[18]; 41,16; 44,7.[9-10]; 73,[16]; 86,[9]; 95,[14]; 107,5; 115,[18-19]; 116,9; 125,5; 129,7. ⲙⲡⲥⲣⲏⲧⲉ 3,31-32; 46,30. ⲁϣ ⲛ ⲣⲏⲧⲉ, see ⲁϣ.

ⲣⲟⲟⲩϣ (306b) nn m. 25,8; 43,4.

ⲣⲱϣⲉ (309a) vb. 25,6-7; 27,24; 30,12. nn m. 37,11.

ⲥⲁ (313a) nn m. 68,23. ⲛⲥⲁ, ⲛⲥⲱ′ 1,27; 2,13; 3,21; 8,9; 13,[13].15; 16,22; 25,4; 27,[18]; 29,29; 43,20; 44,2; 45,26; 46,20; 64,22; 76,11.19; 77,17-18; 79,8-9; 81,21; 82,18; 83,19; 114,19; 124,11; 130,18.23; 131,1. ⲛⲥⲁ ⲥⲁ ⲛⲓⲙ 16,15; 87,17. ⲙⲛⲛⲥⲁ, ⲙⲛⲛⲥⲱ′ 1,6; 12,7; 77,23; 130,3-4.

ⲥⲁ (313a) nn m. 5,3.

ⲥⲃⲱ (319b) nn f. 119,3; 120,22. ⲁⲧⲥⲃⲱ 130,7.

(ⲥⲟⲗⲥⲗ) (331a) vb. ⲥⲉⲗ ⲥⲱⲗ′ 128,13.

ⲥⲙⲏ (334b) nn f. 26,8.

(ⲥⲙⲓⲛⲉ) (337a) vb. ⲥⲉⲙⲛⲏⲩ† 65,11.

ⲥⲙⲟⲧ (340b) nn m, f. 56,22; 59,16.

ⲥⲙⲟⲩ (335a) vb. 6,21; 7,9.[16].[22]; 13,1; 51,6.19; 86,12; 88,9; 99,9; 129,9. ⲣⲉϥⲥⲙⲟⲩ 122,16; 126,18. nn m. 3,17; 44,24.

ⲥⲓⲛⲉ (343b) vb. 5,18.29; 46,30. ⲥⲓⲛⲉ ⲉⲃⲟⲗ ϩⲛ 4,13; 5,17; 8,10.

ⲥⲛⲁⲩ (346b) nn. 7,2; 46,11; 73,[15]; 84,3. ⲥⲛ̄ⲧⲉ 36,17; 82,4; 94,6; 118,22. ⲃ̄ 40,5. ⲙⲉϩⲥⲛⲁⲩ 7,7.{14}.15; 28,[26-27]; 29,6; 39,21; 43,1; 114,15;

115,[19-20]; 116,11; 118,20; 119,6; 120,2.4; 121,2; 126,9.11; 127,[25].[26].
ⲘⲈⲈ̄ 34,4. ⲘⲈⲈⲤⲚⲦⲈ 82,9-10; 84,9; 122,4; 124,2.

(ⲤⲰⲚⲈ) (348b) vb. ⲤⲞⲚⲈ † 3,22; 46,8.10.

(ⲤⲚⲀⲨⲈ) (349a) nn m. ⲤⲚⲀⲈ 131,6.10.25.

ⲤⲞⲠ (349b) nn m. 2,11; 4,[14]; 5,20.23.29; 7,10.17; 11,13; 25,12; 45,14; 53,8.[16]; 54,1. ⲘⲈⲈⲤⲞⲠ 7,2. ⲈⲤ ⲞⲨⲤⲞⲠ 17,17; 19,12; 74,[15-16].16.

ⲤⲠⲓⲢ (351b) nn m. ⲚⲤⲀ ⲤⲠⲓⲢ 46,21.

(ⲤⲰⲢⲘ) (355a) vb. ⲤⲞⲢⲘ † 130,14.

ⲤⲰⲦⲘ (363b) vb. 14,2; 24,6.13; 25,20; 26,9; 35,21; 44,[23]; 60,10.18; 62,16; 64,[11]; 128,15; 129,19; 131,19. nn m. 7,30; 26,9. ⲀⲦⲤⲰⲦⲘ 130,18.

ⲤⲰⲦⲠ (365a) vb. 1,7; 131,7. ⲤⲞⲦⲠ † 2,30; 4,8; 5,1; 14,12; 21,9; 24,9; 26,17; 130,20; 131,5. nn m. 4,17; 45,8-9; 130,4.

(ⲤⲎⲨ) (367b) nn m. ⲤⲎⲞⲨ 132,1.

ⲤⲞⲞⲨ (368b) nn m, f. 28,8. ⲘⲈⲈⲤⲞⲞⲨ 6,1.

ⲤⲞⲞⲨⲚ (369b) vb. 4,6; 121,7.10. ⲤⲞⲨⲰⲚ † 5,11; 60,[21-22]; 66,9; 81,19; 82,16; 83,21; 93,[15]; 94,[8]; 118,[9]. ⲤⲞⲨⲚ † 81,20. nn m. 1,9; 15,8; 22,16-17; 76,20; 96,1.

ⲤⲞⲞⲨⲦⲚ (371a) vb. 1,30. ⲤⲞⲨⲦⲰⲚ † 2,8.

ⲤⲀⲩⲩ (378b) nn. 5,20.

(ⲤⲞⲞⲈ) (380b) vb. ⲤⲞⲈ † 1,16; 130,26.

(ⲤⲰⲈⲦ) (381a) vb. ⲤⲀⲈⲦ † 6,13.

(ⲤⲈⲢⲀⲥ) (381b) vb. ⲤⲈⲀⲥ † 130,1. ⲤⲀⲈⲦ' 129,13.

(ⲤⲈⲓⲘⲈ) (385a) nn f. ⲘⲚⲦⲤⲈⲓⲘⲈ 1,13; 131,6.

ⲤⲀⲈⲚⲈ (385b) vb. ⲞⲨⲈⲈ ⲤⲀⲈⲚⲈ 124,4.

ⲦⲀⲈⲓⲞ (390b) vb. nn m. 123,9.

† (392a) vb. 1,19; 5,3; 9,12; 10,8; 11,8; 13,16; 14,18; 18,2; 37,11.13; 47,11.22; 56,18; 58,23.26; 60,24; 61,23; 65,16; 93,4; 108,1; 115,5; 119,3; 124,12; 130,16; 131,3.16. ⲚⲀⲀ' 3,26-27. ⲢⲈⲨ† 58,22; 121,26. † ⳞⲞⲘ, see ⳞⲞⲘ.

(ⲦⲂⲀ) (399a) nn m. ⲀⲚⲦⲂⲀ 47,14; 123,1.14; 126,1.

ⲦⲂⲂⲞ (399b) vb. 15,[20-21]; 75,23. ⲦⲞⲨⲂⲎⲨ † 61,13; 65,18; 84,21; 129,25. ⲦⲞⲨⲂⲎⲞⲨⲦ † 21,12.14; 22,[25]; 24,14-15; 27,[2-3]; 38,[19]. ⲦⲂⲂⲎⲞⲨⲦ † 10,11. ⲦⲂⲂⲞ ⲈⲂⲞⲖ 6,11. nn m. 21,20; 94,4.

ⲦⲰⲂⲈ (402a) vb. 63,15.

ⲦⲀⲔⲞ (405a) vb. 3,28; 9,12; 46,24; 48,13.16; 73,[22]. ⲦⲈⲔⲞ 116,18. ⲦⲀⲔⲚⲞⲨⲦ † 9,4-5.15; 10,[15]; 26,25. nn m. 4,5; 11,1; 114,8; 132,2.5. ⲀⲦⲦⲀⲔⲞ 116,24. ⲘⲚⲦⲀⲦⲦⲀⲔⲞ 9,6; 114,8.13.

ⲦⲈⲖⲎⲖ (410a) vb. 78,20; 129,20-21.

ⲦⲀⲘⲓⲞ (413a) vb. 10,3. nn m. 108,5.

ⲦⲀⲘⲞ (413b) vb. 45,3; 47,28.

ⲦⲚⲚⲞⲞⲨ (419b) vb. 131,15.

ⲧⲁⲛⲋⲟ (421a) vb. 24,15. ⲣⲉϥⲧⲁⲛⲋⲟ 5,6; 24,[19].

ⲧⲱⲡ (423a) nn m. 3,16; 27,7.

(ⲧⲱⲡⲉ) (423a) ϯⲡⲉ nn f. 9,8.

ⲧⲏⲣ′ (424a) adj. 2,14.21.24.[31-32].33; 3,6.18; 4,26; 5,13.23; 11,21; 12,21; 15,17; 17,12; 18,20; 19,3; 20,17.[26]; 21,3; 22,9.12.21; 23,8.10; 27,10; 28,5; 29,23; 33,9; 36,22; 37,13.24; 38,11; 41,25; 42,14.16.22; 44,16.17.19; 47,28; 48,1.7.15; 49,5; 52,15; 53,[14].22.23; 54,13.14; 55,22.25; 56,5.6.7.[13]; 59,21; 62,12.13.19; 63,10; 64,7.[15]; 65,5.21; 67,4; 73,[3].6; 74,3.19; 75,12.22.25; 77,25; 78,[4]; 79,[17]; 80,16; 81,19; 85,12.24; 86,[20]; 88,16; 91,17.[18].21; 93,1; 108,3; 113,14; 114,10.16.[16]; 115,8.20; 116,1; 117,2.4.8.25; 119,[15].16; 120,[6-7].10.13.20; 121,8.[9].11.14.15.[17].17-18.18-19; 122,6.10; 123,11; 124,1; 125,5.10.14.17; 127,6-7.10.12.14; 128,8.9.16.23; 129,6.9.18-19; 130,9.25. ⲡⲧⲏⲣϥ, ⲡⲓⲡⲧⲏⲣϥ 1,20; 9,24; 20,[2]; 21,18; 22,16.20; 25,15; 27,3; 41,6.19; 42,[5]; 64,19; 85,[19]; 98,3.4; 117,15. ⲛⲓⲡⲧⲏⲣϥ/ⲛⲓⲧⲏⲣϥ 18,22; 23,14; 67,23. ⲟⲩⲧⲏⲣϥ/ⲟⲩⲡⲧⲏⲣϥ 2,17; 65,23; 86,23-24.

(ⲧⲱⲣⲉ) (425a) nn f. ⲧⲟⲟⲧ′ 1,22; 2,24; 5,22; 10,7; 58,21; 131,3.5. ⲋⲁⲧⲟⲟⲧ′ 9,18. ⲋⲓⲧⲛ,ⲋⲓⲧⲟⲟⲧ′ 9,10; 96,15; 100,10. ⲉⲃⲟⲗ ⲋⲓⲧⲛ, ⲋⲓⲧⲟⲟⲧ′ 1,28; 4,12.25; 6,[8].11.14; 7,3-4.12.17; 10,13.29.31; 11,10; 12,4; 21,3; 24,7; 37,14; 44,15; 46,12-13.28; 53,17; 60,19; 78,17; 79,9-10; 81,24; 82,2; 83,9.14.16-17; 85,21; 87,11; 96,14; 98,3-4; 119,16; 124,7-8.10; 125,15-16.

(ⲧⲱⲧ) (438a) vb. ⲁⲧⲧⲱⲧ ⲛ ⲋⲏⲧ 131,24.

(ⲧⲟⲩ) (440b) nn. ϯⲟⲩ 18,18; 53,25. ⲙⲉⲋⲧⲟⲩ 19,11.13.14-15; 24,26; 53,15.[20-21]; 121,1.

(ⲧⲁⲟⲩⲟ) (441b) vb. ⲧⲁⲩⲉ 9,17.

ⲧⲟⲩⲛⲟⲥ (446b) vb. 130,15.18.

(ⲧⲟⲩⲋⲟ) (448b) nn m. ⲧⲟⲩⲋⲉ 25,10.

(ⲧⲱϣ) (449b) vb. ⲧⲏϣ† 24,18; 25,9; 46,16. ϯ ⲧⲟϣ 18,2

ⲧⲁϣⲟ (452b) vb. ⲧⲁϣⲟ ⲟⲉⲓϣ 4,15.

(ⲧⲱⲋ) (453b) vb. 118,2. ⲧⲉⲋ† 45,[6].

ⲧⲁⲋⲟ (455a) vb. 124,18-19; 132,2. nn m. 117,6. ⲁⲋⲉⲣⲁⲧ′ see ⲋⲉ.

ϯⲋⲉ (456b) nn m. 73,15.

ⲑⲃⲃⲓⲟ (457b) vb.. 96,3. ⲑⲉⲃⲓⲏⲟⲩ(ⲧ)† ⲑⲉⲃⲓⲏⲩ† 12,3; 28,18; 42,19; 93,3; 131,4.

ⲧⲱⲋⲙ (458b) vb. 130,25; 131,18.

ⲧⲅⲁ(ⲉ)ⲓⲟ (465b) nn m. 130,[12-13].

ⲧⲱⲅⲛ (466a) 5,10.

ⲟⲩ (467b) pron. 3,4.31; 7,28; 8,5.6.11.14; 13,[12].20; 30,18; 57,17; 85,16.19; 96,4; 131,17.

ⲟⲩⲁ (469a) nn. 5,17; 19,13; 23,16.24; 24,[31]; 25,23; 32,6; 39,10; 44,13;

45,23; 51,24.[25].25; 52,6.[6]; 64,14.19; 66,14; 73,15; 76,12.15; 79,25;
85,16.17.20; 87,17; 88,17.17; 94,5; 96,9; 105,8; 116,2.25; 118,15; 125,7.22;
129,8. ⲕⲁⲧⲁ ⲟⲩⲁ 18,15.[17].[25]; 19,11.16.18; 22,14; 25,14; 32,21;
41,17.19; 48,2; 59,17; 116,3; 117,3; 120,6; 127, 3.12.14; 129,17. ⲡⲟⲩⲁ
ⲡⲟⲩⲁ 5,21; 12,8.10; 18,11; 23,18; 43,6; 44,3; 46,19.[25-26]; 48,3; 55,[13-
14]; 115,11.[17]; 123,12-13 ⲡⲟⲩⲉⲥ 44,11. ⲧⲟⲩⲉⲥ 11,17; 59,9. ⲧⲟⲩⲉⲥ
ⲧⲟⲩⲉⲥ 11,8-9.18; 15,[2]; 21,21; 27,5; 28,10; 30,10-11.
ⲟⲩ (470a) article *passim*.
ⲟⲩⲉ (470b) vb. ⲟⲩⲣⲟⲩ⁺ 43,[16-17]; 96,3. ⲣⲥⲡⲟⲩⲉ 81,9.
ⲟⲩⲃⲉ (476a) prep. ⲉⲧⲟⲩⲃⲏ' 2,33. ⲟⲩⲉ 13,7.
ⲟⲩⲟⲉⲓⲛ (480a) nn m. 1,9; 3,[30]; 4,23.[31]; 5,[3-4].13; 6,3.32; 11,10.11.19;
29,18-19; 30,2; 32,10; 33,[15]; 46,1; 47,[30]; 48,6; 52,19.20; 55,[17];
56,[15-16]; 61,21; 74,14; 76,[6]; 81,5; 83,7; 117,10.11; 132,3.
ⲟⲩⲟⲛ (481a) vb. 33,2; 114,1.4.9.10.[12].14; 116,6; 121,13 ⲟⲩⲛ 8,3-4;
13,17; 20,22; 22,2; 25,9; 44,14; 73,18; 120,16; 127,17; 131,24. ⲟⲩⲛⲧⲉ
35,11. ⲟⲩⲛⲧⲁ', ⲉⲩⲛⲧⲁ' 5,4; 8,11-12; 18,7; 23,[3]; 27,6; 28,22; 39,17;
46,[6]; 48,11; 58,26-27; 82,18; 119,[18-19]; 125,5.
ⲟⲩⲛⲟⲩ (484b) nn f. ⲧⲛⲟⲩ 15,5; 24,11; 25,11-12; 62,17 ⲧⲉⲛⲟⲩ 4,4.
ⲟⲩⲱⲛⲣ (486a) vb. 20,23; 36,3. ⲟⲩⲟⲛⲣ⁺, ⲉⲩⲟⲛⲣ 1,25; 6,[12]; 46,23.
ⲟⲩⲱⲛⲣ ⲉⲃⲟⲗ 2,12; 3,12-13; 9,5; 10,6-7.[31]-11,[1]; 14,4.9.11; 23,1.8;
30,26; 38,22; 39,23; 54,12; 78,[13-14]; 81,24; 82,3-4.5-6; 97,14-15; 104,1;
120,9; 122,11; 127,13. nn m. 8,18; 24,8; 28,26; 29,[26]. ⲣⲛ ⲟⲩⲟⲩⲱⲛⲣ
ⲉⲃⲟⲗ 45,10. ⲛⲥⲟⲩⲟⲛⲣ ⲉⲃⲟⲗ 122,13. ⲁⲧⲟⲩⲱⲛⲣ 119,14.
ⲣⲉϥⲟⲩⲉⲛⲣ 54,21; 118,8.10; 122,10; 126,5.
(ⲟⲩⲟⲡ) (487 a) vb. ⲟⲩⲁⲁⲃ⁺ 1,29; 2,6; 4,[12-13]; 5,5; 7,13; 23,[28]; 24,5;
35,9; 58,24; 82,22; 114,5; 130,17.
ⲟⲩⲏⲣ (488b) pron. 8,6.[13-14]; 44,5.
ⲟⲩⲣⲟⲧ (490a) vb. nn m. 4,22.
ⲟⲩⲱⲧ (494a) adj. 7,4; 11,6.17; 14,5; 18,4; 21,16; 23,9; 27,20; 41,18; 56,23;
64,14; 67,10.19; 74,7; 92,14; 105,10.14; 115,7.9.14; 130,6-7. ⲙⲛⲧⲟⲩⲱⲧ
67,14; 68,26; 75,21; 79,19-20; 84,20; 86,22-23.
ⲟⲩⲱⲧⲃ (496a) vb. 25,17-18; 116,21; 130,21-22. ⲟⲩⲟⲧⲃ⁺ ⲉⲃⲟⲗ 12,9;
43,1. ⲟⲩⲟⲧⲃ⁺ ⲉⲣⲟⲩⲛ 65,[12-13] nn m. 114,7; 123,7. ⲁⲧⲟⲩⲱⲧⲃ
48,[8-9]; 114,6; 116,19; 122,9; 130,24. ⲙⲛⲧⲁⲧⲟⲩⲱⲧⲃ 11,2.
ⲟⲩⲟⲉⲓϣ (499b) nn m. 1,20; 26,29; 46,[10]. ⲟⲩⲁⲉⲓϣ 76,10.
ⲛⲟⲩⲟⲩⲟⲉⲓϣ ⲛⲓⲙ 1,26; 10,15; 23,23.
ⲟⲩⲱϣ (500a) vb. 2,13; 28,7; 44,[17-18]. ⲟⲩⲁϣ' 21,5; 52,13; 77,9. nn m.
29,4
(ⲟⲩⲱϣⲥ) (503b) vb. ⲟⲩⲱϣⲥ ⲉⲃⲟⲗ 56,20; 81,13; 83,2.
ⲟⲩⲱⲣ' (505b) 16,[2].
ⲟⲩⲍⲁⲥ (511b) nn m. 42,15.17; 46,16.25; 73,2; 83,4.5; 131,7.
ⲱⲕ (519b) vb. 1,25.

(ⲱⲕⲙ) (519b) vb. ⲟⲕⲙ[†] 3,24.

(ⲱⲗ) (521a) vb. ⲉⲗ 30,6.

ⲱⲙⲥ (523a) vb. 5,19. ✝ ⲱⲙⲥ 60,24; 61,23. ⲝⲓ ⲱⲙⲥ 6,7; 7,[2].10.16; 24,19-20; 25,12; 62,13-14.

ⲱⲛϩ (525a) vb. 17,18; 55,15.[16]; 130,4. ⲟⲛϩ[†] 1,2.7.7; 3,11; 4,16; 5,21; 6,10; 17,17; 20,1; 21,11; 30,14; 38,4; 42,13; 44,25; 45,9; 46,9; 47,10-11; 48,4.5.17; 66,25; 108,16; 115,3; 118,14.15.15; 125,6; 127,3; 130,16; 131,22. nn m. 3,11; 14,14; 15,4.14; 16,20; 17,8.20; 20,23; 29,22-23; 66,17; 68,4; 73,10; 74,11; 75,9.18; 79,13; 86,17; 90,24; 106,13; 118,14. ⲙⲛⲧⲱⲛϩ 15,5; 66,25; 85,22.

(ⲱⲡ) (526a) vb. ⲏⲡⲉ[†] 113,11.

ⲱⲣ(ⲉ)ⲃ (528a) 9,9.

(ⲱϩⲉ) (536b) vb. ⲁϩⲉ[†] 131,17. ⲟϩⲉ[†] 122,15. ⲁϩⲉⲣⲁⲧ⳿ 3,28; 6,3.19; 7,6.14.20; 12,2; 13,8-9; 16,12-13; 27,9.21-22; 31,14.21; 32,2.9; 45,21; 46,20; 47,12; 53,20; 63,11-12.[14]; 65,12; 74,15; 78,15.19; 81,12; 82,15; 84,10; 97,16-17; 105,[1]; 114,[14-15].22; 115,12; 116,7.15.22; 117,1; 125,17-18; 127,16.

(ⲱϫⲛ) (539a) vb. ⲁⲧⲱϫⲛ 33,10.

ϣⲁ (541a) ϣⲁ ⲉⲛⲉϩ, see ⲉⲛⲉϩ.

ϣⲓ (547b) vb. nn m. 6,7. ⲁⲧ✝ϣⲓ 32,11; 62,22; 64,17.

ϣⲱⲓ (550a) nn m. 29,29.

ϣⲥⲃⲉ (551a) vb. 5,9. ϣⲉⲃⲓⲱ[†], ϣⲉⲃⲓⲏⲟⲩⲧ[†] 3,7; 8,2-3.4.5; 10,9; 13,[19-20].[25-26]; 26,21-22; 27,8; 115,21. nn m. 30,27; 49,2; 116,22.

ϣⲃⲏⲣ (553a) nn. ϣⲃⲏⲣ ⲛ ϣⲱⲡⲉ 27,9-10; 43,12. ⲙⲛⲧϣⲃⲏⲣ 22,[19]; 23,4; 116,4.

ϣⲱⲗϩ (562a) vb. 39,6. nn m. 106,3.

ϣⲙⲙⲟ (565b) nn. 1,21-22; 45,22.

ϣⲙⲟⲩⲛ (566b) nn. 127,4.

(ϣⲟⲙⲛⲧ) (566b) nn. ⲡⲓϣⲙⲧ⳿ 125,19. ϣⲟⲙⲧ 14,2-3; 27,13; 74,15; 118,16.[16-17].17; 125,18; 130,2. ⲡⲓϣⲙⲧⲅⲟⲙ, see ⲅⲟⲙ. ⲙⲉϩϣⲟⲙⲧⲉ 7,[8].10; 25,18-19; 28,10-11; 29,8-9; 40,12; 84,2; 118,19; 119,8; 120,[10-11].15; 126,12-13.15; 128,1.2. ⲡⲓϣⲙⲧϩⲟⲟⲩⲧ, see ϩⲟⲟⲩⲧ. ⲛⲓϣⲙⲧⲅⲉⲛⲟⲥ 57,24; 83,10-11. ⲅ 2,28; 7,14. ⲙⲉϩⲅ 34,6.

ϣⲏⲛ (568b) nn m. 48,12; 55,20; 113,4.24.[25].

ϣⲓⲛⲉ (569a) vb. 7,22; 16,13; 45,26; 129,18. nn m. 43,5.25.

ϣⲱⲡ (574b) vb. 22,3; 26,12.13; 29,20. ⲣⲉϥϣⲱⲡ 68,3.

ϣⲱⲡⲉ (577b) vb. 1,5.28; 2,32; 3,[7]; 5,16; 6,[17]; 7,5.13.18; 9,3; 10,13; 11,12; 12,9; 16,6.9.[23]; 17,10-11.21; 25,15; 26,15; 30,13; 31,17; 35,6; 44,12.16.21; 45,14.21.23.26; 46,1; 49,10; 53,19; 59,[14].15; 61,14; 62,15; 66,[23]; 67,22; 79,19; 81,9.22.23; 82,9.18.22; 83,13.23; 91,24; 96,5; 116,15; 121,20; 122,1.2; 123,5.16; 124,5; 128,12; 129,12. ϣⲟⲟⲡ[†] 2,25.26.31;

3,6.8.12.13; 4,27; 5,6.8.11-12.[24-25].27; 6,4.9.15; 11,3.7.11; 12,6.[12].14-
15.17.20; 15,[13]; 16,1.6.18; 17,1.3; 18,1.11.[16]; 19,1.10.12-13.17.28;
20,6; 21,1.13.15-16; 22,13; 23,3; 24,11.17; 25,23.27; 26,1.[3].3; 27,1;
28,3.14.18-19.23.24; 29,1.13.15.28.28-29; 30,19.[20]; 31,11; 33,16; 35,20;
36,4; 37,[5]; 38,7.10.[14].[15]; 39,[9-10].[14].16.18; 40,15; 41,[7-8]; 42,19;
43,3.13.18.[22]; 44,8.10; 45,27; 46,[17].31; 47,29; 48,22; 52,3; 53,24;
55,22; 56,4.23; 57,23; 59,[11].22; 60,8; 61,12.14; 64,15.16.[19-20]; 66,1.[7-
8].[11].13.19.24; 67,11.[12-13].15.24; 68,7.[8].9.12.13.[15-16].20.21.24-
25; 73,[9-10].17; 74,5.22; 75,8.12.24; 76,12.21-22.24; 77,15; 78,8; 79,25;
80,[6].7.12.15.17.[21]; 81,[6].15.16.{17}.{18}.20-21.22.{23}; 82,1.14;
83,[1].17.19.22; 84,12.22; 90,9; 92,[17].[18]; 94,[18]; 96,17; 97,5; 102,1;
103,2.3; 105,5.[16]; 106,1; 107,4; 108,2; 113,5.8.15.17; 114,3.11.[16-
17].18.24; 115,4.6.[7].8 .12.23.[25]; 116,1.2.6.8.11.[11-12].[13-14].20;
117,3.12.13.[14-15]; 118,6-7; 119,12.[14].17.19; 120,7-8.16.[21]; 121,4.6.8;
122,20; 123,15.17; 124,14.15; 125,6.11.12.24; 126,2.7; 127,10.11.20;
128,8.22.24; 129,7. nn.m. 16,4; 17,3; 25,3; 27,10; 41,17; 124,12. ⲉϢⲱⲡⲉ
11,9; 18,8; 22,7-8.10; 23,6.7.15; 24,30; 31,12.[17-18].[23-24]; 35,3-4;
43,14.20; 44,17; 45,12; 46,15; 58,23; 73,5.[12].[14].22; 93,3-4.[5]; 121,19;
123,3. ⲁⲧϢⲱⲡⲉ 117,14. Ϣⲃⲏⲣ ⲛϢⲱⲡⲉ, see Ϣⲃⲏⲣ.

Ϣⲡⲏⲣⲉ (581a) nn m. ⲣ Ϣⲡⲏⲣⲉ 26,20.

Ϣⲏⲣⲉ (584a) nn m. 6,26; 7,8; 13,10; 16,[12]; 30,9; 51,[14]; 52,23.

(Ϣⲱⲣⲡ) (586b) vb. Ϣⲟⲣⲡ⁺ 42,18(?). nn m., often as adj. before nouns.
3,18; 6,[22].24; 10,11; 17,56; 18,12; 19,7; 20,6.8.11.16-17; 24,12; 29,3;
34,18; 43,25; 60,13; 61,7; 65,7; 77,21.22.25; 79,7; 80,15.17; 84,11.15;
85,11; 88,[20]; 91,13; 97,[4]; 107,6.8; 115,19; 118,18; 119,4.20; 120,2;
121,1; 122,2; 124,2; 126,2.4; 127,19.21. ⲛϢⲟⲣⲡ 14,3; 114,14. ⲣ
Ϣⲟⲣⲡ, ⲣ Ϣⲣⲡ 2,31; 20,6.11; 37,7; 58,20; 74,[4]; 75,24; 82,17.20;
83,1.7.22; 115,25; 123,21.

Ϣⲱⲱⲧ (590b) vb. 39,12. Ϣⲱⲧ 33,12. nn m. 45,18.

Ϣⲧⲟⲣⲧⲣ (597b) vb. 4,30.

(ϢⲱϢ) (606a) vb. ϢⲏϢ 125,1.

ϢϢⲉ (607b) vb. 60,16.

Ϣⲁⲝⲛⲓ (608a) vb. intr. 11,5; 42,15; 43,30.

Ϣⲁⲝⲉ (612b) vb. 22,[2]; 35,16; 94,9. nn m. 1,1; 5,7.10; 9,4.28; 16,21;
17,5.9; 25,28; 26,16; 28,13; 29,14.24.26; 30,8.21-22.[23-24]; 36,5; 38,8;
44,9; 53,4; 66,[20-21]; 120,12. ⲁⲧϢⲁⲝⲉ 5,2-3; 28,13-14; 29,25; 46,4;
74,20; 77,19; 122,7-8; 124,17; 126,10.

Ϣⲟⲝⲛⲉ (615b) vb. 3,14; 57,16.18.

Ϣⲱⲝⲡ (616b) vb. ⲛⲓⲕⲉϢⲱⲝⲡ 10,14; 12,18; 77,24; 113,14; 125,10.

ϥⲓ (620a) vb. 10,7; 25,7; 43,4.

ϥⲧⲟⲟⲩ (625a) nn. 5,[29]; 6,27-29; 18,14-15; 19,10.14; 27,3; 28,17; 29,2.13;

51,17; 54,17-18; 56,[19]; 57,12; 115,15.24; 119,19; 120,16.[23]; 121,4; 125,9; 127,4.17.   ⲙⲉϩⲧⲟⲟⲩ 6,20; 7,20; 28,29; 29,11; 113,14-15.16; 114,23; 119,10; 120,8.18; 124,19-20; 126,17.[19-20]; 128,4.5.   ⲙⲉϩⲁ 7,17.

ϩⲁ   (634b) prep. 29,12; 23,4; 68,25; 127,5; 130,19; 131,4.

ϩⲁⲉ   (635a) nn m. ⲣϩⲁⲉ 42,17; 76,17.18.

ϩⲉ   (637a) vb. ϩⲉ ⲉϩⲣⲁⲓ 45,28.

ϩⲉ   (638b) nn. 84,4.

ϩⲏ   (640b) nn m. 46,8. ϩⲁⲧ', ϩⲏⲧ' 5,5; 47,25. ϩⲁ ⲧⲉⲩⲉϩⲏ 127,6. ϩⲁⲑⲏ 4,30; 64,15; 113,5.

ϩⲓ, ϩⲓⲱ(ⲱ)'   (643b) prep. 17,17; 57,8.20.24; 74,16; 94,18; 120,21; 121,6; 123,15; 124,8.10; 125,6.16; 127,10; 130,7.

ϩⲓⲏ   (646a) nn f. 4,30. †ϩⲓⲏ 19,4; 21,[19]; 25,10. ϩⲓⲏ ⲛⲉⲓ ⲉⲃⲟⲗ 12,7.

ϩⲟ   (646b) nn m. 10,17. ⲛⲁϩⲣⲛ, ⲛⲁϩⲣⲁ' 47,12; 63,12; 78,15-16; 125,18; 129,2. ϩⲁⲗϩⲟ, see ϩⲁⲗ.

ϩⲱⲱ', ϩⲱ'   (651b) pron. 44,9; 45,19; 77,9-10; 81,13; 115,3.

ϩⲱⲃ, ϩⲃⲏⲩⲉ   (653a) nn m. 1,22; 9,11; 25,4; 27,18; 43,17.27; 47,19; 64,10; 121,10. ⲣ ϩⲱⲃ 1,14; 10,5.14.

ϩⲱⲃⲥ   (658b) vb. 64,6.

(ϩⲁⲗ)   (664b) nn. ⲣ ϩⲁⲗ 131,20; 132,4. ϩⲁⲗϩⲟ 10,17.

ϩⲛ, ⲛϩⲏⲧ'   (683a) prep. 1,5.8.12.14.17.19; 2,3.6.15.[15].25.27; 3,11.13.22; 4,5.13.21.[26].28; 5,8.15.17; 6,13; 7,29.30; 8,6.18; 9,3.8; 10,4.10; 11,2.11.11-12.13.[16]; 12,1.6.10.13.20; 15,6.9; 16,2; 17,20; 18,26; 19,13; 21,2.16; 22,13; 23,8.27; 24,2.3.4.8.11.15; 25,10.12.26; 26,3.5.8.9.[16].20; 28,10.14; 30,1; 32,[28]; 33,16; 36,10.20.25; 37,1; 38,9.10.[13].14; 42,9.12; 43,3.13.28; 44,12; 45,10.28; 46,18; 47,[18].29; 48,[22]; 51,1; 58,9.25; 60,14.22; 62,14; 64,2.[16].20; 68,7.8.12; 73,8.10.19; 74,24; 75,8.9.13; 76,24; 78,10.16; 79,11.20; 80,7.9; 89,13.17; 94,6; 96,1; 97,5.[18]; 99,3; 103,4; 105,5; 108,2.12.21; 113,8.[16].17; 114,3.[11].13.[15].[18]; 115,1.4.10; 116,7.8.10.11.12; 117,21; 120,8; 123,17; 124,15; 125,2.2.11.24; 126,3; 127,6.20; 128,8; 129,14; 131,2. ⲉⲃⲟⲗ ϩⲛ 6,4; 9,5-6; 12,[15]; 13,[23]; 14,4.8.[11].16.[22]; 16,16; 17,[14]; 24,22.26; 25,15-16; 26,15-16.24-25; 30,16; 32,14; 36,19; 37,3.4; 38,9; 52,18.19-20.21.22; 54,[5]; 56,13.17; 77,19; 78,14.21; 81,[15-16].17; 93,2-3; 114,[17]; 115,6; 116,21; 124,[19]. ϩⲣⲁⲓ ϩⲛ, ⲛϩⲣⲁⲓ ϩⲛ 1,11; 10,3.10.12; 17,18; 21,1.3-4.6.7; 22,[19-20]; 24,10.11-12; 26,5; 27,[4]; 30,2.3; 41,15; 44,9.26; 45,21-22; 46,[8].11.15.18; 56,21; 60,12; 61,[21].23; 63,16; 66,8.[18].[24]; 67,9.[11-12].16.17-18.22; 68,3-4; 74,17.[17-18]; 76,[2].[8].14; 84,16.18-19.19-20; 85,16; 87,23; 92,16; 94,3; 114,[6-7].[8]; 115,4.8-9.[23-24]; 116,1-2.4; 118,3.4.14; 119,17; 120,15.16-17; 121,[23-24]; 123,3.15; 124,3.7; 125,4.7.8.22; 126,7; 127,7.16.18; 129,8; 132,[1].

ϩⲟⲩⲛ (685b) nn m. ⲉϩⲟⲩⲛ 25,10-11; 26,7; 61,[16]; 65,10.11.13.19; 129,4.

(ϩⲛⲉ) (690a) suffix vb. ϩⲛⲁⲥ 21,5.

ϩⲁⲡ (693b) nn m. ϯ ϩⲁⲡ 9,12; 11,8. ⲣⲉϥϯϩⲁⲡ 47,22; 96,5-6.

ϩⲣⲁⲓ (698a) nn m. 1,17; 4,1; 10,10; 13,1; 17,18; 46,15; 57,13; 67,22. ⲥⲁϩⲣⲁⲓ 13,1. ⲉϩⲣⲁⲓ 1,17; 3,15.28; 4,1; 5,24; 6,[2]; 12,11.14.[16]; 18,3; 19,4; 21,20.22; 23,21.23; 24,18; 30,10; 31,10; 32,8; 45,28; 46,3.16.26; 105,3; 129,23.26.[28]. ⲛϩⲣⲁⲓ 1,11; 10,2-3.12; 21,7; 40,10; 41,6; 43,16; 49,8; 59,12; 63,14; 67,1.9.17; 104,[20]; 107,[1]; 115,3-4; 118,3; 123,2.14-15; 124,7; 127,18.

(ϩⲁⲣⲉϩ) (707b) vb. ⲁⲣⲉϩ 4,24; 24,21. ⲣⲉϥⲁⲣⲉϩ 47,1.15.

ϩⲏⲧ (714a) nn m. 1,25; 3,23.25; 4,[22]; 10,22; 131,24.

ϩⲱⲧⲡ (724b) vb. 22,11; 23,12.[14]; 29,5; 80,10; 129,8-9. ϩⲟⲧⲡ⁺ 23,10; 32,1; 115,7-8; 117,3.

ϩⲟⲟⲩ (731a) vb. 46,13.

(ϩⲓⲟⲩⲉ) (732b) vb. ϩⲓ ⲧⲟⲟⲧ 1,22.

ϩⲟⲩⲟ (735a) nn m. 5,2; 10,19; 14,12.19; 21,[13].14; 24,9; 42,18-19; 55,10.12; 65,15; 81,8; 83,16; 123,10.

ϩⲟⲩⲉⲓⲧ (738a) nn. 6,19; 7,21.

ϩⲟⲟⲩⲧ (738b) 2,[13-14]; 7,6; 13,4; 18,6.21; 19,[18].[22]; 36,[6]; 40,[7-8]; 41,12.20-21; 44,28.30; 52,[10]; 54,15; 57,14; 83,11; 84,[5]; 97,1; 124,22; 125,14-15; 127,9; 129,5. ⲙⲛⲧϩⲟⲟⲩⲧ 131,8. ϣⲙⲧϩⲟⲟⲩⲧ 18,23-24; 24,4; 39,13; 41,12; 44,30; 51,22; 52,16; 53,13; 56,12-18; 61,17-18.

(ϩⲟⲝϩⲝ) (743b) vb ϩⲟⲝϩⲉⲝ⁺ 115,2.

ⲝⲉ (746b) conj. after verbs 4,9.10; 5,12; 23,2.7; 26,21; 83,9. Direct statement or question 2,25; 3,3.31; 8,9.11.13; 9,2; 13,9; 14,1; 22,2; 26,4; 29,28; 30,18-19.20; 44,4; 45,5.7.12; 51,24; 57,17; 62,12; 64,11; 85,17; 86,13.16; 96,4; 118,13; 128,18; 130,16. Explicative 4,18.19; 30,7; 46,24; 76,18.19; 77,24; 80,14; 83,22; 115,8; 126,4. Final 4,4.7.15; 9,7; 16,6; 18,13; 37,16.21; 46,21; 59,13; 81,8; 82,17; 83,14.15.20; 119,15; 123,16; 126,5; 131,13.

ⲝⲓ (747b) vb. 5,4.14.15.25.28; 6,7; 7,[2].[10].16; 9,8; 11,10; 12,5; 13,18; 15,6.9; 16,17; 24,19; 25,12; 26,8; 27,15; 44,11; 46,1.26.27.28; 48,28; 50,7; 55,13; 61,8.10.11.13; 62,[13].[14]; 68,16.17; 73,12.14.16.23; 74,25; 94,2; 96,2.[6]; 116,10; 117,11; 119,15; 123,9; 124,[9]; 129,13.15.22.24; 130,26. ⲝⲓⲙⲕⲁϩ 42,23; 96,15. ⲙⲛⲧⲁⲧⲝⲓ ⲙⲕⲁϩ 11,13-14. ⲣⲉϥⲝⲓ 47,25. ⲝⲓⲟⲟⲣ, see ⲉⲓⲟⲟⲣ. ⲝⲓ ϭⲟⲙ, see ϭⲟⲙ.

ⲝⲱ (754a) vb. 3,17; 14,1; 51,23; 64,10; 86,15; 118,13; 130,15. ⲝⲟ 7,23; 60,24. ⲝⲟⲟⲥ 4,20; 26,9; 45,9; 47,27; 52,25; 63,[9]; 86,12; 128,27.

(ⲝⲱⲥ) (756a) nn m. ⲉⲝⲛ 9,10; 18,8-9; 47,10. ϩⲓⲝⲛ 2,8; 4,24; 5,12; 6,[9].15.19; 7,6-7.14.[20]; 16,5; 27,[22]; 29,3.6.8.10; 31,14.21; 32,9; 33,1-2; 53,20; 61,12; 63,14; 82,15; 122,19. ⲉⲃⲟⲗ ϩⲓⲝⲛ 27,15. ⲉϩⲣⲁⲓ ϩⲓⲁⲛ 24,18-19; 32,8; 46,16.

ϫⲱⲕ (761a) vb. 13,16; 18,13; 93,20. ϫⲏⲕ† 98,2. ϫⲱⲕ ⲉⲃⲟⲗ 22,6; 113,18. ϫⲏⲕ† ⲉⲃⲟⲗ 19,15; 48,2; 116,3; 117,[9]; 123,3.11.

ϫⲱⲕⲙ (763a) vb. 17,4; 22,22; 23,5.16; 25,20; 53,15.25; 131,2. nn. 22,[22]; 23,5.[17]; 24,29; 25,9.19; 62,[12]. nn m. ϫⲓ ϫⲱⲕⲙ 13,18; 15,6.[9].

ϫⲉⲕⲁⲁⲥ (764a) 45,8.

ϫⲡⲟ (778b) vb. 9,15; 27,17; 52,11. nn m. 1,24; 46,3; 48,25; 77,17; 114,3. adj. 9,4; 20,5; 114,2.

ϫⲓⲟⲟⲣ see ⲉⲓⲟⲟⲣ.

ϫⲱⲱⲣⲉ (782a) vb. ϫⲟⲟⲣ† ⲉⲃⲟⲗ 88,15; 115,1. nn. 45,4.

(ϫⲓⲥⲉ) (788b) vb. ϫⲟⲥⲉ† 2,7; 13,5; 19,4; 20,3; 34,15; 60,20; 65,15; 125,3. nn m. 4,8; 8,8; 9,[2].

(ϫⲟⲟⲩ) (793a) vb. ϫⲉⲩ 45,2.

ϫⲱϣ, see ϭⲱϣ.

ϫⲱϩ (797a) vb. 63,22.

ϭⲉ (802a) Particle 24,14; 34,11; 45,24. Adv. 1,14; 62,17.

(ϭⲱ) (803a) vb. ϭⲉⲉⲧ† 118,2; 128,9.

(ϭⲟ(ⲉ)ⲥⲗⲉ) (807b) vb. ϭⲁⲗⲏⲟⲩⲧ† 25,5; 42,11.

ϭⲱⲗⲡ (812a) vb. ϭⲱⲗⲡ ⲉⲃⲟⲗ 62,[23]; 64,[9].

ϭⲟⲙ (815b) nn f. 1,19; 2,23; 3,10.13; 5,4.11; 6,9.15; 7,4.12.12.18.18.29; 8,2; 9,28; 11,5.9; 12,1; 13,17; 14,7.9.10; 15,14; 17,1; 18,3; 20,13; 21,11; 24,7.14; 25,3.16; 27,16; 28,15; 29,7; 32,9.15; 34,[5]; 37,1.4; 41,5.24; 44,5; 45,3.[29]; 46,6.17.24.28; 48,29.29; 53,18.18; 55,24; 58,17; 59,1; 60,14; 63,21; 65,9.21; 66,15; 74,13; 77,19-21; 78,11; 80,10; 85,15; 86,8; 91,14; 100,11; 113,15.18.19; 115,10.[18]; 116,16; 121,12.17; 124,13; 125,2; 128,12; 131,16. ⲁⲧϭⲟⲙ 26,10. ⲙⲛⲧϭⲟⲙ 15,18. ϣⲙ(ⲛ)ⲧϭⲟⲙ 17,7; 20,16; 24,12-13; 38,13; 63,8; 79,[21-22]; 80,18; 87,13; 97,2; 118,11-12; 123,[18-19]; 124,3-4; 128,20. † ϭⲟⲙ 1,31; 4,17; 14,10; 57,21; 58,[12]; 118,9; 130,8.12. ϣϭⲟⲙ 22,2; 32,16.17; 44,[14]; 73,4; 94,2. ϫⲓϭⲟⲙ 50,7; 61,8; 68,17; 96,2; 119,15; 129,13.22. ϭⲙ ϭⲟⲙ 2,6; 26,12; 62,8; 63,22; 83,20-21; 94,1; 123,4.

ϭⲟⲛⲥ (822a) nn. 131,1.

ϭⲉⲡⲏ (825a) vb. 43,24.

ϭⲏⲡⲉ (825b) nn f. 4,31; 47,26.

ϭⲱⲣϭ (831a) nn. 29,12; 53,21.

ϭⲟⲧ (833a) nn f. 1,6; 36,7.

(ϭⲱϣ) (836b) nn m. ϫⲱϣ 113,8.

ϭⲱϣⲧ (837a) vb. 9,16. ϭⲱϣⲧ ⲉⲡⲉⲥⲏⲧ 27,12.

(ϭⲱⲱϫⲉ) (841a) vb. ϭⲱϫⲉ 46,12.

ϭⲓⲛⲉ (820a) vb. 1,15; 3,19; 43,15; 44,3; 66,22. ϭⲙ ϭⲟⲙ, see ϭⲟⲙ.

ϭⲉⲉⲧ, see ϭⲱ.

Greek Words: VIII, I

ἀγαθός 117,16.17. ⲙ̄ⲛ̄ⲧⲁⲅⲁⲑ ⲟⲥ 75,19-20; 124,9-10.

ἀγάπη 36,13.

ἀγαπᾶν ⲁⲅⲁⲡⲁ 28,20; 31,13.

ἄγγελος 3,29; 4,11.28; 6,6.18; 7,5.13.[19]; 13,9-10; 19,8; 28,19; 34,19.25; 35,[7].8; 47,25; 48,22; 51,13; 55,24-25; 95,1-2; 113,1.[21].22; 128,18. ⲙ̄ⲛ̄ⲧⲁⲅⲅⲉⲗⲟⲥ 30,30; 130,10.

ἀγών 4,18.

ἀήρ 5,18; 8,11; 9,3; 48,[5]; 55,16; 113,9; 130,1.

αἰσθάνεσθαι ⲉⲥⲑⲁⲛⲉⲥⲑⲉ 43,7.

αἴσθησις ⲉⲥⲑ ⲏ ⲥ ⲓ ⲥ 2,15; 9,8; 26,16; 48,26; 95,[8]; 98,[9]; 129,[26].

αἰσθητός ⲉⲥⲑ ⲏⲧⲟⲛ 1,19; 3,22; 26,10; 32,19; 42,12; 86,[10]; 95,[14]; 130,6.

αἰτεῖν ⲁⲓⲧⲓ 3,20; 58,8.

αἰών ⲉⲱ ⲛ 2,26; 4,[18].27; 5,19.22; 6,20; 7,7.[15].21; 8,13; 9,29; 11,3; 12,8.22; 13,2; 14,5-6; 18,14.18; 19,8.11-12; 22,1.14; 24,28; 25,18; 28,8; 29,3; 31,12.15; 32,12; 34,11.23; 35,10; 46,19-20.31; 47,30; 48,4; 50,5; 53,21; 55,9.14; 56,14.17.20.21; 59,20; 61,16-17; 62,20; 76,7; 77,25; 78,9; 88,18-19.19; 89,21; 105,2; 113,16; 114,23; 115,9.11-12.14.16.17.24; 116,5; 118,10; 120,3.[8].[15].[23]; 121,14,21,23; 122,2; 123,13.14.16; 124,11.14; 125,4.7.8; 126,2.8.9.13.[17-18]; 127,17.18.[20].[25]; 129,10.23.27; 131,21.22.

ἀλλά 1,26; 16,3.8; 17,15; 29,16; 32,20; 33,23; 37,3; 38,18; 42,18; 43,27; 44,8; 78,13.23; 80,21; 82,[21]; 83,19; 85,18; 91,25; 92,25; 96,12; 115,3; 118,2; 120,6; 124,13; 131,9.

ἀνάγκη 1,24; 21,18.

ἀντίτυπος 5,18-19; 8,13; 11,2-3; 12,4.10-11.13.15-16.[21-22]; 24,27; 31,6; 129,27.

ἀόρατος ⲁⲟⲣⲁⲧⲟⲛ 17,12-13; 20,17-18; 24,9.13; 34,20; 36,[8-9]; 57,25; 58,[16-17]; 80,18-19; 84,14; 87,[14]; 97,[5-6]; 118,11; 122,4; 123,19; 129,11.

ἁπλοῦς ⲣⲁⲡⲗⲟⲩⲛ 3,7; 23,22.[25]; 30,[26]; 39,[7]; 44,[12-13]; 48,8.9-10; 50,2; 59,14.[18]; 66,20; 67,20; 74,6; 76,13; 77,[3]; 79,17-22; 82,23; 83,3.20; 93,9; 113,6.7. ⲙ̄ⲛ̄ⲧⲣⲁⲡⲗⲟⲩⲥ 84,17; 87,11-12; 124,8.

ἁπλῶς 75,22.

ἄρχειν ⲁⲣⲭⲓ 46,14; 78,12.

ἀρχή 2,30; 3,4; 9,14; 14,4.5.7.8.9-10; 20,6; 23,6; 36,12; 41,[23-24]; 45,17; 103,1; 105,9; 113,7; 115,6; 121,18.

ἄρχων 4,29-30; 9,12; 10,17; 19,7; 35,13; 130,11.

αὐτογενής 2,28; 6,5.8.[21-22].24; 7,3.11; 12,16.[17]; 15,6; 17,7; 18,19; 19,6; 20,7; 22,7.22-23; 24,3; 25,11.16; 28,25; 29,21-22; 30,5-6.7.15.21; 33,[18-19]; 34,[16].[17]; 35,[11].[19].22; 41,[9-10].[10]; 44,31; 46,18-19; 47,29; 53,16-17.23; 56,15; 58,14; 125,20; 127,15.19; 129,23-24.

αὐτογενιός ⲀⲨⲦⲞⲄⲈⲚⲒⲞⲚ 18,14; 28,12.

βοηθός 46,29; 47,18.

γάρ 3,19; 4,31; 10,15; 14,3; 17,9.12; 18,14 20.22; 19,9.19; 20,13; 21,9; 27,13; 28,3; 37,15; 39,8; 43,[5].28; 44,13.21; 45,19; 48,29; 50,10; 55,8.25; 59,25; 66,15; 67,6.11; 68,24; 73,7; 77,13; 82,16; 94,16; 95,17; 96,7; 97,8; 115,11; 116,12; 117,21; 121,4; 130,12; 131,19. καὶ γάρ 95,13; 123,12.

γνῶσις 29; 17,[14]; 24,20; 25,[1].7.14; 27,24; 28,15.28; 29,10.15.20; 30,6.11.22.23; 39,15-16; 40,6; 41,8.15.18; 45,15; 62,21; 76,21; 82,10.11.12; 83,12; 84,15; 97,1.15-16; 117,5.5; 118,[10-11].23; 123,22; 124,1.18; 128,10; 129,20; 130,3.

γενεά 4,[15]; 6,[27]; 51,[16].

γένος 2,16; 3,16; 4,[9]; 7,5.{5-6}; 19,2; 20,2; 23,15; 24,23; 26,5; 31,20; 57,12.24; 65,22; 83,[10-11]; 85,14; 114,10-11; 118,1; 126,19.

γυμνάζειν ⲄⲨⲘⲚⲀϨⲈ 12,3.

δαίμων 43,12; 113,1-2.

δέ passim.

διαφορά 19,3; 26,19; 27,26-27; 28,18; 35,15; 94,[25]-95,1.2-3.4; 115,[15-16]; 125,9; 127,17.

εἶδος 2,16; 3,9; 9,22; 18,12; 19,2; 23,15; 27,[3].6.13.19; 28,3.19; 39,29; 40,5; 41,13; 48,17.19; 54,14; 65,22; 66,21; 84,22; 85,15; 101,5; 117,22; 120,12-13.20.

εἴδωλον 10,1.2.4.4-5.6.11; 26,14; 76,25; 107,6.

εἰκών ⲈⲒⲔⲰⲚ 10,16; 79,24; 80,8; 97,3; 125,1.

εἰ μήτι 45,30; 67,7; 68,[25].

ἐλπίς ⲈⲖⲠⲒⳞ 28,21; 31,19.

ἐνάς ⲈⲚⲚⲀⳟ 67,[14-15]; 75,20; 84,19; 85,20; 98,[1].2.

ἐνέργεια 16,19; 68,5.15; 74,10-11; 78,10; 79,11-12.21; 85,13.21; 86,17; 87,20; 88,22; 127,9.13-14. ⲀⲦⲈⲚⲈⲣⲄⲒⲀ 124,16.

ἐνεργεῖν ⲈⲚⲈⲣⲄⳞ 74,19-20; 85,10.

ἔννοια 2,15; 16,3; 20,17; 24,10.12; 52,22.22-23; 60,12.13.19; 63,17; 65,8.19-20; 101,17.

ἐπειδή 60,14; 81,15; 127,11.

ἐπιθυμεῖν ⲈⲠⲒⲐⲨⲘⳞ 43,21-22.

ἐπιθυμία 1,13.

ἐπιστήμη 119,2-3; 120,14.

ἐρῆμος 3,27.

ἔτι yet 128,[19].

ζῷον 48,[9]; 113,3.23.24; 117,2.

ἤ 2,33; 3,4.5.11; 4,10; 8,2.6.10.12.14.15.27; 17.16; 21,18.18; 28,6.6; 30,19; 32,16; 73,15; 96,[6]; 116,10; 119,3;.128,26.

ἤδη 10,12.

θηρίον 3,27.

ἰδέα **ΕΙΔΕΑ** 11,5; 67,13.13; 68,14; 74,9.

ἵνα **ϩΙΝΑ** 4,[6].15; 9,7; 16,6; 18,13; 37,16.21; 46,21; 58,22; 59,13; 81,7; 82,17; 119,15; 123,3.15; 124,5; 131,13.

καθολικός **ΚΑΘΟⲖΙΚΟΝ** 22,5-6.

κακία **ΑΤΚΑΤΙΑ** 1,30; 130,20.

κακῶς 43,18.

καλυπτός **ΚⲀⲤ** see proper name index

κἄν 123,6.

καρπός 48,16.

κατά 3,15; 5,21; 12,1.7-8.10; 15,[14].15.16.22; 18,3.11.15.17.25; 19,1.10-11.14.16.18; 21,18.18-19; 22,14; 23,17; 25,13; 28,9; 32,21; 41,17.19.19; 43,[6]; 46,19; 48,2.3; 51,19; 55,13; 59,16.17; 74,10.12; 92,17; 106,14; 115,11.13.16; 116,3; 117,3; 119,21; 120,6; 126,6; 127,3.12.14; 129,17.

ΚΑΤΑ ΟⲨⲀ see **ΟⲨⲀ**.

κατανόησις 82,23-24.

κοινωνεῖν **ΚΟΙΝⲰΝΙ** share 22,4-5.

κόλασις 131,[23].26.

κοσμικός **ΚΟⲤⲘΙΚΟΝ** 5,2; 8,12.

κοσμοκράτωρ 1,18.

κόσμος 1,5; 2,[32]; 3,23; 4,26; 5,8.26; 8,17; 9,11.13; 10,3.5; 11,1; 12,6-7; 24,31-25,1; 35,7-8; 42,[12]; 46,30; 95,13; 114,12; 130,5.10-11.

κριτής 9,7.

κτίσις 1,17; 8,16; 9,9.29.

μακάριος 11,16; 20,4.24; 40,[16-17]; 68,10.14; 76,[16]; 90,[16]. mnt≠makarios 3,9-10; 14,13; 15,7-8.14-15; 37,22-23; 66,17-18; 73,10-11; 75,11.17-18; 76,13-14; 79,14-15; 80,23; 84,13; 86,[21]; 87,12-13; 97,[4-5]; 123,18; 124,9.

μερικός 1,21; 18,12; 19,3-4; 22,1; 23,19; 66,6; 85,18.

μέρος 2,[16-17]; 19,9.14; 20,1.10; 21,19; 22,15; 23,13-14; 28,6; 66,7; 117,21; 119,1

μετάνοια 5,27; 8,[15-16]; 10,9; 11,29; 12,14-15; 27,22; 31,9.

μετανοεῖν **ⲘΕΤΑΝΟΕΙ** 25,8-9; 28,1.5; 43,19-20.

μόνος **ⲘΟΝΟΝ** 16,2

μορθή form 9,21; 33,4; 45,24-25; 48,19; 61,10; 74,25. at≠morFy 16,7.

νοερός **ΝΟΕ ρΟ Ϲ, ΝΟΕ ρΟΝ** 2,1; 5,7; 22,5; 26,19; 58,18; 74,[13-14]; 79,[12-13].13; 87,8.

νόημα 45,28; 46,23; 92,[17].

νοῦς 1,12; 18,7; 19,22; 24,3; 29,18; 30,8.17; 33,13.20; 36,16; 38,[2].18; 39,15; 41,4.21; 42,2.[21]; 43,22; 44,3.29; 45,16; 48,20; 54,20; 55,21; 67,17; 113,2; 119,1; 124,[22]; 129,6.

ὄντως 5,24.26-27; 6,4; 8,18; 12,12.14.17; 18,1; 25,21; 26,1; 31,7; 37,5; 39,14.18; 41,26; 53,24; 61,[14-15]; 64,16; 66,11-12.[13]; 68,13; 78,8-9;

79,25; 80,6; 81,16.18; 82,14; 84,11.12; 92,18; 95,11; 103,[2]; 104,15; 116,6.14.[20]; 117,12.13; 118,7; 124,15; 125,12; 128,24.

ὁρμή ϩΟΡⲙⲏ 29,11-12; 45,22.

οὐδέ 4,5; 14,7; 73,4; 106,[5]; 119,[21].

οὖν 17,6; 21,19; 24,18; 26,12; 96,5.

οὐσία 2,20;9,20;15,15;17,2;20,20;26,18;68,6;103,3;116,8.9.17. ⲀⲦΟⲨⲤΙⲀ 79,8.

πάλιν 44,18; 82,11.

παντέλειος see τέλειος.

πάντως 21,17.[28]; 73,9.

παραλήμπτωρ 47,24.

παρθενικός 57,[15].

παρθένος 36.[23]; 58,[6]; 63,[6-7]; 83,11; 87,[10]; 125,15; 126,14; 129,11.

παρθενωφωτός 129,3.

παροίκησις 5,25; 8,15; 12,11.12-13; 27,15-16; 43,14.

πηγή 17,11.

πλάσμα 4,24.

πλήρωμα 77,8.

πνεῦμα Π̅Ν̅Ⲁ̅ 2,6.27; 3,21; 5,5.6; 8,[22]; 17,13; 20,18; 21,8; 23,28; 24,5.7.10.13.15; 36,9; 38,3; 47,5.11; 52,18.19;57,18.[22].25; 58,17.22.24; 59,8; 61,13; 63,8.14; 64,17; 66,13; 67,19; 74,7; 75,14; 79,16.[23]; 80,19; 84,[14].18; 87,14; 97,3.6; 118,12; 122,4; 123,[20]; 128,21; 129,12.

πρᾶξις 43,26; 116,10.

προεῖναι Π ΡⲰΟ Ν 10,12.

πρός 10,1; 21,13; 77,16.24; 79,10; 132,5.

πύξος 130,2.

πῶς 2,25.31; 3,6; 22,2; 23,2.8.9.11.13; 128,22.

σιγή 24,11.14; 51,3; 52,[20].21; 124,1.15.

σοφία 9,16; 10,8.16; 27,12; 45,3; 119,2; 120,7.

σπορά 30,13; 47,10; 130,16.

στοιχεῖον 113,6.

σφραγίζειν ⲤⲫΡⲀⲦΙϪⲈ 6,14; 58,24; 129,14.

σφραγίς 57,[8].11.[20].23; 58,13.

σῶμα 2,19; 10,18; 21,15; 26,27; 27,2; 42,22;46,9; 48,24; 65,17.20; 73,25; 81,3; 113,4; 116,[17-18]; 123,7. ⲀⲦⲤⲰⲙⲀ 2,19; 21,8-9.10; 65,18; 116,17.

σωματικός ⲤⲰⲙⲀⲦΙⲔΟ Ν 1,10-11; 26,11; 43,8.

σωτήρ 131,15.

τάξις 18,4; 108,9; 113,13; 114,12; 115,22; 125,3.

τέλειος ⲦⲈⲖΙΟⲤ 2,9; 6,25; 7,19; 10,29; 13,4.11; 14,21; 15,3; 17,6.8-9.10; 18,6.15.17.22-23.[25]; 19,1.5;20,1.3;24,2-3.16.16;25,[14];28,[26];29,[18]; 30,4-5.8.17.29.[30];32,14;33,13.15;36,10;38,1.3.4.16;39,22;40,23;41,14.20;

44,28-29; 46,23; 48,1; 50,3; 54,7.13; 59,18; 60,4.15.20.23; 61,18; 62,[10].[15]; 67,20; 68,11.20.21.[26]; 73,13; 76,16; 79,17; 83,12; 86,14; 87,[9]; 88,[20]; 93,17.18; 94,5; 98,1; 118,12; 121,9; 123,5.17.19; 124,6.22; 127,8.12; 128,21; 129,5.15-16.17. ⲙⲛⲧ̀ⲧⲉⲗⲓⲟⲥ 68,18; 74,12-13.24; 75,[10]; 76,15; 77,[11-12].14; 79,12; 80,22; 81,10; 85,[9]; 86,22. ⲡⲁⲛⲧⲉⲗⲓⲟⲥ 18,16; 20,2-3; 24,17; 25,18; 40,16; 52,14; 59,23; 62,19; 63,19; 86,11; 91,15-16; 119,18; 121,3.11; 124,6; 125,16-17; 129,12-13. ⲙⲛⲧ̀ⲡⲁⲛⲧⲉⲗⲓⲟⲥ 77,13; 80,13; 123,8-9.

τολμᾶν ⲧⲟⲗⲙⲁ 3,26.

τόλμα ⲧⲟⲗⲙⲏ 128,11.19.

τόπος 3,3; 18,9; 21,16; 23,18; 28,9; 67,21; 82,19; 117,[8].

τότε 3,23; 5,11; 7,22; 43,4; 44,13; 45,9.17; 56,24; 61,15; 63,13; 68,19.

τύπος 8,12; 9,13.19; 11,12; 12,5; 22,3-4; 46,24.27; 126,6-7.

ὑλικός ϩⲩⲗⲓⲕⲟⲛ 26,17-18; 42,[24-25].

ὕλη ϩⲩⲗⲏ 1,16; 2,20; 5,9; 9,14; 46,6; 73,24; 105,[13]; 123,8; 128,9.

ὕπαρξις ϩⲩⲡⲁⲣⲝⲓⲥ 2,21.24.30; 3,8-9.11-12; 14,13; 15,10-11.[16-17]; 16,1.11-12; 17,2; 20,[21].[22]; 23,27; 30,18; 34,1; 36,2; 40,[9-10]; 66,16.19; 68,16-17; 73,1.8; 74,[8-9]; 75,7; 79,7-8.11.20; 84.16; 85,13; 86,15-16; 89,[9]; 93,6-7; 95,5.[16]; 98,5; 99,2; 107,3; 124,16.

φαντάζεσθαι ⲫⲁⲛⲧⲁⲍⲉⲑⲁⲓ 10,13-14.

φύσις 26,17; 46,2.

φωστήρ 6,[28]; 29,2; 31,16; 32,[4-5]; 51,17; 54,18; 55,[11]; 62,20; 63,16; 119,4; 120,5.11.[18-19]; 121,5; 126,4.11-12.15-16.[20]; 127,21.26; 128,2.5-6.

χάος 1,12; 117,7.

χρηστός ⲭ̄ⲣ̄ⲥ̄ 131,14. ⲙⲛⲧ̀ⲭⲣⲏⲥⲧⲟⲥ 78,22.

χρόνος 4.19; 26,28; 27,5; 78,13; 131,20.

χωρεῖν ⲭⲱⲣⲓⲛ 21,8; 44,15. ⲁⲛⲁⲭⲱⲣⲓⲛ 44,20.22; 45,12-13

χώρημα 82,8.

ψυχή 1,30; 6,21; 8,4.4; 11,10.29; 12,6.19; 17,8; 24,2; 26,20; 27,1.10.11.13-14; 28,11.30; 29,5.19; 30,11.28; 31,3; 32,18; 33,24; 34,10.13.22.[24]; 35,5; 42,21; 43,2.23; 47,1; 48,18; 55,20; 57,22; 60,22; 73,18; 113,3.22.23; 130,20. ⲁⲧⲯⲩⲭⲏ́ 73.19.

ψυχικός 1,12; 58,17-18.

ὡς 18,8; 30,28; 39,9.10; 114,2.9; 115,5; 116,8.

(ⲉϭ ϩⲧ) (60a) nn m. ⲉⲡⲉⲥ ϩⲧ 10,20; 27,12; 65,[10]; 89,15.

ⲉⲧ, ⲉⲧⲉ, ⲉⲑ passim.

ⲉⲧⲃⲉ (61a) prep. 3,24.31; 4,[15]; 7,22; 8,5.10-11.1], 12-13,14,15,16-19; 9,6; 10,19; 13,[12].20; 14.2,17; 18,2; 28,15; 34,6.12,25,[27]; 26,19,27,11; 28,8; 29,27; 30,12.17.20.24.29; 36,4; 39,18; 46,11]; 57,16.17,[10]; 58,20-21; 60,17; 64,12; 68,20; 73,17.[20],21.23.28; 74,[21]; 75,[1]; 81,[11]; 82,15-16; 94,2.9; 96.4; 122,3; 123,2.6.8; 124,[ ]. ⲉⲧⲃⲉ ⲡⲁⲓ 35,[15-16], 39,5; 43,24.26; 46,3; 75,1[ ]; 98,5. ⲉⲧⲃⲉ ⲡⲁ 1,[2] ; 25,[2]; 29,12.20.24; 46,[15]; 94,2; 123,2.6.

ⲉⲟⲟⲩ (62a) nn m. 4,25; 5,15; 6,6.33; 11,6,24; [18]; 44,20[ ]; 47,12, 17,16; 48,23; 51,[9].[21]; 52,[12]; 53,[13-14]; 54,[ ].16.17; 55,18, 56,[16]; 57,[14]; 62,[11]; 63,[9-10].[21]; 73,[13]; 86,20; 88,[14-15].18; 93,~, 115,22; 127,[ ].12,[13],22; 121,[8]; 122,5.10.15.16; 123,[ ]. ; 125,2,13,14; 129,14.

ⲉϣⲁⲝ ⲉ (63b) conjunct. 8,3.

ⲉⲓ (70a) vb. 37,25; 58,2; 131,4.16. ⲉⲓ ⲉⲝ ⲡⲁ[ ]1a 28[ ]48[6] ; ⲛⲁ.1 57,13; 129,2. ⲉⲓ ⲉⲃⲟⲗ 12,7; 24,8; 41,8; 83,16; 121,16; 124,[14]; 129,16-17.28. ⲉⲓ ⲉϩⲣⲁⲓ, ⲉⲓ ⲉϩⲁⲡⲓ ⲉ 5,24.28; 6,2; 129,23.29; 130,5. ⲛ ⲧ ⲉⲓ (ⲛⲓ) 9,6; 46,8; 65,13.

ⲉⲓⲉ (74a) conjunct. 43,[18].

ⲉⲓⲙⲉ (77b) vb. 3,14; 13.13; 20,12; 21-22,8.14.17-18; 23,2,7,16; 40,14; 41,1; 44,6-7; 45,8,16,29; 58,20; 78,8; 80,17,21; 82,7; 85,8; 85,[ ]; 37.15.16.19.21.22; 88,15; 97,9; 99,5; 120,1.5; 121,19; 124,6.7; 130,16. ⲁⲙⲉ 17,15; 26,6; 67,4; 81,11. ⲙⲉ 73,11; 88,16; 120,29; 123,26. ⲉⲓⲙⲉ nn m. 53,22. ⲁ ⲛ ⲧ ⲉⲓⲙⲉ (ⲁⲙⲧⲙⲉ) nn f. 29,23; 30,9; 43,16; 44,20; 67,5; 75,[10-11].[11].12. ⲁ.ⲧⲉⲓⲙⲉ (ⲁⲧⲙⲙⲉ) 3,32; 50,20; 81,[ ]; 128,13.17. ⲁ ⲛ ⲧ.ⲣⲉⲓⲙⲉ 117,6.7. ⲡⲉϥⲉⲓⲙⲉ 58,19.

ⲉⲓⲛⲉ (79b) vb. ⲉⲓⲛⲉ ⲉϩ ⲡ[ ]15 15[ ].[ ].ⲛ ⲧ ⲓ,21, 17 78 ⲛⲧ ⲉⲓ ⲟⲩ ⲟ ⲛ 129,4. [ ]

ⲉⲓⲛⲉ (80b) vb. 28,4.22; 43,24; 81,[ ] [ ] ⲟ nn. 3,[28,2]; 17,14-18 ; 22,13, 26,5.8; 27,7; 88,21; 55,3; 96,1; ; 88,21; 39,24; 118,8.13.

(ⲉⲓⲟⲟⲣ) (82a) ⲁⲓ ⲟ ⲟ ⲣ nn m. 14,2; 37,[25; 61,11; 1-3.]

ⲉⲓⲣⲉ (83a) vb. 3,26; 25,6; 28,4; [ ].26; ⲟ nn. [18]; 1,16; 7,[23]; 8,3.29.32; 10,5.14; 27,9.27; 41,16,17; [ ] [ ] ⲁ[ ]; 85,[ ]; ; ; 77,27; 80,[19]; 81,1.20; 82,[ ] 12,38; 40,1 [ ] ⲛ [ ]; ; ; [ ] ; 131,[ ],12; 131,20; 132,4. ⲣ ⲛ [ ] ⲉ[ ] 16,6.18; 18,3; 30,4; ; ; ; 12,16.25,3; 31,23,19; 43.[7],8.19.21; 44,[ ]; 2; 45,12; 68,14; ; ; 26,14; 28,12; 129,14. ⲣ ⲧ 10,12; 26,16; 47,9.45.56; 58,20; 130,[ ] ; ; ; 131,23. ⲁⲓⲧ 46,9,14.

ⲉⲓⲱⲣ ϩ (84b) vb. 31,[9,20]; 63,[20].[7].9.

(ⲉⲓⲥ) (85a) interject. 81,[ ]; 93,28 ; ; 120,14,18.

(ⲓ ⲙⲥ) (86a) ar.[ ]; 1, 1[ ] [ ]; [ ]

PROPER NAMES: VIII, *I*

ⲁⲃⲣⲁⲥⲁⳍ 47,13.

ⲁⲇⲁⲙⲁⲥ 6,26; 30,4.10.25; 33,17; 51,14.

ⲁⲕⲣⲁⲙⲁⲥ 47,3.

ⲁⲕⲣⲉⲙⲱⲛ 126,9.

ⲇⲕⲣⲱⲛ 52,15.

ⲁⲗⲫⲗⲉⲧⲉ 88,12.

ⲁⲙⲃⲟⲣⲥⲓⲟⲥ 126,13-14.

ⲁⲛⲧⲓⲫⲁⲛⲧⲉⲥ 54,24; 126,16-17.

ⲁⲡⲟⲫⲁⲛⲧⲉⲥ 129,2.

ⲁⲣⲁⲙⲉⲛ 88,[11].

(ⲕ)ⲁⲣⲙⲉⲇⲣⲟⲛ 86,19; 119,[5]; 120,3; 126,[23]; 127,9.

ⲁⲣⲙⲟⳍⲏⲗ 29,3; 32,[5]; 51,[17]; 100,[6]. ⲁⲣⲙⲟⳍⲏⲗ ⲟⲣⲛⲉⲟⲥ
  ⲉⲧⲉⲣⲟⲩⲛⲓⲟⲥ 127,[22-23].

ⲁⲣⲣⲟⲥ 128,1.

ⲁⲧⲇⲁⲏⲗ 47,13.

ⲁⲧⲉⲣⲟⲩⲛⲓⲟⲥ 8,8; 9,2; 47,21-22; 127,22-23.

ⲁⲫⲣⲏⲇⲱⲛ 86,[13]; 88,18; 122,6.

ⲁⲫⲣⲟⲡⲁⲓⲥ 129,3.

ⲃⲁ-[ ]-ⲙⲟⲥ 47,19.

ⲃⲁⲣⲃⲏⲗⲱ 14,6; 36,14 20; 37,20; 53,10; 62,21; 63,6; 83,9; 87,10; 91,19;
  118,10; 119,23; 122,1; 124,11; 129,10.

ⲃⲁⲣⲅⲁⲣⲁⲧⲧⲏⲥ 6,12.

ⲃⲏⲣⲓⲑⲉⲧⲥ 88,10.

ⲅⲁⲃⲣⲓⲏⲗ 57,9; 58,[21-22].

ⲅⲁⲙⲁⲗⲓⲏⲗ 47,2.

ⲅⲉⲣⲁⲇⲁⲙⲁⲥ, ⲡⲓⲅⲉⲣⲁⲇⲁⲙⲁⲥ 6,23; 13,6; 51,7.

ⲇⲁⲧⲉⲓⲟⲑⲉ 29,9; 51,18. ⲇⲁⲧⲑⲉⲓⲟⲑⲉ ⲗⲁⲣⲁⲛⲉⲧⲥ
  ⲉⲡⲓⲫⲁⲛⲓⲟⲥ ⲉⲓⲇⲟⲥ 128,3-4.

ⲇⲏⲓ̈ⲫ[86,16; 119,7-8.

ⲇⲟⳍⲟⲙⲉⲇⲱⲛ 126,8.

ⲉⲓⲇⲉⲁ 119,13.

ⲉⲓⲇⲟⲙⲉⲛⲉⲧⲥ 47,21.

ⲉⲓⲣ[.]ⲛ 47,20.

ⲉⲗⲉⲛⲟⲥ 6,[16]; 54,25; 126,21.

ⲉⲡⲓⲫ[86,20.

ⲉⲣⲓⲅⲉⲛⲁⲟⲣ 88,[10].

ⲉⲧⲕⲣⲉⲃⲱⲥ 47,23.

ⲉⲧⲣⲓⲟⲥ 47,15.

ⲉⲧⲣⲧⲙⲉⲛⲉⲧⲥ 47,17.

ⳍⲁⲣⲉⲧ[54,[4].

ʒⲁⲭⲑⲟⲥ 54,22; 126,12.
ʒⲱⲧⲉⲛⲉⲑⲗⲟⲥ 6,17.
ʒⲟⲥⲧⲣⲓⲁⲛⲟⲥ 1,[3-4]; 3,31; 14,1; 64,11; 128,15; 132,6.
ⲏⲗⲏⲗⲏⲑ 29,11; 31,16-17; 51,18. ⲏⲗⲏⲗⲏⲑ ⲕⲟⲣⲇⲏⲣⲏ
   ⲉⲥⲧⲓⲫⲁⲛⲓⲟⲥ ⲁⲗⲗⲟⲅⲉⲛⲓⲟⲥ 128,6-7.
ⲏⲗⲓⲗⲓⲟⲩⲫⲉⲩ 88,[12].
ⲏⲫⲏⲥⲏⲭ 13,8; 45,2.11.
ⲑⲉⲟⲡⲉⲙⲡⲧⲟⲥ 47,16-17.
ⲑⲟⲩⲣⲱ 47,27.
ⲓ̈ⲁⲧⲟ[52,2.
ⲓ̈ⲁⲭⲑⲟⲥ 54,23; 126,12.
ⲓ̈ⲉⲥⲉⲩⲥ ⲙⲁʒⲁⲣⲉⲩⲥ ⲓ̈ⲉⲥⲥⲉⲇⲉⲕⲉⲩⲥ 47,5-6; 57,5-6.
ⲓ̈ⲁⲟⲗⲁⲟⲥ 1,4; 4,10.
ⲓ̈ⲥⲁⲩⲏⲗ 47,13.
ⲓ̈ⲟⲩⲏⲗ 53,14; 54,17; 63,10; 125,14. ⲓ̈ⲱⲏⲗ 57,15; 62,12.
ⲕⲁⲩⲡⲧⲟⲥ 15,12; 20,4; 22,12. ⲕⲁⲥ 2,23; 13,2; 18,10; 19,5; 23,17; 24,6;
   33,21; 36,21; 39,25; 40,25; 41,22.22; 44,26; 58,16; 82,12; 85,11; 88,21;
   92,21; 97,4; 101,12; 115,9.13; 119,12; 121,3.5; 122,17; 124,18; 125,12;
   126,7; 129,10.
ⲕⲉⲥⲗⲁⲣ 47,23.
ⲗⲁⲗⲁⲙⲉⲛⲥ 47,20; 88,13.
ⲗⲱⲏⲗ 47,4.
ⲙⲁⲗⲥⲏⲇⲱⲛ 119.[9]; 120,17.
ⲙⲁⲣⲥⲏⲇⲱⲛ 122,[16-17].
ⲙⲓⲣⲟⲑⲉⲁ 6,30; 30,14.
ⲙⲓⲭⲁⲣ 6,10.15.
ⲙⲓⲭⲉⲩⲥ 6,[10].16.
ⲙⲛⲏⲥⲓⲛⲟⲩⲥ 47,4.
ⲛⲉⲫ[86,14.
ⲛⲟⲏⲑⲉⲩ[88,13.
ⲟⲗⲙⲓⲥ 119,11; 120,24.
ⲟⲗⲥⲏⲛ 47,18.
ⲟⲣⲙⲟⲥ 47,9.
ⲡⲓⲅⲉⲣⲁⲇⲁⲙⲁⲥ, see ⲅⲉⲣⲁⲇⲁⲙⲁⲥ.
ⲡⲗⲏⲥⲓⲑⲉⲁ 51,12.
ⲡⲣⲟⲫⲁⲛⲓⲁ 6,31.
ⲡⲣⲱⲛⲏⲥ 53,12.
ⲡⲣⲱⲧⲟⲫⲁⲛⲉⲥ 13,3; 15,9-10; 18,5; 20,9; 22,9-10; 23,5-6; 24,5-6; 29,16;
   38,17; 40,[6-7]; 41,[3-4].30-31; 41,[31-42,1]; 44,27; 54,19; 58,15; 63,12-
   13; 124,21; 127,8; 129,4-5.
ⲥⲁⲗⲁⲙⲉʒ 62,18; 63,18; 64,8.

ⲥⲁⲙⲃⲗⲱ 47,24.

ⲥⲁⲫⲫⲱ 47,26.

ⲥⲉⲗⲇⲁⲱ 6,16; 54,24-25; 126,[20].

ⲥⲉⲗⲙⲉⲛ 54,20.

ⲥⲉⲙⲉⲗⲉⲗ 52,7.

ⲥ ⲏ ⲑ 7,[9]; 30,10; 130,17. ⲥ ⲏ ⲑ ⲉⲙⲙⲁⲭⲁ ⲥ ⲏ ⲑ 6,25; 51,14-15.

ⲥ ⲏ ⲑ ⲉ ⲩ ⲥ 54,23; 126,16.

ⲥ ⲓ ⲟ ⲩ 88,17.

ⲥ ⲟ ⲗ ⲙ ⲓ ⲥ 122,12; 126,4.

ⲥ ⲟ ⲫ ⲓ ⲁ 9,16; 10,8.16; 27,12; 45,3; 119,2; 120,7.

ⲥ ⲧ ⲏ ⲑ ⲉ ⲩ ⲥ 47,16.

ⲥ ⲧ ⲣ ⲉ ⲙ ⲯ ⲟ ⲩ ⲭ ⲟ ⲥ 47,3.

ⲥ ⲩ ⲙ ⲫ ⲑ ⲁ ⲣ 47,22.

ⲧ ⲉ ⲗ ⲙ ⲁ ⲭ ⲁ ⲏ [52,8.

ⲫ ⲁ ⲗ ⲉ ⲣ ⲓ ⲥ 47,14.

ⲫ ⲁ ⲗ ⲥ ⲏ ⲥ 47,14.

ⲱ ⲙ ⲱ ⲑ ⲉ ⲙ [52,9.

ⲱ ⲣ ⲓ ⲙ ⲉ ⲛ ⲓ ⲟ ⲥ   88,11.

ⲱ ⲣ ⲟ ⲓ ⲁ ⲏ ⲗ 29,6-7; 51,[18]; 127,[26-27].

45,20. ⲁⲧⲙⲟⲩⲣⲉ 37,19; 61,13; 68,22; 79,19 . . . ⲁⲛⲧⲁⲧⲙⲟⲩⲣⲉ 75,13.

(ⲯⲓⲥ) (273b) an m. ⲡⲉⲥⲉ . . . 27,5 . . .

ⲡⲱⲧ (274a) vb. 131,5; 132,5 . . .

ⲡⲱϣ (277a) vb. 15,7; 98,9; 121,5. ⲁⲧⲡⲱϣ . . . 3,27-28; 21,10; 53,14; 101,13 .

ⲡⲱϧ (282a) vb. 130,1. ⲡⲓⲛⲉ . . . 76,9; 115,13 . . .

(ⲡⲉⲥⲉ) (285a) vb. ⲡⲉⲥ . . . . . . 62;9,1; . . . 35,1; 52,17; 62,11; 96,4; 128,19 . . .

(ⲣⲟ) (286b) nn m. ⲕⲁⲣⲱϥ 12,24 . . .

ⲣⲱ (290a) particle 3,25; 4,4; 6,13; 7; 8,22 . . .

ⲣⲓⲕⲉ (291b) vb. 42,2 . . .

ⲣⲱⲕϧ (293a) vb. 74 . . . 15,19 . . .

ⲣⲱⲙⲉ (294b) nn m. 4,12; 6;[24]; 8[1];5,8-7,13;11-12,24; 40,5; 42,7,20; 43,2,13,[19]; 94,1 . . . [1]; 45, . . . 9,1; 93,21; 95,2 . . .

ⲣⲁⲛ (297b) nn m. 5,[7];6,4 . . . 6,3;2;12-13; 19;4,25;25,32-26,1;51,19;53,16; 88,14. † . . ⲣⲁⲛ . . . 1,18; . . . 19,6 . . . ⲣⲁⲛ . . .

ⲣⲁⲧ⸗ (302b) nn m⸗ . . . 15,16. ⲁϫⲉⲛⲣⲁⲧ⸗ see ⲱϧⲉ . . .

ⲣⲏⲧⲉ (304b) nn m. 9,15 . . . 9,1; 11;95,2. ⲛⲉⲓⲣⲏⲧⲉ 2,12,21;4;16,4- 5; 18,9;10,13; 19, . . . 25;[23]; 26,1-3;[1]; 29,1; 40,2; 48,15; 94,3. ⲙⲡⲣⲏⲧⲉ [25];5,7;16-14;[17];18;118;19,3;21;15,23,121;25,25;26,11; 28,[18]; 41,16; 44,7[19-10]; 78;[16]; 86,[9]; 95,[14]; 107,8; 115,[18-19]; 116,9; 135,5; 139,7. ⲁⲡⲉ . . . 3,21-2;9,16 . . . ⲙⲁ . . . 9,15 . . . see ⲁⲩ . . .

ⲣⲟⲟⲩϣ (7 . . .) . . .

ⲣⲱⲙⲉ (3 . . .) . . . an m. 37,4 . . .

ⲥⲁ (31 . . .) nn . . . ⲙⲉⲥ . . . 1,7; 14; . . . 60,13;[19]13; 16,22; . . . 27, . . . 27, . . . 44,24; 4 . . . 45, ... 25,23; 70,11,19; 77,17,18; 77;3,9; 81,21;8 . . . 6,[2]; 112,[8]; 124,11; 130,15,23; 131,1. ⲙⲉⲥ . . . ⲥⲁ . . . . . . 40, . . . ⲙⲁⲩⲙⲉϧ; ⲙⲁⲛ . . . 1,6; 12,7; 77,25; 130,3⸗.

ⲥⲁ (313a) nn m⸗ . . .

ⲥⲉⲱ (315b) vb. . . .

(ⲥⲟⲟⲩ⸗) (317 . . .) . . .

ⲥⲙⲏ (315b) nn f. . . .

(ⲥⲁⲓⲛⲉ) (337a) vb. ⲥⲉⲁⲛⲓⲛⲉ 115,11.

ⲥⲁⲟⲧ (340b) nn m. 3, . . . 62; 40,5 . . .

ⲥⲱⲧ (343a)[4]b. 63; 70 . . . [1];[1];51,8 . . . 25,11 95,7 . . . 139,9. ⲡⲉⲩϭ . . . 12 . . . 122,18. nn m. 5,17; 4 . . .

ⲥⲓⲙⲉ (345)a vb . . . 16,21. ⲥⲓⲙⲉ ⲥⲟⲟⲩ . . . 13,5;[21];10.

ⲥⲛⲁⲩ (346a) . . . 14;[1];7;[15];84,3. ⲥⲛ . . . 19,23; 49,6; 58,22. ⲃ 19,5 . . . 97,[8],13,26;[2];22],29,[1] . . .

COPTIC WORDS: VIII,2

ⲁⲗⲟⲩ (5a) nn m. 133,25.

(ⲁⲙⲟⲩ) (7b) vb. ⲁⲙⲏⲉⲓⲧⲛ 137,23-24.

ⲁⲙⲁϧⲧⲉ ((9a) vb. 134,23-24; 135,18; 137,5.

ⲁⲛ (10b) part. 136,1; 137,12; 138,28.

(ⲁⲛⲁⲓ) (11a) vb. ⲣ ⲁⲛⲁˢ 133,6.

ⲁⲛⲟⲕ (11b) pron. ⲁⲛⲟⲛ 134,17; 136,16.[21]; 138,16; 139,22; 140,6.
ⲛⲧⲟⲕ 133,1. ⲛⲧⲱⲧⲛ 135,4-5; 137,5.10.20.22.26. ⲛⲧⲟϥ 133,6;
136,5.23; 137,28; 138,15; 139,12. ⲛⲧⲟⲟⲩ 135,28; 136,20; 137,[11].

ⲁⲩ (22a) interrog pron. 137,15. ⲛ ⲁⲩ ⲛⲣⲏⲧⲉ 134,26. ⲛ ⲁⲩ ⲛϧⲉ
133,4-5.

(ⲁϫⲛˊ) (25b) prep. ⲉϫ ⲛˊ 133,13; 135,13.

ⲃⲱⲕ (29a) vb. 134,25; 140,19. ⲃⲱⲕ ⲉⲣⲁⲧˢ 133,10. ⲃⲱⲕ ϧⲛ 140,26-
27. ⲃⲱⲕ ⲉϫ ⲛˊ 133,3.

ⲉⲃⲣⲏⲅⲉⲥ (53b) nn f. 138,4.

ⲉⲛⲉϧ (57a) nn m. ϧⲁ ⲉⲛⲉϩ 134,18; 140,23.

ⲉⲣϧⲧ (58a) vb. 132,22. nn m. 137,25.

ⲉⲣⲏⲩ (59a) nn m,f. 138,122; 140,14.

ⲉⲧ, ⲉⲑ, ⲉⲧⲉ (61a) rel pref. 132,15; 133,14.15.22-23.25; 134,5.17;
135,5.10.12.15.17.21.22.26; 136,15.18.19.23.25; 137,6.7.8.10.19.22;
138.12-13.18.28; 139,21.23; 140,18.19.

ⲉⲧⲃⲉ (61a) prep. 134,16; 135,2.7.8; 136,16.17-18; 137,3-4; 138,12.14.20;
139,25. ⲉⲧⲃⲏⲏⲧˢ 138,18. ⲉⲧⲃⲉ ⲡⲁⲓ 137,3; 139,25. ⲉⲧⲃⲉ ⲟⲩ
134,16; 135,2.

ⲉⲟⲟⲩ (62a) nn m. 139,26.

ⲉⲩϫⲉ (63b) conjunct. 133,6; 138,15.

ⲉⲓ (70a) vb. 133,7; 134,25. ⲉⲓ ⲉⲩⲙⲁ 132,19; 133,3.18;. ⲉⲓ ⲉϧⲟⲩⲛ ⲉˊ
136,27. ⲉⲓ ⲉϧⲣⲁⲓ 139,13.16. ⲉⲓ ⲉϧⲣⲁⲓ ⲉˊ 136,19; 139,5.6.

ⲉⲓⲙⲉ (77b) vb. 133,4; 134,21. ⲓⲙⲉ 132,16.

ⲉⲓⲛⲉ (80b) nn m. 139,25. ⲙⲛⲧⲁⲧⲉⲓⲛⲉ 136,14.

ⲉⲓⲣⲉ (83a) 139,24; 140,7.11. ⲣ + Gk. vb. 137,29.30; 139,16; 140,14. ⲣ +
nn. 134,11; 135,5; 136,1; 138.1.2; 139,8; 140,20-21.

(ⲉⲓⲱⲣϧ) (84b) vb. ⲓⲱⲣϧ nn m. 134,12.

ⲉⲓⲥϧⲏⲧⲉ (85a) interj. 140,22.

(ⲉⲓⲱⲧ) (86b) nn m. ⲓⲱⲧ 133,21.21.22; 135,14; 136,1; 137,27,28-29;
139,2.26. ⲙⲛⲧⲉⲓⲱⲧ 136,28.

(ⲉⲓⲩⲉ) (88b) vb. ⲁⲱⲧˢ 139,16. ⲁⲱⲧˢⲉϫ ⲛ 139,[19].

ⲕⲉ (90b) nn m,f. 133,13; 140,8. ⲛⲕⲉⲥⲟⲡ 134,2; 135,8; 137,14; 140,2.

(ⲕⲟⲩⲓ) (92b) nn m,f. ⲙⲛⲧⲕⲟⲩⲓ 138,20.

ⲕⲱ (94b) vb. ⲕⲱ ⲉϩⲣⲁⲓ̈ ⲉϫⲱ⸍ 135,23-24.

(ⲕⲱⲕ) (100b) vb. ⲕⲁⲕ⸍ ⲕⲁϩⲏⲟⲩ 137,6-7.

ⲕⲁⲕⲉ (101b) nn m. 134,1.

ⲕⲗⲟⲙ (104b) nn m. 139,17.

ⲕⲱⲧⲉ (124a) vb. ⲕⲱⲧⲉ ⲛⲥⲱ⸍ 134,9. ⲕⲟⲧ⸍ 134,2. ⲕⲟⲧ⸍ ⲉϩⲣⲁⲓ̈ ⲉ⸍ 138,10.

(ⲕⲱϩ) (132b) vb. ⲣⲉϥⲕⲱϩ 136,8.

ⲙⲁ (153a) nn m. 133,15; 134,25; 138,7. ⲉⲩⲙⲁ 132,[19-20]; 133,3.18; 137,24. ⲙⲁ ⲛϣⲱⲡⲉ 134,24. ⲉⲡⲙⲁ ⲛ⸍ 136,9.10.

(ⲙⲉ) (156a) nn m. ⲙⲉⲣⲉ⸍ 133,3. ⲙⲉⲣⲓⲧ 132,14.

(ⲙⲟⲩ) (159a) nn m. ⲙⲟⲟⲩⲧ† 135,26; 136,13.20.22; 137,9; 139,20. ⲙⲛⲧⲁⲧⲙⲟⲩ 134,5.7.

ⲙⲕⲁϩ (163a) vb. ϫⲓ ⲙⲕⲁϩ 138,16.24.27.28. ϫⲓ ⲙⲕⲁϩ ⲉⲧⲃⲉ (ⲉⲧⲃⲏⲏⲧ⸍) 138,18.20. ϫⲓ ⲙⲁⲕϩ ϩⲛ 139,23. ϫⲓ ⲙⲕⲁϩ nn m. 139,22.

ⲙⲛ (169b) prep. 133,16; 137,10.16.22; 137,10.16.22. ⲛⲙⲙⲁ⸍ 132,2.15; 137,21.

ⲙⲛ (170a) conj. 132,14.15.18; 138,4.26; 140,8.18.21.

ⲙⲁⲉⲓⲛ (170b) vb. † ⲙⲁⲉⲓⲛ 139,13.

ⲙⲛⲧⲣⲉ (177a) vb. ⲣ ⲙⲛⲧⲣⲉ 135,5.

(ⲙⲁⲧⲉ) (189a) vb, ⲙⲧⲱⲟⲩ 133,25.

(ⲙⲁⲧⲉ) (190a) adv. ⲉⲙⲁⲧⲉ 139,[5].

ⲙⲏⲧⲉ (190b) 137,9.

ⲙⲟⲩⲧⲉ (191b) vb. 133,14.

ⲙⲧⲟⲛ (194b) nn m. 137,11; 140,4.

(ⲙⲁⲩ) (196b) nn. ⲉⲙⲁⲩ 133,16. ⲉⲧⲙⲙⲁⲩ 138,7.

ⲙⲁⲟⲩ (197a) nn f. 135,12; 139,23.

ⲙⲉⲉⲩⲉ (199a) vb. 136,21.

ⲙⲏⲏϣⲉ (202a) nn m. 139,9.

ⲙⲟⲟϣⲉ (203b) vb. ⲙⲟⲟϣⲉ ⲉϩⲣⲁⲓ̈ ϩⲛ 139,30.

ⲙⲟⲩϩ (208a) vb. ⲙⲟⲩϩ ⲉⲃⲟⲗ ϩⲛ 137,1; 139,14; 140,9.

(ⲙϩⲁⲁⲩ) (212b) nn m. ⲙϩⲁⲟⲩ 139,20.

ⲛ⸍,ⲙⲙⲟ⸍,ⲙⲙⲱ⸍ (215a) part. 132,22; 133,2.11; 134,3.14.16-17; 134.20.24; 135.4.18; 136,3; 137,5.14-15.20; 138,15.18.22; 140,[3].14.15.16-17.24.

(ⲛⲟⲩ) (219a) vb. ⲛⲏⲩ† 138,9-10.

ⲛ⸍,ⲛⲁ⸍ (216a) prep. 132,22; 133,27; 134,8; 135,3; 136,25.26; 138,6; 139,12; 140,25.

ⲛⲓⲙ (225b) adj. 138,9; 139,12.24.

ⲛⲧⲉ (230a) part. 132,12.[18]; 133,7.22; 134,4.6.12.22; 135,1.9.12.14.21.27; 136,7.28; 139,26.28.

ⲚⲞⲨⲦⲈ (230b) nn m. 133,8.

ⲚⲀⲨ (233b) vb. 140,8.

(ⲚⲞⲨⲀⲈ) (241b) vb. ⲚⲞⲀ⸍ ⲈⲬⲚ 133,19.

ⲚⲞⲨⲢⲘ (243b) vb. 137,13.

ⲚⲀⲢⲦⲈ (246a) vb. 140,18. ⲘⲚⲦⲚⲀⲢⲦⲈ nn f. 135,7.

ⲚⲞⳠ (250a) adj. 134,10. ⲘⲚⲦⲚⲞⳠ nn f. 135,13-14.

ⲚⳠⲒ (252a) part. 133,18; 134,10; 135,16.18.27; 138,4.13-14.17; 140,26.20.

ⲞⲈⲒⲰ (257b) nn m. ⲦⲀⲰⲈ ⲞⲒⲈⲰ 132,20-21; 140,12.26.

ⲠⲀ'Ⲓ, ⲦⲀ'Ⲓ, ⲚⲀ'Ⲓ (259a) pron. 133,8;.22; 134,5; 135,6.9.20; 136,3.25; 137,3.7; 139,24.27. ⲠⲈ'Ⲓ⸍ 139,22; ⲚⲈ'Ⲓ⸍ 139,29.

ⲠⲈ (259a) nn f. 138,5.7. ⲚⲦⲠⲈ Ⲛ⸍ 137,17.

ⲠⲰ⸍ (260b) pron. 136,23.

ⲠⲰⲢⲀ (271b) vb. ⲠⲰⲢⲀ ⲈⲂⲞⲖ 133,2; 140,11-12.24.

ⲠⲀⲦ (273b) nn f. 133,20.

ⲠⲀⲢⲢⲈ (282b) nn m.f. Ⲣ ⲠⲀⲢⲢⲈ 139,8.

(ⲠⲈⲀⲈ) (285a) vb. ⲠⲈⲀⲀ⸍ 137.10.[15].

(ⲢⲞ) (288b) nn m. ⲢⲰ⸍ 139,9.

ⲢⲰⲘⲈ (294b) nn. m,f. 136,22; 137,9.22.

ⲢⲀⲚ (297b) nn m. 139,7; 140,19.

ⲢⲠⲈ (298b) nn m. 139,7.

ⲢⲀⲰⲈ (308b) vb. 135,26; 139,5. nn m. 133,11; 140,20.

ⲤⲂⲰ (319b) nn f. ✝ ⲤⲂⲰ 132,20. ✝ ⲤⲂⲰ ⲢⲚ 137,24; 139,6-7.

ⲤⲘⲎ (334b) nn f. 134,13; 135,3; 137,18; 138,21. ⲀⲒ ⲤⲘⲎ 134,15; 139,14.

ⲤⲘⲞⲨ (335a) vb. 136,5. nn m. 136,7; 138,9

ⲤⲞⲚ (342b) nn m. 132,13.16; 133.6. ⲤⲚⲎⲨ 132,15; 139,13.21.28.

ⲤⲞⲠ (349b) nn m. 138,23. See also ⲔⲈ.

ⲤⲈⲈⲠⲈ (351a) nn m. 133,13; 140,2-3.

(ⲤⲰⲦⲈ) (362a) vb. ⲢⲈϤⲤⲰⲦⲈ 134,7.

ⲤⲰⲦⲘ (363b) vb. 133,24; 134,1; 136,23-24.25. ⲤⲰⲦⲘ ⲚⲤⲀ⸍, 139,29. ⲘⲚⲦⲀⲦⲤⲰⲦⲘ nn f. 135,10-11.

ⲤⲞⲞⲨⲚ (369b) vb. 136,1. ⲤⲞⲨⲰⲚ⸍ 136.[20-21].

ⲤⲰⲞⲨⲢ (372b) vb. 133,12.16; 140,[2].13.

(ⲤⲀⲢⲚⲈ) (385b) vb. ⲞⲨⲀⲢ ⲤⲀⲢⲚⲈ nn m. 135,13.

✝ (392a) 134,8; 136,26; 137,23.24; 139,6.27; 140,5. ✝ ⲚⲘ⸍, 135,2; 137,10.16;.20.21. ✝ ⲢⲒⲰⲰ⸍, 139,[17-18].

ⲦⲰⲂⲢ (402a) nn m. 137,28.

(ⲦⲀⲔⲞ) (405a) vb. ⲦⲀⲔⲎⲞⲨⲦ✝ 137,7.

ⲦⲈⲖⲎⲖ (410a) vb. 133,11.

ⲦⲀⲖⳠⲞ (411b) nn m. 140,11.

ⲦⲀⲘⲒⲞ (413a) vb. 136,8-9.

(ⲧⲁⲙⲟ) (413b) vb. ⲧⲁⲙⲟⲥ 137,15.

(ⲧⲱⲙⲥ) (416a) vb. ⲧⲟⲙⲥⲥ 139,19.

(ⲧⲛⲛⲟⲟⲩ) (419b) vb. ⲧⲛⲛⲟⲟⲩⲥ ⲉϩⲣ︦ⲓ ϩⲛ 136,17.

ⲧⲏⲣⲥ (424a) adj. 132.19' 135.6.27; 140,[17-18].

(ⲧⲱⲣⲉ) (425a) nn f. ⲉⲃⲟⲗ ϩⲓⲧⲛ 132,22-133,[1].

ⲧⲱⲣⲡ (430b) vb. ⲧⲱⲣⲡ ⲉⲃⲟⲗ 138,6.

ⲧⲟⲟⲩ (440b) nn. 133,14; 134,11.

ⲧⲁⲩⲟ (441b) vb. 137,30.

(ⲧⲱⲟⲩⲛ) (445a) vb. ⲧⲱⲛⲥ ⲉⲃⲟⲗ ϩⲛ 139,20.

ⲧⲟⲩⲛⲟⲥ (446b) vb. 135,15.

(ⲧⲱϣ) (449b) vb. ⲧⲟϣⲥ 133,4. nn m. 136,11.

(ⲟⲩⲁ) (469a) nn. ⲡⲟⲩⲁ ⲡⲟⲩⲁ 140,10. ⲟⲩⲁⲧⲥ 135,5.

ⲟ ⲩ (470a) indefinite art. 132,17; 133,27; 134,8.10.22.23.24; 136,2.8.[9].10.12.14.26; 137,9.11.25; 138,4.4.14; 139,7.[17].18.[20].[20]; 140,5.7.9.11.20.21.21.27.27.

ⲟⲩⲟⲉⲓⲛ (480a) nn m. 133,22; 134,6.10; 135,4; 138,12. ⲣ ⲟⲩⲟⲉⲓⲛ ⲉⲃⲟⲗ ϩⲛ 134,11-12..

(ⲟⲩⲟⲛ) (481a) vb. ⲟⲩⲛⲧⲁⲥ, ⲉⲩⲛⲧⲁⲥ 133,23; 134,26. ⲙⲛⲧⲁⲥ 137,11.

ⲟⲩⲟⲛ (482a) pron. ⲟⲩⲟⲛ ⲛⲓⲙ 140,18.

ⲟⲩⲱⲛ (482b) vb. 139,9.

ⲟⲩⲱⲛϩ (486a) vb. ⲟⲩⲱⲛϩ ⲉⲃⲟⲗ 134,10.12-13; 135,12.16; 137,19.27-28; 138,6; 140,16.

(ⲟⲩⲟⲡ) (487a) vb. ⲟⲩⲁⲁⲃ† 133,26; 139,14; 140,10.

ⲟⲩⲏⲣ (488b) interrogative pron. ⲁⲟⲩⲏⲣ 138,16.

ⲟⲩⲱϣ (500a) vb. 132,16; 134,21; 135,14; 136,[8]; 137,12.

ⲟⲩⲱϣⲃ (502b) vb. 134,19; 138,17.

ⲟⲩⲱϣⲧ (504a) vb. 137,14.

(ⲟⲩⲱϩ) (505b) vb. ⲟⲩⲁϩⲥ 135,13. See also ⲥⲁϩⲛⲉ.

ⲟⲩⲝⲁⲓ (511b) nn m. 132,21; 137,2.25; 139,7.

(ⲱⲗ(ⲉ)ⲙ) (522b) vb. ⲟⲗⲥ ⲉϩⲟⲩⲛ 135,25.

ⲱⲛϩ (525a) nn m. 134,4; 139,28.

ⲱϣ (533a) vb. ⲱϣ ⲉⲃⲟⲗ ϣⲁⲣⲟⲥ 134,13-14. ⲟϣⲥ 133,9-10.

ϣⲁ (541b) prep. 134,14; 137,18; 138,21; 140,13.

ϣⲉ (546a) nn m. 139,19.

(ϣⲓ) (547b) vb. ⲁⲧϯϣⲓ 139,27.

(ϣⲃⲏⲣ) (553a) nn m. qbyⲁⲡⲟⲥⲧⲟⲗⲟⲓ 132,14-15.

ϣⲗⲏⲗ (559a) vb. 133,20; 134,3.

ϣⲙⲙⲟ (565b) nn. 136,2-3; 139,21.

ϣⲙϣⲉ (567a) vb. 136,4.

ϣⲓⲛⲉ (569a) 134,16. ϩⲓ ϣⲙⲛⲟⲩϥⲉ 133,5.

ϣⲟⲛⲧⲉ (573a) nn f. 139,<17>.

ϢⲰⲠⲈ (577b) vb. 133,27; 135,19; 136,[7].15; 137,4.8; 138,13.13; 140,20.
    ϢⲰⲠⲈ ⲈⲂⲟⲗ ϨⲚ 135,3-4; 136,13-14; 138,4-5. ϢⲰⲠⲈ ϢⲀⲣⲟ'
    138,21. ϢⲟⲟⲠ⁺ 134,5.17-18; 136,2. nn m. 134,24. ⲈϢⲰⲠⲈ 137,6.
ⲰⲎⲣⲈ (584a) nn m. 134,3-4.4.6; 139,26.
(ϢⲰⲣⲠ) (586b) vb. ⲣ ϢⲣⲠ ⲚⲀⲟⲟ' 138,2.
(ϢⲰⲰⲦ) (590b) vb. 134,21-22; 135,[9].10.20.20; 137,3.
ϢⲀⲬⲈ (612b) vb. 135,8.16. ϢⲀⲬⲈ ⲘⲚ 136,22-23; 138,11. nn m.
    134,15; 138,14; 140,25.
(ϢⲟⲬⲚⲈ) (615b) vb. ⲘⲚⲦⲀⲦϢⲟⲬⲚⲈ 135,11.
ϢⲰⲬⲠ (616b) vb. 135,17.
Ϥⲓ (620a) vb. 136,28.
ϤⲦⲟⲟⲨ (625a) nn. 140,25.
(ϨⲀⲈⲓⲟ) (636b) interj. ⲀⲈⲓⲟ 134,1.
ϨⲈ (637a) vb. ϨⲈ ⲈⲂⲟⲗ 136,18.
ϨⲈ (638b) nn f. ⲚⲦϨⲈ 133,20; 137,21.23; 139,15. ⲐⲈ 137,16. ⲔⲀⲦⲀ ⲐⲈ
    133,24; 136,24; 137,11-12; 138,2.
(Ϩⲓ) (643b) prep. ϨⲓⲰⲰ' 139,17-18.
ϨⲓⲈ (645b) part. 138,16.
(ϨⲓⲎ) (646a) nn f. ϨⲓⲦⲈϨⲓⲎ 138,12.
ϨⲰⲰ' (651b) pron. 138,19; 140,6. ϨⲰ' 136,24.
ϨⲰⲂ (653a) nn m. 139,12.24.
(ϨⲰⲰⲔ) (661b) vb. ϨⲰⲔ' ⲚϨⲣⲀⲓ̈ ϨⲚ 137,26.
ϨⲘⲟⲦ (681a) nn m. 140,21. ϢⲠ ϨⲘⲟⲦ ⲚⲀ' 138,8.
ϨⲚ (683a) prep. 133,1.25; 134,1.5.24; 136,6; 137,9.25; 138,3; 139,7.11.19.23;
    140,27.27. ⲈⲂⲟⲗ ϨⲚ 134,12; 135,3-4; 136,14.14-15; 137,[18-19]; 138,5;
    139,4.20; 140,9. ϨⲣⲀⲓ̈ ϨⲚ 132,21; 136,11; 137,2.26; 138,9; 139,7.25.30.
    ⲈϨⲣⲀⲓ̈ ϨⲚ 136,17.
(ϨⲟⲨⲚ) (685b) nn m. ⲈϨⲟⲨⲚ Ⲉ' 13,25; 136,27. ⲤⲀϨⲟⲨⲚ 137,22.
ϨⲀⲠⲤ (696a) vb. 138,19.23.24-25.
(ϨⲣⲀⲓ̈) (698a) nn m. ⲈϨⲣⲀⲓ̈ Ⲉ' 136,6.19; 138,7.10.11; 139,6.16; 140,25.
    See also ϨⲚ.
(ϨⲣⲟⲟⲨ) (704b) nn m. ϨⲣⲟⲨⲘⲠⲈ 138,5.
(ϨⲰⲦⲂ) (723b) vb. ϨⲟⲦⲂ' 134,9.
(ϨⲟⲟⲨ) (730a) nn m. ⲠⲟⲟⲨ 136,25.
(ϨⲓⲟⲦⲈ) (732b) vb. Ϩⲓ' 133,5.
ϨⲀϨ (741b) nn. 138,23.
ⲬⲈ (746b) conjunction. 132,19.20; 133,4.6.15.21; 134,3.14.15.20.23;
    135,4.6.28; 136,12.21.26; 137,3.5.5.10.11.15.15.20; 138,15.18.22.23;
    139,10.15; 140,[3].6.12.15.17.25.

ⲀⲒ (747b) vb. 135,22; 138,16.18.20.24.27.28; 139,13.22.23. ⲀⲒⲦˢ 133,8.
 ⲀⲒ ⲚⲦⲞⲞⲦˢ 132,17. See also ⲘⲔⲀⲐ.
ⲀⲞ (752a) vb. 135,22.
ⲀⲰ (754a) vb. 133,21; 134,3.14.20; 135,4; 137,14.19; 138,14.17.22;
 140,3.15.16. ⲀⲞˢ 133,15; 138,2.22. ⲀⲈˊ 135,6.
(ⲀⲰ)(756a) nn m. ⲈⲀⲚ 133,13.19; 135,24; 139,19. ⲈⲐⲢⲀⲒ ⲈⲀⲚ 136,6.
ⲀⲈⲔⲀⲀⲤ (764a) conjunct. 139,3.
(ⲀⲠⲞ) (778b) vb ⲀⲠⲞˢ 135,28.
ⲀⲞⲈⲒⲤ (787b) nn m,f. 132,18; 133,1; 134,20-21; 137,15; 138.9.14.[15];
 139,8.11.25; 140,3.12-13.
ⲀⲒⲤⲈ (788b) vb. ⲀⲒⲤⲈ ⲚⲐⲎⲦ 136,6.
ⲀⲞⲈⲒⲦ (790b) nn m. 133,15.
(ⲀⲞⲞⲨ) (793a) vb. ⲀⲞⲞⲨˢ 132,11.
(ⲀⲰⲰϬⲈ) (800b) vb. ⲀⲎϬⲈ 139,18.
ϬⲈ (802b) part. 135,22; 138,16.
(ϬⲂⲂⲈ) (805a) vb. ⲣ ϬⲀⲂⲐⲎⲦ 138,1; 140,22.
ϬⲞⲘ (815b) nn f. 135,2.23.27; 136,7.11; 137,10; 140,7.27. ϬⲀⲘ 134,8;
140,21. ✝ ϬⲞⲘ 136,4; 137,26.

Greek Words: VIII,2

αἰών **ⲉⲱⲛ** 134,22; 135,9.15.21.25.

ἀλλά 135,[7]; 136,3; 139,22.

ἀμήν 140,15.

ἄνομος 139,29-30.

ἀπόστολος 132,12; 133,18-19; 134,19; 137,13-14; 138,8; 139,4; 140,8.23-24.
  fellow 132,14-15.

ἀσπάζεσθαι **ⲁⲥⲡⲁ3ⲉ** 140,14.

ἀρχηγός 139,27; 140,4.

ἄρχων 137,16.17.21.

αὐθάδης 135,16-17.19.21; 136,5-6.

ἀφθαρσία 133,23.

βοήθειν **ⲃⲟⲏⲑⲓ** 137,29.30.

γάρ 133,26; 137,21; 139,12.26.

δέ 132,16; 133,1; 135,11.17; 136,1.5.11.16.20.23; 137,[3].10.20.[23]; 138,11.27;
  139,5.10.; 140,19.22.

εἰκών **ⲟⲓⲕⲱⲛ** 136,9.[9].

εἰρήνη 140,27. **ϯⲣⲏⲛⲏ** 140,17.

ἐντολή 132,17; 133,7.

ἐξουσία 135,[1].24; 136,12.26.

ἐπειδή 134,8; 136,2; 137,2.12.16.

ἐπιστήμη 140,5.6.

ἐπιστολή 132,10.

ἤ 134,25.25 .26; 135,[2].

ἡγεμών 138,26.

ἰδέα 136,15.

ἵνα **ⲟⲓⲛⲁ** 137,[13]; 140,6.

κατά 133,7.24; 136,2-4; 137,11-12; 138,2; 139,25.

κληρονομία 136,27.

κόσμος 132,19; 135,27-28; 137,24.25.

μαθητής 139,10.

μακάριος 133,16.

μέν 135,9.

μέρος 135,15.22.

μή (interrog.) 139,[11].

μορφή 136,10.[11].

ὅταν **ⲟⲟⲧⲁⲛ** 133,17; 138,3; 139,11.

οὐδέ not 138,28.

οὖν 133,6; 139,29.

παράβασις 139,23.

παρρησία 135,1.

πλάσμα 136,19.

πλάσσειν ⲡⲗⲁⲥⲥⲁ 136,12.

πλήρωμα 134,22-23; 136,16.19; 137,4.

πνεῦμα ⲡⲚⲀ 139,14; 140,5.9.

πῶς 134,23.25.26.

σπέρμα 136,18.

στολή 139,18.

συναγωγή 138,25-26.

σῶμα 133,17; 136,13.17; 138,3; 139,11.

σωτήρ 132,18.

τότε 133,12.17-18; 134,9.18; 135,3; 137,7-8.13.17; 138,3.7.21; 140,[1].7.15.23.

φορεῖν ⲫⲟⲣⲉⲓ 139,16.[17-18].

φωστήρ 133,27; 137,8; 139,16.

χαίρειν ⲭⲉⲣⲉ 132,[15].

ὡς 137,29.

ὥστε ϩⲱⲥⲧⲉ 134,11; 138,27.

PROPER NAMES: VIII, 2

ïєроυϲⲁⲗⲏⲙ: Ⲑⲗⲏⲙ 138,10; 139,7.

(ïⲏϲоυϲ) ⲓⲥ 139,22.23.27; 140,16.27. ⲓⲥ ⲡⲉⲭⲥ 132,12-13; 133,26; 134,17; 140,3. ⲡⲉⲛⲛоυⲧⲉ ⲓⲥ 133,7-8. ⲡⲉⲛⲫⲱϲⲧⲏⲣ ⲓⲥ 139,16. ⲡ(ⲉⲛ)ⲍоⲓⲥ ⲓⲥ 139,11; 140,12-13. ⲡ(ⲉⲛ)ⲍоⲓⲥ ⲓⲥ ⲡⲉⲭⲥ 133,1; 139,8; 140,[3-4].

ⲡⲉⲧⲣоⲥ 132,10.12; 133,10.12; 138,17; 139,10; 140,[1-2].[7].

ⲫⲓⲗⲓⲡⲡоⲥ 132,11.13; 133,9.

ⲭⲣⲓϲⲧоⲥ: ⲭⲥ 133,17; 134,6. ⲓⲥ ⲡⲉⲭⲥ   132,12-13; 133,26; 134,17; 140,3.

REFERENCES TO ANCIENT WORKS

Note: References to Nag Hammadi tractates cited in their own introductions and footnotes are omitted. References to a tractate or work as a whole are listed "general."

A. NHC and BG Tractates; Other Gnostic and Related Literature

I,2: *Ap. James*		13,4	239
4,37-6,21	247	13,14	239
6,15-17	247	13,22-23	241
14,35-36	243	13,27	241
general	227	13,28	239
		13,30	239
I,3: *Gos. Truth*		13,32	239
31,1-4	247	14,24-15,13	240
31,13-16	237	15,1-19	241
		19,8-10	11
I,4: *Treat. Res.*		25,11-16	243
46,34-38	245	30,20-21	243
general	227	30,33-35	237
		general 11, 15, 16, 17, 217, 230,	
I,5: *Tri. Tac.*			231
115,3-11	245		
		II,2: *Gos. Thom.*	
II,I: *Ap. John*		37,4-6	243
1,17-29	239	37,20-23	245
2,1-9	237	37,31-37	241
2,12-13	239	37,34	240
2,25-9,25	16	41,1012	245
4,1-2	239		
6,15	239	II,3: *Gos. Phil.*	
9.25ff	230, 239	61,29-32	243
10,6-7	239		
10,14ff	3	II,4: *Hyp. Arch.*	
10,18	239	87,12	241
10,19	241	87,15-20	241
10, 19-28		87,21	241
10,21	239	90,29	241
11,9-10	23	92,27	241
12,8	239	93,32-94,2	239

94,14	241	64,20	41
94,17	241	64,21	42, 127
94,32	241	64,24-27	114
general	17	65,1-5	116
		65,6-8	114
II,5: *Orig. World*		66,8-22	123
100,10-19	241	66,10-15	115
114,15-115,3	241	67,17	123
		general	15, 16, 217
III,I: *Ap. John*			
14,9ff	237	III,4: *Soph. Jes. Chr.*	
		90,14-91,20	237
III,2: *Gos. Eg.*		91,2-9	239
41,13-16	215	91,10-13	237
41,23-48,8	16	104,17-18	239
44,3-9	123	114,14-15	239
44,23	16	119,1-8	249
44,27	125		
49,1-7	38, 43	III,5: *Dial. Sav.*	
50,2	54	121,5-9	237
50,10	40	132,11-12	243
50,16-56,2	16	138,11-14	243
51,5-9	16	139,13-15	239
52-53	114	140,14-19	243
52,1-54,11	16		
52,19-20	114	IV, I: *Ap. John*	
52,19ff	131	15,1ff	237
52,26-53,1	116	21,16	241
53,25	54		
56,4-13	121	IV, 2: *Gos. Eg.*	
56,6	121	59,19ff	123
56,22-57,5	16	61,10	42
60,2	115	75,18-19	38
61,23-62,11	16	76,4	
62-65	114	41	
64,4	38	76,9-10	41
64,9-20	16	76,11	42
64,13	116		
64,15-20	41	V,I: *Eugnostos*	
64,15-16	115	9,4-5	239
64,15	41	general	227

V,2: *Apoc. Paul*
19,8-13 — 237
general — 10

V,3: *1 Apoc. Jas.*
24,27ff — 31

V,4: *2 Apoc. Jas.*
55,15-20 — 243
56,7-14 — 243

V,5: *Apoc, Adam*
64,15 — 36
64,16-19 — 33
69,17-18 — 247
75,22-26 — 114, 116
77,27ff — 38
78,5 — 62
84,5-8 — 115
85,28-31 — 237
85,29-31 — 115
general — 17

VI, I: *Acts Pet. 12 Apost.*
3,4-11 — 247

VI,8: *Asclepius*
69,14ff — 150

VII,I: *Para. Shem*
7,11ff — 38
general — 10, 18

VII,2: *Treat. Seth*
52,8-10 — 243
54,4 — 245
54,10 — 245
59,9-11 — 243
69,11-12 — 245

VII,3: *Apoc. Pet.*
71,32-72,2 — 237

82,26-83,8 — 33
83,6-15 — 237
83,31ff — 106
84,12-13 — 113

VII,5: *Steles Seth*
118,10-11 — 221
118,13 — 16
118,17 — 16
118,26 — 42
118,28 — 42
121,25-30 — 15
121,31 — 15
122,4-123.5 — 15
125,6-25 — 15
125,23-25 — 16,122
126,1-17 — 15
126,10-12 — 205
126,10 — 167
126,12 — 167
general — 15

VIII,I: *Zostrianos*
2,24-3,13 — 239
general — 227

IX,I: *Melch.*
5,17-20 — 114
6,1 — 215
16,30 — 215
general — 17, 217

IX,2: *Norea*
general — 17

X: *Marsanes*
2,12-4,23 — 16
4,15-17 — 15
6,15-16 — 16
6,18-19 — 15
8,18-25 — 16
9,1-13 — 15

42,24-25	72	BG 8502,2: *Ap. John*	
64,19-20	114	36,16ff	230
general	15	46,1	241
XI,3: *Allogenes*		Cod. Bruce *Untitled*	
45,13-16	61	234	127
45,28-30	15	238,26-239,27	17
45,31-46,35	15	252,21ff	205
47,8-11	61	255,15-26	17
47,9	15	263,11-264,6	17
50,20-25	16	264	127
50,20	125	general	15, 17
52,13-15	16		
52,13-33	218	*Ex. Theod.*	
52,21-25	16	78.2	239
54,6-13	205	23,2	239
54,7	205		
54,17-20	170	*Kephalia*	
54,12	167	general	237
54,20	116		
54,22-23	122	*Pist. Soph.*	
54,23	167	2-5	237
54,26-31	15	6	237
54,35	122	8	237
55,17-20	16	44	235
58,26-69,20	16	77	237
66,34	15	general	251
68,16-20	16		
general	15	*Poimandres*	
		24-26	243
XIII,I: *Trim. Prot.*			
47,28-29	237		
48,18-21	41		
48,19-20	115		
48,25-30	114		
general	17, 217		
BG 8502, I: Gos. Mary			
8,12	237		

B. Biblical and Related Literature

1. Old Testament

Gen		Ps	
3:1	239	39:8	41
		43	38
Num		74:19	36
1:10	114	89:26	37
2:20	114	138:16	41
Deut		Isa	
32:6	37	6:9-10	77
		42:1-4	237

2. OLD TESTAMENT APOCRYPHA AND PSEUDEPIGRAPHA

Adam and Eve		2 Enoch	
general	10	22:8-10	39
		33:47-54	221
Apoc Seth		65:8	223
general	10	general	10, 217
1 Enoch		Jubilees	
6	47	4:15	47
17-36	10		
80	218	Wis	
82:1	223	9:9-11	111
general	217		

3. NEW TESTAMENT

Matt		3:18	235
10:17-18	247	9:2-8	237
12:18-21	237	9:7	38
17:5	237	10:13-16	245
27	247	13:9	247
28:18-20	249	15	247
28:20	239	16:15-18	249
		shorter ending	247
Mark			
1:11	237		

Luke			1:13	235
1:9	36		2:1-4	249
1:80	32		2:14-40	247
15:17	113		2:38	247
19:29	237		2:42-47	247
21:12	247		3:6	247
21:37	237		3:13	237
22:39	237		3:15	247
22:41	237		4:8	247
23	247		4:10	247
24:44-49	235, 249		4:27	237
24:46	247		4:29	239
24:47	247		4:30	237
24:49	82		4:31	239, 247
24:51	245		5:12-16	247
24:52-53	245,247		5:30	247
			5:31	247
John			5:42	247
1:1-18	237, 243		6:5	235
1:10	243		7:60	237
1:11	243		7:55	247
1:12	243		8:4-40	235
1:43-48	235		9:1-9	237
6:5-7	235		9:3	129
7:33	245		9:22	237
12:21-22	235		9:40	237
14:8-9	235		10:16	245
16:5	245		10:39-41	247
19	229, 245, 247		13:9	247
19:5	247		13:29-30	247
20:19-23	229, 249		13:52	247
20:28	235		14:22	247
			15:23	235
Acts			20:36	237
1-12	229		21:5	237
1:1-8	235, 249		21:8-9	235
1:8	249		22:4-11	237
1:9	38, 245		22:6	129
1:12	237, 245, 247		26:1	237

26:9-18	237	1 Thess	
26:13	129	3:3-4	247
27:24	36	4:17	38
Rom		2 Thess	
1:7	235	1:5-8	247
4:20	32		
16:16	249	1 Tim	
		2:14	239
1 Cor		3:12-13	247
2:6	44		
10:1-2	38	Heb	
13	28, 80	2:10	247
15	237	7:3	66
15:3-5	247	12:2	247
15:49	241		
16:20	249	1 Pet	
		1:12	218
2 Cor			
1:1	235	2 Pet	
5:1-5	221	1:16-19	237
5:2-3	243	1:17	237
12:2-3	38		
13:12	249	1 John	
		1:5	237
Eph			
4:15	31	Rev	
6:10-20	245	1:12-16	237
		11:17	38
Phil		14:1	41
2:15	243	17:8-41	41

4. New Testament Apocrypha

Acts of Philip		109	247
21	237	111	237, 243
97	239		
		Ep. Apost.	
Acts of Thomas		30	251
28	251		
80	237	Gos. Eb.	
		frg. 4	237

C. Patristic Literature

Barn.		Iren.	
12.5	239	*Adv. Haer.*	
		I.2.1-2	239
Clem. Alex.		I.2.2	239
Strom.		I.21.4	245
I.15	11	I.29	17
V.14	12	I.29.1-4	230
		I.29.4	239, 241
1 Clem.		I.30	17
59.2-4	237	I.9.4	116
		III.11.8	251
2 Clem.			
20.5	247	Justin	
		Mart. Pol.	
Did.		14.1-3	237
1:4	44	20.2	237
9.2,3	237		
10.2,3	237	Orig.	
		de Princ.	
Epiphanius		II.11	40
Pan.			
I.30	17	Ps.-Clem.	
II.40	18	*Epistula Petri*	
		general	227, 228
Hipp.			
Ref.			
V.8.44	243		
VI.34	239		
VII.27.6	245		
Ign.			
Eph.			
19	73		
Rom.			
3.3	235		
Smyrn.			
1.1	235		
3.2	247		

D. MISCELLANEOUS GREEK AND LATIN WORKS

Arnobius
  Contra. Gentes
    2.15   11,12
    general   11, 12

Diog. Laert.
    VIII.9-11   237
    IX.1   237

Plato
  Phaedo
    83A   20
  Phaedrus
    240A   20
  Resp.
    X   10
    X,614b-621d   12
  Symp.
    210a-212   19
  Tim.
    28C   24

Plot.
  Enn.
    I.1.2-3.7   117
    II.1.8.1-15   22

II.1.31-40   63
II.7.20-50   22
II.9   21
II.9.5.23ff   21, 40
II.9.5,25-26   46
II.9.6   40
II.9.6,1-6   21
II.9.6.28-62   21
II.9.6.59-63   21
II.9.10   21
II.9.10.19-24   21
II.9.13   22
II.9.14.37-43   22
II.9.16.15-33   23
II.9.27-28   21
III.8   20
general   21

Porphyry
  Vit. Plot.
    16   11, 19, 36

Ptolemy
  Letter to Flora
    general   227

REFERENCES TO MODERN AUTHORS

Anderson, F. 10

Angus, S. 15

Armstrong A.H. 23

Barns, J.W.B., Brown, G.M. and Shelton, J.C. 3,4

Bauer, W. 15

Baynes, C.A. 40, 41

Berliner Arbeitskreis 11

Bethge, H.-G. 227, 229, 230, 232

Bidez, J. and Cumont, F. 11

Böhlig, A. and Wisse, F. 16

Bousset, W. 15

Bultmann, R. 81

Collins, J. 10

Colpe, C. 11, 18, 55, 118

Crum, A. 109, 111

Davidson, G. 114, 115

Dillon, J. 20,23

Dodds, E.R. 23, 25, 28

Doresse, J. 3, 7, 11, 224

Emmel, S. 3, 30, 43, 232

Fallon, F. 10

Foester, W. 227

Hadot, P. 25

Hedrick, C.W. 16

Hengel, M. 10, 11

Henry, P., and Schwyzer, H.-R. 19

Hinz, W. 11

Jackson, A.V. 11

Jonas, H. 13,14

Klijin, A. F. J. 47

Koschorke, K. 227, 229

Krause, M. and Labib,P. 5

Lampe, G. 237

Layton, B. 7, 20, 27

Luttikhuizen, G.P. 227

McCracken, G.E. 11

MacDermott, V. see Schmidt-McDermott

Ménard, J.-É. 227

Meyer, M.W. 227, 229, 230, 231, 232, 235

Nickelsburg, G.W.E. 15

Orelli (in PL), 12

Pagels, E. 18

Parrott, D. M. 227

Pearson, B. 7, 15, 18, 20, 25, 38, 67

Perkins, P. 7, 10, 20, 23, 26, 27, 32, 36

Puech, H.-Ch. 3, 7, 11, 227

Robinson, J.M. 3, 4, 5, 7, 15, 25, 232

Rudolf, K. 13

Schenke, H.-M. 15, 18, 39, 42, 115, 236

Schmidt, C. 17, 18, 19, 20, 25

Schmidt, C., ed. and MacDermott, V. 17, 127, 205

Schneemelcher, W. 232

Scholer, D.M. 4

Schweizer, E. 24, 117

Scopello, M. 7, 10, 15, 39

Sevrin, J.-M. 7, 15

Sieber, J.H. 7, 11, 15, 25, 28

Tardieu, M. 20

Tröger, K.-W. 227

Tuckett, C.M. 28

Turner, J. 7, 15, 18, 25, 28

Wallis, R. T. 20, 23

Widengren, G. 13, 14, 218

Williams, M. A. 7, 20, 42

Wire, A. and Turner, J. 25

Wisse, F. 17, 18, 227

Zaehner, R. C. 117

Zandee, J. 20

Ziegler, K. 11